Lecture Notes in Computer Science 13798

Founding Editors

Gerhard Goos
Juris Hartmanis

Editorial Board Members

The series Lecture Notes in Computer Science (LNCS), including its subseries Lecture Notes in Artificial Intelligence (LNAI) and Lecture Notes in Bioinformatics (LNBI), has established itself as a medium for the publication of new developments in computer science and information technology research, teaching, and education.

LNCS enjoys close cooperation with the computer science R & D community, the series counts many renowned academics among its volume editors and paper authors, and collaborates with prestigious societies. Its mission is to serve this international community by providing an invaluable service, mainly focused on the publication of conference and workshop proceedings and postproceedings. LNCS commenced publication in 1973.

Hiroyuki Takizawa · Hong Shen ·
Toshihiro Hanawa · Jong Hyuk Park · Hui Tian ·
Ryusuke Egawa
Editors

Parallel and Distributed Computing, Applications and Technologies

23rd International Conference, PDCAT 2022
Sendai, Japan, December 7–9, 2022
Proceedings

Springer

Editors
Hiroyuki Takizawa
Tohoku University
Aoba-ku, Japan

Toshihiro Hanawa
The University of Tokyo
Tokyo, Japan

Hui Tian
Griffith University
Queensland, QLD, Australia

Hong Shen
Sun Yat-sen University
Guangzhou, China

Jong Hyuk Park
Seoul National University of Science
and Technology
Seoul, Korea (Republic of)

Ryusuke Egawa
Tokyo Denki University
Tokyo, Japan

ISSN 0302-9743   ISSN 1611-3349 (electronic)
Lecture Notes in Computer Science
ISBN 978-3-031-29926-1   ISBN 978-3-031-29927-8 (eBook)
https://doi.org/10.1007/978-3-031-29927-8

This Springer imprint is published by the registered company Springer Nature Switzerland AG
The registered company address is: Gewerbestrasse 11, 6330 Cham, Switzerland

Preface

This volume contains the papers from the 23rd International Conference on Parallel and Distributed Computing, Applications, and Technologies (PDCAT 2022). PDCAT is a forum for scientists, engineers, and practitioners worldwide to present the latest research, results, ideas, developments, and applications in all parallel and distributed computing areas.

The conference started in Hong Kong in 2000, and PDCAT 2022 took place in Sendai, Japan, after 22 years of success in different countries/regions, including Taiwan, Japan, China, South Korea, Singapore, Australia, and New Zealand. Like the previous conference, due to the COVID-19 pandemic, the event was held in a hybrid manner with over 90 participants from 11 different countries.

This year we received 95 submissions from authors in 21 countries and regions worldwide. Out of these submissions, we have accepted 24 regular papers and 16 short papers. This represents an acceptance rate of 25% for regular papers and 42% for all papers, including short papers. The submission quality was high, and the selection of papers was extremely tough. The paper review process involved all Program Committee members, and to ensure a high-quality program and provide sufficient feedback to authors, we made a great effort to have each paper single-blind reviews by three independent reviewers on average. In these proceedings, all accepted and presented papers are included.

It would not have been possible for PDCAT 2022 to take place without the help and support of various people. The proceedings editors wish to thank all authors, exhibitors, participants, Organizing Committee members, dedicated Scientific Committee members, and all the other reviewers for their contributions. We also thank all sponsors, especially the Cyberscience Center of Tohoku University and Sendai City, for their support. We would like to express our most profound appreciation to Michael Sheng of Macquarie University, Australia; Geoffrey Fox from the University of Virginia, USA; Masaaki Kondo from Keio University and RIKEN Center for Computational Science, Japan; Michael Resch from High Performance Computing Center Stuttgart, Germany; who delivered excellent keynotes and helped attain the objectives of the conference. We also thank Springer for their trust and for publishing the post-proceedings of PDCAT 2022.

Finally, again, we would like to thank all the authors for submitting their latest research efforts and all the participants of the conference. We sincerely hope that these post-proceedings will contribute to the further development in their research field.

Hiroyuki Takizawa
Hong Shen
Toshihiro Hanawa
Jong Hyuk Park
Hui Tian
Ryusuke Egawa

Organization

General Chairs

Hiroyuki Takizawa	Tohoku University, Japan
Hong Shen	Sun Yat-sen University, China

Program Chairs

Toshihiro Hanawa	The University of Tokyo, Japan
Jong Hyuk Park	Seoul National University of Science and Technology, South Korea
Hui Tian	Griffith University, Australia

Poster Chair

Yohei Miki	The University of Tokyo, Japan

Publications Chair

Ryusuke Egawa	Tokyo Denki University, Japan

Publicity Chair

Keichi Takahashi	Tohoku University, Japan

Local Arrangements Chair

Yoichi Shimomura	Tohoku University, Japan

Registration and Finance Chair

Kazuhiko Komatsu   Tohoku University, Japan

Program Committee

Hamid Arabnia   University of Georgia, USA
Ritu Arora   University of Texas at San Antonio, USA
Costin Badica   University of Craiova, Romania
Susumu Date   Osaka University, Japan
Toshio Endo   Tokyo Institute of Technology, Japan
Arata Endo   Nara Institute of Science and Technology, Japan
Karl Fürlinger   Ludwig Maximilian University of Munich,
                           Germany
Hajime Fujita   Fastly, Inc., USA
Norihisa Fujita   University of Tsukuba, Japan
Keiichiro Fukazawa   Kyoto University, Japan
Masaru Fukushi   Yamaguchi University, Japan
Teofilo Gonzalez   University of California, Santa Barbara, USA
Jose Gracia   High Performance Computing Center Stuttgart,
                           Germany
Huaxi Gu   Xidian University, China
Longkun Guo   Qilu University of Technology, China
Tetsuya Hoshino   The University of Tokyo, Japan
Fumihiko Ino   Osaka University, Japan
Yasushi Inoguchi   Japan Advanced Institute of Science and
                           Technology, Japan
Mirjana Ivanovic   University of Novi Sad, Serbia
Haibin Kan   Fudan University, China
Yamin Li   Hosei University, Japan
Weifa Liang   City University of Hong Kong, China
James Lin   Shanghai Jiao Tong University, China
Marin Lujak   University Rey Juan Carlos, Spain
Manu Malek   Stevens Institute of Technology, USA
Shintaro Momose   NEC Corporation, Japan
Chawanat Nakasan   Kasetsart University, Thailand
Takeshi Nanri   Kyushu University, Japan
Satoshi Ohshima   Nagoya University, Japan
Marcin Paprzycki   Systems Research Institute, Polish Academy of
                           Sciences, Poland
Yingpeng Sang   Sun Yat-sen University, China

Masayuki Sato	Tohoku University, Japan
Michael Sheng	Macquarie University, Australia
Yuanquan Shi	Huaihua University, China
Toyotaro Suzumura	The University of Tokyo, Japan
Jubee Tada	Yamagata University, Japan
Atsuko Takefusa	National Institute of Informatics, Japan
Thi Hong Tran	Osaka Metropolitan University, Japan
Miwako Tsuji	RIKEN Center for Computational Science, Japan
Vadim Voevodin	Lomonosov Moscow State University, Russia
Yasutaka Wada	Meisei University, Japan
Xian Wang	Xi'an Jiaotong University, China
Jigang Wu	Guangdong University of Technology, China
Jingjing Yu	Beijing Jiaotong University, China
Filip Zavoral	Charles University in Prague, Czech Republic
Yong Zhang	Shenzhen Institutes of Advanced Technology, China
Haibo Zhang	University of Otago, New Zealand
Cheng Zhong	Guangxi University, China

Contents

Deep Learning

Quantum Computing and Programming Language

Best Papers

Optimization (2)

Privacy

Workflow

Heterogeneous System (1)

Heterogeneous states (I)

Towards Priority-Flexible Task Mapping for Heterogeneous Multi-core NUMA Systems

Yifan Jin[1](✉), Mulya Agung[2], Keichi Takahashi[1], Yoichi Shimomura[1],
and Hiroyuki Takizawa[1]

[1] Cyberscience Center, Tohoku University, Sendai, Japan
`jinyifan@hpc.is.tohoku.ac.jp`, {`keichi,shimomura32,takizawa`}`@tohoku.ac.jp`
[2] Institute of Genetics and Cancer, University of Edinburgh, Edinburgh, Scotland
`mulya.agung@ed.ac.uk`

Abstract. With the rapid development of heterogeneous multi-core processors, a new High Performance Computing (HPC) system architecture combining the heterogeneous multi-core architecture and NUMA architecture will emerge in the future. However, existing task mapping methods are ineffective on such systems because they do not simultaneously consider multiple performance factors caused by the heterogeneity in memory access and core performance. In a parallel application, one factor can affect performance more than another depending on the communication and computation load imbalances among parallel tasks. In this case, a task mapping method must prioritize one factor over another when calculating the mapping. To solve this problem, this paper proposes a new mapping method with two task mapping priority options: the memory-aware priority option (MPO) and the heterogeneity-aware priority option (HPO). A priority option switching mechanism (POSM) selects the appropriate priority option for the combination of a system and an application by analyzing their characteristics. Compared with other methods that do not switch mapping priorities, the proposed method achieves overall performance improvement when dealing with a set of applications with different characteristics.

Keywords: Task mapping · NUMA architecture · Heterogeneous multi-core architecture

1 Introduction

Due to power budget constraints, a multi-core processor has evolved to employ a heterogeneous multi-core architecture integrating some kinds of cores with different performance and energy characteristics on a single chip. Heterogeneous multi-cores can potentially save energy by assigning the most suitable task to each core. Given that modern HPC systems are tightly constrained by energy consumption, the heterogeneous multi-core architecture that improves energy efficiency shows a significant practical value in HPC. In addition, the Non-Uniform Memory Access (NUMA) architecture has become a de facto standard

H. Takizawa et al. (Eds.): PDCAT 2022, LNCS 13798, pp. 3–15, 2023.
https://doi.org/10.1007/978-3-031-29927-8_1

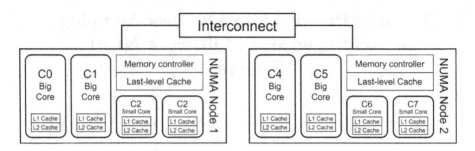

Fig. 1. A NUMA system with heterogeneous multi-core processors.

in modern HPC systems. Based on the above facts, the deployment of a new HPC system architecture combining the heterogeneous multi-core architecture and NUMA architecture is foreseeable.

Figure 1 shows an example system consisting of two NUMA nodes, each of which contains two different types of cores. The high-performance cores are hereinafter called "Big cores" and the low-performance cores are called "Small cores." Due to these differences, mapping tasks generated by parallel applications to cores, called task mapping, can affect performance and energy efficiency [9]. However, the combined use of the heterogeneous multi-core architecture and NUMA architecture poses new challenges for task mapping on this new system configuration. Inefficient task mapping not only results in computation power wastage but also causes performance degradation due to memory latency variations. Therefore, an efficient task mapping method is necessary to effectively utilize such systems.

The main contributions of this paper are as follows:

1. This paper identifies the challenges of task mapping posed by adopting heterogeneous multicore processors to NUMA systems.
2. This paper proposes a task mapping method to address the challenges by selecting between two priority options to determine the best mapping for applications on NUMA systems built with heterogeneous multi-core processors.
3. This paper investigates the key performance characteristics of applications that can be used to select the mapping priority.

2   Motivation and Objective

Task mapping is an important part of resource management because it could significantly affect the usage of heterogeneity and memory resources in systems. A proper task mapping will be a key to achieve high performance on heterogeneous multi-core NUMA systems.

For different system architectures and different applications, task mapping needs to consider the impact of different factors [9]. On heterogeneous multi-core systems, inappropriate task mapping causes serious load imbalance and waste of system resources. Particularly for applications involving tasks with different loads, choosing the wrong core type for each task significantly increases execution time. On NUMA systems, inappropriate task mapping causes memory access load imbalance and remote access penalty. For applications with high communication loads between tasks, these issues will affect performance more than the computation load imbalance. In this case, a task mapping method that prioritizes a mapping algorithm to reduce the memory access imbalance and remote access penalty will significantly improve performance. On the other hand, the task mapping will hardly affect applications with a low memory access intensity. Therefore, to achieve a high performance for different applications, a task mapping method must adjust the mapping priority according to the application's computation and communication behaviors.

Most of the conventional studies on NUMA awareness consider homogeneous processors and/or processor cores. These studies focus on improving the locality of memory access or reducing memory congestion, and they assume the use of homogeneous processors in the target system. Jeannot *et al.* [8] proposed TreeMatch algorithm to decrease the communication costs in parallel applications. Diener *et al.* [7] presented a mapping technique that increases locality while maintaining the balance of memory access. Agung *et al.* [1] proposed a task mapping technique, DeLoc, to address both locality and memory congestion. On the other hand, most of the conventional studies on heterogeneous multi-core architectures mainly assume a homogeneous interconnection among cores. This is because those studies do not consider the large-scale use of heterogeneous multicore processors in HPC environments and assume that a single multicore processor is used independently. Chen *et al.* [6] presented a technique to map an application to its optimum core by analyzing the microarchitecture-independent characteristics of that application. Yu *et al.* [12] presented a COLAB scheduling framework that targets on heterogeneous multicore processors by making collaborative decisions on multiple factors. Saez *et al.* [10] presented AID, a set of three new loop-scheduling methods specifically tailored to data-parallel OpenMP applications on heterogeneous multicore processors. AID distributes iterations unevenly across worker threads to efficiently cater to performance asymmetry across cores.

This paper extends the previous studies by developing a new task mapping method that simultaneously considers both NUMA memory awareness and core heterogeneity.

3   Task Mapping with Priority Option Switching

3.1   Overview

Considering the diversity of application characteristics and system configuration on heterogeneous multi-core NUMA systems, this paper proposes a task mapping method that switches between two priority options to determine the best mapping for the target application on the target system.

Figure 2 shows the workflow of the proposed method. It first analyzes the application characteristics and system configuration from the profiling results,

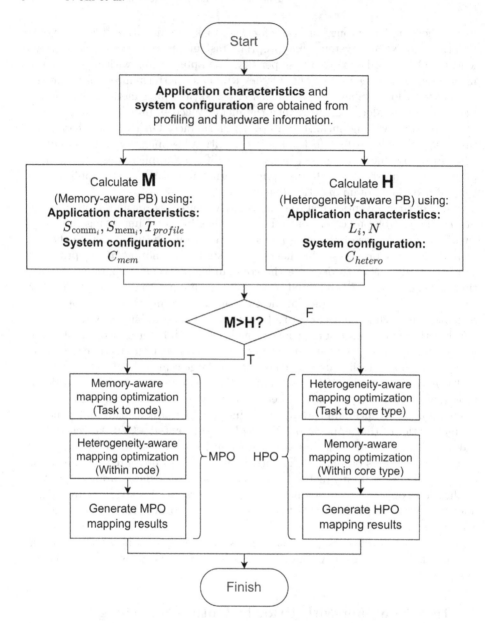

Fig. 2. Workflow of the proposed task mapping method.

then selects an appropriate priority option for the current situation, and finally uses the selected priority option to perform task mapping. The two proposed priority options are the memory-aware priority option (MPO) and the heterogeneity-aware priority option (HPO). The proposed priority option switching mechanism (POSM) selects appropriate priority options for individual sys-

tems and applications considering their performance characteristics. Choosing
one of the priority options prioritizes the impact of the respective factor at the
task mapping. However, the influence of the other factor on the mapping result
is not completely ignored because some applications might be sensitive to both
memory and core performance characteristics.

3.2   Potential Benefit Metrics and POSM

To select an appropriate priority option, it is necessary to investigate the key performance characteristics of applications. To achieve this, this paper proposes two
potential benefit (PB) metrics that characterizes an application: the memory-
aware potential benefit referred to as M and heterogeneity-aware potential benefit referred to as H. These two metrics are used to quantify the impact of a
mapping factor on performance. A higher value of each PB means a higher performance improvement gained from the mapping optimization associated with
the PB.

To obtain M, we calculate the communication throughput (TP_{comm}) and
memory access throughput (TP_{mem}) of the application. Higher values of these
throughputs indicate a higher memory intensity of an application. Hence, the
memory intensiveness is positively correlated with M. TP_{comm} and TP_{mem} are
defined by Eqs. (1) and (2), respectively. S_{comm_i} represents the sum of the communication size between task i and all other tasks. S_{mem_i} represents the sum of
the memory read and write sizes of task i. N represents the total number of tasks
and $T_{profile}$ represents the execution time of the application when obtaining the
task communication and memory access information.

$$TP_{comm} = \frac{\sum_{i=1}^{N} S_{comm_i}}{T_{profile}}. \tag{1}$$

$$TP_{mem} = \frac{\sum_{i=1}^{N} S_{mem_i}}{T_{profile}}. \tag{2}$$

Then, the memory-aware PB value, M, is calculated by

$$M = C_{mem} \times (TP_{comm} + TP_{mem}), \tag{3}$$

where C_{mem} represents the memory coefficient, which is used to adjust the magnitude of M so that it can be fairly compared with H, and to reflect the impact
of the memory device capacity in the system on M.

To obtain H, we calculate the coefficient of variation of the task load of
the application. Hence, H represents the load heterogeneity of the tasks in the
application. The coefficient of variation of the task load (CV_{load}) is defined by
Eq. (4).

$$CV_{load} = \frac{\sqrt{\frac{1}{N}\sum_{i=1}^{N}(L_i - \bar{L})^2}}{\bar{L}}, \tag{4}$$

where L_i represents the load of task i, $\bar{L}$ represents the arithmetic mean of the load of all tasks, and N represents the total number of tasks. Then, the heterogeneity-aware PB value, H, is calculated by

$$H = C_{hetero} \times CV_{load}, \tag{5}$$

where C_{hetero} represents the heterogeneity coefficient, which is used to adjust the magnitude of H so that it can be fairly compared with M, and is also used to reflect the influence of the core heterogeneity in the system on H.

C_{mem} and C_{hetero} are empirical constants, and they can be obtained from simulations for application profiling. In our experiments, we found that C_{mem} is negatively correlated with the system memory capacity while C_{hetero} is positively correlated with the core performance difference. Hence both values need to be readjusted when the system configuration is changed to ensure that POSM can make accurate selections based on the PBs.

M and H are used to guide POSM proposed in this paper. For a combination of an application and a system, the two PB values are calculated, and the POSM selects the priority option corresponding to the larger PB value.

3.3   HPO and MPO Mapping Algorithms

Using the selected priority option, the proposed method then applies HPO or MPO mapping algorithm to emit a mapping of tasks to cores. These two algorithms work as follows.

The MPO algorithm first pairs two tasks heavily communicating with each other and maps the tasks in a pair to the same NUMA node to improve the locality. Then it distributes high-intensity communications evenly among NUMA nodes to reduce memory access load imbalance, which is similar to DeLoc [1]. Within a NUMA node, the algorithm assigns tasks to the Big and Small cores greedily from high to low L_i values.

The HPO algorithm first sorts tasks based on their L_i values and divides them into two groups: high-load and low-load, which correspond to the Big and Small cores, respectively. Within each group, it then maps tasks to the cores on different NUMA nodes with the same approach as the first step of MPO.

The two-step procedure of these two algorithms ensures that both mapping factors are considered and that the primary factor is not influenced by the secondary factor.

Table 1. The simulated heterogeneous system.

Parameter	Value
NUMA node (processor)	1× 8-core heterogeneous processor;
	L1I/L1D cache per core;
	L2 cache per core;
	L3 cache shared between 8 cores;
	1× memory controllers;
Processor core	8× 2.4 GHz cores; 8× 1.2 GHz cores;
	Nehalem performance model
L1I/L1D cache	256 KB; 8-way; 64-byte line size; LRU policy
L2 cache	2 MB; 8-way; LRU policy
L3 cache	8 MB; 16-way; LRU policy
Memory controller	45 ns latency; 36 GB/s bandwidth;
	8-way interleaved; DRAM directory model
Interconnect	25.6 GB/s bandwidth; network bus model

4 Evaluation

4.1 Experimental Environment

In the evaluation, the target heterogeneous multi-core NUMA system consists of two NUMA nodes and 16 processor cores. Each NUMA node consists of eight processor cores with two different clock frequencies, four of which run at 2.4 GHz and the other four run at 1.2 GHz. Table 1 shows the processor, cache and memory controller parameters for this system. To the best of our knowledge, there is no real system that exactly matches the target system at present, though such a system is promising and foreseeable. Therefore, we use the Sniper [4] simulator to simulate the target system.

As workloads, the following evaluations use the OpenMP version of the fluidanimate application from the PARSEC benchmark [3], the lavaMD application from the Rodinia benchmark [5], the FFT application from the SPLASH-2 benchmark [11] and the BT and MG applications from the NAS Parallel Benchmarks [2]. The characteristics of each application are shown in Table 2. The PARSEC-fluidanimat and Rodinia-lavaMD applications generate threads with different loads, while the SPLASH-2-FFT application generates threads with the same load. The NPB-BT and NPB-MG applications have a high memory intensity and can be used to evaluate the benefit of MPO.

Table 2. Benchmark application characteristics.

Benchmark Name	Task Load Difference	Memory Access Intensity
PARSEC-fluidanimate	High	Low
Rodinia-lavaMD	High	Low
NPB-BT	High	High
NPB-MG	Low	High
SPLASH-2-FFT	Low	Low

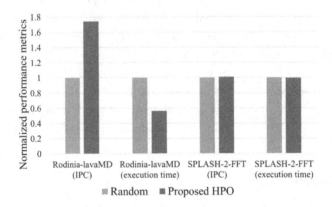

Fig. 3. Performance improvements from HPO.

4.2 Evaluation of HPO and MPO

The goal of this evaluation is to demonstrate the effectiveness of the mapping method proposed in this paper. The two priority options of this mapping method include HPO and MPO. We discusses the effectiveness of these two priority options separately. To show the performance improvements of the two options, this evaluation compares the execution time with HPO or MPO to the average execution time of multiple executions with random mapping. In the random mapping, the task mapping is calculated randomly and independently for each execution. The mapping results given by the proposed mapping optimization method or random mapping are used as the inputs for the simulator. We have developed an extended version of the Sniper simulator that provides an option to use a thread mapping configuration for the simulation [1].

The experimental results in Fig. 3 show that when using HPO, only some applications show an improvement over random mapping. Rodinia-lavaMD can obtain performance improvements in terms of instructions per cycle (IPC) and execution time. This is due to the high CV_{load} value in this application. In contrast, SPLASH-2-FFT shows a CV_{load} value close to zero, indicating that the computation loads among this application's tasks are similar. Therefore, changing the task mapping has no impact on the performance of SPLASH-2-FFT.

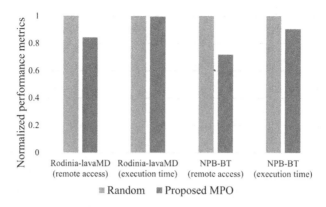

Fig. 4. Performance improvements from MPO.

The experimental results in Fig. 4 show that MPO is also not suitable for all applications. Both of the benchmarks, Rodinia-lavaMD and NPB-BT, can gain a certain performance improvement from the reduction in the number of remote memory accesses. However, Rodinia-lavaMD exhibits almost no change in the execution time, while NPB-BT shows about 10% shorter execution time. This is due to the different intensities of memory accesses between the two applications. The communication and memory access intensities of Rodinia-lavaMD cannot saturate the capacity of the memory device on a single NUMA node. Therefore, although Rodinia-lavaMD can achieve a certain reduction in number of remote memory accesses, the overall execution time does not decrease significantly.

These two results show that one priority option cannot provide a suitable mapping for all kinds of applications. This fact shows the necessity of the two mapping priority options and the switching mechanism proposed in this paper.

4.3   Evaluation of POSM

To show the benefits of POSM, we evaluate the impacts of different mapping methods on the performance of a set of applications with different characteristics. Our mapping method is expected to improve performance consistently by switching the priority according to each application's characteristics. In this evaluation, the application set consists of the following five benchmark kernels: PARSEC-fluidanimate, Rodinia-lavaMD, NPB-BT, NPB-MG, and SPLASH-2-FFT. First, the simulator uses the default Packed mapping, which maps the neighboring tasks to the same NUMA node, to get the baseline execution time for each application. The performance improvements of tested mapping methods are obtained by measuring their execution times relative to the baseline results.

To evaluate the accuracy of POSM, we first calculate the M and H values for the five applications, respectively. Figure 5 shows M and H for each application, normalized to range between 0 and 1. Then, we execute each application twice and observe the actual execution time. From the results in Fig. 6, the appropriate priority option for each application can be determined. By observing the

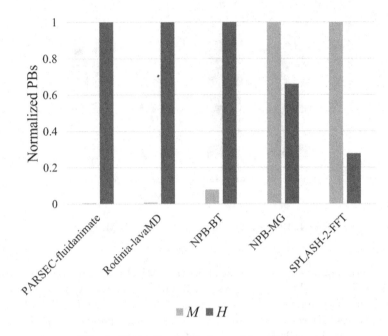

Fig. 5. Normalized PBs for each application.

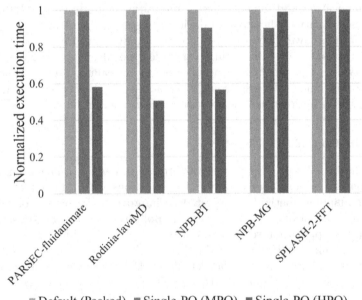

Fig. 6. Normalized execution time for each application.

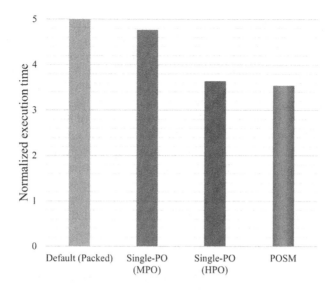

Fig. 7. The overall performance of the application set.

calculated PBs in Fig. 5 and the execution time in Fig. 6, it can be found that a larger PB value results in a shorter execution time. These results show that the proposed PB metrics can accurately predict which priority option will yield a better performance, which means that POSM can use them to determine the best mapping algorithm for a target application. Therefore, POSM can consistently improve performance across the set of applications.

By selecting the best mapping algorithm for each application, POSM can achieve a higher total performance improvement. We verify this point by comparing the total execution time of the application set obtained using four different mapping methods including Packed, MPO, HPO and POSM. As shown in Fig. 7, although close to HPO, POSM still shows a marginal improvement compared with HPO and achieves the shortest total execution time. This is due to the small improvement of the applications suitable for MPO in this evaluation. This result demonstrates the benefit of the HPO algorithm and the importance of not ignoring the memory factor. As a result, compared to other methods that do not switch mapping priorities, the proposed method can achieve higher overall improvements in execution time when dealing with a set of applications with different characteristics.

5 Conclusions

In heterogeneous multi-core NUMA systems, task mapping becomes more challenging due to the heterogeneity in memory access and core performance. In order to take into account the diversity of system configuration and application characteristics, this paper proposed a task mapping method that switches between two priority options to determine the best mapping for the target application on the target system. This method includes two priority options, MPO and HPO, and a priority option switching mechanism, POSM. We also introduced metrics to estimate the benefit of each mapping priority option.

The evaluation results showed that the proposed POSM can accurately select appropriate mapping priority options by analyzing application characteristics and system configurations. In the evaluation with a set of different applications, POSM can consistently improve performance for each application. Compared with other methods that do not switch mapping priorities, our method can achieve higher overall improvements in execution time when dealing with applications with different characteristics.

Our future work will extend POSM to use online profiling. By obtaining the profiling information online, POSM can be applied during the application runtime.

Acknowledgements. This work was partially supported by MEXT Next Generation High-Performance Computing Infrastructures and Applications R&D Program "R&D of A Quantum-Annealing-Assisted Next Generation HPC Infrastructure and its Applications," Grant-in-Aid for Scientific Research(A) #20H00593, Grant-in-Aid for Challenging Research (Exploratory) #22K19764, and JST, the establishment of university fellowships towards the creation of science technology innovation, Grant Number JPMJFS2102.

References

1. Agung, M., Amrizal, M.A., Egawa, R., Takizawa, H.: DeLoc: a locality and memory-congestion-aware task mapping method for modern NUMA systems. IEEE Access **8**, 6937–6953 (2020)
2. Bailey, D., Harris, T., Saphir, W., Van Der Wijngaart, R., Woo, A., Yarrow, M.: The NAS parallel benchmarks 2.0. Technical report, Technical Report NAS-95-020, NASA Ames Research Center (1995)
3. Bienia, C., Kumar, S., Singh, J.P., Li, K.: The parsec benchmark suite: characterization and architectural implications. In: Proceedings of the 17th International Conference on Parallel Architectures and Compilation Techniques, pp. 72–81 (2008)
4. Carlson, T.E., Heirman, W., Eeckhout, L.: Sniper: exploring the level of abstraction for scalable and accurate parallel multi-core simulation. In: Proceedings of 2011 International Conference for High Performance Computing, Networking, Storage and Analysis, pp. 1–12 (2011)
5. Che, S., et al.: Rodinia: a benchmark suite for heterogeneous computing. In: 2009 IEEE International Symposium on Workload Characterization (IISWC), pp. 44–54. IEEE (2009)
6. Chen, J., Nayyar, N., John, L.K.: Mapping of applications to heterogeneous multicores based on micro-architecture independent characteristics. In: Third Workshop on Unique Chips and Systems, ISPASS2007 (2017)
7. Diener, M., Cruz, E.H.M., Alves, M.A.Z., Alhakeem, M.S., Navaux, P.O.A., Heiß, H.-U.: Locality and balance for communication-aware thread mapping in multicore systems. In: Träff, J.L., Hunold, S., Versaci, F. (eds.) Euro-Par 2015. LNCS, vol.

9233, pp. 196–208. Springer, Heidelberg (2015). https://doi.org/10.1007/978-3-662-48096-0_16

8. Jeannot, E., Mercier, G., Tessier, F.: Process placement in multicore clusters: algorithmic issues and practical techniques. IEEE Trans. Parallel Distrib. Syst. **25**(4), 993–1002 (2013)

9. Mittal, S.: A survey of techniques for architecting and managing asymmetric multicore processors. ACM Comput. Surv. (CSUR) **48**(3), 1–38 (2016)

10. Saez, J.C., Castro, F., Prieto-Matias, M.: Enabling performance portability of data-parallel OpenMP applications on asymmetric multicore processors. In: 49th International Conference on Parallel Processing-ICPP, pp. 1–11 (2020)

11. Woo, S.C., Ohara, M., Torrie, E., Singh, J.P., Gupta, A.: The splash-2 programs: characterization and methodological considerations. ACM SIGARCH Comput. Architect. News **23**(2), 24–36 (1995)

12. Yu, T., et al.: Collaborative heterogeneity-aware OS scheduler for asymmetric multicore processors. IEEE Trans. Parallel Distrib. Syst. **32**(5), 1224–1237 (2020)

Multi-GPU Scaling of a Conservative Weakly Compressible Solver for Large-Scale Two-Phase Flow Simulation

Kai Yang[1]([✉]) and Takayuki Aoki[2]

[1] Department of Mechanical Engineering, Tokyo Institute of Technology,
2-12-1 i7-3, O-okayama, Meguro-ku, Tokyo 152-8550, Japan
`yang@sim.gsic.titech.ac.jp`
[2] Global Scientific Information and Computing Center, Tokyo Institute of Technology,
2-12-1 i7-3, O-okayama, Meguro-ku, Tokyo 152-8550, Japan
`taoki@gsic.titech.ac.jp`

Abstract. To address the demand for high-performance large-scale simulation of two-phase flows, a momentum-conserving weakly compressible Navier-Stokes solver with multi-GPU computation is proposed. Following the principle of consistent transport, the phase-field model and VOF method are coupled with the momentum equation respectively. Combined with the evolving pressure projection method to damp the acoustic wave, this solver aims at a robust and accurate computation of violent two-phase flows with a high density ratio, while taking advantage of fully explicit time integration of the weakly compressible Navier-Stokes equations. Factors affecting the performance and scalability of multi-GPU computing, including domain partitioning, communication hiding, and solver choice, are discussed and analyzed. Finally, the conservative solver is used to simulate the Rayleigh-Taylor instability, milk crown and liquid jet atomization problems. Accurate and delicate evolution process of the two-phase interface is demonstrated.

Keywords: Multiple GPUs · Explicit method · Momentum conservation · Two-phase flow · Volume of fluid

1 Introduction

In recent years, the use of GPU as computational accelerator has attracted wide attention. Powerful computing performance and high bandwidth for data transfer are the main features of GPU. At the same time, general programming environments such as OpenCL and CUDA have emerged, which greatly promote the application of GPU in many fields including scientific computing. In order to make the best use of the increasing computing performance of modern supercomputers with heterogeneous architecture, new demand on scalability is put forward for the numerical methods. In the simulation of incompressible flow, a Poisson equation should be solved implicitly. This poses a great challenge for massively parallel and scalable computing because of the complexity in the iteration algorithms [5] and the slow convergence rate for two-phase flows with a high density contrast [20].

H. Takizawa et al. (Eds.): PDCAT 2022, LNCS 13798, pp. 16–27, 2023.
https://doi.org/10.1007/978-3-031-29927-8_2

On the other hand, weakly compressible Navier-Stokes equations are becoming a popular alternative for simulation of incompressible fluid flows. An independent pressure evolution equation can be derived under the low Mach number and isothermal condition [13], and it can be explicitly integrated in time. Benefiting from the hyperbolic-parabolic system of weakly compressible Navier-Stokes equations, excellent performance and scalability can be expected for large-scale computing. Recently, a weakly compressible scheme combined with adaptive mesh refinement has been successfully applied to simulating two-phase flows [8].

However, several major problems remain in weakly compressible method including the oscillation of the velocity and pressure induced by the acoustic wave, momentum conservation and consistent transport for two-phase flows and the accuracy of interface capturing and curvature estimation. Meanwhile, the strong scaling and performance of weakly compressible solves on the multi-GPU cluster should be evaluated.

The remainder part of this paper briefly presents the equations and our numerical methods, followed by the study on multi-GPU computation. Finally, numerical results of large-scale computation of two-phase flows are shown.

2   Numerical Methods

2.1   Con-CAC-LS

The first conservative solver for two-phase flow simulation introduced here is referred as Con-CAC-LS, which represents the combination of the conservative Navier-Stokes equation, conservative Allen-Cahn equation and level-set method. The momentum equation in conservative form is

$$\frac{\partial \rho \boldsymbol{u}}{\partial t} + \nabla \cdot (\rho \boldsymbol{u} \otimes \boldsymbol{u}) = -\nabla p + \nabla \cdot \left(\mu \left(\nabla \boldsymbol{u} + \nabla \boldsymbol{u}^T\right)\right) + \boldsymbol{F}. \tag{1}$$

We simulate an immiscible two-phase fluid system by using the one-fluid model. An indicator function ϕ is used to distinguish the different fluid regions in the domain, and the motion of the interface between two fluids is governed by the conservative Allen-Cahn equation of the phase-field model [3],

$$\frac{\partial \phi}{\partial t} + \nabla \cdot (\phi \boldsymbol{u}) = \nabla \cdot \left[M \left(\nabla \phi - \frac{4\phi(1-\phi)}{W} \boldsymbol{n} \right) \right], \tag{2}$$

where M is the mobility, $W = 3\Delta x$ is the width of interface, and $\boldsymbol{n}$ is the unit outward-normal vector of the interface. Fluid properties such as the density and viscosity can be evaluated on the basis of the phase-field function, as $\rho = \phi \rho_h + (1-\phi) \rho_l$, $\mu = \phi \mu_h + (1-\phi) \mu_l$, where the physical properties of the heavy and light fluids are indicated by the subscripts h and l, respectively.

In order to achieve the consistent and conservative transport of mass and momentum, the convective parts of Eq. (1) and Eq. (2) are coupled in the finite-volume formulation. A collocated grid system is used for spatial discretization, which means all primitive variables are defined at the center of each cell. Different with the VOF method, the volume flux crossing a cell face in the conservative Allen-Cahn equation is given by

$$\mathcal{F}^V = u_f\phi - M\left(\nabla\phi - \frac{4\phi(1-\phi)}{W}\boldsymbol{n}\right),\tag{3}$$

where the subscript f denotes an arbitrary cell face. u_f is a face-centered advection velocity, and its construction will be described in the Sect. 2.3. Next, the mass and momentum fluxes can be calculated sequentially based on the volume flux by using the same method as in our previous work [17]. A third-order MUSCL scheme is applied for the spatial reconstruction of the convective terms. We use a three-stage third-order strong-stability-preserving Runge-Kutta (SSP-RK-3) scheme for the time integration of the transport equations. The viscous part of Eq. (1) is solved by the second-order central difference scheme in space and first-order Euler forward scheme in time.

Since the level-set function has a superior geometric representation of the interface, we use the level-set method as a complementary tool for calculating the interface normal and curvature with better accuracy. The time evolution of level-set function ψ follows the advection equation:

$$\frac{\partial\psi}{\partial t} + \boldsymbol{u}\cdot\nabla\psi = 0.\tag{4}$$

The advection term is calculated by a third-order WENO scheme and the temporal derivative is integrated by the SSP-RK-3 scheme. The coupling between the phase-field function and level-set function is realized by the hyperbolic tangent and its inverse function.

The surface tension force in the two-phase flow is formulated by a density-scaled continuum surface force (CSF) model [19], F_s has the following form:

$$F_s = \frac{2\rho}{\rho_h + \rho_l}\sigma\kappa\nabla\phi,\tag{5}$$

where σ is the coefficient of surface tension, and κ is the curvature of the interface. The normal vector in Eq. (2) and the curvature in Eq. (5) are calculated by using the level-set function with the second-order central difference scheme.

2.2 Con-PLIC-HF

The second conservative solver combines the momentum equation Eq. (1), PLIC and height function method. Therefore, it is referred as Con-PLIC-HF. In this solver, the motion of the interface between two fluids is governed by the volume of fluid (VOF) equation

$$\frac{\partial f}{\partial t} + \nabla\cdot(\boldsymbol{u}f) = f\nabla\cdot\boldsymbol{u},\tag{6}$$

where f represents the volume fraction of the heavy fluid. Different with the conservative Allen-Cahn equation Eq. 2, the above VOF equation cannot be used as a substitute for the continuity equation representing conservation of mass. Hence additional continuity equations for heavy and light fluids need to be solved simultaneously:

$$\frac{\partial f\rho_h}{\partial t} + \nabla\cdot(\boldsymbol{u}f\rho_h) = 0,\tag{7}$$

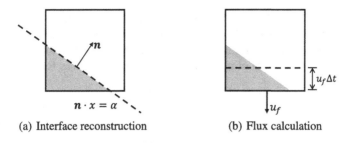

(a) Interface reconstruction   (b) Flux calculation

Fig. 1. PLIC method.

$$\frac{\partial(1-f)\rho_l}{\partial t} + \nabla \cdot [\boldsymbol{u}(1-f)\rho_l] = 0. \tag{8}$$

Similarly, the convective part of Eq. (1) is also split into two equations for heavy and light fluids, respectively:

$$\frac{\partial f\rho_h \boldsymbol{u}}{\partial t} + \nabla \cdot (f\rho_h \boldsymbol{u} \otimes \boldsymbol{u}) = 0, \tag{9}$$

$$\frac{\partial(1-f)\rho_l \boldsymbol{u}}{\partial t} + \nabla \cdot [(1-f)\rho_l \boldsymbol{u} \otimes \boldsymbol{u}] = 0. \tag{10}$$

The average density and momentum of the fluid can be obtained directly by summing the two components.

As one of the geometric VOF methods, the piecewise linear interface calculation (PLIC) method approximates the interface in each interfacial cell as a line in two dimensions or a plane in three dimensions, as illustrated in Fig. 1(a). The linear interface is defined by the equation

$$\boldsymbol{n} \cdot \boldsymbol{x} = \alpha, \tag{11}$$

where α is a constant that enforces the volume fraction cut by the interface is f. Here, the interface normal $\boldsymbol{n}$ is computed by the mixed Youngs-centered (MYC) method [1]. Based on the orthogonal grid, we apply the analytical method [12] to solve the interface reconstruction and flux calculation process as illustrated in Fig. 1.

We use the Weymouth & Yue method [15] to solve the VOF equation Eq. (6), where the multi-dimensional advection of Eq. (6) is split into a series of one-dimensional advection problem. In order to make the transport of mass and momentum consistent with that of volume fraction, Eq. (7)–(10) are also solved by the dimensional-splitting method. The density and momentum at the cell face are reconstructed by the Bell-Collela-Glaz (BCG) second-order upwind scheme [2,4]. To couple the transport equations, the numerical fluxes of mass and momentum are evaluated through multiplying the reconstructed value by the flux of volume fraction $\mathcal{F}^V$ which is computed by the PLIC method:

$$\mathcal{F}^{Y_h} = \boldsymbol{Y}_{h,f}\mathcal{F}^{V,h}, \tag{12a}$$

$$\mathcal{F}^{Y_l} = \boldsymbol{Y}_{l,f}\mathcal{F}^{V,l}, \tag{12b}$$

where $Y = (\rho, \rho u)$ and Y_f represents the reconstructed quantities at the cell face by the BCG scheme. $\mathcal{F}^{Y_h}$ and $\mathcal{F}^{Y_l}$ denote the amount of mass and momentum transported across the cell face during the time step. As illustrated in Fig. 1(b), the volume flux of the heavy phase $\mathcal{F}^{V,h}$ and that of the light phase $\mathcal{F}^{V,l}$ are related as follows:

$$\mathcal{F}^{V,l} = u_f \Delta t - \mathcal{F}^{V,h}. \tag{13}$$

In the case of geometric VOF method, it is straightforward to apply the height function method for the estimation of interface curvature:

$$\kappa = \frac{H_{xx} + H_{yy} + H_{xx}H_y^2 + H_{yy}H_x^2 - 2H_{xy}H_xH_y}{\left(1 + H_x^2 + H_y^2\right)^{3/2}}, \tag{14}$$

where H is the height function. An improved height function technique is adopted here with a new discretization of the partial derivatives of the height function [7], which has a better accuracy than the standard central difference scheme.

2.3 Evolving Pressure Projection Method

Instead of the pressure Poisson equation derived from the incompressible Navier-Stokes equation, the pressure evolution equation for weakly compressible and isothermal fluid flow can be written as [13]:

$$\frac{\partial p}{\partial t} + \rho c_s^2 \nabla \cdot u = 0, \tag{15}$$

where c_s is an artificial speed of sound, which is required to be large enough to satisfy the low Mach number condition $Ma = |u|_{\max} / c_s \ll 1$. The diffusion term of pressure is neglected because our proposed new method is more effective in suppressing acoustic waves.

Following the Chorin's projection method for solving incompressible Navier-Stokes equations, an intermediate velocity u^* is updated from u^n at time step n by solving the momentum equation, Eq. (1), without the pressure gradient term. The intermediate velocity needs to be corrected by a pressure projection step, which gives the solution at the next time step u^{n+1}:

$$\frac{u^{n+1} - u^*}{\Delta t} = -\frac{1}{\rho}\nabla p^{n+1}. \tag{16}$$

In the weakly compressible flow simulation, we have proposed an evolving pressure projection method [16] to alleviate the undesirable effect of the acoustic wave and consequently diminish the fluctuations in the velocity and pressure fields. In our previous formulation, the pressure and velocity are corrected by a two-step iteration, which can be simplified to a new pressure evolution equation as follows:

$$\frac{\partial p}{\partial t} + \rho c_s^2 \left[\nabla \cdot u^* - \nabla \cdot \left(\frac{1}{\rho}\nabla p\right)\Delta t\right] = 0. \tag{17}$$

This hyperbolic equation for pressure can be explicitly advanced in time by using a local spatial stencil. It significantly benefits scalability of computation in spite of the

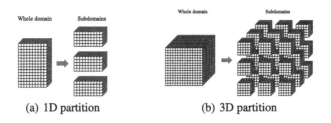

(a) 1D partition   (b) 3D partition

Fig. 2. Domain partition for multi-GPU computation.

speed-of-sound restriction on the time step. It is worth noting that the Eq. (17) reduces to the Poisson equation when the speed of sound is infinite or when the evolution of pressure converges with time. This means that in the limit case, the proposed method will converge to the incompressible fluid flow. To avoid pressure-velocity decoupling when the pressure projection is performed on the collocated grid, we apply the method of the approximate pressure projection [10].

3   Multi-GPU Computation

Stencil-based numerical methods such as the finite volume method naturally fit the framework of CUDA which is the programming interface on GPU. The idea for parallel computing on multiple GPUs is to decompose the whole computational domain into several subdomains, each of them is computed by one GPU respectively, as shown in Fig. 2. However, in practical problems, the subdomains are not completely independent of each other. The general situation is that the data at boundaries of adjacent subdomain need to be accessed. A common approach for data communication between GPUs is the message passing interface (MPI). While only pointers to CPU (host) memory is accepted in a regular MPI implementation, the buffers for communication allocated in the device memory of GPU can be passed by using CUDA-aware MPI.

An effective approach to improve the performance of multi-GPU computation is hiding the communication time [14], which is realized by overlapping the kernel execution for inner cells and the data transfer for outer cells of the subdomain. With the help of CUDA stream technique, the outer cells that account for only a small fraction of the total number of grids are first computed by the CUDA stream with the higher priority. And the computing kernel for inner cells is launched with a low-priority stream. Once the computation of the high-priority stream is completed, the communication process for outer cells is performed simultaneously with the inner computation. We have implemented the overlapping technique for the program with 1D domain partition which corresponds to Fig. 2(a). Currently, our 3D domain partition program corresponding to Fig. 2(b) does not support overlapping communication and computation.

In this work, we use the NVIDIA Tesla V100 SXM2 on the FLOW Type II supercomputer to perform all of the computation. NVLink and InfiniBand EDR are deployed in this supercomputer for the intra-node and inter-node connection, respectively. The HPC SDK 21.2 is employed to compile the MPI+CUDA program.

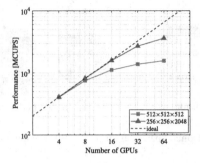

Fig. 3. Strong scaling of Con-CAC-LS with 1D domain partition (overlapping).

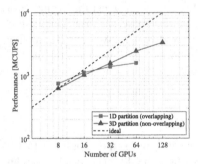

Fig. 4. Comparison between 1D domain partition (overlapping) and 3D domain partition (non-overlapping) for the strong scaling of Con-CAC-LS on a $512 \times 512 \times 512$ grid.

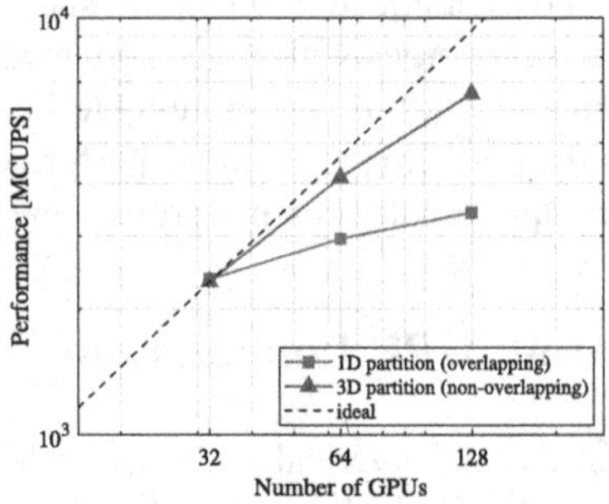

Fig. 5. Comparison between 1D domain partition (overlapping) and 3D domain partition (non-overlapping) for the strong scaling of Con-CAC-LS on a $1024 \times 1024 \times 1024$ grid.

3.1 Performance of Con-CAC-LS

In this section, the strong scaling, which concerns the speedup for a fixed problem size with respect to the number of processors, is evaluated for our multi-GPU solvers. The performance is measured by the mega cells update per second (MCUPS). In the case of 1D domain partition with the overlapping technique, the amount of computation of each subdomain keeps decreasing as the number of GPUs increases, but the amount of data communication does not change. Hence the communication cannot be hidden anymore. As shown in Fig. 3, the computational performance does not increase proportionally with the number of GPUs. Moreover, different domain shapes with the same total number of meshes also affect the performance of 1D domain partition. The results show that strong scaling from 4 to 16 GPUs achieves even ideal performance in the rectangular domain, but behaves much worse in the cubic domain.

Figure 4 and Fig. 5 show the comparison between 1D domain partition and 3D domain partition for the strong scaling of Con-CAC-LS in the cubic domain with different resolutions. Although the overlapping technique is not implemented in the program

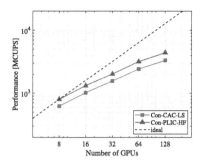

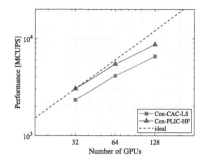

Fig. 6. Comparison between Con-PLIC-HF and Con-CAC-LS with 3D domain partition (non-overlapping) for the strong scaling on a $512 \times 512 \times 512$ grid.

Fig. 7. Comparison between Con-PLIC-HF and Con-CAC-LS with 3D domain partition (non-overlapping) for the strong scaling on a $1024 \times 1024 \times 1024$ grid.

with 3D domain partition, the 3D partition demonstrates better scalability and higher performance on a large number of GPUs. This significant advantage comes from the variation of the surface area-to-volume ratio with the number of GPUs at different partitioning methods. When the computational domain is partitioned in multiple dimensions at the same time, each subdomain not only decreases in computation with smaller volume, but also decreases in data communication with smaller surface area instead of remaining constant as in the one-dimensional partition.

3.2 Performance of Con-PLIC-HF

For the dimensional-splitting method used in the transport part of the Con-PLIC-HF, we optimize the data communication accordingly. When the transport equation is solved in a certain dimension, data communication is performed only in the direction of this dimension. The strong scaling of Con-PLIC-HF with 3D domain partition in Fig. 6 and Fig. 7. Compared to Con-CAC-LS, Con-PLIC-HF has almost identical scalability but with higher overall performance. Although Con-PLIC-HF solves more transport equations, on the one hand, the analytical method greatly simplifies the computation of the interface geometry reconstruction, and on the other hand, it does not use the higher-order Runge-Kutta time integration, which multiplies the computational effort, as Con-CAC-LS does.

4 Numerical Results

4.1 Rayleigh-Taylor Instability

The first numerical result is to discuss the mesh dependency of the two-phase flow simulation. A classical two-phase flow phenomenon known as Rayleigh-Taylor instability is simulated. We follow the computation conditions described in a reference paper [9]. Initially the heavy fluid with density $\rho_h = 1.225$ is placed on top of the light fluid with

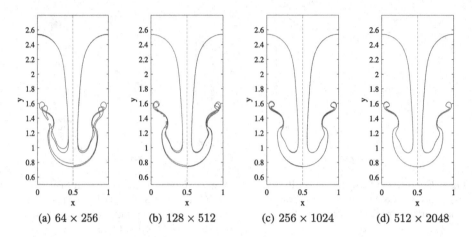

(a) 64 × 256   (b) 128 × 512   (c) 256 × 1024   (d) 512 × 2048

Fig. 8. Interface location of the Rayleigh-Taylor instability at $t = 0.9$ predicted by Con-CAC-LS (red line), Con-PLIC-HF (blue line) and the reference solution (black line) with different mesh resolutions. (Color figure online)

density $\rho_l = 0.1694$. The viscosity of both fluids is $\mu_h = \mu_l = 0.00313$. The two-phase interface is horizontally positioned at the center of a 1×4 rectangular domain and perturbed with a cosine wave of amplitude 0.05. This problem is free of the surface tension force, and only the gravity $g = 9.81$ is applied. At the beginning, the fluid in the whole domain is at rest. Slip conditions are imposed on the enclosing walls.

The interface location of the Rayleigh-Taylor instability at $t = 0.9$ is depicted in Fig. 8 with four different mesh resolutions including 64×256, 128×512, 256×1024 and 512×2048. The results indicate that Con-PLIC-HF has a better mesh convergence than Con-CAC-LS and is more accurate when the mesh resolution is insufficient.

4.2 Drop Impacting on a Thin Liquid Film

To demonstrate the accuracy of our method in resolving three-dimensional interface topology, we solve the problem of a drop impacting on a thin liquid film and a classical phenomenon known as milk crown is reproduced. This problem has been extensively studied by numerical simulation, experiment and theoretical analysis [18]. The water tank considered measures 60 mm × 60 mm × 20 mm. Considering the symmetry of this computation, only a quarter of the water tank is calculated and discretized by a $768 \times 768 \times 512$ uniform grid. The depth of the thin liquid film is 0.82 mm. Initially the liquid film and air are at rest. A droplet of diameter $D = 7.04$ mm is falling with the speed of 1.61 m/s. The physical properties of the liquid and gas are $\rho_h = 1000$ kg/m³, $\rho_l = 1$ kg/m³, $\mu_h = 1.0 \times 10^{-3}$ Pa·s, $\mu_l = 1.0 \times 10^{-5}$ Pa·s, and surface tension coefficient $\sigma = 0.07275$ N/m. The Weber number is 250 in this case. No-slip conditions are imposed on all walls. This computation is performed on 18 V100 GPUs.

The time evolution of the liquid surface is depicted in Fig. 9 and Fig. 10 for two solvers, respectively. By comparing the results, Con-PLIC-HF solver can resolve the

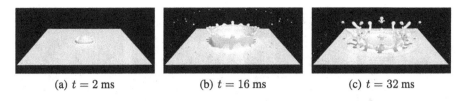

(a) $t = 2$ ms   (b) $t = 16$ ms   (c) $t = 32$ ms

Fig. 9. Results of 3D drop impacting on liquid film by Con-CAC-LS solver.

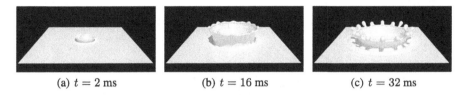

(a) $t = 2$ ms   (b) $t = 16$ ms   (c) $t = 32$ ms

Fig. 10. Results of 3D drop impacting on liquid film by Con-PLIC-HF solver.

fingering structure of the interface very well. Con-CAC-LS solver produces a lot of splashing drops and the free rim breaks up. But they should not occur at this low Weber number case.

4.3   Liquid Jet in Gas Cross-Flow

The last simulation presented in this paper is a three-dimensional liquid jet in gas cross-flow. This problem has been studied in a existing literature [6] and also used by us to verify the importance of consistent transport and momentum conservation [17]. The jet column predicted by a non-conservative method will break up within a short distance after leaving the nozzle, affected by the gas cross-flow. And the droplets formed after breaking up are quickly blown to the downstream region with the gas. On the contrary, our conservative solver can produce more accurate simulation results on the interface shape and trajectory of the jet.

The computational domain size measures 2.0 cm $\times$ 1.5 cm $\times$ 3.5 cm and is discretized by a $1024 \times 768 \times 1792$ uniform grid. The liquid nozzle of diameter 0.8 mm is placed on the bottom wall and centered at $(0.2$ cm$, 0.75$ cm$, 0$ cm$)$. The gas blows in from the left boundary in the positive x direction with a constant velocity V_g, and the liquid is injected from the nozzle along the positive z direction with a constant velocity V_l. The physical properties are listed in Table 1. No-slip conditions are imposed on

Table 1. Physical parameters and fluid properties for liquid jet in gas cross-flow simulations.

ρ_l [kg/m^3]	ρ_g [kg/m^3]	μ_l [Pa·s]	μ_g [Pa·s]	σ [N/m]	V_l [m/s]	V_g [m/s]
118	1.18	0.000307	0.0000186	0.0708	51.45	54.8

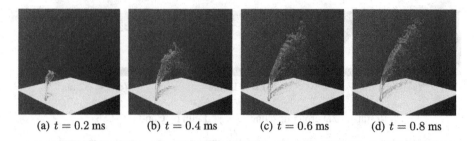

(a) $t = 0.2$ ms   (b) $t = 0.4$ ms   (c) $t = 0.6$ ms   (d) $t = 0.8$ ms

Fig. 11. Time evolution of liquid jet surface in gas cross-flow.

the bottom wall $z_{\min}$ except for the nozzle. The outflow conditions are applied to the right boundary $x_{\max}$. Other walls at $y_{\min}$, $y_{\max}$ and $z_{\max}$ have the slip conditions. This computation is performed on 42 V100 GPUs by using the Con-PLIC-HF solver.

Numerical results for the time evolution of the liquid jet are depicted in Fig. 11. In the large-scale simulation with our conservative solver, a great number of liquid drops with different sizes are successfully resolved. The trajectory of the liquid column is also in good agreement with other numerical simulations and an experimental study [11].

5 Conclusion

This paper presents the multi-GPU computation for simulating two-phase flows with our original conservative weakly compressible Navier-Stokes solvers which are fully explicit and inherently parallel. Con-CAC-LS that involves conservative Allen-Cahn equation and level-set method and Con-PLIC-HF that involves PLIC and height function method are proposed under the principle of consistent transport and momentum conservation. For multi-GPU computation, the strong scaling with two types of domain partition is evaluated and a better scalability is exhibited by the 3D partition. The technique for overlapping communication and computation is implemented and discussed. The scaling test also shows that Con-PLIC-HF has a overall higher performance.

After demonstrating the superior mesh convergence of Con-PLIC-HF through simulations of the Rayleigh-Taylor instability, we use this solver to perform large-scale simulations of milk crown and liquid jet problems. In these two-phase flow computations with high density ratio and high Reynolds number, we present high fidelity results with detailed reproduction of the complex interface structures. The simulations have shown the excellent applicability of our solver.

Acknowledgements. This research was partly supported by a Grant-in-Aid for Scientific Research (S) 19H05613, from the Japan Society for the Promotion of Science (JSPS), and Joint Usage/Research Center for Interdisciplinary Large-scale Information Infrastructures (JHPCN), jh200018 and jh210013, and High Performance Computing Infrastructure (HPCI) hp210129 projects, and JST SPRING, grant number JPMJSP2106. The authors thank the Global Scientific Information and Computing Center, Tokyo Institute of Technology for use of the computing resources of the TSUBAME 3.0 supercomputer and the Information Technology Center of Nagoya University for use of the computing resources of the Flow Type II supercomputer.

References

1. Aulisa, E., Manservisi, S., Scardovelli, R., Zaleski, S.: Interface reconstruction with least-squares fit and split advection in three-dimensional cartesian geometry. J. Comput. Phys. **225**(2), 2301–2319 (2007)
2. Bell, J.B., Colella, P., Glaz, H.M.: A second-order projection method for the incompressible Navier-Stokes equations. J. Comput. Phys. **85**(2), 257–283 (1989)
3. Chiu, P.H., Lin, Y.T.: A conservative phase field method for solving incompressible two-phase flows. J. Comput. Phys. **230**(1), 185–204 (2011)
4. Fuster, D., Popinet, S.: An all-Mach method for the simulation of bubble dynamics problems in the presence of surface tension. J. Comput. Phys. **374**, 752–768 (2018)
5. Ha, S., Park, J., You, D.: A GPU-accelerated semi-implicit fractional-step method for numerical solutions of incompressible Navier-Stokes equations. J. Comput. Phys. **352**, 246–264 (2018)
6. Li, X., Soteriou, M.C.: High fidelity simulation and analysis of liquid jet atomization in a gaseous crossflow at intermediate weber numbers. Phys. Fluids **28**(8), 082101 (2016)
7. Lopez, J., Zanzi, C., Gomez, P., Zamora, R., Faura, F., Hernandez, J.: An improved height function technique for computing interface curvature from volume fractions. Comput. Methods Appl. Mech. Eng. **198**(33–36), 2555–2564 (2009)
8. Matsushita, S., Aoki, T.: Gas-liquid two-phase flows simulation based on weakly compressible scheme with interface-adapted AMR method. J. Comput. Phys. **445**, 110605 (2021)
9. Mirjalili, S., Ivey, C.B., Mani, A.: Comparison between the diffuse interface and volume of fluid methods for simulating two-phase flows. Int. J. Multiph. Flow **116**, 221–238 (2019)
10. Popinet, S.: An accurate adaptive solver for surface-tension-driven interfacial flows. J. Comput. Phys. **228**(16), 5838–5866 (2009)
11. Sallam, K., Aalburg, C., Faeth, G.: Breakup of round nonturbulent liquid jets in gaseous crossflow. AIAA J. **42**(12), 2529–2540 (2004)
12. Scardovelli, R., Zaleski, S.: Analytical relations connecting linear interfaces and volume fractions in rectangular grids. J. Comput. Phys. **164**(1), 228–237 (2000)
13. Toutant, A.: General and exact pressure evolution equation. Phys. Lett. A **381**(44), 3739–3742 (2017)
14. Wang, X., Aoki, T.: Multi-GPU performance of incompressible flow computation by lattice Boltzmann method on GPU cluster. Parallel Comput. **37**(9), 521–535 (2011)
15. Weymouth, G.D., Yue, D.K.P.: Conservative volume-of-fluid method for free-surface simulations on cartesian-grids. J. Comput. Phys. **229**(8), 2853–2865 (2010)
16. Yang, K., Aoki, T.: Weakly compressible Navier-Stokes solver based on evolving pressure projection method for two-phase flow simulations. J. Comput. Phys. **431**, 110113 (2021)
17. Yang, K., Aoki, T.: A momentum-conserving weakly compressible Navier-Stokes solver for simulation of violent two-phase flows with high density ratio. Submitted (2022)
18. Yarin, A.L., et al.: Drop impact dynamics: splashing, spreading, receding, bouncing. Ann. Rev. Fluid Mech. **38**(1), 159–192 (2006)
19. Yokoi, K.: A density-scaled continuum surface force model within a balanced force formulation. J. Comput. Phys. **278**, 221–228 (2014)
20. Zaspel, P., Griebel, M.: Solving incompressible two-phase flows on multi-GPU clusters. Comput. Fluids **80**, 356–364 (2013)

Improving the Performance of Lattice Boltzmann Method with Pipelined Algorithm on A Heterogeneous Multi-zone Processor

Qingyang Zhang[1,2], Lei Xu[3], Rongliang Chen[3], Lin Chen[1,2], Xinhai Chen[1,2], Qinglin Wang[1,2], Jie Liu[1,2], and Bo Yang[1,2(✉)]

[1] Science and Technology on Parallel and Distributed Processing Laboratory, National University of Defense Technology, Changsha 410000, People's Republic of China
`yangbo78@nudt.edu.cn`
[2] Laboratory of Software Engineering for Complex Systems, National University of Defense Technology, Changsha 410000, People's Republic of China
[3] Shenzhen Institutes of Advanced Technology, Chinese Academy of Sciences, Shenzhen 518055, People's Republic of China

Abstract. Lattice Boltzmann method (LBM) has become a powerful method in computational fluid dynamics and has drawn more and more attention in high-performance computing due to its particulate nature and local dynamics, especially on recent multi-core or many-core platforms. This paper develops a parallel software framework for 3D LBM simulation on a heterogeneous multi-zone processor, MT-3000. An improved pipelined algorithm named *Pencil-H* is proposed, which can not only fully exploit the advantages of each component of MT-3000 but also overlap the time of calculation and communication. Moreover, an architecture-aware multi-level parallelization algorithm is developed to fully utilize the computational performance of MT-3000. A benchmark test is performed to verify the reliability and test the performance of the LBM code. Experimental results show that the optimized code achieves a 32.02× speedup compared with using 16 CPU cores and achieves a performance of 286.03MLUPS which reaches 72.3% of the theoretical peak performance.

Keywords: Lattice Boltzmann method (LBM) · Heterogeneous · MT-3000 · Parallel algorithm

1 Introduction

Lattice Boltzmann method (LBM) has become a powerful method in computational fluid dynamics to solve incompressible flow problems, such as thermo-

This work was partially supported by the National Key Research and Development Program of China (2021YFB0300101), NSFC (Nos. 62161160312, 12071461 and 12101588), and Shenzhen Fund (No. RCYX20200714114735074).

dynamics, biomechanics, aerodynamics, and environmental science [1–4]. LBM solves the discrete velocity Boltzmann equation by modeling the fluids at the mesoscopic level. In the LBM, the fluid domain is discretized into lattices corresponding to the uniform Cartesian grids, and the motion of particles is described by the evolution of particle distribution functions, which are divided into collision and stream operations. The macroscopic variables are computed by accumulating the particle distribution functions. The simulation of fluid problems with complex boundaries demands excessive computing time and high memory requirements, especially in 3D cases [5]. Fortunately, the rapid development of high-performance computing technologies provides a reliable platform for LBM.

From a programming point of view, LBM is a kind of stencil computational pattern that is easy to implement [6]. Due to its particulate nature and local dynamics, LBM has a remarkable advantage in parallelization, especially on recent multi-core or many-core platforms. Many scholars are committed to employing graphics processing units (GPUs) in LBM simulations, which have shown impressive speedups over general-purpose CPU versions. Bailey et al. improved upon prior single-precision GPU LBM results for the D3Q19 model by increasing GPU multiprocessor and introduced a space-efficient storage method [7]. Kraus et al. implemented the LBM code on a single-GPU system and optimized its performance on parallel multi-GPU systems on one node [8]. They broke the one double-precision Tflops barrier on a single-host system with two GPUs using the most compute-intensive part of the code. Tran et al. parallelized the LBM on a GPU by incorporating memory-efficient techniques, and developed optimization techniques to reduce the register uses [9]. Herschlag et al. studied the GPU data access patterns on complex geometries for LBM and presented the first near-optimal strong results for LBM with arterial geometries running on GPUs [10]. Vardhan and Gounley et al. proposed a new regularized LBM implementation that can reduce the memory footprint by only storing the macroscopic moment-based data and demonstrating the effectiveness of the moment representation on a GPU architecture [12,13]. These studies have shown that the graphics-dedicated high-bandwidth memory of GPU provides a suitable platform for LBM. However, the low capacity of local memory inhibits optimization techniques for data prefetching and data sharing between cores [6].

Some researchers devote themselves to optimizing the performance of LBM on other multi-core or many-core processors. Biferale et al. implemented and optimized a state-of-the-art LBM code on the prototype of the application-driven AuroraScience machine [14]. Fu et al. designed both sequential and parallel memory-aware algorithms to optimize the performance of LBM on the Intel Haswell system and the Intel Skylake system [15]. Fan et al. proposed an adaptive parallel optimization algorithm for LBM so that it can get automatically optimized on different hardware platforms [16]. Robertsén et al. implemented the LBM on the Knights Landing generation of Xeon Phi processor [17]. It is worth noting that Ho et al. improved the 3D LBM stencil by using local memory and asynchronous prefetching on the Kalray MPPA-256 many-core processor [6]. And Liu et al. proposed some techniques to boost the simulation speed and improve the scalability of LBM on the SW26010 processor [18]. Their works show that the clustered many-core architectures are also a suitable platform for larger-scale LBM simulations.

Notably, Lu et al. proposed a heterogeneous multi-zone processor for HPC named MT-3000, which achieves 11.6TFLOPS double-precision performance [19]. Moreover, they also elaborated on the possibility of constructing a large-scale supercomputer with MT-3000 chips, which motivates our implementation in developing a high-performance 3D LBM algorithm on MT-3000. The present research aims to improve the pipelined algorithm for LBM and develop an architecture-aware multi-level parallelization algorithm for LBM on MT-3000. More specifically, some possible contributions of the current paper are summarized as follows.

A parallel software framework for 3D LBM simulation is developed on an advanced heterogeneous multi-zone processor MT-3000 in this paper. A three stages pipelined algorithm named *Pencil-H* is proposed for 3D LBM simulations in heterogeneous architectures. In the *Pencil-H* algorithm, accelerator, CPU, and MPI are respectively responsible for the three stages in the pipeline, which realizes the overlapping of calculation time and communication time. Moreover, an architecture-aware multi-level parallelization algorithm is developed to fully release the computational performance of MT-3000. The optimization is described in detail, and the performance improvement brought by different optimizations is evaluated. Our algorithm and optimization method could also be helpful for the performance improvement of LBM on similar heterogeneous processors.

The rest of the paper is organized as follows. Section 2 describes the overview architecture of MT-3000. Section 3 introduces the LBM model, the data storage schemes, the improved pipelined algorithm, and the multi-level parallelization strategy. Section 4 shows the numerical results and performance results. Finally, Sect. 5 presents the conclusion and the future working plan.

2   MT-3000

The heterogeneous multi-zone processor MT-3000, designed for compute-intensive tasks, has an ultra-high double-precision performance of 11.6 TFLOPS, which provides another choice for supercomputers [19]. As presented in Fig. 1, MT-3000 includes 16 general-purpose CPU cores, 96 acceleration control cores (Ctrl), and 1536 computation-oriented accelerator cores (ACCs). The acceleration zone consists of four autonomous acceleration clusters. There are 24 control cores, 384 ACCs, one on-chip global shared memory (GSM), one high bandwidth shared memory (HBSM), and one off-chip double data rate (DDR) memory space in each cluster. The 16 general-purpose CPU cores can access all the HBSM and DDR space of all acceleration clusters, while the control cores and ACC can only access GSM, HBSM, and DDR within their cluster. The general-purpose CPU cores can control the overall task. And the acceleration clusters run independently of each other.

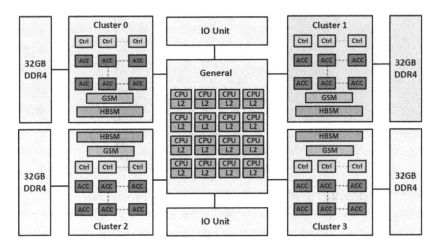

Fig. 1. The architecture of MT-3000.

Twenty-four control cores and 384 ACCs are grouped into 24 acceleration arrays in each cluster. The control core in an acceleration array serves as a computational engine, while 16 ACCs are driven by single instruction and work in lockstep. Such an arrangement provides excellent convenience for data-level parallelism. Moreover, the computation units in each ACC are organized in a very long instruction word manner that can further improve efficiency. There is an on-chip array memory (AM) that can support two load/stores to each ACC at most in each acceleration array. Each AM has a vector memory capacity of 864 KB, where 96 KB is occupied by a cyclic redundancy check, and 768 KB can be used for data storage.

2.1   Programming Environment

As shown in Fig. 2, a hierarchical software stack with four layers is employed to ease the use of MT-3000. The first layer includes the Linux operating system (OS) and the driver responsible for the interactions between CPUs and acceleration arrays. The second layer contains a low-level interface (i.e., LibMT) that can manage acceleration arrays, the compiler (i.e., M3CC) that can translate C codes into binaries, and the high-performance math libraries (HPML). A heterogeneous threading model (i.e., Hthreads) for programming and an OpenCL standard of v1.2 for MT-3000 is implemented on the third layer and last layers, respectively.

3   Methodology

3.1   Lattice Boltzmann Method

LBM is a mesoscopic approach in CFD to simulate fluid flow problems. Typically, there are three parts in LBM: an evolution equation for the particle distribution

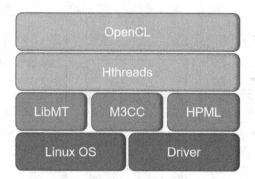

Fig. 2. The schematic of programming environment.

function, a lattice velocity model, and the equilibrium distribution [20–22]. The evolution equation can be expressed by

$$f_\alpha(\mathbf{x},t) - f_\alpha(\mathbf{x} - \mathbf{e}_\alpha \Delta t, t - \Delta t) = \Omega_\alpha(\mathbf{x} - \mathbf{e}_\alpha \Delta t, t - \Delta t), \tag{1}$$

where $f_\alpha(\mathbf{x},t)$ is the particle distribution function at point $\mathbf{x}$ and time t, Δt is the length of a time step, $\mathbf{e}_\alpha$ is the lattice velocity model, and Ω_α is the collision operator.

In this paper,

$$\Omega_\alpha(\mathbf{x},t) = -\frac{1}{\tau}\left[f_\alpha(\mathbf{x},t) - f_\alpha^{eq}(\mathbf{x},t)\right], \tag{2}$$

where τ is the relaxation time. It is related to the kinematic viscosity ν and can be calculated by

$$\nu = c_s{}^2\left(\tau - 0.5\right). \tag{3}$$

where the lattice sound speed $c_s = 1/\sqrt{3}$ for D3Q19 lattice velocity model. f_α^{eq} is the local equilibrium distribution function in the following form

$$f_\alpha^{eq} = \rho\omega_\alpha\left[1 + \frac{\mathbf{e}_\alpha \cdot \mathbf{u}}{c_s^2} + \frac{(\mathbf{e}_\alpha \cdot \mathbf{u})^2}{2c_s^4} - \frac{\mathbf{u}^2}{2c_s^2}\right]. \tag{4}$$

Here, ω_α is the weight coefficient, ρ and $\mathbf{u}$ are the macroscopic density and velocity, respectively calculated by

$$\rho = \sum_\alpha f_\alpha, \rho\mathbf{u} = \sum_\alpha f_\alpha \mathbf{e}_\alpha. \tag{5}$$

The D3Q19 lattice velocity model is adopted to simulate 3D fluid problems in this paper. With this pre-defined model, the particle distribution functions in each lattice node will stream to 18 neighboring nodes after updates.

3.2   Data Storage Schemes

Various memory storage techniques have been studied to track geometric information and data at each lattice point. The memory storage strategy influences not only the memory consumption but also the performance of the algorithm [10,11]. There are two primary ideas for laying out the particle distribution functions in memory [10]. One is the array of structures (AOS) layout, in which the particle distribution functions in one lattice point are stored adjacently, and all the lattice points are stored in turn. The other one is the structure of arrays (SOA) layout, in which the particle distribution functions in the same direction are stored in the same array in order of grid points. Considering that LBM updates each lattice point with the same set of rules during each time step, we stored the data in SOA layout to fully exploit the computational advantages of the vector SIMD architecture in MT-3000.

We employed the lexicographical order (i.e., dictionary order) to store the information of 3D lattice points in a single dimension in the memory. With such order, the lattice points are arranged by comparing the coordinate value of each point. Meanwhile, the pipelined algorithm that we used demands the domain to be cut into chunks along the z direction. To preserve the continuity of the data, we checked the x coordinate first and checked the z coordinate last. Therefore, given a lattice cuboid with dimensions (M, N, O), the qth particle distribution function of the lattice point with relative position (i, j, k) will be stored at the memory location:

$$g(i, j, k, q) = qMNO + (kN + j)M + i, \tag{6}$$

Physically, LBM consists of a collision step and a streaming step at each time step. In the collision step, 19 particle distribution functions at a lattice point need to be updated, and the updated functions need to be migrated to the neighboring lattice point during the streaming step. We combined the loop of collision step and streaming step to reduce the time of memory access and employed the ping-pong buffering pattern (i.e., A-B memory access pattern) [23] to avoid the memory traffic. With the ping-pong buffering pattern, only $19 \times 2 \times sizeof(double)$ bytes of memory is required to update one lattice point.

3.3   An Improved Pipelined Algorithm

Pencil, proposed by Wang and Chandramowlishwaran for practical CFD problems, is a pipelined stencil algorithm for distribution memory machines [24]. In this algorithm, the domain is cut into chunks along one dimension, and the computation and communication of chunks at different layers can be overlapped. For example, the calculation of the C_nth layer and the communication of the C_{n-1}th layer can be overlapped in the form of *Pencil*. Given that MT-3000 is a heterogeneous multi-zone processor, we added one more stage for *Pencil* to adapt to the heterogeneous architectures. As illustrated in Fig. 3, the domains in *process m* and *process n* are cut into several chunks in rectangular shapes. ACC, CPU, and MPI are respectively responsible for different stages in the algorithm. ACC deals with the update calculation, CPU runs the boundary processing, and MPI performs the communications among processes. These three stages are running at the same time in the algorithm. When the chunk C_{n+1} is being computed by

ACC, the chunk C_n has been computed and is being processed by the CPU. The chunk C_{n-1}, on the other hand, has already been updated, and the communication of its halo layers is being performed by MPI. Therefore, the calculation time of ACC, the running time of CPU, and the communication time of MPI can be overlapped. To simplify the description, we name the improved pipelined algorithm *Pencil-H* (a Heterogeneous version of Pencil).

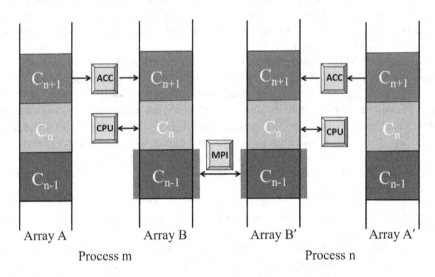

Fig. 3. *Pencil-H*: A three-stage pipelined algorithm with ping-pong buffering memory pattern for LBM in heterogeneous architectures. ACC, CPU, and MPI are respectively responsible for the three stages in the pipeline.

As described in Sect. 3.2, we combined the loop of the collision step and the streaming step by employing the ping-pong memory pattern. Therefore, in each stage of *Pencil-H*, ACC should load the particle distribution functions from *Array A* and stream the updated functions to the neighboring lattice point. Given that a specified particle distribution function in D3Q19 model is migrated with the same rules in every time step, we add 18 address offsets into DMA put operation to complete the streaming of 18 directions. The offsets of 18 directions can be pre-computed according to the data storage scheme mentioned in Sect. 3.2. And we can use the CPU to correct the lattice points in which the particle distribution functions may not need to be migrated. The correction is easy to implement since all the computed data are written to the DDR4, and the CPU can access all the DDR4 data in different acceleration clusters. In addition, we also employ the CPU to perform the boundary treatment since the treatment requires almost no calculations but a lot of branch judgments.

3.4   Multi-level Parallelization Strategy

To fully release the performance of MT-3000, with a deep study of the heterogeneous architecture, we implement a three-level parallelism strategy by using the multi-layer programming environment. See Fig. 4 for details. The LBM code is written in $C++$ language. Given that there are four acceleration clusters in one MT-3000 processor, we first divided the computational domain into four subdomains and stored the subdomains in four DDR4 memories. Four MPI processes are employed to perform the local computations of four subdomains and the communications among processes, and this is the *first* level of parallelism. And as the demand of the *Pencil-H* algorithm, the subdomains should be cut into several chunks in rectangular shape along the z dimension. The size of each chunk should suit loop tiling and DMA transfer.

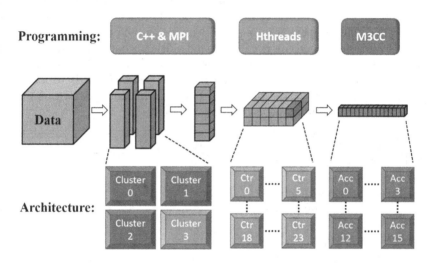

Fig. 4. The data division for the three-level parallelism strategy. The first row and the third row respectively illustrate the programming environment and the architecture corresponding to each parallelism level.

Given that there are 24 control cores in each cluster to handle the single instruction stream, we further divide each chunk into 24 data blocks. With the help of the heterogeneous threading model (i.e., Hthreads), we assign 24 blocks to 24 acceleration arrays in one cluster. And the data blocks can be loaded to AM of each acceleration array through the DMA component. Moreover, since one MT-3000 processor has 16 CPU cores, 4 CPU cores are assigned to one MPI process to perform the boundary treatment, and this is the *second* level of parallelism.

Since the computation units in each ACC are organized in a very long instruction word, we also implement the data-level parallelism to fully utilize the multizone micro-architecture of MT-3000, which corresponds to the *third* level of parallelism. Since the control cores can drive 16 ACCs by one single instruction stream, we pack 16 double-precision float points as a vector. Therefore, each control core can compute with 16 ACCs simultaneously. Moreover, we have rewritten the kernels by using assembly language to improve their performance fully. By unrolling loops manually and scheduling instructions carefully, the execution time of kernels has reached the minimum.

With the data storage schemes mentioned in Sect. 3.1, the particle distribution functions are accessed only once during each time step. Moreover, there is only 768 KB for data storage in each AM, so the data are not necessary to stay in the AM long. MT-3000 supports DMA parallel access operations, which provides a high memory access bandwidth. Based on this feature, we employ a double buffering technology to overlap the time of computations and memory access. As illustrated in Algorithm 1, there are two buffers in AM, and the computation of each buffer is divided into two pipelines. Note that the step of *preload* and *prestore* is non-blocking, so the time for such steps can be considered negligible. The time spent in *compute* depends on the performance of ACCs, while the *wait* time depends on the DMA bandwidth. As computations are much faster than data transfers, the computations can be fully overlapped by DMA data transfer. In addition, by employing different DMA channels to load and store, and with the help of the ping-pong buffering memory pattern, data can be loaded and stored simultaneously without conflicts.

Algorithm 1: Compute with double buffering.

1: /*The first load instruction.*/
2: $Buffer(0)\_preload(0)$;
3: $Buffer(1)\_preload(0)$;
4: /*Loop of Double buffering*/
5: **for** $i = 0$; $i < N$; $i++$ **do**
6:    **for** $j = 0$; $j < 2$; $j++$ **do**
7:       $Buffer(j)\_load\_wait(i)$;
8:       $Buffer(j)\_compute(i)$.
9:       $Buffer(j)\_prestore(i)$.
10:       **if** $i < N - 1$ **then**
11:          $Buffer(j)\_preload(i + 1)$;
12:       **end if**
13:    **end for**
14:    $Buffer(0)\_store\_wait(i)$;
15:    $Buffer(1)\_store\_wait(i)$;
16: **end for**

---

4   Numerical and Performance Results

A flow around a single building that described in [25] is simulated as a benchmark problem in this paper. The fluid domain is initialized by a horizontal wind velocity, which is a power function of the vertical height. In this experiment, the statistics are measured on a vertical cross-section $y = 0$ and a horizontal cross-section at $\frac{1}{16}$ of the model building height. The space size is set to be 1 m. The numerical results are presented in Fig. 5, the measuring points are located at the longitudinal dotted lines, and the values of the velocity at the measuring points are denoted as the distance from the original positions. Positive and negative values are plotted on the right and left sides of the measuring lines, respectively. Results show that the simulation results agree well with the measured wind tunnel data.

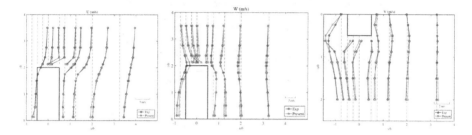

Fig. 5. Results of benchmark test. (Left) The x-velocity U at $y = 0$. (Middle) The z-velocity W at $y = 0$. (Right) The y-velocity V at $z = \frac{b}{16}$.

The performance of LBM software is usually measured in MLUPS, which means million lattices updates per second [26]. The performance can be calculated as [18]:

$$P = M/t_s, \tag{7}$$

where, P is the performance measured in MLUPS, M is the total number of the lattice cells, t_s is the physical time for a single time step.

We utilized the benchmark model with a mesh size of $1440 \times 960 \times 100$ to test the performance of our code. We test the performance of the code with all the optimizations described in this paper. Figure 6 presents the performance improvements brought by different optimization methods. In the figure, "CPU" illustrates the compute time when 16 CPU cores are used. "CPU+ACC" shows the compute time with the acceleration of ACCs. Similarly, "Stream Combine", "Double Buffering", and "Pencil-H" refer to those using the stream combine method, double buffering strategy, and the *Pencil-H* algorithm, respectively. With all these optimization methods, we can achieve a superb performance of 286.03MLUPS and a 32.02 times speedup compared with using 16 CPU cores.

In our algorithm, at least 19 elements of the particle distribution function are needed to load from and store them back to DDR4 to update one lattice, which means that at least 304 bytes need to be transferred between DDR4 and AM. Given that LBM is extremely limited by memory bandwidth [27], we first measure the DMA bandwidth utilizing our code without any calculations. Since the number of lattices per chunk in our simulation is between 3.0×10^6 and

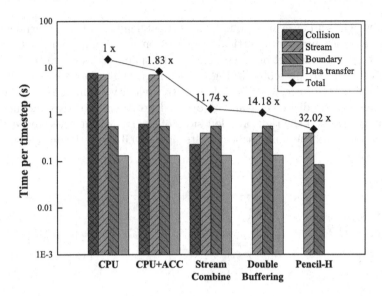

Fig. 6. The performance improvement brought by different optimization methods. Here "Data transfer", "Boundary", "Stream" and "Collision" refer to the different parts of the code.

3.5×10^7, the peak DMA bandwidth available for 1 cluster of our simulator is 28 GB/s. Therefore, we can get the upper bound of the performance for our code in MT-3000 by using the roofline performance model [27]:

$$\frac{28GB/s \times 4}{304bytes} = 395.59MLUPS, \tag{8}$$

where, 4 refers to the 4 cluster in MT-3000. Therefore, we reached 72.3% of the the theoretical peak performance of LBM on MT-3000 processor:

$$\frac{286.03MLUPS}{395.59MLUPS} = 72.3\%, \tag{9}$$

5   Conclusions

This paper developed a parallel software framework for 3D LBM simulation on MT-3000, an advanced heterogeneous multi-zone processor for high-performance computing. Firstly, we carefully designed the data storage scheme for heterogeneous architecture. After that, we introduced an improved pipelined algorithm named *Pencil-H*. In *Pencil-H*, the subdomain in each process is cut into chunks along the z dimension. And accelerator cores, CPU, and MPI are running at three different stages in the algorithm. ACC deals with the update calculation, CPU runs the boundary treatment, and MPI performs the communications among processes. *Pencil-H* can not only give full play to the advantages of each component in heterogeneous architecture but also overlap the time of calculation and communication. In addition, we deeply studied the architecture of MT-3000 and developed a three-level parallelism strategy with the multi-layer programming environment to fully release its computational performance.

A flow around a single building was simulated as a benchmark to verify the reliability of the LBM framework. And the simulation results agreed well with the experimental data. We then tested the performance of LBM on MT-3000. After employing all the optimization methods introduced in this paper, the LBM code achieved a 32.02 times speedup compared with using 16 CPU cores. Moreover, it achieved a superb performance of 286.03MLUPS which reached 72.3% of the theoretical peak performance of LBM on MT-3000.

It should be noted that the algorithm and optimization method proposed in this paper could also be helpful for the performance improvement of LBM on similar heterogeneous processors. And the numerical results in this paper show that heterogeneous processors like MT-3000 are also excellent platforms for LBM simulation. Notably, Lu et al. have elaborated on the possibility of a large-scale supercomputer construction based on MT-3000. Future work will be devoted to improving the scalability of the LBM software on supercomputers and simulating the large-scale physical problems with this software.

References

1. Reyhanian, E., Dorschner, B., Karlin, I.V.: Thermokinetic lattice Boltzmann model of nonideal fluids. Phys. Rev. E **102**(2), 020103 (2020)
2. Feiger, B., Vardhan, M., Gounley, J., et al.: Suitability of lattice Boltzmann inlet and outlet boundary conditions for simulating flow in image-derived vasculature. Commun. Numer. Methods Eng. **35**(6), e3198 (2019)
3. Han, M., Ooka, R., Kikumoto, H.: Lattice Boltzmann method-based large-eddy simulation of indoor isothermal airflow. Int. J. Heat Mass Transf. **130**, 700–709 (2019)
4. Xu, L., Chen, R., Cai, X.C.: Parallel finite-volume discrete Boltzmann method for inviscid compressible flows on unstructured grids. Phys. Rev. E **103**(2), 023306 (2021)
5. Guo, W., Jin, C., Li, J.: High performance lattice Boltzmann algorithms for fluid flows. In: 2008 International Symposium on Information Science and Engineering, pp. 33–37. IEEE, Shanghai (2008)
6. Ho, M.Q., Obrecht, C., Tourancheau, B., et al.: Improving 3D Lattice Boltzmann method stencil with asynchronous transfers on many-core processors. In: IEEE 36th International Performance Computing and Communications Conference (IPCCC), pp. 1–9. IEEE, San Diego (2017)
7. Bailey, P., Myre, J., Walsh, S.D.C., et al.: Accelerating lattice Boltzmann fluid flow simulations using graphics processors. In: 2009 International Conference on Parallel Processing, pp. 550–557, Vienna (2009)
8. Kraus, J., Pivanti, M., Schifano, S.F., et al.: Benchmarking GPUs with a parallel Lattice-Boltzmann code. In: 2013 25th International Symposium on Computer Architecture and High Performance Computing, pp. 160–167, Porto de Galinhas (2013)

9. Tran, N.P., Lee, M., Choi, D.H.: Memory-efficient parallelization of 3D lattice Boltzmann flow solver on a GPU. In: 2015 IEEE 22nd International Conference on High Performance Computing (HiPC), pp. 315–324. IEEE, Bengaluru (2015)
10. Herschlag, G., Lee, S., Vetter, J.S., et al.: GPU data access on complex geometries for D3Q19 lattice Boltzmann method. In: 2018 IEEE International Parallel & Distributed Processing Symposium, vol 32, pp. 2400–2414. IEEE, Vancouver (2018)
11. Chen, D., Ken, K.: Improving effective bandwidth through compiler enhancement of global cache reuse. J. Parallel Distrib. Comput. **64**(1), 108–134 (2004)
12. Vardhan, M., Gounley, J., Hegele, L., et al.: Moment representation in the lattice Boltzmann method on massively parallel hardware. In: International Conference for High Performance Computing. Networking, Storage and Analysis, pp. 1–21. IEEE, Denver (2019)
13. Gounley, J., Vardhan, M., Draeger, E.W., et al.: Propagation pattern for moment representation of the lattice Boltzmann method. IEEE Trans. Parallel Distrib. Syst. **33**(3), 642–653 (2021)
14. Biferale, L., Sbragaglia, M., Scagliarini, A., et al.: Lattice Boltzmann method simulations on massively parallel multi-core architectures. In: the 19th High Performance Computing Symposia, pp. 73–80, San Diego (2011)
15. Fu, Y., Li, F., Song, F., et al.: Designing a parallel memory-aware lattice Boltzmann algorithm on manycore systems. In: 2018 30th International Symposium on Computer Architecture and High Performance Computing (SBAC-PAD), pp. 97–106, Lyon (2018)
16. Fan, S., Guo, X., Li, C., et al.: Apoal: an adaptive parallel optimization algorithm for LBM fluid simulations. In: 2019 IEEE 21st International Conference on High Performance Computing and Communications; IEEE 17th International Conference on Smart City; IEEE 5th International Conference on Data Science and Systems (HPCC/SmartCity/DSS), pp. 834–840. IEEE, Zhangjiajie (2019)
17. Robertsén, F., Mattila, K., Westerholm, J.: High-performance SIMD implementation of the lattice Boltzmann method on the Xeon Phi processor. Concurrency Comput.: Pract. Experience **31**(13), e5072 (2019)
18. Liu, Z., Chu, X.S., Lv, X., et al.: SunwayLB: enabling extreme-scale lattice Boltzmann method based computing fluid dynamics simulations on sunway taihulight. In: 2019 IEEE International Parallel and Distributed Processing Symposium, pp. 557–566. IEEE, Rio de Janeiro (2019)
19. Lu, K., Wang, Y., Guo, Y., et al.: MT-3000: a heterogeneous multi-zone processor for HPC. CCF Trans. High Perform. Comput. **4**(2), 1–15 (2022). https://doi.org/10.1007/s42514-022-00095-y
20. Guo, Z., Shu, C.: Lattice Boltzmann Method and its Applications in Engineering. World Scientific Publishing, Singapore (2013)
21. Kruger, T., Kusumaatmaja, H., Kuzmin, R.A., et al.: The Lattice Boltzmann Method: Principles and Practice. Springer, New York (2017)
22. Succi, S.: The lattice Boltzmann Equation for Complex States of Flowing Matter. Oxford University Press, Oxford (2019)
23. Pohl, T., Kowarschik, M., Wilke, J., et al.: Optimization and profiling of the cache performance of parallel lattice Boltzmann codes. Parallel Process. Lett. **13**(4), 549–560 (2003)
24. Wang, H., Chandramowlishwaran, A.: Pencil: a pipelined algorithm for distributed stencils, In: SC 2020: Proceedings of the International Conference for High Performance Computing, Networking, Storage and Analysis, pp. 1–16. ACM, Atlanta (2020)

25. Yoshiea, R., Mochidab, A., Tominagac, Y., et al.: Cooperative project for CFD prediction of pedestrian wind environment in the architectural institute of Japan. J. Wind Eng. Ind. Aerodyn. **95**(9–11), 1551–1578 (2007)
26. Wellein, G., Zeiser, T., Hager, G., Donath, S.: On the single processor performance of simple lattice Boltzmann kernels. Comput. Fluids **35**(8–9), 910–919 (2006)
27. Godenschwager, C., Schornbaum, F., Bauer, M., et al.: A framework for hybrid parallel flow simulations with a trillion cells in complex geometries. In: SC 2013: Proceedings of the International Conference on High Performance Computing, Networking, Storage and Analysis, pp. 1–12. ACM, Denver (2013)

FPGA

DEEPFAKE CLI: Accelerated Deepfake Detection Using FPGAs

Omkar Bhilare$^{(\boxtimes)}$, Rahul Singh, Vedant Paranjape, Sravan Chittupalli,
Shraddha Suratkar, and Faruk Kazi

Department of Electrical Engineering, V.J.T.I, Mumbai, India
{oabhilare_b19,rsingh_b18,vvparanjape_b18,schittupalli_b18,
fskazi}@el.vjti.ac.in, sssuratkar@ce.vjti.ac.in

Abstract. Because of the availability of larger datasets and recent improvements in the generative model, more realistic Deepfake videos are being produced each day. People consume around one billion hours of video on social media platforms every day, and that's why it is very important to stop the spread of fake videos as they can be damaging, dangerous, and malicious. There has been a significant improvement in the field of deepfake classification, but deepfake detection and inference have remained a difficult task. To solve this problem in this paper, we propose a novel DEEPFAKE C-L-I (Classification - Localization - Inference) in which we have explored the idea of accelerating Quantized Deepfake Detection Models using FPGAs due to their ability of maximum parallelism and energy efficiency compared to generalized GPUs. In this paper, we have used light MesoNet with EFF-YNet structure and accelerated it on VCK5000 FPGA, powered by state-of-the-art VC1902 Versal Architecture which uses AI, DSP, and Adaptable Engines for acceleration. We have benchmarked our inference speed with other state-of-the-art inference nodes, got 316.8 FPS on VCK5000 while maintaining 93% Accuracy.

Keywords: Generative Models · Deepfake Detection · Deepfake Classification · Machine Learning · Quantized · FPGAs · MesoNet · EFF-YNet · VCK5000 · VC1902 · Versal Architecture · AI · DSP · Adaptable Engines

1 Introduction

Deepfake is artificially created media in which a frame is created synthetically using someone else's features like face, structure, lip movements, etc. They are usually created by leveraging a Generative Adversarial Network to create a picture or video which looks realistic enough to deceive any person. While Deepfakes were initially created to prank individuals, they started getting attention due to their use in illegal activities like celebrity pornographic videos, fake news, and

---

O. Bhilare, R. Singh, V. Paranjape and S. Chittupalli—These Authors contributed equally to this work.

© The Author(s), under exclusive license to Springer Nature Switzerland AG 2023
H. Takizawa et al. (Eds.): PDCAT 2022, LNCS 13798, pp. 45–56, 2023.
https://doi.org/10.1007/978-3-031-29927-8_4

bullying. Hence, detecting deepfakes has become a very important issue in recent years.

Upon going through relevant literature and existing methods of deepfake classification, we observed that it is essentially an image classification problem, but the catch here is that pathological differences between the real and fake images are quite small, as a result existing convolutional neural networks (CNN) models need to be modified and tuned to detect these minute differences.

MesoNet is a CNN architecture which is used to detect Face2Face and Deep-fakes manipulations accurately [1]. It is designed in such a way that it uses cropped faces from videos and analyses mid-level features. The model focuses on the right amount of details by using an architecture with small number of layers. XceptionNet is a complex model originally designed for working with 2D Images which uses depthwise separable convolutional layers with residual connections [2], as a result it gives higher performance than MesoNet [1]. However, this model takes a lot of time to train. EfficientNets which are relatively a newer family of CNN models aimed at providing efficient resource management by balancing model parameters like width, depth, and resolution, outperform models which have a similar number of parameters [3]. Researchers have taken a step further and proposed classifying each pixel of the image as real or fake. The U-Net architecture addresses this issue by employing an encoder-decoder based network with skip connections [4]. To improve classification accuracy, Eff-Ynet describes a novel architecture which combines EfficientNet encoder with a classification and segmentation branch [5]. It is designed to classify an image and also find regions where the image is real and where it is fake. The job of segmentation helps train the classifier, and at the same time it also produces useful segmentation masks.

The inference of neural networks is usually slow on general-purpose GPUs [6]. One way to accelerate the inference of these networks is to use soft cores emulating on the FPGAs, which allows the user to utilize the task and data level parallelism to reach the performance of ASIC implementations while taking reduced design time [7]. It is also possible to make RNN or CNN specific hardware architectures. In this paper, they have accelerated Deep Recurrent Neural Network (DRNN) on a hardware accelerator running on XILINX ZYNQ FPGA [8]. These ZYNQ boards are heterogeneous in nature, which means it has a hardcore CPU besides FPGA. In one of the paper, researchers have mapped BNNs (Binarized neural networks) onto an FPGA device while FP32 networks are mapped to the CPU, this hybrid mapping increases overall neural network efficiency while maintaining inference speed [9]. Researchers have found these ZYNQ boards perform better than CPUs and GPUs [10].

One of the paper, transforms the model into FP8[1] format for speed up [11]. Upon evaluating this, we decided to go with INT8[2] in our implementation, thus quantized our model to INT8 precision. This means that our model, which was

---

[1] FP8 means 8-bit floating point representation.
[2] INT8 means 8-bit integer representation.

originally trained on FP32[3] precision, was converted to INT8 (See footnote 1) precision. By reducing the precision, the number of bits required to store the model parameters are reduced, which means it requires less amount of memory to store and reduces the number of clock cycles to transfer data between memory and the accelerator over the PCIe bus.

We propose U-YNet, a combined segmentation, and classification model which consists of UNet Encoder and Decoder responsible for producing a segmentation map to show the altered regions in the deepfake content and a classification branch present at the end of the UNet Encoder branch responsible for classifying if the media content is real or deepfake origin. The segmentation map is a novel way to identify the regions of a face that have been mangled to create the deepfake, giving an insight into the construction of a deepfake and paving the way for creating models to reverse a deepfake as well. This model runs on a Deep Learning Processing Unit (DPU)[4] present in the AMD-XILINX VCK 5000 Versal FPGA device. It consists of dedicated processing units like hardware accelerated convolution engine which enables convolution based model like UNet (and U-YNet) to run with higher inference speeds, enabling real-time classification of deepfake content.

2   Motivation and Background

Improvement in generative models and abundance of datasets has led to evolution of models that can generate realistic looking deepfake videos, deceiving the human eye and machines as well (Fig. 1). There is a huge potential to spread deepfaked videos by malicious actors for their gains, as more than 100 million hours of video content is watched every day on social media.

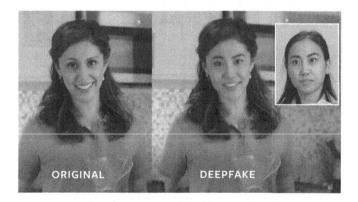

Fig. 1. Completely believable deepfakes can be generated with ease nowadays.

---

[3] FP32 means 32-bit floating point representation.
[4] DPU stands for Deep Learning Processor Unit. Read more: https://www.xilinx.com/products/intellectual-property/dpu.html.

Looking at this with the perspective of computation, faster computation speeds and easily available compute resources means that deepfake videos can be generated with ease. This makes fast and effective detection of these videos very crucial to stop the malicious use of deepfake videos.

On March 16, 2022, a video claiming to show Ukraine President Volodymyr Zelensky calling for the Ukrainian people to surrender to Russia was aired on news channel Ukraine 24, and circulated on social media. Such events clearly show how potent of a tool, deepfakes are for creating social chaos. Thus, there is a need for faster detection of such deepfake videos so that they can be taken down even before reaching the social media users. This paper aims to leverage the massively parallel nature of FPGAs to efficiently run Deep Neural networks that power the deepfake detection algorithms.

3   Implementation

Deepfake C-L-I (Classification - Localization - Inference) is a novel system that we are proposing in this paper, which consists of an optimum combination of software and hardware tools to accelerate deepfake detection on FPGAs. The block diagram of Deepfake CLI is shown in Fig. 2. The software part of the acceleration system consists of a deep learning model comprised of a UNet Segmentation and a Classification Model. As for the hardware part, these models are first quantized to INT8 for DPU Architecture supported by VCK5000 to achieve maximum performance, then later on it is run on the FPGA.

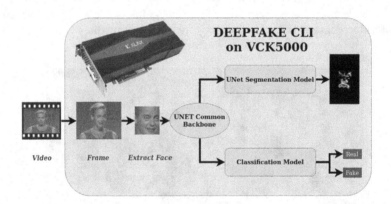

Fig. 2. Flowchart of Deepfake CLI

The implementation of Deepfake C-L-I is divided into two parts as software and hardware as follows:

3.1   Software Implementation

We implemented a multitask model called U-YNet, that can produce classification (real or fake) and segmentation results on deepfake content. The backbone which is the UNet Encoder takes a frame as the input and then the encoded features are passed to the classification branch and the UNet decoder simultaneously. The reason for doing this is that the combination of loss of classification and segmentation tasks may help the classification branch to learn from the segmentation branch features during training.

3.1.1   Dataset

Currently, there are many deepfake detection datasets available, which include both real and manipulated videos and images. To name a few, we have Face-Forensics++ [12], UADFV, Google DFD, CelebDF [13] and the DFDC dataset [14]. The source of videos for all datasets is different, and the fake videos are generated from the real frames using various deepfake generation models. DFDC is currently the largest available deepfakes dataset (Fig. 3) with the most number of videos and faces. So we trained the model using DFDC. The dataset does not ship with the segmentation masks that we need for training the segmentation branch of the U-YNet model. To create the mask, we find the absolute difference between the real frame and the fake frame, which encodes one for a manipulated pixel and a zero for the real one.

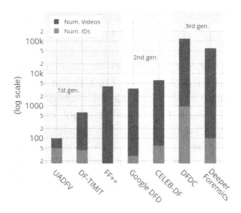

Fig. 3. Comparison of current deepfakes datasets [15]

Data Leakage Challenge: Initially, while training we were getting 99% accuracy on the DFDC dataset, which meant that the model was overfitting. After insinuating on this problem, we found that DFDC has 1:124 videos per subject. So, while randomly splitting the dataset into testing, training, and validation datasets, the training dataset had examples of all the faces in the dataset. So the model was basically learning the faces and not classifying the deepfake features, giving high accuracy on the test dataset. This problem is called data leakage.

Solution: We solved this by clustering similar faces together and then segregating the dataset such that a face in the training dataset does not repeat in the testing dataset. This prevented overfitting, and the model focused on learning features rather than faces.

3.1.2   Loss Function and Training
For the segmentation task we used Cross Entropy Loss and for the classification task we used Binary Cross Entropy Loss (BCE).

Cross-entropy is used to measure the difference between two probability distributions, and it is used for both classification and segmentation tasks. We use the average of both losses as the final loss.

The model was trained using the final loss. Finally, Adam Optimiser was used for converging the model. The model was trained for 40 epochs on the created DFDC dataset on NVIDIA DGX-1.

3.2   Hardware Implementation

The hardware setup of Deepfake CLI consists of Dell R740 Server which is a two socket machine with two Intel Xeon processor installed and paired with 32 GB DDR4 RAM running Ubuntu Server 20.04 LTS, kernel version 5.4.0. The server was installed with VCK5000[5] an FPGA development card built on XILINX 7 nm Versal ACAP[6] Architecture which is ideal for acceleration of AI models for cloud and edge application.

In the previous chapter, we have described the changes that had to be done in the dataset to overcome the challenges. For efficient usage of FPGA resources, it is crucial to train a hardware centric model with ideal weights for the model. Since earlier the model was in FP32, and it is not optimal to run this on the FPGA [11], we used the Vitis-AI toolchain to convert the FP32 model to INT8. The entire vitis flow is show in Fig. 4a which consists of three steps which are Quantization, Compilation, and Inference explained as follows:

3.2.1   Quantization
Neural nets after being trained on some dataset store all the weights and biases in the FP32 format in the model. If this model is directly used for inference, it will be compute and memory intensive and might not be able to serve the real-time processing demands. Since detecting deepfake videos in real-time is a crucial goal of this project, to get better inference speed we have quantized our model to be more hardware-centric using Vitis AI Quantizer. This used the

[5] Read more: https://www.xilinx.com/products/boards-and-kits/vck5000.html.

[6] ACAP stands for Adaptive Compute Acceleration Platform. Read more: https://www.xilinx.com/products/silicon-devices/acap/versal.html.

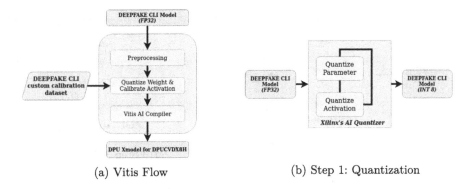

(a) Vitis Flow   (b) Step 1: Quantization

Fig. 4. Vitis Flow & Step 1: Quantization

Post Training Quantization method to quantize Deepfake CLI model suitable for our real-time needs. Post Training model is less demanding in terms of runtime, being done by running few inference cycles on a dataset known as the calibration dataset. This calibration dataset can be from a training or testing set, and it has to be around 100–1000 images. As shown in Fig. 4b, we were able to quantize the Deepfake CLI model from FP32 format to INT8 with Quantize parameters and Quantize activations modules.

3.2.2   Compilation

Once the model quantization step has been completed which generates a .xmodel file, we are ready for the final steps to deploy our model onto VCK5000. We will need to compile our model weights file by using the compiler provided by Vitis-AI. Vitis-AI provides a compiler tool that acts as an interface for optimization of deep neural networks for specific DPUs (See footnote 4). With a range of compiler option present due to different DPUs (See footnote 4) available by Xilinx, it will transform the neural network to the targeted platform DPU instruction set for efficient optimization.

Every DPU variant designed by Xilinx to be run on their FPGA board has its own set of optimized instruction to ensure efficient execution of the neural network on hardware. To adhere to this demand, we need to compile our quantized model for the DPU variant it will run on. An overview of Vitis AI compiler framework is described in Fig. 5a. After it has completed topology parsing of the neural network obtained by quantization, the Vitis AI compiler will construct a computational graph as Intermediate Representation. The compiler will also be responsible for further optimization such as fusion of computational nodes which provides higher performance and reduces memory footprint, using the existing parallelism to make sure the instructions are scheduled efficiently.

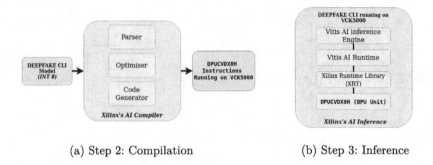

(a) Step 2: Compilation   (b) Step 3: Inference

Fig. 5. Hardware Implementation flow

3.2.3   Inference

Now that compilation of our model weights has been completed, we are ready to use it for Inference. We use the Vitis AI Runtime Library(VART) available in Python and C++. We pre-process the input image by resizing the image to 224×224, and then scale the values from 0–255 to 0–1. The images also have a scaling operation applied to them to convert them to INT8 format as required by the model. We then append the images to a list and pass it to the DPU running on the VCK5000 loaded with our quantized model.

VCK5000 takes the images in batches of eight and gives us two outputs, the segmented mask, and a classification label that tells us if the image or video is a deepfake content or not. The segmented output is stored in a .npy format for post-processing, so we could visualize the output in a Jupyter notebook.

The classification output is given at the end of the inference code, which tells us how well the model performed on unseen data. A JSON file contains the label for unseen data, we compare it with the model output and print the accuracy of how well it performs. The inference process was explained in the Fig. 5b.

4   Results

4.1   Software Results

The Deepfake CLI model was evaluated on a testing dataset which had around 2,00,000 frames. These frames have faces that were never seen by the model before. Our main task was classification, hence segmentation results are not presented here. As we can see from the Table 1, we were able to increase the accuracy of the model by almost 6% using a multitask learning model.

Table 1. Module Accuracy Comparison

Model	Accuracy
U-YNet model	94.12%
U-YNet model without segmentation branch	88.27%

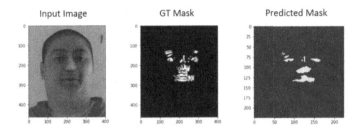

Fig. 6. (Left to Right) Input Image, Ground Truth, Predicted Mask

4.2 Hardware Results

The Deepfake CLI model was first quantized, compiled and then inferenced on the VCK5000 FPGA card. We have tested the model on the FPGA with various deepfake videos and images. In the Fig. 6, the predicted mask by Deepfake CLI model matches with the Ground Truth Mask for the given input image. Now for the hardware results, as shown in Fig. 7 the segmentation output of VCK5000 also matches with the Ground Truth Mask. Deepfake CLI's main aim was to increase the inference speed of the deepfake detection. Here are the results of the classification branch, shown in the Table 2. We have obtained 316.80 FPS for the classification model of deepfake detection on VCK5000. Because of quantization of the model to INT8, there was around 1% loss in accuracy, but we got better inference speeds than other inference nodes.

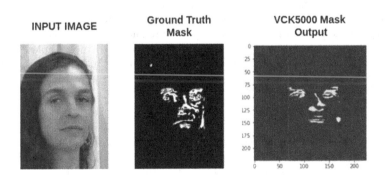

Fig. 7. (Left to Right) Input Image, Ground Truth, FPGA Output

Table 2. Classification Results

Parameter	Value
Total Images	5001
Correct Predictions	4851
Wrong Predictions	350
Accuracy	93.001%
FPS	**316.80**

4.3 Benchmarking Deepfake CLI with Other Nodes

We had created a dedicated hardware centric model and inferenced it on
VCK5000. We had compared the results of the segmentation model on different
state-of-the-art inference nodes available in the market.

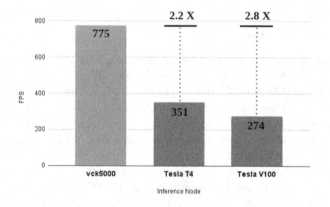

Fig. 8. FPS vs Inference Nodes (All nodes were running INT8 Deepfake CLI Unet
model, TensorRT SDK was used to quantize INT8 model for Tesla T4 and V100 while
for VCK5000 we have used Vitis AI Flow.). (In this benchmarking test, we have compared the inference speed of simpler Deepfake CLI model which only consists of Unet
model (segmentation branch). This was done due to the TensorRT quantization limitation for Tesla T4 and V100 nodes. We have also obtained the complete Y-UNet
Inference speed for VCK5000, which was 316.80 FPS (Table 2). When both branches
are included in Deepfake CLI, the layers in the network gets approximately doubled
and thus reduces inference speed by half.)

As shown in Fig. 8, we have obtained 775 FPS for the segmentation model of
deepfake detection on VCK5000. For the same model, we had got a much lower
FPS on other inference nodes, like Nvidia's Tesla T4 and V100. This result shows
that with proper model preprocessing, quantization, and compilation for FPGA
architecture will give better inference speeds than its counterpart GPUs.

5   Conclusion

Because of the rapid increase in computation speeds, deepfake detection will be one of the concerns in the upcoming era. In this paper, we implemented a novel architecture that combined segmentation and classification models, which were trained on DGX A100 and inferred on VCK5000. We used a modified DFDC dataset to reduce data leakage and solve the over fitting problem. The Deepfake CLI software model was designed from a hardware-centric point of view, and it was quantized and compiled for the VCK5000 AI inference versal card. We were able to classify the deepfake images as well as videos on the Accelerated FPGA fabric. **We have obtained a 120% gain on the inference speed on the VCK5000 FPGA fabric compared to state-of-the-art Tesla T4 inference node.**

6   Future Work

The ever-increasing research in deepfake generation demands better and faster techniques to decode and detect these deepfake images and videos in real-time. The future goals of Deepfake C-L-I are as follows:

– Modeling and Training more generalized model for deepfake detection.
– Restoring the deepfaked region of the frame.
– Adding AWS FPGA support for easy access.
– Adding accelerators for pre and post-processing of images and videos for ML model.

Acknowledgment. We are grateful to the Centre of Excellence in Complex and Non-Linear Dynamical Systems, V.J.T.I. (*CoE-CNDS*) for support in the project. Also, we would like to thank the entire hackster.io and AMD-Xilinx Team for shipping us the VCK5000 board, and the technical support to get it up and running.

References

1. Afchar, D., Nozick, V., Yamagishi, J., Echizen, I.: MesoNet: a compact facial video forgery detection network. In: IEEE International Workshop on Information Forensics and Security (WIFS), vol. 2018, pp. 1–7 (2018). https://doi.org/10.1109/WIFS.2018.8630761
2. Chollet, F.: Xception: deep learning with depthwise separable convolutions. In: IEEE Conference on Computer Vision and Pattern Recognition (CVPR), vol. 2017, pp. 1800–1807 (2017). https://doi.org/10.1109/CVPR.2017.195
3. Tan, M., Le, Q.V.: Efficient net: rethinking model scaling for convolutional neural networks. ArXiv, vol. abs/1905.11946 (2019)
4. Ronneberger, O., Fischer, P., Brox, T.: U-Net: Convolutional Networks for Biomedical Image Segmentation. In: Navab, N., Hornegger, J., Wells, W., Frangi, A. (eds.) MICCAI 2015. LNCS, vol. 9351. Springer, Cham (2015). https://doi.org/10.1007/978-3-319-24574-4_28

5. Tjon, E., Moh, M., Moh, T.S.: Eff-YNet: a Dual task network for Deepfake detection and segmentation. In: 2021 15th International Conference on Ubiquitous Information Management and Communication (IMCOM), pp. 1–8 (2021). https://doi.org/10.1109/IMCOM51814.2021.9377373

6. Boutros, A., et al.: Beyond peak performance: comparing the real performance of AI-optimized FPGAs and GPUs. In: International Conference on Field-Programmable Technology (ICFPT), vol. 2020, pp. 10–19 (2020). https://doi.org/10.1109/ICFPT51103.2020.00011

7. Amiri, M., Siddiqui, F.M., Kelly, C., Woods, R., Rafferty, K., Bardak, B.: FPGA-based soft-core processors for image processing applications. J. Signal Process. Syst. **87**(1), 139–156 (2016). https://doi.org/10.1007/s11265-016-1185-7

8. Hao, Y., Quigley, S.F.: The implementation of a deep recurrent neural network language model on a Xilinx FPGA. ArXiv, abs/1710.10296 (2017)

9. Amiri, S., Hosseinabady, M., McIntosh-Smith, S., Nunez-Yanez, J.: Multi-precision convolutional neural networks on heterogeneous hardware. In: 2018 Design, Automation & Test in Europe Conference & Exhibition (DATE), pp. 419–424 (2018). https://doi.org/10.23919/DATE.2018.8342046

10. Mahjoub, A.B., Atri, M.: Implementation of convolutional-LSTM network based on CPU, GPU and pynq-zl board. In: IEEE International Conference on Design & Test of Integrated Micro & Nano-Systems (DTS) **2019**, 1–6 (2019). https://doi.org/10.1109/DTSS.2019.8915287

11. Sun, X., et al.: Hybrid 8-bit floating point (HFP8) training and inference for deep neural networks. NeurIPS (2019). https://proceedings.neurips.cc/paper/2019/file/65fc9fb4897a89789352e211ca2d398f-Paper.pdf

12. Rössler, A., Cozzolino, D., Verdoliva, L., Riess, C., Thies, J., Nießner, M.: Face-Forensics++: learning to detect manipulated facial images (2019). arXiv:1901.08971

13. Li, Y., Yang, X., Sun, P., Qi, H., Lyu, S.: Celeb-df: a largescale challenging dataset for deepfake forensics. In: Proceedings of the IEEE/CVF Conference on Computer Vision and Pattern Recognition, pp. 3207–3216 (2020)

14. Dolhansky, B., et al.: The deepfake detection challenge dataset. arXiv preprint. arXiv:2006.07397 (2020)

15. Das, S., Seferbekov, S., Datta, A., Islam, M.S., Amin, M.R.: Towards solving the deepfake problem: an analysis on improving DeepFake detection using dynamic face augmentation. arXiv (2021)

Memory Access Optimization for Former Process of Pencil Drawing Style Image Conversion in High-Level Synthesis

Honoka Tani and Akira Yamawaki[✉]

Department of Electrical Engineering and Electronics, Kyushu Institute of Technology, Kitakyushu, Japan
tani.honoka795@mail.kyutech.jp, ya-ma@ecs.kyutech.ac.jp

Abstract. To effectively use high-level synthesis, which automatically converts software to hardware, it is necessary to create software programs considering hardware configuration. This paper attempts to automatically generate high-performance and power-saving hardware from software for pencil drawing style image conversion. The former process of the pencil drawing style image conversion reads the input image for each window and generates a lot of middle images. Automatic generation of better hardware requires an optimization of those memory accesses. The proposed method optimizing memory accesses achieves a performance improvement of about 65 times over the base hardware. As a result, the proposed method improved performance by about 1.4 times and 50 times compared to the software execution on a PC and an embedded CPU respectively.

Keywords: High-Level Synthesis · Memory access · FPGA

1 Introduction

The advance of virtual space technology will further accelerate the development of image processing systems. In particular, further development of smart glasses is expected, and it is desirable to achieve higher performance and power saving in high-level image processing, such as non-photorealistic rendering that synthesizes, processes, and transforms real images in the field of view. In this paper, we focus on a pencil drawing style image conversion process [1, 2], which is one of non-photorealistic rendering, and develop hardware for it. To develop high-performance and power-saving hardware, we use high-level synthesis (HLS) tools. The HLS is a technology that automatically converts software to hardware and can significantly reduce the burden of hardware design [3–6]. However, to use HLS effectively, it is necessary to create software programs considering the structure of hardware. The HLS technology is used to develop hardware modules of several software applications [7, 8]. However, we cannot find previous research applying HLS to the pencil drawing style image conversion of non-photorealistic rendering.

The whole processing flow of the pencil drawing style image conversion briefly consists of the former process and the latter process. Since the whole processing flow is

H. Takizawa et al. (Eds.): PDCAT 2022, LNCS 13798, pp. 57–68, 2023.
https://doi.org/10.1007/978-3-031-29927-8_5

large, we would like to focus on the former process as a first step. The former process of the pencil drawing style image conversion reads the input image for each window and generates a lot of middle images. So, we attempt to optimize those memory accesses so that the HLS generates a well-organized hardware module.

This paper is organized as follows. Section 2 briefly explains the whole processing flow of the pencil drawing style image conversion. Then, the algorithm intuitive source code is shown. Section 3 describes the proposed software description method considering the nature of hardware module. Section 4 show the experimental results and discusses them. Finally Sect. 5 concludes this paper.

2   Pencil Drawing Style Conversion Process

The pencil drawing style conversion process in this paper is designed to imitate the characteristic that when a person draws an outline with a pencil, multiple lines are overlapped along the edge and in the same direction. Figure 1 shows an overview of the process.

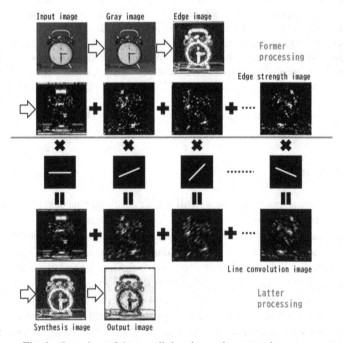

Fig. 1. Overview of the pencil drawing style conversion process

A color input image is converted to a gray image. Next, a Sobel filter is applied to the gray image to extract edges. When the Sobel filter is applied, the edge strengths are given in the x- and y-directions, and the direction of the vector is the direction of the edge. This is separated into eight directions of 22.5° each to obtain an edge strength image. The line convolution image is then obtained by convolving the line images corresponding to each edge strength image. These images are synthesized, and the luminance is inverted to output a pencil-drawing style image.

First, pure software was created to implement the algorithm in an intuitive manner. Figure 2 shows the former processing software program.

The GetGray function grays a single pixel, the GetSobel function applies a Sobel filter, and the angle function separates edge strength in eight directions.

```
void PencilFormer( u32 *src, u8 dst[8][1280 * 720], u16 w, u16 h )
{
  int i, j, k, l, a;
  u8 s;
  u8 win[3][3];

  for( i = 3/2; i < h - 3/2; i++ ){
    for( j = 3/2; j < w - 3/2;j++ ){
      for( k = (-3/2); k <= 3/2; k++ ){
        for( l = (-3/2); l <= 3/2; l++ ){
          win[(3/2) + k][(3/2) + l]
              = GetGray(src[((i + k) * w) + (j + l)]);
        }
      }
      int x,y;
      s = GetSobel(win, &x, &y);
      a = angle(x, y);

      for( k = 0 ; k < 8 ; k++ ){
        if( k == a ) dst[k][ i * w + j] = s;
        else         dst[k][ i * w + j] = 0;
      }
    }
  }
}
```

Fig. 2. Pure software program

3 Proposal Method

High-level synthesis can directly convert to hardware for a simple algorithm. However, the pencil drawing style conversion process in this paper is a window-based process, so memory access is complex. In addition, the input/output of edge strength images in eight directions may increase memory access and adversely affect hardware performance. Therefore, the pure software shown in Fig. 2 is not suitable for effective use of high-level synthesis. In this paper, we divide the overall processing into two parts and reconstruct the former processing software within the smaller target into software that considering the hardware configuration, based on the following policies.

(1) Instead of using an image-size array of eight edge intensity images, use an image-size array of 64 bits per element, with each element containing the strength of one byte in each of the eight directions, to reduce the number of memory outputs.
(2) The window-based memory access is changed to a pixel-based raster scan method so that the memory access becomes a one-dimensional continuous access.

The software program for high-level synthesis will be developed in the following sections.

3.1 Reconstruction of Edge Strength Image Input/output

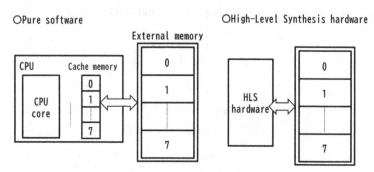

Fig. 3. Output of the edge strength image

As images become larger, it is not possible to store all the image data inside the hardware, so they are generally placed in large external memory. The pure software shown in Sect. 2 is compiled and executed by the CPU. The CPU usually accesses the high-speed memory called cache memory, as shown on the left side of Fig. 3, and accesses external memory only when necessary. Therefore, preparing individual edge strength images is not predicted to have a significant impact on performance. On the other hand, the high-level synthesis hardware needs to access external memory directly, as shown on the right side of Fig. 3, so an increase in memory accesses directly leads to performance degradation. Therefore, the software that serves as the input to the high-level synthesis hardware is restructured to minimize memory accesses for high-level synthesis. In the pure software, when outputting the eight edge strength images, the edge strengths were written in separate two-dimensional arrays corresponding to the direction of the edge strength. As a result, the number of elements required for output is eight times that of the input image. Figure 4 shows the hardware configuration and program that improves on this point

```
void PencilFormer( u32 *src, u64 *dst, u16 w, u16 h )
{
    int i, j, k, l, a;
    u8 s, win[3][3], class[8];

    for( i = 3/2; i < h - 3/2; i++ ){
        for( j = 3/2; j < w - 3/2;j++ ){
            for( k = (-3/2); k <= 3/2; k++ ){
                for( l = (-3/2); l <= 3/2; l++ ){
                    win[(3/2) + k][(3/2) + l] = GetGray(src[((i + k) * w) + (j + l)]);
                }
            }
            int x,y;
            s = GetSobel(win, &x, &y);
            a = angle(x, y);

            for( k = 0 ; k < 8 ; k++ ){
                if( k == a ) class[k] = s;
                else         class[k] = 0;
            }
            u64 dst val = 0;
            for( k = 0 ; k < 8 ; k++ ) dst val |= (u64) class[k] << (k * 8);
            dst[ i w + j] = dst val;
        }
    }
}
```

Fig. 4. Change to 64-bit array of edge strength images

The output is an image-size array of 64 bits per element, and the 8-directional intensities are written one byte at a time. Depending on the direction of the edge strength, either the edge strength or '0' is written. Thus, it is possible to write the edge intensities for eight directions in one element, reducing the number of writes to the edge intensity image.

3.2 Reconstruction of Memory Access Unit

Software is a sequential process, completing one process at a time, so that one process is not started until the next process is completed. In contrast, hardware is a parallel process and performs pipeline processing, allowing multiple processes to be performed in parallel. Figure 5 shows the pipeline processing for the program shown in Fig. 4.

Figure 5 shows a conceptual diagram of three-stage pipeline operation. The vertical direction represents the processing stages (St.1, 2, and 3), and the processing data moves horizontally through each stage. St.1 is the window readout, St.2 is the Sobel filter processing, and St.3 is the output of the edge intensity image.

Ideally, the pipeline would advance one clock at a time, so processing of the entire image would be expected to be completed in the number of image-size clocks. However, in the case of window-by-window processing, as shown in Fig. 5, all pixels in a 3 × 3

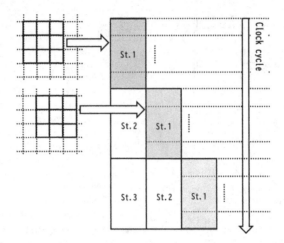

Fig. 5. Concept of operation of pipeline processing

```
int i, j, k, l;
u8 win[3][3];
for( i = 3/2; i < h - 3/2; i++ ){
  for( j = 3/2; j < w - 3/2; j++ ){
    for( k = (-3/2); k <= 3/2; k++ ){
      for( l = (-3/2); l <= 3/2; l++ ){
        win[(3/2) + k][(3/2) + l] = GetGray(src[((i + k) * w) + (j + l)]);
      }
    }
  }
}
```

```
int i, j, k, l;
static u8 buf_r[3][1280];
u8 pix, pixel[3], win[3][3];
for( i = 0 ; i < h ; i++ ){
  for( j = 0 ; j < w ; j++ ){
    pix = GetGray(src[i * w + j]);
    for( k = 0 ; k < 2 ; k++ ){
      buf_r[k][j] = buf_r[k + 1][j];
      pixel[k] = buf_r[k][j];
    }
    pixel[2] = buf_r[2][j] = pix;
    for( k = 0 ; k < 3 ; k++ ){
      for( l = 0 ; l < 2 ; l++ ){
        win[k][l] = win[k][l + 1];
      }
    }
    for( k = 0 ; k < 3 ; k++ ){
      win[k][2] = pixel[k];
    }
  }
}
```

Fig. 6. Program Description for High-level Synthesis

window must be read before the next stage of processing can proceed. Therefore, it takes 9 clocks to complete Stage 1, and as a result, the pipeline advances only every 9 clocks, which means that the processing of the entire image requires approximately 9 times the number of clocks of the image size. This means that processing the entire image requires approximately nine times the number of clocks of the image size. Figure 6 shows the program improvements that can be made to achieve ideal pipelining even for window processing.

In Fig. 6, the memory access is changed from window-by-window to pixel-by-pixel raster scan. This is made possible by using buffers, which are temporary storage locations for data. A schematic diagram is shown in Fig. 7.

First, the input image is read one pixel at a time and written to a buffer (St.1). Next, the buffer row data is written to a 3 × 3 window function (St.2). Then, filter processing is performed (St.3). In this way, one-dimensional sequential memory access can be realized.

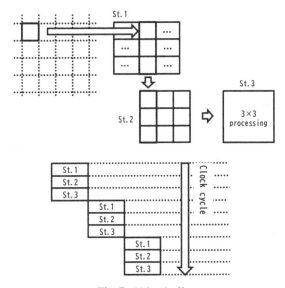

Fig. 7. Using buffer

4   Experiments and Discussions

The terms used in the experiment are defined in Table 1 below.

Table 1. Definition of Terms

terms	Program Contents
program1	Pure software(Fig.2)
program2	Merges edge strength images into a single 64-bit, single-pixel image(Fig.4)
program3	Memory access changed to raster scan method(Fig.6)

In addition, the input images used in this study are shown in Fig. 8. Figure 8 (a) shows a relatively large-size image used for verification, and (b) shows a smaller-size image for logic circuit simulation.

(a) For verification (1280×720)

(b) For logic circuit simulation
(64×64)

Fig. 8. Experimental image

4.1 Software Execution Time

The execution time of software programs was measured using cygwin64 on a PC. The results are shown in Fig. 9. The CPU of the PC is Intel's Core i5, operating at 3.7 GHz. The compiler used was gcc, and the optimization option was-O3.

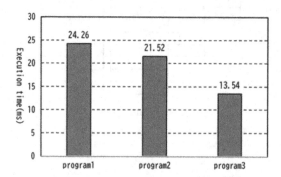

Fig. 9. Execution time on the PC

Figure 9 shows that the software performance on the PC was almost the same for program1 and program2. It can be seen that the reconstruction of multiple images packed into a single image with long and large pixels has almost no negative effect on software performance. One possible reason is that the cache memory worked effectively. It is assumed that the effect of the cache memory masked the effects of both the access to the eight individual edge-enhanced images and the window-by-window memory accesses.

On the other hand, the reconstruction to program3 achieved a performance improvement of approximately 1.8 times compared to program1. Raster-scanning of continuous accesses against windowed reads of discontinuous accesses is also effective for cache memory.

4.2 Simplified Estimate of the Number of Cycles After High-Level Synthesis

Next, the software was high-level synthesized and converted to high-level synthesis hardware using Xilinx's high-level synthesis tool, Vitis HLS 2021.1. After applying high-level synthesis to the software, the high-level synthesis tool generates a hardware module and reports an estimate of the total number of clock cycles required by the hardware module for the entire process. The results are shown in Fig. 10.

The programs were restructured for higher-level synthesis, which is expected to reduce the estimated number of clocks. However, there is no difference in the number of clocks between programs 1 and 2, and there is no effect of integrating edge intensity images. On the other hand, the estimated number of clocks for program 3 was significantly reduced, and a value close to 921,600 (=1280 × 720) total pixels was obtained.

For programs 1 and 2, the high-level synthesis tool is unclear about the details of the memory addresses and seems to report only the number of clocks required for the internal processing of the functions. Therefore, to measure the processing time considering more detailed data input/output, we performed logic circuit simulations on the automatically generated hardware in the high-level synthesis tool.

4.3 Performance Estimation in Logic Circuit Simulation

In logic circuit simulation, the operation of high-level synthesis hardware is simulated at the clock cycle level, taking even data input/output into account, so the processing time is predicted to be close to that of the actual device to some extent.

In this experiment, we attempted to simulate a logic circuit with a large image size, as shown in Fig. 8(a), but the simulation did not complete even after several hours. Therefore, to speed up the experiment, the image size was set to 64 × 64 as shown in Fig. 8(b) through trial experiments. The number of clock cycles obtained from the experiment is shown in Fig. 11.

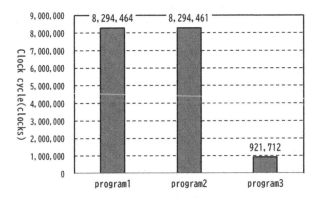

Fig. 10. Estimated clock count value after high-level synthesis

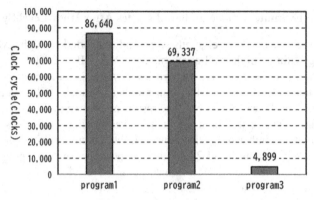

Fig. 11. Simulation Results

Figure 11 shows that more detailed and accurate logic simulation shows that the processing time decreases as the program is reconstructed. The performance improvement from program1 to program2 is about 1.25 times (=86640/69337), which represents the effect of consolidating 8 image arrays into 1 image array with 64 bits per pixel and increasing the pixel size by 8 times. This represents the effect of reducing the number of memory accesses to 1/8 by integrating eight image arrays into one image array, even though the pixel size is increased by a factor of eight by increasing the number of bits per pixel to 64 bits. The total number of pixels in the image in Fig. 8(b) is 4,096 (= 64 × 64), and the total number of clock cycles in program 3 is approximately ideal. This is because, as shown in Fig. 5, program 3 has achieved an ideal pipelining of 1 data/ 1 clock by the high-level synthesis tool.

4.4   Performance Measurement on Actual Equipment

The generated high-level synthesis hardware was converted into circuit data to be written into an FPGA using Xilinx's FPGA implementation tool Vivado 2021.1. The FPGA to be implemented was Xilinx's Zynq-7000, and the FPGA board ZYBO Z7 from DIGI-LENT, which is equipped with the FPGA, was used for verification on the actual device. A display was connected to the HDMI port on the FPGA board for visual verification, and images before and after processing were directly displayed there. Figure 8(a) was used to measure the number of clocks on the actual device and the number of clocks of the software on the PC, and the execution time was calculated. The operating frequencies were PC (3.7 GHz), embedded processor (650 MHz), and FPGA (100 MHz). The verification results are shown in Fig. 12.

The same trend as the results obtained from the logic circuit simulation (Fig. 11) was observed in the verification on the actual device. In the verification on the actual device, the proposed method with memory access optimization achieved a performance improvement of approximately 65 times at the hardware level. The hardware generated from the program3 achieved a performance improvement of about 54 times and power efficiency of about 350 times over the software on the embedded CPU, and a performance improvement of about 1.4 times and power efficiency of about 50 times over the software on the PC.

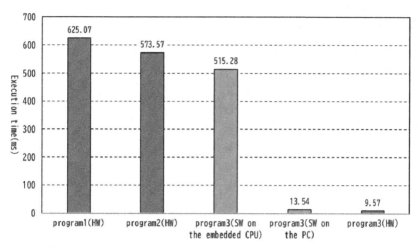

Fig. 12. Actual equipment verification results

5 Conclusion

In this paper, we propose a method of describing memory access for software in which high-level synthesis produces high-performance hardware. Experimental results show that the software reconstruction is an effective method for improving hardware performance. In the future, we plan to implement the entire hardware by applying the same description as in this paper to the later stage of the pencil-drawing style image conversion process.

References

1. Kumar, M.P.P., Poornima, B., Nagendraswamy, H.S., Manjunath, C.: A comprehensive survey on non-photorealistic rendering and benchmark developments for image abstraction and stylization. Iran J. Comput. Sci. **2**(3), 131–165 (2019). https://doi.org/10.1007/s42044-019-000 34-1
2. Lu, C., Xu, L., Jia, J.: Combining sketch and tone for pencil drawing production. In: Proceedings of International Symposium on Non-Photorealistic Animation and Rendering 2012, pp. 65–73 (2012)
3. Nane, R., Sima, V.-M., Olivier, B., Meeuws, R., Yankova, Y., Bertels, K.: DWARV 2.0: a CoSy-based C-to-VHDL hardware compiler. In: FPL, pp. 619–622 (2012)
4. Ferrandi, F., et al.: Invited: Bambu: an open-source research framework for the high-level synthesis of complex applications. In: 2021 58th ACM/IEEE Design Automation Conference (DAC), pp. 1327–1330 (2021)

5. Özkan, M.A., et al.: AnyHLS: high-level synthesis with partial evaluation. IEEE Trans. Comput. Aided Des. Integr. Circuits Syst. **39**(11), 3202–3214 (2020)
6. Petrou Mousouliotis, P.G., Petrou, L.P.: CNN-grinder: from algorithmic to high-level synthesis descriptions of CNNs for low-end-low-cost FPGA SoCs. Microprocess. Microsyst. **73** (2020). https://doi.org/10.1016/j.micpro.2020.102990
7. Younes, H., Ibrahim, A., Rizk, M., Valle, M.: Algorithmic-level approximate tensorial SVM using high-level synthesis on FPGA. Electronics **10**(2), 205 (2021). https://doi.org/10.3390/electronics10020205
8. Sjövall, P., Lemmetti, A., Vanne, J., Lahti, S., Hämäläinen, T.D.: High-level synthesis implementation of an embedded real-time HEVC intra encoder on FPGA for media applications. ACM Trans. Des. Autom. Electron. Syst. **27**(4), Article No. 35, 1–34 (2022). https://doi.org/10.1145/3491215

Word2Vec FPGA Accelerator Based on Spatial and Temporal Parallelism

Hasitha Muthumala Waidyasooriya$^{(\boxtimes)}$, Shutaro Ishihara, and Masanori Hariyama

Graduate School of Information Sciences, Tohoku University, 6-3-09, Aramaki-Aza-Aoba, Aoba, Sendai, Miyagi 980-8579, Japan
{hasitha,hariyama}@tohoku.ac.jp, shutaro.ishihara.p5@dc.tohoku.ac.jp

Abstract. Word2vec is a word embedding method that converts words into vectors in such a way that the semantically and syntactically relevant words are close to each other in the vector space. Acceleration is required to reduce the processing time of Word2vec. We propose a power-efficient FPGA accelerator exploiting temporal and spatial parallelism. The proposed FPGA accelerator has the highest power-efficiency compared to existing top-end GPU accelerators. It is more power efficient and nearly two times faster compared to a previously proposed highly power-efficient FPGA accelerator.

Keywords: Word embedding · FPGA · machine learning · natural language processing

1 Introduction

Word embedding is a method of mapping words onto vectors in such a way that semantically and syntactically relevant words are closed to each other in the vector space. Word2vec [10,11] is one of such word embedding methods. It is already used in many applications such as NLP [8], sentiment classification [16,17] and big data processing [9]. Many accelerators are already proposed using high-end CPUs such as [6,7,14,15] and using GPUs such as [2,3,5]. However, the power consumption of such high-end processors is very high. To solve this problem, FPGA accelerators such as [12] are also proposed.

In this paper, we propose an FPGA accelerator design using OpenCL for Word2vec acceleration. It is based on a novel scheduling method that exploits both temporal an spatial parallelism. We achieved a high power efficiency compared to existing top-end GPU-based accelerators. The proposed accelerator is more power-efficient and nearly two times faster compared to one of the previous power-efficient FPGA accelerator.

2 Previous Work

2.1 Word2vec Algorithm

Word2vec produces a vector space for a large corpus of text. A vector is assigned to each unique word in the corpus. Words that share common context are located

H. Takizawa et al. (Eds.): PDCAT 2022, LNCS 13798, pp. 69–77, 2023.
https://doi.org/10.1007/978-3-031-29927-8_6

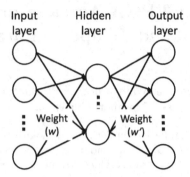

Fig. 1. Neural network of Word2vec.

close to each other in the vector space. There are two methods to compute vectors. One is to use the context to predict a target word, which is known as *continuous bag of words* (CBOW). The other is to use a word to predict a target context, which is called *skip-gram*.

Let us consider a corpus that contain the words $w_1, w_2, ..., w_T$. Let us denote w_t as the word at the position t. The set of words form $t - b$ and $t + b$ are given by the set $w_{t-b}, w_{t-b+1}, ..., w_{t-1}, w_{t+1}, ..., w_{t+b}$. When the word w_t in a corpus is appeared, the probability of finding a near-by word w_{t+j} is given by $P(w_{t+j}|w_t)$. We consider the minimization of the objective function L given by Eq.(1), using two-layer neural network, shown in Fig. 1. The input and output layers consist of v-dimensional vocabulary, where the number of unique words of the corpus is v. The weights of the hidden layer and the output layer are $W = [v_1 v_2 v_3 ... v_v]$ and $W\prime = [v\prime_1 v\prime_2 v\prime_3 ... v\prime_v]$, respectively.

$$L = \sum_{t=1}^{T} \sum_{-b \leq j \leq b, j \neq 0} log(P(w_{t+j}|w_t)) \tag{1}$$

In order to find the probability P, *skip-gram with negative sampling* (SGNS) model is proposed in [10,11]. Since this paper is focused on hardware implementation of the Word2vec, we limit our explanation to the data-flow of the algorithm.

FPGA accelerator for word2vec has been proposed in [12]. This method is based on the Hogwild method [13] by executing multiple processing units simultaneously. However, when more processing units are added, the required memory access bandwidth increases. After adding a certain number of processing units, we will no longer get any processing speed increase. To solve this problem, we propose a new scheduling method to increase the temporal parallelism. The proposed systolic array architecture employs temporal parallelism by reusing intermediate data. As a result, we can reduce the required memory bandwidth while accessing more data in parallel.

```
1  for all words in a sentence do
2  |    outputword ← select from sentence
3  |    for all words in a window do
4  |    |    inputword ← select from window
5  |    |    li = inputword× LAYERSIZE
6  |    |    for x ← 1 to LAYERSIZE do
7  |    |    |    temp[x] = 0
8  |    |    end
9  |    |    for k ← 1 to NEGATIVE +1 do
10 |    |    |    if k == 0 then
11 |    |    |    |    targetword ← outputword
12 |    |    |    |    label = 1
13 |    |    |    else
                      // negative samples
14 |    |    |    |    targetword ← select from negative words
15 |    |    |    |    label = 0
16 |    |    |    end
17 |    |    |    lo = targetword× LAYERSIZE
18 |    |    |    f = 0
19 |    |    |    for x ← 1 to LAYERSIZE do
20 |    |    |    |    f+ = W[li + x] × W'[lo + x]
21 |    |    |    end
22 |    |    |    g = ALPHA ×(label − σ(f))
23 |    |    |    for x ← 1 to LAYERSIZE do
24 |    |    |    |    temp[x]+ = g × W'[lo + x]
25 |    |    |    end
26 |    |    |    for x ← 1 to LAYERSIZE do
27 |    |    |    |    W'[lo + x]+ = g × W[l1 + x]
28 |    |    |    end
29 |    |    end
30 |    |    for x ← 1 to LAYERSIZE do
31 |    |    |    W[li + x]+ = temp[x]
32 |    |    end
33 |    end
34 end
```

Algorithm 1: An extract of the SGNS algorithm

2.2 Acceleration of Word2vec

Algorithm 1 shows the word2vec computation using skip-gram model. The computation is highly data dependent and difficult to parallelize. The most popular method of acceleration is to use Hogwild method [13]. It computes the outer loop in parallel in multiple threads. The data dependency among multiple threads is ignored. However, when we increase the number of threads, we also have to access more data in parallel. As we can see in Algorithm 1, the *outputword* in line 2, *inputword* in line 5, negative words in line 14 and weight vectors W and W' are accessed from the main memory. The required bandwidth to access vector W is relatively small since the value of li does not change rapidly. However, the value of l_o changes for each loop iteration in line 9 due to different negative words. Since the negative words are selected randomly, the value of l_o is also decided randomly. As a result, access of W' requires a large memory bandwidth. To solve this problem, [6] proposes a method to share negative samples. This method use the same set of negative words inside a window. It has been proven in many studies that the method in [6] does not have a noticeable impact on the accuracy of the algorithm.

2.3   Data-Flow of Word2vec

As shown in Algorithm 1, data dependency exists only among arrays W and W'. The data of the array W are read in line 20 and written back in line 31. Similarly, data of the array W' are read in lines 20 and 24, and written back in line 27. All the other data are read-only, so that no data dependency exists. Note that, $LAYERSIZE$ number of elements are accessed from arrays W and W' from the base addresses li and lo respectively. The values of li and lo are decided by *inputword* and *targetword*. The *targetword* equals either to an *outputword* or to a *negativeword*. Since the data access is already complex, we focus only on *inputword* and *outputword*.

Algorithm 2 shows an extremely simplified version of the SGNS method, that only focus on the updates of the W and W' arrays. For the simplicity, let us denote $W[li]$ as W_i and $W'[lo]$ as W'_o where $i, o \in \{1, 2, 3, ...\}$. When the window size is $2 \times b$, the access sequence in Algorithm 2 is (W_{k-b}, W'_k) ,(W_{k-b+1}, W'_k), ... , (W_{k+b}, W'_k), (W_{k+1-b}, W'_k). Within a window, different elements of array W are accessed, so that there is no data dependency. On the other hand, the same element of W' is accessed, and the computation of each element is dependent on the value of the same element accessed earlier.

We rearrange the access order in such a way that the data accessed at the same time are different and the data dependency is preserved. Figure 2 shows and example of such a scheduling scheme. In this case, window size is 6. Data in the same horizontal direction are processed in parallel. In each control step, new data are accessed to compute W and W'. Computed results of W and W' are reused two and one control steps later, respectively. Therefore, W and W' are reused 6 times, which equals to the window size. However, as we can see in Fig. 2, W_i, W'_i (such as $(W_4 W'_4), (W_5 W'_5), ...$) are not calculated. Therefore, we can skip this calculation.

As shown in Algorithm 1, W' is updated after the calculation of each sample. Similarly, W is updated after the calculation of each window. The updated data are written to the external memory and read back when those are required again. In the proposed scheduling in Fig. 2, a new data of W and W' are accessed in each control step, without waiting for the previous data to be written to the external memory. In order to work this method accurately, $W_i \neq W_j$ and $W'_i \neq W'_j$ for $i \neq j$. This is usually true since we purposely schedule the data flow in such a way that $i \neq j$ in every control step. However, we have assumed that *inputwords* (and/or *outputwords*) shown in Algorithm 1 are different at different positions.

```
1  for all words in a sentence do
2  |    outputword ← select from sentence
3  |    lo = outputword× LAYERSIZE
4  |    for all words in a window do
5  |    |    inputword ← select from window
6  |    |    li = inputword× LAYERSIZE
7  |    |    update(W[li])
8  |    |    update(W'[lo])
9  |    end
10 end
```

Algorithm 2: The data access of SGNS algorithm. Negative sample data access and computations are omitted for simplicity. The computations in the inner-most loops are also omitted.

However, there is a possibility that the same *inputword* (and/or *outputword*) is found at different positions. In such cases, the previous values of the data are accessed from the external memory before those were updated. We can minimize this affect by processing in small batches, rather than the whole sentence. After each batch, the data are written back to the external memory and accessed again in the next batch. Therefore, the data dependency among batches is preserved. The smaller the batch sizes are, lesser the possibility of violating data dependency. However, it also increases the external memory access.

Temporal parallelism refers to compute multiple windows in parallel while preserving the data dependency as shown in the horizontal direction of each time step in Fig. 2. Spatial parallelism refers to the data parallel computation of multiple vector values. For example, we can apply spatial parallelism to the lines 19, 23, 26 and 30 in Algorithm 1, so that part of those loops are processed in parallel.

3   Systolic Array Architecture for Word2vec

Figure 3 shows the proposed 1-D systolic array architecture. The number of PEs equals to the window size and each PE corresponds to the computation of a position of the window. That is, each PE corresponds to the computation belonging to the nodes shown horizontally in each time step in Fig. 2. In the next time step, PEs are reused. PEs are connected through shift-registers and those shift-registers are used to transfer intermediate results between PEs. Only the first and the last PEs access the external memory while the rest of the PEs reuse the intermediate results of the previous PEs. Therefore, the memory access is reduced.

Figure 4 shows the scheduling of the operations inside a PE. The data access and computation are done in parallel so that the data access overhead is negligible compared to the computation time. The computation is done with the degree of spatial parallelism. Increasing this parallelism will increase the memory access bandwidth.

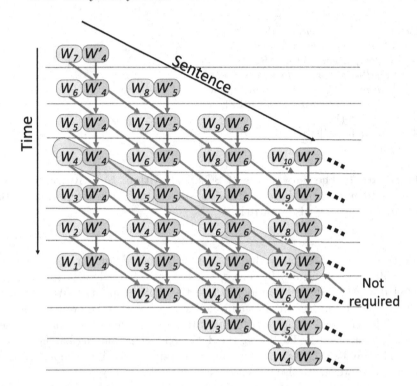

Fig. 2. Scheduling scheme to process multiple window positions in parallel.

4 Evaluation

For the evaluation, we use 'BittWare 520N-MX FPGA board [1] that contains a Stratix 10 SX FPGA. We use ntel FPGA SDK for OpenCL version 19.4. Host codes are compiled using gcc version 10.2.0. The training data set is "news.shuffled.en.2010 2.1 GB" sample in "one billion word benchmark" [4].

Figure 5 shows the processing speed comparison against a previous FPGA-based accelerator [12] that has very high performance. The proposed accelerator is faster than the previous one and achieved nearly 2 times speed-up when the negative sample size is 10. Table 1 shows the resource utilization. The most critical one is logic resources with a utilization of 44%. Moreover, memory bandwidth is 34 GB/s, and it is only 6% of the theoretical maximum. Therefore, we can increase the speed-up further by increasing the spatial parallelism.

Figure 6 shows the power-efficiency comparison against previous accelerators that use GPUs and FPGAs. Power-efficiency is given by "kilo words per second per Watt" ($kWord/s/W$). Note that we use the maximum TDP (thermal dissipation power) values of GPUs to compute the power-efficiency, since actual values are not available. With our practical experience, we can say that the actual power consumption of GPUs are much close to their maximum TDP values for the applications optimized for the highest performance. FPGA power consump-

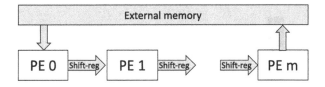

Fig. 3. Neural network of Word2vec.

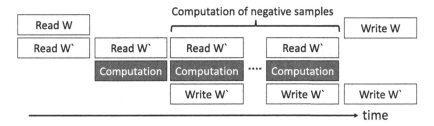

Fig. 4. Neural network of Word2vec.

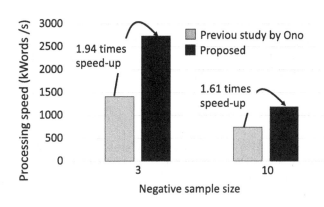

Fig. 5. Comparison of processing speed against previous FPGA accelerators.

Table 1. Comparison of resource usage.

Negative samples	Logic	Registers	DSP (%)	RAM block (%)	Clock frequency
3	307,637 (44%)	656,314	515 (13%)	2000 (29%)	254 MHz
10	305,642 (43%)	645,893	515 (13%)	2101 (31%)	260 MHz

tion is measured directly from the board. The proposed accelerator consumes 90 W, which is smaller compared to those of high-end GPUs. Our FPGA-based implementation has the highest power-efficiency compared to all previous GPU-based implementations such as [2,3,5] and [15]. In addition, we achieved better power-efficiency compared to CPU-based implementations such as [6] and [14]

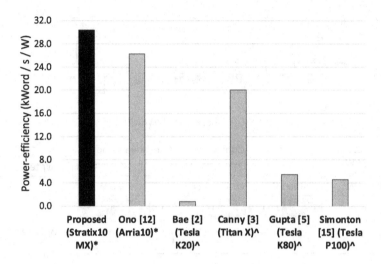

Fig. 6. Comparison of power-efficiency. ^Calculated using max TDP. *Calculated using measured power.

and also the previous FPGA implementation [12]. We measure the accuracy using "Google analogy dataset". The accuracy of the FPGA implementation is similar to that of CPU implementation.

5   Conclusion

In this paper, we proposed an FPGA-based accelerator for Word2vec exploiting temporal ans spatial parallelism. It has the best power-efficiency and nearly two times faster compared to previously proposed FPGA implementation [12]. Since less than 50% of the resources and only 6% of the bandwidth are used, it is possible to further increase performance by allowing more spatial parallel operations. Temporal parallel operations can be mapped to multiple FPGAs in a pipeline. There is a huge potential to increase the speed-up further.

Acknowledgment. This research is partly supported by MEXT KAKENHI, grant number 19K11998.

References

1. 520N-MX (2022). https://www.bittware.com/fpga/520n-mx/
2. Bae, S., Yi, Y.: Acceleration of Word2vec using GPUs. In: Hirose, A., Ozawa, S., Doya, K., Ikeda, K., Lee, M., Liu, D. (eds.) ICONIP 2016. LNCS, vol. 9948, pp. 269–279. Springer, Cham (2016). https://doi.org/10.1007/978-3-319-46672-9_31
3. Canny, J., Zhao, H., Jaros, B., Chen, Y., Mao, J.: Machine learning at the limit. In: 2015 Big IEEE International Conference on Big Data (Big Data), pp. 233–242. IEEE (2015)

4. Chelba, C., et al.: One billion word benchmark for measuring progress in statistical language modeling. arXiv preprint arXiv:1312.3005 (2013)
5. Gupta, S., Khare, V.: BlazingText: scaling and accelerating Word2Vec using multiple GPUs. In: Proceedings of the Machine Learning on HPC Environments, p. 6. ACM (2017)
6. Ji, S., Satish, N., Li, S., Dubey, P.: Parallelizing word2vec in multi-core and many-core architectures. arXiv preprint arXiv:1611.06172 (2016)
7. Ji, S., Satish, N., Li, S., Dubey, P.: Parallelizing word2vec in shared and distributed memory. arXiv preprint arXiv:1604.04661 (2016)
8. Kiros, R., et al.: Skip-thought vectors. In: Advances in Neural Information Processing Systems, pp. 3294–3302 (2015)
9. Ma, L., Zhang, Y.: Using Word2Vec to process big text data. In: 2015 IEEE International Conference on Big Data (Big Data), pp. 2895–2897. IEEE (2015)
10. Mikolov, T., Chen, K., Corrado, G., Dean, J.: Efficient estimation of word representations in vector space. arXiv preprint arXiv:1301.3781 (2013)
11. Mikolov, T., Sutskever, I., Chen, K., Corrado, G.S., Dean, J.: Distributed representations of words and phrases and their compositionality. In: Advances in Neural Information Processing Systems, pp. 3111–3119 (2013)
12. Ono, T., et al.: FPGA-based acceleration of word2vec using OpenCL. In: 2019 IEEE International Symposium on Circuits and Systems (ISCAS), pp. 1–5. IEEE (2019)
13. Recht, B., Re, C., Wright, S., Niu, F.: Hogwild: a lock-free approach to parallelizing stochastic gradient descent. In: Advances in Neural Information Processing Systems, pp. 693–701 (2011)
14. Rengasamy, V., Fu, T.Y., Lee, W.C., Madduri, K.: Optimizing Word2Vec performance on multicore systems. In: Proceedings of the Seventh Workshop on Irregular Applications: Architectures and Algorithms, p. 3. ACM (2017)
15. Simonton, T.M., Alaghband, G.: Efficient and accurate Word2Vec implementations in GPU and shared-memory multicore architectures. In: High Performance Extreme Computing Conference (HPEC), 2017 IEEE, pp. 1–7. IEEE (2017)
16. Su, Z., Xu, H., Zhang, D., Xu, Y.: Chinese sentiment classification using a neural network tool-Word2vec. In: 2014 International Conference on Multisensor Fusion and Information Integration for Intelligent Systems (MFI), pp. 1–6. IEEE (2014)
17. Xue, B., Fu, C., Shaobin, Z.: A study on sentiment computing and classification of sina weibo with word2vec. In: 2014 IEEE International Congress on Big Data (BigData Congress), pp. 358–363. IEEE (2014)

HPC and AI

Analyzing I/O Performance
of a Hierarchical HPC Storage System
for Distributed Deep Learning

Takaaki Fukai[1]([✉])[ID], Kento Sato[2][ID], and Takahiro Hirofuchi[1][ID]

[1] National Institute of Advanced Industrial Science and Technology (AIST),
Tokyo, Japan
{takaaki.fukai,t.hirofuchi}@aist.go.jp
[2] RIKEN Center for Computational Science, Kobe, Japan
kento.sato@riken.jp

Abstract. Deep learning is a vital technology in our lives today. Both
the size of training datasets and neural networks are growing to tackle
more challenging problems with deep learning. Distributed deep neural
network (DDNN) training technique is necessary to train a model with
large datasets and networks. For large-scale DDNN training, HPC clusters are excellent computation environments. I/O performance is critical
in large-scale DDNN on HPC clusters because it is becoming a bottleneck. Most flagship-class HPC clusters have hierarchical storage systems. It is necessary to quantify the performance improvement effect
of the hierarchical storage system on the workloads to design future
HPC storage systems. This study demonstrates the quantitative performance analysis of the hierarchical storage system for DDNN workload
in a flagship-class supercomputer. Our analysis shows how much performance improvement and storage volume increment will be required to
achieve the performance goal.

Keywords: Deep neural network · Distributed deep neural network
training · I/O performance · Hierarchical storage system · High
performance computing

1 Introduction

Today, there is a substantially higher demand for large-scale deep learning. The
sizes of training models and datasets for the training are expanding to satisfy
the demand. For example, datasets, like OpenImage [10], are used for training
image classification models like EfficientNet [19]. Some computational science
applications also use deep learning methods, such as CosmoFlow [12] and Deep-
Cam [9]. These heavy workloads are beyond a single machine's processing and
memory capabilities. Therefore, it must use the distributed deep neural network
(DDNN) training technique, which enables training models on multiple machines

connected via a network. HPC, optimized for huge and distributed workloads, is a favorable environment for large training workloads.

I/O is becoming a bottleneck in the training workloads for the following reasons [14,16]. The first reason is dataset growth. For training higher-quality models, dataset sizes are growing [5,11]. Training applications generate many I/O requests when dealing with large datasets that cannot fit in memory. The second reason is expanding performance gap between computation and I/O. Although computation time is becoming shorter using distributed execution techniques, I/O performance is not improved. This expands the performance gap. Therefore, the I/O performance of future HPC clusters is crucial.

It is essential but challenging to determine what improvements to storage systems would result in a target I/O intensive DDNN workload performance goal for developing a storage system for future HPC. The first reason it is difficult is that most storage systems in flagship-class HPC clusters are hierarchical, combining fast but small storage, and a slow but extensive storage system [17,20]. Therefore, it is unclear whether our costs—the volume for the local file system or the throughput of the global or local filesystems—should be covered. The second reason is that tuning a DNN application for distributed execution requires several weeks or months for a new cluster or processor architecture. Therefore, much cost and time would be required to determine the I/O bottleneck in the DDNN training workload.

This study demonstrates a case study on the performance analysis of a hierarchical storage system for DDNN workload and the estimation of necessary improvement of the storage systems to meet a performance goal. The I/O operations time of synthetic I/O intensive training workload would first be measured with various proportions of fast and slow storage sizes to reveal the effect of faster storage. Next, based on the findings of the I/O performance analysis, the impact of storage system improvement on training performance will be estimated. The method can estimate the contribution of various improvements of a hierarchical storage system to overall training performance.

The contributions of this work are: (1) A methodology to study the I/O bottleneck of DDNN training workloads in the hierarchical storage system; (2) A methodology to explore options for improvement of a storage system to satisfy the performance goal of DDNN training workloads.

The remaining part of this study is organized as follows. The background is explained in Sect. 2. The related work is reviewed in Sect. 3. Section 4 describes our method, which is illustrated on a supercomputer of the flagship class in Sect. 5. The method's potential is covered in Sect. 6 of the text. Finally, conclusions are presented in Sect. 7.

2   Background

2.1   File Access in Distributed Neural Network Workloads

The file access pattern in DNN training applications differs from that in scientific computational applications. In training, stochastic gradient descent (SGD) is a common technique to improve training speed and accuracy [3,13,22]. In SGD, a program splits a training dataset into a mini-batch and inputs a mini-batch to the neural network. It shuffles the order of the dataset's files whenever inputting all samples to the neural network to avoid the degradation of training accuracy due to a fixed input order. Therefore, the program accesses each file once an epoch in random order. Due to less temporal and spatial locality, it is hard to apply general cache policies. The reading file frequently experiences a cache miss if the dataset is larger than the memory volume for page caches. I/O is prone to becoming the bottleneck for this reason.

In distributed training, multiple compute nodes read the dataset simultaneously. In data-parallel, which is one of the common parallelizing techniques, each compute node has a part of the dataset and calculates it. There are two ways to shuffle data: local shuffle and global shuffle. Local shuffle means that each process only shuffles and reads a part of the dataset. On the other hand, global shuffle means that the application shuffles the whole dataset and splits it for each computer every epoch. Local shuffling makes it easy to use local storage for each computer because the computer needs to access only the initial allocated part of the dataset. However, it reduces the training accuracy because it reduces the randomness of the input dataset. Therefore, in some cases, the local shuffle approach is not suitable because of the accuracy degradation. In contrast, the global shuffling does not affect the training accuracy, but replacing the part of the dataset for each epoch is a heavy I/O workload, especially training with a large dataset and many computers. Therefore, we focus on global shuffling in this study.

2.2   Storage System in HPC

Recent flagship-class HPC clusters provide a hierarchical storage system typically consisting of a small but fast storage system and a large but slow storage system. HPC clusters often provide the former as a local file system (LFS) and the latter as a global file system (GFS). For example, Summit [20] provides node-local burst buffers (node-local NVMe SSD) and a parallel file system (IBM's SpectrumScale GPFS^{TM}). Fugaku [17] also provides a hierarchical storage system that consists of the 1st level storage (an SSD for every 16 nodes) and the 2nd level storage (a Global storage system). We assume that DDNN applications in a global shuffle manner use the local storage in the hierarchical storage as the cache of global storage. Therefore, an important question to answer for designing future storage systems in HPC for machine learning workload is what is the optimum balance of fast and slow storage from the viewpoint of size and performance?

3   Related Work

Numerous studies have been conducted to analyze and model the DNN performance. Wang et al. proposed a modeling method for the DNN training workload based on the Roofline model [21]. They focus on the computation and memory accesses; however, the I/O performance is not considered.

Numerous works are available for analyzing and optimizing I/O performance for DDNN workloads. Several studies [14, 16] have analyzed the I/O performance of the DDNN and proposed optimization methods. For example, Devarajan et al. proposed a benchmark to measure the I/O performance for DDNN and find the opportunity for tuning I/O parameters [6, 7]. The storage system targeted in these studies is not hierarchical. We focus on the I/O performance of hierarchical storage systems.

Several studies [8, 18, 23, 24] assume hierarchical storage systems in their I/O optimization method for DDNN workloads. They focus on application-level optimization to solve the I/O bottleneck. In contrast, our work is toward performance improvement of storage systems.

Paul et al. analyzed the I/O log produced by the jobs on Supercomputer Summit during a year [15]. They showed the tendency of ML jobs and their usage of the storage system, especially the usage of the burst buffer. The 23,389 ML jobs of 845,036 jobs in 2020 on Summit were analyzed in this study. The analysis showed a rapid increment in the use of ML technologies in HPC, and some ML jobs used the burst buffer in addition to the GPFS. This study analyzes the actual ML workload from the viewpoint of usage of the hierarchical storage system in the HPC environment. In-depth I/O performance analysis of hierarchical storage systems is done in our work.

4   Methodology

4.1   Overview

Our analysis method is composed of three steps, (1) measuring I/O performance, (2) analyzing measurement results, and (3) estimating the impact of the speed-up of global and local storage on training performance.

We execute a DDNN benchmark in the measurement while profiling the I/O on a hierarchical storage system. The benchmark reads a dataset from the hierarchical storage system and uses LFS as the cache of GFS. We measure the I/O performance with various proportions of the size of the cached data on LFS to reveal how LFS contributes to overall I/O performance. We expect that the performance characteristics depend on a performance balance of GFS and LFS as well as the sizes of files in a dataset. Therefore, we combine various performance balances with the file size to assess the I/O performance.

In the analyzing step, the profiling data were analyzed separately using the file system and the type of I/O operation. To do this, we break down the I/O time into the following four I/O classes according to the I/O profiling data obtained in the benchmark execution. *GFS-READ* is a class for reading operations on a GFS, *GFS-META* is a class for metadata operations (`open()`, `close()`) on a GFS, *LFS-READ* is a class for reading operations on an LFS, and *LFS-META* is a class for metadata operations on an LFS. Note that file operations on the dataset in DNN training are only `open()`, `close()`, and `read()` because applications do not make any modifications and new samples. We target the I/O time of the slowest process among all parallel processes, because it is the most dominant for the overall training time.

In the estimating step, we extrapolate from the above results the expected training time enabled by the speed-up of global and local storage. We first calculate the expected overall I/O operation time assuming that a given ratio improves the speed of an I/O class. We also calculate the expected impact on training time by the performance improvement of multiple I/O classes and which combination would satisfy the performance goal.

4.2   Measuring I/O Performance by Benchmark

We use DLIO [7] benchmark, an I/O benchmark for distributed deep neural network workloads, to measure the I/O performance. DLIO benchmark supports distributed execution and generating the synthetic dataset for the benchmark. It does not, however, support hierarchical storage. Therefore, we add the three functions to DLIO to measure the performance of hierarchical storage systems. The functions are (1) reading the dataset from both GFS and LFS in a specified proportion, (2) global shuffling, and (3) generating the synthetic files on the local filesystem by each compute node.

Cached files are not evicted in the benchmark execution. That is, the cache policy is pinning. As described in Sect. 2, the training application accesses all samples at equal times. Therefore, the cache hit rate with the pinning policy is the same as the percentage of the cached file [14].

Two datasets were prepared: a small file dataset and a large file emulating ImageNet dataset and CosmoFlow dataset, respectively. The small file dataset consists of 128 KiB files and the large file dataset consists of 12 MiB files. The number of files in the small and large datasets is 589824 and 6144, respectively. The total size of both datasets is 72 GiB, so that the entire dataset can be on the LFS. All of the processes read the same number of files. Since the entire dataset cannot be put on the memory of each compute node (32 GiB), the benchmark application reads the files from the filesystem. The file format in both datasets is tfrecord, and the number of samples in each file is one.

We measure the I/O performance with different numbers of the object storage targets (OSTs) of the lustre-based GFS to determine the I/O performance with multiple performance balances of the GFS and LFS. The number of OSTs can be limited to 1 by using `lfs` command. Therefore, we measure the I/O performance with all provided OSTs (faster GFS) and 1 OST (slower GFS).

Darshan [2], a profiling tool for I/O, was used to measure the I/O performance in the benchmark execution. Darshan can capture and record each file operations such as `open()`, `close()`, and `read()`.

4.3 Analyzing the I/O Performance

The I/O time of the slowest process is broken down into the four I/O classes defined in Sect. 4.1 to reveal the bottleneck in detail and recognize which I/O class is a bottleneck. We calculate the I/O time for each process and find the slowest one, which dominates the training performance. Then, we analyze the I/O performance from the log generated by darshan using `darshan-parser` command [1]. Finally, we calculate each I/O time based on `POSIX_F_READ_TIME` and `POSIX_F_META_TIME`.

4.4 Estimate Performance by Storage Improvement

We calculate $\times \frac{100}{100+N}$ of the measured time of the I/O class to estimate the impact of $N\%$ throughput improvement of an I/O class. The improvement may not directly influence the total I/O time since the improvement may change the bottleneck to another I/O class. Therefore, we calculate the total I/O time for each process with the improvement of a class, then pick the slowest process.

5 Experiment Results

5.1 Setup for Experiment

The experiments were conducted on Supercomputer Fugaku [17]. The compute nodes of Fugaku have 48 computing cores of A64FX and 32 GiB HBM2 memory. Fugaku has a hierarchical filesystem comprising the 1st- and 2nd-level filesystems named LLIO and FEFS, respectively. In our measurement, we regard the LLIO as an LFS and the FEFS as a GFS. FEFS is a lustre-based parallel filesystem with 60 OSTs in Fugaku. One per 192 compute nodes were connected to the FEFS by InfiniBand EDR. The other compute nodes connected by TofuD access FEFS through the network and the compute node. For LLIO, one per 16 compute nodes has an NVMe SSD, and the other compute nodes are connected access to the SSD through the network and the compute node. LLIO provides three areas, "node temporary area", "shared temporary area", and "2nd-layer cache area" [4]. In our measurement, we only use "node temporary areas", a dedicated area for a compute node, since the transparent cache does not allow us to regulate the caching files of the dataset on LLIO.

We run the DLIO benchmark as batch jobs over Supercomputer Fugaku's 768 compute nodes for our measurement. The four processes execute every compute node, so the total number of processes is 3072. The node layout is $8 \times 6 \times 16$ in the TofuD torus network. An option was also passed to the job scheduler to strict the position of the node connected to the GFS.

The datasets on the GFS are generated before executing the benchmark job. Because the system removes data on LFS after finishing the job, every benchmark job produces the same dataset on LFS as on GFS. Note that the job generates the dataset instead of copying the dataset from GFS to reduce the setup time.

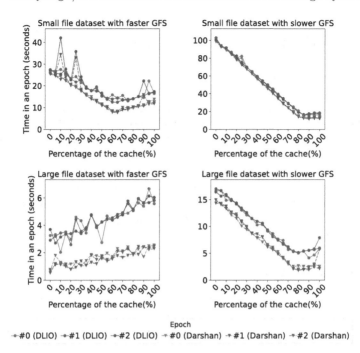

Fig. 1. Execution time of DLIO benchmark and I/O time reported by Darshan ("Percentage of the cache" means percentages of the files in the dataset put on the LFS).

The benchmark was executed every 5% from 0% to 100% cache rate. The calculation time in the DLIO was set to zero. Therefore, the DLIO reports only the I/O and data processing time. The number of epochs is three to avoid making the darshan log files huge. The prefetch of the dataloader is enabled so that it is not synchronized for each iteration, even if the computation threads are synchronized for all-reduce communication. The batch size is 12 for the small file dataset and 2 for the large file dataset.

5.2   Measuring Execution Time for Epochs

In our experiments, the execution time of the DLIO benchmark and I/O time in the benchmark execution with various settings were first measured, as mentioned in Sect. 4.2. Then, the difference in the performance was revealed based on file sizes in the datasets and speeds of GFS. Additionally, by comparing the execution time reported by the benchmark and the total I/O time reported by the I/O profiler, it was verified that the benchmark is I/O intensive.

Figure 1 shows the execution time and I/O time for each epoch in a job. The x-axis of the graphs shows the percentage of the files on the LFS. The y-axis shows the execution time of an epoch. The graph shows the results of 3 epochs in a benchmark execution. The lines with round markers are the execution time reported by the DLIO benchmark, and those with triangular markers are the I/O time reported by Darshan. Since the I/O time of the slowest I/O process is dominant, they are calculated and plotted as I/O time on the graph.

The results show that the influence of the LFS on the training performance is based on the file sizes and the performance balance of GFS and LFS. The effect of the LFS with the 1 OST of GFS is more significant than that with the 60 OSTs. The reason is the performance difference between LFS and GFS on the 1 OST is larger than that on 60 OSTs. In 12 MiB file workload with 60 OST of GFS, the LFS does not contribute to the performance improvement, and using only the GFS with the 60 OST is the best.

About the I/O time, the graph indicates that the execution time is constantly longer about 2 s, but it is strongly related to the I/O time. This finding shows a high correlation between training performance and the I/O time of the slowest process in each epoch.

5.3   Analyzing I/O Performance

Next, the Darshan records are classified into the four I/O classes, and the I/O time for each class is computed. Figure 2 illustrates the result of the breakdown of the #2 epoch in the previous graphs. Each line demonstrates the total I/O time, the same as in Fig. 1. Based on these findings, the bottleneck is different depending on the setup.

In 128 KiB file workload with the faster GFS, the bottleneck is GFS-META when less than 60% of the data is on the LFS. However, the bottleneck is changed to LFS-READ with more than 60% cached data on LFS. When more than 60% of the data is put on LFS, LFS throughput is saturated. Therefore, the read time from LFS increases linearly with the percentage of the cached data. So putting more than 60% of data in the cache in the workload does not add to the training performance. For example, in training with the ImageNet dataset, whose size is almost 150 GB, almost 90 GiB LFS for each compute node is enough to achieve the best I/O performance by the hierarchical storage system. With the 60% cached data, both GFS-META and LFS-READ are included in the I/O time of the slowest process.

Compared with the faster GFS, the I/O bottleneck in the workload with the slower GFS is quite different. The upper-right graph in Fig. 2 shows that the bottleneck is GFS-READ instead of GFS-META with small percentages of the LFS (less than 80%). The reason GFS-META time becomes shorter is reducing the load on the metadata server of FEFS because of the lower throughput of the GFS.

Compared with the small file workload, the I/O bottleneck in the large file workload with the faster GFS is also very different. The lower-left graph in Fig. 2 illustrates that the bottleneck is the LFS-READ in most cases. Because the number of metadata operations is much smaller than the small file workload, the GFS fully provides its bandwidth without the bottleneck by the metadata operation. Therefore, the total bandwidth of the GFS is higher than that of the LFS. This indicates that the 768 compute nodes are not enough to use the

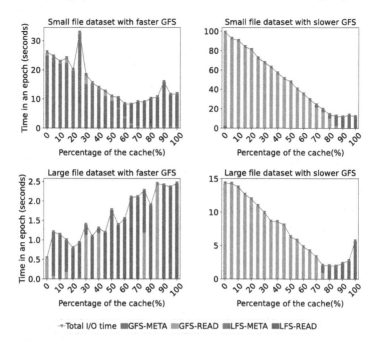

Fig. 2. Break down the I/O time of the slowest process for each epoch (Note: Range of y-axis are different)

LFS's scalability fully. Note that the 768 nodes are not so large scale as workload in Fugaku. However, from the viewpoint of the machine learning workload, the number of nodes is large enough to lead to a large-batch problem.

The tendency of the performance in the large file workload with the slower GFS is similar to that in the small file workload with slower GFS. Although the LFS-READ time in caching 100% case significantly increases in the lower-left graph in Fig. 2, we think it is an impact of noise because the spike does not appear in the other epochs in Fig. 1.

From the viewpoint of exploration of storage design for a performance goal, the result on a small file dataset and faster GFS (the left side graph in Fig. 2) is a challenging situation since multiple I/O class is are included in the I/O time in the fastest result (cache rate = 65%). This implies that improving only one I/O class processing will not be enough to improve the entire I/O performance. Therefore, we use the outcome to illustrate how we estimate the impact of I/O improvement.

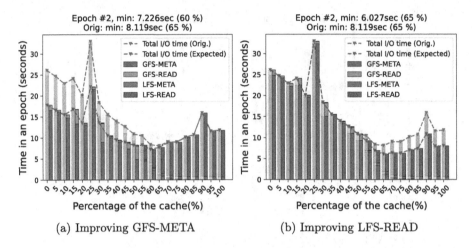

(a) Improving GFS-META   (b) Improving LFS-READ

Fig. 3. Expectation of the I/O time with 50% improvement with a small file dataset and 60 OSTs of the GFS

5.4 Estimating the Impact of the Storage Improvements

As mentioned in Sect. 4.4, the performance improvement is estimated from the analysis result using a simple calculation. Figure 3 illustrates the result of the estimation of the impact of a 50% improvement in GFS-META (Fig. 3a) and LFS-READ (Fig. 3b). The axes in the graph are the same as those in Fig. 2.

The estimated outcome of improving the GFS-META by 50% is shown in Fig. 3a. The best combination of the GFS and LFS is changed from 65% to 60% LFS, and the slowest I/O time is reduced by almost 12.8% in the best case. Figure 3b shows the estimation result of improving the LFS-READ by 50%. The best cache rate is not changed, and the slowest I/O time in the best case is reduced by 24%.

Next, we estimate of the impact of the improvement of two operations classes simultaneously. There are many parameters and values, such as the improvement rate for each operation, the cache rate, and the I/O time. All of them are too many to put on a single graph. Again, the system's architect needs knowledge of the given performance goal. Therefore, we present the estimate by indicating which improvement combination would meet the performance goal.

Figure 4 shows the sufficient combinations of the performance improvement on two classes, GFS-META and LFS-READ, on the small file dataset and the faster GFS workload. The result in the graph is based on the measurement of I/O time in the #2 epoch. The x and y axes show the improvement rate. The graph plots the dot if the improvement combination meets the performance goal. For example, the graph indicates a result for the performance goal of 4 s I/O time in an epoch. Additionally, the colors of the dots indicate the minimum cache rate to meet the goal. For example, achieving 4 s I/O time in an epoch with a 65% cache rate requires at least 120% improvement in LFS-READ. In that case, a 140% improvement of the GFS-META is required. The architect can explore the option of the improvement choice by the plot.

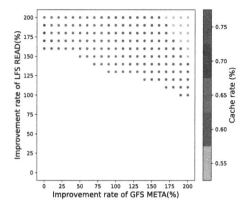

Fig. 4. The estimation of performance improvement of GFS-META and LFS-META for meeting the performance goal of 4 sec/epoch (128 KiB, 60 OST GFS)

6   Discussion

We used the global shuffling technique to exploit GFS in our evaluation. However, we can also consider intermediate technique. Training applications with the local shuffle can combine the LFS and GFS to allocate larger chunks of the dataset to each compute node than that with only the LFS. In this case, the LFS is regarded as the cache of the GFS, and the size of the chunk and randomness of the shuffling are a trade-off. Therefore, the application user can also use our method to find the contributions to the performance of the LFS to consider how large chunks are preferred from the viewpoint of cache rate.

In our evaluation, we assume a pinning cache policy on the LFS. However, our analysis can be applied to the other cache policies if the cache hit rate can be calculated. You can replace the "cache rate" with "cache hit rate" in the analysis result because both are the same in DNN workloads with the pinning policy. Then you can find the required size of the LFS from the relation between the cache hit rate and the cache size in your better cache policy.

In our evaluation, we estimate the improvement by a simple calculation. However, their performance characteristics may not be straightforward. For example, the estimation from the measurement results with 1 OST of the GFS with the simple calculation does not fit that with the 60 OSTs of GFS. The computation process can be improved by modeling the characteristics for a more accurate estimation. The considerable approaches are based on machine learning or queueing theory. Even if the calculation method is improved, our plot method shown in Fig. 4 is helpful for the storage system architect.

7   Conclusion

This study presented a case study on the performance analysis of a hierarchical storage system for the DDNN workload in a flagship-class HPC cluster, discussing potential performance improvement enabled by the speed-up of the storage system. It also estimated the improvement of training performance through various improvements to the hierarchical filesystem. The analysis results showed that the I/O bottleneck in the training workload depends on the performance balance between global and local storage and file sizes in a dataset.

Our estimation indicated that the performance improvement of a global filesystem would reduce the necessary volume size of a LFS, and the performance improvement of the LFS will reduce the fastest I/O time. Our estimation method can help architects of HPC file systems determine the volume size and performance requirements for local and global file systems to achieve a specific performance objective.

Because our proposed method needs the measurement of I/O performance at least once, one of our future works is exploring a simpler or no measurement-required method. The other future work is to build the performance modeling of the storage system for more accurate estimation.

Acknowledgements. This research used computational resources of the supercomputer Fugaku provided by the RIKEN Center for Computational Science. The authors would like to thank Enago (www.enago.jp) for the English language review.

References

1. Darshan-util installation and usage. https://www.mcs.anl.gov/research/projects/darshan/docs/darshan-util.html
2. Darshan - HPC I/O Characterization Tool. https://www.mcs.anl.gov/research/projects/darshan/
3. Akiba, T., et al.: Extremely large minibatch SGD: training ResNet-50 on ImageNet in 15 minutes (2017). https://arxiv.org/abs/1711.04325
4. Akimoto, H., et al.: File system and power management enhanced for supercomputer Fugaku. Fujitsu Tech. Rev. **3**, 2020-03 (2020)
5. Beal, J., et al.: Billion-scale pretraining with vision transformers for multi-task visual representations. In: Proceedings of the IEEE/CVF Winter Conference on Applications of Computer Vision, pp. 564–573 (2022)
6. Devarajan, H.: DLIO Benchmark. https://github.com/hariharan-devarajan/dlio_benchmark
7. Devarajan, H., et al.: DLIO: a data-centric benchmark for scientific deep learning applications. In: 2021 IEEE/ACM 21st International Symposium on Cluster, Cloud and Internet Computing (CCGrid), pp. 81–91 (2021)
8. Dryden, N., et al.: Clairvoyant prefetching for distributed machine learning I/O. In: Proceedings of the International Conference for High Performance Computing, Networking, Storage and Analysis, SC 2021. Association for Computing Machinery, New York (2021)
9. Kurth, T., et al.: Exascale deep learning for climate analytics. In: SC18: International Conference for High Performance Computing, Networking, Storage and Analysis, pp. 649–660. IEEE (2018)
10. Kuznetsova, A., et al.: The open images dataset V4. Int. J. Comput. Vision **128**(7), 1956–1981 (2020). https://doi.org/10.1007/s11263-020-01316-z

11. Mahajan, D., et al.: Exploring the limits of weakly supervised pretraining. In: Proceedings of the European Conference on Computer Vision (ECCV), pp. 181–196 (2018)
12. Mathuriya, A., et al.: CosmoFlow: using deep learning to learn the universe at scale. In: Proceedings of the International Conference for High Performance Computing, Networking, Storage, and Analysis, SC 2018. IEEE Press (2018)
13. Mikami, H., et al.: Massively distributed SGD: ImageNet/ResNet-50 training in a flash (2018). https://arxiv.org/abs/1811.05233
14. Mohan, J., et al.: Analyzing and mitigating data stalls in DNN training. Proc. VLDB Endow. **14**(5), 771–784 (2021)
15. Paul, A.K., et al.: Characterizing machine learning I/O workloads on leadership scale HPC systems. In: 2021 29th International Symposium on Modeling, Analysis, and Simulation of Computer and Telecommunication Systems (MASCOTS), pp. 1–8 (2021)
16. Pumma, S., et al.: Scalable deep learning via I/O analysis and optimization. ACM Trans. Parallel Comput. **6**(2) (2019)
17. Sato, M., et al.: Co-design for A64FX manycore processor and "Fugaku". In: SC20: International Conference for High Performance Computing, Networking, Storage and Analysis, pp. 1–15 (2020)
18. Serizawa, K., Tatebe, O.: Accelerating machine learning I/O by overlapping data staging and mini-batch generations. In: Proceedings of the 6th IEEE/ACM International Conference on Big Data Computing, Applications and Technologies, BDCAT 2019, pp. 31–34. Association for Computing Machinery, New York (2019)
19. Tan, M., Le, Q.: EfficientNet: rethinking model scaling for convolutional neural networks. In: Chaudhuri, K., Salakhutdinov, R. (eds.) Proceedings of the 36th International Conference on Machine Learning. Proceedings of Machine Learning Research, vol. 97, pp. 6105–6114. PMLR (2019). https://proceedings.mlr.press/v97/tan19a.html
20. Vazhkudai, S.S., et al.: The design, deployment, and evaluation of the CORAL pre-exascale systems. In: SC18: International Conference for High Performance Computing, Networking, Storage and Analysis, pp. 661–672 (2018)
21. Wang, Y., et al.: Time-based roofline for deep learning performance analysis. In: 2020 IEEE/ACM Fourth Workshop on Deep Learning on Supercomputers (DLS), pp. 10–19 (2020)
22. Yamazaki, M., et al.: Yet another accelerated SGD: ResNet-50 training on ImageNet in 74.7 seconds (2019). https://arxiv.org/abs/1903.12650
23. Zhu, Y., et al.: Entropy-aware I/O pipelining for large-scale deep learning on HPC systems. In: 2018 IEEE 26th International Symposium on Modeling, Analysis, and Simulation of Computer and Telecommunication Systems (MASCOTS), pp. 145–156 (2018)
24. Zhu, Y., et al.: Efficient user-level storage disaggregation for deep learning. In: 2019 IEEE International Conference on Cluster Computing (CLUSTER), pp. 1–12 (2019)

An Advantage Actor-Critic Deep Reinforcement Learning Method for Power Management in HPC Systems

Fitra Rahmani Khasyah[1], Kadek Gemilang Santiyuda[1], Gabriel Kaunang[1], Faizal Makhrus[1], Muhammad Alfian Amrizal[1(✉)], and Hiroyuki Takizawa[2]

[1] Department of Computer Science and Electronics, Universitas Gadjah Mada, Yogyakarta 55281, Indonesia
muhammad.alfian.amrizal@ugm.ac.id
[2] Cyberscience Center, Tohoku University, Sendai 980-8578, Japan

Abstract. A primary concern when deploying a High-Performance Computing (HPC) system is its high energy consumption. Typical HPC systems consist of hundreds to thousands of compute nodes that consume huge amount of electrical power even during their idle states. One way to increase the energy efficiency is to apply the backfilling method to the First Come First Serve (FCFS) job scheduler (FCFS+Backfilling). The backfilling method allows jobs that arrive later than the first job in the queue to be executed earlier if the starting time of the first job is not affected, therefore increasing the throughput and the energy efficiency of the system. Nodes that are idle for a specific amount of time can also be switched off to further improve the energy efficiency. However, switching off nodes based only on their idle time can also impair the energy efficiency and the throughput instead of improving them. As an example, new jobs may immediately arrive after nodes are switched off, hence missing the chance of directly executing the jobs via backfilling. This paper proposed a Deep Reinforcement Learning (DRL)-based method to predict the most appropriate timing to switch on/off nodes. A DRL agent is trained with Advantage Actor-Critic algorithm to decide which nodes must be switched on/off at a specific timestep. Our simulation results on NASA iPSC/860 HPC historical job dataset show that the proposed method can reduce the total energy consumption compared to most of the conventional timeout policies that switch off nodes after they became idle for some period of time.

Keywords: HPC · Power management · Energy consumption · Deep reinforcement learning · Advantage actor-critic

1 Introduction

High energy consumption is one of the main problems when deploying High-Performance Computing (HPC) systems [2,7]. One of the causes of the high energy usage is because production-level HPC systems have to provide a particular Quality of Service (QoS) to their users [4]. Nodes of these systems are

H. Takizawa et al. (Eds.): PDCAT 2022, LNCS 13798, pp. 94–107, 2023.
https://doi.org/10.1007/978-3-031-29927-8_8

often configured to always be on standby-mode so that they can immediately run users' jobs as soon as the jobs enter the queue. The energy consumed by an HPC node during standby-mode is still quite high [3]. Thus, the total wasted energy when the nodes are waiting for the jobs is still very large considering that the number of nodes of HPC systems can reach hundreds to thousands of compute nodes [1].

One way to improve energy efficiency in HPC systems is to implement the FCFS+Backfilling scheduler [20,22]. The FCFS scheduler refers to the scheduler with an allocation method based on the order of the job arrival in the queue, while the Backfilling scheduler refers to the scheduler with an allocation method that allows the first job in the queue to be preceded by smaller jobs farther back in the queue as long as the starting time of the first job is not delayed. In addition to improving energy efficiency, the FCFS+Backfilling scheduler can also reduce the average job waiting time.

The FCFS+Backfilling scheduler can be combined with other methods to further reduce energy usage, one of which is by exploiting the different power states of the node. Each node can have multiple power states, such as active and sleep. Energy usage can be significantly reduced by moving idle nodes (active but not running any job) to sleep state if they have been idle for some period of time [6,12,23]. However, the methods of switching off nodes (or putting them to sleep) has the potential to reduce the efficiency of the FCFS+Backfilling scheduler if the nodes are switched off at inappropriate time. For example, if some nodes are switched off and then a job that can be backfilled arrives, the job might be unable to run immediately due to an insufficient number of available nodes. This is because, unlike the case on a single computer, switching on/off nodes on a large-scale HPC system may take longer period of time. In some cases, these processes may take 30–60 min or more [21]. Therefore, determining the right timing to switch off nodes will be crucial and will have a significant impact on the efficiency of FCFS+Backfilling scheduler.

Machine Learning (ML) is one method that can be used to predict the timing to switch on/off nodes of an HPC system. The best timing can be estimated if the dynamics of job arrivals in an HPC system can be predicted. One of the ML branches that has been recently investigated and proven to have good performance for predicting the dynamics of job arrivals is Reinforcement Learning (RL) [25]. Mao et al. [17] developed an RL-based multi-resource cluster scheduler that allocates jobs to various HPC clusters and concluded that the RL approach can be applied to job scheduling on large-scale HPC systems. Zhang et al. [28] developed an RL-based generic HPC batch job scheduler that was trained on one HPC system and used on other systems. They showed that the approach can adapt to various jobs from other systems with different characteristics and requires relatively low computational overhead. Kumar et al. [15] developed a scheduler that uses Deep Reinforcement Learning (DRL) and successfully minimizes average job waiting time on the system. Liang et al. [16] also proposed a DRL-based model that can reduce the average job waiting time, as well as ensuring fairness between large and small jobs without starvation. Based on these studies, RL in general, or DRL in particular, has recently emerged as an effective solution for performing prediction in dynamic and complex computing environment such as in HPC systems. Therefore, we hypothesized that RL/DRL also has the potential to identify the best timing to switch the power state of each node in the HPC systems because it correlates with job arrival times which are also dynamic in nature. To the best of our knowledge, no work has investigated RL/DRL's potential on determining when is the best time to switch on/off nodes of HPC systems and its effect to the energy consumption of the systems.

In this paper, the core algorithm that is used in several state-of-the-art DRL, called Advantage Actor-Critic (A2C) [19], is utilized to develop a model for predicting the best timing for switching on/off multiple nodes of an HPC system. A2C consists of two agents named Actor and Critic. Actor is responsible for learning when to switch on/off the nodes and Critic reduces the prediction error. In this paper, we make the following three contributions:

- We formulate the problem to be solved as Power State Management Problem (PSMP) and present the energy consumption and energy waste models for nodes with multiple power states.
- We design an A2C-DRL method to switch on/off the nodes.
- We provide simulation-based evaluation results using real-world job history dataset demonstrating that the proposed method is able to outperform most of the conventional timeout policies (policies in which nodes are switched off when they have been idle for some specific amount of time).

The rest of this paper is organized as follows. In Sect. 2, we formally describe the PSMP considered in this paper. In Sect. 3, an A2C deep reinforcement learning method is presented, and its performance in terms of energy consumption and energy waste is evaluated in Sect. 4. Finally, the conclusions and the future works of this paper are stated in Sect. 5.

2   Power State Management Problem

This section formally describes PSMP considered in this paper. In PSMP, there are N jobs to be submitted to an HPC system that comprises M compute nodes. The incoming jobs will enter a queue and are allocated to the nodes by the FCFS+backfilling scheduler. The i-th job requests m nodes to be run, has runtime e_i and is submitted at t_i^{sub}, with $1 \leq i \leq N$ and $1 \leq m \leq M$. Based on the number of requested nodes, a job can be allocated to several nodes, but each node can only be allocated one job at a time. If the i-th job has been allocated the nodes it requested, then its starting time is denoted as t_i^{start}. After a job is started, it cannot be canceled, paused, or reallocated to other nodes until it is finished. Therefore, preemptive job allocation and switching off nodes with a running job are prohibited.

Each node has four power states, namely active, sleep, switching on, and switching off. An active node consumes p_a power and a sleeping node consumes p_s power with $p_a > p_s$. A job can be allocated to any available node, whether it is active or sleep, and the job can be immediately started if all of its allocated nodes are active. On the other hand, sleeping nodes needs to be switched on first prior to starting its allocated job, hence increasing the job's waiting time. Switching on a node takes T_{son} second and consume p_{son} power, meanwhile switching off a node takes T_{soff} second and consumes p_{soff} power. A node being switched off cannot be switched on immediately before it is completely switched off. A node being switched on also needs to be completely switched on before being able to be switched off again.

The state of M nodes at time t is represented by an M dimensional vector $\mathbf{u}_t = (u_{t1}, \ldots, u_{tM})$. If the m-th node is active at time t, then $u_{tm} = 0$, and $u_{tm} = 1$ if it is in the sleep state. If the m-th node is switching on, then $u_{tm} = 2$, and $u_{tm} = 3$ if it is switching off.

The nodes allocation of the i-th job is represented by an M dimensional vector $\mathbf{l}_i = (l_{i1}, \ldots, l_{iM})$ with $l_{im} = 1$ if the i-th job is allocated to the m-th node. As an example, if $M = 4$ and $\mathbf{l}_i = (1, 0, 1, 0)$, then the i-th job is allocated to the first and third nodes.

The objective of the problem is to switch on and switch off the nodes at the appropriate time so that the total energy consumption is minimized. The total energy consumption is given as

$$F(\mathbf{U}) = \sum_{m=1}^{M} \sum_{t=1}^{T} (\llbracket u_{tm} = 0 \rrbracket p_a + \llbracket u_{tm} = 1 \rrbracket p_s + \llbracket u_{tm} = 2 \rrbracket p_{son} + \llbracket u_{tm} = 3 \rrbracket p_{soff}),$$
(1)

with T is the time when the last job finishes its execution and $\mathbf{U} = (\mathbf{u}_1, \ldots, \mathbf{u}_T)$.

A more specific energy-related metric, the energy waste, can also be derived. The energy is deemed to be wasted if used other than for computing, i.e., when a node is active but idle, when it is switching on, and when it is switching off. An M dimensional vector $\mathbf{c}_t = (c_{t1}, \ldots, c_{tM})$ is used to represent the two different active states of M nodes at time t, i.e., active-idle or active-computing. The value of c_{tm} is given as

$$c_{tm} = \llbracket \exists i, 1 \leq i \leq N, l_{im} = 1 \wedge t_i^{start} \leq t \leq (t_i^{start} + e_i) \rrbracket$$
(2)

with $\llbracket . \rrbracket$ is the Iverson bracket. If the m-th node is idle at t, then $c_{tm} = 0$. Otherwise, it is computing and denoted as $c_{tm} = 1$. Formally, the energy waste is given as

$$F'(\mathbf{U}, \mathbf{C}) = \sum_{m=1}^{M} \sum_{t=1}^{T} (\llbracket u_{tm} = 0 \wedge c_{tm} = 0 \rrbracket p_a + \llbracket u_{tm} = 2 \rrbracket p_{son} + \llbracket u_{tm} = 3 \rrbracket p_{soff}),$$
(3)

with $\mathbf{C} = (\mathbf{c}_1, \ldots, \mathbf{c}_T)$.

Equations (1) and (3) must be minimized without violating two constraints. First, a node must always be active when a job is allocated to it as given in (4),

$$l_{im} = 1 \Rightarrow u_{tm} = 0, \text{for } t_i^{start} \leq t \leq t_i^{start} + e_i, \forall i,$$
(4)

and second, no nodes are running more than one job at a time as given in (5),

$$\sum_{i=1}^{N}(l_{im}[\![t_i^{start} \leq t \wedge t \leq (t_i^{start} + e_i)]\!]) \leq 1, \forall m, \forall t. \tag{5}$$

The notations used in this section are summarized in Table 1.

Table 1. Notations in the PSMP formulation

Variables	Definition
N	Number of jobs to be submitted
M	Number of nodes
i	Job ID
m	Number of requested nodes
e_i	Runtime of job i
t_i^{sub}	Submit time of job i
t_i^{start}	Starting time of job i
p_a	Power consumed by an active node
p_s	Power consumed by a sleeping node
p_{son}	Power consumed when a node is switching on
p_{soff}	Power consumed when a node is switching off
T_{son}	Time needed for a node to switch on
T_{soff}	Time needed for a node to switch off
T	Time when last job finished its execution
t	Current time
u_{tm}	State of the m-th node at time t
$\mathbf{u}_t = (u_{t1}, \ldots, u_{tM})$	State vector of M nodes at time t
l_{im}	Allocation status of m-th node for i-th job
$\mathbf{l}_i = (l_{i1}, \ldots, l_{iM})$	Allocation vector of M node for i-th job
c_{tm}	Computing status of m-th node at t
$\mathbf{c}_t = (c_{t1}, \ldots, c_{tM})$	Computing status vector of M nodes at t

3 A2C Deep Reinforcement Learning for Power State Management Problem

In this section, PSMP described in Sect. 2 is formulated as a Markov Decision Process (MDP) based on the formulation given in [25]. The MDP formulation of PSMP is given in Subsect. 3.1. Afterward, architecture and training method of the DRL agent using Advantage Actor-Critic (A2C) are described in Subsect. 3.2.

3.1   MDP Formulation of PSMP

In MDP, a decision maker or an agent interacts with the environment by observing the state of the environment and taking action based on the observed state. The environment then returns a reward signal to the agent based on its state and the action taken by the agent.

MDP can formally be described by the tuple $\langle \mathcal{S}, \mathcal{A}, \mathcal{P}, R, \gamma \rangle$ with $\mathcal{S}$ is the set of all states, $\mathcal{A}$ is the action space of the agent, $\mathcal{P}$ is the state transition probability of the environment, R is the reward function, and γ is the reward discount factor. In this paper, the agent is designed to perform an action regarding which nodes to switch on/off every constant time interval Δt. The agent performs its k-th action, $\mathbf{a}_k \in \mathcal{A}$, after observing the state of the environment denoted as $s_k \in \mathcal{S}$. This action is based on the policy $\pi(\mathbf{a}_k \mid s_k)$ that maximizes the expected return of the environment, $\mathrm{E}_\pi[G_k]$, with the return G_k is given in (6),

$$G_k = \sum_{i=0}^{K-k} \gamma^i r_{k+i}. \tag{6}$$

Here, r_k is the reward after the agent observes the state s_k and performs $\mathbf{a}_k$, and the K-th action is the last action of the agent.

In this paper, we propose to represent the state s_k as the system features $\mathbf{X}_k = (\mathbf{x}_{k1}, \ldots, \mathbf{x}_{kM})$, with $\mathbf{x}_{km}$ denotes the features of the m-th node right before $\mathbf{a}_k$ is performed, and $\dim(\mathbf{x}_{km}) = 11$. The 11 features used in this paper are given in Table 2. The action space is denoted as $\mathcal{A} = \{0,1\}^M$, so that $\mathbf{a}_k = (a_{k1}, \ldots, a_{kM}) \in \mathcal{A}$. The action $a_{km} = 0$ represents the k-th action to switch off the m-th node, and $a_{km} = 1$ represents the action to switch it on.

Table 2. The features used to represent the state of the system

No.	Features
1	Number of jobs in the queue
2	Current Arrival Rate
3	Average waiting time of the jobs currently in the queue
4	Total wasted energy
5	Average requested runtime of the jobs currently in the queue
6	u_{tm}
7	$[\![u_{tm} = 0 \wedge c_{tm} = 0]\!]$
8	The m-th node's current idle time
9	The m-th node's release time
10	The m-th node's wasted energy
11	The m-th node's total time used to switch on and switch off

Given the state s_k, the action $\mathbf{a}_k$ is performed based on a policy $\pi(\mathbf{a}_k \mid s_k)$. In this paper, we use a policy parametrized by a deep neural network. The parameters are denoted as $\boldsymbol{\theta}$; therefore, the parametrized policy is denoted as $\pi(\mathbf{a}_k \mid s_k; \boldsymbol{\theta})$. There might be actions that can lead to the violation of constraints given in (5) and (4). Therefore, the action needs to be masked so that only feasible nodes are switched on or off.

The reward signal r_k corresponds to the action $\mathbf{a}_k$ performed by the agent must then be returned. We formulate the reward signal based on the system's total energy waste and the total waiting time of jobs in the queue during the time between the k-th and the $(k+1)$-th actions. Thus, the agent will get the reward from its previous action before it performs the next action. The wasted energy component of the reward is given in (7),

$$R_1(k, k+1) = \sum_{t=\Delta t \times k}^{t=\Delta t \times (k+1)} F'\left((\mathbf{u}_t), (\mathbf{c}_t)\right), \tag{7}$$

with F' is the wasted energy given in (3). The jobs' waiting time component of the reward is given in (8),

$$R_2(k, k+1) = \sum_{i=1}^{N} \sum_{t=\Delta t \times k}^{t=\Delta t \times (k+1)} q_{ti}, \tag{8}$$

with $q_{ti} = 1$ if the i-th job is still in the queue at time t and $q_{ti} = 0$ otherwise. The two components have difference scale, therefore they have to be normalized before being aggregated as the reward signal. Finally, the reward r_k is given in (9),

$$r_k = -\alpha \frac{R_1(k, k+1)}{M p_a \Delta t} - \beta \frac{R_2(k, k+1)}{J(k, k+1)}, \tag{9}$$

with $\alpha, \beta \in [0, 1], \alpha + \beta = 1$, and $J(k, k+1)$ is the maximum waiting time of jobs which are in the queue between k-th and $(k+1)$-th actions as given in (10),

$$J(k, k+1) = (\sum_{i=1}^{N}[[t_i^{sub} \leq \Delta t \times (k+1) \wedge t_i^{sub} \geq \Delta t \times k]]) \times \Delta t. \tag{10}$$

3.2   A2C-DRL for PSMP

The architecture of the Actor comprises two parts, a feature encoder and an action's probability head. Similarly, the Critic also comprises a feature encoder and a value head. The feature encoder used for the Actor and the Critic is the encoder used in the Transformer architecture [26] without the positional encoding which is firstly introduced in [14]. The difference in ordering the system features has no significant meaning as the input for the Actor and Critic, therefore the positional encoding is not used. The probability head of the Actor is a multi-layer Feed-forward (FF) or Multi-layer Perceptron (MLP) with two outputs, one for each action's probability with softmax activation function in the final layer to normalize the probabilities. Similarly, the Critic's value head is also an MLP with one output at the final layer for the estimation of the state value function. The Actor's learned parameters are denoted as $\boldsymbol{\theta}$, and the Critic's learned parameters are denoted as $\boldsymbol{\theta}_v$. The illustration of the architecture is given in Fig. 1.

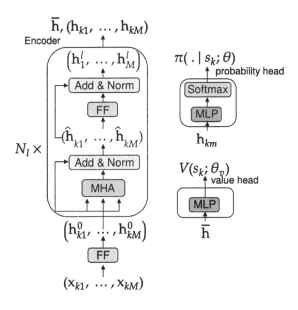

Fig. 1. Architecture illustration

For the k-th action, the system features $\mathbf{X}_k = (\mathbf{x}_{k1}, \ldots, \mathbf{x}_{kM})$, that represent the state s_k, are embedded via linear projection producing $\mathbf{h}_{km}^0 = W^x \mathbf{x}_{km} + \mathbf{b^x}$, with W^x and $\mathbf{b^x}$ are the learned linear projection parameters and $1 \leq m \leq M$. The produced embeddings are then updated by an attention layer, which consists of two sublayers, i.e., Multi-Head Attention (MHA) and an FF layer. The updated embeddings are denoted as $\mathbf{h}_{km}^l$, with $1 \leq l \leq N_{att}$, where N_{att} is the number of attention layers employed. Each sublayer has a skip-connection [11] and a Batch Normalization (BN) layer [13]. For each attention layer, the embeddings update is given in (12),

$$\hat{\mathbf{h}}_{km} = \text{BN}^l \left(\mathbf{h}_{km}^{(l-1)} + \text{MHA}_m^l \left(\mathbf{h}_{k1}^{(l-1)}, \ldots, \mathbf{h}_{kM}^{(l-1)} \right) \right), \tag{11}$$

$$\mathbf{h}_{km}^l = \text{BN}^l \left(\hat{\mathbf{h}}_{km} + \text{FF}^l(\hat{\mathbf{h}}_{km}) \right). \tag{12}$$

The MHA sublayers use N_h heads with dimensionality $\frac{d_h}{N_h}$, with d_h is the embeddings' dimensionality. The encoder outputs the embeddings produced by the final attention layer, $\mathbf{h}_{km}^{N_{att}}$, and their average, $\bar{\mathbf{h}}_k^{N_{att}} = \frac{1}{M} \sum_{m=1}^M \mathbf{h}_{km}^{N_{att}}$. For ease of readability, the N_{att} index is omitted from the embeddings, $\mathbf{h}_{km}$, and the aggregated embedding, $\bar{\mathbf{h}}_k$.

The Actor takes the final embedding for each node, $\mathbf{h}_{km}$, as the input to the probability head to compute the probability to either switch off or switch on the corresponding node, $\pi(a_{km} = 0 \mid s_k; \boldsymbol{\theta})$ and $\pi(a_{km} = 1 \mid s_k; \boldsymbol{\theta})$ for $1 \leq m \leq M$. In the training phase, the action taken for the m-th node is sampled from the computed probability, $a_{km} \sim \pi(a_{km} \mid s_k; \boldsymbol{\theta})$, to encourage action exploration. However, in the testing phase, the action with the highest probability is taken for each node, $a_{km} = \arg\max_{\mathcal{A}} \pi(. \mid s_k; \boldsymbol{\theta})$. The Critic takes the aggregate of the final embeddings, $\bar{\mathbf{h}}_k$, as the input to the value head to compute the estimated state value function, $V(s_k; \boldsymbol{\theta}_v)$.

The parameters of the Actor and the Critic are updated everytime N_b observations, represented by the tuple $\langle s_k, \mathbf{a}_k, r_k \rangle$, have been collected. The parameters update method in the A2C [19] is used in this paper. Firstly, the estimation of the advantage function is computed as given in (13),

$$A(s_k, \mathbf{a}_k; \boldsymbol{\theta}, \boldsymbol{\theta}_v) = \sum_{j=0}^{N_b-1} \gamma^j r_{k+j} + \gamma^k V(s_{k+N_b}; \boldsymbol{\theta}_v) - V(s_k; \boldsymbol{\theta}_v). \tag{13}$$

If the last observation out of N_b collected observations is a terminal state, then $V(s_{k+N_b}; \boldsymbol{\theta}_v) = 0$ in (13).

The update for the Actor parameters is given in (14),

$$d\boldsymbol{\theta} = \nabla_\theta \sum_{k=1}^{N_b} \log \pi(\mathbf{a}_k \mid s_k; \boldsymbol{\theta}) A(s_k, \mathbf{a}_k; \boldsymbol{\theta}, \boldsymbol{\theta}_v). \tag{14}$$

The update for the Critic parameters is obtained based on the mean squared error between the estimation produced by the Critic and the computed estimate of the advantage function as given in (15),

$$d\boldsymbol{\theta}v = \nabla_\theta v \frac{1}{N_b} \sum_{k=1}^{N_b} (A(s_k, \mathbf{a}_k; \boldsymbol{\theta}, \boldsymbol{\theta}_v) - V(s_k; \boldsymbol{\theta}_v))^2. \tag{15}$$

4 Evaluation

In this section, we explain how we conduct the experiment and discuss the results of the DRL agent we have trained compared to timeout policies in terms of energy. Here, timeout policies refer to the conventional methods where nodes are regularly switched off based on the amount of time they have spent in idle state.

4.1 Experimental Setup

Batsim-py [5] simulator is used to simulate resource and job management. The platform is configured based on [12] where a node takes 45 min to switch off and 30 min to switch on. Every second when a node is in computing, idle, and switching on state, it consumes 190 W. Meanwhile, when it is in sleep or switching off state, it only consumes 9 W. The watt consumption is based on the experimental settings found in [8], and it is adjusted to PSMP formulation. The simulation was run on a 32 GB RAM Intel Core i9-9820X CPU @ 3.30 GHz (20 CPUs) hardware.

The dataset used for this research is from NASA Ames iPSC/860 log [9], accessible through Parallel Workloads Archive [10]. The log contains three months worth of sanitized records for the 128-node iPSC/860 at NASA Ames Research Center. It contains 18,239 jobs in total from October 1993 to December 1993. This dataset has been used in several researches [18,24,27]. It includes basic information about the number of nodes, runtime, start time, user, and command. However, based on the scope of this research; only jobs information about the number of requested nodes, runtime, and start time are utilized. The log is preprocessed to remove any jobs requesting 0 nodes as it is not compatible with the simulator.

The log was split 80:20 for training and testing the DRL agent. During the training process, the DRL agent would make decisions by sampling the action based on the computed probability, and in the testing process, it would pick the maximum value between switching the nodes on or off. The agent was trained on one epoch and the hyperparameter settings of the Actor-Critic architecture are based on the settings used in [14] without further hyperparameter tuning. The list of hyperparameters used in the experiment is shown in Table 3.

Table 3. The hyperparameter settings for the experimental study

Hyperparameter	Value
Number of head in MHA, N_h	8
Number of layers in MHA N_{att}	3
The embedding size, d_h	128
Learning rate	0.0001
Discounted return gamma	0.99
Gradient clipping norm	2
N_b	64
α	0.5
β	0.5
Δt	1800

We compared the trained agent with the baseline method and several timeout policies. The baseline method represents the condition where no power state switching is performed: each of the compute node is always kept at idle state when it is not allocated any job. A total of 12 different timeout policies are used in the experiment. The timeout configuration is ranging from 5 min up to 60 min (in the multiples of 5). To test the agent, first we run 80% of the dataset with the baseline method, then running the rest 20% with each of the method to be compared so as not to lose continuity in the time-series dataset. We then collected metrics of total energy consumption and total energy waste.

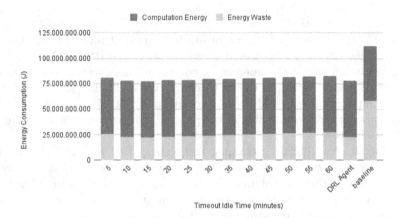

Fig. 2. Total energy consumption

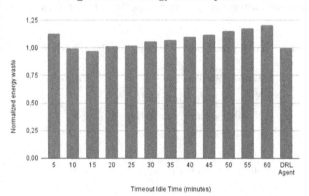

Fig. 3. Normalized energy waste vs timeout policies

4.2   Results and Discussion

In this section the results obtained by the experimental study are discussed. The total energy, comprises energy waste and computation energy, used by the 12 configurations of timeout policy, the baseline method, and the proposed DRL-based method is given in Fig. 2. As shown in this figure, the proposed method using the DRL agent has significantly lower total energy consumption than the baseline method. In addition, it also outperforms 10 out of the 12 timeout policy configurations.

To further highlight the difference in performance between the proposed method and the timeout policies, Fig. 3 shows the zoomed-in version of the energy waste of each method normalized to the proposed method's energy waste. From the timeout policies results in this figure, we can see that, as we decrease the timeout interval, the energy waste also decreases until it reaches an optimal interval in which decreasing the interval further will result in the increase of the energy waste. In this experiment, the optimal timeout interval is found to be the

15 min configuration. It can be observed from the figure that the energy waste gradually increases as the timeout is set bigger or smaller than 15 min.

As previously mentioned, the proposed DRL-based method outperforms 10 out of 12 configurations of the timeout policy. The worst configuration of timeout policy, namely with 60 min timeout, produces 20% higher energy waste compared to the proposed method. On the other hand, the optimal configuration of the timeout policy produces only 3% lower energy waste compared to the proposed DRL-based method. This is an arguably remarkable result produced by the proposed method without prior hyperparameter tuning and trained only for one epoch.

5 Conclusion

Conventional methods that regularly switch off nodes based only on their idle time, called timeout policies, might reduce the efficiency of FCFS+Backfilling scheduler. This work proposed an A2C-based A2C method to determine when is the best timing to switch on/off a particular node in an HPC system. Our simulation results on NASA iPSC/860 HPC historical job dataset show that the proposed method achieves more than 60% reduction in wasted energy compared to the baseline and up to 20% reduction compared to the other timeout policies. Out of the 12 policies, only two policies, namely 10 and 15 min timeout policies, were slightly better than the proposed method, marginally exceeding it by 0.3% and 3%, respectively. However, since the DRL agent was only trained with one epoch, it is reasonable to expect that the proposed method will outperform all the timeout policies when the number of training epochs is bigger.

Our future work will focus on further improving the performance of the proposed A2C-based DRL method. This includes training the model with more epochs as well as testing it with different hyper-parameters. Note that in the experiments discussed in this paper, both of the reward's weights α and β are set equally. The actions of the agent may change if the values of α and β are not equal. The impact on changing these weights on the energy consumption/energy waste of the HPC system will be discussed in our future work. In addition, the number of power states considered in this paper is only two, active and sleep, since some systems may have more than two power states, we will extend the PSMP for arbitrary number of states. Finally, the superiority of the proposed method will be evaluated on various system configurations and job history data.

Acknowledgement. This work was partially supported by the grant of Penelitian Dosen Dana Masyarakat Alokasi Fakultas MIPA-UGM under Contract No. 91/J01.1.28/PL.06.02/2022, Grant-in-Aid for Challenging Research (Exploratory) #22K19764, and Joint Usage/Research Center for Interdisciplinary Large-scale Information Infrastructures jh220025.

References

1. Top500 lists. https://www.top500.org/

2. Amrizal, M.A., Takizawa, H.: Optimizing energy consumption on HPC systems with a multi-level checkpointing mechanism. In: 2017 International Conference on Networking, Architecture, and Storage (NAS), pp. 1–9. IEEE (2017)
3. Barroso, L.A., Hölzle, U.: The case for energy-proportional computing. Computer **40**(12), 33–37 (2007)
4. Bridi, T., Bartolini, A., Lombardi, M., Milano, M., Benini, L.: A constraint programming scheduler for heterogeneous high-performance computing machines. IEEE Trans. Parallel Distrib. Syst. **27**(10), 2781–2794 (2016)
5. Casagrande, L.C.: Batsim-py (2020). https://github.com/lccasagrande/batsim-py
6. Chen, H., Lu, Y., Zhu, Q.: A power-aware job scheduling algorithm. In: 2012 International Conference on Cloud and Service Computing, pp. 8–11. IEEE (2012)
7. Dayarathna, M., Wen, Y., Fan, R.: Data center energy consumption modeling: a survey. IEEE Commun. Surv. Tutor. **18**(1), 732–794 (2015)
8. Dutot, P.-F., Mercier, M., Poquet, M., Richard, O.: Batsim: a realistic language-independent resources and jobs management systems simulator. In: Desai, N., Cirne, W. (eds.) JSSPP 2015-2016. LNCS, vol. 10353, pp. 178–197. Springer, Cham (2017). https://doi.org/10.1007/978-3-319-61756-5_10
9. Feitelson, D.G., Nitzberg, B.: Job characteristics of a production parallel scientific workload on the NASA Ames iPSC/860. In: Feitelson, D.G., Rudolph, L. (eds.) JSSPP 1995. LNCS, vol. 949, pp. 337–360. Springer, Heidelberg (1995). https://doi.org/10.1007/3-540-60153-8_38
10. Feitelson, D.G., Tsafrir, D., Krakov, D.: Experience with using the parallel workloads archive. J. Parallel Distrib. Comput. **74**(10), 2967–2982 (2014)
11. He, K., Zhang, X., Ren, S., Sun, J.: Deep residual learning for image recognition. In: 2016 IEEE Conference on Computer Vision and Pattern Recognition (CVPR), pp. 770–778 (2016)
12. Hikita, J., Hirano, A., Nakashima, H.: Saving 200 kw and $200 k/year by power-aware job/machine scheduling. In: 2008 IEEE International Symposium on Parallel and Distributed Processing, pp. 1–8. IEEE (2008)
13. Ioffe, S., Szegedy, C.: Batch normalization: accelerating deep network training by reducing internal covariate shift. In: Proceedings of the 32nd International Conference on International Conference on Machine Learning, ICML 2015, vol. 37, pp. 448–456. JMLR.org (2015)
14. Kool, W., van Hoof, H., Welling, M.: Attention, learn to solve routing problems! In: 7th International Conference on Learning Representations, ICLR 2019, New Orleans, LA, USA, 6–9 May 2019. OpenReview.net (2019)
15. Kumar, V., Bhambri, S., Shambharkar, P.G.: Multiple resource management and burst time prediction using deep reinforcement learning. In: Eighth International Conference on Advances in Computing, Communication and Information Technology CCIT, pp. 51–58 (2019)
16. Liang, S., Yang, Z., Jin, F., Chen, Y.: Data centers job scheduling with deep reinforcement learning. In: Lauw, H.W., Wong, R.C.-W., Ntoulas, A., Lim, E.-P., Ng, S.-K., Pan, S.J. (eds.) PAKDD 2020. LNCS (LNAI), vol. 12085, pp. 906–917. Springer, Cham (2020). https://doi.org/10.1007/978-3-030-47436-2_68
17. Mao, H., Alizadeh, M., Menache, I., Kandula, S.: Resource management with deep reinforcement learning. In: Proceedings of the 15th ACM Workshop on Hot Topics in Networks, pp. 50–56 (2016)
18. Meng, J., McCauley, S., Kaplan, F., Leung, V.J., Coskun, A.K.: Simulation and optimization of HPC job allocation for jointly reducing communication and cooling costs. Sustain. Comput.: Inform. Syst. **6**, 48–57 (2015). https://doi.org/

10.1016/j.suscom.2014.05.002. https://www.sciencedirect.com/science/article/pii/ S2210537914000237. Special Issue on Selected Papers from 2013 International Green Computing Conference (IGCC)

19. Mnih, V., et al.: Asynchronous methods for deep reinforcement learning. In: Proceedings of the 33rd International Conference on International Conference on Machine Learning, ICML 2016, vol. 48, pp. 1928–1937. JMLR.org (2016)

20. Mu'alem, A.W., Feitelson, D.G.: Utilization, predictability, workloads, and user runtime estimates in scheduling the IBM SP2 with backfilling. IEEE Trans. Parallel Distrib. Syst. **12**(6), 529–543 (2001)

21. Ohmura, T., Shimomura, Y., Egawa, R., Takizawa, H.: Toward building a digital twin of job scheduling and power management on an HPC system. In: Klusáček, D., Julita, C., Rodrigo, G.P. (eds.) JSSPP 2022. LNCS, vol. 13592, pp. 47–67. Springer, Cham (2023). https://doi.org/10.1007/978-3-031-22698-4_3

22. Pinedo, M.L.: Scheduling, vol. 29. Springer, Heidelberg (2012)

23. Pinheiro, E., Bianchini, R., Carrera, E.V., Heath, T.: Load balancing and unbalancing for power and performance in cluster-based systems. Technical report, Rutgers University (2001)

24. Shirani, M.R., Safi-Esfahani, F.: Dynamic scheduling of tasks in cloud computing applying dragonfly algorithm, biogeography-based optimization algorithm and Mexican hat wavelet. J. Supercomput. **77**(2), 1214–1272 (2020). https://doi.org/ 10.1007/s11227-020-03317-8

25. Sutton, R.S., Barto, A.G.: Reinforcement Learning: An Introduction. MIT Press, Cambridge (2018)

26. Vaswani, A., et al.: Attention is all you need. In: Guyon, I., et al. (eds.) Advances in Neural Information Processing Systems, vol. 30. Curran Associates, Inc. (2017)

27. Yang, S.: Online scheduling with migration cost. In: 2012 IEEE 26th International Parallel and Distributed Processing Symposium Workshops & PhD Forum, pp. 2168–2175 (2012). https://doi.org/10.1109/IPDPSW.2012.268

28. Zhang, D., Dai, D., He, Y., Bao, F.S., Xie, B.: RLScheduler: an automated HPC batch job scheduler using reinforcement learning. In: SC20: International Conference for High Performance Computing, Networking, Storage and Analysis, pp. 1–15. IEEE (2020)

An AutoML Based Algorithm for Performance Prediction in HPC Systems

Amit Mankodi$^{(\boxtimes)}$, Amit Bhatt, and Bhaskar Chaudhury

Dhirubhai Ambani Institute of Information and Communication Technology,
Gandhinagar, India
amit_mankodi@daiict.ac.in

Abstract. Neural networks are extensively utilized for building performance prediction models for high-performance computing systems. It is challenging to construct the neural network architecture that provides accurate performance (runtime) predictions by exploring the number of layers and neurons in each layer. Automated machine learning (AutoML) using neural architecture search (NAS) frameworks such as Auto-Keras have been proposed to tune neural networks automatically. Researchers have utilized AutoML frameworks for many application domains to build neural networks automatically, providing accurate predictions. However, AutoML has not been explored for performance prediction domain based on our literature survey. Hence, our goal is to show the feasibility of AutoML-based algorithm for performance prediction of HPC systems. In this paper, we propose a novel AutoML based algorithm that builds a neural network model layer-by-layer for performance prediction. Our algorithm takes decisions based on prediction accuracy metric values to add a new layer to tune the network. We have performed extensive experiments utilizing applications from SPEC CPU 2006, SPEC CPU 2017 benchmark suites. Performance prediction accuracy results of RMSE (Root Mean Squared Error), MedAE (Median Absolute Error) and MedAPE (Median Absolute Percentage Error) from our experiments demonstrate superior performance of our algorithm compared to the state-of-the-art Auto-Keras framework.

Keywords: Performance Prediction · High Performance Computing · Automated Machine Learning · Neural Architecture Search

1 Introduction

Performance prediction is an active area of research for high-performance computing (HPC) systems. In performance prediction, models are built using application-specific actual runtimes called application's performance and the HPC systems' features on which the application was executed. The constructed models are then provided with features of new HPC system to predict the performance. Machine learning methods are widely used in building performance

H. Takizawa et al. (Eds.): PDCAT 2022, LNCS 13798, pp. 108–119, 2023.
https://doi.org/10.1007/978-3-031-29927-8_9

prediction models. In particular, there is a surge in the use of neural network models for performance prediction [2,14,16,18–20]. The performance evaluation of the Tianhe-3 prototype using convolution neural network is performed in [2]. Various deep neural network workloads have been used by [14] to test the gShare framework proposed to share GPU memory in containers. Performance prediction of SPEC benchmark applications using artificial neural networks for more than 50000 machine configurations is carried out in [16]. The work in [18] used neural network models to implement transfer learning to predict the performance of the target HPC system from the data collected from the source HPC system. Our work in [19] evaluates various configurations of neural network models for performance prediction on HPC systems for NPB benchmark applications. Performance of SPEC and NPB benchmark applications is predicted for cloud environment before deployment in [20] wherein one of the models are built using neural network.

Developing a neural network model manually that provides high prediction accuracy is challenging due to complexity in parameter selection, such as the number of hidden layers and the number of neurons in each layer. Work in [13] first surveyed constructive algorithms with structured learning that applies various techniques to build neural networks automatically using search space for regression tasks such as performance prediction. Neural Architecture Search (NAS) is the process of automating neural network architecture, i.e., to select the number of layers and neurons, is thus a logical next step in automated machine learning. Automated machine learning (AutoML) using NAS is active research area recently [4,24,33]. Various frameworks [5–7,11,32] have been developed to build automated neural network models. Auto-Keras [11] framework built on a Python library Keras that uses Bayesian Optimization to automatically tune the number of dense layers, units, and other parameters. Auto-PyTourch [32] uses multi-fidelity optimization to tune the neural network architecture automatically. Auto-Sklearn [7] is built on top of the widely used Scikit-Learn ML framework and takes advantage of Bayesian optimization, meta-learning, and Ensemble Learning to automate the model. AutoGluon-Tabular [5] focuses on providing an automated machine learning model for structured data.

Researchers have either developed specialized automated machine learning frameworks or have used existing tools for the application domains of their expertise. The first open-source and extensible AutoML framework is proposed in [8] for object detection. AutoML framework for ensemble learning in recommender systems to automate the process of generating the ensembles is proposed in [9]. Work in [28] proposed AutoML model that leverages reinforcement learning to predict the quantization policy to reduce the size of neural network model for embedded systems. AutoML tools are developed in [15,31] for genomic research. Automated machine learning is utilized to perform information retrieval in [23] to select relevant publications. For the medical domain, image and tabular data classifications are performed in [12,30] for diabetes prediction and disease detection from images. Proximity detection using crowdsensing classification is performed in [1] to gather information about which mobile devices are in proximity to one another. The work in [10] investigates the robustness of AutoML systems for time series forecasting in sensor networks using temperature data. Regression and classification tasks on image and tabular datasets from various non-performance prediction application domains are performed in [21,27]. Our literature review shows that although automated machine learning (AutoML) is utilized for various application domains, AutoML is not much explored for performance prediction.

In the performance prediction domain, research works have been carried out to either manually tune the neural network or select the hardware systems that run the constructed neural network in an optimized way. For example, work in [25] performs a selection of efficient hardware or kernel or tune neural networks manually to improve the accuracy for a given task. Similarly, [29] tunes the neural network manually to improve the performance of the network. Work in [26] automates performance prediction by automatically instrumenting the code; however, the neural network is built manually. Automated machine learning GoldenNAS is implemented in [17] for hardware-aware selection of neural network model for non-performance prediction tasks. Hence, the motivation of our work in this paper is to propose an algorithm based on automated machine learning (AutoML) to construct a neural network automatically, focusing only on the performance prediction domain. The contribution of this work is summarized as follows:

– We propose an AutoML based algorithm to automatically build a neural network layer-by-layer for the performance prediction task.
– We first evaluate the accuracy of our algorithm by validating that the prediction accuracy metric values improve at each layer of a neural network as it is built.
– We compare the accuracy and efficiency of our algorithm with the state-of-the-art AutoML framework Auto-Keras.

The remainder of this paper is structured as follows: In Sect. 2 we explain the proposed algorithm. Section 3 provides details about performance dataset construction for each of the benchmark applications used for the experiments. Section 4 shows results from the evaluation of our algorithm. Finally, we present conclusions and future work in Sect. 5.

2   Algorithm

In this section, we describe the proposed AutoML based algorithm as shown below. Our algorithm constructs a neural network automatically layer-by-layer for performance prediction. The decision of adding a new layer is taken based on the current and previous metric values. For the current implementation of our algorithm, we have considered the root mean squared error (RMSE) metric for making the decision whether to add a new layer or not; however, it can be modified to utilize any other metric.

Our AutoML based algorithm considers HPC system hardware features as input (independent) features (X) and performance (runtime) (y) as an output (dependent) feature (line 2, 3). For our implementation, we have considered nine hardware features: CPU clock, number of cores, instruction-set architecture (ISA), sizes of three cache levels, memory type, memory clock, and memory size (line 1); however, we can modify the input features depending on feature availability. We use the OneHotEncoder encoding technique from category encoders python package to convert memory type and ISA, text (categorical) data features, to real-valued features because neural network requires all input features in numerical format (line 4). We then split the performance dataset $[X, y]$ into training and testing set $[X_{train}, y_{train}]$ and $[X_{test}, y_{test}]$ using the train_test_split() function from scikit-learn [22] python machine learning library (line 5). The train_test_split() function internally calls ShuffleSplit() function to randomize the selection of samples for training and testing sets. We use 80% performance dataset samples for training and the remaining 20% samples for testing (prediction).

Our AutoML based algorithm constructs a neural network only using a training dataset. We standardize the input and output features of the training dataset from $[X_{train}, y_{train}]$ to $X_{train\_std}, y_{train\_std}$ using StandardScaler() function from scikit-learn before using it (line 8). StandardScaler applies $(X - \mu(X))/\sigma(X)$ to standardize each feature with a mean (μ) of zero and a standard deviation (σ) of one (line 6, 7). We have used Keras [3], an open-source python library for neural networks, to build a neural network in our algorithm. The algorithm starts with an input layer with the number of neurons equal to the number of input features in standardized training set $|X_{train\_std}|$ (line 11). In the first iteration (L=0), algorithm adds the output layer directly connected to the input layer using the linear activation function (line 16 condition is false). Hence, the first neural network model has only two layers, input and output, without any hidden layer. The algorithm trains the neural network using the training set $X_{train\_std}, y_{train\_std}$ and also perform prediction using only the input features X_{train_std} from the same training set to get the predicted performance $y_{\hat{train}\_std}$ (line 22). It then calculates the metric root mean squared error (RMSE) using the actual and predicted performance values $RMSE \leftarrow \sqrt{\frac{1}{n} \sum_{i=1}^{n} (y_{train\_std} - y_{\hat{train}\_std})^2}$ (line 23). In the second iteration (L=1), algorithm adds the first hidden layer between the input and output layers with the number of neurons equal to the previous iteration's RMSE*100 (line 16 condition is true). The hidden layer is connected using the ReLU activation function with the input and linear activation to the output layer. The algorithm trains neural network from L=1 with a single hidden layer using the training dataset and performs prediction (line 22). Again algorithm calculates the RMSE value for the neural network from the current iteration (L = 1)(line 23) and compares it with RMSE from the previous iteration (L = 0) (line 24). The algorithm continues to the next iteration and adds an additional hidden layer if the current iteration's RMSE is lower than the previous iteration's RMSE; otherwise, the algorithm stops (line 24). For each subsequent iteration, the algorithm follows the same iterative process. Our Algorithm

Algorithm 1: AutoML Based Algorithm for Performance Prediction of HPC Systems

---

1 Let HPC Systems Hardware Feature Set be $X \leftarrow$ $cpu\_clock, isa, l1\_size, l2\_size, l3\_size, num\_cpus, mem\_type, mem\_clock, mem\_size$;

2 Let Performance (Runtime) of HPC Systems be y;

3 Let Performance Dataset be $[X, y]$;

4 Encode Text Data Features to Real Valued Features $X \leftarrow Encode(X)$;

5 Split Performance Dataset $[X, y]$ into Training and Testing Sets $[X_{train}, y_{train}]$ and $[X_{test}, y_{test}]$;

6 Standardize Training Set Systems Hardware Features $X_{train\_std} \leftarrow \frac{(X_{train} - \mu(X_{train}))}{\sigma(X_{train})}$;

7 Standardize Training Set Performance (Runtime) $y_{train\_std} \leftarrow \frac{(y_{train} - \mu(y_{train}))}{\sigma(y_{train})}$;

8 Standardized Training Dataset be $[X_{train\_std}, y_{train\_std}]$;

9 Assign Largest Possible Value To Metric $RMSE \leftarrow \infty$;

10 $L \leftarrow 0$;

11 Create Neural Network Input Layer $NN \leftarrow [layer = L, neurons = |X_{train\_std}|]$;

12 $prev\_NN \leftarrow NN$;

13 **do**

14 | $NN \leftarrow prev\_NN$;

15 | $prev\_RMSE \leftarrow RMSE$;

16 | **if** $L \geq 1$ **then**

17 | | Add Hidden Layer $NN.add \leftarrow [layer = L, neurons = RMSE * 100]$;

18 | **end**

19 | $L \leftarrow L + 1$;

20 | $prev\_NN \leftarrow NN$;

21 | Add Output Layer $NN \leftarrow [layer = L + 1, neurons = |y_{train\_std}|]$;

22 | $\hat{y_{train\_std}} \leftarrow NN.predict(X_{train\_std})$;

23 | $RMSE \leftarrow \sqrt{\frac{1}{n} \sum_{i=1}^{n} (y_{train\_std} - \hat{y_{train\_std}})^2}$;

24 **while** $RMSE \leq prev\_RMSE$;

25 $NN \leftarrow prev\_NN$;

26 Output NN

---

behaves similar to gradient descent to find the minima of RMSE value to converge. However, similar to gradient descent problem, the algorithm can converge early or overshoot and may find different convergence point of RMSE value rather than the actual.

3   SPEC Benchmark Applications Performance Dataset

SPEC CPU 2006 and SPEC CPU 2017 benchmark suites consist of industry-standard, CPU intensive applications to measure and compare compute-intensive performance, stressing a system's processor and memory subsystem. Both suites are divided into four sub-suites; integer speed, integer rate, floating-point speed

Table 1. SPEC Benchmark Applications Used

SPEC 2017 Float	SPEC 2006 Float	SPEC 2017 Int	SPEC 2006 Int
603.bwaves_s	416.gamess	600.perlbench_s	401.bzip2
607.cactuBSSN_s	433.milc	602.gcc_s	456.hmmer
619.lbm_s	434.zeusmp	605.mcf_s	458.sjeng
621.wrf_s	435.gromacs	620.omnetpp_s	462.libquantum
627.cam4_s	437.leslie3d	623.xalancbmk_s	473.astar
628.pop2_s	447.dealII	625.x264_s	
638.imagick_s	450.soplex	631.deepsjeng_s	
644.nab_s	453.povray	641.leela_s	
649.fotonik3d_s	454.calculix	648.exchange2_s	
654.roms_s		657.xz_s	

and floating-point rate, out of which we use integer speed (Int) and floating-point speed (Float) suites. Table 1 shows 19 applications selected from SPEC CPU 2006 and 2017 floating-point speed suites and 15 applications selected from SPEC CPU 2006 and 2017 integer speed suites. Systems manufacturers execute these benchmark suites and publish the results, including the performance (runtime) and system features, in various file formats, including comma-separated values (CSV). Using the BeautifulSoup python package, we downloaded CSV files with results of 2000 systems uploaded on the SPEC website. We then extracted nine hardware features (cores, instruction-set, cpu clock, memory speed, memory type, memory size and L1, L2 L3 Cache sizes) and the performance (runtime) from CSV files to build a performance dataset for each application required by our AutoML based algorithm.

4 Experiments and Results

For each of the applications, we have already constructed a performance dataset as explained in Sect. 3. We then built a neural network using our AutoML based algorithm as described in Sect. 2. To build the neural network, we first prepared an application-specific performance dataset by encoding text data features memory type and ISA to real value, dividing the dataset into training and testing datasets using 80:20 ratio and scaling the features of the datasets. We scaled both hardware features and performance (runtime) for the training dataset, while we scaled only hardware features for the testing dataset. Our algorithm trained a neural network while constructing it for each application-specific scaled training dataset. We predicted the runtimes for the scaled testing dataset using an application-specific trained neural network.

We evaluated the neural network constructed utilizing our AutoML based algorithm in two ways. First, we measure the accuracy at each iteration as the hidden layers are added to the neural network to evaluate the effectiveness of our

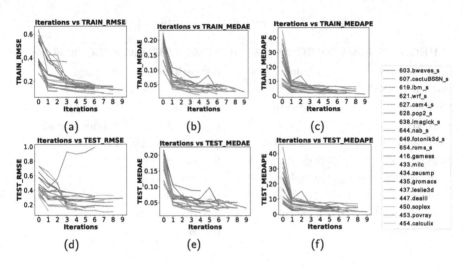

Fig. 1. SPEC Float Benchmark: Our AutoML Based Algorithm Accuracy

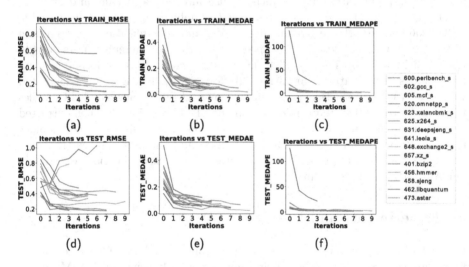

Fig. 2. SPEC Int Benchmark: Our AutoML Based Algorithm Accuracy

algorithm. Second, we compare the accuracies between two neural networks, one built by our AutoML based algorithm and the other with the state-of-the-art Auto-Keras, built for the same application.

4.1   Evaluation of Algorithm Effectiveness

We used RMSE metric in our algorithm to build neural network automatically; hence, we evaluated the accuracy using RMSE metric. In addition, we evaluated the accuracy using two other important metrics, median absolute error (MedAE)

Table 2. Neural Networks Runtime Comparison

Benchmark	Our Algorithm	Auto-Keras
SPEC Float	20 mins	33 mins
SPEC Int	16 mins	26 mins

and median absolute percentage error (MedAPE). Figures 1a and 2b depicts the
RMSE metric at each iteration for training dataset of SPEC Float and SPEC Int
applications. We observe that as the hidden layers are added in each iteration
RMSE reduces. The effectiveness of our algorithm lies in the fact that number
of neurons at each added hidden layer in iteration N is directly proportional to
RMSE calculated in previous iteration N-1. For example, neural network built for
638.imagick_s has 56, 45 38, 15 and 13, neurons in respective hidden layers due to
RMSE values 0.5682, 0.4552, 0.3818, 0.1573, 0.1399 in iterations zero to four. We
also observe from Figs. 1d and 2d that RMSE for testing datasets also reduces
with each iteration for all applications except for 627.cam4_s, 631.deepsjeng_s,
625.x264_s. We can confirm from the MedAE and MedAPE plots that the metric
value gradually reduces with each iteration for training as well testing datasets
for each application. We observe that for some applications all 9 iterations are
not required because RMSE of last iteration for that application is optimal and
any additional iteration causes increase in RMSE.

4.2   Accuracy Comparison with the State-of-the-Art

To compare the results from our AutoML based algorithm with the state-of-the-
art, we built neural networks for each of the applications in Auto-Keras using
StructuredDataRegressor(max_trials=3). Figures 3 and 4 displays the comparison of RMSE, MedAE and MedAPE from the neural network model build from
our algorithm versus Auto-Keras. We observe that for all applications except
627.cam4_s, 631.deepsjeng_s, 625.x264_s, the neural network built by our algorithm outperforms the one from Auto-Keras. Our algorithm outperforms Auto-
Keras because we believe that the Auto-Keras StructuredDataRegressor class
uses two hidden layers, each with 32 neurons statically for all applications. In
contrast, our algorithm dynamically determines the number of hidden layers and
neurons in each layer based on metric value. Furthermore, upon comparing the
running time of the neural network on Google Colaboratory, we found that our
model took less time to run compared to Auto-Keras, as shown in Table 2.

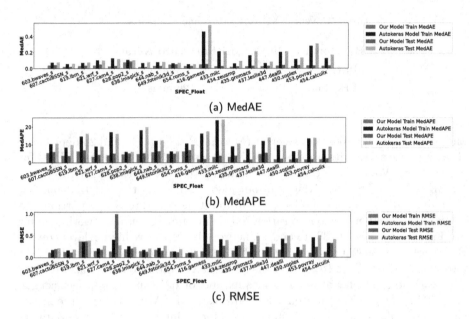

(a) MedAE

(b) MedAPE

(c) RMSE

Fig. 3. SPEC Float Benchmark: Train and Test Accuracy of Our AutoML Based Algorithm vs Auto-Keras

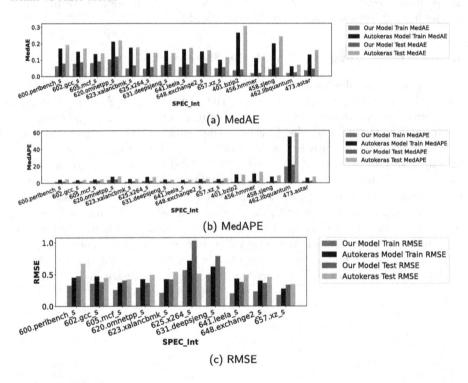

(a) MedAE

(b) MedAPE

(c) RMSE

Fig. 4. SPEC Int Benchmark: Train and Test Accuracy of Our AutoML Based Algorithm vs Auto-Keras

5 Conclusions and Future Work

In this paper, we proposed the first AutoML based algorithm to automatically construct a neural network for performance prediction. We have shown that the neural network model built using our algorithm provides higher accuracy than the state-of-the-art. In the future, we plan to evaluate our AutoML based algorithm with a larger number of automated machine learning tools. We also plan to evaluate our algorithm with performance datasets with other input features.

References

1. Agarwal, R., Chopra, S., Christophides, V., Georgantas, N., Issarny, V.: Detecting mobile crowdsensing context in the wild. In: Proceedings - IEEE International Conference on Mobile Data Management, June 2019, pp. 170–175. Institute of Electrical and Electronics Engineers Inc. (2019). https://doi.org/10.1109/MDM.2019.00-60
2. Chen, W., Dong, X., Chen, H., Wang, Q., Yu, X., Zhang, X.: Performance evaluation of convolutional neural network on tianhe-3 prototype. J. Supercomput. **77**(11), 12647–12665 (2021). https://doi.org/10.1007/S11227-021-03759-8/FIGURES/10, https://link.springer.com/article/10.1007/s11227-021-03759-8
3. Chollet, F., et al.: Keras. https://keras.io (2015)
4. Elsken, T., Metzen, J.H., Hutter, F.: Neural architecture search: a survey. J. Mach. Learn. Res. **20**, 1–21 (2019). https://doi.org/10.5555/3322706.3361996, http://jmlr.org/papers/v20/18-598.html
5. Erickson, N., et al.: AutoGluon-tabular: robust and accurate AutoML for structured data (2020). https://arxiv.org/abs/2003.06505v1
6. Ferreira, L., Pilastri, A., Martins, C.M., Pires, P.M., Cortez, P.: A comparison of automl tools for machine learning, deep learning and XGBoost. In: Proceedings of the International Joint Conference on Neural Networks, July 2021. Institute of Electrical and Electronics Engineers Inc. (2021). https://doi.org/10.1109/IJCNN52387.2021.9534091
7. Feurer, M., Eggensperger, K., Falkner, S., Lindauer, M., Hutter, F.: Auto-sklearn 2.0: hands-free AutoML via meta-learning (2020). https://arxiv.org/abs/2007.04074v2
8. García-Domínguez, M., Domínguez, C., Heras, J., Mata, E., Pascual, V.: UFOD: an AutoML framework for the construction, comparison, and combination of object detection models. Pattern Recogn. Lett. **145**, 135–140 (2021). https://doi.org/10.1016/J.PATREC.2021.01.022
9. Gupta, G., Katarya, R.: EnPSO: an AutoML technique for generating ensemble recommender system. Arab. J. Sci. Eng. **46**(9), 8677–8695 (2021). https://doi.org/10.1007/S13369-021-05670-Z/FIGURES/8, https://link.springer.com/article/10.1007/s13369-021-05670-z
10. Halvari, T., Nurminen, J.K., Mikkonen, T.: Robustness of AutoML for time series forecasting in sensor networks. In: 2021 IFIP Networking Conference, IFIP Networking 2021. Institute of Electrical and Electronics Engineers Inc. (2021). https://doi.org/10.23919/IFIPNETWORKING52078.2021.9472199
11. Jin, H., Song, Q., Hu, X.: Auto-Keras: an efficient neural architecture search system. In: Proceedings of the 25th ACM SIGKDD International Conference on Knowledge Discovery & Data Mining. ACM, New York, NY, USA (2019). https://doi.org/10.1145/3292500, https://doi.org/10.1145/3292500.3330648

12. Kulkarni, G.N., Ambesange, S., Vijayalaxmi, A., Sahoo, A.: Comparision of diabetic prediction AutoML model with customized model. In: Proceedings - International Conference on Artificial Intelligence and Smart Systems, ICAIS 2021, pp. 842–847. Institute of Electrical and Electronics Engineers Inc. (2021). https://doi.org/10.1109/ICAIS50930.2021.9395775

13. Kwok, T.Y., Yeung, D.Y.: Constructive algorithms for structure learning in feedforward neural networks for regression problems. IEEE Trans. Neural Netw. 8(3), 630–645 (1997). https://doi.org/10.1109/72.572102

14. Lee, M., Ahn, H., Hong, C.H., Nikolopoulos, D.S.: gShare: a centralized GPU memory management framework to enable GPU memory sharing for containers. Future Gener. Comput. Syst. 130, 181–192 (2022). https://doi.org/10.1016/J.FUTURE.2021.12.016, https://linkinghub.elsevier.com/retrieve/pii/S0167739X21004970

15. Liu, D., et al.: AutoGenome: an AutoML tool for genomic research. Artif. Intell. Life Sci. 1, 100017 (2021). https://doi.org/10.1016/J.AILSCI.2021.100017

16. Lopez, L., Guynn, M., Lu, M.: Predicting computer performance based on hardware configuration using multiple neural networks. In: Proceedings - 17th IEEE International Conference on Machine Learning and Applications, ICMLA 2018, pp. 824–827. Institute of Electrical and Electronics Engineers Inc. (2019). https://doi.org/10.1109/ICMLA.2018.00132

17. Luo, X., Liu, D., Huai, S., Kong, H., Chen, H., Liu, W.: Designing efficient DNNs via hardware-aware neural architecture search and beyond. IEEE Trans. Comput. Aided Des. Integr. Circuits Syst. (2021). https://doi.org/10.1109/TCAD.2021.3100249

18. Malakar, P., Balaprakash, P., Vishwanath, V., Morozov, V., Kumaran, K.: Benchmarking machine learning methods for performance modeling of scientific applications. In: Proceedings of PMBS 2018: Performance Modeling, Benchmarking and Simulation of High Performance Computer Systems, Held in conjunction with SC 2018: The International Conference for High Performance Computing, Networking, Storage and Analysis, pp. 33–44. Institute of Electrical and Electronics Engineers Inc., Dallas, Texas, USA (2019). https://doi.org/10.1109/PMBS.2018.8641686

19. Mankodi, A., Bhatt, A., Chaudhury, B.: Evaluation of neural network models for performance prediction of scientific applications. In: IEEE Region 10th Annual International Conference, Proceedings/TENCON. November 2020, pp. 426–431. Institute of Electrical and Electronics Engineers Inc. (2020). https://doi.org/10.1109/TENCON50793.2020.9293788

20. Mariani, G., Anghel, A., Jongerius, R., Dittmann, G.: Predicting cloud performance for HPC applications before deployment. Futur. Gener. Comput. Syst. 87, 618–628 (2018). https://doi.org/10.1016/j.future.2017.10.048

21. Nikitin, N., et al.: Automated evolutionary approach for the design of composite machine learning pipelines. Futur. Gener. Comput. Syst. 127, 109–125 (2022). https://doi.org/10.1016/J.FUTURE.2021.08.022

22. Pedregosa, F., et al.: Scikit-learn: machine learning in python. J. Mach. Learn. Res. 12, 2825–2830 (2011). http://scikit-learn.sourceforge.net

23. Rakhshani, H., et al.: Automated machine learning for information retrieval in scientific articles. In: 2020 IEEE Congress on Evolutionary Computation, CEC 2020 - Conference Proceedings. Institute of Electrical and Electronics Engineers Inc. (2020). https://doi.org/10.1109/CEC48606.2020.9185893

24. Ren, P., et al.: A comprehensive survey of neural architecture search. ACM Comput. Surv. (CSUR), 54(4), 76 (2021). https://doi.org/10.1145/3447582

25. Srivastava, A., Zhang, N., Kannan, R., Prasanna, V.K.: Towards high performance, portability, and productivity: lightweight augmented neural networks for performance prediction. In: Proceedings - 2020 IEEE 27th International Conference on High Performance Computing, Data, and Analytics, HiPC 2020, pp. 21–30. Institute of Electrical and Electronics Engineers Inc. (2020). https://doi.org/10.1109/HIPC50609.2020.00016

26. Sun, J., Sun, G., Zhan, S., Zhang, J., Chen, Y.: Automated performance modeling of HPC applications using machine learning. IEEE Trans. Comput. **69**(5), 749–763 (2020). https://doi.org/10.1109/TC.2020.2964767

27. Wang, K., Guo, P.: A robust automated machine learning system with pseudoinverse learning. Cogn. Comput. **13**(3), 724–735 (2021). https://doi.org/10.1007/S12559-021-09853-6, https://link.springer.com/article/10.1007/s12559-021-09853-6

28. Wang, K., Liu, Z., Lin, Y., Lin, J., Han, S.: Hardware-centric AutoML for mixed-precision quantization. Int. J. Comput. Vis. **128**(8–9), 2035–2048 (2020). https://doi.org/10.1007/S11263-020-01339-6/FIGURES/11, https://link.springer.com/article/10.1007/s11263-020-01339-6

29. Wang, C.C., Liao, Y.C., Kao, M.C., Liang, W.Y., Hung, S.H.: Toward accurate platform-aware performance modeling for deep neural networks. ACM SIGAPP Appl. Comput. Rev. **21**(1), 50–61 (2021). https://doi.org/10.1145/3477133.3477137, https://dl.acm.org/doi/abs/10.1145/3477133.3477137

30. Yang, J., Shi, R., Ni, B.: MedMNIST classification decathlon: a lightweight automl benchmark for medical image analysis. In: Proceedings - International Symposium on Biomedical Imaging, April 2021, pp. 191–195. IEEE Computer Society (2021). https://doi.org/10.1109/ISBI48211.2021.9434062

31. Zhang, L., et al.: AutoGGN: a gene graph network AutoML tool for multi-omics research. Artif. Intell. Life Sci. **1**, 100019 (2021). https://doi.org/10.1016/J.AILSCI.2021.100019

32. Zimmer, L., Lindauer, M., Hutter, F.: Auto-pytorch tabular: multi-fidelity metalearning for efficient and robust AutoDL. IEEE Trans. Pattern Anal. Mach. Intell. **43**(9), 3079–3090 (2020). https://doi.org/10.1109/TPAMI.2021.3067763, https://arxiv.org/abs/2006.13799v3

33. Zöller, M.A., Huber, M.F.: Benchmark and survey of automated machine learning frameworks. J. Artif. Intell. Res. **70**, 409–472 (2021). https://doi.org/10.1613/JAIR.1.11854, https://dl.acm.org/doi/abs/10.1613/jair.1.11854

Embedded Systems and Communication

Edge-Gateway Intrusion Detection for Smart Home

Zhiming Sun[1], Jingjing Yu[1(✉)], and Xingchun Liu[2]

[1] School of Electronic and Information Engineering, Beijing Jiaotong University,
Beijing 100044, China
`{21125078,jjyu}@bjtu.edu.cn`
[2] Taikang Life Insurance Co., Ltd., Beijing 110000, China
`liuxc51@taikanglife.com`

Abstract. With the development of Internet of Things (IoT) and intelligent sensing technology, smart devices and smart home applications have been widely applied to benefit human life. However, due to the increasing number and diversity of smart home devices, they are vulnerable to be attacked that might cause serious security threats and user's privacy disclosure. In addition, large-scale distributed and heterogeneous sensing devices have different requirements for the low latency and reliability of intrusion detection algorithms. Therefore, this paper proposes an edge-gateway intrusion detection system for smart home, including edge intrusion detection model based on Gaussian distribution for smart devices and gateway intrusion detection model based on graph sampling and aggregation with random features (RF-GraphSAGE). The edge intrusion detection algorithm is directly monitoring the data of important smart devices, such as surveillance camera, to realize real-time detection of various malicious attacks. The gateway-level centralized intrusion detection algorithm monitors the traffic data of overall network to further reduce the undetected rate of anomalies and improve the detection accuracy for various attacks. Experimental results demonstrated that proposed framework achieves superior intrusion detection performance on average recall rate, average precision rate and average F1-score, when compared with prior state-of-the-art algorithms.

Keywords: Edge-gateway · Gaussian distribution · RF-GraphSAGE · Intrusion detection

1 Introduction

With the development of Internet of Things (IoT) and intelligent sensing technology, various smart home devices are widely used to improve the quality of daily life, such as surveillance cameras, environment monitor, smart lights and doorbells [1, 2]. However, with the rapid growth of device number and device-type diversification, the smart home network faces a large variety of network attacks, serious security threats and privacy leaks, which makes it urgent to develop reliable intrusion detection algorithms to

---

Supported by Fundamental Research Funds for Central Universities (Grant No. 2021JBM004).

H. Takizawa et al. (Eds.): PDCAT 2022, LNCS 13798, pp. 123–135, 2023.
https://doi.org/10.1007/978-3-031-29927-8_10

improve the security of devices and data-transmission procedure. In smart home system, because the data capacity of sensor nodes is usually limited, the sensing data of devices is generally uploaded to the cloud center through gateway for processing, which can be accessed by all devices and users, thus increasing the risk of information leakage [3, 4]. In addition, current smart home system contains large-scale distributed and heterogeneous sensing devices. Different types of devices have different date volume, encoding format and sensing speed, which make them suffer from different vulnerable attacks and show different importance for network security [5–7]. All above bring great challenges to intrusion detection for smart home, and heterogeneous devices have different requirements for the low latency and reliability of intrusion detection algorithms, which cannot be handled very well by traditional intrusion detection algorithms for IoT [8–17].

Therefore, to solve these problems, this paper proposes an edge-gateway two-level intrusion detection system based on Gaussian distribution model and RF-GraphSAGE model. Device-level detection algorithm based on Gaussian distribution is deployed on the important smart devices, such as surveillance cameras, to facilitate timely detection of anomalies and improve the real-time performance of intrusion detection. The gateway-level centralized intrusion detection algorithm based on RF-GraphSAGE is deployed on the gateway to monitor the traffic data of overall network for comprehensive anomaly detection, realize the detection of various attack types and improve the detection reliability.

This paper is structured as follows. Related work is presented in Sect. 2. Section 3 proposes our edge-gateway intrusion detection system for smart home. In Sect. 4, experiments based on smart home dataset are performed and results of proposed intrusion detection system are analyzed. Section 5 summarizes the conclusions of this paper.

2   Related Work

Smart home devices have multiple cross-device characteristics and diverse deployment environments. The computing power of edge devices is not as good as that of cloud servers, and they are closer to sensitive data and users [9, 10]. These are the reasons for security vulnerabilities. In response to these problems, Amouri, Alaparthy and Morger [11, 12] used machine learning to cultivate an intrusion detection system for IoT networks. Verma et al. [13] used convolutional neural network (CNN) to design intrusion detection system. Through adaptive synthetic sampling algorithm, they mainly dealt with the problem of data imbalance and improved the detection rate of imbalanced data sets, but the detection rate of Dos and Probe attack types was low. Sinha et al. [14] combined the unique advantages of convolutional neural network and bidirectional long short-term memory network (LSTM). This algorithm learns both spatial and temporal characteristics of the data to improve detection rates. Besides, since 2020, with the vigorous development of graph neural networks and their applications, graph neural network (GNN) has achieved state-of-the-art network topology modeling performance in cybersecurity tasks [15, 16]. Lo, Wai Weng et al. [17] proposed an GNN network called graph sampling and aggregation based on edges (E-GraphSAGE), which can capture edge features and topology information of graphs for network intrusion detection in the Internet of Things and improve the performance of network intrusion detection. However, the dataset applied in this paper contains much more abnormal data than normal data, which does not match the data characteristics of the actual smart home network traffics. Therefore, this paper proposes an edge-gateway intrusion detection system for smart home to detect various malicious attacks timely and accurately. A novel GNN model called RF-GraphSAGE is applied as the gateway-level intrusion detection model to effectively improve the detection reliability.

3   Edge-Gateway Intrusion Detection System for Smart Home

3.1   System Framework

Considering the node heterogeneity and diversification of anomaly detection requirements for smart home devices, a two-stage edge-gateway intrusion detection system is proposed. The system framework is shown in Fig. 1.

At the first stage, for the smart devices with better computation capacity, which could have more serious threat of privacy disclosure once attacked, the device-level edge intrusion detection algorithm based on Gaussian distribution is deployed to bring more sensitivity and better real-time capability of intrusion detection. A Gaussian distribution model using two-dimensional features of device sensing data is applied to determine the threshold through ten-fold cross-validation and discover malicious traffic data in time at the data source to improve the real-time performance of malicious attack detection.

For the traffic data from lightweight devices without processing and storage capacity, a gateway-level centralized intrusion detection algorithm based on RF-GraphSAGE is deployed as the second-stage detection. It monitors the multi-source heterogeneous

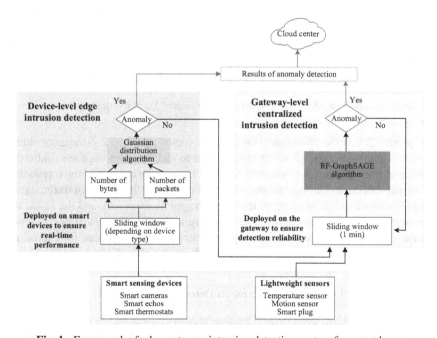

Fig. 1. Framework of edge-gateway intrusion detection system for smart home

network traffic data at gateway, performs traffic anomaly analysis by exploring the correlation pattern between key features of network traffic data and network anomalies through proposed RF-GraphSAGE graph neural network, then achieves cross-device detection of multiple attack types and improve the comprehensive detection reliability.

3.2 Edge Intrusion Detection of Smart Device Based on Gaussian Distribution

A device-level edge intrusion detection algorithm is deployed on smart devices to realize the real-time detection for serious attacks at the device end. The lightweight edge intrusion detection algorithm uses two-dimensional features of device traffic data (number of packets and number of bytes) for abnormal detection where the threshold is computed by Gaussian distribution model. This device-level edge intrusion detection algorithm is applied with the sliding window to establish a Gaussian distribution model for the two-dimensional characteristics of the number of packets and the number of bytes in an IoT device traffic and obtain intrusion detection thresholds through normal traffic data training, thereby realizing abnormal data discovery in real case.

Assuming $\mathcal{D}$ represents the set of smart home devices, $d_i \in \mathcal{D}$ is the i-th device identified by its IP and port number, where $i = 1, 2, \ldots, N$. T_{cpu} is the threshold of CPU capacity of each device to judge whether this device can install the edge intrusion detection algorithm. The traffic data generated by IoT devices is a time stream composed of data packets, including user information, device information, byte information, data packet information etc. For each smart device, two-dimensional features are extracted from the traffic data based on sliding window with fixed size, which is set according to different device type. In the experiment, we choose 1 min for smart camera to ensure the real-time intrusion detection. A multivariate Gaussian distribution model is established for the features of traffic data to perform density estimation and decide the detection threshold. Assuming $x = \{x^1, x^2\}$ as the two-dimensional features of traffic data in smart device, each feature contains m samples as $x^1 = \{x_1^1, x_2^1, \ldots, x_m^1\}$ and $x^2 = \{x_1^2, x_2^2, \ldots, x_m^2\}$. Based on the study of [18], x follows multidimensional Gaussian distribution, as:

$$N(x|\mu, \Sigma) = \frac{1}{2\pi |\Sigma|^{\frac{1}{2}}} \exp\left\{-\frac{1}{2}(x - \mu)^{\mathrm{T}} \Sigma^{-1}(x - \mu)\right\} \tag{1}$$

where μ and Σ are the two-dimensional mean vector and 2×2 covariance matrix of x. After establishing the Gaussian distribution model, we then used ten-fold cross-validation to train the model to generate the best F1 score to determine the threshold φ for intrusion detection. During the edge intrusion detection, the unknown traffic data x' are fed into the model. If $p(x') \leq \varphi$, it will be judged as abnormal, and the result will be uploaded to the cloud center for users to query and taking actions. If $p(x') > \varphi$, it is normal data and it will be transmitted to the gateway level algorithm for centralized intrusion detection. The flowchart and pseudocode are given in Table 1 and Fig. 2.

3.3 Gateway-Level Centralized Intrusion Detection Based on RF-GraphSAGE

The gateway-level RF-GraphSAGE algorithm is applied to centrally examine network traffic data for intrusion detection. It is a graph neural network which mapping IPs

Table 1. Pseudocode of device-level edge intrusion detection algorithm

Input: the raw traffic of the devices$\{S_{d_1}, \dots, S_{d_2}, \dots, S_{d_N}\}$
Device's CPU: $\{d_1.CPU, d_2.CPU, \dots, d_N.CPU\}$
The threshold of CPU capacity: T_{cpu}
1 for i in $\{d_1.CPU, d_2.CPU, \dots, d_n.CPU\}$:
2   if $(d_i.CPU \geq T_{cpu})$:
3   d_G.append(d_i)
4   return $d_G = \{d'_1, d'_2, \dots, d'_i\}$
5 For device d'_i, the traffic data is $S_{d'_i}$. $dataset1$ represents the normal data traffic generated by device d'_i . $dataset2$ represents a mix of normal and abnormal data traffic generated by device d'_i.
6 The two-dimensional features of the number of packets and the number of bytes of traffic are extracted from traffic data.
7 Initialize anomaly threshold: φ
8 for i in range (10):
9   μ, Σ= GuassianParamEstimation$(dataset1.\{x^1, x^2\})$
6    $x = dataset2.\{x^1, x^2\}$
7    $p(x) = \frac{1}{2\pi|\Sigma|^{\frac{1}{2}}} \exp\left\{-\frac{1}{2}(x-\mu)^T(\Sigma)^{-1}(x-\mu)\right\}$
8   if $(p(x) \leq \varphi)$:
9          $TP = TP + 1$
10   else:
11         $FN = FN + 1$
12   precision $= TP/(TP + FP)$, recall$= TP/(TP + FN)$
13   where TP, TN, FP and FN represent the number of True Positives, True Negatives, False Positives and False Negatives respectively.
14   F1=2* precision* recall / (precision+ recall)
15   $\varphi = \varphi + 0.01$
16 return max(F1), φ
17 For new traffic data x'
18 $p(x') = \frac{1}{2\pi|\Sigma|^{\frac{1}{2}}} \exp\left\{-\frac{1}{2}(x'-\mu)^T(\Sigma)^{-1}(x'-\mu)\right\}$
19 if $(p(x') \leq \varphi)$:
20   abnormal
21 else:
22   normal
Output: precision rate, recall rate, F1-score

and ports to graph nodes and network flows to graph edges to capture network traffic data features by the node information, edge information and topology of graph, thereby improving the accuracy of intrusion detection. The framework is shown in Fig. 3.

In our algorithm, a graph is defined as $\mathcal{G}(\mathcal{V}, \mathcal{E})$, where $\mathcal{V}$ is the set of devices and $\mathcal{E}$ is the set of graph edges representing message passing between two devices. The IP address and port number form a string to represent the device node. Vector $x_v = \{1, \dots, 1\}, \forall v \in \mathcal{V}$ are used to initialize the features of the node v. The dimension of the vector in each node depends on the number of edge features in graph. These messages can be characterized by

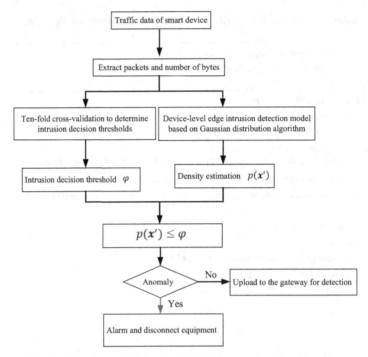

Fig. 2. Flowchart of device-level edge intrusion detection algorithm

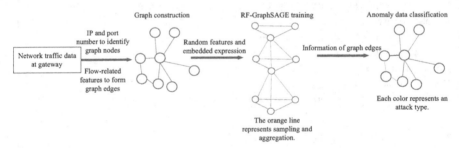

Fig. 3. Framework of gateway-level RF-GraphSAGE algorithm

the feature vector of edge $e_{uv} = \{length\ of\ packet, \ldots, end\ time\}, \forall uv \in \mathcal{E}$, where e_{uv} represents the message from device u to device v. Based on the GraphSAGE network structure [17], random features are introduced to enhance the robustness of intrusion detection. One-dimensional random features are added to each node and each edge. That is, $e_{uv} = \{length\ of\ packet, \ldots, end\ time, r\}, \forall uv \in \mathcal{E}, x_v = \{1, \ldots, 1, r\}, \forall v \in \mathcal{V},$ where r represents the one-dimensional random features.

RF-GraphSAGE training procedure are shown in Table 2. Expressed by the aggregation function AGG(·), we aggregate the information of all adjacent edges of the node, and then take the average, which can reduce the loss of information as much as possible. The information is aggregated based on the mean of the sampled neighborhood $\mathcal{N}(v)$ at the node v of the k-th ($k = 1, \ldots, K = 2$) layer, as:

$$h^k_{\mathcal{N}(v)} = \frac{\text{AGG}_k(\{e^{k-1}_{uv}, \forall u \in \mathcal{N}(v), uv \in \mathcal{E}\})}{|\mathcal{N}(v)|_e} \tag{2}$$

where e^{k-1}_{uv} is the edge information of u and v nodes at layer $k - 1$. $|\mathcal{N}(v)|_e$ represents the number of edges in the sampled neighbor. The information aggregated by the nodes at layer k is concatenated with the embedded information of the nodes in the previous layer. After multiplying the connected information with the trainable parameter $\mathbf{W}^k$ and passing the result through a nonlinear activation function σ, the embedding information of node v at layer k is calculated as:

$$h^k_v = \sigma\left(\mathbf{W}^k \cdot \text{CONCAT}\left(h^{k-1}_v, h^k_{\mathcal{N}(v)}\right)\right) \tag{3}$$

The where h^k_v is the embedding feature of the current node v at layer k. $\mathbf{W}^k$ is the weight matrix. σ is the ReLu activation function. CONCAT(·) is the concatenating operation along features. The embedded information of node v in the final layer K is h^K_v and the specific network parameters are given in Table 3. The embedded feature of the edge uv is formed by concatenating the information of the nodes u and v, as:

$$z^K_{uv} = \text{CONCAT}(h^K_u, h^K_v), uv \in \mathcal{E} \tag{4}$$

Then, z^K_{uv} is input into the softmax layer which normalizes the embedded feature to obtain a probability value. This value is compared with the real label to obtain the classification result of the edge and the attack type corresponding to the current data stream.

Table 2. Training of gateway-level RF-GraphSAGE algorithm

Input: $\mathcal{G}(\mathcal{V}, \mathcal{E})$
edge features: $e_{uv} = \{length\ of\ packet, \ldots, end\ time, r\}, \forall uv \in \mathcal{E}$
node features: $x_v = \{1, \ldots, 1, r\}, \forall v \in \mathcal{V}$
1 node v initialization: $h^0_v = x_v$
2 for k in K:
3   for v in $\mathcal{V}$:
4      $h^k_{\mathcal{N}(v)} = \frac{\text{AGG}_k(\{e^{k-1}_{uv}, \forall u \in \mathcal{N}(v), uv \in \mathcal{E}\})}{|N(v)|_e}$
5      $h^k_v = \sigma(\mathbf{W}^k \cdot \text{CONCAT}(h^{k-1}_v, h^k_{\mathcal{N}(v)}))$
6 h^K_v
7 for uv in $\mathcal{E}$:
8    $z^K_{uv} = \text{CONCAT}(h^K_u, h^K_v), uv \in \mathcal{E}$
Output: precision rate, recall rate, F1-score, and the attack type corresponding to each edge.

Table 3. Parameter settings for the network layer

Number of network layers	K=2
Sampling method	full neighborhood sampling
Learning rate	0.001
Edge embedding dimension	256
Node embedding dimension	128
Activation function	ReLU
Dropout	0.2
Loss function	CrossEntropyLoss
Optimizer	Adam optimizer

4 Results and Discussion

4.1 Experimental Setup

To simulate the smart home environment, IoT Security dataset [18, 19] is applied in our experiments. The dataset builds an intelligent environment with 28 types of home devices for continuous 26 weeks, including smart camera, lightbulb, power switch, motion sensor and amazon echo. The attack types included in this dataset are ARP spoofing, TCP SYN flooding, UDP flooding, Ping of Death, SNMP, TCP SYN, SSDP, Smurf. Each type of attack contains three different attack rates as 1pps, 10pps, and 100pps. The intrusion detection results are measured by precision rate, recall rate and F1-score.

4.2 Results of Device-Level Edge Intrusion Detection

Results of Device-level edge intrusion detection based on Gaussian distribution are given in Fig. 4. The traffic data of Samsung smart camera with three different attack rates are selected for anomaly detection. The lightweight two-dimensional feature extraction is carried out on the camera data with three sliding windows of 1 min, 3 min, and 5 min, respectively.

As shown in Fig. 4, even only examining two simple traffic date features of smart camera (number of packets and the number of bytes), our edge instruction detection algorithm can effectively detect high-rate abnormal traffic data. However, it has poor performance on low-rate abnormal traffic, especially with 1pps attack rate. Also, the selecting of time window length is critical for the performance of abnormal detection, that should be decided based on the type of device, sensing data rate and data volume. Considering the limited computation and storage capability of edge devices, in order to bring better real-time performance of abnormal detection and minimize the threat of intrusion, the sliding window size of feature extraction for smart camera is set to 1 min in our later experiments. And the comprehensive gateway-level centralized intrusion detection should be added at the next stage to improve the reliability of intrusion detection for multiple device and attack types.

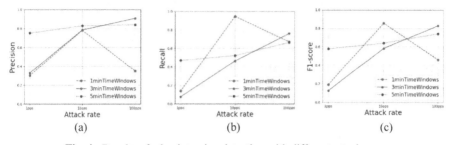

Fig. 4. Results of edge intrusion detection with different attack rates.

4.3 Results of Gateway-Level Centralized Intrusion Detection

RF-GraphSAGE centralized intrusion detection algorithm are applied at gateway of smart home to monitor mixed traffic data from lightweight devices and smart devices that have been identified as normal by edge intrusion detection algorithm, with the purpose to improve the comprehensive detection reliability toward multiple attack types.

Table 4, 5 and 6 show the performance comparison of proposed RF-GraphSAGE intrusion detection algorithm with E-GraphSAGE [17], CNN [13] and CNN-BiLSTM [14]. It can be seen that proposed RF-GraphSAGE shows optimal performance in average precision, average recall rate, and average F1-score values. When compared with the optimal CNN-BiLSTM model, the average recall rate of our RF-GraphSAGE is increased by 2.82%, the average precision rate increased by 0.70%, and the average F1-score increased by 3.23%. In addition, when considering different attack types, the average recall rate, average precision rate, and average F1-score of proposed RF-GraphSAGE overall nine attack types are all above 90.93%, 84.52%, and 87.79%. Therefore, our proposed gateway-level centralized detection algorithm based on RF-GraphSAGE is demonstrated to have higher detection accuracy over all smart home devices, when compared with current CNN, CNN-BiLSTM and E-GraphSAGE algorithms.

Table 4. Average recall rate of different intrusion detection algorithms

Type of attack	CNN	CNN-BiLSTM	E-GraphSAGE	RF-GraphSAGE
Normal	0.9755	0.9589	0.9552	0.9639
Ssdp100W2D2W	0.9969	0.9917	0.9941	0.9891
Ssdp10W2D2W	0.9950	0.9560	0.9869	0.9718
Ssdp1W2D2W	0.9746	0.9093	0.8928	0.9370
TcpSynReflection100W2D2W	0.9653	0.8912	0.9138	0.9217
TcpSynReflection10W2D2W	0.9624	0.8795	0.8319	0.9214
TcpSynReflection1W2D2W	0.9489	0.8368	0.8188	0.9093
UdpDevice100W2D	0.8577	0.9551	0.9668	0.9755
UdpDevice10W2D	0.7565	0.9427	0.9515	0.9585

(*continued*)

Table 4. (*continued*)

Type of attack	CNN	CNN-BiLSTM	E-GraphSAGE	RF-GraphSAGE
UdpDevice1W2D	0.5600	0.9140	0.9207	0.9480
Average	0.8993	0.9235	0.9232	0.9496

Table 5. Average precision rate of different intrusion detection algorithms

Type of attack	CNN	CNN-BiLSTM	E-GraphSAGE	RF-GraphSAGE
Normal	0.9360	0.9519	0.9632	0.9700
Ssdp100W2D2W	0.9891	0.9907	0.9962	0.9966
Ssdp10W2D2W	0.9843	0.9747	0.9898	0.9937
Ssdp1W2D2W	0.9605	0.9106	0.7798	0.8452
TcpSynReflection100W2D2W	0.9400	0.9068	0.9111	0.9508
TcpSynReflection10W2D2W	0.9547	0.8910	0.9227	0.9070
TcpSynReflection1W2D2W	0.9705	0.8590	0.7253	0.8524
UdpDevice100W2D	0.8635	0.9478	0.9568	0.9639
UdpDevice10W2D	0.8394	0.9364	0.9428	0.9581
UdpDevice1W2D	0.8695	0.9510	0.9262	0.9469
Average	0.9307	0.9320	0.9114	0.9385

Table 6. Average F1-score of different intrusion detection algorithms

Type of attack	CNN	CNN-BiLSTM	E-GraphSAGE	RF-GraphSAGE
Normal	0.9553	0.9558	0.9558	0.9668
Ssdp100W2D2W	0.9930	0.9930	0.9951	0.9928
Ssdp10W2D2W	0.9896	0.9896	0.9879	0.9845
Ssdp1W2D2W	0.9672	0.9675	0.8450	0.8974
TcpSynReflection100W2D2W	0.9521	0.9526	0.9019	0.9367
TcpSynReflection10W2D2W	0.9578	0.9586	0.8624	0.9160
TcpSynReflection1W2D2W	0.9589	0.9597	0.7355	0.8779
UdpDevice100W2D	0.8567	0.8606	0.9630	0.9694

(*continued*)

Table 6. (*continued*)

Type of attack	CNN	CNN-BiLSTM	E-GraphSAGE	RF-GraphSAGE
UdpDevice10W2D	0.7870	0.7980	0.9478	0.9573
UdpDevice1W2D	0.6641	0.7148	0.9230	0.9473
Average	0.9082	0.9150	0.9118	0.9446

The intrusion detection results over different device types are shown in Table 7. No matter smart devices or lightweight devices, proposed RF-GraphSAGE algorithm can provide good detection results on the abnormal traffic data. The precision detection rates reach more than 83.81%. And the average recall rate, average precision rate and average F1-score reach more than 93.70%, 93.12% and 93.17%. Therefore, proposed gateway-level intrusion detection algorithm is effective and feasible for the detection of abnormal traffics in heterogeneous smart home network.

Table 7. Results of gateway-level centralized intrusion detection algorithm over devices

Smart home devices	Recall rate	Precision rate	F1-score
Lifx Lightbulb	0.9837	0.9748	0.9702
Hue bulb	0.9780	0.8381	0.9029
TPLink switch	0.9841	0.9953	0.9897
Amazon echo	0.8379	0.9025	0.8690
Samsung smart camera	0.8513	0.9654	0.9048
Netatmo camera	0.9706	0.9542	0.9623
Chromecast ultra	0.9662	0.9431	0.9545
WEMO Motion Sensor	0.9260	0.8498	0.8862
WEMO Power Switch	0.9353	0.9576	0.9463

5 Conclusion

With wide application of smart home devices in people's daily life, they excessively access and utilize users' private data, such as habits, health data, home location, daily routine and monitoring videos. However, current smart home devices rarely deploy intrusion detection algorithms due to their limited computational capacity, various manufacturers, and different requirements for the real time and reliability of abnormality detection, which make them be vulnerable and face with serious security threats. To solve these problems, this paper proposes an edge-gateway intrusion detection system for smart home, including device-level Gaussian distribution algorithm and gateway-level

RF-GraphSAGE algorithm, which are respectively deployed on smart devices and gateways to realize two-stage anomaly detection of heterogeneous network traffic against multiple attacks. The experiment results prove that proposed edge-gateway intrusion detection system provides high real-time performance and good accuracy for intrusion detection over multiple attack types and devices in smart home.

References

1. Yuan, D., et al.: Intrusion detection for smart home security based on data augmentation with edge computing. In: 2020 IEEE International Conference on Communications (ICC), ICC 2020, pp. 1–6 (2020)
2. Saxena, U., Sodhi, J.S., Singh, Y.: An analysis of DDoS attacks in a smart home networks. In: 2020 10th International Conference on Cloud Computing, Data Science & Engineering (Confluence), pp. 272–276 (2020)
3. Al-Kadi, O., Moustafa, N., Turnbull, B.P., Choo, K.R.: A deep blockchain framework-enabled collaborative intrusion detection for protecting IoT and cloud networks. IEEE Internet Things J. **8**(12), 9463–9472 (2021)
4. Shen, S., Huang, L., Zhou, H., Yu, S., Fan, E., Cao, Q.: Multistage signaling game-based optimal detection strategies for suppressing malware diffusion in fog-cloud-based IoT networks. IEEE Internet Things J. **5**(2), 1043–1054 (2018)
5. Graf, J., Neubauer, K., Fischer, S., Hackenberg, R.: Architecture of an intelligent intrusion detection system for smart home. In: 2020 IEEE International Conference on Pervasive Computing and Communications Workshops (PerCom Workshops), pp. 1–6 (2020)
6. Kang, B., Jeong, J., Choo, H.: Docker swarm and Kubernetes containers for smart home gateway. IT Prof. **23**, 75–80 (2021)
7. Khare, S., Totaro, M.W.: Ensemble learning for detecting attacks and anomalies in IoT smart home. In: 2020 3rd International Conference on Data Intelligence and Security (ICDIS), pp. 56–63 (2020)
8. Lourme, O., Hauspie, M.: Toward a realistic intrusion detection system dedicated to smart-home environments. In: 2021 17th International Conference on Wireless and Mobile Computing, Networking and Communications (WiMob), pp. 80–85 (2021)
9. Haddadpajouh, H., Dehghantanha, A., Parizi, R.M., Aledhari, M., Karimipour, H.: A survey on internet of things security: requirements, challenges, and solutions. Internet Things **14**, 100129 (2021)
10. Nizzi, F., Pecorella, T., Esposito, F., Pierucci, L., Fantacci, R.: IoT security via address shuffling: the easy way. IEEE Internet Things J. **6**(2), 3764–3774 (2019)
11. Amouri, A., Alaparthy, V.T., Morgera, S.D.: Cross layer-based intrusion detection based on network behavior for IoT. In: 2018 IEEE 19th Wireless and Microwave Technology Conference (WAMICON), pp. 1–4 (2018)
12. Alghayadh, F., Debnath, D.: HID-SMART: hybrid intrusion detection model for smart home. In: 2020 10th Annual Computing and Communication Workshop and Conference (CCWC), pp. 0384–0389 (2020)
13. Verma, A., Kaushik, P., Shrivastava, G.: A network intrusion detection approach using variant of convolution neural network. In: 2019 International Conference on Communication and Electronics Systems (ICCES), pp. 409–416 (2019)
14. Sinha, J., Manollas, M.: Efficient deep CNN-BiLSTM model for network intrusion detection. In: Proceedings of the 2020 3rd International Conference on Artificial Intelligence and Pattern Recognition (2020)

15. Chang, L., Branco, P.: Graph-based solutions with residuals for intrusion detection: the modified E-GraphSAGE and E-ResGAT algorithms. arXiv abs/2111.13597 (2021)
16. Dong, G., et al.: Graph neural networks in IoT: a survey. arXiv abs/2203.15935 (2022)
17. Lo, W.W., Layeghy, S., Sarhan, M., Gallagher, M.R., Portmann, M.: E-GraphSAGE: a graph neural network based intrusion detection system for IoT. In: 2022 IEEE/IFIP Network Operations and Management Symposium, NOMS 2022, pp. 1–9 (2022)
18. Xing, L.: Intrusion detection for internet of things based on network traffic anomaly analysis (2021). https://doi.org/10.26944/d.cnki.gbfju
19. Hamza, A., Gharakheili, H.H., Benson, T.A., Sivaraman, V.: Detecting volumetric attacks on IoT devices via SDN-based monitoring of MUD activity. In: Proceedings of the 2019 ACM Symposium on SDN Research (2019)

Energy-Delay Tradeoff in Parallel Task Allocation and Execution for Autonomous Platooning Applications

Liang Dai[1,2]([⊠]) [iD], Hangyu Tian[1,2], Dingxuan Ju[1,2], and Hongke Xu[1]

[1] School of Electronics and Control Engineering, Chang'an University, Xi'an, China
{ldai,hangyutian,dingxuanju,xhk}@chd.edu.cn
[2] Joint Laboratory for Internet of Vehicles, Ministry of Education-China Mobile
Communications Corporation, Chang'an University, Xi'an, China

Abstract. Aiming to guarantee the Makespan of data-intensive tasks in autonomous platooning applications and improve the system energy utilization, we proposed a parallel task allocation and execution algorithm using divisible load theory for energy-delay tradeoff in autonomous platooning applications in this paper. Assuming that the autonomous vehicles in the platoon support the dynamic voltage and frequency scaling technology, the autonomous vehicles adjust the processing capacity and communication capacity of the vehicles to the optimal level without exceeding the maximum completion time based on dynamic programming theory, so as to minimize the total energy consumption of the autonomous platoon. In order to calculate the allocation strategy conveniently in large-scale autonomous platoon,the Markov chain model is used to analyze the parallel task allocation and execution process in autonomous platooning applications, which is equivalent to queuing model. Then the Little theorem is used to analyze the total Makespan in the parallel task allocation and execution process, which modelled as a serially divisible load scheduling process. The simulation results show that the proposed parallel task allocation and execution algorithm for autonomous platooning applications can adjust the voltage and frequency of the autonomous vehicles to the most suitable level under the premise of meeting the total Makespan constraint, so as to reduce the total energy consumption in the task allocation and execution process. At the same time, the equivalence of the parallel task allocation and execution process and Markov chain model is verified.

Keywords: Autonomous platooning applications · Energy consumption-delay tradeoff · Divisible load scheduling · Dynamic voltage and frequency scaling · Dynamic programming · Markov chain model

Supported by National Key Research and Development Program of China (2021YFB2601401).

H. Takizawa et al. (Eds.): PDCAT 2022, LNCS 13798, pp. 136–146, 2023.
https://doi.org/10.1007/978-3-031-29927-8_11

1 Introduction

Autonomous platooning applications have the minimum node degree and the maximum topology length. Autonomous Vehicle Platooning technology is still in the technical test stage all over the world, but its positive impact and practical significance on the transportation system are self-evident [1]. Our current research is to realize the automatic driving and platoon driving of large trucks on the highway, improve the traffic flow and reduce the air resistance by shortening the vehicles' distance, so as to improve energy efficiency and safety [2].

With the improvement of the integration and performance of high-precision and high-performance sensors, such as a camera, Millimeter Wave Radar, LIDAR, and ultrasonic radar, on autonomous vehicles and the further development of application business, the problem of computing and communication energy consumption of on-board computing facilities has gradually become prominent and has become a new bottleneck in system design. Dynamic voltage and frequency scaling (DVFS) adjusts energy consumption from hardware by simultaneously changing the power supply voltage and frequency of on-board computing facilities [3]. The new sound, video, radar, ultrasonic and other sensors mounted on the autonomous vehicles need to perform data-intensive tasks such as image and video processing, large-scale signal processing, high-dimensional matrix operation and so on. Although the data scale is very large, it has the characteristics of parallel processing and arbitrary divisibility. The divisible load scheduling model distributes the tasks to the network nodes according to the processing capacity and communication capacity of the nodes in the network. It reduces the total Makespan and improves the utilization of network resources by removing the idle and waiting in the process of task execution. The divisible load scheduling model can obtain the analytical solution of the optimal solution [4–6]. Alfaqawi et al. studied the distributed divisible load scheduling problem in star topology wireless networks with energy harvesting function. A constrained partially observable Markov decision process is used to describe the divisible load scheduling model of star topology wireless networks with energy constraints [5]. Wang et al. designed a divisible load scheduling strategy for large-scale star topology network computing platform considering execution time, available resources and energy efficiency. A heuristic algorithm proposed by the author based on this strategy can run in a short time [6]. Liu proposed a divisible load scheduling algorithm based on energy balance in bus topology networks, which can effectively reduce the standard deviation of energy consumption under the premise of time relaxation [7]. Suresh studied the separable load scheduling problem in linear topology sensor networks, but did not consider the energy problem of sensor nodes [8].

Nowadays, the research on task planning and cooperation in the autonomous vehicles platooning has received great attention. Autonomous vehicles can maintain a relatively stable geometric posture and motion state between themselves and other autonomous vehicles in the platoon by adjusting their driving speed and steering in a complex and changeable environment [9]. At the same time, it meets the task requirements and adapts to the constraints of the surrounding environment, so as to realize the cooperative driving behavior between multiple autonomous vehicles linked by wireless communication [10]. Generally, we have the reasons to believe that the autonomous vehicles' spacing in platoon will remain stable during the normal operation of autonomous vehicles platooning in the future, and the divisible load theory can be used in task allocation and execution in autonomous platooning applications. Due to the location relationship of vehicles in autonomous platooning applications, the execution order of inter-vehicles communication, task scheduling and instruction issuance are limited [2]. The task allocation and execution process in autonomous platooning applications is modeled using the divisible load theory, and the optimal scheduling strategy based on the divisible load theory is solved. Further, based on the dynamic programming theory, according to the computing power and communication capacity of each autonomous vehicle in autonomous platooning applications and the maximum computing delay that can be tolerated by data-intensive task. Based on the divisible load theory, the optimal task allocation and execution strategy under the current maximum computing delay is obtained.

2   Divisible Load Scheduling Model

The system model of autonomous platooning applications is shown in Fig. 1. There are $N+1$ vehicles in the platoon, i.e. $v_0, v_1, \ldots, v_N$. v_0 is located at the head of the autonomous platoon, and the divisible load is distributed from v_0 to the downstream vehicles, and v_0 undertakes the task of load division.

Fig. 1. Schematic diagram of autonomous platooning applications.

For any vehicle in the autonomous platoon, v_i is within the communication coverage of its upstream and downstream vehicles. l_i $(i \in [1, N])$ represents the communication link from v_i to v_{i+1} in the autonomous platoon. v_0 divides the load into $N+1$ sub tasks and distributes them to other vehicles one way through the links in the platoon. The load percentage allocated to vehicle v_i is expressed in α_i $(i \in [0, N])$. Each vehicle can transmit and process the subtask at the same time. A vehicle can only accept the subtask sent by one vehicle at the same time. The time sequence diagram of the load scheduling model in the autonomous platoon is shown in Fig. 2.

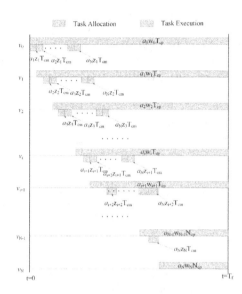

Fig. 2. Sequence diagram of serial divisible load model.

At the starting time, v_0 adjusts the voltage and frequency corresponding to each vehicle according to the Makespan limit of the current service, so that the communication capacity and computing capacity of the vehicles can minimize energy consumption under the condition of meeting the Makespan limit. Vehicle v_0 divides the total load into $N + 1$ parts according to the currently selected voltage and frequency level and transmits it to the downstream vehicle, as shown in Fig. 2. Then, load α_1 is transmitted to v_1 through link l_1, v_1 starts processing data after receiving the load, while v_1 transmits load α_2 to v_2 after receiving the load, v_2 processes data after receiving the load, and so on until load α_N is transmitted to v_N and v_N receives and completes the final data processing. When $v_0, v_1 \ldots v_N$ completes its sub tasks at the same time, the total Makespan of the autonomous platoon is the shortest [4–6]. According to the divisible load theory [4–6], the sum of the load percentages distributed on each vehicle is 1:

$$\sum_{i=0}^{m} \alpha_i = 1 \tag{1}$$

The time taken by the vehicle to transmit the unit load on the standard link is T_{cm}, and the time taken by the vehicle to process the unit load on the standard link is T_{cp}. For vehicle v_i, the allocated processing speed relative to the standard vehicle is represented by ω_i according to the needs of the Makespan limit. As shown in Fig. 2, the vehicle's processing frequency is equal to the reciprocal of the vehicle' processing unit load cycle, so the size of w_i is expressed as the reciprocal of the product of the vehicle's operating frequency and T_{cp}, and the communication speed allocated relative to the standard vehicle on the communication link l_i is expressed by z_i. Then the processing time of load α_i on s_i can be expressed as $\alpha_i w_i T_{cp}$, the communication time of load α_i on communication link l_i can be expressed as $\alpha_i z_i T_{cm}$, and T_f represents the total time of load completion, as shown in Fig. 2, it can be seen that $T_f = \alpha_0 w_0 T_{cp}$. The processing time of downstream vehicles is $\alpha_{i+1}(z_i + z_{i+1})T_{cm}$ different from that of upstream vehicles. It can be seen from Fig. 2 that the processing time of the vechile is:

$$T_{i,cp}(\alpha) = \begin{cases} \alpha_0 w_0 T_{cp}, i = 0 \\ \alpha_{i+1}(z_i + z_{i+1})T_{cm} + \alpha_{i+1}w_{i+1}T_{cp}, i > 0 \end{cases} \quad (2)$$

According to the divisible load theory, all vehicles complete the load processing at the same time. At this time, the result of linear topology serial divisible load scheduling is optimal and the total Makespan is the shortest. The following time series recurrence functions and constraint inequalities can be obtained:

$$\alpha_i w_i T_{cp} = \alpha_{i+1}(z_i + z_{i+1})T_{cm} + \alpha_{i+1}w_{i+1}T_{cp} \quad (3)$$

$$\alpha_{j+1}z_i \leq \alpha_j z_{i+1}, i = 1,2,\ldots,N-1, j = i+1, i+2,\ldots,N \quad (4)$$

It can be seen from Fig. 2 that $z_0 = 0$, where the constraint inequality (4) is to ensure that the adjacent vehicles continuously send the load, and there will be no waiting between the completion time of the upstream vehicle sending the load and the time of the downstream vehicle receiving the load. The recursive expression of the serial divisible load scheduling result can be obtained from Eq. (3):

$$\alpha_i x_i = \alpha_{i+1} \quad (5)$$

where x_i is:

$$x_i = \frac{w_i T_{cp}}{(z_i + z_{i+1})T_{cm} + w_{i+1}T_{cp}}, i \in [0, N-1] \quad (6)$$

From Eqs. (1) and (5–6), we can obtain:

$$\alpha_0 = \frac{1}{1 + \sum_{k=0}^{N-1}\prod_{j=0}^{k} x_j} \quad (7)$$

The recursive expression of load percentage α_i about α_0 distributed by vehicle v_i can be obtained through Eq. (7):

$$\alpha_i = \alpha_0 \prod_{j=0}^{i-1} x_j, i \in [1, N-1] \quad (8)$$

According to the sequence diagram in Fig. 2, the total makespan T_f of serial divisible load is as follows:

$$T_f = \alpha_0 w_0 T_{cp} \quad (9)$$

In order to ensure that the load scheduling constraint inequality (4) of adjacent vehicles is true, the closed expressions of load percentage and processing time are valid, that is, $x_i < 1$, and $z_i \leq z_{i+1}$. From $x_i < 1$, i.e. Eq. (6), $\omega_i \leq \omega_{i+1}$ satisfies the constraint equation at this time.

3   Markov Chain Model

In this paper, Markov chain model is introduced in order to analyze the divisible load scheduling model of large-scale autonomous platooning applications. Taking the vehicles of the autonomous platooning applications as the state of the Markov chain and the combination of the communication and computing capabilities of adjacent vehicles constrained by the optimization principle of the divisible load scheduling model of the autonomous platooning applications as the transition probability in the chain, the state transition diagram of the optimal allocation mode of the Markov chain and vehicles as shown in Fig. 3 can be obtained.

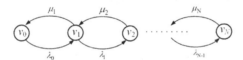

Fig. 3. Load distribution proportion state transition diagram.

As can be seen from the sequence diagram of serial divisible load model in Fig. 2, the total makespan T_f is the sum of the waiting time from the start time to the time when the vehicle v_i receives the task and the processing time used by vehicle v_i. Let the average speed of the vehicle v_i when receiving tasks on link l_i be τ_i. The expression of τ_i is as follows:

$$\tau_i = \frac{1}{\mu_i - \lambda_i} i \in [1, N-1] \tag{10}$$

where λ_i is the data arrival rate of vehicle v_i and μ_i is the data processing rate. Taking the combination of communication and computing power of adjacent vehicles constrained by the optimization principle of the divisible load scheduling model of autonomous platooning applications as the transition probability λ_i, μ_i in the Markov chain as shown in Fig. 3, the steady-state distribution of Markov process can be calculated. The steady-state probability is the percentage of load allocated to vehicles. That is:

$$\lambda_i = \omega_i T_{cp}, \mu_{i+1} = (z_i + z_{i+1}) T_{cm} + \omega_{i+1} T_{cp} \tag{11}$$

Let the waiting time of vehicle v_i from the start time to the time when it receives the task be t_i. according to Little's theorem, t_i is:

$$t_i = \sum_{j=1}^{i} \frac{1}{\tau_j} \alpha_j \tag{12}$$

Therefore, the total makespan in autonomous platooning applications is:

$$T_f = T_{i,cp} + t_i = \alpha_i \omega_i T_{cp} + t_i \tag{13}$$

4   Energy Consumption Model

4.1   Energy Consumption Model for Task Execution

According to the dynamic voltage and frequency scaling technology, the vehicles' hardware power consumption is related to the selection of voltage and frequency. For vehicle v_i in the autonomous platooning applications, the vehicle's processing frequency is equal to the reciprocal of the vehicle's processing unit load cycle, so the size of ω_i is the reciprocal of the product of the operating frequency and T_{cp}, and its operating frequency is expressed as $\frac{1}{\omega_i T_{cp}}$ by its processing rate ω_i. if the processing speed level that the vehicle can support relative to the standard vehicle is $\Omega_1, \ldots, \Omega_M$, $\Omega_i < \Omega_{i+1}, i \in [1, M-1]$, then there is: $\Omega_1 \leq \omega_i \leq \Omega_M$. Since the vehicle's energy consumption is directly proportional to the load size, operating frequency and switching capacitor [11], the energy consumption of vehicle v_i to process the load can be expressed as:

$$E_{p,i} = \alpha_i \varepsilon_i \left(\omega_i T_{cp} \right)^{1-\varphi} \tag{14}$$

where $\varepsilon_i \geq 0$ is the size of the switching capacitor and $\varphi \geq 1$ is the constant. Then the total energy consumption E_p used by all vehicles in the autonomous platooning applications to process the load is:

$$E_p = \sum_{i=0}^{N} E_{p,i} \tag{15}$$

4.2   Energy Consumption Model for Load Transmission

If the communication rate level supported by link l_i is $Z_1, \ldots, Z_M$, $Z_i < Z_{i+1}, i \in [1, M-1]$, there are: $Z_1 \leq z_i \leq Z_M$. The transmission power of vehicle v_i can be expressed as [2]:

$$P_i \approx \frac{\pi_2^{-1} \ln \frac{\pi_1}{\varepsilon_i}}{h_{i,i+1}^2} \left(2^{z_i^{-1}} - 1 \right) \tag{16}$$

where $h_{i,i+1}$ is the channel amplitude of adjacent vehicles v_i and v_{i+1}, Rayleigh fading channel model is adoptedc [12], and π_1 and π_2 are channel correlation constants. It can be seen from Fig. 2 that the total time $T_{cm,i}$ of data transmission on link l_i is $T_{cm} z_i \sum_{n=i}^{N} \alpha_n$. According to the basic definition of energy consumption, the transmission energy consumption on link l_i is:

$$E_{c,i} = T_{cm,i} P_i \tag{17}$$

Then the total energy consumption of task transmission on the link is:

$$E_c = \sum_{i=1}^{N} E_{c,i} \tag{18}$$

5 Energy Consumption-Delay Tradeoff Task Allocation and Execution Algorithm

Dynamic voltage and frequency scaling technology can adjust the operating frequency of the vehicles by controlling the voltage and frequency, so as to control the makespan and energy consumption. The processing rate set is $\omega_i \in \{\Omega_1, \Omega_2, \ldots, \Omega_M\}$. Under the constraint of given makespan $T_f \leq T_{given}$, the processing capacity Ω_j and communication capacity Z_j, $1 \leq j \leq M$ of vehicle v_i are dynamically adjusted. Vehicle v_0 calculates the optimal task allocation and execution strategy corresponding to $N + 1$ sets of computing and communication capabilities that can minimize the system energy from the M voltage and frequency levels of each vehicle according to the maximum makespan limit of divisible load. The sum of the energy consumption of vehicle v_i in the processing task and its communication on link l_i is $E_i = E_{p,i} + E_{c,i}$. It is defined that the total energy consumption from v_i to all subsequent vehicles $v_{i+1}, v_{i+2}, \ldots, v_N$ to complete their assigned tasks is C_i, where $C_{N+1} = 0$. Then the update expression of this scheduling process can be obtained from Bellman equation:

$$C_i\left(\omega_i\right) = \min\left\{E_i\left(\omega_i\right) + C_{i+1}\left(\omega_{i+1}\right) \middle| T_f \leq T_{given}\right\} \tag{19}$$

If the optimal processing speed allocated by vehicle v_i is ω_i^*, the selection strategy of the optimal processing speed can be obtained according to the dynamic programming theory as follows:

$$\omega_i^* = argmin\left\{C_0\left(\omega_i\right) \middle| T_f \leq T_{given}\right\} \tag{20}$$

The pseudo code of the dynamic programming algorithm for energy consumption-delay tradeoff task allocation and execution algorithm is shown in algorithm 1.

Algorithm 1: Energy-delay tradeoff task allocation and execution algorithm in autonomous platooning applications

---

Input: initializing $C_i\left(0\right) = 0$, $C_i\left(\omega_i\right) = \infty$, N,$C_{N+1} = 0$, $C_{total} = 0$, T_{given}
Output: C_{total}

1 some description;
2 **for** $i \to [N, 0]$ **do**
3   **if** $\omega_i \to [\Omega_1, \Omega_M]$ **then**
4          $C_i\left(\omega_i\right) = \min\left\{E_i\left(\omega_i\right) + C_{i+1}\left(\omega_{i+1}\right) \middle| T_f \leq T_{given}\right\}$;
5   Save results $E_i\left(\omega_i\right)$;
6   to update ω_i^*;
7   **end**
8 **end**
9 Optimal allocation processing speed of vehicles:
    $\omega_i^* = argmin\left\{C_0\left(\omega_i\right) \middle| T_f \leq T_{given}\right\}$
10 **for** $i \to [0, N]$ **do**
11      $C_{total} = C_{total} + E_i\left(\omega_i^*\right)$;
12 **end**
13 Calculated optimal energy consumption: C_{total};

---

6   Simulation and Analysis

The experimental analysis consists of two parts. Firstly, the energy-delay trade-off task allocation and execution algorithm (EDTD) proposed in this paper is compared with the maximum transmit rate protocol (MTRP) and the lowest transmit rate protocol (LTRP). MTRP is that all vehicles use the highest processing speed and communication speed to schedule divisible load, while LPRT is that all vehicles use the lowest processing speed and communication speed. Secondly, the total task processing time of MTRP, LTRP and EDTD is compared. In addition, the Markov chain equivalent model of task allocation and execution process is verified by simulation. The total makespan of the three strategies is calculated by the Little theorem. In Fig. 5, MC-LPRT, MC-MPRT and MC-EDTD represent the total makespan of LPRT, MPRT and EDTD calculated by the Little theorem. In the process of simulation verification, the simulation parameters are shown in Table 1.

Table 1. Simulation parameter table

Parameter	Symbol	Parameter value	Unit
Given deadline	T_{given}	0.4	s
Switch Capacitor	ε_i	0.1	F
Bit error rate	ε_i	0.05	%
Channel parameters	π_1	0.2	-
Channel parameters	π_2	3	-
Number of nodes	N	[3,10]	-
Frequency coefficient	φ	3	-

The selectable set of vehicles' processing speed Ω and communication speed Z is 0.3, 0.4, 0.5..., 1, $T_{cm} = T_{cp} = 1$. Figure 4(a) shows the change trend of total energy consumption of autonomous platooning applications under three strategies. It can be seen from the figure that the energy consumption of EDTD and LPRT is less than that of MTRP because MTRP uses the highest processing and communication speed. LPRT consumes less energy than EDTD because LPRT selects the minimum processing speed and communication speed, which reduces the total energy consumption and prolongs the total makespan. In Fig. 4(a), the change trend of total energy consumption finally tends to a fixed value, because when the divisible load scheduling model reaches a certain number of vehicles, the load allocated by subsequent increased vehicles is too small, resulting in little change in total energy consumption.

Figure 4(b) show the relationship between the number of vehicles and the total makespan of the divisible load scheduling model in different scale autonomous platoons. The total makespan of LPRT obviously exceeds the setting parameter 0.4 of the given time limit T_{given}. Combined with Fig. 4(a) and

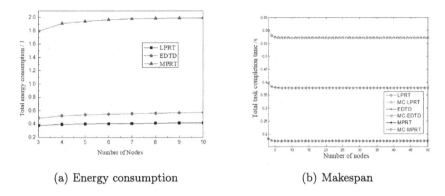

(a) Energy consumption   (b) Makespan

Fig. 4. Total energy consumption and Makespan of different platooning scale conditions.

Fig. 4(b), the total makespan of EDTD algorithm is larger than that of MTRP because it is the optimal combination of processing capacity and communication capacity calculated according to the maximum completion time limit of load, However, it ensures the minimum total energy consumption without exceeding the given time limit T_{given}. As can be seen from Fig. 4(b), with the increase of platooning vehicles in the platoon, the three strategies all reflect the reduction of the total makespan due to the increase of parallel computing scale. Overall, MTRP can get a shorter total task completion time, and LPRT can lead to the minimum total energy consumption. EDTD algorithm focuses on finding the optimal energy consumption without exceeding a given time limit. From Fig. 4(b), the Markov chain model is suitable for calculating the total task completion time of autonomous platooning applications with linear topology of different scales, and the divisible load model has the same total task completion time as the Markov chain model. Using the transition probability between Markov chain states and Eq. (3) can also conveniently analyze the task allocation proportion and total energy consumption of divisible load scheduling in autonomous platooning applications under different platooning scale conditions.

7   Conclusion

In this paper, we study the energy-delay tradeoff of task allocation and execution algorithm for autonomous platooning applications. Based on the dynamic programming theory, the algorithm can minimize the energy consumption through dynamic voltage and frequency scaling technology when the maximum Makespan is relaxed. In terms of calculating the divisible load scheduling scheme and the minimum total Makespan of large-scale autonomous platooning applications, we studied the Markov chain model equivalent to the task allocation and execution of autonomous platooning applications to improve the analysis and calculation efficiency of large-scale platoonings.

References

1. Zeng, T., Semiari, O., Saad, W., Bennis, M.: Joint communication and control for wireless autonomous vehicular platoon systems. IEEE Trans. Commun. **67**(11), 7907–7922 (2019)
2. Li, K., Ni, W., Tovar, E., Guizani, M.: Optimal rate-adaptive data dissemination in vehicular platoons. IEEE Trans. Intell. Transp. Syst. **21**(10), 4241–4251 (2020)
3. Kostrzewa, A., Kadeed, T., Nikoli B., Ernst, R.: Supporting dynamic voltage and frequency scaling in networks-on-chip for hard real-time systems. 2018 IEEE 24th International Conference on Embedded and Real-Time Computing Systems and Applications (RTCSA), pp. 125–135 (2018)
4. Chen, C.: Divisible nonlinear load distribution on complete b-Ary trees. IEEE Trans. Aerosp. Electron. Syst. **56**(2), 998–1013 (2020)
5. Alfaqawi, M., Habaebi, M.H., Islam, M.R., Siddiqi, M.U.: Energy harvesting network with wireless distributed computing. IEEE Syst. J. **13**(3), 2605–2616 (2019)
6. Wang, X., Veeravalli, B., Ma, H.: On the design of a time, resource and energy efficient multi-installment large-scale workload scheduling strategy for network-based compute platforms. IEEE Trans. Parallel Distrib. Syst. **30**(5), 1120–1133 (2019)
7. Liu, D., Yang, X., Cheng, Z.: An energy-aware scheduling algorithm for divisible loads in a bus network. Concurrency Comput. Pract. Experience **28**(5), 1612–1628 (2016)
8. Suresh, S., Mani, V., Omkar, S.N., et al.: A new load distribution strategy for linear network with communication delays. Math. Comput. Simul. **79**(5), 1488–1501 (2009)
9. Wang, J., Luo, X., Wong, W., Guan, X.: Specified-time vehicular platoon control with flexible safe distance constraint. IEEE Trans. Veh. Technol. **68**(11), 10489–10503 (2019)
10. Pfadler, A., Jornod, G., Assaad, A. E. Jung, P.: Predictive quality of service: adaptation of platoon inter-vehicle distance to packet inter-reception time. In: 2020 IEEE 91st Vehicular Technology Conference (VTC2020-Spring), pp. 1–5 (2020)
11. Cho, H., Cui, Y., Lee, J.: Energy-efficient computation task splitting for edge computing-enabled vehicular networks. In: 2020 IEEE International Conference on Communications Workshops (ICC Workshops), pp. 1–6 (2020)
12. Yang, K., et al.: High-speed vehicle-to-vehicle radio channel characteristics for subur-ban and municipal lake region at 5.9 GHz. In: 2019 13th European Conference on Antennas and Propagation (EuCAP), pp. 1–5 (2019)

A Reservation-Based List Scheduling for Embedded Systems with Memory Constraints

Kai-Siang Wang and Jerry Chou[✉]

National Tsing Hua University, Hsinchu, Taiwan
{kswang,jchou}@lsalab.cs.nthu.edu.tw

Abstract. Many embedded systems have hard resource constraints that make schedules found by list scheduling heuristics infeasible. One of the main challenges yielded by memory constraints and the high degree of parallelism is deadlock. In this paper, our primary goal is to find a feasible solution given the memory constraints. We propose a reservation-based solution, an extension for list scheduling algorithms, that can be integrated into those algorithms and make them aware of memory constraints. We show our technique prevents deadlock and significantly reduces the required memory size. The experimental results on randomly generated graphs and real world applications show that our proposed solution can obtain relatively high-quality solutions with up to 10% makespan improvement and 30% memory reduction on average.

Keywords: DAG scheduling · Memory Constraints · Optimization

1 Introduction

Task scheduling problem has been presented for a long time and is usually formatted as a DAG(Directed Acyclic Graph). Since it has been proved to be NP-hard, many scheduling heuristics have been proposed, and variations based on them have emerged. They can be formulated into three categories: List Scheduling Heuristics, Clustering Heuristics, and Task Duplication Heuristics. Among them, list scheduling is relatively common, and because of its effectiveness, many applications have adopted this group of algorithms.

List scheduling usually has two phases. The first phase consists of calculating the priority of each task in a given metric, the average bottom level in HEFT [11], for example. After that, we sort the tasks with their priorities in descending order. Then, in the second phase, we follow the order of the list and assign each task to the processor with another predefined metric. i.e., EFT(Earliest Finish Time) in HEFT. At the end of this process, a static schedule is generated as illustrated with Algorithm 1.

Traditionally, there are a few limitations in real-world applications, such as network delay and heterogeneity cause people to make some modifications. For example, HEFT [11] takes the communication costs and different computation

© The Author(s), under exclusive license to Springer Nature Switzerland AG 2023
H. Takizawa et al. (Eds.): PDCAT 2022, LNCS 13798, pp. 147–157, 2023.
https://doi.org/10.1007/978-3-031-29927-8_12

costs based on each processor into account. In multi-processor systems or cloud computing, such scheduling algorithm has greatly succeeded.

Nowadays, however, deep learning applications have emerged drastically. Those applications adopt one or multiple huge DNN models to help people solve significant tasks, e.g., Object-detection and NLP. However, although GPUs often carry out model training, given their massive parallelism, simple control flow, and high energy efficiency, model inference in the market includes FPGA and ASIC chips. Since those devices often have scarce memory resources, scheduling in embedded devices could be challenging and is not a trivial problem. The scheduling algorithms that do not take memory into account may lead to poor schedules. Furthermore, a schedule could occur **deadlocks** if it's not aware of **memory constraints**.

In this paper, we propose a reservation-based solution that addresses the issues caused by memory constraints. This solution can be integrated into most list scheduling algorithms. We validate our solutions in terms of effectiveness with two examples: HEFT and CPOP.

2   Related Work

2.1   Scheduling with Shared Memory Constraints

One way to improve general list scheduling algorithms such as HEFT is to adjust their priority functions. Since in HEFT, priorities are only decided by the rank of each task, it may inevitably fail to address the problem caused by additional requirements such as memory constraints. This applies to most list scheduling algorithms whose objectives are to minimize makespan only. Due to the aggressiveness of finding shorter makespan, they usually require more memory and thus fail to conform to memory constraints. Therefore, in [1], the main goal of their priority adjustment is to find a priority list in which no two sets of tasks in different memory clusters overlap. This action prevents the algorithm from finding the schedule that uses multiple memory sets simultaneously. Based on the original priorities, they give priority bonuses to the tasks that follow the conditions they define. However, although the priority adjustment may lead to a good priority list, the processor selection phase could still cause deadlocks. In addition, it is more suitable for computation-bound workflows where it can partition the graph easier. We show that when the workflows are memory bound, the case in our definitions, this method might perform worse than *delaying*, a naive solution we provide in Sect. 5.

2.2   Analysis

There are several works [2,3,9] that discuss what is the maximal memory size required given a DAG. When scheduling algorithms are scheduling with the memory of maximal size, they can eventually find a feasible solution. They all use the max-cut algorithm to find maximum memory usage given any timestamp to find the maximum memory size. Once they find the maximum size, they can promise any workflow to be free from deadlock. Furthermore, they even consider the number of processors to make this bound more accurate. Although we know the boundary it provides, in real-world applications, the memory usage is usually less than that bound due to the schedule found by scheduling algorithms.

3   Challenges: Scheduling with Memory Constraints

3.1   Memory Constraints

Generally, if the memory required by the tasks in a DAG is considerable enough, memory size is one of the challenges of scheduling the graph on embedded devices. For example, deploying a large DNN model on embedded devices. Embedded devices usually have smaller memory than clustering servers or even regular PCs. The objective of most traditional scheduling algorithms is to find the minimized makespan. Since their goals are the minimized execution time and they are unaware of memory constraints, they may inevitably sacrifice the optimization opportunity toward memory usage. As a result, this prevents them from finding better solutions or even feasible solutions under memory size limitations. For this purpose, it is crucial to design a specific optimization method to reduce the execution time as much as possible and conform to the given memory constraint. Many previous works [6,10] have already taken memory as their primary objective. For instance, Abraham [10] adopts a graph coloring algorithm with an overlapping technique to minimize total memory usage. In this situation, coloring can impact the schedule since two tasks with the same color cannot execute at the time. Even with memory allocation optimizations, however, we found that many dedicated devices are designed to run a single workflow in the real world. Therefore, it makes no sense to reduce memory usage, and minimized memory usage should not be the primary goal. Instead, we try to maximize the memory usage while such usage doesn't exceed the device's memory size.

3.2   Motivation Example

In embedded systems, scheduling algorithms which follow the precedence constraints are not necessary to find a feasible solution due to memory constraints. We show the example in Fig. 1b. In this graph, each task has the internal buffer and output buffer represented $(Buffer, Output)$. Considering HEFT, the algorithms we use, the priority list found by the algorithm is $[1, 2, 3, 4, 6, 5, 7]$. With this sequence, we will first run and allocate the first fourth tasks, $[1, 2, 3, 4]$. At this moment, if we cannot allocate the memory for task 4, even with *delaying*, the deadlock happens. Since tasks 1, 2, and 3 have to keep their memory usage until task 5 has finished, task 4 cannot be executed until one of them is complete.

4   Problem Modeling

We consider the problem of scheduling dependent tasks on n processors with different computing power, denoted by p_1, ..., p_n. As proposed in previous

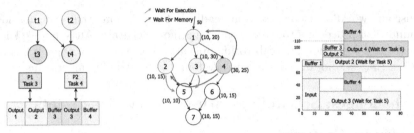

(a) Memory and task dependency constraints

(b) Schedule that causes deadlock

(c) Memory snapshot in deadlock condition

Fig. 1. Illustration of DAG scheduling problem with memory constraint.

works [5,8], this type of workflow is often modeled as a directed acyclic graph(DAG). Given a DAG, $G = (V, E)$, where V represents a set of tasks and E represents a set of edges between two adjacent tasks. Each $v \in V$ represents a task and has a weight that represents the buffer size, denoted by mb_v, needed when computing such a task(e.g., weight parameters of a convolution). Each $(i, j) \in E$ represents a precedence constraint that v_i has to complete before v_j can start. In addition, the weight of the edge (i, j), denoted by mo_i, represents the output produced by task i. In our target environments, the communication cost is neglectable since the processors are either on the same chip or located closely. Our computing environment is described by a $|V| * |P|$ matrix where $|V|$ and $|P|$ represent the number of the tasks, and processors, respectively. For each $v \in V$, it has $|P|$ independent computation cost running on different processors.

4.1   Memory Model

Our target environment includes a shared memory that has a fixed size m, from address 0 to $m - 1$. All memory slots created during the schedule are stored on this single memory. Each slot can be allocated to an arbitrary address but cannot be partitioned, which may introduce fragmentation. In this work, we simply adopt the best-fit strategy and do not further optimize it. We consider the memory constraint as that the total memory usage at any moment in the schedule should be less than m. This usage also considers the fragments, which implies that the actual amount of memory used is less than it.

To run a task v, we need first to allocate two memory slots, internal buffer mb_v and output buffer mo_v occupying a certain amount in the shared memory. mb_v is only used for this task and can be free as soon as this task has finished. On the other hand, mo_v is shared by its direct successors and cannot be free until all its successors are completed. This implies that when this task is running, the input memory mi_p, which is the output memory from its predecessor p, should also be kept in the shared memory. Although this model seems to be simple, this characteristic can affect the schedule results significantly. We use Fig. 1a to illustrate. We can see that even though tasks 1 and 2 have finished the execution, since their output still occupies the memory, tasks 3 and 4 cannot be executed at the same time.

Algorithm 1. List Scheduling with Memory Allocation

Require: $(tasks, M_s)$
Ensure: $schedule$
 1: $schedule \leftarrow []$
 2: $tasks \leftarrow readInput("file")$
 3: $calculatePriority(tasks)$
 4: $sortedTasks = sortByPriority(tasks)$
 5: **for** $task \in sortedTasks$ **do**
 6:     $est, eft, pid \leftarrow findProcessor(task, schedule)$
 7:     $ast, aft \leftarrow allocateMemory(task, est, eft)$
 8:     $freeMemory(task)$
 9:     $updateTask(pid, ast, aft)$
10:     $schedule[pid].append(task)$
11: **end for**

Objective. The objective function of the problem is to find a schedule that the memory usage at any time is under C_m while its makespan is minimized.

4.2 List Scheduling Definition

In this section, we define the general list scheduling algorithms referred to in this paper as Algorithm 1. First of all, we calculate the priorities for each task in the graph by the function provided by different algorithms, e.g., HEFT calculates *Rank* bottom-up and assigns tasks a higher priority if they have a larger rank, and sort the tasks by the priority in a non-ascending order, *sortedTasks* in Algorithm 1. For each task in *sortedTasks*, we schedule them on the processor by the function provided by the specified algorithm. For example, HEFT chooses the processor that has EFT(Earliest Finish Time). Note that in this step, we also need to allocate the memory needed for running this task and release the memory when it is done. A schedule fails when there exists a task that cannot allocate the memory.

5   Proposed Solution

In this section, we propose a reservation-based algorithm. Before introducing the solution, we outline certain desired behaviors we want our solution to have. First of all, we know that due to the memory constraint, a schedule may be infeasible due to the ignorance of the memory capacity, leading to the deadlock condition. We will also show that a deadlock could still easily occur even with *delaying* if the sequence isn't changed during the processor selection step. As a result, we hope that our solution will be able to slightly rearrange the sequence. Furthermore, in order to avoid the deadlock, we might potentially decrease the degree of parallelism. Therefore, we want our solution to be adaptable to the degree of parallelism.

List scheduling with memory constraints can be slightly different from that without such limitations. During the execution, tasks might not be able to execute as soon as all of their dependencies have been resolved due to memory constraints. A straightforward solution is to delay its execution until there is enough memory. For this reason, we call this naive solution *delaying*.

First, we discuss why the solution by *delaying* is far from a "good" solution. From our observation, we found that although it follows the ordering from list scheduling algorithms, the effect brought by delaying could be huge. That is, the total delay time is way more significant than the consequence that we reorder the tasks. Furthermore, *delaying* may require a larger memory due to its inflexibility and fixed ordering. We then design our method based on the features mentioned above with the following description. First of all, we should know why the original schedule might be infeasible. The primary goals of most list scheduling algorithms are minimal makespan, which runs the tasks as many as possible if there are any idle processors. For instance, if the tasks in the same layer run simultaneously and occupy all the memory, their successors would never have a chance to be executed. Therefore, we have to reorder the sequence of the task executions. For this purpose, we reserve its successors, which means that we also allocate the memory needed and the schedule slots for its processors, with depth k to ensure that it can be executed with no deadlock and that the memory it uses can be freed since we also guarantee the executions of the successors when looking at a task. The depth k represents that it will reserve for all successors with distance k. The reservation can fail, though. In this case, we will skip to the next task given by the list scheduling algorithm's preordering phase and follow the same steps repeatedly. During this procedure, we achieve the goal of reordering while following the list scheduling algorithm's order as similarly as we can. Though aggressive, this leads to good-quality schedules (the one with a shorter makespan while respecting memory constraints). In addition, we will try different reservation depths k when scheduling a DAG. Since the larger k conceptually leads to lower memory usage and a longer makespan, our method provides an extensive solution set that can fit different use cases.

In Algorithm 2, we first calculate the priority based on different list scheduling algorithms and sort them by their priorities. After that, we iterate through the task in the sorted task list and reserve each of them. We skip the task if it cannot be reserved. In *reserve* function, we have to check if all the predecessors of the task have been allocated yet. If not, we have to allocate them first. Depending on the depth k, we recursively reserve the successors of this task if k does not equal -1. In the function *checkDeps*, we still have to first recursively check the allocation of the dependencies has been done. If it is done, we can now allocate the memory for the current task and schedule it. Here, we use the function *scheduleTask* to represent the code from line 6 to line 10 in Algorithm 1.

It is important to note that we solve potential deadlocks in the processor selection phase, which means that we do not modify the priority list, probably the best sequence for tasks' execution. While respecting memory constraints, we still find schedules with comparably shorter makespan values. Please note

---

Algorithm 2. Reservation-based heuristic

Require: $(tasks, M_s)$
Ensure: $schedule$
1: $schedule \leftarrow []$
2: $calculatePriority(tasks)$
3: $sortedTasks = sortByPriority(tasks)$
4: **for** $task \in sortedTasks$ **do**
5:     $reservable \leftarrow$ RESERVE$(task, k)$
6:     **if not** $reservable$ **then**
7:         $rollback(task)$
8:     **end if**
9: **end for**
10: **function** RESERVE$((task, k))$
11:     **if** $depth == -1$ **then**
12:         **return** True
13:     **end if**

14:     $reservable \leftarrow$ CHECKDEPS$(task)$
15:     **for** $edge \in task.outEdges$ **do**
16:         $reservable \leftarrow reservable$ &
    RESERVE$(edge.target, k - 1)$
17:     **end for**
18: **end function**
19: **function** CHECKDEPS$(task)$
20:     $checked \leftarrow$ True
21:     **for** $edge \in task.inEdges$ **do**
22:         $checked \leftarrow checked$ &
    CHECKDEPS$(edge.target)$
23:     **end for**
24:     **return** $checked$ &
    $scheduleTask(task)$
25: **end function**

---

that our solution is not deadlock-free. It is possible that our solution cannot find feasible solution. However, we will show the effectiveness of reducing the chance of deadlock in the Sect. 6. In addition, we can see that our proposed solution is totally independent of the list scheduling algorithm we choose, and thus it can be easily integrated into existing list scheduling algorithms.

We illustrate our solution with reservation depth $k = 1$ step by step shown in Fig. 2. In the following graphs, the tasks colored with blue represent reserving tasks. The green ones represent the successors of the reserving task with distance k. The red ones represent the tasks that fail to allocate the memory. Lastly, the grey ones represent the dependencies that are needed to be resolved before the reservation. In addition, the bottom of the Fig. 2 represents the memory snapshots of the corresponding reservation step. In these graphs, the blocks are labeled by B or O, representing the internal buffer and output buffer produced by a task.

1. Initially, the entry task, task 1, is selected and reserve the memory for its direct successors in Fig. 2a. When it tries to allocate for task 4, the memory is insufficient, and thus, the reservation fails.
2. During the reservation process, we also need to ensure every dependency is fulfilled. For example, In Fig. 2b, task 1, 3 need to be allocated first.
3. We then have to roll back all tasks allocated by task 1, including itself, i.e., tasks 1, 2, 3, and 4. When task 2 starts its reservation, both memory slots and schedule slots are empty.
4. Then, we find the next task following the priority list and do the same thing again.

After performing our algorithm, we can see that the order of the tasks selecting the processor is actually 1, 2, 3, 5, 4, 6, 7, slightly different from the original priority list. We can also see that in the memory allocation graph, due to the

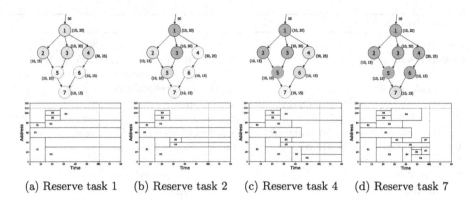

(a) Reserve task 1   (b) Reserve task 2   (c) Reserve task 4   (d) Reserve task 7

Fig. 2. Scheduling example.

early execution of task 5, we can free the memory occupied by tasks 2 and 3 early. As a result, tasks 4 and 6 can be scheduled afterward.

6   Experimental Results

In this section, we evaluated our solution with randomly generated graphs and 5 real world applications. To our best knowledge, SBAC [1] is the latest work that also considers hard memory constraints. We compared our solution with SBAC and showed that our solution outperforms it.

6.1   Random Workflows Generator

To evaluate our work, we need a random graph generator. For this purpose, we used the synthetic DAG generation program [7] with three different parameters:

- n: number of DAG nodes. Four different values are used $n = (20, 50, 100, 200)$.
- max_out: maximal number of out degrees of a node. This value leads to different densities of the graphs. $max\_out = (1, 2, 3, 4)$.
- α: this parameter affects the height and the width of the DAG. The depth of the DAG is set as $\sqrt{n}/\alpha$. A small value will lead to a thin DAG, whereas a large value induces a fat DAG. The following values are used $\alpha = (0.5, 1.0, 1.5)$.

6.2   Impact of Depth k

This section shows the impact of different reservation depth k on the degree of parallelism in Fig. 3. We ran our experiment with 100 random graphs and $k = (0, 1, 2, 3, 4, 5)$. Apparently, we can see that when k is larger, the degree of parallelism goes down. The reason behind this is that with a larger k, it may reserve more memory for more predecessors and therefore makes its siblings

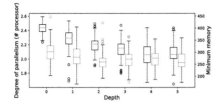

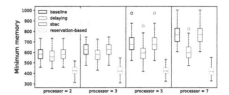

Fig. 3. Degree of parallelism with different k

Fig. 4. Evaluation of reservation-based
algorithm on CPOP

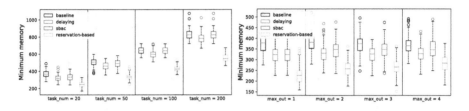

Fig. 5. Minimum memory usage boxplot

have less memory to allocate and therefore reduces the degree of parallelism.
Meanwhile, the minimum memory decreases along with the depth in the range
of $[0, 3]$ while increasing when the depth is $[3, 5]$. It is because when the depth is
too large, the reservation may contain too many tasks where the order of them
is fixed and therefore has little impact on improving the minimum memory.

6.3   Minimum Memory Usage

In this section, we apply our solution to find minimized memory by setting the
memory constraints in the range from the usage found by HEFT to the smallest
memory usage we can find. The results are shown in Fig. 5. HEFT represents
the scheduler that does not consider the memory size at all and works as the
baseline. We compared our solution with *delaying* and SBAC.

Randomly Generated Workflows. The randomly generated workflows are
controlled by the DAG parameters mentioned above and different processor numbers. We ran each parameter setting with 100 iterations. The results are shown
in Fig. 5 We found that except *max_out*, our solution can have a larger improvement when the value of the other parameters increases, as shown in the left
figure. We only show the results of *task_num*, for example, due to conserving
space. These parameters are directly related to the higher degree of parallelism
the schedule could have. Therefore, if an algorithm is too aggressive to optimize
for the shorter makespan, it will always try to run as many tasks as possible
at the same time, which leads to higher memory usage. On the other hand,

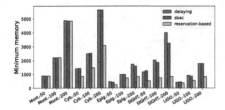
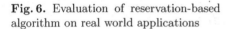

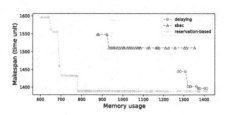

Fig. 6. Evaluation of reservation-based algorithm on real world applications

Fig. 7. Trade-off between memory usage and makespan

our solution takes the memory constraint into account and can effectively minimize memory usage. On the other hand, regarding the max_out, our solution has less improvement when it increases, shown in the right figure. The reason behind the result might be the fact that when max_out increases, the number of edges will also increase. In this situation, the room for our solution to make an improvement is relatively small.

Real World Applications. We evaluated our solution on five real world applications: Montage, CyberShake, Epigenomics, SIGHT, and LIGO [4]. We validated our solution with three different graph sizes: 50, 100, and 200. To our best knowledge, there is no such an ML workflow generator for the research purpose; therefore, we chose these workflows to show the generalization of our method. The result is shown in Fig. 6. Apparently, our solution requires much less memory compared with the other two algorithms, except in the case of Montage. One observation is that Montage workflows have a pattern that high parallelism nodes are followed by a bottleneck node(synchronization node). In this case, we have to execute all the nodes in the previous layer before executing such a node. This pattern decreases the effectiveness of the reservation. It is also clear our solutions are way more efficient for large DAGs. This result is similar to the result from the random graphs. A larger DAG provides more opportunities for our solution to make the reservation that can reduce memory usage at some stage of the schedule.

6.4 Minimized Makespan Value Under Memory Constraints

In this section, we show that the reservation-based algorithm can not only minimize memory usage but also provide better makespan value under certain memory constraints. Besides, the trade-off between the makespan and the memory usage also helps users to determine their desired performance with a certain memory size. In Fig. 7, we can easily see that the points from our method are all equally close or closer to the origin than *delaying* and SBAC. Furthermore, we can see that even with a memory size under around 603, our solution can still find solutions in which *delaying* could only find one with a memory size larger than around 1272 and 876 for SBAC. Furthermore, our solution also has a shorter or equal makespan value when we fix the memory usage.

6.5 Applicability

Since our solution is an extension of list scheduling algorithms, we need to prove that our solution could provide a similar result on algorithms other than HEFT. Therefore, we integrated our solution into Critical-Path-on-a-Processor (CPOP) [11] without modifying its priority and processor selection functions. In Fig. 4, we can see the reservation-based algorithm outperforms the other two methods, and the improvement is more significant when the number of processors increases.

7 Conclusions

In this paper, we have addressed the scheduling problem under memory constraints and presented a reservation-based algorithm. Our solution prevents deadlock from happening effectively by reordering the sequence in the processor selection phase only when needed. In addition, the experimental results show that our solution can provide a relatively better solution set compared with *delaying* and SBAC in both minimized memory and shorter makespan. Although our approach is mainly designed and evaluated based on the original HEFT, our solution can be generalized to all list-based scheduling.

References

1. Arras, P.-A., Fuin, D., Jeannot, E., Stoutchinin, A., Thibault, S.: List scheduling in embedded systems under memory constraints. Int. J. Parallel Prog. **43**(6), 1103–1128 (2015)
2. Bathie, G., Marchal, L., Robert, Y., Thibault, S.: Revisiting dynamic DAG scheduling under memory constraints for shared-memory platforms. In: IEEE IPDPS, pp. 597–606 (2020)
3. Bathie, G., Marchal, L., Robert, Y., Thibault, S.: Dynamic DAG scheduling under memory constraints for shared-memory platforms. Int. J. Netw. Comput. **11**(1), 27–49 (2021)
4. Deelman, E., et al.: The evolution of the Pegasus workflow management software. Comput. Sci. Eng. **21**(4), 22–36 (2019)
5. Fu, H., Yu, C., Sun, J., Wang, M., Du, J.: A list scheduling algorithm for DAG-based parallel computing models. In: Wang, G., Zomaya, A., Perez, G.M., Li, K. (eds.) ICA3PP 2015. LNCS, vol. 9529, pp. 406–419. Springer, Cham (2015). https://doi.org/10.1007/978-3-319-27122-4_28
6. Lin, W.-F., et al.: ONNC: a compilation framework connecting ONNX to proprietary deep learning accelerators. In: IEEE AICAS, pp. 214–218 (2019)
7. Livioni. Dag_generator (2022). https://github.com/Livioni/DAG_Generator.git
8. Luo, J., Zhou, Y., Li, X., Yuan, M., Yao, J., Zeng, J.: Learning to optimize DAG scheduling in heterogeneous environment (2021)
9. Marchal, L., Nagy, H., Simon, B., Vivien, F.: Parallel scheduling of DAGs under memory constraints. In: IEEE IPDPS, pp. 204–213 (2018)
10. Miniskar, N.R., Pasupuleti, S.K., Rajagopal, V., Vishnoi, A., Ramasamy, C.K., Gadde, R.N.: Optimal SDRAM buffer allocator for efficient reuse of layer IO in CNNs inference framework. In: IEEE ISCAS, pp. 1–5 (2018)
11. Topcuoglu, H., Hariri, S., Wu, M.-Y.: Performance-effective and low-complexity task scheduling for heterogeneous computing. IEEE TPDS **13**(3), 260–274 (2002)

Formalization and Verification of SIP Using CSP

Zhiru Hou[1], Jiaqi Yin[2], Huibiao Zhu[1]($\boxtimes$), and Ningning Chen[1]

[1] Shanghai Key Laboratory of Trustworthy Computing,
East China Normal University, Shanghai, China
hbzhu@sei.ecnu.edu.cn
[2] School of Software, Northwestern Polytechnical University, Xi'an, China

Abstract. As one of the most popular multimedia communication protocol, Session Initiation Protocol (SIP) has lots of interesting features, such as extensible and open communication. However, with its rapid development, load balance problem and security risks are exposed. Finding the suitable method to solve the two problems has become an important issue. In this paper, we first apply Communicating Sequential Processes (CSP) to model SIP, then adopt the model checking tool Process Analysis Tookit (PAT) to verify the internal properties and the safety properties of our model. The verification results show that the SIP model has load balance problem and it cannot assure the security of data with malicious users. So we enhance it by adding Software Defined Networking (SDN) architecture and identity authentication mechanism in the process. In the light of new verification results, it can be found that the improved model can satisfy the internal properties and we succeed in improving the security of the SIP model.

Keywords: Session Initiation Protocol (SIP) · CSP · Modeling · Verification · Software Defined Networking (SDN)

1 Introduction

Session Initiation Protocol (SIP) [1] is developed by the Internet Engineering Task Force (IETF) and published as Request for Comments (RFC) 3261 in 2002. With its increasing popularity and importance in VoIP applications, some experts found some problems with SIP, such as security problems and load problem [6,14,15]. With such invovled researches on SIP, formalizing and verifying this protocol effectively is of great significance.

In recent years, some work has already carried out on SIP. From the formal perspective, some researches [2–4,11] proposed the formalization of SIP using Coloured Petri Net, and their purposes were to establish a model of verified and validated SIP components, but these researches did not involve the load or security problems of SIP. Montazerolghaem et al. [5] presented OpenSIP technology, which used Software Defined Networking (SDN) to upgrade the SIP network

© The Author(s), under exclusive license to Springer Nature Switzerland AG 2023
H. Takizawa et al. (Eds.): PDCAT 2022, LNCS 13798, pp. 158–171, 2023.
https://doi.org/10.1007/978-3-031-29927-8_13

framework to achieve resource management. Montazerolghaem [6] also proposed to use SDN to solve the overload problem of SIP with three algorithms. Some work [5,6] made efforts on load problem of SIP protocol with SDN, as well as simulating and analyzing them. For security problems of SIP, an efficient SIP authentication protocol has been proposed by the researchers [12]. However, they did not give verifications in a very strict way. To the best of our knowledge, there are few work on the formalization of load or security problems on SIP. Thus, we utilize the process algebra CSP to model the architecture of SIP and use the model checker PAT to verify several internal properties and security properties.

In this paper, we use classical process algebra language Communicating Sequential Processes (CSP) [7,8] to model SIP. CSP is a formal modeling language for describing the concurrent and distributed interactive, it has been successfully applied to model and verify diverse concurrent systems and protocols [8,17]. Moreover, we also use the model checking tool Process Analysis Toolkit (PAT) [9,10] to verify some interesting properties, including *Deadlock Freeness* and *Load Balance*. These are internal properties of the model, and we also discuss security properties, including *Register Faking*, *Server Faking* and *Client Faking*. The verification results demonstrate that the load problem and authentication problems exist in SIP. On the basis, we construct a new model for SIP where SDN architecture and identity authentication mechanism are adopted. In addition to the above five properties, we also verify three other properties in the new model, including *Data Consistency*, *Order Property* and *Reliability*. From the new verification results, we can believe that the new model can effectively solve the load problem and the authentication problems.

The remainder of this paper is organized as follows. Section 2 first gives a brief introduction to SIP protocol and SDN architecture, and then analyzes the load and security problems. Section 3 is denoted to formalizing the model of SIP using CSP. In Sect. 4, we apply the model checker PAT to verify the properties and analyze the verification results. Further, Sect. 5 is about the new model of SIP for the improvement which adopts the SDN architecture and identity authentication mechanism. At last, we give a conclusion and make a discussion on the future work in Sect. 6.

2   Background

In this section, we first give an overview of SIP protocol, especially its communication process, load problem and security problems. We also give an introduction to SDN architecture, and analyze how it solves the problems mentioned before.

2.1   SIP

A SIP session involves four main components: SIP user agent, SIP register, SIP proxy server, and SIP redirect server. SIP user agent includes user agent client and user agent server. In this paper, we mainly model user agent client, user agent server and register under reliable mechanism.

SIP messages are mainly divided into request messages and response messages. The request messages have different types, including *invite, ack, bye, cancel, direction* and *register*. When the client wants to communicate with the server, the following sequence of actions occurs:

(1) The client sends registration request *regist* to the register.
(2) The register returns the response *regresp* to tell client whether its registration is successful.
(3) After receiving successful registration, the client sends *request* to the server.
(4) Finally, the server returns *response* to the client.

But when more clients want to communicate with server at the same time, there will be a load problem on SIP. Because the capacity of SIP server is limited, the large number of the SIP user agents could cause the servers overload. Given the challenge and enlightened by [6], SDN architecture can be used to solve the load problem.

Except the load problem, SIP protocol can be attacked by the intruder easily. The security problems of SIP mainly concentrate on identity authentication and DDoS attacks. In this paper, we focus on the identity authentication problem as below:

(1) Register faking: The intruder can pretend to be a legal register to randomly communicate with the client. There is no register authentication on the client.
(2) Agent server faking: The intruder can pretend to be a legal agent server to randomly communicate with other components.
(3) Register interception attack: The intruder can pretend to be a legal client to randomly communicate with the register, then the intruder can send wrong registration message to the register.

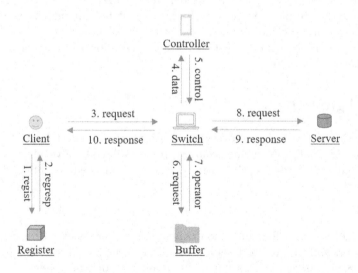

Fig. 1. Formal Communications of SIP with SDN

2.2 SDN

SDN [13] is a network architecture which has two main components, including forwarding elements (SDN switches) and SDN controllers. Based on SDN architecture, we can use the controller to control the distribution of the server with the least request algorithm and switch is used to transfer messages. The least request algorithm [6] indicates that the server with the minimum load is allocated first. The formal communications of SIP with SDN are shown in Fig. 1, and we will introduce more details of the formal communication in Sect. 5.

For the security problem of SIP mentioned before, we can also use this model to solve them with authentication mechanism. The main enhancement here is the pre-validation of the related components. If the ability of verification is not enough, it is easy to cause information leakage and leads to be faked by intruder. Here we propose the method as below, we use how to prevent the agent server faking for an instance:

(1) We assume that each related component has a public and private key. For the agent server, it has the public key K_i and the private key K_i^{-1}.
(2) The server can use K_i to communicate with the switches, because the switches have the verification algorithm to get the corresponding verification code. In addition, the intruders have their own verification algorithm to get the verification code.
(3) At last we have to test whether the two verification codes are matched. If the two verification codes match, the components can communicate normally; otherwise, the corresponding communication will be discarded.

3 Modeling SIP

In this section, we apply CSP to formalize the model of SIP. The model mainly has three components, including *Register*, *Client* and *Server*. Besides, in order to reflect safety issues, we also add *Intruder* into this model.

3.1 Sets, Messages and Channels

For more convenience, we give the definitions of sets used in the model. We define the set of *Register* of register component, *Client* of client component and *Server* of server component. In addition, we define the set: *EID* is the identifier of server and *UID* is the identifier of client.

Besides, we define the sets of messages: *Regist* means the registration message, *Registok* means the registration response. *RespT* represents the response sent from server. *inviteT* represents the request sent from client, and it has four kinds of requests here, including *invite, ack, cancel* and *bye*. *Content* is the message including the address or something else. Based on the definitions above, we model the messages used in the model as below:

$$MSGS =_{df} Msg_{invite1} \cup Msg_{resp1} \cup Msg_{regi} \cup Msg_{regr},$$

- $Msg_{invite1} =_{df} \{uid, inviteT, content, registok | uid \in UID, inviteT \in InviteT, content \in Content, registok \in Registok\}$,
- $Msg_{resp1} =_{df} \{uid, eid, respT, content | uid \in UID, eid \in UID, respT \in RespT, content \in Content\}$,
- $Msg_{regi} =_{df} \{uid, regist | uid \in UID, regist \in Regist\}$,
- $Msg_{regr} =_{df} \{uid, registok | uid \in UID, registok \in Registok\}$.

Then, we define two kinds of channels to model the communications among components: $ComUR$, $ComUE$; besides, channels of intruders who fake register, client, and agent server as follows: $FakeR$, $FakeC$, $FakeS$. Interprocess communications between the processes are illustrated in Fig. 2.

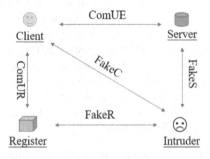

Fig. 2. Channels of SIP

3.2 Overall Modeling

For the model of SIP, system process is composed of three subprocesses running in parallel through their own corresponding channels, including $Register_1$, $Server_1$ and $Client_1$. Besides, we introduce a process $Intruder$ used to fake messages in communication. The behavior of SIP is modeled as below. Due to the limited space, $Server_1$ is not introduced in detail.

$$SIP =_{df} Register_1 \parallel Server_1 \parallel Client_1 \parallel Intruder(Fact);$$

3.3 Register

The client sends the registration message to the register firstly, then waits to return the response. The behavior of $Register_1$ is modeled as below.

$$Register_1 =_{df} ComUR?Msg_{regi} \rightarrow ComUR!Msg_{regr} \rightarrow Register_1$$

Based on the given model $Register_1$, we need to consider the behaviors of the intruder. On account of the vulnerability of the register, communications on the channels involved the register is not safe and it can be faked by the intruder. As shown in Fig. 2, the register can receive the fake messages from the intruder. We achieve the description of the intruder by means of renaming [8]. The renaming of $Client_1$, $Server_1$ and $Register_1$ is similar, here we only give $Register_1$'s renaming $RegisterI_1$ as below.

$$RegisterI_1 =_{df} Register_1[[$$
$$ComUR?\{|ComUR|\} \leftarrow ComUR?\{|ComUR|\},$$
$$ComUR?\{|ComUR|\} \leftarrow FakeR?\{|ComUR|\},$$
$$ComUR!\{|ComUR|\} \leftarrow ComUR!\{|ComUR|\},$$
$$ComUR!\{|ComUR|\} \leftarrow FakeR!\{|ComUR|\}]]$$

Here, $\{|c|\}$ stands for the set of all communications over channel c. The first two formulas mean that the process $RegisterI_1$ performs either a $ComUR?Msg$ or $FakeR?Msg$ event, whenever $Register_1$ performs a corresponding $ComUR?Msg$ event. In PAT, we realize the renaming by replacing common communications with faked communications, and combining them with common communcations using the general choice $\Box$. The remaining formulas have similar meanings.

3.4 Client

The client is one of the important components in SIP. The requests have different types, so we can use the general choice $\Box$ to depict this process. When the client wants to send invite message, it should register firstly. After the registration, the client can send request messages to the server directly, and the request messages include *invite, ack, cancel* and *bye* messages. Then the client waits for the response from the server. The detailed behavior is modeled as below.

$$Client_1 =_{df} ComUR!Msg_{regi} \rightarrow ComUR?Msg_{regr} \rightarrow leng(uid);$$
$$ComUE!Msg_{invite1} \rightarrow ComUE?Msg_{resp1} \rightarrow Client_1$$
$$\Box ComUE!Msg_{invite1} \rightarrow ComUE?Msg_{resp1} \rightarrow Client_1$$

3.5 Intruder

Now, we introduce the intruder entity. If the intruder has sufficient knowledge, it may be able to affect a faking attack. Once the process $Intruder$ is added into the whole system, the system is not secure anymore.

$$Intruder(Fact) =_{df} Fake?m \rightarrow Intruder(Fact \cup Info(m))$$
$$\Box Fake!m \rightarrow Intruder(Fact)$$

$Fact$ denotes the messages what $Intruder$ already knows. m contains $regi$, $regr$ and $resp$ messages. Function $Info$ is used to make $Intruder$ get different parts of the message. $Info(m)$ means that $Intruder$ can get information included in m.

4 Verification

In this section, we conduct verification of the model through model checker PAT to verify five properties in *SIP*, including *Deadlock Freeness, Load Balance, Register Faking, Server Faking* and *Client Faking*.

4.1   Verification in PAT

Property 1: Deadlock Freeness
The first property is deadlock freeness which means the system should avoid the deadlock. PAT provides us with a primitive:

$\#assert\ SIP\ deadlockfree;$

Property 2: Load Balance
This property means that the system should satisfy the load balancing finally. We use the LTL (Linear Temporal Logic) formula to describe this property. <> is the symbol of "eventually" and [] is the symbol of "always". We combine these two notations to denote that the process eventually always satisfies this property. In this paper, we set two servers, so we can verify this property by seeing whether the load of each server is equal. The assertion about this property is defined as below:

$$\#define\ LoadBalance(loaN[0] == loaN[1]);$$
$$\#assert\ SIP\ \models <>\ []LoadBalance;$$

Property 3: Register Faking
This property means that the system is unware that an intruder has succeeded in posing as a legal register. *register_fake_success* is a Boolean variable defined to verify whether the intruder has succeeded in the corresponding communication. So we have:

$$\#define\ Register\_Fake\_Success\ register\_fake\_success == true;$$
$$\#assert\ SIP\ reaches\ Register\_Fake\_Success;$$

Property 4: Server Faking
If the intruder has the ability to pretend to be a server and communicate with other entities, we consider this problem as server faking. We have:

$$\#define\ Server\_Fake\_Success\ server\_fake\_success == true;$$
$$\#assert\ SIP\ reaches\ Server\_Fake\_Success;$$

Property 5: Client Faking
Supposing the intruder successfully disguises itself as a client and communicates with other entities, we run into the problem of client faking. We have:

$$\#define\ Client\_Fake\_Success\ client\_fake\_success == true;$$
$$\#assert\ SIP\ reaches\ Client\_Fake\_Success;$$

4.2   Results

The verification results of SIP are illustrated in Fig. 3. From Fig. 3, we can see *Deadlock Freeness* is valid, but *Load Balance* is invalid, which indicates the loads are not balanced in SIP. Besides, the three safety properties including *Register Faking*, *Server Faking* and *Client Faking* are valid, the results represent that the intruder can succeed in posing as a legal register, server or client.

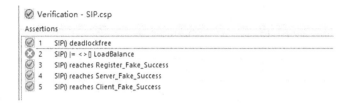

Fig. 3. Verification Results of SIP

5 Improvement

Since SIP cannot satisfy the *Load Balance* property and it also has the authentication problems, we improve the model of SIP. In this section, the new model is called $SIPS$. $SIPS$ adds SDN architecture and identity authentication mechanism to SIP, and we model it using similar methods and feed the improved model to PAT again.

5.1 Modeling SIPS

5.1.1 Sets, Messages and Channels

Considering the sets defined in Sect. 3, we define: *Switch, Controller* and *Buffer*. In addition, we also define the sets: *CID* is the identifier of *Controller, errorCode* represents the types of errors that may occur and *Operator* represents operations of *Buffer*. To prevent the threat of the intruder, we use the authentication mechanism to enhance the security and there are some variables as shown in Table 1. Based on the definitions above, we model the messages as below:

- $Msg_{data} =_{df} \{cid, uid, content | cid \in CID, uid \in UID, content \in Content\}$,
- $Msg_{control} =_{df} \{cid, uid, eid, content | cid \in CID, uid \in UID, eid \in EID, content \in Content\}$,
- $Msg_{operator} =_{df} \{cid, uid, eid, operator, errorcode, content | cid \in CID, uid \in UID, eid \in EID, operator \in Operator, errorcode \in errorCode, content \in Content\}$.

Except *ComUR*, we also define four kinds of channels to model the communications among components: *ComSU, ComCS, ComSE, ComSB*.

Table 1. Variables of Authentication

Variables	Definitions
K_i	Public Key
K_i^{-1}	Private Key
K_r	Authentication Key
a	Authentication Algorithm
M	Verification Code
$E(K_r,K_i)$	Encryption Cipher
$D(E(K_r,K_i),K_i^{-1})$	Decryption Cipher

5.1.2   Overall Modeling

System process is composed of all six subprocesses running in parallel through their own corresponding channel. The subprocesses are *Register, Client, Switch, Controller, Server* and *Buffer*. Besides, we also introduce a process *Intruder*, the behavior of system process is modeled as below.

$$SIPS =_{df} Register \parallel Server \parallel Client \parallel Switch \parallel Controller \parallel Buffer \parallel Intruder(F);$$

Due to the limited space, *Register*, *Server* and *Buffer* are not introduced in detail.

5.1.3   Client

In this model, the client sends the request message with encryption cipher to the switch firstly, then the client waits to receive the response from the switch. *Client* can be formalized as follows.

$$Client =_{df} ComUR!Msg_{regist}.E(K_c, K_i) \rightarrow$$
$$ComUR?Msg_{regresp}.D(E(K_r, K_i), K_i^{-1}) \rightarrow$$
$$\left(\begin{pmatrix} ComSU!Msg_{invite} \rightarrow \\ ComSU?Msg_{resp} \rightarrow Client \end{pmatrix} \right)$$
$$\lhd (M_c' == M_c) \rhd Skip$$
$$\Box \; ComSU!Msg_{invite} \rightarrow ComSU?Msg_{resp} \rightarrow Client$$

5.1.4   Switch

The switch process plays an important role in the SDN architecture. The main function of switch is to coordinate the messages among the remaining components. Firstly, it receives the request from the client. Then, the switch confirms the specific type of the received request message. If its *inviteT* type is *invite*, the switch will send the message to the controller, waiting for the controller to return the control message. At last, the switch will send the request message to the server, waiting for the server to respond. In addition, the request message will also be sent to the buffer. If the type is not *invite*, the switch will check whether the session exists in buffer firstly and if the session does not exist, the session will be discarded; if it exists, it will be sent to the server directly. The detailed behavior is modeled as below.

$$Switch =_{df} ComSU?Msg_{invite} \rightarrow ComSB!Msg_{invite} \rightarrow ComSB?Msg_{operator} \rightarrow$$

$$\left(\left(\begin{array}{l} \left(\begin{array}{l} ComCS!Msg_{data} \rightarrow ComCS?Msg_{control} \rightarrow \\ \left(\begin{array}{l} ComSE!Msg_{invite} \rightarrow ComSE?Msg_{resp}.D(E(K_s, K_i), K_i^{-1}); \\ \left(ComSU!Msg_{resp} \lhd (M_s' == M_s) \rhd Skip \right) \end{array} \right) \\ \lhd (operator == ok) \rhd Skip \end{array} \right) \right) \right)$$

$$\lhd inviteT == invite \rhd$$

$$\left(\left(\begin{array}{l} \left(\begin{array}{l} ComSE!Msg_{invite} \rightarrow ComSE?Msg_{resp}.D(E(K_s, K_i), K_i^{-1}) \rightarrow \\ \left(ComSU!Msg_{resp} \lhd (M_s' == M_s) \rhd Skip \right) \end{array} \right) \\ \lhd (operator == ok) \rhd Skip \end{array} \right) \right)$$

5.1.5 Controller

The controller receives data message from switch, then it checks the load of each server. We use the least request algorithm *Validate* to allocate server, which represents finding the server of minimum load. Then, the controller sends the control message to switch. Next, we formalize the process *Controller* as below.

$$Controller =_{df} ComCS?Msg_{data} \rightarrow Validate(uid, cid, eid) \rightarrow$$
$$ComCS!Msg_{control} \rightarrow Controller$$

5.1.6 Intruder

In this model, we use identity authentication mechanism to ensure safety, therefore in addition to the modeling part of *Intruder* in Sect. 3, we will cover a few more things as following.

$$FACT =_{df} Fact \cup Key \cup MSG \cup \{k, c | k \in Key, c \in content\}$$
$$\cup \{k, E(k, c) | k \in Key, c \in content\}$$

We also need to define how the intruder deduces new facts from the facts that it already knows.

$$\{k, c\} \mapsto E(k, c) \quad \{k, E(k, c)\} \mapsto c \quad F \mapsto f \wedge F \subseteq F' \Rightarrow F' \mapsto f$$

We define F represents the facts intruder has learned, set f means that the new facts deduced from F and $\mapsto$ represents the deducing process. The first rule represents the encryption process, and the second rule indicates the decryption process. The last rule shows that if intruder can deduce the fact f from the set F, then the intruder can deduce the fact f from the bigger set F', and F' includes F. Then we define channel $Deduce$ to describe the behaviors above.

New facts can be deduced from the known facts of the intruder. Thus, if the intruder knows all the messages and submessages, it will send fake messages to other entities. We formalize $Intruder$ as below.

$$Intruder(F) =_{df} {}_{m \in MSG} Fake?m \rightarrow Intruder(F \cup Info(m))$$

$$_{m \in MSG \cap Info(m) \subseteq F} Fake!m \rightarrow Intruder(F)$$

$$_{f \in FACT, f \notin F, F \mapsto f} Deduce.f.F \rightarrow Intruder(F \cup \{f\})$$

The first rule means that the intruder can get messages via a channel of $Fake$. The second rule represents that the intruder can send the fake message to other entities. The last one means that the intruder can deduce some new facts from its known knowledge via channel $Deduce$.

5.2   Verification

In this section, we verify the five properties in $SIPS$ mentioned before with the aid of the model checker PAT. In order to better reflect the availability of the new model, we also verify three properties in $SIPS$, including $Data\ Consistency$, $Order\ Property$ and $Reliability$.

5.2.1   Verification in PAT

Property 6: Data Consistency
By verifying that number of messages in the buffer are consistent with the server, the result can test whether the data consistency is satisfied in the model. If this property is valid, we can also know that the message reaches the server smoothly. The assertion is defined as below:

$$\#define\ consistency(aplN[0] == isApplied[0] \&\& aplN[1] == isApplied[1]\ \&\&$$

$$msgN[0] == isInvited[0] \&\& msgN[1] == isInvited[1]);$$

$$\#assert\ SIPS \models consistency;$$

Property 7: Order Property
Besides, we can use the $Order\ Property$ to verify the SDN architecture between the switch and the controller. If the switch satisfies this property, it should strictly commit the messages according to the order they added. We use array $cmtNum$ to represent whether the message is committed. There are three valid conditions listed as follows. $NoApl$ represents none of the messages is committed. $prevApl1$ represents the former message is committed and the latter one is not.

prevApl2 represents all of the messages are committed. The assertion about this property is defined as below:

$$\#define\ NoApl(CmtNum[0] == 0\ \&\&\ CmtNum[1] == 0);$$
$$\#define\ prevApl1(CmtNum[0] == 1\ \&\&\ CmtNum[1] == 0);$$
$$\#define\ prevApl2(CmtNum[0] == 1\ \&\&\ CmtNum[1] == 1);$$
$$\#define\ Order(NoApl\ ||\ prevApl1\ ||\ prevApl2);$$
$$\#assert\ SIPS \models Order;$$

Property 8: Reliability

This paper models SIP protocol under reliable mechanism, that is to say the retransmission rule is not in this model. Here we use array $buf[uid][eid]$ to represent whether the message has been transmitted. If $buf[uid][eid]$ is 1, this indicates the message has been transmitted. The assertion is defined as below:

$$\#define\ NoTran(buf[0][0] == 1||buf[0][1] == 1||buf[1][0] == 1||buf[1][1] == 1);$$
$$\#assert\ SIPS\ reaches\ NoTran;$$

5.2.2   Verification Results

As illustrated in Fig. 4, the new verification results of $SIPS$ show that the internal properties are valid, including *Deadlock Freeness*, *Load Balance*, *Data Consistency*, *Order Property* and *Reliability*, we can see that SDN with least request algorithm can solve the load balance problem on SIP effectively and also satisfy other internal properties. For safety properties, we enhance the authentication between the entities with verification algorithm. From Fig. 4, we can see our method is correct and the intruder cannot successfully pretend to be legal entities.

Fig. 4. Verification Results of $SIPS$

6   Conclusion and Future Work

In this paper, we have formalized the model of SIP protocol using classical process algebra CSP. Then we verified the constructed model in the model checker PAT. The verification results show that the SIP protocol has load problem and potential security risk of authentication. To solve the problems, we proposed an improved method for SIP model by combining SDN architecture and using identity authentication mechanism, then verified the improved model again. The verification results of the improved model illustrate that the load problem can be coped and the problem of identity authentication will not occur again; besides, the improved model can also satisfy other three internal properties.

In the future, for multipoint communication problems of SIP, we will consider the combination of SIP and H.323 [16] to explore more functional properties. Furthermore, we will also focus on other security problems, such as DDoS attacks.

Acknowledgements. This work was partially supported by the National Natural Science Foundation of China (Grant Nos. 62032024, 61872145), the "Digital Silk Road" Shanghai International Joint Lab of Trustworthy Intelligent Software (Grant No. 22510750100), Shanghai Trusted Industry Internet Software Collaborative Innovation Center, and the Dean's Fund of Shanghai Key Laboratory of Trustworthy Computing (East China Normal University).

References

1. Rosenberg, J.D., et al.: SIP: session initiation protocol. RFC 3261: 1-269 (2002)
2. Liu, J., Liu, L.: A coloured Petri Net approach to the functional and performance analysis of SIP non-INVITE transaction. Trans. Petri Nets Other Model. Concurr. **9**, 147–177 (2014)
3. Gehlot, V., Nigro, C.: Colored Petri Net model of the session initiation protocol (SIP). In: IECON, pp. 2150–2155 (2010)
4. Yang, P., Yuan, Z., Wang, J.: Petri Net model of session initiation protocol and its verification. In: WICOM 2007, pp. 1861–1864 (2007)
5. Montazerolghaem, A.R., Moghaddam, M.H.Y., Leon-Garcia, A.: OpenSIP: toward software-defined SIP networking. IEEE Trans. Netw. Serv. Manag. **15**(1), 184–199 (2018)
6. Montazerolghaem, A.: SIP server load balancing based on SDN. CoRR abs/1908.04047 (2019)
7. Hoare, C.A.R.: Communicating Sequential Processes. Prentice-Hall, Hoboken (1985). ISBN 0-13-153271-5
8. Lowe, G., Roscoe, B.: Using CSP to detect errors in the TMN protocol. IEEE Trans. Software Eng. **23**(10), 659–669 (1997)
9. PAT: Process analysis toolkit. http://pat.comp.nus.edu.sg
10. Si, Y., et al.: Model checking with fairness assumptions using PAT. Front. Comput. Sci. **8**(1), 1–16 (2014)
11. Bai, Y., Ye, X., Ma, Y.: Formal modeling and analysis of SIP using colored Petri Nets. In: WICOM (2011). https://doi.org/10.1109/wicom.2011.6040445

12. Lu, Y., Li, L., Peng, H., Yang, Y.: A secure and efficient mutual authentication scheme for session initiation protocol. Peer-to-Peer Netw. Appl. **9**(2), 449–459 (2016)
13. Kreutz, D., Ramos, F.M.V., Veríssimo, P., Rothenberg, C., Azodolmolky, S., Uhlig, S.: Software-defined networking: a comprehensive survey. Proc. IEEE **103**(1), 14–76 (2015)
14. Salsano, S., Veltri, L., Papalilo, D.: SIP security issues: the SIP authentication procedure and its processing load. IEEE Netw. **16**(6), 38–44 (2002)
15. Chaudhry, S.A., Naqvi, H., Sher, M., Farash, M.S., Hassan, M.U.: An improved and provably secure privacy preserving authentication protocol for SIP. Peer-to-Peer Netw. Appl. **10**(1), 1–15 (2017)
16. International Telecommunication Union: Packet-base Multimedia Communication Systems. ITU-T Recommendation H.323 (1999)
17. Roscoe, A.W., Huang, J.: Checking noninterference in timed CSP. Formal Aspects Comput. **25**(1), 3–35 (2013)

Blockchain

Towards a Blockchain and Fog-Based Proactive Data Distribution Framework for ICN

Somnath Mazumdar[1]([✉])[ID] and Thomas Dreibholz[2][ID]

[1] Department of Digitalization, Copenhagen Business School,
Solbjerg Plads 3, 2000 Frederiksberg, Denmark
sma.digi@cbs.dk
[2] Centre for Digital Engineering, Simula Metropolitan,
Pilestredet 52, 0167 Oslo, Norway
dreibh@simula.no

Abstract. Most of today's IP traffic is cloud traffic. Due to a vast, complex and non-transparent Internet infrastructure, securely accessing and delegating data is not a trivial task. Existing technologies of Information-Centric Networking (ICN) make content distribution and access easy while primarily relying on the existing cloud-based security features. The primary aim of ICN is to make data independent of its storage location and application. ICN builds upon traditional distributed computing, which means ICN platforms also can suffer from similar data security issues as distributed computing platforms. We present our ongoing work to develop a secure, proactive data distribution framework. The framework answers the research question, i.e., *How to extend online data protection with a secure data distribution model for the ICN platform?* Our framework adds a data protection *layer* over the content distribution network, using blockchain and relying on the fog to distribute the contents with low latency. Our framework is different from the existing works in multiple aspects, such as *i)* data are primarily distributed from the fog nodes, *ii)* blockchain is used to protect data and *iii)* blockchain allows statistical and other information sharing among stakeholders (such as content creators) following access rights. Sharing statistics about content distribution activity can bring transparency and trustworthiness among the stakeholders, including the subscribers, into the ICN platforms. We showed such a framework is possible by presenting initial performance results and our reflections while implementing it on a cloud/fog research testbed.

Keywords: Blockchain · Cloud · Data · Distribution · Fog · ICN · Security

1 Introduction

Data[1] distribution technologies, e.g. Information-Centric Networking (ICN), primarily use data caching and data replication to distribute the contents [3].

---

[1] We use the term content and data interchangeably in this paper.

H. Takizawa et al. (Eds.): PDCAT 2022, LNCS 13798, pp. 175–186, 2023.
https://doi.org/10.1007/978-3-031-29927-8_14

Named Data Networking (NDN) [21] and Content-Centric Networking (CCN) are two popular ICN framework implementations. Using the existing IP ecosystem, ICN facilitates content access only by name. A scalable name-based routing and an efficient name-resolution process are required to support data-centric communication because it can improve network bandwidth utilization. ICN applies content-focused security rather than on the communication process [25]. The ICN framework generally suffers from multiple security attacks, such as unauthorized content access, denial-of-service and network-cache pollution [12]. In cache attacks, node caches are filled with unpopular content, decreasing throughput and increasing delay. As a result of such attacks, ICN infrastructure suffers from lower performance and higher energy consumption. ICN lacks data confidentiality and employs cryptography protocols to authenticate the name-to-content binding [24]. However, such cryptographic techniques can be computationally expensive, and name-to-content verification does not guarantee the quality and trustworthiness of the requested data. For efficient data distribution in ICN, in-network caching is introduced, allowing the content to be copied and distributed across [2] without strong authentication and authorization mechanism. Overall, it complicates ICN content access control management, but it is highly required for better performance.

Applying blockchain on top of ICN can reduce security-related issues. Blockchain can inherently support content tamper resistance and integrity checking, thanks to hashing. Data immutability is also supported by blockchain. It can further offer added security checks via the private blockchain platform. Blockchain is attack-resistant but not attack-proof and can bring performance benefits to ICN platforms. For instance, blockchain-based data distribution in NDN platforms is more efficient than IP networking [23]. In some cases, blockchain fits better to NDN than IP, offering better message delay [11]. Blockchain has found its way into secure media content delivery over the Internet [19] and is also used for ICN to trace malicious nodes thanks to its traceability feature [14].

In a traditional ICN network, only the content service providers (CSPs) manage everything. There are multiple cases where CSPs are non-transparent to content creators. It is arguable whether the current content distribution platforms are skewed towards the network owner's profit and non-transparent. However, the current content distribution platforms are out of the reach of content creators. Existing non-blockchain-based decentralized access control schemes for ICN-based content distribution and protection lack multi-level security and content access audits [1,15,18]. In this paper, we are presenting one blockchain and fog-based data distribution framework. It relies on blockchain for content protection and access delegation among the subscribers and other stakeholders, while fog can offer lower latency. Our framework differs from existing works in many ways. First, we rely on fog to enhance the content-delegation performance of latency-sensitive ICN applications. Second, we are using blockchain to protect the data and also incorporated a two-tier access control policy via the smart contract. The proposed two-tier access delegation model allows ICN stakeholders and subscribers to securely and legitimately access the data. We have implemented the framework using our cloud/fog research testbed. Furthermore, we have also reported our results on delegating the media files and the data distribution capacity of the testbed.

2   Related Work

Multiple works propose decentralized access control schemes to overcome content access problems without blockchain [1,15,18]. Mishra et al. offer an access control framework for ICN to guarantee trusted content to legitimate subscribers [18] and aim to increase content availability and quality of experience. Abdallah et al. propose a decentralized access control protocol for subscribers and nodes using the self-certifying naming scheme [1], while for the content provider, Li et al. developed an integrity verification process by distributing integrity verification tokens to authorized nodes [15].

Asaf et al., in their survey, show how blockchain is implemented in NDN and presents some challenges concerning blockchain over NDN [5]. Authors in [23] propose an NDN-based Ethereum client to enhance the data delivery with in-network caching and multicasting features of NDN. Lyu et al. propose a blockchain-based access control model to achieve hierarchical access for a content provider and present an access token mechanism [17]. It aims to find a balance between privacy and audit. In another work, blockchain is implemented over NDN to support transactions broadcasting by switching from the IP-based push protocol to NDN-based pull protocol [9]. Li et al. propose a blockchain-based tracing mechanism for content delivery in ICN [14], which stores the behaviours of ICN nodes to trace the malicious nodes. However, the authors have not completely clarified how much data blockchain and the cloud will store. A blockchain-based data life-cycle protection framework is proposed to offer a trusted ICN. The framework can exploit transactions and smart contracts after identifying the attack patterns and design requirements [16]. Conti et al. propose a blockchain-based authentication technique for mobility management in ICN [6]. Tan et al. propose an access control mechanism for ICN, where the contents are divided into multiple original blocks [22]. Next, the model applies the XOR-coding algorithm to encode blocks for recovering original contents later. Blockndn shows that a blockchain-based NDN is better for data broadcasting regarding message delay and traffic generation [11]. A name-based security mechanism to secure content distribution in ICN is also proposed to counter the key escrow problem by leveraging hierarchical identity-based encryption [7].

Finally, our work proposes a blockchain-based data/content distribution framework for a content provider. Fog will store frequently accessed content, and the rest will be in the cloud. Fog will reduce access latency, and the blockchain will store the metadata of the contents. The blockchain-based two-tier model supports a content access control policy. Here, one tier is dedicated to the subscriber, and the other allows the stakeholders (e.g. content creators) to view transactions related to their content. Such information can help stakeholders to understand the content's popularity and associated financial transactions.

3   Proposed Framework

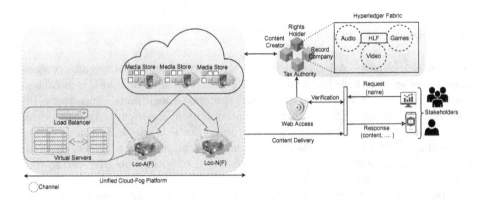

Fig. 1. Architecture of the proposed secure data/content distribution framework.

Figure 1 presents the proposed blockchain- and fog-based secure content distribution framework. It aims to complement the existing ICN by *i)* increasing the content's security (from the current security level) using blockchain and *ii)* improve the performance by relying on fog for a better subscriber experience, while cloud platforms are a good fit for applications that can tolerate delays up to 100 ms [20]. We have considered this framework from a CSP's perspective. CSPs will maintain the whole distribution platform. However, it will be tough for CSPs to manipulate the stored blockchain records without informing other stakeholders. Such a blockchain-based ICN solution adds content protection and access control while delegating content to the subscribers/stakeholders. Blockchain can make the ICN platform more transparent. For instance, stakeholders can access content-related details, such as content access statistics, content popularity, revenue from content, and others. It is worth noting that customizing the smart contract can also allow access to more detailed information. The current framework considers six stakeholders, but more can be added easily. The current list of stakeholders is as follows: *i)* CSP, *ii)* Subscribers, *iii)* Content Creator(s), *iv)* Right Holder(s), *v)* Record Companies or Labels, *vi)* Public authority for tax and copyright protection (and violation). Adding more stakeholders can make it more transparent and a more acceptable solution.

3.1   Framework Overview

The framework (refer to Fig. 1) has two primary components. They are *i)* cloud/-fog platform to host content (off-chain storage), and *ii)* blockchain to provide data protection and access delegation. We can see from Fig. 1 that after successfully checking subscribers' credentials (by the blockchain), their request is routed based on the designated access tiers. We have considered protected visibility as tier one[2] and private visibility as tier zero[3]. The level of content visibility as per tiers should be decided before the network implementation. The subscribers belong to tier one, and stakeholders are associated with tier zero. A subscriber requests content (e.g. a movie) by sending the content name. Next, a relevant REpresentational State Transfer (REST) API call will be generated to process the viewer's request. The related smart contract will be invoked, and after successful access rights verification, another API call will be made to initiate the media file transfer via the nearby fog nodes. Users can have only age-appropriate content access (thanks to a tier-based access control policy), while inappropriate content related to explicit content, violence, and other inappropriate documentaries is filtered out via the rules embedded into the smart contracts. Such content delegation based on the access control policy feature makes our framework *proactive*. Generally, content fragmentation is done at the transport layer. From the content delivery request side, ICN supports *Name packets* for request, and *Data packets* for the response. The ICN uses protocol data units to distribute the contents larger than standard maximum transmission units. Data transmission can be based on a pull protocol (such as HTTP Live Streaming) instead of widely used push protocols to achieve higher efficiency in the application layer. Content data authenticity and encryption are automatically performed (at an off-chain storage level) by the blockchain using the hashing and digital signature. The proposed platform is private, which means all the network subscribers, including the stakeholders, are verified before conducting any network activity. Thus, content added to the framework is always trusted. After adding metadata to the content, manipulating content (or viewing manipulation) is tough. We have used the Hyperledger Fabric (HLF) blockchain platform for the implementation [4]. HLF applies a more traditional byzantine fault-tolerant consensus mechanism, which does not require mining and is one of the few platforms to develop enterprise-level applications. HLF also offers channels which are a secure form of communication. Each channel can be dedicated per content type (refer to the top right of Fig. 1). Finally, primary contents are stored in the cloud/fog platform, and the metadata is stored in the blockchain, which helps to preserve the content's integrity.

3.2 Framework Data Flow

Figure 2 shows how data flows inside the framework. It is worth mentioning that such a seamless information flow can improve the service optimization of the platform. All important events are recorded on the blockchain. The flow starts when movie 'X' is listed on the platform after buying the media rights by a CSP. The file of the movie 'X' will be stored in the cloud storage, but the movie's metadata (including the storage location) will be stored in the blockchain. The storage location is also added to the metadata and later hashed before adding to the blockchain to ensure no changes can be made to the media content. After

---

[2] allows access services based on the subscribed plan.

[3] allows stakeholders to access the blockchain.

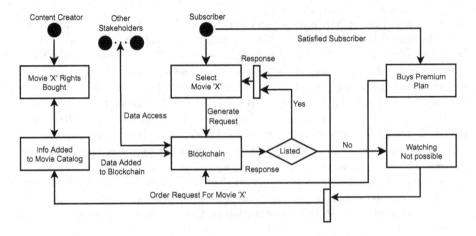

Fig. 2. Seamless data flow inside the framework.

the movie is listed on the network, subscribers can watch the movie. Later, media usage metrics can be accessible to the stakeholders, including the original content creator. If a subscriber subscribes to a premium plan, the stakeholders can also see such information. Based on the implementation, stakeholders can see how much revenue is generated using the advertisement and subscription plans. Finally, if any movie is not listed (rare at this time), the framework can also inform the CSP to include it.

3.3 Security-Related Advantages

ICN wraps all network functionalities around the content name by supporting the name resolution system. It builds upon traditional distributed computing, which means ICN also suffers from similar security issues as distributed computing platforms. Here, we will qualitatively discuss how blockchain offers better security than legacy ICN platforms following the STRIDE model [13]. Spoofing-related events result from low physical security measures of nodes, but taking down the whole network using one blockchain node is technically not possible. Next, data tampering and repudiation are very hard to achieve, thanks to the employed hashing and digital signature of data blocks. The hash connects data blocks. HLF uses the SHA-256 hashing algorithm and the elliptic curve digital signature algorithm as the digital signature to counter such issues. Information disclosure leads to user data compromise, which is hard because of employed blockchain-based access control. Denial-of-service forces the ICN platform to be temporarily unavailable. In such cases, an attacker needs enormous computing power relative to the blockchain-based ICN network size. Finally, elevation of privilege cannot be done easily on the private platform because a network administrator verifies all network users before delegating access rights to them. So, overall, blockchain brings advantages primarily related to content security compared to non-blockchain-based ICN platforms. Data integrity is maintained by employing a hashing algorithm, and a digital signature is used to authenticate the subscribers.

3.4 Block Structure

```
{
"content_data": {
    "content_name": "file_name",
    "content_type": "video",
    "content_id": "2ede927-..-8a26a2665aea",
    "content_owned_by": "content owner/copyright owner name",
    "content_location": "list of caching locations/storage locations/urls",
    "content_manifest": " list of connected payloads",
    "content_length": "value",
    "content_price": "current price",
    "content_misc_name": "other partial content names",
    "content_meta_data": {
        "content_rating": "general/parental guidance/mature/...",
        "content_genre": "genre name",
        "content_timestamp": "adding to blockchain",
        "content_added_by": "content service provider",
        "content_format": "MP4/MOV/AVCHD"
        }
    }
}
```

Fig. 3. Representation of current block structure for managing a video/movie file.

Blockchain is a linear-linked-list representation of a distributed ledger and is primarily a collection of distributed transactions. Here, a transaction represents one named content accessed by viewers, while a data block holds n transactions. n is implementation-dependent, but it should not be too large because larger block sizes reduce the scalability of the network. Figure 3 shows our customized block structure to wrap the content's information (work in progress). Such customization speeds up video content processing (access and delegation). Our current version of the block structure holds both content-specific data and metadata. content_id is the message digest after applying an SHA-256 function on the content's primary name and the content itself. Such an approach ensures that no modification can go unnoticed after adding the content to the blockchain (i.e. supporting data immutability). One of the problems with the named content in ICNs is that the content might have multiple partial names. The name might be partial when a viewer requests the content via its name. In that case, content_misc_name will hold a list of possible words that can help to look up the content faster. content_price is also a piece of important information for the content creator. Generally, the CSPs use dynamic pricing models so that price manipulation can be visible to the relevant stakeholders. It is worth noting that the framework does not support any cryptocurrency (or tokens). Similar to video content, it is possible to create other blocks for audio, games and other content. We keep the meta information in data blocks, while primary content (such as video or audio files) is stored in the cloud/fog.

4   Performance Results

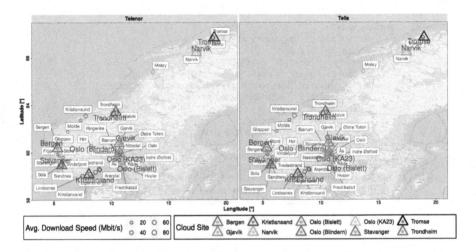

Fig. 4. Fog nodes and their cloud mappings with their average downloading speed.

To showcase the feasibility of our framework, we created the setup shown in Fig. 4, which is an extended part of our cloud/fog research testbed distributed over Norway [8]. The cloud sites are marked with triangles, and the fog nodes are shown as circles. Each fog node is connected using 4G modems relying on broadband connections. These connections are from two Internet service providers (ISPs), i.e., Telenor and Telia. The left-hand part of Fig. 4 presents the Telenor-based layout, while the right-hand part shows the Telia-based layout. The circle size corresponds to the average download speed. To show the fog performance, we had chosen three typical media sizes[4]: 1 GiB for standard definition (SD), 3 GiB for high definition (HD), and 7 GiB for ultra-high definition (4K). Table 1 presents the resulting average download time for each media file size per fog site location (municipality-level aggregation) over each of the two ISPs (if available) for municipalities with a population of at least 10,000. Furthermore, the table contains the mapping to the geographically nearest cloud.

As shown in Table 1, streaming the 4K media to Telenor-backed fog nodes took just more than 14:28 min (as best case, for Telenor in Trondheim) and a maximum of 167 min (worst case, for Telenor in Malvik), while the other ISP can stream 4K video in 19:17 min (best case, for Telia in Trondheim) to almost 167 min (worst case, for Telenor in Malvik). Theoretically, our cloud setup (all

---

[4] https://help.netflix.com/en/node/87/us (accessed Oct. 20, 2022).

Table 1. Content downloading time (minutes:seconds) from fog nodes (only for locations with population of at least 10,000).

Cloud Loc.	Fog Loc.	Telenor			Telia		
		SD	HD	4K	SD	HD	4K
Bergen	Bergen	11:34	34:44	81:02	5:02	15:07	35:17
	Stord	11:33	34:40	80:54	12:44	38:12	89:09
Gjøvik	Gjøvik	6:16	18:50	43:57	8:50	26:30	61:50
	Østre Toten	13:15	39:47	92:50	3:18	9:54	23:07
Kristiansand	Arendal	3:52	11:38	27:09	4:38	13:54	32:26
	Eigersund	2:50	8:30	19:51	3:32	10:36	24:44
	Kristiansand	2:59	8:58	20:55	4:40	14:01	32:43
	Lindesnes	3:39	10:59	25:39	6:39	19:58	46:35
Narvik	Narvik	2:51	8:34	20:00	5:51	17:34	41:01
Oslo (Bislett)	Oslo	3:48	11:24	26:38	4:21	13:03	30:29
Oslo (Blindern)	Bærum	11:48	35:25	82:40	–	–	–
	Nittedal	2:10	6:32	15:15	2:45	8:16	19:17
	Ringerike	6:00	18:01	42:04	12:48	38:25	89:39
Oslo (KA23)	Ås	5:48	17:24	40:36	6:00	18:01	42:04
	Bærum	–	–	–	9:00	27:01	63:04
	Fredrikstad	9:11	27:33	64:17	10:39	31:59	74:38
	Indre Østfold	5:44	17:12	40:09	6:07	18:22	42:51
	Nesodden	14:36	43:48	102:14	8:11	24:35	57:23
Stavanger	Sandnes	12:59	38:59	90:58	5:03	15:10	35:24
	Sola	2:30	7:32	17:36	8:33	25:39	59:53
	Stavanger	3:00	9:01	21:03	5:46	17:18	40:22
Tromsø	Tromsø	3:19	9:58	23:17	5:20	16:01	37:22
Trondheim	Kristiansund	3:38	10:56	25:31	2:47	8:21	19:30
	Malvik	23:50	71:32	166:56	13:10	39:30	92:10
	Molde	9:34	28:44	67:04	9:04	27:13	63:31
	Trondheim	2:04	6:12	14:28	2:47	8:21	19:30

Table 2. Content downloading time (minutes:seconds) from public cloud providers.

Cloud	Region	Avg. Download Speed (Mbit/s)	SD	HD	4K
Amazon Cloud	Stockholm	100.95	1:27	4:22	10:11
Microsoft Azure	Norway East	113.55	1:17	3:53	9:04
Google Cloud	Finland	102.62	1:25	4:17	10:01

sites; not shown in the table) can deliver the same 4K file in 61 s (best case) to a maximum of 10 min (worst case). The actual download time significantly varies in rural areas, leading to increased download times. Caching and more intelligent content distribution can improve the network performance (e.g. by avoiding unnecessary transfers during peak hours, trying to utilise non-peak hours, and using nearby download locations). We also have reported the content downloading time from public cloud service providers in Table 2. These values reflect the CDN service network performance offered by the three popular cloud service providers. It is worth noting that they do not offer any fog-based services. For all three video file types, the Trondheim facility (Telenor as ISP) is the best among all our testbed facilities compared to the Microsoft Azure CDN service (Norway).

Table 3. Average network latency of compute services of three public cloud service providers and the testbed.

Cloud	Region	Avg. Latency (ms)
Amazon Cloud	Stockholm	32
Microsoft Azure	Norway East	41
Google Cloud	Finland	40
NorNet Cloud	Norway	27
NorNet Fog	Norway	59

Table 3 compares the average network latency (round trip times using IPv4 packets) among all platforms and the cloud/fog testbed. Our fog testbed units are slower than the cloud because the fog nodes are connected via 4G mobile broadband. We can see that the NorNet Cloud has an average latency of 27 ms for a 4G-based connection and 12.75 ms for a fibre-based link (not reported in the table). It is worth noting that commercial infrastructures are highly resourceful and professionally maintained compared to a research testbed. Our aim was never to beat the commercial providers but to show that our framework has been implemented on a realistic testbed, and the comparison proves it. We can also infer that adding fog by the commercial facility will surely improve the latency of content delegation, and adding blockchain will distribute content securely.

4.1   Lesson Learned

To offer a better viewing experience, the Open Connect program[5] from Netflix aims to develop a better content caching infrastructure using ISPs' resources. Here, we aim to build a framework to offer better content security and improved cache coordination with effective network storage management. While working

---

[5] https://openconnect.netflix.com/en/ (accessed Oct. 20, 2022).

on the performance data, we also started looking into *How to optimize storage cost by intelligent fog-level content caching?* In such a scenario, machine learning (ML) can lower content access latency and storage costs by predicting content popularity. ML is already used for predicting popular video contents [10]. Currently, an ML module is being developed using user-ID (hashed value/anonymous for privacy), content viewing patterns (such as genre, content type) and other information (model-dependent) related features to improve the quality of experience.

5   Conclusion and Future Work

ICN aims to offer location-independent data access via improved caching and replication. We propose a blockchain-based content distribution framework to provide better content security and make the distribution process transparent to the relevant stakeholders. We do not use blockchain for content storage but to protect it. All content-related metadata in hashed format is stored in the blockchain. We reported performance results related to our content distribution while handling video files. We aim to complete the benchmarking of our platform before implementing ML for smart caching of popular content as future work. To the best of our knowledge, there is no prototype similar to ours which uses blockchain to secure ICN and is implemented using a cloud/fog testbed.

References

1. AbdAllah, E.G., Zulkernine, M., Hassanein, H.S.: DACPI: a decentralized access control protocol for information-centric networking. In: IEEE International Conference on Communications, pp. 1–6. IEEE (2016)
2. Abdullahi, I., Arif, S., Hassan, S.: Survey on caching approaches in information-centric networking. J. Netw. Comput. Appl. **56**, 48–59 (2015)
3. Ahlgren, B., Dannewitz, C., Imbrenda, C., Kutscher, D., Ohlman, B.: A survey of information-centric networking. IEEE Commun. Mag. **50**(7), 26–36 (2012)
4. Androulaki, E., et al.: A distributed operating system for permissioned blockchains. In: 13th EuroSys Conference, EuroSys'18. Association for Computing Machinery (2018)
5. Asaf, K., Rehman, R.A., Kim, B.S.: Blockchain technology in named data networks: a detailed survey. J. Netw. Comput. Appl. **171**, 1–15 (2020)
6. Conti, M., Hassan, M., Lal, C.: BlockAuth: blockchain-based distributed producer authentication in ICN. Comput. Netw. **164**, 1–15 (2019)
7. Fotiou, N., Polyzos, G.C.: Decentralized name-based security for content distribution using blockchains. In: IEEE Conference on Computer Communications Workshops, pp. 415–420. IEEE (2016)
8. Gran, E.G., Dreibholz, T., Kvalbein, A.: NorNet core - a multi-homed research testbed. Comput. Netw. **61**, 75–87 (2014)
9. Guo, J., Wang, M., Chen, B., Yu, S., Zhang, H., Zhang, Y.: Enabling blockchain applications over named data networking. In: International Conference on Communications, pp. 1–6. IEEE (2019)

10. Jeon, H., Seo, W., Park, E., Choi, S.: Hybrid machine learning approach for popularity prediction of newly released contents of online video streaming services. Technol. Forecast. Soc. Chang. **161**, 1–17 (2020)
11. Jin, T., Zhang, X., Liu, Y., Lei, K.: Blockndn: a bitcoin blockchain decentralized system over named data networking. In: International Conference on Ubiquitous and Future Networks, pp. 75–80. IEEE (2017)
12. Kim, D., Bi, J., Vasilakos, A.V., Yeom, I.: Security of cached content in NDN. IEEE Trans. Inf. Forensics Secur. **12**(12), 2933–2944 (2017)
13. Kohnfelder, L., Garg, P.: The Threats to Our Products. Microsoft Interface, Microsoft Corporation **33** (1999)
14. Li, H., Wang, K., Miyazaki, T., Xu, C., Guo, S., Sun, Y.: Trust-enhanced content delivery in blockchain-based information-centric networking. IEEE Netw. **33**(5), 183–189 (2019)
15. Li, Q., Zhang, X., Zheng, Q., Sandhu, R., Fu, X.: LIVE: lightweight integrity verification and content access control for named data networking. IEEE Trans. Inf. Forensics Secur. **10**(2), 308–320 (2014)
16. Li, R., Asaeda, H.: A blockchain-based data life-cycle protection framework for information-centric networks. IEEE Commun. Mag. **57**(6), 20–25 (2019)
17. Lyu, Q., Qi, Y., Zhang, X., Liu, H., Wang, Q., Zheng, N.: SBAC: a secure blockchain-based access control framework for information-centric networking. J. Netw. Comput. Appl. **149**, 1–17 (2020)
18. Misra, S., Tourani, R., Natividad, F., Mick, T., Majd, N.E., Huang, H.: AccConF: an access control framework for leveraging in-network cached data in the ICN-enabled wireless edge. IEEE Trans. Dependable Secure Comput. **16**(1), 5–17 (2017)
19. Nazarian, A., Arana, M., Prestegard, D.L.: Blockchain configuration for secure content delivery. Patents (2021)
20. Pelle, I., Czentye, J., Dóka, J., Sonkoly, B.: Towards latency sensitive cloud native applications: a performance study on AWS. In: IEEE 12th International Conference on Cloud Computing, pp. 272–280. IEEE (2019)
21. Saxena, D., Raychoudhury, V., Suri, N., Becker, C., Cao, J.: Named data networking: a survey. Comput. Sci. Rev. **19**, 15–55 (2016)
22. Tan, X., Huang, C., Ji, L.: Access control scheme based on combination of blockchain and XOR-coding for ICN. In: 5th International Conference on Cyber Security and Cloud Computing/4th International Conference on Edge Computing and Scalable Cloud, pp. 160–165. IEEE (2018)
23. Thai, Q.T., Ko, N., Byun, S.H., Kim, S.M.: Design and implementation of NDN-based ethereum blockchain. J. Netw. Comput. Appl. **200**, 1–18 (2022)
24. Wissingh, B., Wood, C.A., Afanasyev, A., Zhang, L., Oran, D., Tschudin, C.: Information-centric networking (ICN): content-centric networking (CCNx) and named data networking (NDN) terminology. Informational RFC 8793, IETF (2020)
25. Zhang, Z., et al.: An overview of security support in named data networking. IEEE Commun. Mag. **56**(11), 62–68 (2018)

Research on User Influence Weighted Scoring Algorithm Incorporating Incentive Mechanism

Jingya Xu[2,4], Lina Ge[1,3,4(✉)], Wei Zhou[1,3], Liang Yan[1,4], and Zheng Hu[1,4]

[1] School of Artificial Intelligence, Guangxi Minzu University, Nanning, China
66436539@qq.com
[2] School of Electronic Information, Guangxi Minzu University, Nanning, China
[3] Guangxi Key Laboratory of Hybrid Computation and IC Design Analysis, Nanning, China
[4] Key Laboratory of Network Communication Engineering, Guangxi Minzu University, Nanning, China

Abstract. Overall product ratings are an important basis for users when shopping online or using online services. However, some sellers and web service providers put a large amount of false rating data into the rating system to improve their own rankings, which seriously damages the interests of users. In this paper, two methods are used to reduce the impact of false ratings on overall ratings. First, a user influence weighted scoring algorithm is proposed to analyze user behavior and build a user influence model. The influence of different users on the rating is considered when calculating the overall rating to improve the accuracy of the project's overall rating. Secondly, a blockchain-based rating incentive mechanism is designed to correlate users' rating behavior with their interests, which effectively constrains their rating behavior and further makes them consciously, as well as proactively provide more authentic ratings. Comparing the proposed algorithm with the rating algorithms used on Douban and IMDB, the simulation shows that the algorithm performs best in terms of resistance to interference. The experimental results also show that the rating incentive mechanism can reward high-impact users and punish low-impact malicious users, and can effectively defend against malicious users.

Keywords: User influence model · Weighted scoring algorithm · Incentive mechanism · Blockchain

1 Introduction

In recent years, a series of online services represented by online shopping, online movie viewing, and online reading has risen rapidly. When users use online websites or mobile apps, they will take the comprehensive score of goods or virtual services as an important basis [1]. According to the survey data of Jupiter Research, an American market research company, 77% of Internet users will refer to product reviews written by other people on the Internet before purchasing a product [2]. Online ratings are a form of credit guarantee that emerged at the beginning of the construction of Internet platforms [3]. The establishment of a rating mechanism not only proves the commercial value of the

H. Takizawa et al. (Eds.): PDCAT 2022, LNCS 13798, pp. 187–198, 2023.
https://doi.org/10.1007/978-3-031-29927-8_15

information but is also an important means to overcome the "lemon puzzle" [4]. However, some sellers and online service providers are putting a lot of untrue rating data into the rating system to improve the rating and ranking of their products. This seriously harms the interests of users and other merchants. The lack of constraints has led to a serious decline in the accuracy and authenticity of rating data on virtual service sites and e-commerce sites. The issue of trust in the Internet is one of the most important issues that need to be urgently addressed for the continued healthy development of online services today.

Currently, major websites with evaluation needs have established their own set of evaluation systems to provide online reviews and rating functions [5]. Douban uses a simple weighted rating algorithm where the weight is a percentage of the number of users rating the site; the rating algorithm used in the IMDB TOP250 is a Bayesian statistical algorithm. To a certain extent, it has alleviated the credit crisis of online transactions and increased the confidence of users in online transactions [6]. However, there are still some problems with the current scoring algorithms and evaluation rules. It lacks a mechanism to discern whether users' ratings are genuine and objective. It also does not take into account the impact that different users have on the overall rating. It is not possible to effectively constrain user behavior and motivate users to make realistic evaluations. Therefore, it is necessary to construct a user influence model by analyzing users' evaluation behavior. The influence of the different users is used as a weight in the weighting algorithm when calculating the overall rating.

Improving the overall accuracy and authenticity of ratings requires not only a weighting algorithm but also an effective rating incentive mechanism. Current traditional scoring incentives are based on the system giving users tokens or financial rewards when they rate a project. To a certain extent, this incentive policy has served to encourage users to rate. However, due to the drawback of its undifferentiated rewards, it also brings a large number of low-quality ratings to the rating system. As blockchain technology continues to mature, blockchain incentives are also widely used in privacy protection [7–10], data sharing [11–14], and supply chains [15–18]. The characteristics of blockchain technology, such as non-tamperability and openness and transparency, can guarantee the reliability of the scoring incentive mechanism.

To solve the above problems, the following research and work are carried out in this paper. (1) Construct a user influence model, analyzing the characteristics of user evaluation behavior in four aspects: authenticity, objectivity, honesty, and user participation enthusiasm of user ratings. And using the Analytic Hierarchy Process to select appropriate weights for these four factors. (2) A user influence weighted evaluation algorithm is proposed to calculate the comprehensive rating taking into account the influence of different users on the rating. It effectively solves the problem of malicious users injecting a large amount of false evaluation information and improves the accuracy of the comprehensive rating of the project. (3) Propose a rating incentive mechanism to closely link the quality of users' ratings with their interests. Effectively restrain users' rating behaviour, guide users to consciously and actively maintain the network ecological environment of the rating system and improve the authenticity of comprehensive project ratings.

2   User Influence Weighting Algorithm

2.1   User Influence Model

By analyzing the characteristics of user rating behavior, the influence of users is modeled in terms of four factors: authenticity, objectivity, honesty, and active participation of users. The weights of these four factors were determined using the AHP (Ana-lytic Hierarchy Process). This is used to distinguish between users who are more influential in the overall rating of the project and those who are less influential. Table 1 summarises commonly used parameters in the algorithm.

Table 1. Important parameters and meanings in the algorithm.

Variables	Implication
U	The set of users involved in the evaluation, $U_i \in U$
S	The set of categories of evaluation items, $S_j \in S$
$P(U_i, S_j)$	Degree of preference of user U_i for items of category S_j
N_i	Total number of times user U_i has reviewed all items
$N(U_i, S_j)$	Number of times user U_i has evaluated category S_j items
$M_{i,j}$	Average rating of items in category S_j by user U_i
M_i	Average rating of all items by user U_i
$M_{i,a}$	Average rating of user U_i for the item with the highest type of preference
M_a	Average rating of all users of this item
$M_{i,b}$	Average rating of user U_i for the item with the lowest type of preference
M_b	Average rating of all users of this item

Authenticity of User Ratings: There are differences in user preferences for different types of projects, and this difference is reflected in the user ratings for different types of projects. The authenticity of users' ratings of items has a direct impact on the authenticity of the overall item ratings. The degree of truthfulness of user ratings is indicated by calculating the dispersion of user ratings for different types of items. If a user's scores for different types of items are relatively concentrated, it means that the user's scores for all items are relatively single, and the range of score changes is relatively small. Whether or not they like the item, the ratings are relatively close. In this case, the ratings of users of this type are less informative. In contrast, if a user's ratings vary significantly between the different types of items, they are based on their preferences and the real situation of the items. These user ratings are of high reference value to other users who have not used the item. The authenticity of the rating of user U_i is denoted as $F(U_i)$, which is calculated by formulation (1).

$$F(U_i) = \frac{\sum\limits_{j \in S} \left(M_{i,j} - M_i\right)^2}{|S|} \tag{1}$$

Objectivity of User Rating: Some users rate items more subjectively, and others rate items more objectively. User ratings with more objective ratings are more valuable for reference. The objectiveness index is used to measure whether the user's rating of the item is objective. To evaluate the objectivity of user ratings, users' preferences for various types of items should be considered. By calculating the number of user evaluations for different types of items, users' preferences can be more intuitively understood. A user preference calculation formulation is introduced to show a user's preference for different types of items, and the preference degree of user U_i for items of category S_j can be calculated by formulation (2). If the average rating of the user for the item with the highest type of preference and the item with the lowest type of preference is closer to the average rating scored by all users of the item, it means that the user's rating is more accurate and objective. The user's rating has a higher reference value. The objectivity of the user's rating is noted as $C(U_i)$, which is calculated by formulation (3).

$$P\left(U_i, S_j\right) = \frac{N\left(U_i, S_j\right)}{|N_i|} \tag{2}$$

$$C(U_i) = \frac{1}{\ln\left(\frac{\sqrt{\left(M_{i,a}-M_a\right)^2+\left(M_{i,b}-M_b\right)^2}}{2} + 2\right)} \tag{3}$$

Honesty of User Ratings: The honesty of user ratings is calculated based on the user's last eight rating behaviors. The design of the honesty vector draws on the P2P credit vector mechanism proposed by A.A.Selcuk, E.Uzun, etc. [19]. The integrity vector is represented as an eight-bit binary vector of integrity from left to right, depending on the order in which the evaluation actions occur. The initial value of the eight bits is 0. This design can pay more attention to the user's recent rating behavior. Set a threshold for extreme evaluations, and determine whether the number of users who rated the item accounts for less than 30% of the total number of users who rated the item. If it is less than 30%, it is judged as a malicious evaluation. The non-malicious evaluation behavior is recorded as 1, and the malicious evaluation behavior is recorded as 0. After a non-malicious evaluation by the user, the leftmost binary bit is marked as 1. The honest vector is updated as shown in Fig. 1. The flag bit represents the subscript of the user's first recorded evaluation.

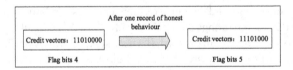

Fig. 1. Update of the credit vector after one honest act by the user

m is the sign bit. Converts the honest vector from the first m binary digits of the left digit to decimal, denoted by the parameter $(\gamma)_2$. The converted decimal number is used as the numerator and 2^m as the denominator. The two are divided to obtain a number in the range $[0, 1)$, which is the user's honesty coefficient. The honesty of the user's rating is written as $H(U_i)$ and is calculated by the formulation (4).

$$H(U_i) = \frac{(\gamma)_2}{2^m} \tag{4}$$

Active Participation of User Ratings: Actually, some users are more active and willing to express their opinions and feelings about projects. And others who rarely or hardly ever evaluate the project, these users tend to have low engagement motivation and gradually lose the trust of other users. User participation enthusiasm is considered from two aspects: the total number of user evaluations of all items and the number of user evaluation item types. Suppose user A has watched 50 movies of the same type, and user B has watched 5 different types of movies, 10 of each type. At this time, only considering the total number of user evaluations cannot distinguish the user's participation enthusiasm. The user's participation enthusiasm is recorded as $I(U_i)$, and it is calculated by formulation (5).

$$I(U_i) = 1 - \frac{1}{\ln\left(\sum_{j \in S} |S| \times N\left(U_i, S_j\right)\right)} \tag{5}$$

User Influence: The user influence is composed of the above four factors, i.e. the authenticity, objectivity, honesty, and active participation of the user's rating, which is denoted as $T(U_i)$ and calculated by the formulation (6). The value of λ has the property as in formulation (7).

$$T(U_i) = \lambda_1 F(U_i) + \lambda_2 C(U_i) + \lambda_3 H(U_i) + \lambda_4 I(U_i) \tag{6}$$

$$\lambda_1 + \lambda_2 + \lambda_3 + \lambda_4 = 1 \tag{7}$$

Use AHP to obtain the weight λ. Firstly, a hierarchical structure model is established, with the target level being user influence, represented by A1. The four criteria of the criterion layer are the authenticity of user rating B1, the objectivity of user rating B2, the honesty of user rating B3, and the active participation of user B4. The method of constructing the judgment matrix in AHP is the consensus matrix method. Make a pairwise comparison of each scheme under a certain criterion and rate it according to the degree of importance. The pairwise comparison matrix P between the criterion layer and the target layer is constructed by pairwise comparison, as in the formulation (8).

$$P = \begin{bmatrix} 1 & 3 & 5 & 4 \\ \frac{1}{3} & 1 & 5 & 4 \\ \frac{1}{5} & \frac{1}{5} & 1 & 2 \\ \frac{1}{4} & \frac{1}{4} & \frac{1}{2} & 1 \end{bmatrix} \tag{8}$$

Because the construction of the judgment matrix is greatly affected by subjective factors, it is necessary to check the consistency of the calculation results [20]. Among them, the random consistency index RI is related to the order of the judgment matrix.

The larger the order of the matrix, the greater the possibility of random deviation of consistency [21]. The corresponding index RI of the fourth-order matrix is 0.9. Considering that deviations from consistency may be due to random reasons, it is also necessary to compare the CI with the random consistency indicator RI when testing whether the judgment matrix has satisfactory consistency, to derive the test coefficient CR, as in formulation (9).

$$CR = \frac{CI}{RI} \qquad (9)$$

When the consistency ratio $CR < 0.1$, the judgment matrix passes the consistency test. The maximum characteristic root λ_{max} of the judgment matrix and its corresponding eigenvector was solved by the arithmetic mean method and judged for consistency. The eigenvector was normalized and noted as W_1. Matrix P: $\lambda_{max} = 4.261$, $W_1 = (0.5231, 0.3003, 0.0984, 0.0782)$, $CI = 0.0872$, calculated as $CR = 0.0968 < 0.10$, and the consistency test passed. Therefore, the judgment matrix constructed is considered reasonable and feasible. The weights corresponding to the four influencing factors of the user influence model were calculated as shown in Table 2 below.

Table 2. The corresponding weights of the four factors affect the user's credit.

Influencing factors	Authenticity of user ratings	Objectivity of user ratings	Accuracy of user ratings	Active participation of user ratings
Weighting	0.508	0.303	0.106	0.083

The user influence calculation is therefore communicated as shown in formulation (10).

$$T(U_i) = 0.508F(U_i) + 0.303C(U_i) + 0.106H(U_i) + 0.083I(U_i) \qquad (10)$$

2.2 Weighted Rating Algorithm

To minimize the impact of malicious users on the overall rating, this paper proposes a user influence weighted scoring algorithm. The design of the weighting in terms of user influence is intended to prevent users with lower quality ratings from having a disproportionate impact on the ratings. The numerator of the formulation is the sum of the product of the users' ratings and their influence, and the denominator is the sum of each user's influence. The final settlement score for the tth cycle is denoted as W_t, which represents the overall rating of n users for the item at moment t, as in formulation (11). $T(i)$ is the influence of user i, G_i is the rating of the item by user i.

$$W_t = \frac{\sum\limits_{i=1}^{n} T(i) \times G_i}{\sum\limits_{i=1}^{n} T(i)} \qquad (11)$$

The rating cycle begins with the user rating the item. After a user submits a rating, the rating cannot be modified and the rating cycle ends. At the end of a rating cycle, the settlement of this period begins. Analyze the user's rating behavior, and update the user's influence according to the user's influence calculation formulation. The blockchain issues corresponding rewards to users according to their influence. According to the updated user influence, the item score is updated through the influence weighted rating algorithm, and the next rating cycle begins.

3 Rating Incentive Mechanism

To constrain user behavior, this paper proposes a differentiated rating incentive mechanism based on blockchain. Unlike traditional centralized rating systems, blockchain technology is immutable, open and transparent, making the distribution of scoring rewards more credible. Each user is associated with a unique Ethereum account address, and the smart contract issues token rewards to users at intervals of each rating cycle. The total amount of rewards issued by the blockchain to users in a cycle consists of two parts: each rating user pays an admission fee of 5 tokens to the blockchain prize pool; the blockchain provides the same number of tokens as the total entry fee paid by all participating scoring users in a cycle.

The advantage of this design is that the number of ratings in a rating cycle is proportional to the total amount of rewards issued by the blockchain, saving the overhead of the rating system. The number of rewards issued by the blockchain to users is determined by the proportion of user influence to the total influence of rated users. Users with large influence will receive higher rewards than paying the admission fee. And users with low influence will have a portion of the admission fee confiscated. The reward obtained by user U_i is shown in formulation (12). R_i denotes the number of rewards received by user U_i in a cycle, $T(i)$ is the influence of user i, and n denotes the number of users participating in rating in a cycle. The total amount of rewards issued by the blockchain to users consists of an entrance fee of 5 tokens paid by each user and an equal amount of tokens provided by the system, which is 10n in total.

$$R_i = \frac{T(i)}{\sum\limits_{i=1}^{n} T(i)} \times 10n \tag{12}$$

4 Experiments and Analysis

To verify the validity and universality of the user influence weighting algorithm and the blockchain rating incentive mechanism proposed in this paper. This section designs relevant experiments based on the algorithms proposed in the previous section.

4.1 Experimental Environment

The experiment selects the public dataset MovieLens 1M, which contains 1,000,209 ratings of 3,900 movies by 6,040 users, with a score ranging from 1 to 5, and also includes movie genre information. The dataset required for this paper is constructed in the following ways: (1) filter out the movie with the largest number of ratings (2) calculate the number of ratings owned by all users who rated the movie and filter out the 100 users with the largest number of ratings. (3) Traverse the database and filter out all the movies reviewed by these 100 users. The filtered normal user data set contains 101,559 ratings of 3,462 movies by 100 users.

4.2 Experimental Protocols

The performance of the influence weighted scoring algorithm in real scenarios are tested by gradually adding abnormal users among normal users. The following typical non-normal users were added to give an initial insight into the resistance of the rating algorithm to interference. Add 5 to 50 abnormal users to the data 10 times, and divide the data into 11 groups. The non-normal users are divided into three categories, as shown in Table 3.

Table 3. Categories of non-normal users added in three experiments.

Experiment	Categories of non-normal users
Experiment 1	Rated 2 for all movies
Experiment 2	Rated 10 for all movies
Experiment 2	Rated only one type of movie with a score of 2

Take ten types of movies, the one with the largest number of ratings for each type, and the arithmetic average of the comprehensive scores of ten movies in total, and compare them with the evaluation algorithms of mainstream websites (take the Douban movie scoring algorithm and IMDB TOP250 movie scoring algorithm as examples). Compare the experiment and analyze the trend of score change. The Douban movie scoring algorithm is calculated according to formulation (13).

$$W = \sum_{i=1}^{10} N_i \times i \tag{13}$$

where i denotes the different scores given to the film from 1 star to 5 stars (the number of stars correspondingly multiplied by 2 to convert to a ten-point scale), and N_i denotes the percentage of people who scored i out of the total number of people who scored the film. The scoring algorithm used in the IMDB TOP250 is the Bayesian statistical algorithm, with the formulation (14).

$$W = \frac{V}{V + m} \times R + \frac{m}{V + m} \times C \tag{14}$$

R is the arithmetic mean score of the movie. V is the total number of people who reviewed the movie. m is the minimum number of reviews needed to enter the IMDB Top 250. C is the arithmetic mean score of all movies so far.

4.3   Analysis of Experimental Results

Ratings Immunity Test Results and Analysis

(1) Add 5 to 50 users who rated all movies as 2 to the data in 10 steps, and divide the data into 11 groups. The trend of movie scores is shown in Fig. 2(a). The experimental data shows that before adding non-normal users, the movie scores calculated by the influence weighting algorithm were similar to those calculated by the Douban rating algorithm, with a difference of only 0.015. It shows that the movie score calculated by the influence weighting algorithm is almost equal to the score calculated by the current mainstream movie scoring websites, and has a certain authority. After adding non-normal users to the group, the movie score calculated by the influence weighted algorithm decreased from 8.29 at the beginning to 7.702, a drop of only 0.588. While the score calculated by the Douban algorithm decreased by 2.375 and the IMDB algorithm decreased most significantly, with a 2.414 decrease. From Fig. 2(a), it can be seen that the influence weighted scoring algorithm (red line) has a gentle downward trend with the increase in the number of non-normal users. While the downward trend of the Douban scoring algorithm (black line) and the IMDB scoring algorithm (blue line) is steeper. This shows that the influence weighted scoring algorithm has better anti-interference characteristics than the Douban scoring algorithm and the IMDB scoring algorithm. The calculated score is more realistic.

(2) Add 5 to 50 users who rated all movies as 10 to the data in 10 steps. The trend of movie scores is as follows shown in Fig. 2(b). The experimental data shows that the movie score calculated by the influence weighting algorithm increased from 8.29 at the beginning to 8.49 after adding non-normal users to the group, which only increased by 0.2. While the score calculated by the Douban scoring algorithm increased by 0.693. The IMDB scoring algorithm changed most significantly, with a 1.372 increase in score. As can be seen from Fig. 2(b), the influence weighted scoring algorithm (red line) has a significantly slower score increase trend than the Douban scoring algorithm (black line) and the IMDB scoring algorithm (blue line) as the number of abnormal users increases. This shows that the increase in the proportion of non-normal users has the least impact on the influence weighted scoring algorithm.

(3) Add 5 to 50 users who only rated one type of movie to the data in 10 steps, and the score is 2 points. The trend of movie scores is shown in Fig. 2(c). The experimental results show that the influence weighted scoring algorithm reduces the score from 8.29 to 7.742, only 0.53, with the increase in the proportion of non-normal users. While the Douban scoring algorithm and the IMDB scoring algorithm decreased by 1.375 and 1.506, respectively. As shown in Fig. 2(c), when the number of non-normal users gradually increases, the influence weighted scoring algorithm (red line) has the most gentle decreasing trend and the strongest anti-interference. The

three different scoring algorithms in the three experiments with the increase of the proportion of non-normal users and the comparison of score changes are shown in Fig. 2(d). The influence weighted scoring algorithm (blue) showed the least change in score.

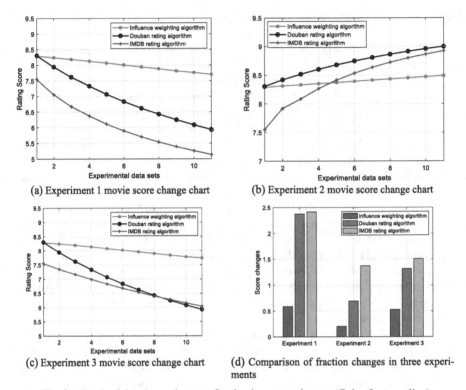

(a) Experiment 1 movie score change chart

(b) Experiment 2 movie score change chart

(c) Experiment 3 movie score change chart

(d) Comparison of fraction changes in three experiments

Fig. 2. Graph of the change in score for the three experiments (Color figure online)

Results and Analysis of the Rating Incentive Mechanism Experiment

According to the above incentive mechanism and experimental method design, use Python for data visualization. Add 10 non-normal users of three different types to the 100 normal users. Do three experiments to compare the income of normal and abnormal users. This proves the feasibility and effectiveness of the incentive mechanism. The income amount of different users are shown in Fig. 3. The experimental results show that in the three experiments, the income amount of normal users (blue histogram) is higher than that of non-normal users (red histogram), and the income amount of normal users is 5 tokens higher than the admission fee. In contrast, the non-normal users all gained less than 5 tokens, suggesting that the incentive mechanism effectively constrains non-normal rating behavior and improves the quality of the overall score.

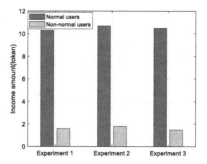

Fig. 3. Amount of revenue for different users in three experiments (Color figure online)

4.4 Safety Analysis

The user's personal information, the user's influence value, and the comprehensive score of each cycle project need to be stored on the chain to achieve the security and reliability of the key data. It is very expensive to open up storage space on the blockchain, so store pictures and text descriptions of projects on IPFS. IPFS is a blockchain-based, permanent, decentralized method of saving and sharing files. It is a point-to-point distributed protocol to solve the redundancy and security of data storage and reduce the pressure on data storage on the chain. A large number of ordinary data such as user ratings are stored on the non-relational database MongoDB, which is more scalable.

5 Conclusion

This paper proposes a user influence weighted rating algorithm, which takes into account the influence of different users on the scoring when calculating the overall score of an item. It effectively improves the anti-interference capability of the rating algorithm. A user influence weighted rating algorithm that includes an incentive mechanism is proposed. While rewarding users who rate seriously, malicious users who interfere with the normal operation of the system are punished. The quality of the ratings is improved to ensure the healthy development of the system ecology. And the effectiveness and feasibility of the algorithm are proved through experiments. The next step can be to carry out research work in the following two aspects: (1) The current influence model in this paper is based on AHP to design the weights of the four factors. But the user rating behavior is greatly influenced by subjective factors, which can be studied with the help of machine learning in the future. (2) The evaluation algorithm only considers the user's rating of the item, not considering the textual content of the user's comments on the item. The next step needs to use a neural network model to identify the textual content and classify it to improve the system's ability to identify malicious users.

Acknowledgement. This work was supported by the National Natural Science Foundation of China under Grant 61862007, Guangxi Natural Science Foundation (No. 2020GXNSFBA297103).

References

1. Lisi, A., De Salve, A., Mori, P., et al.: Rewarding reviews with tokens: an Ethereum-based approach. Futur. Gener. Comput. Syst. **120**, 36–54 (2021)
2. Tang, X., Zhang, K., Su, H.: A research on product innovation performance in the virtual brand community of the internet. Sci. Res. Manage. **40**(06), 224–234 (2019)
3. Liu, X.H.: Current situation and prospect of consumer credit scoring under digital finance. Credit Reference (5), 65–72 (2020)
4. Nie, W.: On film evaluation mechanism in the context of "internet+": a case study of Chinese mainstream film grading websites. Contemp. Cinema (4), 128–133 (2016)
5. Zhigang, W.U., Anjie, S.U., Huijie, L.I., et al.: Comprehensive evaluation method based on analytic hierarchy process and data fusion. J. Henan Univ. (Nat. Sci.) **43**(05), 567–572 (2013)
6. Xiu, Y.N.: The influence of refined cedit evaluation system on consumers' purchase intention. Co-Oper. Econ. Sci. (21), 118–120 (2013)
7. Wang, Y., Shen, H., Tian, Y.B.: Blockchian-based collaborative location privacy protection mechanism. J. Chin. Comput. Syst. (06), 1–10 (2022)
8. Zhu, J.M., Zhang, Q.N., Gao, S., et al.: Privacy preserving and trustworthy federated learning model based on blockchain. Chin. J. Comput. **44**(12), 2464–2484 (2021)
9. Xu, J., Wen, M., Zhang, K.: Improved K-anonymous incentive mechanism scheme combined with blockchain technology. Comput. Eng. Appl. **56**(06), 111–116 (2020)
10. Yang, S.J., Zheng, K., Zhang, H., et al.: K-anonymous location privacy protection scheme based on game theory and blockchain fusion. Appl. Res. Comput. **38**(05), 1320–1326 (2021)
11. Guo, J.P., Li, S.H.: Research on incentive mechanism of public security information sharing based on blockchain under the background of big data. Jiangsu Sci. Technol. Inf. **39**(12), 30–33 (2022)
12. Shi, Q.S., Qin, R., Qiao, P., et al.: Incentive mechanism for data sharing of power material procurement based on consortium blockchain. Electr. Power **55**(03), 87–96 (2022)
13. Du, Y., Wang, H.Y., Hu, Z.X.: Co-construction and sharing of literature and information resources in regional colleges and universities based on blockchain incentive mechanism. J. Libr. Inf. Sci. Agric. **34**(04), 74–83 (2022)
14. Xiong, X., Li, L.X., et al.: Research progress of blockchain in internet of vehicles data sharing. J. Front. Comput. Sci. Technol. **16**(5), 1008 (2022)
15. Yang, X.C., Li, Y.Q.: Study on the willingness of sharing multi-agent data of supply chain from the perspective of blockchain technology. Sci. Technol. Manage. Res. **41**(23), 181–192 (2021)
16. Zhang, L.: Research on financial innovation of supply chain driven by blockchain from the perspective of game theory. Econ. Probl. (04), 48–54 (2019)
17. Bai, Y.F., Zhai, D.X., Wu, D.L., et al.: Blockchainbased optimization strategies for supply chain finance platforms. Financ. Econ. Res. **35**(04), 119–132 (2020)
18. Zhou, L., Deng, Y., Zhang, Y.Y.: Game analysis of supply chain finance for small and micro enterprises' financing based on blockchian. Financ. Theory Pract. (09), 21–31 (2021)
19. Selcuk, A.A., Uzun, E., Pariente, M.R.: A reputation-based trust management system for P2P networks. In: 2004 IEEE International Symposium on Cluster Computing and the Grid, CCGrid 2004, pp. 251–258. IEEE (2004)
20. Wang, S.S.: Discussion on supplier selection of manufacturing enterprise in supply chain. Anhui University of Technology (2010)
21. Sheng, J., Xu, Z.W., Li, R.: A brief discussion on the construction of apost-evaluation model for the operation effect of banking internet online marketing activities. Commer. Econ. Rev. (21), 78–80 (2021)

BloodMan-Chain: A Management of Blood and Its Products Transportation Based on Blockchain Approach

Trieu Hai Le[1]([✉]), Phuc Nguyen Trong[2], Khiem Huynh Gia[2], Hong Khanh Vo[2], Luong Hoang Huong[2], Khoa Tran Dang[2], Hieu Le Van[2], Nghia Huynh Huu[2], Tran Nguyen Huyen[2], The Anh Nguyen[2], Loc Van Cao Phu[2], Duy Nguyen Truong Quoc[2], Bang Le Khanh[2], and Kiet Le Tuan[2]

[1] Can Tho University of Technology, Can Tho City, Vietnam
lhtrieu.0127@gmail.com
[2] FPT University, Can Tho City, Vietnam

Abstract. Today's rapidly increasing demand, product severity, strict age and handling requirements, and operational system preservation requirements, make blood and its products supply chain management become a complex but fundamental matter. On the other hand, blood and its products are one of the products that have not found an alternative and play a massive role in the treatment of diseases today. The current supply is obtained from only the blood of volunteers (known as donors). In particular, depending on the type of product extracted from the blood (e.g. red blood cells, white blood cells, platelets, plasma). They require different procedures and storage environments (e.g. time, temperature, humidity). However, the current blood management processes are done manually - where all data entry is done by medical staff. Furthermore, data related to the entire blood donation process (e.g., blood donors, blood recipients, blood inventories) are centrally stored and are difficult to assess reliably. Ensuring centralised data security is extremely difficult because of stealing personal information or losing data. To address these limitations, in this paper, we introduce the blood management process based on blockchain technology and store data in a decentralized distributed ledger called BloodMan-Chain. Specifically, we target two main contributions: i) we design the BloodMan-Chain model to manage all relevant information about blood and its products based on blockchain technology, and ii) we implement the proof-of-concept of BloodMan-Chain by Hyperledger Fabric and evaluate this in the two scenarios (i.e., data creation and data access).

Keywords: Blood donation · Blockchain · Hyperledger Fabric · blood products supply chain

1 Introduction

Blood consists of many components such as red blood cells, white blood cells, platelets, plasma, and other components extracted from whole blood. Each blood component serves a specific function in the human body; for example, red blood cells help transport oxygen to cells/parts of the body. Therefore, products extracted from the blood have many different uses in medical treatment. Blood is an important medical resource in long-term treatment as well as in emergencies; for instance, blood is often required for trauma victims, types of surgery, organ transplants, childbirth and for patients being treated for cancer, leukemia and anemia. Each unit of blood is very precious and gives a lot of hope to the patients; for example, a liter of blood can sustain the life of a premature baby for two weeks; 40 or more units of blood may be required for the survival of an accidental blood loss trauma victim, or 8 units of platelets per day are the minimum for the treatment regimen of blood cancer patients.

However, all blood collected must be analysed before being transferred to the recipient. One important part of this work is reducing the risk of infection by transmission [1]. Specifically, the common infection mechanism is hepatitis B virus (HBV), human immunodeficiency virus (HIV) and hepatitis C virus (HCV). Besides, new infectious risks continue to emerge, with the more recent identification of mad cow disease, West Nile virus and Creutzfeldt-Jakob disease (vCJD). Reducing this risk increases the complicated process and the blood supply chain management cost.

It can be argued that optimizing the blood supply chain management process is the key to solving the current blood shortage problem in medical facilities. Specifically, the blood donation center will directly contact donors (i.e., in case of emergency) or organize events calling for community blood donations. Donors must undergo a health assessment before donating blood. Then, this raw blood is converted into different components such as red blood cells, white blood cells, platelets, and plasma. The amount of blood and its products after censorship will be partially transferred to medical/health care centers (periodically) or in case of emergency, the rest will be stored in the warehouse. The distribution and storage of blood and its products are also worth considering as each has different requirements and different duration of use.

Besides, the information of blood, recipients, and donors is stored in a centralized server. Specifically, information about donors is divided into many areas. If those donors are not at their residence address, they cannot participate in the system. Also, the stored information is extremely sensitive (i.e., it contains information outside of blood diseases) for both donors and recipients. Centralized storage can lose information or be exploited by malicious users.

Several approaches address these problems by applying Blockchain techniques in the other environment (e.g., cash-on-delivery [2–4], healthcare [5–7], supply chain [8–10], and others [11–13]). In order to solve a series of important issues mentioned above, this paper focuses on building BloodMan-Chain: the management transportation of blood and its products based on blockchain technology. The main contributions of BloodMan-Chain are two-fold. i) we design the BloodMan-Chain model to manage all relevant information about blood and its products based on blockchain technology, ii) we implement the proof-of-concept of BloodMan-Chain by Hyperledger Fabric and evaluate this in several scenarios.

In this paper, the structure is organized as follows. The next section of the paper presents a literature review of relevant issues. The BloodMan-Chain overall architecture is shown in Sect. 3. Section 4 describes the framework and benefits of the proposed system via evaluation. Finally, Sect. 5 dedicates for the conclusions and future research opportunities.

2 Related Work

2.1 Blood Supply Chain Management Systems Not Based on Blockchain Technology

The blood supply chain management integrates core business processes and information. These processes use a central server to handle visibility and traceability issues. The system combines a very complex process that requires synchronization of different operations, leading to randomness and supply chain risk [14,15]. For example, Nagurney et al. [16] proposed a model to minimize costs and risks by expressing the breakdown properties of blood as a supply factor. Armaghan and Pazani [17] introduced a blood supply chain to handle urgent requests from blood units during the Iran earthquake. The main contribution of [17] is to reduce the cost of the blood supply chain network and maximize reliability.

One disadvantage of centralized storage in the above approaches is transparency [18]. To address this issue, Lam et al. [19,20] demonstrated the implementation of a micro services-oriented software architecture for middleware that collects, stores, and traces data in a centralized manner in order to provide data analysis. To apply these advantages, a centralized blood donation management solution has been proposed in [21].

However, the above approaches face many inherent risks for systems based on centralized management. Verifying the reliability of the data is admissible to this approach. In particular, any data displayed is only taken from the data available in the database provided by the central server. Besides, important information that affects the treatment process can be lost if the central server is hacked. This is an extremely dangerous thing for medical/healthcare organizations Due to these dangers, it is urgent to find a decentralized storage solution and increase data authenticity. Blockchain technology can fulfill both of these requirements. The next two sections will summarize blockchain-based management models as well as focus on the blood supply chain management model.

2.2 Blood Supply Chain Management Systems Based on Blockchain Technology

Trieu [22], and Nga [23] propose a cold-blooded supply chain system based on Hyperledger Fabric called BloodChain. The proposed system supports the verification of blood-related transactions from donors to recipients. Moreover, Blood-Chain allows displaying the necessary information during the blood donation process. Similarly, Lakshminarayanan et al. [24] proposed a blood supply chain management system based on Hyperledger Fabric. Similar to BloodChain, it also ensured transparency of donated blood by tracking blood units between donors and recipients. On the other hand, Toyoda et al. [25] have integrated the RFIDs into the blood bags using the EPC stored in the tag. This integration helps to ensure reliability and avoid tampering by tracking products and checking their tags. However, there are some limitations to the solutions above. For example, the verification of the system proposed in [22,23] is incomplete due to the lack of evaluation analysis. Furthermore, the monitoring solution proposed in [25] is limited to monitoring blood bags only, and it does not guarantee the traceability of blood components (i.e., red blood cells, platelets, white blood cells, platelets and plasma). Since different blood components have other shelf lives and storage temperatures, the order of the usage preference should also be considered.

Moreover, the authors in [26] have proposed a decentralized solution based on an Ethereum-based blockchain for blood transport. In their design, certified blood donation centers (CBDCs) are the only privileged members with the right to create smart contracts to manage the entire system. Donors were recognized through an identifier such as their social security number and password. Besides, Peltoniemi et al. [27] discussed how decentralized blockchain was for plasma tracking and management. In more detail, the system stores donors' information before separating their plasma. They then maintain the origin of the plasma and identify poor blood quality. Another solution based on Hypeledger was proposed by Kim et al. [28] to build a blockchain-based blood supply chain management system. In addition to the fact that this solution is based on a private blockchain, to protect the privacy of donors, it only focuses on tracing information related to the supply chain, but it does not track the identity of the donors as well as the part of a blood unit.

To sum up, none of the above blockchain-based solutions guarantees data privacy while providing a robust system for tracking and managing the donated blood supply chain. In addition, the above methods focus only on managing blood information rather than considering their products (i.e., red blood cells, white blood cells, platelets and plasma). This is extremely important because each product has different management conditions and usage times. Our proposed solution captures various aspects of the blood donation system such as collection, distribution, request and delivery of blood units. It ensures that all these aspects are captured decentralized, traceable, accountable, transparent, secure, and auditable. Our solution tracks all necessary stages of the donated blood unit cycle, from donation until consumption.

3   BloodMan-Chain Architecture

To address the traditional approach drawbacks (see Sect. 2), we introduce a blockchain-based blood supply chain management model called BloodMan-Chain. This section will present an overview model including actors and a detailed model of BloodMan-Chain.

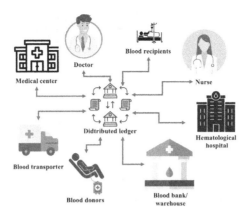

Fig. 1. The overall architecture of the BloodMan-Chain

3.1   Overview Model

The most significant difference between BloodMan-Chain and the traditional model is that all data and retrieval requests are stored in a distributed ledger. Specifically, Fig. 1 shows the actors who have a role in the system. All data related to blood/blood products are stored, but also all requests for data retrieval from medical staff and transporters are stored in a distributed ledger. This increases transparency for the whole system. Data owners quickly know which users can access their data. As for blood records, all information about donors is stored in a distributed ledger. Information about blood type, number of blood donations, time, location, and other personal information are all stored and processed in a decentralized approach. Thereby, medical facilities can retrieve and confirm data related to the treatment process.

Figure 2 details the process of collecting blood donors and blood records decentralized instead of local like traditional approaches. Besides, the data of medical centers/hospitals is also very important. Instead of local storage, BloodMan-Chain aims for a decentralized model where data can be shared for healthcare purposes. Specifically, medical centers/hospitals can exchange information on blood volume and blood products that can be shared in an emergency, reducing requirements for hematology hospitals. In addition, information about patients treated at one healthcare facility in the past can be easily retrieved by another facility, thereby increasing the quality of treatment for patients. Figure 3 shows the steps for storing information of healthcare facilities (i.e., medical records) into a distributed ledger.

3.2   Detailed Model

BloodMan-Chain is presented in Fig. 4 with 8 main actors including medical staff (nurses, doctors), recipients, donors, hospitals (i.e., clinic, medical clinic, mobile blood collection unit), hematology hospital, blood bank, blood transporter, and

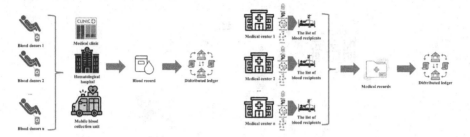

Fig. 2. The storage process of the donor's information in distributed ledger

Fig. 3. The storage process of the medical center's information in distributed ledger

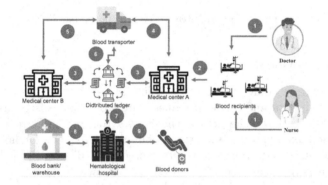

Fig. 4. The detailed architecture of the BloodMan-Chain

distributed ledger. BloodMan-Chain focuses on building a Blockchain-based blood supply chain model, where the transport of blood between medical facilities plays an important role and reduces the pressure on the hematology hospital in the blood collection process from donors. Specifically, step 1 collects the treatment history of recipients through the records of nurses and doctors (i.e., medical staff). All this information will be updated to the hospital where the recipients are being treated (step 2). In the event that the amount of blood and blood products is insufficient during treatment, the hospital will submit a request by updating the current status of blood amount on the distributed ledger. All information about blood volume, blood type and other special requirements are shared with relevant parties in BloodMan-Chain (step 3). At this step, the data of medical facilities is also updated. Blood volumes in a medical facility's system can be shared with other facilities to optimize blood availability. To do that, the establishment needs to update the status and send a request to the transporter about the collection and receipt locations of blood and blood products (steps 4 & 5). After that, the transporter must always update the progress of the shipment on the distributed ledger (step 6). All information about location, time, and order information can be verified and moderated by the stakeholders.

We continue to consider another case where the requested amount of blood and blood products is not available in the system, i.e., the state of blood and blood products is not available. This request is forwarded to the hematology hospital (step 7). Step 8 describes the procedure for checking the amount of blood and blood products in stock. Step 9 contacts the donors to schedule a blood test and donation if the requested amount of blood is unavailable. The list of donors is gathered from previous blood donation sessions and selected the candidates with the closest addresses.

4   Evaluation Scenarios

4.1   Environment Setting

Our paradigm is deployed on the Hyperledger Fabric network maintained inside docker containers. In this section, we measure the performance of chaincode in the two scenarios: initializing (i.e., creating data) and accessing data. The experiments are deployed on Ubuntu 20.01 configuration, core i5 2.7 Ghz, and 8 GB RAM.

To prove the effectiveness of our model, we also define several experiments by exploiting the Hyperledger Caliper[1] that is used to design the test scenarios and collect all the information regarding the performance.

4.2   Results

4.2.1   Data Creation

In this scenario, the study measures the performance of the data initialization function/data created (e.g., blood record) performed through smart contracts. The number of requests sent simultaneously from 2 users[2]. Table 1 shows the execution results of the data initialization/creation function (e.g., blood record). The data initialization/creation script is conducted with two users concurrently making 1000–10000 requests to the system. We measure the parameters of command success/failure, send rate (transaction per second), system latency (i.e., max, min, avg), and throughput (transaction per second) Based on the execution results in Table 1, it can be seen that the number of successful and failed requests is stable (except in the case of 10000 requests). In the first nine scenarios (1000–9000 requests), the number of failed requests ranges from 14861–22283, while the number of successful requests is maintained at a much higher rate, from 27970–34831 requests. However, in the last scenario, the failure rate is higher than the success rate, 37894 and 23672, respectively. This proves that the system works well with the scenario from 9000 requests (i.e., two users - 2 peers). In addition, we also evaluate the latency of the whole system. Specifically, the maximum delay value ranges from 840.33 to 1366.83 s. Besides, the value of send rate ranges from 163.5 to 173.5 (TPS) in the first nine scenarios

---

[1] https://www.hyperledger.org/use/caliper.

[2] We set up one organization with two users and two peers.

and the highest in the tenth scenario with 205.2 (TPS). Similarly, throughput measurements ranged from 30.3 to 38.8 (TPS) in the first nine scenarios and reached a maximum value of 54.1 (TPS) in the last one.

Table 1. Data creation/initialization (e.g., blood record) results in the BloodMan-Chain

#requests	Succ	Fail	Send Rate (TPS)	Max Latency(s)	Min Latency(s)	Avg Latency(s)	Throughput (TPS)
1000	30505	18607	163.7	1251.62	1.21	780.6	31.9
2000	32196	18494	169	1324.05	11.62	831.13	31.3
3000	29776	22283	173.5	1186.66	12.63	762.59	35.2
4000	28269	21524	165.9	1138.24	7.24	722.93	35.1
5000	34362	17087	171.5	1366.83	6.85	837.88	31.5
6000	32828	16485	164.4	1306.1	6.29	818.69	30.8
7000	34831	14861	165.6	1347.43	5.6	843.07	30.3
8000	27970	21070	163.5	1015.16	8.1	666.99	37.4
9000	30158	21698	172.9	1043.7	0.92	677.78	38.8
10000	23672	37894	205.2	840.33	6.17	600.35	54.1

4.2.2 Data Access (Retrieving/Querying)

In the second experiment, we consider the data access (e.g., blood record). We also setup 10 scenarios from 1000 to 10000 requests which access the blood record from 2 users. Table 2 shows the execution results of the data access function (e.g., blood record). Compared with the first solution, the results of 10 scenarios to evaluate the data accessibility of BloodMan-Chain are more balanced. Specifically, the successful data retrieval commands rate accounted for 95% (ranging from 85194 to 111384 requests). The system's latency is also minimal, with a maximum of 8.36 s and a minimum of 0.01 s. The send rate value achieves very high performance from 289.5 to 388.7 (TPS). Similarly, throughput values range from 289.1 to 387.4 (TPS).

Table 2. Data access (e.g., blood record) results in the BloodMan-Chain

#requests	Succ	Fail	Send Rate (TPS)	Max Latency(s)	Min Latency(s)	Avg Latency(s)	Throughput (TPS)
1000	107654	5646	377.7	8.36	0.01	5.79	376.2
2000	108426	5639	380.2	7.9	0.01	6.1	378.8
3000	109370	5964	384.4	8.04	0.01	6.17	382.8
4000	109103	5940	383.5	7.98	0.01	6.17	382
5000	110939	5240	387.3	7.68	0.02	6.02	385.9
6000	110992	5452	388.1	7.86	0.01	6.08	386.9
7000	110769	5271	386.8	7.7	0.01	6	385.2
8000	110329	5844	387.2	8.02	0.01	6.04	385.8
9000	111384	5235	388.7	7.82	0.01	5.95	387.4
10000	85194	1643	289.5	8.09	0.01	2.89	289.1

5   Conclusion

The paper applies the benefits of Blockchain technology (i.e. transparency, decentralized storage) to propose BloodMan-Chain: blood and its products transportation management process based on the limitations of the traditional system. The paper provides a proof of concept based on the Hyperledger Fabric platform, which stores information about blood and blood products during storage and transport. Information is transparently stored for easy verification during transportation and storage. Detailed assessments of the number of successful and failed requests, latency, send rate (TPS), as well as throughput (TPS), analyzed based on the Hyperledger Caliper platform, proved the feasibility of our approach.

In future work, we aim to build an authorization mechanism for stakeholders [29,30] based on ABAC [31–33]. Specifically, users (e.g., donors) are allowed to design policies to manage their personal data (e.g., what data to share and with whom). Moreover, this research result is only the first step toward building a system based on blockchain technology in a real environment. We, therefore, aim to implement the proposed model for export in more complex scenarios where healthcare facility processes have multiple roles and execute off-chain (i.e. out of scope for the current version) of medical facilities.

References

1. Sullivan, P.: Developing an administrative plan for transfusion medicine–a global perspective. Transfusion **45**, 224S-240S (2005)
2. Duong-Trung, N., et al.: Multi-sessions mechanism for decentralized cash on delivery system. Int. J. Adv. Comput. Sci. Appl **10**(9), 563–617 (2019)
3. Ha, X.S., et al.: DeM-CoD: novel access-control-based cash on delivery mechanism for decentralized marketplace. In: 2020 IEEE 19th International Conference on Trust, Security and Privacy in Computing and Communications (TrustCom), pp. 71–78. IEEE (2020)
4. Le, N.T.T., et al.: Assuring non-fraudulent transactions in cash on delivery by introducing double smart contracts. Int. J. Adv. Comput. Sci. Appl. **10**(5), 677–684 (2019)
5. Duong-Trung, N., et al.: On components of a patient-centered healthcare system using smart contract. In: Proceedings of the International Conference on Cryptography, Security and Privacy, pp. 31–35 (2020)
6. Duong-Trung, N., et al.: Smart care: integrating blockchain technology into the design of patient-centered healthcare systems. In: Proceedings of the 2020 4th International Conference on Cryptography, Security and Privacy. ICCSP 2020, pp. 105–109 (2020)
7. Son, H.X., Le, T.H., Quynh, N.T.T., Huy, H.N.D., Duong-Trung, N., Luong, H.H.: Toward a blockchain-based technology in dealing with emergencies in patient-centered healthcare systems. In: Bouzefrane, S., Laurent, M., Boumerdassi, S., Renault, E. (eds.) MSPN 2020. LNCS, vol. 12605, pp. 44–56. Springer, Cham (2021). https://doi.org/10.1007/978-3-030-67550-9_4

8. Khoi, N.H.T., et al.: VBlock - blockchain based traceability in medical products supply chain management: case study in Vietnam. In: International Conference on Artificial Intelligence for Smart Community (2020)

9. Le, H.T., et al.: Patient-chain: patient-centered healthcare system a blockchain-based technology in dealing with emergencies. In: Shen, H., et al. (eds.) PDCAT 2021. LNCS, vol. 13148, pp. 576–583. Springer, Cham (2022). https://doi.org/10.1007/978-3-030-96772-7_54

10. Son, H.X., et al.: Towards a mechanism for protecting seller's interest of cash on delivery by using smart contract in hyperledger. Int. J. Adv. Comput. Sci. Appl. **10**(4), 45–50 (2019)

11. Luong, H.H., Huynh, T.K.N., Dao, A.T., Nguyen, H.T.: An approach for project management system based on blockchain. In: Dang, T.K., Küng, J., Chung, T.M., Takizawa, M. (eds.) FDSE 2021. CCIS, vol. 1500, pp. 310–326. Springer, Singapore (2021). https://doi.org/10.1007/978-981-16-8062-5_21

12. Khoi, N.H.T., et al.: Domain name system resolution system with hyperledger fabric blockchain. In: International Conference on Inventive Computation and Information Technologies (2022)

13. Ha, X.S., Le, T.H., Phan, T.T., Nguyen, H.H.D., Vo, H.K., Duong-Trung, N.: Scrutinizing trust and transparency in cash on delivery systems. In: Wang, G., Chen, B., Li, W., Di Pietro, R., Yan, X., Han, H. (eds.) SpaCCS 2020. LNCS, vol. 12382, pp. 214–227. Springer, Cham (2021). https://doi.org/10.1007/978-3-030-68851-6_15

14. Shahbaz, M.S., et al.: What is supply chain risk management? A review. Adv. Sci. Lett. **23**(9), 9233–9238 (2017)

15. Lavastre, O., et al.: Effect of firm characteristics, supplier relationships and techniques used on supply chain risk management (SCRM): an empirical investigation on French industrial firms. Int. J. Prod. Res. **52**(11), 3381–3403 (2014)

16. Nagurney, A., Masoumi, A.H., Yu, M.: Supply chain network operations management of a blood banking system with cost and risk minimization. Comput. Manage. Sci. **9**(2), 205–231 (2012)

17. Armaghan, N., Pazani, N.: A model for designing a blood supply chain network to earthquake disasters (Case Study: Tehran City). Int. J. Qual. Res. **13**(3), 605–624 (2019)

18. Luong, H.H., et al.: IoHT-MBA: an internet of healthcare things (IoHT) platform based on microservice and brokerless architecture (2021)

19. Thanh, L.N.T., et al.: SIP-MBA: a secure IoT platform with brokerless and microservice architecture (2021)

20. Lam, N.T.T., et al.: BMDD: a novel approach for IoT platform (Broker-less and microservice architecture, decentralized identity, and dynamic transmission messages). In: PeerJ (2022)

21. Alharbi, F.: Progression towards an e-management centralized blood donation system in Saudi Arabia. In: 2019 International Conference on Advances in the Emerging Computing Technologies, pp. 1–5. IEEE (2020)

22. Le, H.T., et al.: BloodChain: a blood donation network managed by blockchain technologies. Network **2**(1), 21–35 (2022)

23. Quynh, N.T.T., et al.: Toward a design of blood donation management by blockchain technologies. In: Gervasi, O., et al. (eds.) ICCSA 2021. LNCS, vol. 12956, pp. 78–90. Springer, Cham (2021). https://doi.org/10.1007/978-3-030-87010-2_6

24. Lakshminarayanan, S., Kumar, P.N., Dhanya, N.M.: Implementation of blockchain-based blood donation framework. In: Chandrabose, A., Furbach, U., Ghosh, A., Kumar M., A. (eds.) ICCIDS 2020. IAICT, vol. 578, pp. 276–290. Springer, Cham (2020). https://doi.org/10.1007/978-3-030-63467-4_22

25. Toyoda, K., et al.: A novel blockchain-based product ownership management system (POMS) for anti-counterfeits in the post supply chain. IEEE Access **5**, 17465–17477 (2017)

26. Çağlıyangil, M., Erdem, S., Özdağoğlu, G.: A blockchain based framework for blood distribution. In: Hacioglu, U. (ed.) Digital Business Strategies in Blockchain Ecosystems. CMS, pp. 63–82. Springer, Cham (2020). https://doi.org/10.1007/978-3-030-29739-8_4

27. Peltoniemi, T., Ihalainen, J.: Evaluating blockchain for the governance of the plasma derivatives supply chain: How distributed ledger technology can mitigate plasma supply chain risks. In: Blockchain in Healthcare Today (2019)

28. Kim, S., Kim, D.: Design of an innovative blood cold chain management system using blockchain technologies. ICIC Express Lett. Part B: Appl. **9**(10), 1067–1073 (2018)

29. Xuan, X.S., et al.: Rew-XAC: an approach to rewriting request for elastic ABAC enforcement with dynamic policies. In: 2016 International Conference on Advanced Computing and Applications, pp. 25–31. IEEE (2016)

30. Son, H.X., Dang, T.K., Massacci, F.: REW-SMT: a new approach for rewriting XACML request with dynamic big data security policies. In: Wang, G., Atiquzzaman, M., Yan, Z., Choo, K.-K.R. (eds.) SpaCCS 2017. LNCS, vol. 10656, pp. 501–515. Springer, Cham (2017). https://doi.org/10.1007/978-3-319-72389-1_40

31. Hoang, N.M., Son, H.X.: A dynamic solution for fine-grained policy conflict resolution. In: Proceedings of the 3rd International Conference on Cryptography, Security and Privacy, pp. 116–120 (2019)

32. Son, H.X., Hoang, N.M.: A novel attribute-based access control system for fine-grained privacy protection. In: Proceedings of the 3rd International Conference on Cryptography, Security and Privacy, pp. 76–80 (2019)

33. Thi, Q.N.T., Dang, T.K., Van, H.L., Son, H.X.: Using JSON to specify privacy preserving-enabled attribute-based access control policies. In: Wang, G., Atiquzzaman, M., Yan, Z., Choo, K.-K.R. (eds.) SpaCCS 2017. LNCS, vol. 10656, pp. 561–570. Springer, Cham (2017). https://doi.org/10.1007/978-3-319-72389-1_44

Deep Learning

A Systematic Comparison on Prevailing Intrusion Detection Models

Jianxuan Liu, Haotian Xue, Junfeng Wang, Shuo Hong, Hao Fu,
and Omar Dib$^{(\boxtimes)}$

Department of Computer Science, Wenzhou-Kean University, Wenzhou, China
{liujia,xueha,wangjunf,hongs,fuh,odib}@kean.edu

Abstract. Modern vehicles have become connected via On-Board Units
(OBUs) involving many complex embedded and networked devices
with steadily increasing processing and communication resources. Those
devices exchange information through intra-vehicle networks to implement various functionalities and perform actions. Vehicles' connectivity has also been extended to external networks through vehicle-to-
everything technologies, enabling communications with other vehicles,
infrastructures, and smart devices. In parallel to the significant increase
in quality of service, the connectivity of modern vehicles raises their
vulnerabilities to cyber-attacks targeting both intra-vehicle and external
networks. To secure communications in vehicular networks, there has
been a consistent effort to develop intrusion detection systems based on
machine learning techniques to detect and ultimately react to malicious
cyber-attacks. In this article, we study several machine learning algorithms, deep learning models, and hyper-parameter optimization techniques to detect vulnerability attacks on vehicular networks. Experimental results on well-known data sets such as CICIDS2017, NSL-KDD,
IoTID20, KDDCup99, and UNSW-NB15 indicate that learning-based
algorithms can detect various types of intrusion detection attacks with
significant performance.

Keywords: Intelligent Transportation Systems · Intrusion Detection
Systems · Machine Learning · Deep Learning · Security

1 Introduction

The Internet of Things (IoT) has shown its vitality in the past decade in many
areas such as the agricultural, medical, transport, and automobile industries [27].
With Covid 19, the connectivity trend has accelerated at a rapid pace driven
by human's need for collaboration, competition, and entertainment through IoT
services. This unprecedented rise in digital connectivity is estimated to soar to an
astonishing 906 billion dollars market value by 2025, with 75.44 billion connected
devices generating 79 Zettabytes (ZB) of data. That said, IoT has been identified
as a crucial component of digital transformation across all sectors. Nowadays,
IoT devices collect, store and process confidential data, making the latter a
precious target for cyber threats [8]. The problem is aggravated by the openness

© The Author(s), under exclusive license to Springer Nature Switzerland AG 2023
H. Takizawa et al. (Eds.): PDCAT 2022, LNCS 13798, pp. 213–224, 2023.
https://doi.org/10.1007/978-3-031-29927-8_17

and distributed nature of the network architecture and the insufficiency of digital security measures. Therefore, there has been a seamless need to develop novel and robust cyber-security measures to monitor, manage and control the security of services and data across the digital domain boundaries.

The Intrusion Detection System (IDS) is developed to examine the IoT network traffic, and identify potential cyber-attacks. An IDS is a monitoring system that analyzes network traffic for suspicious behaviors and issues notifications accordingly. IDSs are used to identify abnormalities with the goal of apprehending hackers before they cause significant network harm. Under its multiple categories, a network-based intrusion detection system (NIDS) is installed at a critical location or points inside the network to monitor incoming and outgoing traffic and search for any suspicious patterns. With the correct placement, NIDS shows critical performance among these aspects:

— monitoring the functioning of routers, firewalls, key management servers, and files used by security controls to detect, prevent, or recover from assaults; — providing administrators with effective methods to tune, arrange, and comprehend essential OS audit trails and other logs that are otherwise tough to monitor or analyze; — establishing a user-friendly interface to ease the system security maintenance process; — including an extensive attack signature database against which patterns from the system can be matched; — recognizing and reporting when the IDS detects that data files have been altered with; — generating instant alerts and notifications when the security is compromised or at risk; — blocking and stopping network intruders or isolating the server under attack.

In recent years, most IDS systems have primarily been based on blockchain technology [7], machine learning (ML) and deep learning (DL) frameworks, established by implementing mature models and algorithms. Due to their dynamic learning nature, those models can be generalized to cope with new types of cyber-attacks, even with complicated and high-dimensional patterns [25]. Furthermore, DL models allow for the training of nonlinear relationships on big datasets in a systematic way. Motivated by their solid capacity and robust behaviors, this work studies the prevailing ML and DL models for detecting various types of network intrusions in vehicular networks. This paper analyses multiple combinations of feature-selection techniques, hyper-parameters optimization, and tuning methods on five frequently referred IDS data sets respectively, aiming at:

(1) discussing the development of traditional ML algorithms and advanced DL models for intrusion detection; (2) presenting a comprehensive analysis of how technical factors such as the optimization algorithm, feature-selection technique, and hyper-parameters affect the intrusion detection results; (3) analyze the robustness of models across several intrusion data sets; (4) proposing a more general and integral IDS solution.

The rest of the paper is organized as follows: Sect. 2 provides a comprehensive review on critical IDS studies (2016–2022). Section 3 elaborates on the research methodology adopted in this study. Section 4 presents the test results of our experimental study with various ML, DL, and HPO methodologies adopted. Section 5 provides conclusions and future directions.

2   Related Work

Machine Learning (ML) models have been widely used for Intrusion Detection (ID) tasks in vehicular ad hoc networks (VANETs). For example, Alshammari et al. [3] applied two ML techniques, K-Nearest Neighbors (KNN) and Support Vector Machine (SVM), to cluster and classify the intrusions in VANETs; the authors demonstrated the ability of their method to detect two specific types of attacks, the DoS and Fuzzy attacks; two car-hacking datasets were used: "DoS dataset" and "fuzzy dataset" provided by the Hacking and Countermeasure Research Lab (HCRL) [13]; authors argued that the intrusion detection technique relies heavily on the analysis of the offset ratio and time interval between the messages request and the response in the CAN. Similarly, Aswal et al. [4] analyzed the applicability of six traditional ML algorithms: Naive Bayes (NB), KNN, Logistic Regression (LR), Linear Discriminant Analysis (LDA), Classification And Regression Trees (CART), and SVM to bot attack detection on the Internet of vehicles (IoV); their performance assessment was done on one dataset (CICIDS2017), with a single type of attacks "bot attack." The authors indicated that the CART model outperforms other algorithms in terms of True Positive Rate (TPR) and False Positive Rate (FPR) and mentioned that the algorithm might not perform uniformly on new configurations and datasets.

Deep Learning (DL) models have also been widely used in IDSs. For example, Yang and Shami [30] proposed a transfer learning and ensemble learning-based IDS for IoV systems; an architecture based on CNN and advanced hyper-parameter optimization techniques were presented; authors demonstrated the high detection rates and F1-scores of their method in both intra-vehicle and external vehicular networks; two well-known public IDS datasets: the Car-Hacking and the CICIDS2017 were considered. In addition, Aloqaily et al. [2] proposed a novel method (D2H-IDS) based on a Deep belief and Decision Tree-based for ID in innovative connected vehicle cloud environments; the deep belief function was interestingly used for data dimensionality reduction, while an ID3-based decision tree technique was used for feature selection and attacks classification purposes. Authors demonstrated via ten simulations the effectiveness of their system through real cyber-security attack scenarios; more specifically, their solution achieved an overall accuracy of 99.43%, with a 99.92% detection rate and 0.96% false positive and a false negative rate of 1.53%. NSL-KDD [5] was the only dataset used in the simulation, and only four types of attacks (DoS, Probe, R2L, U2R) were considered. Motivated by the superiority of ensemble methods, Rashid et al. [20] introduced a tree-based stacking ensemble technique (SET) and tested its effectiveness on two ID datasets (NSL-KDD and UNSW-NB15); the authors highlighted the impact of feature selection techniques on the performance of their model, as well as the additional computation overhead induced by the stacking method. Furthermore, Alkahtani and Aldhyani [1] applied three DL algorithms in the context of a robust ID framework: a CNN, a long short-term memory (LSTM), and a hybrid CNN-LSTM model; the three models were evaluated on the IoTID20 dataset and achieved accuracy as follows: CNN = 96.60%, LSTM = 99.82%, and CNN-LSTM = 98.80%. Intriguingly, the authors enforced dimensionality reduction and employed particle swarm optimization (PSO) to select a subset of relevant features from the network dataset.

To address the availability issue in (VANETs) and to mitigate DDoS attacks, Gao et al. [12] proposed a scalable, reliable, and robust distributed NIDS; authors claimed that handling DDoS attacks requires scalable methods to capture, store and process the big data; to achieve that, they proposed a real-time network traffic collection module and a network traffic detection module; Spark was used to speed up data processing, HDFS to store massive suspicious attacks, and micro-batch data processing model to improve the real-time performance of traffic feature collection. To perform the classification, the authors adopted an RF classifier; NSL-KDD and UNSW-NB15 datasets were used for testing; the experimental results showed that their system reached an accuracy rate of 99.95% and 98.75% and the false alarm rate (FAR) of 0.05% and 1.08%. To tackle the computational complexity issue, Injadat et al. [14] proposed a novel multi-stage optimized ML-based NIDS framework. The authors studied the impact of oversampling and feature selection techniques on their model's performance and time complexity. Their work was evaluated using two ID datasets, the CICIDS 2017 and the UNSW-NB 2015 datasets. Their experiments showed that their model could reduce the training sample size (up to 74%) and feature set size (up to 50%) without compromising the model's accuracy. Likewise, Basati et al. [6] introduced a novel NIDS that uses a lightweight and efficient neural network based on the idea of deep feature extraction. In their model, the input vector of the network is permuted in a 3D space, and its individual values are brought close together, allowing for highly discriminative feature extraction using a small number of layers and convolution filters. As a result, their model significantly consumed less computational power; this feature was relevant for real-time intrusion detection in the context of IoT devices with limited processing capabilities. The model's efficiency was assessed using three popular datasets UNSW-NB15, CICIDS2017, and KDDCup99.

To select the best hyper-parameters for ML and DL models, several optimization techniques have been recently proposed. Unarguably, using the best parameter values for the model significantly impacts the model's performance; however, it often requires deep algorithmic knowledge and appropriate optimization techniques. In this connection, Yang and Shami [29] discussed several available frameworks for hyper-parameter optimization (HPO) problems; the authors presented the application of HPO to ML algorithms and conducted experiments on benchmark datasets to compare different HPOs. To summarize, Bayesian Optimization HyperBand (BOHB) [11] is the recommended choice for optimizing an ML model if randomly selected subsets are highly-representative of the given dataset; otherwise, Bayesian Optimization models (BO) [9] such as Gaussian process (BO-GP), random forest (BO-RF), and tree-structured Parzen estimators (BO-TPE) models [10] are recommended for small hyper-parameter configuration space. Lastly, despite their high computational time, heuristic approaches [16] such as Genetic Algorithm (GA) and PSO [17] are usually the best choice for ample configuration space.

3   Methodology

Since previous studies have partial consideration of IDS development due to the consideration of specific types of cyber-attacks or evaluation of a limited number of datasets [28], this study employs several widely-used datasets for IDS development known as CICIDS2017 [23], NSL-KDD [24], IoTID20 [26], KDDCup99 [15] and UNSW-NB15 [18] to evaluate ML algorithms and advanced DL models. The selected datasets are comprehensive and cover modern network traffic patterns [15,18,23,24,26], which were also proven by some previous IDS studies [19,22]. A taxonomy of the five datasets is presented in Fig. 1.

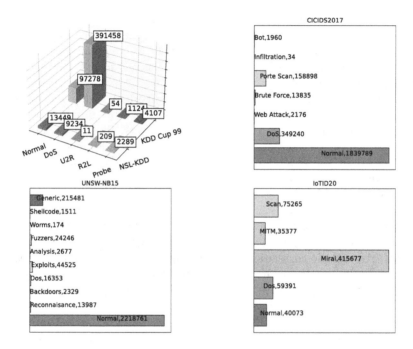

Fig. 1. Distribution of Datasets

The applied learning models fall under two categories: a) traditional ML techniques involving Decision Tree (DT), Random Forest (RF), Ensemble Tree (ET), and XGboost (XG), and b) advanced DL models comprising CNN, VGG16, VGG19, Xception, ResNet, Inception, and InceptionResnet. As for the ML algorithms, the ID framework built in this paper is based on MTH-IDS, A Multitiered Hybrid Intrusion Detection System for the Internet of Vehicles, proposed by Li et al. [28]. This framework includes four stages 1) data processing, 2) features engineering, 3) a signature-based IDS, and 4) an anomaly-based IDS. The steps are intrinsically linked to improving the model accuracy and training efficiency.

In the first stage, a k-means-based cluster sampling method is applied to generate a highly representative subset, followed by a Synthetic Minority Over-sampling Technique (SMOTE) as a means to avoid class imbalance. The cluster sampling consists of grouping the original data points into multiple clusters; then, a proportion of data is sampled from each cluster to form a representative subset. Among clustering algorithms, k-means is used due to its simple implementation and low computational complexity. After clustering, random sampling is applied to each cluster to select a subset of the data as the sampled subset.

To avoid class imbalance, resampling methods are used. This includes random sampling and SMOTE, which can create new instances for the minority classes. Unlike random sampling, which simply replicates the instances and may cause overfitting, SMOTE can synthesize high-quality instances based on the concept of KNN; thus, SMOTE is chosen in the proposed IDS to solve the class imbalance. After obtaining a representative and balanced data set, several additional data preprocessing steps are completed, including transforming categorical features into numerical features using a label encoder and using Z-score to normalize data that often have vastly different ranges.

Data preprocessing can generate a high-quality and highly representative data set; however, obtaining an optimal feature list by appropriate feature engineering can also improve the quality of data sets. Stage two employs an information-gain-based (IG) and a Fast Correlation Based Filter (FCBF) [21] to remove irrelevant and redundant features and then passed to the KPCA model to reduce dimensionality and noisy features further.

The IG method is used as a typical Feature Selection (FS) due to its low computational complexity. Based on the changes in entropy, IG measures how much information a feature can bring to the targeted variable. Although the IG-based FS method eliminates the unimportant features, redundant features may still exist. Among the correlation-based FS algorithms, the FCBF algorithm is selected since it has shown remarkable performance on high-dimensional data sets while retaining informative features. In FCBF, the symmetrical uncertainty (SU) is calculated to measure the correlations between features by normalizing the IG values. Although utilizing IG-FCBF can return a better feature set than only using IG, FCBF has a major limitation: it only calculates the correlation between pairs of features. Still, it does not consider correlations among multiple features. Hence, KPCA is worth to be utilized after implementing the IG-FCBF method. In the third stage, a signature-based IDS is developed to detect known attacks via four-tree-based ML models DT, RF, ET, and XGboost. Subsequently, BO-TPE, PSO, and GA HPO techniques are used and compared to improve the ID accuracy further. In addition to BO-TPE, PSO, and GA techniques [29]. Lastly, an anomaly-based IDS is employed to detect unknown attack patterns, passing the suspicious instances to a CL k-means model to separate attack samples from standard samples effectively. K-means is selected for this task due to the real-time requirements of vehicle-level systems. Ultimately, the detection result of each test sample is returned, which could be a known attack with its type, or a normal packet (see Fig. 1 for the different types of attacks).

A CNN and transfer learning-based IDS is used to apply advanced DL models [30]. This process is divided into three parts orderly data pre-processing, models development, and ensemble models. The first stage transforms datasets into image forms to fit the input requirements. The transformation process starts with data normalization. Since the pixel values of images range from 0 to 255, the data should also be normalized to the scale of 0–255. Quantile normalization is used as the min-max normalization method does not handle outliers well and may cause most data samples to have minimal values. After normalization, the data samples are converted into chunks based on the timestamps and feature sizes of network traffic datasets. Next, the transformed images are labeled based on the attack patterns in the data chunks.

After the pre-processing data procedures, the final transformed image set is generated as the input of CNN models. In the second phase, pretrained but fitted to our datasets CNN, VGG16, VGG19, Xception, ResNet, Inception, Inception-Resnet, and CNN DL models are applied. Similar to ML algorithms, HPO techniques are used to improve the performance of models. After that, phase 3 is executed to select the best DL models as a base for the ensemble learning models. To evaluate the generalizability of models and avoid overfitting, cross-validation and hold-out methods are used in the known attack detection experiments. Moreover, several metrics, including accuracy, precision, recall, and F1-score are used to comprehensively evaluate the performance of the proposed models.

4 Experimental Study

To evaluate our work, the data pre-processing steps and various learning modes were implemented using the Pandas, Scikit-learn, Keras, TenserFlow, and XGBoost libraries in Python3. In contrast, the HPO algorithms were implemented based on Scikit-optimize, Hyperopt, Optunity, and TPOT libraries. Matplotlib and seaborn libraries were used for visualization. The experiments were carried out on a cloud server having the following properties: Ubuntu 20.04.3 LTS, 160 GB of RAM, with Intel(R) Xeon(R) Gold 6330 CPU @ 2.00GHz, and GPU: NVIDIA(R) GeForce(R) RTX 3090 24GB. We have applied the different machine learning and deep learning models on five ID datasets: CICIDS2017, NSL-KDD, IoTID20, KDDCup99, and UNSW-NB15. Each simulation is repeated five times to minimise the bias in the results. The average accuracy of models is presented in Fig. 2. We plot the accuracy in % for the five datasets for each of the models on the X-axis. In addition, for each dataset, we add hatches to the model with the highest accuracy. As can be seen from the Figure 2, machine learning models have, in general, better accuracy than deep learning models. More specifically, the Extra Tree (ET) model has the highest accuracy (99.86%) for the CICIDS2017 dataset. However, VGG16 has the highest accuracy on datasets IoTID20, UNSW-NB15, NSL-KDD, and KDDCup99 with the following accuracy of 100%, 98.23%, and 100.0%, and 99,8%, respectively. Deep learning models such as Resnet, Inception, and Inception-Resnet showed under-fitting behavior and thus mediocre performance due to the lack of training data. It is known that those models are very complex regarding their parameters and thereby require a large amount of data to be efficiently trained. For instance, the stacking model implemented [28] showed less performance than ET, as the stacking does not always guarantee superior performance. Indeed, using one model's output as an input for another might decrease the total efficiency due to local minima issues.

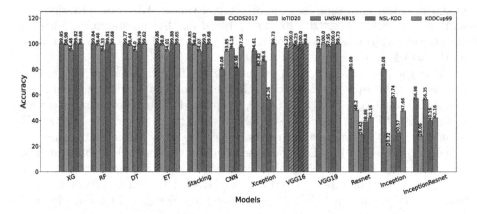

Fig. 2. Average Accuracy of all Models on Different Datasets

We apply BO-TPE, PSO, and GA following the search settings indicated in [29] to assess the impact of Hyper-Parameter Optimisation (HPO) techniques on the various ML models. The effect of HPO techniques on the accuracy of models is presented in Fig. 3 for all datasets; five simulations are used, and the average is computed and plotted for each combination of model, dataset, and HPO technique. As indicated in Fig. 3, the impact of HPO varies and closely depends on the model itself and the characteristics of the dataset. For example, BO-TPE significantly improved the accuracy of XGBoost on the IotID20 dataset; however, it did not help for the UNSW-NB15 dataset. The negative impact (i.e., below 0) in the accuracy means that HPO is acting like a random selection of input parameters; that is, using an HPO or random values for hyper-parameters is equivalent. Having that said, we conclude that non of the HPO techniques is robust enough to handle many algorithms or various datasets. Nonetheless, BO-TPE showed superior or equivalent performance compared to GA and PSO.

For an IDS to be relevant for real-world usage, classifying a typical scenario as normal or attack must be done in real-time. Failure to do so may retard the decision-making process and consequently be dangerous for the application's environment. To tackle this problem, we study the relationship between the model's accuracy and its prediction time for each dataset. Specifically, we plot the time needed for the model to classify an instance against its average accuracy using its corresponding best HPO technique and present the results in Fig. 4. Results indicate that the prediction time for all models is in milliseconds (<0.08

ms), which is suitable for real-time contexts. Interestingly, results also point out a trade-off between accuracy and prediction time. For example, for CICIDS2017, the ET model has the highest accuracy, 99.86; however, XGBoost and DT are the fastest. Similarly, VGG16 and VGG19 have 100% accuracy on the NSL-KDD dataset; however, XGBoost and DT are the fastest. Generally, DL models have the highest accuracy at the expense of higher prediction time due to the complexity of the model (Table 1).

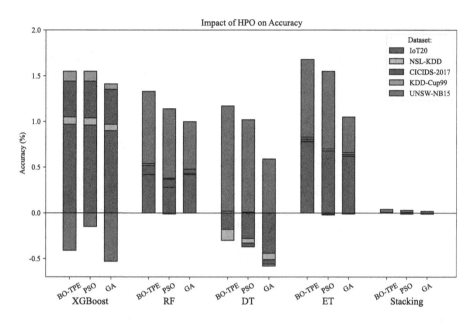

Fig. 3. Comparison of Accuracy Change after Hyper-parameter Optimization

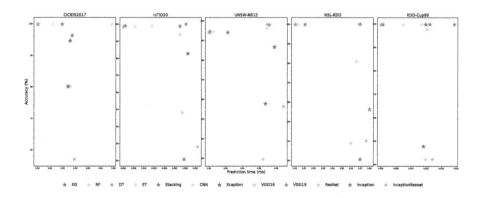

Fig. 4. Average Accuracy and Prediction Time of all Models across Datasets

Table 1. Performance of Best Algorithms for each Dataset

Dataset	Model	Accuracy	Precision	Recall	F1-Score
CIC	ET	99.82±0.03	99.82±0.03	99.82±0.03	99.82±0.03
	VGG16	96.74±0.03	95.87±0.01	96.26±0.03	96.02±0.03
NSL	Stacking	99.88±0.0119	99.88±0.0179	99.88±0.0119	99.88±0.0132
	VGG16	100±0.03	99.86±0.03	99.83±0.02	99.83±0.02
IoT	Stacking	98.82±0.18	98.70±0.17	98.69±0.18	98.69±0.17
	VGG16	100±0.04	93.46±0.03	95.49±0.04	94.18±0.04
KDD	Stacking	99.68 ± 0.06	99.80 ± 0.04	99.61 ± 0.06	99.69 ± 0.04
	VGG16	99.8±0.01	99.82±0.05	99.79±0.04	99.79±0.04
UNS	XGBoost	94.46±0.18	93.79±0.1	93.73±0.18	93.57±0.11
	VGG16	98.23±0.05	96.84±0.04	96.77±0.03	96.44±0.02

To better assess the performance of the two categories of models, ML and DL, we report the three crucial metrics for classification tasks: precision, recall, and F1-score metrics. For each dataset, we only show the metrics of the best model, applied after tuning the parameters with respect to the best HPO technique for each model and dataset. We shorten the name of the dataset in the first column to three letters for presentation purposes. Interestingly, for some datasets such as IotID20, the F1-score does not reflect the high accuracy of the VGG-16 model, which might be a sign of over-fitting or triggered due to imbalanced data. Nevertheless, all the three assessment metrics show the ability of ML and DL to significantly isolate the intrusions even though their robustness is not guaranteed across all the datasets. Evaluating the standard deviations shed light on the steady performance of one particular model on a specific dataset. In this convention, once a dataset is fixed, the performance of a learning model, either ML, or DL, will be robust.

5   Conclusions

The cyber-security field has recently amassed particular focus from the industry and academia due to the increasing reliance of particulars and establishments on the Internet and their rising concerns about the security of their network infrastructures and the privacy of their digital activities. Consequently, substantial resources have been dispensed and allocated to enforce security measures against likely cyber-threats or malicious activities. In this respect, various types of network intrusion detection systems (NIDSs) have been proposed in the literature, mainly based on Machine Learning (ML) and Deep Learning (DL) models. This paper studied several ML and DL algorithms and Hyper-Parameter Optimization (HPO) techniques to detect vulnerability attacks in vehicular networks. Five data sets, CICIDS2017, NSL-KDD, IoTID20, KDDCup99, and UNSW-NB15, were used to assess the performance of models. Results indicate that recent DL models could achieve accuracy close to 100%; however, learning-based models do not automatically inherit the robustness feature. Besides, HPO techniques, despite their expensive computation time, are essential to unleash the notable performance of learning models. Compared to PSO and GA, BO-TPE optimiser performed the best for the HPO. Other models can be explored for future works, particularly combining supervised and unsupervised ML techniques may result in a more remarkable performance in detecting novel types of intrusions. And exploring more feature selection techniques, such as information gain and correlation-based, might be relevant for real-time NIDSs.

References

1. Alkahtani, H., Aldhyani, T.H.: Intrusion detection system to advance internet of things infrastructure-based deep learning algorithms. Complexity **2021** (2021)
2. Aloqaily, M., Otoum, S., Al Ridhawi, I., Jararweh, Y.: An intrusion detection system for connected vehicles in smart cities. Ad Hoc Netw. **90**, 101842 (2019)
3. Alshammari, A., Zohdy, M.A., Debnath, D., Corser, G.: Classification approach for intrusion detection in vehicle systems. Wirel. Eng. Technol. **9**(4), 79–94 (2018)
4. Aswal, K., Dobhal, D.C., Pathak, H.: Comparative analysis of machine learning algorithms for identification of bot attack on the internet of vehicles (IoV). In: 2020 International Conference on Inventive Computation Technologies (ICICT), pp. 312–317. IEEE (2020)
5. Bala, R., Nagpal, R.: A review on KDD CUP99 and NSL NSL-KDD dataset. Int. J. Adv. Res. Comput. Sci. **10**(2) (2019)
6. Basati, A., Faghih, M.M.: DFE: efficient IoT network intrusion detection using deep feature extraction. Neural Comput. Appl. 1–21 (2022)
7. Diallo, E.H., Dib, O., Agha, K.A.: The journey of blockchain inclusion in vehicular networks: a taxonomy. In: 2021 Third International Conference on Blockchain Computing and Applications (BCCA), pp. 135–142 (2021). https://doi.org/10.1109/BCCA53669.2021.9657050
8. Diallo, EH., Dib, O., Al Agha, K.: A blockchain-based approach to track traffic messages in vehicular networks. In: Gupta, G., Wang, L., Yadav, A., Rana, P., Wang, Z. (eds.) Proceedings of Academia-Industry Consortium for Data Science. AISC, vol. 1411, pp. 345–362. Springer, Singapore (2022). https://doi.org/10.1007/978-981-16-6887-6_28
9. Eggensperger, K., et al.: Towards an empirical foundation for assessing bayesian optimization of hyperparameters. In: NIPS workshop on Bayesian Optimization in Theory and Practice, vol. 10 (2013)
10. Eggensperger, K., Hutter, F., Hoos, H., Leyton-Brown, K.: Efficient benchmarking of hyperparameter optimizers via surrogates. In: Proceedings of the AAAI Conference on Artificial Intelligence, vol. 29 (2015)
11. Falkner, S., Klein, A., Hutter, F.: BOHB: robust and efficient hyperparameter optimization at scale. In: International Conference on Machine Learning, pp. 1437–1446. PMLR (2018)
12. Gao, Y., Wu, H., Song, B., Jin, Y., Luo, X., Zeng, X.: A distributed network intrusion detection system for distributed denial of service attacks in vehicular ad hoc network. IEEE Access **7**, 154560–154571 (2019)
13. Hacking, Lab, C.R.: Can intrusion dataset (2017). http://ocslab.hksecurity.net/Dataset/CAN-intrusion-dataset

14. Injadat, M., Moubayed, A., Nassif, A.B., Shami, A.: Multi-stage optimized machine learning framework for network intrusion detection. IEEE Trans. Netw. Serv. Manag. **18**(2), 1803–1816 (2020)
15. Lippmann, R., Haines, J.W., Fried, D.J., Korba, J., Das, K.: The 1999 DARPA off-line intrusion detection evaluation. Comput. Netw. **34**(4), 579–595 (2000). https://doi.org/10.1016/S1389-1286(00)00139-0
16. Nan, Z., Wang, X., Dib, O.: Metaheuristic enhancement with identified elite genes by machine learning. In: Chen, J., Hashimoto, T., Tang, X., Wu, J. (eds.) Knowledge and Systems Sciences. KSS 2022. CCIS, vol. 1592, pp. 34–49. Springer, Singapore (2022). https://doi.org/10.1007/978-981-19-3610-4_3
17. Nematzadeh, S., Kiani, F., Torkamanian-Afshar, M., Aydin, N.: Tuning hyperparameters of machine learning algorithms and deep neural networks using metaheuristics: a bioinformatics study on biomedical and biological cases. Comput. Biol. Chem. **97**, 107619 (2022)
18. Nour, M., Slay, J.: UNSW-NB15: a comprehensive data set for network intrusion detection systems (UNSW-NB15 network data set). In: IEEE Military Communications and Information Systems Conference (MilCIS), pp. 1–6 (2015)
19. Panigrahi, R., Borah, S.: A detailed analysis of cicids2017 dataset for designing intrusion detection systems. Int. J. Eng. Technol. **7**(3.24), 479–482 (2018)
20. Rashid, M., Kamruzzaman, J., Imam, T., Wibowo, S., Gordon, S.: A tree-based stacking ensemble technique with feature selection for network intrusion detection. Appl. Intell. 1–14 (2022)
21. Senliol, B., Gulgezen, G., Yu, L., Cataltepe, Z.: Fast correlation based filter (FCBF) with a different search strategy. In: 2008 23rd International Symposium on Computer and Information Sciences, pp. 1–4 (2008). https://doi.org/10.1109/ISCIS.2008.4717949
22. Sharafaldin, I., Habibi Lashkari, A., Ghorbani, A.A.: A detailed analysis of the CICIDS2017 data set. In: Mori, P., Furnell, S., Camp, O. (eds.) Information Systems Security and Privacy. ICISSP 2018. CCIS, vol. 977, pp. 172–188. Springer, Cham (2019). https://doi.org/10.1007/978-3-030-25109-3_9
23. Sharafaldin, I., Lashkari, A.H., Ghorbani, A.A.: Toward generating a new intrusion detection dataset and intrusion traffic characterization. ICISSp **1**, 108–116 (2018)
24. Tavallaee, M., Bagheri, E., Lu, W., Ghorbani, A.A.: A detailed analysis of the KDD CUP 99 data set. In: 2009 IEEE Symposium on Computational Intelligence for Security and Defense Applications, pp. 1–6. IEEE (2009)
25. Thakkar, A., Lohiya, R.: A survey on intrusion detection system: feature selection, model, performance measures, application perspective, challenges, and future research directions. Artif. Intell. Rev. 1–111 (2021)
26. Ullah, I., Mahmoud, Q.H.: A scheme for generating a dataset for anomalous activity detection in IoT networks. In: Goutte, C., Zhu, X. (eds.) Advances in Artificial Intelligence. Canadian AI 2020. LNCS, vol. 12109, pp. 508–520. Springer, Cham (2020). https://doi.org/10.1007/978-3-030-47358-7_52
27. Ullah, I., Mahmoud, Q.H.: Design and development of a deep learning-based model for anomaly detection in iot networks. IEEE Access **9**, 103906–103926 (2021)
28. Yang, L., Moubayed, A., Shami, A.: MTH-IDS: a multitiered hybrid intrusion detection system for internet of vehicles. IEEE Internet Things J. **9**(1), 616–632 (2021)
29. Yang, L., Shami, A.: On hyperparameter optimization of machine learning algorithms: theory and practice. Neurocomputing **415**, 295–316 (2020)
30. Yang, L., Shami, A.: A transfer learning and optimized CNN based intrusion detection system for internet of vehicles. arXiv preprint arXiv:2201.11812 (2022)

Enhancing Resolution of Inferring Hi-C Data Integrating U-Net and ResNet Networks

Fengjiao Zhao[1,2], Na Li[1,2], and Cheng Zhong[1,2(✉)]

[1] School of Computer, Electronics and Information, Guangxi University, Nanning 530004, Guangxi, China
1913392073@st.gxu.edu.cn, {lina123,chzhong}@gxu.edu.cn
[2] Key Laboratory of Parallel and Distributed Computing Technology in Guangxi Universities, Nanning 530004, Guangxi, China

Abstract. The Hi-C data is the basis of three-dimensional chromosome structure reconstruction. In this paper, a method integrating U-Net and ResNET network is proposed to infer high resolution Hi-C data from existing low-resolution Hi-C data. Firstly, the U-Net is used as the backbone network to make full use of the shallow layer details and deep layer essential features of Hi-C data. Secondly, the residual module is introduced into the coding path and decoding path of the network to increase the depth of the model and prevent network degradation. Finally, the down sampling is used to reduce the calculation amount to decrease the required running time for the network model. The experimental results on real datasets showed that the proposed method had better performance than existing methods, and the inferred high resolution Hi-C data was closer to the real Hi-C data.

Keywords: Chromosome 3D structure · Hi-C data · Convolution neural network · Inferring algorithm

1 Introduction

Studying gene expression mechanism has become an important issue in modern molecular biology [1]. The 3D structure and function of genes are mutually unified. The spatial interaction of gene loci on chromosomes is an important factor affecting gene expression [2]. Advance of high-throughput chromosome conformation capture (Hi-C) technology makes it possible to systematically study the spatial structure of chromosomes [3]. The interaction frequency data obtained from Hi-C experiment is usually represented by a two-dimensional matrix whose rows and columns denote the number of sub-boxes of DNA sequence and values represent total amount of interaction frequencies of corresponding sub-boxes. The resolution of an interaction frequency matrix is equal to the size of a sub-box, and its common value range is from 1Kb to 1Mb. Chromosome substructures such as A/B chromatin compartment [4], topological association domain [5], and chromatin ring [6] can be observed from heat map for the interaction frequency matrix,

H. Takizawa et al. (Eds.): PDCAT 2022, LNCS 13798, pp. 225–237, 2023.
https://doi.org/10.1007/978-3-031-29927-8_18

which significantly expands people's understanding of 3D structure of chromosomes and gene regulation mechanism.

The Hi-C data with high resolution will provide more in-depth insights for studying chromosome three-dimensional structure. However, the linear increase of resolution of Hi-C data requires the quadratic increase of sequencing depth [7]. It means that the cost of obtaining high-resolution Hi-C data will be very expensive. Currently, the Hi-C data with high resolution is only available in a limited number of cell lines [8]. In practical applications, most available Hi-C data are of low resolution [3]. It is necessary to develop computing methods to infer high-resolution Hi-C data from existing low-resolution Hi-C data.

Over the years, researchers have proposed some methods for inferring high-resolution Hi-C data. The HiCPlus [9] infers high-resolution Hi-C data from low-resolution Hi-C data by constructing a three-layer convolution neural network (CNN) model and the mean square error for supervised learning. The Boost-HiC [10] uses length of the shortest path in interaction frequency matrix to express relationship for the Euclidean distance between chromosome segments and interaction frequency value to infer the unknown interaction frequency value according to the known value in the matrix. The HiCNN [11] consists of global and local residual modules and it uses GPU computing to accelerate network convergence for inferring Hi-C data. The hicGAN [12] uses the generative countermeasure network (GAN) [13] and cross entropy as the backbone network and loss function respectively to achieve better inferring results via the game confrontation between the discriminator and generator. The DeepHiC [14] uses the mixture of Mean Square Error (MSE) loss, total change loss, perception loss, and cross entropy loss as the loss function and Swish function as the incentive layer of the network to infer Hi-C data. The HiCSR [15] infers HiC data by combining GAN with denoising self-encoder. The denoising self-encoder performs unsupervised learning, uses the interaction frequency matrix randomly added with white noise as the input, and outputs the predicted matrix with no noise. The SRHiC [16] improves the residual module to strengthen the nonlinearity of the network and applies small convolution kernel to multiple convolution to reduce the network parameters when inferring HiC data. The inferring HiC data method CEHiCLE [17] applies conditional generative confrontation network and variational self-encoder as backbone network and generator respectively, and uses antagonism loss, variational loss, insulation loss inspired by chromosome topology, and MSE loss as loss function.

In recent years, some inferring Hi-C data methods use convolutional neural network models, which have better reconstruction performance than traditional methods. However, most of these inferring methods using a single network model have long training period and difficult to converge. In order to solve the above problems and obtain high-resolution Hi-C data more quickly and accurately, this paper proposes an inferring method integrating two kinds of network models.

2 Method

2.1 Data Preprocessing

The experimental data used are from the dataset registered with GSE63525 in the high-throughput gene expression database, which contains Hi-C data of multiple different types of cells [8]. The Hi-C data of chromosomes labeled with no. 1, 2, and 422 in human B lymphocyte dataset GM12878 were selected as the training set of our model SR-UNet and Hi-C data of chromosome labeled with no.3 were selected as validation set. Three datasets were selected as test sets in the experiment. They are human erythroleukemia cell K562 dataset, human embryonic lung fibroblast IMR90 dataset, and mouse B lymphocyte ch12-lx data set, in which each human cell data set contains 22 autosomes and mouse cell dataset contains 19 autosomes. The resolution of all above datasets is 100 kb, and the comparison quality is larger or equal to 30.

The GSE63525 dataset includes paired terminal sequences generated in the Hi-C experiment and their corresponding interaction frequency values. In this paper, all paired terminal sequences are first traversed to determine size of the interaction frequency matrix, all known interaction frequency values are filled into corresponding positions in the matrix in turn, and the original interaction frequency matrix is generated. Our method SR-UNet conducts supervised learning to infer high-resolution interaction frequency matrix from low-resolution interaction frequency matrix. In order to obtain labeled samples for model training and evaluation, the original interaction frequency matrix is regarded as the real high-resolution interaction frequency matrix, and the original matrix is randomly down sampled to simulate the low-resolution interaction frequency matrix. During training process, the network model first infers the simulated high-resolution matrix from the down sampled matrix, and adjusts the network parameters by comparing difference between the simulated high-resolution matrix and real high-resolution matrix. In principle, the resolution of the original matrix is the same as that of the random down sampled matrix. But in the practical application of Hi-C data, people think that after down sampling, the interaction frequency matrix is sequenced in shallower depth, which is usually processed as low-resolution data [18]. Similar to [9], the down sampling rate is set to 1/16.

Because the number of chromosomes is small and the size of a single chromosome is large, all interaction frequency matrices are partitioned into smaller sub-matrices to expand the dataset, in which the size of the sub-matrix is set to 40 × 40. There is no overlap between any two sub-matrices. After partitioning, the high-resolution sub-matrix and low-resolution sub-matrix corresponding to the training set and verification set are spliced, and their order is disordered so that the distribution of each batch of samples in the model training process is as close as possible to the real data to achieve better training results.

2.2 Structure of Network Model

The details of the network model constructed by our method SR-UNet are shown in Fig. 1, in which its input data and output data are low and high resolution interaction frequency sub-matrixes respectively, n is the number of sub-matrixes for one training, $p \times p$ is size of each sub-matrix, "1" means that input channel is single one.

The SR-UNet comprises of five network layers. In the first layer, a convolution kernel of size 3×3 is used to expand the number of input channels to 64, the residual module is connected to deepen the network, and the maximum pooled core of size 2×2 with stride of 2 is used to perform down sampling to reduce the scale of characteristic map to $p/2 \times p/2$. The structure of the second layer is the same as that of the first layer, the number of its channels is enlarged to 128 via the same network layer, and the scale of characteristic diagram is reduced to $p/4 \times p/4$. In the third layer, a convolution kernel of size 3×3 is used to enlarged the number of its channels to 256, and four residual modules are added to further enhance the network depth for better feature extraction. In the fourth layer, the up sampling is performed by the deconvolution kernel of size 2×2 with stride of 2 and 128 channels, the scale of characteristic image is enlarged to $p/2 \times p/2$, the output characteristic graph of the second layer is spliced with the output of deconvolution kernel through jump connection, the number of channels is enlarged to 256 and the number of channels is reduced to 128 by the convolution kernel of size 3×3 again, and the data fusion details and essential features are realized by following a residual module to deepen the network. In the fifth layer, its structure is the same as that of the fourth layer, the number of its channels is reduced to 64 and the scale of the characteristic map is restored to $p \times p$. Finally, the convolution kernel of scale 1×1 is used to reduce the number of channels to 1, and the inferred high-resolution Hi-C data are outputted. The residual module is consisted of two convolution kernels of size 3×3 each, and the input and output characteristic maps are superimposed through jump connection to prevent degradation problems with increase of network depth. Each convolution layer in the model is followed by ReLU as a nonlinear activation function to slow down disappearance of the gradient and accelerate convergence of the network.

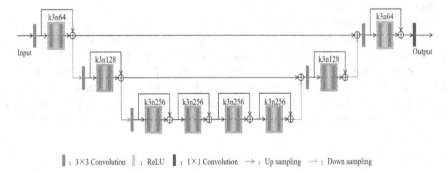

■ : 3×3 Convolution ▌ : ReLU ▎ : 1×1 Convolution → : Up sampling → : Down sampling

Fig. 1. Model architecture of the SR-UNet

The SR-UNet uses the early stop mechanism [19] to prevent over fitting to ensure that the trained model has good performance in both training set and test set. When the training period exceeds 20, the loss function value of the model is tested on the verification set every other period. If the loss function value is greater than the last test result, the training is stop. The mean square error function (MSE) has the advantages of smooth continuity, everywhere derivability, and unique stable solution, etc. The SR-UNet uses MSE as the loss function to measure difference between the data inferred from the network model and the real data during training process. Given a set $\{x_i, x_i' | i = 1,2,...,k\}$, where x_i is the i-th low resolution interaction frequency sub-matrix, x_i' is the i-th real high resolution interaction frequency sub-matrix related to x_i, $i = 1,2,...,k$. The value of MSE loss function value is computed by formula (1).

$$loss = \frac{1}{k} \sum_{i=1}^{k} (F(x_i) - F(x_i')) \tag{1}$$

where $F(x_i)$ is a mapping function to be learned from x_i, to x_i', $i = 1,2,...,k$.

2.3 Algorithm

Let *model* represent the network model to be trained in SR-UNet, D denote the number of network layers, C_i be the number of convolution cores of the i-th layer network, K_i^2 represent the size of convolution kernel of the i-th layer network, M_i^2 denote the scale of the output characteristic graph of the i-th layer network, D_{train} and D_{valid} represent the training set and validation set respectively, in which they contain multiple one-to-one low and high-resolution interaction frequency matrices for training model parameters, D_{test} denote the test set which contains multiple low resolution interaction frequency matrices to test generalization ability of the model, D_{result} represent the result inferred by the trained model on D_{test}, $p \times p$ denote size of the partitioned sub-matrix, E be the maximum training times, and S indicate the training times of starting early stop detection. By integrating U-Net [20] and ResNet [21], the algorithm SR-UNet describes the procedure for enhancing resolution of inferring Hi-C data.

Algorithm 1 SR-UNet

Input: *Model*, D_{train}, D_{valid}, D_{test}, p, B, E, S;

Output: D_{result};

Begin

1: Partition matrix pair in $D_{train} = \{(L_i, H_i)|i = 1,2,...,n\}$ and $D_{valid} = \{(L_j, H_j)|j = 1,2,...,m\}$ to sub-matrix pairs of size $p \times p$, (L_i, H_i) represents the i-the low resolution interaction frequency matrix in D_{train}, (L_j, H_j) denotes the j-th high-resolution interaction frequency matrix in D_{valid}, n and m denote the number of D_{train} and D_{valid} respectively;

2: Initialize the model parameters in *model*;

3: $Max\_Loss \leftarrow 10^{20}$;

4: for $i=0$ to E-1 do

5:   $i \leftarrow i+1$;

6:   $head \leftarrow 0$;

7:   while $head<n-B$ do

8:     $tail \leftarrow head+B$;

9:     Select samples between (L_{head}, H_{head}) and (L_{tail}, H_{tail}) in D_{train} to train *Model*;

10:    Update the model parameters in *model*;

11:    $head \leftarrow tail+1$;

12:   end while

13:   if $i \geq S$ then

14:     Compute *Loss* with D_{valid} as input in *Model* according to formula (1);

15:     if $Loss<Max\_Loss$ then $Max\_Loss \leftarrow Loss$ else break;

19:   end if

20:   end if

21: end for

22: Partition each matrice in D_{test} into sub-matrices $D_{test} = \{L_i|i = 1,2,...,q\}$ of size $p \times p$, L_i is the i-th low resolution interaction frequency sub-matrix and q is the amount of D_{test};

23: The trained *Model* is used to predict the samples in D_{test} and then the inferred high resolution interaction frequency matrix dataset D_{result} is reported

End.

3 Experiment

The experiment was carried out on computing node CX50-G30 with CPU 2 × Intel Xeon Gold 6230 and main memory 192 GB DDR4 of Sugon 7000A parallel cluster system at Guangxi University. The running operating system is CentOS 7.4. The algorithm was implemented by Python3.7 programming. The Tensorflow2.0 was used to train and test the network model.

In the experiment, we evaluated our method SR-UNet with other methods HiCNN [11], SRHiC [16], and U-Net [20] without ResNet [21] fusion. Similar to [11], we used the loss function value (*loss*) and Pearson correlation coefficient value (*PCC*) [22] to evaluate the convergence of these inferred methods on the verification dataset, and we applied the root mean square error (*RMSE*) [23], *PCC*, and running time to evaluate the result accuracy and efficiency of the inferred methods on the test dataset. The *RMSE* and *PCC* are used to measure the difference and correlation between high-resolution

Hi-C data obtained by inferred methods and real Hi-C data, respectively. The smaller the *RMSE*, and the larger the *PCC*. It indicates that the inferred high-resolution Hi-C data have higher accuracy, they are more similar to real Hi-C data.

3.1 Experiment of Training Network Model

Similar to [24], Xavier was used to initialize the parameters of SR-UNet and U-Net, the random gradient descent method SGD [25] was applied to update the weights and offsets for the models, the learning rate during training was set to 0.001, the number of samples in each batch was set to 128, and the maximum number of training times was set to 100. When the maximum number of training times is reached or the early stop mechanism is triggered, the training model will be stopped. For HiCNN and SRHiC, their default parameter values were used to conduct the experiment, and the early stop mechanism similar to SR-UNet was also used to prevent over fitting.

Firstly, the human B lymphocyte data set GM12878 was used to train SR-UNet, HiCNN, SRHiC, and U-Net, in which the interaction frequency matrix of chromosomes labeled with no. 1, 2, 4–22 was used as the training set and the interaction frequency matrix of chromosome labeled with no. 3 was used as the verification dataset. During training process, the values of *loss* and *PCC* of the four methods on the verification dataset are shown in Fig. 2 and Fig. 3 respectively.

It can be seen from Fig. 2 that in first nine training periods, the *loss* values of the four inferring methods on the verification dataset were decreased rapidly, in which the decreased speed of the values *loss* of SR-UNet was the fastest, followed by the decreased speed of the *loss* values of U-Net, HiCNN, and SRHiC respectively.

On the other hand, with increase of training times, the decline trend of *loss* value of the four inferring methods has become slow, and the descending and ascending are carried out alternately in the process of decline, but the overall trend remains declining. In this process, the *loss* value of SR-UNet is totally lower than that of other three methods, and the up-down floating change of SR-UNet is also smaller that of the other three methods. After several times of training, the four methods, especially the SR-UNet, converged to a stable state, the *loss* value remained basically unchanged, and finally finished training. Compared with HiCNN, SRHiC, and U-Net, the final *loss* value of SR-UNet on the verification dataset is smaller. It illustrates that SR-UNet has faster convergence speed, stronger stability, and better training results.

Figure 3 shows that with increase of training times, the values of *PCC* obtained by SR-UNet, HiCNN, SRHiC, and U-Net on the verification dataset are first increased rapidly, then are slowed down, and finally are approached to 1. On the other hand, the values of *PCC* of SR-UNet are always greater than that of the other three methods. This indicates that the high-resolution interaction frequency matrix inferred by SR-UNet is more similar to the real interaction frequency matrix on the verification dataset. This is because the SR-UNet makes full use of the shallow layer details and deep layer essential characteristics of low resolution Hi-C data and applies the residual module to increase the network depth and prevent network degradation.

From Figs. 2 and 3, we can see that at beginning of training, our method SR-UNet and other three methods HiCNN, SRHiC, and U-Net were converged quickly and the training effect of the model was also greatly improved, with advancement of the training process,

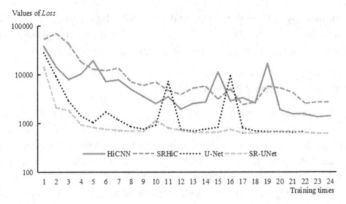

Fig. 2. Values of Loss of the four inferring methods on the verification dataset

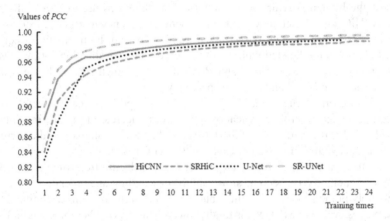

Fig. 3. Values of *PCC* of the four inferring methods on the verification dataset

the convergence speed of the four inferring methods was decreased and the improvement of the training effect also became slow, and finally the convergence was stopped and the training effect was no longer improved. This illustrates that the convergence of *loss* value during training of inferring methods is positively correlated with the quality of training effect.

3.2 Experimental Results on Human Cell Datasets

In order to evaluate the performance of the network model, 22 autosomes in the K562 dataset of human red and white blood disease cells were used as the test dataset to compare the inferred quality and running speed of the method SR-UNet with other three methods HiCNN, SRHiC, and U-Net. Table 1 shows the values of *RMSE* and *PCC* for the high-resolution Hi-C data inferred by four methods and real Hi-C data and Table 2 shows the required time for running the four inferred methods on the K562 dataset, in which "chr" represents "chromosome".

Table 1. Values of *RMSE* and *PCC* obtained by four inferring methods on dataset K562

Method	chr1		chr2		chr3		chr4		chr5		chr6		chr7		chr8	
	RMSE	*PCC*	*RMSE*	*PCC*	*RMSE*	*PCC*	*RMSE*	*PCC*	*RMSE*	*PCC*	*RMSE*	*PCC*	*RMSE*	*PCC*	*RMSE*	*PCC*
HiCNN	17.92	0.996	12.87	0.994	13.90	0.995	11.87	0.994	14.85	0.994	18.49	0.996	19.65	0.995	16.39	0.994
SRHiC	27.45	0.995	18.39	0.994	20.39	0.995	16.65	0.994	21.37	0.994	27.80	0.995	28.74	0.995	23.36	0.994
U-Net	10.30	0.997	7.96	0.996	8.75	0.996	7.94	0.995	9.17	0.996	10.96	0.997	11.25	0.997	9.92	0.996
SR-UNet	10.06	0.997	7.78	0.996	8.50	0.996	7.76	0.995	8.98	0.996	10.65	0.997	10.95	0.997	9.64	0.996

Method	chr9		chr10		chr11		chr12		chr13		chr14		chr15		chr16	
	RMSE	*PCC*	*RMSE*	*PCC*	*RMSE*	*PCC*	*RMSE*	*PCC*	*RMSE*	*PCC*	*RMSE*	*PCC*	*RMSE*	*PCC*	*RMSE*	*PCC*
HiCNN	22.60	0.995	18.87	0.995	19.58	0.995	18.51	0.995	16.16	0.992	16.81	0.994	25.26	0.995	29.58	0.995
SRHiC	33.90	0.994	27.34	0.994	29.20	0.995	27.61	0.995	21.34	0.992	23.76	0.993	37.61	0.995	44.09	0.994
U-Net	11.20	0.998	11.38	0.996	11.64	0.997	11.15	0.996	10.04	0.995	11.25	0.995	15.00	0.997	16.04	0.997
SR-UNet	10.88	0.998	11.07	0.997	11.47	0.997	10.91	0.997	9.65	0.995	10.97	0.995	14.62	0.997	15.75	0.997

Method	chr17		chr18		chr19		chr20		chr21		chr22	
	RMSE	*PCC*	*RMSE*	*PCC*	*RMSE*	*PCC*	*RMSE*	*PCC*	*RMSE*	*PCC*	*RMSE*	*PCC*
HiCNN	29.15	0.995	20.01	0.995	37.73	0.996	30.44	0.995	42.45	0.996	86.79	0.995
SRHiC	44.10	0.995	29.49	0.995	61.64	0.995	47.05	0.994	64.87	0.995	130.03	0.994
U-Net	16.25	0.997	13.27	0.996	21.12	0.998	19.05	0.997	22.66	0.997	38.82	0.999
SR-UNet	15.91	0.997	12.91	0.996	20.78	0.998	18.43	0.997	22.41	0.997	35.88	0.999

It can be seen from Table 1 that among the four inferred methods, for the chromosomes labeled with no. 1–22 of K562 dataset, the method SR-UNet obtained the lowest value of *RMSE*, the method U-Net achieved the second lowest value of *RMSE*, the method HiCNN obtained the third lowest value of RMSE, and the method SRHiC had the highest value of *RMSE*. For the Pearson correlation coefficient, the four inferring methods had good performance for the chromosomes labeled with no. 1–22 of K562 data set, all the *PCC* values were greater than 0.99. Although the *PCC* of U-Net is almost the same as that of SR-UNet, on the whole, the *PCC* of SR-UNet was still higher than that of the other three methods. This is because the SR-UNet combines the advantages of RESNet and UNet, and increasing network depth will better fit the data characteristics and pay attention to the low and high-level information of Hi-C data at the same time. This indicates that the method SR-UNet can infer high resolution Hi-C data with higher quality from the dataset K562.

We can see from Table 2 that for the chromosomes labeled with no. 1–20 of the dataset K562, the required time for running U-Net was the least, the required time for running SR-UNet was the second least, the required time for running SRHiC was the third least, and the required time for running HiCNN was the most among the four inferring methods. In addition, for the chromosomes labeled with no. 21 and 22 of the dataset K562, the required time for running SR-UNet was the same as that of running U-Net, which was remarkably less than that of running SRHiC and HiCNN. Because the SR-UNet integrates RESNet in U-Net to increase the number of network layers to improve inferring quality, it spends more running time than the U-Net as a whole. The

Table 2. Required time (s) of running four inferring methods on dataset K562

Method	chr1	chr2	chr3	chr4	chr5	chr6	chr7	chr8	chr9	chr10	chr11
HiCNN	168.9	186.2	131.6	121.9	105.0	96.3	83.4	68.2	39.6	55.8	55.6
SRHiC	84.8	93.7	63.3	57.9	51.7	46.9	43.9	35.0	18.9	27.9	28.0
U-Net	47.9	53.5	34.9	32.8	29.2	25.5	21.8	18.5	11.0	15.5	16.3
SR-UNet	53.5	59.4	39.2	36.1	32.8	28.5	24.7	20.9	12.3	17.3	17.5

Method	chr12	chr13	chr14	chr15	chr16	chr17	chr18	chr19	chr20	chr21	chr22
HiCNN	55.5	28.4	25.1	20.6	19.0	19.1	17.6	9.5	10.3	3.8	3.7
SRHiC	28.1	14.5	12.7	10.3	9.5	9.6	8.7	4.7	5.1	1.8	1.8
U-Net	15.5	8.0	7.3	6.1	5.6	6.3	5.0	2.5	3.2	1.1	1.1
SR-UNet	17.4	9.1	8.2	6.8	6.2	6.2	5.6	2.9	3.3	1.1	1.1

SR-UNet uses down sampling to reduce the complexity of the model, so it spends much less inferring time than SRHiC and HiCNN.

To further compare the inferred quality and efficiency of running the four methods, Tables 3 and 4 show their values of *RMSE* and *PCC* and running time on the human embryonic lung fibroblast IMR90 dataset, where "chr" denotes "chromosome". From Table 3 we can see that the performance of the four methods on dataset IMR90 was similar to that on dataset K562. Among the four methods, SR-UNet obtained the lowest *RMSE* for chromosomes labeled with no. 1–22 of dataset IMR90. In addition, The *RMSE* of SR-UNet are close to that of U-Net, which were significantly lower than those of HiCNN and SRHiC. The *PCC* of SR-UNet were close to that of U-Net for chromosomes labeled with no.1–22 of dataset IMR90. On the whole, the *PCC* of SR-UNet was the highest, followed by that of U-Net and HiCNN, and the *PCC* of SRHiC was the lowest. The reason why the performance of HiCNN is better than that of SRHiC is that its network depth is greater than that of SRHiC, and it can better fit the data characteristics. The results show that the Hi-C data inferred by SR-UNet from dataset IMR90 had higher accuracy and is more similar to the real Hi-C data.

The results in Table 4 show that for the chromosomes labeled with no. 122 of dataset IMR90, the required time of running U-Net and SR-UNet was the least and the second least respectively among the four inferring methods. Although the running time of SR-UNet was a little more than that of running U-Net, SR-UNet improved the inferred quality by building a network model with more layers. The running time of SRHiC was much less than that of running HiCNN because the number of network model layers of SRHiC was less and its structure was simpler than that of HiCNN.

To sum up, compared with three methods HiCNN, SRHiC and U-Net, the method SR-UNet can obtain the minimum values of *RMSE* and the maximum values of *PCC*, its inferred high-resolution Hi-C data was closer to the real Hi-C data, and its running speed was also faster. This is because the method SR-UNet full plays to the advantages

Table 3. Values of RMSE and PCC obtained by four inferring methods on dataset IMR90

Method	chr1 RMSE	PCC	chr2 RMSE	PCC	chr3 RMSE	PCC	chr4 RMSE	PCC	chr5 RMSE	PCC	chr6 RMSE	PCC	chr7 RMSE	PCC	chr8 RMSE	PCC
HiCNN	21.16	0.994	19.31	0.994	20.52	0.994	19.48	0.993	22.03	0.994	22.34	0.994	22.43	0.994	24.33	0.994
SRHiC	28.15	0.993	25.87	0.993	27.46	0.993	25.56	0.993	29.00	0.993	30.12	0.993	29.83	0.992	32.45	0.993
U-Net	9.44	0.997	8.91	0.997	9.58	0.997	9.42	0.996	10.22	0.996	10.55	0.997	10.61	0.996	11.29	0.997
SR-UNet	9.27	0.997	8.80	0.997	9.45	0.997	9.28	0.996	10.05	0.996	10.44	0.997	10.47	0.996	11.21	0.997

Method	chr9 RMSE	PCC	chr10 RMSE	PCC	chr11 RMSE	PCC	chr12 RMSE	PCC	chr13 RMSE	PCC	chr14 RMSE	PCC	chr15 RMSE	PCC	chr16 RMSE	PCC
HiCNN	28.28	0.995	26.59	0.994	28.12	0.994	26.14	0.994	27.78	0.994	31.42	0.994	35.06	0.995	36.05	0.994
SRHiC	38.14	0.993	35.63	0.993	37.65	0.993	35.55	0.993	36.85	0.994	42.78	0.993	48.65	0.994	46.81	0.992
U-Net	12.74	0.997	12.28	0.997	12.51	0.997	12.29	0.997	13.33	0.996	14.10	0.997	15.51	0.997	15.39	0.997
SR-UNet	12.62	0.997	12.07	0.997	12.31	0.997	12.08	0.997	13.21	0.996	13.98	0.997	15.30	0.997	15.26	0.997

Method	chr17 RMSE	PCC	chr18 RMSE	PCC	chr19 RMSE	PCC	chr20 RMSE	PCC	chr21 RMSE	PCC	chr22 RMSE	PCC
HiCNN	40.36	0.994	32.23	0.994	43.16	0.993	44.91	0.994	50.37	0.995	66.58	0.994
SRHiC	54.75	0.992	43.30	0.993	58.49	0.992	61.11	0.992	67.81	0.994	90.16	0.992
U-Net	16.84	0.997	15.46	0.996	18.58	0.997	20.24	0.997	22.63	0.997	26.20	0.997
SR-UNet	16.49	0.997	15.25	0.997	18.27	0.997	19.48	0.997	22.19	0.997	25.87	0.997

Table 4. Required time (s) of running four inferring methods on dataset IMR90

Method	chr1	chr2	chr3	chr4	chr5	chr6	chr7	chr8	chr9	chr10	chr11
HiCNN	172.5	190.1	126.0	114.2	100.8	90.9	79.4	65.5	41.6	57.2	56.9
SRHiC	85.2	93.6	63.4	57.5	51.1	46.0	39.9	33.0	21.0	28.1	28.2
U-Net	49.2	54.6	36.2	32.9	29.9	25.7	22.0	18.5	11.8	16.0	15.9
SR-UNet	53.9	59.5	39.2	35.8	32.9	28.5	24.5	20.9	13.3	17.5	17.5

Method	chr12	chr13	chr14	chr15	chr16	chr17	chr18	chr19	chr20	chr21	chr22
HiCNN	56.5	29.5	25.7	21.2	19.3	19.6	18.1	9.7	10.4	3.3	3.2
SRHiC	28.1	14.4	12.8	10.5	9.4	9.4	8.7	4.9	5.3	1.5	1.7
U-Net	15.9	8.4	7.7	6.6	5.6	6.0	5.1	2.7	3.0	1.0	1.0
SR-UNet	17.4	9.0	8.2	6.9	6.2	6.1	5.5	2.9	3.2	1.1	1.1

of U-Net and RESNET, and constructs a network model with a large number of layers but low complexity, it can make full use of the surface layer details and deep layer essential characteristics of low resolution Hi-C data in the training process, and its inferred high-resolution Hi-C data has higher accuracy and less running time.

4 Conclusion

The proposed inferring method uses U-Net as the backbone network to make full use of shallow layer details and deep layer essential features of Hi-C data, introduces the residual module to coding and decoding paths of network to increase the depth of the model and prevent network degradation, and the down sampling is used to reduce the amount of calculations to decrease the required running time for the network model. The proposed method had better performance than existing methods, and the inferred high-resolution Hi-C data was closer to real Hi-C data. The work will provide support of higher resolution Hi-C data for chromosome 3D structure reconstruction. The future work is to investigate impact of different loss functions, network model layers, and residual module structure on quality of inferring high-resolution Hi-C data.

Acknowledgments. This work is supported by the National Natural Science Foundation of China under Grant No. 61962004, and the Innovation Project of Guangxi Graduate Education (No.YCSW2021020).

References

1. Armingol, E., Officer, A., Harismendy, O., et al.: Deciphering cell-cell interactions and communication from gene expression. Nat. Rev. Genet. **22**(2), 71–88 (2021)
2. Cao, C., Hong, P., Huang, X., et al.: HPV-CCDC106 integration alters local chromosome architecture and hijacks an enhancer by three-dimensional genome structure remodeling in cervical cancer. J. Genet. Genomics **47**(8), 437–450 (2020)
3. Oluwadare, O., Highsmith, M., Cheng, J.: An overview of methods for reconstructing 3-D chromosome and genome structures from Hi-C data. Biol. Proced. Online **21**, 7 (2019)
4. Zheng, X., Zheng, Y.: CscoreTool: fast Hi-C compartment analysis at high resolution. Bioinformatics **34**(9), 1568–1570 (2018)
5. Szabo, Q., Bantignies, F., Cavalli, G.: Principles of genome folding into topologically associating domains. Sci. Adv. **5**(4), eaaw1668 (2019)
6. Grubert, F., Srivas, R., Spacek, D.V., et al.: Landscape of cohesin-mediated chromatin loops in the human genome. Nature **583**(7818), 737–743 (2020)
7. Eagen, K.P.: Principles of chromosome architecture revealed by Hi-C. Trends Biochem. Sci. **43**(6), 469–478 (2018)
8. Rao, S.S.P., Huntley, M.H., Durand, N.C., et al.: A 3D map of the human genome at kilobase resolution reveals principles of chromatin looping. Cell **159**(7), 1665–1680 (2014)
9. Zhang, Y., An, L., Xu, J., et al.: Enhancing Hi-C data resolution with deep convolutional neural network HiCPlus. Nat. Commun. **9**(1), 750 (2018)
10. Carron, L., Morlot, J.B., Matthys, V., et al.: Boost-HiC: computational enhancement of long-range contacts in chromosomal contact maps. Bioinformatics **35**(16), 2724–2729 (2019)
11. Liu, T., Wang, Z.: HiCNN: a very deep convolutional neural network to better enhance the resolution of Hi-C data. Bioinformatics **35**(21), 4222–4228 (2019)
12. Liu, Q., Lv, H., Jiang, R.: hicGAN infers super resolution Hi-C data with generative adversarial networks. Bioinformatics **35**(14), i99–i107 (2019)
13. Creswell, A., White, T., Dumoulin, V., et al.: Generative adversarial networks: an overview. IEEE Signal Process. Mag. **35**(1), 53–65 (2018)
14. Hong, H., Jiang, S., Li, H., et al.: DeepHiC: a generative adversarial network for enhancing Hi-C data resolution. PLoS Comput. Biol. **16**(2), e1007287 (2020)

15. Dimmick, M.: HiCSR: a Hi-C Super-Resolution Framework for Producing Highly Realistic Contact Maps. University of Toronto, Toronto (2020)
16. Li, Z., Dai, Z.: SRHiC: a deep learning model to enhance the resolution of Hi-C data. Front. Genet. **11**, 353 (2020)
17. Highsmith, M., Cheng, J.: VEHiCLE: a variationally encoded Hi-C loss enhancement algorithm for improving and generating Hi-C data. Sci. Rep. **11**(1), 8880 (2021)
18. Kong, S., Zhang, Y.: Deciphering Hi-C: from 3D genome to function. Cell Biol. Toxicol. **35**(1), 15–32 (2019). https://doi.org/10.1007/s10565-018-09456-2
19. Raskutti, G., Wainwright, M.J., Yu, B.: Early stopping and non-parametric regression: an optimal data-dependent stopping rule. J. Mach. Learn. Res. **15**(1), 335–366 (2014)
20. Ronneberger, O., Fischer, P., Brox, T.: U-net: convolutional networks for biomedical image segmentation. In: Navab, N., Hornegger, J., Wells, W., Frangi, A. (eds) Proceedings of 2015 International Conference on Medical Image Computing and Computer-assisted Intervention, pp.234–241 (2015) https://doi.org/10.1007/978-3-319-24574-4_28
21. He, K., Zhang, X., Ren, S., et al.: Deep residual learning for image recognition. In: Proceedings of the 2016 IEEE Conference on Computer Vision and Pattern Recognition. IEEE, pp.770–778 (2016)
22. Asuero, A.G., Sayago, A., Gonzalez, A.: The correlation coefficient: an overview. Crit. Rev. Anal. Chem. **36**(1), 41–59 (2006)
23. Chai, T., Draxler, R.R.: Root mean square error (RMSE) or mean absolute error (MAE)?- arguments against avoiding RMSE in the literature. Geoscientific Model Develop. **7**(3), 1247–1250 (2014)
24. Cai, N.: Study and Application of Convolution Kernel Weight Initialization Method in Convolution Neural Network (in Chinese). Ningxia University, Yinchun (2019)
25. Li, X., Orabona, F.: On the convergence of stochastic gradient descent with adaptive stepsizes. In: Proceedings of the 22nd International Conference on Artificial Intelligence and Statistics, Naha, Okinawa, Japan. PMLR, vol. 89, pp. 983–992 (2019)

Detecting Network Intrusions with Resilient Approaches Based on Convolutional Neural Networks

Fatin Neamah Ridha Al-Sarray[1,2] and Maslina Zolkepli[2(✉)]

[1] Directorate of Studies and Planning and Follow-Up, Ministry of Higher Education and Scientific Research, Baghdad, Iraq
[2] Department of Computer Science, Faculty of Computer Science and Information Technology, Universiti Putra Malaysia, 43400 Serdang, Selangor, Malaysia
masz@upm.edu.my

Abstract. An anomaly-dependent network intrusion detection method is proposed by presenting a hybrid of Convolutional Neural Network (CNN) and Long Short Term Memory (LSTM) approaches where it detects various network attacks by training a CNN on the NSL-KDD dataset. The proposed approach is able to automatically discovers significant traits without human intervention and achieves higher accuracy in detecting attacks which can improve the performance of intrusion detection systems. The CNN-LSTM approach is applied to detect attacks such as DoS, Probe, U2R, and R2L, and identify normal traffic at the same time. The experimental result reached a low false-positive rate, a high accuracy rate, and a low time average. The results show that the proposed approach outperformed the current state-of-the-art by 4.69% in terms of accuracy and conventional CNN achieved a greater accuracy of roughly 3% compared to the current approach, which amounted to 98.95%, 97.81%, and 94.26% respectively. The consistency of the simulated attacks is unequal which leads to issues in the prediction, therefore, additional efforts to collect more consistent traffic on unusual attacks are required. The proposed approach is targeted to be applied as an effective tool for solving complex classification problems such as NIDS.

Keywords: Intrusion Detection System · Deep Learning · CNN · LSTM · NSL-KDD Dataset

1 Introduction

An Intrusion Detection System (IDS) manages networks by detecting network intrusions, which is a necessary component of today's network security systems [1]. IDSs can detect networks that have previously been breached, as well as networks that are currently being breached [2]. Suspicious activity on the network is flagged and alerted to the network administrator. IDSs may be split into two categories: anomaly and normal detection. An efficient detection system must first set the intrusion's characteristics, then match the criteria to find the intrusion. Normal detection technique relies on knowledge, where

H. Takizawa et al. (Eds.): PDCAT 2022, LNCS 13798, pp. 238–248, 2023.
https://doi.org/10.1007/978-3-031-29927-8_19

it has a high degree of accuracy and a low proportion of false alarms. However, the development of a feature library is needed in order to identify unknown threats.

Anomaly detection has a baseline that specifies the network's usual behavior. Anomaly detection is able to quickly identify any deviations in network activity induced by an intrusion. Detection of innovative and unknown assaults is more effective using anomaly detection. Before an alert is triggered, it compares the violation to the baseline [3].

IDSs are categorized into 3 categories, namely the host intrusion detection system (HIDS), network intrusion detection system (NIDS) [1], and hybrid intrusion detection system (HYIDS). The two intrusion detection systems may be combined to create an all-encompassing solution. The hybrid system is more efficient than traditional intrusion detection systems previous. NIDS and HIDS are often combined by organizations [4].

In order to construct an effective IDS, an ideal IDS must be able to identify each attack type precisely. Therefore, the dataset should include a large variety of attack types in common [5].

2   Deep Learning Applications in Network Intrusion Detection

Malware assaults are detected using machine learning techniques such as instance-based learning that use certain similarity measures to classify data. Other approaches include the K-Nearest Neighbor (KNN) and Self Organizing Map (SOM) families as well as support vector machine (SVM) [6].

The application of deep learning methods in intrusion detection has lately gained a lot of attention as it outperforms more traditional methods. There are few papers in the literature demonstrating the effectiveness of deep learning in multiclass classification, making it an uncommon problem [7]. CNN [8] and LSTM [2] are two popular deep learning algorithms. The ability of CNN to extract local characteristics from data and use spatial abstraction and generalization to its advantage is one of its greatest strengths. The combination of CNN and LSTM models is more stable than the use of CNN and LSTM models independently [9].

Deep-learning techniques are employed to implement the CNN model using the CSE-CIC-IDS2018 dataset [10]. The evaluation method was by comparing the proposed model with the RNN model. Whereas the results of the experiment indicated that the proposed CNN model performs better than the RNN model on the CSE-CIC-IDS2018 dataset.

By combining an N-gran technique with Deep Convolutional Neural Network, a method for detecting DGA-based domain names by evaluating the domain's character strings was introduced [11] where they used bigram and trigram representations to produce evaluation findings for several forms of DGA. The average accuracy was 94.15% for 2-g and 98.29% for 3-g. N-gram-based techniques, on the other hand, are computationally costly and language-dependent.

Intrusion Detection System (IDS) based on deep learning [12] customizes the parameters of the IDS on the NSL-KDD dataset utilizing a cluster configured with Spark to shorten the training process. For the intrusion detection model, Bidirectional Long Short

Term Memory (LSTM) networks are utilized. BiDLSTM leverages every available information in the network and also offers context to the network, which is not possible with a traditional LSTM. The suggested model's accuracy was compared to that of regular LSTM and GRU networks, BiDLSTM beat several other newly presented techniques by 91.36% and 82.05%.

RNNIDS [13] uses RNN to detect and produce difficult patterns in assaults showing that RNNs may be used to produce novel, previously undetected variants of assaults as well as the most complicated malware's synthetic signatures to improve detection rates. RNNs may also be used to produce harmful datasets including unknown malware variants, which can be used to improve the design of an NIDS.

One of the main issues in the intrusion detection field is the low accuracy of identifying possible attacks. Another major issue is the long and complex procedures used to identify attacks. For example several CNN models [2, 14, 15] have been introduced with high accuracy but are more complex and require additional time to identify attacks. Furthermore, the proposed CNN-LSTM model reaches higher accuracy with less processing time and less complexity which makes it advantageous in production environments.

3   Application of CNN-LSTM on NSL-KDD Dataset

CNN model architecture is used for intrusion detection binary classification. An input layer, two levels of convolution and pooling, three completely connected layers, and an output layer make up the single model. VGG-19 is a trained Convolutional Neural Network from the Visual Geometry Group at the University of Oxford's Department of Engineering Science. The number of layers with trainable weights is represented by VGG 19. VGG-19 is made up of 16 convolutional layers and three fully linked layers (Input Layer, Hidden Layer, and Output Layer). The convolution neural network receives a fixed-size (224 * 224 RGB) picture as input, indicating that the matrix was of shape (224, 224, 3). The picture is passed through a series of convolutional (Conv.) layers, each of which contains filters with a very narrow receptive field of (3 * 3), the smallest size that can capture the concepts of left/right, up/down, and center portion.

The proposed method implements a model to classify the network traffic into five categories, and they are as follows: (DoS, U2R, R2L, Probe, and Normal). The traffic can be one of these categories. Since these attacks are large and many small attacks can be a type of attack that matches one of these well-known attacks. Attacks are categorized into one of the 5 classifications mentioned earlier. In addition, the model will classify (Normal and Abnormal) network traffic which enables administrators to identify assaults even if they are unknown.

3.1   NSL-KDD Dataset Overview

The dataset contains many attacks that are binary and multiclass. For the binary classification, the dataset contains 52.16% records of normal traffic and 47.84% of abnormal traffic (i.e. malicious traffic) with regards to multiclass attacks, the dataset contains attacks of four different categories of attacks, such as DoS, R2L, Probe, and U2R.

Since the 4 attacks are well-known attacks and they have always innovative methods to compromise networks, the attacks are categorized into one of the mentioned attacks (DoS, Probe, U2R, and R2L) and the list will assist in identifying the attacks into one of these categories.

Prior to the proposed model, there is a need to perform preprocessing techniques to enhance the data quality before introducing it to the model. This will reduce processing time and increase the accuracy of the model. The technique used in this research for preprocessing the data before feeding it to the model is the "StandardScaler" technique. This technique subtracts the mean from the features and scales to unit variance [16]. The mathematical equation for this approach is:

$$S = \frac{x - m}{Std} \tag{1}$$

where m resembles the training samples' mean when it's available but if the mean is not available (i.e. mean = False) then $m = 0$, the Std refers to the standard deviation of the training samples. If the standard deviation = False, then the value of $Std = 1$.

In addition to the standard scaler, labeling the categories and changing the labeling to numeric labeling is key to properly identifying the categorization done by the model in later stages. For example, in multi-classification 5 categories were added (Normal, Dos, Probe, R2L, and U2R) to the data frame and each category is represented in a number from 0–4 respectively.

Moreover, some column features were excluded from the training as they are not considered. For example, the difficulty column was dropped and not taken into consideration as it is not helpful in categorizing the network traffic. Additionally, certain records were eliminated since they were not regarded to be part of any assault, such as entries with the following values in the service column; (aol, harvest, http_2784, http_8001, red_i, urh_i, printer, and rje).

3.2 Proposed CNN-LSTM Model

The model characteristics used for both CNN and CNN-LSTM models are batch size, epoch number, loss, and optimizer. The size of the batch denotes the number of data inserted in each iteration, whereas the epoch number represents the number of times the model train on the dataset, there is a premium number that can give the best training accuracy. Loss is used to measure the model performance using one of several algorithms. Finally, the optimization algorithm is shown in Table 1.

The proposed model is based on the Convolutional Neural Network approach. The model contains two convolutional layers, max-pooling and dropout layers after each convolutional, and finally, flatten and dense layers for the output classification. IDS network traffic data will be given as input to CNN models.

The first layer starts with the input layer which accepts 32 input and gives output 32 × 1 i.e. the same as the input. However, in the second layer, the input is 32 × 1 but the output is a 32 × 64 matrix. For the subsequent layers, some of the input and output data for each layer is changing and some are still the same. However, unlike the previous layers, the output layer (flatten, dense, and what follows that) converts the matrix into one-dimensional data for preparing it for the final classification in the last Dense layer.

Table 1. Model Parameters

Parameter	Value
Batch size	32
Epoch number	20
Optimization algorithm	Adam
Loss	Categorical_crossenthropy

Table 2 depicts the details of the proposed model. The Layer column describes which layer was added to the model. The parameter column describes the parameter customized in that particular layer. Lastly, the value column describes the assigned value for that particular parameter. For example, with stride = 3 and a kernel size of 32 whereas padding = "same" and relu for activation function.

Table 2. Proposed model parameters settings.

Layer	Parameter	Value
Conv1D	kernel_size	64
	strides	3
	padding	Same
	activation	relu
MaxPooling1D	pool_size	2
Convolution1D	kernel_size	128
	strides	3
	padding	same
	activation	relu
LSTM	Output size	70
Dropout	rate	0.1
Dense	units	5
	activation	softmax
Total Parameters		81,035

CNN Model Architecture

The model is implemented for evaluation purposes and Table 3 describes the parameters and the layers used to implement the model similar to the proposed model details mentioned above.

The proposed CNN model is used to train each sub-dataset. The testing set is made up of 20% of the NSL-KDD train. Whereas another CNN model is used to compare the

Table 3. CNN Model Parameter Settings

Layer	Parameter	Value
Conv1D	kernel_size	32
	strides	3
	padding	Same
	activation	relu
MaxPooling1D	pool_size	2
Dropout	rate	0.5
Convolution1D	kernel_size	64
	strides	3
	padding	same
	activation	relu
MaxPooling1D	pool_size	2
Dropout	rate	0.5
Flatten		
Dense	units	256
	activation	relu
Dropout	rate	0.5
Dense	units	5
	activation	softmax
Total Parameters		138,949

outcome to each other to evaluate the performance of the proposed model. The NSL-KDD is divided into 80% training and 20% testing, the testing part is used to perform the validation. The classification's output will be in the form of four different formats. Accuracies, Confusion Matrix, Classification Report (Accuracy, Precision, Recall, support, and F1-score).

To properly test the proposed model, this part compares the LSTM proposed model to more sophisticated approaches for both CNN models and traditional machine learning algorithms. The proposed CNN-LSTM Model is compared mainly to both the CNN model and the highest accuracy reached by other studies like BiDLSTM, STL, RNN, and more.

Accuracy is the main criteria used to compare to other machine learning and CNN approaches, but for the state-of-the-art approach that has the highest accuracy, additional criteria are also considered for evaluation (which is mentioned in the Evaluation section).

4 Experiment and Results

4.1 CNN Model Experiment

After implementing the CNN model, Table 4 describes the summary of that particular model. The training of the NSL-KDD dataset is performed where the total number of layers in the model is 2 layers. Each layer has maxpooling and dropout layer. Whereas the last layer contains Flatten and Dense layers to flatten the data for the final classification.

Table 4. Custom CNN model summary.

Layer (type)	Output Shape	Param #
conv1d 6 (Conv1D)	(None, 32, 32)	128
max_pooling1d_3 (MaxPooling 1D)	(None, 16, 32)	0
dropout_1 (Dropout)	(None, 16, 32)	0
convid_7 (Conv1D)	(None, 16, 64)	6208
max_poolingid_4 (MaxPooling 1D)	(None, 8, 64)	0
dropout_2 (Dropout)	(None, 8, 64)	0
flatten (Flatten)	(None, 512)	0
dense_1 (Dense)	(None, 256)	131328
dropout_3 (Dropout)	(None, 256)	0
dense_2 (Dense)	(None, 5)	1285
Total params: 138,949 Trainable params: 138,949 Non-trainable params: 0		

After constructing the CNN model using Keras library, the summary of each layer is shown above. The total parameters used in the detection is 138,949 parameters.

The results presented in Table 5 show the correct classifications for each metric, namely Precision, Recall, F1-score, and Accuracy. It is the report summary of the CNN model after performing the evaluation metrics for each category in the dataset. For example, Normal traffic has a precision of 97% in the model results, whereas DoS has a 96% precision.

Table 5. Evaluation metrics CNN model.

	Precision	Recall	F1-score	Accuracy
Normal	97%	99%	98%	97.81%
DoS	96%	97%	96%	
Probe	99%	98%	99%	
R2L	0%	0%	0%	
U2R	93%	71%	81%	

4.2 CNN-LSTM Model Experiment

The first layer contains a Conv1D layer with maxpooling without a dropout layer unlike the previous CNN model which had a dropout layer. Another difference is the final conv1D layer contains LSTM, dropout and dense layers, whereas the previous model contains two dense and 2 dropout layers. Finally, the total number of parameters is less than the previous CNN model which is 81,035 parameters. Table 6 shows the summary of the CNN-LSTM model.

Table 6. CNN-LSTM model summary.

Layer (type)	Output Shape	Param #
conv1d_8 (Conv1D)	(None, 32, 64)	256
max_pooling1d_5 (MaxPooling 1D)	(None, 16, 64)	0
conv1d_9 (Conv1D)	(None, 16, 128)	24704
max_poolingid_6 (MaxPooling 1D)	(None, 8, 128)	0
lstm_1 (LSTM)	(None, 70)	55720
dropout_4 (Dropout)	(None, 70)	0
dense_3 (Dense)	(None, 5)	355
Total params: 81,035 Trainable params: 81,035 Non-trainable params: 0		

4.3 Models' Results Comparison

Figure 1(A) describes the number of network traffic classified by the CNN model as Normal, Abnormal attacks and unknown attacks. Whereas Fig. 1(B) describes the CNN-LSTM.

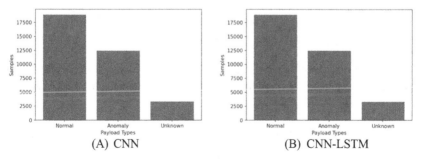

(A) CNN   (B) CNN-LSTM

Fig. 1. Traffic identification

Table 7 shows a comparison between CNN and CNN-LSTM models' classifications for each metric in terms of precision, recall, f1-score, and accuracy.

Table 7. Evaluation Metrics CNN-LSTM and CNN Models.

		Precision	Recall	F1-score	Accuracy
CNN-LSTM	**Normal**	99%	99%	99%	98.95%
	Dos	98%	99%	98%	
	Probe	100%	100%	100%	
	R2L	92%	37%	52%	
	U2R	97%	81%	88%	
CNN	**Normal**	97%	99%	98%	97.81%
	Dos	96%	97%	96%	
	Probe	99%	98%	99%	
	R2L	0%	0%	0%	
	U2R	93%	71%	81%	

Table 8 shows the accuracy of each machine learning and other CNN approaches compared to the proposed method to detect possible attacks in network traffic. As demonstrated the proposed approach gives higher accuracy than any other approach.

Table 8. Accuracy comparison between the proposed approach and other approaches.

Approach	Accuracy
RNN [17]	83.28%
STL [18]	88.39%
BiDLSTM [2]	94.26%
Proposed LSTM	**98.95%**

Table 9 shows the results of the highest study which is BiDLSTM and it has 94.26% accuracy. The proposed model provides higher accuracy with 98.95% which is 4.69% higher than existing studies. Furthermore, Table 9 compares all the classification categories (i.e. Normal, DOS, Probe, R2L, and U2R). However, accuracy is the final measurement criterion that is considered between this study and the BiDLSTM approach.

Table 9. Metric comparison between BiDLSTM and Proposed LSTM Model.

Metric	BiDLSTM					Proposed Approach LSTM				
Accuracy	94.26%					98.95%				
	Normal	DOS	Probe	R2L	U2R	Normal	DOS	Probe	R2L	U2R
Precision	91.07	99.43	53.65	98.43	48.42	99	98	100	92	97
Recall	90.25	96.36	87.32	75.05	46.00	99	99	100	37	81
F1-Score	91.66	92.44	66.47	85.17	47.18	99	98	100	52	88

5   Conclusion

The findings indicated that the proposed CNN-LSTM approach is more accurate than the highest accuracy in the state-of-the-art which reached 98.95% accuracy which is about 4.69% higher than the BiDLSTM approach at 94.26% accuracy. Moreover, the traditional CNN also reached a higher accuracy with about 3% more than the best approach in the literature.

CNN-LSTM model is implemented to detect different attacks, mainly, DoS, Probe, U2R, and R2L, but also identify Normal traffic at the same time. It is able to automatically discovers significant traits without the need for human intervention and achieves higher accuracy in detecting attacks which can improve the performance of intrusion detection systems.

The proposed approach is targeted to be integrated into existing networks, and the database regularly. The consistency of the simulated attacks is unequal which leads to issues in the prediction, therefore, additional efforts need to be done to collect more data on unusual attacks.

References

1. Kumar, D.A.: Intrusion detection systems: a review. Int. J. Adv. Res. Comput. Sci. **8**(8), 356–370 (2017)
2. Imrana, Y., Xiang, Y., Ali, L., Abdul-Rauf, Z.: A bidirectional LSTM deep learning approach for intrusion detection. Expert Syst. Appl. **185**, 115524 (2021)
3. Halim, Z., et al.: An effective genetic algorithm-based feature selection method for intrusion detection systems. Comput. Secur. **110**, 102448 (2021)
4. Rao, K.N., Rao, K.V., Prasad, P.R.: A hybrid intrusion detection system based on sparse autoencoder and deep neural network. Comput. Commun. **180**, 77–88 (2021)
5. Thakkar, A., Lohiya, R.: A review of the advancement in intrusion detection datasets. Procedia Comput. Sci. **167**, 636–645 (2020)
6. Maniriho, P., Mahmood, A.N., Chowdhury, M.J.M.: A study on malicious software behaviour analysis and detection techniques: taxonomy, current trends and challenges. Futur. Gener. Comput. Syst. **130**, 1–18 (2022)
7. El-Telbany, M.E.: Prediction of the electrical load for Egyptian energy management systems: deep learning approach. In: Hassanien, A.-E., Azar, A.T., Gaber, T., Oliva, D., Tolba, F.M. (eds.) AICV 2020. AISC, vol. 1153, pp. 237–246. Springer, Cham (2020). https://doi.org/10.1007/978-3-030-44289-7_23

8. Alkahtani, H., Aldhyani, T.H.H.: Botnet attack detection by using CNN-LSTM model for internet of things applications. Secur. Commun. Netw. **2021**, 1–23 (2021)

9. Zhou, X., Feng, J., Li, Y.: Non-intrusive load decomposition based on CNN–LSTM hybrid deep learning model. Energy Rep. **7**, 5762–5771 (2021)

10. Kim, J., Shin, Y., Choi, E.: An intrusion detection model based on a convolutional neural network. J. Multimed. Inf. Syst. **6**(4), 165–172 (2019)

11. Xu, C., Shen, J., Du, X.: Detection method of domain names generated by DGAs based on semantic representation and deep neural network. Comp. Sec. **85**, 77–88 (2019)

12. Haggag, M., Tantawy, M.M., El-Soudani, M.M.S.: Implementing a deep learning model for intrusion detection on apache spark platform. IEEE Access **8**, 163660–163672 (2020)

13. Sohi, S.M., Seifert, J.P., Ganji, F.: RNNIDS: enhancing network intrusion detection systems through deep learning. Comput. Secur. **102**, 102151 (2021)

14. Kottapalle, P.: A CNN-LSTM model for intrusion detection system from high dimensional data. J. Inf. Comput. Sci. **10**(3), 1362–1370 (2020)

15. Halbouni, A., Gunawan, T.S., Habaebi, M.H., Halbouni, M., Kartiwi, M., Ahmad, R.: CNN-LSTM: hybrid deep neural network for network intrusion detection system. IEEE Access **10**, 99837–99849 (2022)

16. Batchu, R.K., Seetha, H.: A generalized machine learning model for DDoS attacks detection using hybrid feature selection and hyperparameter tuning. Comput. Netw. **200**, 108498 (2021)

17. Yin, C., Zhu, Y., Fei, J., He, X.: A deep learning approach for intrusion detection using recurrent neural networks. IEEE Access **5**, 21954–21961 (2017)

18. Niyaz, Q., Sun, W., Javaid, A.Y., Alam, M.: A deep learning approach for network intrusion detection system. EAI Endorsed Tran. Secur. Saf. **3**, e2 (2015)

Quantum Computing and Programming Language

Analysis of Precision Vectors for Ising-Based Linear Regression

Kaho Aoyama$^{(\boxtimes)}$, Kazuhiko Komatsu$^{(\boxtimes)}$ iD, Masahito Kumagai iD, and Hiroaki Kobayashi iD

Tohoku University, Sendai, Miyagi 980-8579, Japan
{kaho.aoyama.t1,kuma}@dc.tohoku.ac.jp, {komatsu,koba}@tohoku.ac.jp

Abstract. Quantum computing has been much attention as one of the new computational principles. In particular, annealing machines that use the Ising model of statistical mechanics are emerging and feasible next-generation computational technology. Annealing machines can solve combinatorial optimization problems that have been considered difficult to solve in classical computing principles. Currently, Ising-based algorithms are being vigorously developed to perform various applications such as machine learning by solving them as combinatorial optimization problems. On the other hand, the amount of data, such as sensor data and simulation data, used in machine learning applications is drastically increasing. It becomes difficult to handle large amounts of data. In particular, since the number of qubits of annealing machines is limited, Ising-based algorithms independent of data size are strongly required.

This paper focuses on Ising-based linear regression that utilizes a precision vector instead of each data element of target data. Although the use of a precision vector is a key point that can reduce the number of qubits against the amount of data, detail such as how many elements of a precision vector is necessary and how these elements are set to be is not clarified yet. This paper discusses the characteristics of a precision vector through performance evaluation of Ising-based linear regression with a practical data set in empirical ways.

The experimental results show that a proper precision vector considering the input data set can improve the quality of the linear regression.

Keywords: Linear Regression · Precision Vector · Simulated Annealing · Ising Machines

1 Introduction

Recently, since the performance improvement of conventional computers has slowed down, *Ising machines* that employ a new principle of computing have been getting attracted attention. Ising machines are computers dedicated to the optimization problem of the Ising model, one of the magnetic models of physics. Ising machines can often be considered an *accelerator* for combinatorial optimization problems. Thus, Ising-based algorithms have been vigorously developed to

H. Takizawa et al. (Eds.): PDCAT 2022, LNCS 13798, pp. 251–261, 2023.
https://doi.org/10.1007/978-3-031-29927-8_20

expand applications that can be calculated using Ising machines by converting an original target problem to a combinatorial optimization problem. For example, various machine learning applications can be converted to a combinatorial optimization problem and solved by an annealing machine [1,3–5,11].

Although several Ising-based machine learning algorithms have been developed, the number of qubits in Ising machines becomes easily a limiting factor. Since the number of qubits of annealing machines is limited, it is difficult to handle the large amounts of data required for high-precision machine learning. As a result, Ising-based algorithms independent of data size are strongly required.

There have been several approaches to the limitation of the number of qubits. One approach is to reduce a size of a problem to fits the number of qubits of annealing machines [6,10]. The other approach is to essentially transform a problem into another problem [9]. For example, instead of using the number of data in a classical linear regression algorithm, the number of other metrics is utilized for Ising machines.

This paper focuses on Ising-based linear regression that utilizes a precision vector instead of each data element of target data because this approach can solve the large problem size of the input data in machine learning applications.

Although a precision vector is an essential factor that represents the characteristics of its input data in the Ising-based linear regression, the detailed behavior of a precision vector has not been discussed yet. For example, how many elements of a precision vector is necessary and how these elements set to be are not clarified yet, resulting in the difficulty of using the algorithm in practical.

This paper evaluates the performance with various settings of a precision vector to clarify the characteristics and behaviors of a precision vector. Thus, the number of elements in an appropriate precision vector and how to set these elements are examined. The experimental results show that a proper precision vector considering the input data can improve the quality of the linear regression.

The main contributions of this paper are as follows.

1. The effects of a precision vector on the performance of the linear regression are clarified.
2. The guideline on how to choose a precision vector.

The remainder of the paper is organized as follows. Section 2 describes an overview of Ising-based linear regression. Section 3 describes the details of a precision vector of the Ising-based linear regression. Section 4 evaluates various precision vectors using a practical dataset to clarify the characteristics of a precision vector. Finally, Sect. 6 gives conclusions and future work for this paper.

2   Ising-Based Linear Regression

2.1   Linear Regression

Linear regression is one of the most basic regression algorithms [7]. The regression fits of data to the model $y = f(x)$.

A multidimensional linear function used for linear regression is represented by the following equation.

$$\mathbf{y} = w_0 + w_1\mathbf{x_1} + ... + w_d\mathbf{x_d}, \tag{1}$$

$$\mathbf{x_i} = \{x_i^1, x_i^2, ...x_i^N\}, \tag{2}$$

where w_is indicate weight variables and x_is explanatory variables, and y is a target variable.

A squared error function is defined as the difference between the left- and right-hand sides of Eq. (1).

$$\min E(w) = ||Xw - Y||^2. \tag{3}$$

In the linear regression for the present procedure, the squared error function is minimized as shown in Eq. (3). Minimizing Eq. (3) guarantees that Eq. (1) is the best linear function to represent a given dataset.

Here, $X(\in \mathbb{R}^{N\times d+1})$ is a training dataset, X contains N data points. Each data point has d features and is augmented by unity. Thus, the overall size of the data points is $d + 1$. $Y(\in \mathbb{R}^N)$ is the regression label, and $w(\in \mathbb{R}^{d+1})$ is the regression weight to be learned. Expanding Eq. (3) and excluding the constant term, the following equation is derived.

$$\min E(w) = w^T X^T X w - 2w^T X^T Y. \tag{4}$$

The weight w_i in Eq. (4) should be a continuous value. However, since variables in an Ising machine can only take binary values, it is required to represent a continuous value in an Ising machine.

2.2 A Precision Vector

A precision vector is used for representing multiple values by binary variables. Although it is difficult to represent continuous values in an Ising machine, multiple values can be represented by using binary values of an Ising machine. The following equation represents a multiple variable w_i by binary variables $\hat{w}_{ik}$ and a precision vector $P = [p_1, p_2, ..., p_K]^T (K \in \mathbb{N})$.

$$w_i = \sum_{k=1}^{K} p_k \hat{w}_{ik}(\forall i = 1, 2, ..., d + 1). \tag{5}$$

For example, when the precision vector $P = [-1, -\frac{1}{2}, \frac{1}{2}, 1]$, the weight w_i can take values $\{-\frac{3}{2}, -1, -\frac{1}{2}, 0, \frac{1}{2}, 1, \frac{3}{2}\}$ by the combinations of the weights $\hat{w}_{ik} \in \{0, 1\}$.

A precision vector used in this study has 4 features.

1. Each element in a precision vector P can be an integral power of 2.
   - This value has been used in the previous study [9].
2. Each element in a precision vector P can be positive or negative.

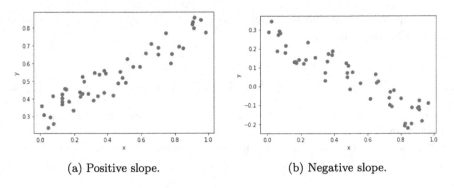

(a) Positive slope.   (b) Negative slope.

Fig. 1. Positive and negative slope.

- Since weights $\hat{w}_{ik}$ must be able to take both positive and negative values, the elements in a precision vector P can take positive and/or negative values. Figure 1 shows a simple example of the slope. From this figure, it can be said that the slope of the data you want to use for linear regression can be positive or negative.

3. A precision vector P is symmetrical.
   - This is not an essential constraint. Symmetric precision vectors are used in this paper because the previous study used symmetric ones [9].
4. A precision vector P does not need to include zero.
   - Even though a precision vector contains zero or not, the weight value w_i becomes the same. Therefore, the result of the regression does not change at all. As a result, from the standpoint of reducing the number of variables, the precision vector should not contain zero.

Features 2 and 4 are to be confirmed in Sect. 4.

2.3   A Precision Vector of Ising-Based Linear Regression

The matrix form of Eq. (5) can be described as the following equation.

$$w = \mathscr{P}\hat{w}. \tag{6}$$

Here, $\mathscr{P} = I_{d+1} \otimes P^T$ is the precision matrix, where $\otimes$ represents a Kronecker product, and $\hat{w} = [\hat{w}_{11}, ..., \hat{w}_{1K}, \hat{w}_{21}, ..., \hat{w}_{2K}, ..., \hat{w}_{(d+1)1}, ..., \hat{w}_{(d+1)K}]$.

By using Eq. (6), Eq. (4) can be rewritten to the following equation.

$$\min E(\hat{w}) = \hat{w}^T \mathscr{P}^T X^T X \mathscr{P}\hat{w} - 2\hat{w}^T \mathscr{P}^T X^T Y. \tag{7}$$

This equation is in the form of a Quadratic Unconstrained Binary Optimization (QUBO) problem. A QUBO problem is a problem that can be solved by Ising machines. The QUBO problem is solved with $\hat{w}$ as variables.

Giving a training dataset X, a regression label Y, and an appropriate precision vector P, the solution of a linear regression problem can be obtained.

The detailed procedure to construct a QUBO matrix is the following steps.

1. Calculate $\mathcal{P}^T X^T X \mathcal{P}$ in the first term of Eq. (7).
2. Since the QUBO matrix should be an upper triangular matrix, the lower triangular component needs to be transformed into the upper triangular component. Since $\mathcal{P}^T X^T X \mathcal{P}$ is a symmetric matrix, the lower triangular component can be set to 0 by doubling the upper triangular component. The symmetry component keeps unchanged.
3. Calculate $-2\mathcal{P}^T X^T Y$ in the second term of Eq. (7). This is a one-dimensional vector. Extend this vector to a two-dimensional vector with only diagonal components.
4. Add the first term and the second term.

To solve the QUBO problem, an appropriate precision vector P needs to be provided to achieve a highly accurate linear regression. However, discussions and analyses of how a precision vector affects performance have not been done. It is not easy to decide how many elements are necessary for a precision vector and what values and a value range are used.

3 Analysis of a Precision Vector for Efficient Ising-Based Linear Regression

To determine a precision vector, it is needed to decide what values should be included and how many elements it has. Since each element in a precision vector can be an integral power of 2, the range of values should be determined to decide the value and the number of elements.

The range of values is determined by setting the absolute maximum value of a precision vector. For example, if the absolute maximum value is 2^{-1}, the range of the precision vector becomes $[-2^{-1}, 2^{-1}]$. This range affects the range of weights. If the range of weights is not sufficient, the weights required for accurate regression are not represented. As a result, the performance of the regression suffers. Therefore, the absolute maximum value needs to be carefully defined.

Next, let us think about setting the absolute minimum value. The absolute minimum affects the fineness of a precision vector. The fineness of the precision vector affects the fineness of weights, which means how fine weights can be expressed. If weights take only sporadic values, regression is less accurate. Therefore, the absolute minimum value must be also carefully defined.

To achieve accurate regression, the absolute maximum value should be set to a large value and the absolute minimum value to a small value. However, the larger the absolute maximum value, the greater the number of elements in the precision vector. The number of elements in the precision vector is K, and the number of variables is $(d+1)K$. As a result, the greater the number of elements in the precision vector, the greater the number of variables. Variables consume the limited qubit of annealing. Therefore, it is needed to set an appropriate precision vector to perform highly accurate regression with a small number of variables.

Our method to generate an appropriate precision vector is setting the absolute maximum value and the absolute minimum value of the precision vector. The detailed procedure is as follows.

1. First, set an absolute maximum value.
2. Second, set an absolute minimum value.

If we set 2^0 as the absolute maximum value and 2^{-2} as the absolute minimum value, the precision vector becomes $[-2^0, -2^{-1}, -2^{-2}, 2^{-2}, 2^{-1}, 2^0]$. Here, both positive and negative value is necessary.

4   Evaluation

4.1   Experimental Environments

This section clarifies the characteristics of a precision vector to find an appropriate setting for its range and its fineness. First, how the range of a precision vector affects the mean squared error (MSE) is examined by changing the absolute maximum and minimum values under the following conditions.

The mean squared error is used as an evaluation metric for the regression. The MSE is the sum of the squares of the differences between the actual and predicted values for each data point, divided by the total number of data. The smaller the value of the MSE, the smaller the error of the model.

The Ising-based linear regression can be performed on simulated annealing machines and/or quantum annealing machines. In this experiment, D-wave Neal 0.5.9 is used for the evaluation. D-wave Neal is provided as a library for simulated annealing in Python [2]. The machine used in this experiment is Xeon Gold 6256 with a 768 GB main memory. In addition, scikit-learn 1.1.2 is used for the evaluation.

The dataset used in this experiment is the California Housing dataset [8]. The number of data points in this dataset is 20,640 and the number of features is 8. In this experiment, the input data is standardized.

Two experiments are mainly conducted. One is that the absolute maximum value is flexible when the absolute minimum value is fixed. By changing the absolute maximum value, the range of a precision vector is examined.

The other is that the minimum value is changed when the maximum value is fixed. By changing the absolute minimum value instead of the absolute maximum value, the fineness of a precision vector is examined.

The MSE is used as the evaluation metric when the absolute maximum value of the precision vector is changed from 2^{-3} to 2^2 and when the absolute minimum value is fixed at 2^{-4}. For example, the precision vector becomes $P = [-2^{-3}, -2^{-4}, 2^{-4}, 2^{-3}]$ when the maximum value is 2^{-3}. When the maximum value is 2^{-2}, $P = [-2^{-2}, -2^{-3}, -2^{-4}, 2^{-4}, 2^{-3}, 2^{-2}]$.

In the second case, the minimum value of the precision vector changes from 2^{-2} to 2^{-8} when the maximum value was fixed at 2^{-1}. For example, the precision vector becomes $P = [-2^{-1}, -2^{-2}, 2^{-2}, 2^{-1}]$ when the minimum value is 2^{-2}. When the minimum value is 2^{-3}, $P = [-2^{-1}, -2^{-2}, -2^{-3}, 2^{-3}, 2^{-2}, 2^{-1}]$.

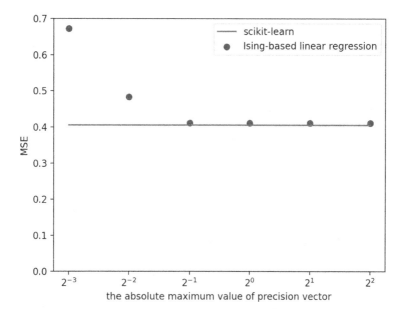

Fig. 2. MSE with various absolute maximum values in a precision vector.

4.2 Results and Discussions

Figure 2 shows the results when the absolute maximum values of the precision vector change. The figure shows that the MSE becomes smaller as the number of the absolute maximum value increase and the MSE saturates around 0.4 when the absolute maximum value is 2^{-1} or larger. The larger the maximum value, the greater the range of weights that can be represented, and the smaller the MSE. This is reasonable because the search range becomes wide as the absolute maximum value increases. As a result, a more suitable result can be obtained as the increase of the absolute maximum value. This means that appropriate weights are not represented when the maximum value is 2^{-2} or smaller. It seems the required range of weights is represented by the precision vector and the MSE changes little as the maximum value is changed when the absolute maximum value is 2^{-1} or larger. The green line is the MSE obtained by using scikit-learn. The MSE obtained by the Ising-based algorithm and the MSE obtained by using scikit-learn are consistent.

From this experiment, it is clarified that the larger absolute maximum value does not contribute to the reduction in the MSE. Therefore, considering the number of qubits consumed by the precision vector, 2^{-1} is the most desirable absolute maximum value in this case.

Figure 3 shows the results when the absolute minimum values change. The figure shows that the MSE becomes smaller as the number of the absolute minimum value decrease and the MSE saturates around 0.4 when the absolute minimum value of the precision vector is 2^{-5} or smaller. The smaller the minimum

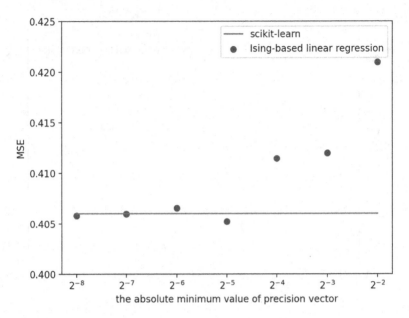

Fig. 3. MSE with various absolute minimum values in a precision vector.

value, the finer the precision vector that can be represented, and the smaller the MSE. This is reasonable because the fineness of the precision vector is not sufficient, the weights take only sporadic values. As a result, the regression becomes less accurate. Therefore, a more suitable and precise result can be obtained as the absolute minimum value decreases. This means that appropriate weights are not represented when the minimum value is 2^{-4} or larger. The MSE changes little as the absolute minimum value is changed when the absolute minimum value of the precision vector is 2^{-5} or smaller. This is because the fineness of the precision vector is sufficient. Although there are some variations in the MSE, this is because the MSE is calculated based on the test data, with the model trained on the training data.

From this experiment, it is clarified that the smaller absolute minimum value does not contribute to the reduction in the MSE. Therefore, considering the number of qubits consumed by the precision vector, 2^{-5} is the most desirable absolute minimum value in this case.

Next, to examine how the zero value in a precision vector affects the result, the MSE between the precision vector with zero and the precision vector without zero is compared. As the precision vector with 0, the following vector $[-2^{-1}, -2^{-2}, -2^{-3}, -2^{-4}, -2^{-5}, 0, 2^{-5}, 2^{-4}, 2^{-3}, 2^{-2}, 2^{-1}]$ is used. As the precision vector without 0, the vector $[-2^{-1}, -2^{-2}, -2^{-3}, -2^{-4}, -2^{-5}, 2^{-5}, 2^{-4}, 2^{-3}, 2^{-2}, 2^{-1}]$ is used. Since the absolute maximum value needs to be at least 2^{-1} from the previous experiment, 2^{-1} is used as the absolute maximum value.

Since the absolute minimum value needs to be at most 2^{-5} from the previous experiment, 2^{-5} is used as the absolute minimum value.

As a result of the experiment, the MSE is 0.4058 for both precision vectors.

This result clarifies that the MSE does not change whether the precision vector contains 0 or not. Therefore, from the standpoint of reducing the number of variables, the precision vector should not contain 0.

Next, to examine whether both positive and negative values are required for a precision vector, the performances of the precision vector with both positive and negative values and the precision vector with only positive values are compared. The precision vector with positive and negative values $[-\frac{1}{2}, -\frac{1}{4}, \frac{1}{4}, \frac{1}{2}]$ is used. For the precision vector with only positive values, $[\frac{1}{16}, \frac{1}{8}, \frac{1}{4}, \frac{1}{2}]$ is used. Since the absolute maximum value needs to be at least 2^{-1} from the previous experiment, 2^{-1} is used as the absolute maximum value. If the absolute minimum value is fixed, the number of elements of the precision vector with only positive values is half of it of the other. Therefore, the absolute minimum value is not fixed, and the two precision vectors have the same number of elements.

As a result of the experiment, the MSE is 0.42098 with the precision vector with positive and negative values. The MSE is 0.51481 with the precision vector with only positive values.

The MSE of the precision vector with only the positive values is lower than that with the positive and negative values. This result clarifies that both positive and negative values are required for a precision vector.

5   Related Work

The number of qubits in Ising machines is limited. In Ising-based linear regression, a precision vector is an important key factor that seriously affects the number of qubits. For this reason, the research in this paper focuses on precision vectors. In the method of this paper, the number of qubits is $(d + 1)K$. Since the number of elements in a precision vector is K, the number of elements in a precision vector directly affects the number of qubits. In addition, the number of features d affects the number of qubits.

The maximum size of all-to-all connections in D-wave 2000Q is 64 variables. If $(d+1)K \leq 64$, must be $d+1 \leq 32$ when K is fixed at 2. This limit is expected to be improved in future annealing machines [9].

Another method has been proposed to reduce the Hamiltonian to a smaller equivalent Hamiltonian, in order to solve large problems with existing quantum annealing machines [10]. However, this method has limited adaptable applications. On the other hand, the idea of the proposed method can be applied to a wide range of applications.

6   Conclusions

This paper has investigated precision vectors of Ising-based linear regression. Ising-based linear regression has an advantage for the number of data N over conventional linear regression. In addition, by using a precision vector, it can be computed with a limited number of qubits, since the number of variables is limited to $(d+1)K$ that does not depend on the number of data N.

Although a precision vector is an important key factor, the characteristics of a precision vector have not been clarified yet. This paper has clarified the characteristics to determine what a precision vector should be. The experimental results of this paper have shown how the absolute maximum and minimum values contribute to the result of Ising-based linear regression. In addition, it has been clarified that a precision vector should contain both positive and negative values and does not need to contain 0.

As future work, more evaluations with other data sets are required. Additionally, more evaluations can be conducted by using multiple annealing machines. In this paper, D-wave Neal is used. The Ising-based linear regression can be performed not only on simulated annealing machines but also on quantum annealing machines. Furthermore, discussion on values of a precision vector is also a future research issue. In this paper, each element in a precision vector is an integral power of 2, and a precision vector is symmetrical. By changing these constraints, it may be possible to achieve high accuracy with fewer elements.

Acknowledgments. This research was partially supported by MEXT Next Generation High-Performance Computing Infrastructures and Applications R&D Program, entitled "R&D of A Quantum-Annealing-Assisted Next Generation HPC Infrastructure and its Applications," Japan-Russia Research Cooperative Program between JSPS and RFBR, Grant number JPJSBP120214801, Grants-in-Aid for Scientific Research (A) #19H01095, and Grants-in-Aid for Scientific Research (C) #20K11838.

References

1. Arthur, D., Pusey-Nazzaro, L., et al.: QUBO formulations for training machine learning models. Sci. Rep. **11**(1), 1–10 (2021)
2. Kirkpatrick, S., Gelatt, C.D., Vecchi, M.P.: Optimization by simulated annealing. Science **220**(4598), 671–680 (1983)
3. Komatsu, K., Kumagai, M., Qi, J., Sato, M., Kobayashi, H.: An externally-constrained Ising clustering method for material informatics. In: 2021 Ninth International Symposium on Computing and Networking Workshops (CANDARW), pp. 201–204. IEEE (2021)
4. Kumagai, M., Komatsu, K., Takano, F., Araki, T., Sato, M., Kobayashi, H.: Combinatorial clustering based on an externally-defined one-hot constraint. In: 2020 Eighth International Symposium on Computing and Networking (CANDAR), pp. 59–68 (2020). https://doi.org/10.1109/CANDAR51075.2020.00015
5. Kumagai, M., Komatsu, K., Takano, F., Araki, T., Sato, M., Kobayashi, H.: An external definition of the one-hot constraint and fast QUBO generation for high-performance combinatorial clustering. Int. J. Netw. Comput. **11**(2), 463–491 (2021)
6. Liu, X., Shaydulin, R., Safro, I.: Quantum approximate optimization algorithm with sparsified phase operator. arXiv preprint arXiv:2205.00118 (2022)
7. Montgomery, D.C., Peck, E.A., Vining, G.G.: Introduction to linear regression analysis. John Wiley & Sons, Hoboken (2021)

8. Pace, R.K., Barry, R.: Sparse spatial autoregressions. Stat. Probab. Lett. **33**(3), 291–297 (1997)
9. Potok, T., et al.: Adiabatic quantum linear regression. Sci. Rep. **11**(1), 1–10 (2021)
10. Thai, P., Thai, M.T., Vu, T., Dinh, T.N.: FastHare: fast Hamiltonian reduction for large-scale quantum annealing. arXiv preprint arXiv:2205.05004 (2022)
11. Wu, N., Xie, Y.: A survey of machine learning for computer architecture and systems. ACM Comput. Surv. **55**(3), 1–39 (2022). https://doi.org/10.1145/3494523

Evaluating and Analyzing Irregular Tree Search in the Tascell and HOPE Parallel Programming Languages

Yusuke Shiki[1]([envelope]) [iD], Masahiro Yasugi[1] [iD], and Tasuku Hiraishi[2] [iD]

[1] Kyushu Institute of Technology, Fukuoka, Japan
shiki@pl.ai.kyutech.ac.jp, yasugi@csn.kyutech.ac.jp
[2] Kyoto Tachibana University, Kyoto, Japan
hiraishi@tachibana-u.ac.jp

Abstract. Well-designed parallel programming languages are useful for safely parallelizing irregular tree search. The Tascell language can speed up a tree search with work stealing; every Tascell worker mostly performs a computation sequentially, promoting long-term sequential (re)use of workspaces. We comprehensively examine techniques for reusing a workspace among siblings of a depth-first search, sequential update of a single partial solution in a backtracking search, and direct merging of search results. The HOPE fault-tolerant language can also speed up a tree search; every HOPE worker executes the entire computation redundantly and sequentially in its own planned order and exchanges partial results sophisticatedly at runtime to omit redundant subcomputations. For HOPE, we propose an adaptive workspace-sharing technique for unmerged distinct search results. In this study, we evaluate and analyze individual techniques by using the UTS benchmark and multiple backtracking search algorithms, optionally combined with histogram generation; Tascell and HOPE show better performance than Cilk Plus and OpenMP.

Keywords: parallel programming languages · irregular tree search · workspaces · work stealing · work omission · evaluation

1 Introduction

Dynamic load balancing is useful for parallelizing irregular tree search. For safe dynamic load balancing, well-designed parallel programming languages are useful as they can internally use elaborate techniques such as subtle but controllable races among workers and other underlying low-level threads. Manually writing low-level protocols is error-prone, causing deadlocks and undefined behaviors.

Sequential programs that perform an irregular tree search may use techniques for long-term (re)use of workspaces. For example, in a backtracking search over a dynamically traversed unknown irregular tree, a sequential program can hold only a single complete or partial solution; starting from the root node (vertex),

© The Author(s), under exclusive license to Springer Nature Switzerland AG 2023
H. Takizawa et al. (Eds.): PDCAT 2022, LNCS 13798, pp. 262–272, 2023.
https://doi.org/10.1007/978-3-031-29927-8_21

the partial solution is extended with in-place updates to satisfy more conditions along a parent-child path of a depth-first search (DFS). A complete solution is found if all conditions are met. For backtracking along the parent-child path (after a complete solution is found or no further depth-first path remains), the sequential program can undo the previous in-place updates.

In most parallel languages for irregular applications, parallelized programs can perform DFS in parallel by recursively spawning potential concurrent search tasks for work-sharing or work-stealing at the cost of copying extended solutions; two or more workers cannot extend a single solution with an in-place update.

The Tascell language [4] can speed up a tree search with work stealing; every Tascell worker mostly performs a computation sequentially, promoting long-term sequential (re)use of workspaces. We comprehensively examine techniques for reusing a workspace among siblings of a depth-first search, sequential update of a single partial solution in a backtracking search, and direct merging of search results.

The HOPE fault-tolerant language [7] can also speed up a tree search; every HOPE worker executes the entire computation redundantly and sequentially in its own planned order and exchanges partial results sophisticatedly at runtime to omit redundant subcomputations.

The contributions of this paper are as follows:

- We evaluate and analyze parallel languages Tascell and HOPE by using the UTS benchmark [5].
- The effectiveness of long-term (re)use of workspaces is comprehensively evaluated in Tascell and HOPE. We evaluate and analyze individual techniques by mainly using multiple backtracking search algorithms, optionally combined with histogram generation.
- For HOPE, we propose an adaptive workspace-sharing technique for unmerged distinct search results.
- For shared memory environments, Cilk Plus and OpenMP are examined. In most cases, Tascell and HOPE show better performance.

The remainder of this paper is organized as follows. Section 2 examines irregular tree search. Section 3 describes the irregular tree search in conventional languages. In Sect. 4, the irregular tree search is described in Tascell [4] and HOPE [7]. Section 5 presents the evaluations of our implementations. Finally, we conclude this paper in Sect. 6.

2 Irregular Tree Search

In this section, we describe irregular tree searches with sequential C programs. Table 1 summarizes the execution times of C programs with their short names and problem sizes. Workspace long-term (re)use levels are explained in this section except L1 of Histogram(n), which is shown in Sect. 4.

Figure 1 shows a C program that originates from uts_dfs.c (which orgUTS in Table 1 stands for) in the UTS benchmark [5] and performs a depth-first

Table 1. Sequential Execution Time in seconds

Name(size)	Workspace long-term (re)use levels		
	L0	L1	L2
Pen(13)	39.63	32.71	26.75
Pen(15)	3364	2799	2275
Nq(15)	66.08	58.30	28.83
Nq(17)	3129	2769	1378
Histogram(25)	26.63	24.83	22.57
Histogram(40)	554.0	515.8	475.4
orgUTSg(13)	20.90	—	—
orgUTSb(20)	27.76	—	—
orgUTSg(16)	564.0	—	—
orgUTSb(400)	542.1	—	—
UTSg(13)	20.56	20.58	—
UTSb(20)	27.15	27.14	—
UTSg(16)	554.9	554.5	—
UTSb(400)	530.2	530.0	—

Table 2. UTS trees and their resulting depths and sizes in millions of nodes.

Tree	Type	r	b_0	d	q	m	Depth	MNodes
g(13)	Geometric	19	3	13	–	–	13	7.780
b(20)	Binomial	42	200000	–	0.123	8	477	12.91
g(16)	Geometric	19	3	16	–	–	16	209.8
b(400)	Binomial	42	4000000	–	0.123	8	660	252.0

search (DFS). Starting from `root` of type `Node`, `serTreeSearch(&root)` performs an irregular tree search and returns the number of visited `Nodes` for simplicity[1]. The irregular tree determines a partial order among tree nodes. Every node has zero or more child nodes. Every node except the root node has a unique parent node. The number of child nodes for a (potential) `parent` node is unknown until the tree search visits the `parent` node (in this case, by calling `uts_numChildren(parent)`). A `child` node is allocated as a local variable of `serTreeSearch` and initialized on the basis of the `parent` node and an index between 0 (inclusive) and the number of child nodes (exclusive).

In Table 1, g(13), b(20), g(16), and b(400) are UTS trees with their parameters shown in Table 2. Table 2 also shows their resulting depths and sizes. According to [5], nodes in a *geometric* tree have a branching factor that follows a geometric distribution with an expected value that is specified by the parameter

---

[1] Note that orgUTS also returns the maximum tree depth and the number of leaves.

```
int serTreeSearch(Node *parent) {
  int numChildren, childType;
  counter_t parentHeight = parent->height;
  int r = 1;
  numChildren = uts_numChildren(parent);
  childType   = uts_childType(parent);
  parent->numChildren = numChildren;
  if (numChildren > 0) {
    int i, j;
    for (i = 0; i < numChildren; i++) {  // Recurse on the children
      Node child;
      child.type = childType; child.height = parentHeight + 1;
      child.numChildren = -1;     // not yet determined
      for (j = 0; j < computeGranularity; j++)
        rng_spawn(parent->state.state, child.state.state, i);
      r += serTreeSearch(&child);
    }
  }
  return r;
}
```

Fig. 1. C program for UTS depth-first search (only returning # of tree nodes). Originating from uts_dfs.c in the UTS benchmark.

$b_0 > 1$; the parameter d specifies its maximum depth. The expected size of a geometric tree is $(b_0)^d$. A node in a *binomial* tree has m children with probability q and has no children with probability $1 - q$, where m and q are parameters of the class of binomial tree. When $qm < 1$, this process generates a finite tree with expected size $\frac{1}{1-qm}$. The variation of subtree sizes increases dramatically as qm approaches 1. The root-specific branching factor b_0 can be set sufficiently high to generate an interesting variety of subtree sizes below the root.

By rewriting the C program shown in Fig. 1, we obtain TreeSearch0 shown in Fig. 2 that performs a UTS DFS without long-term workspace (re)use (UTS with L0 in Table 1). TreeSearch0 is called with an already visited node and the number (and type) of children for that node so that TreeSearch0 can immediately iterate over the children.

On the basis of TreeSearch0, we obtain TreeSearch1 shown in Fig. 2 that performs the UTS DFS by reusing a workspace (for *child) among siblings of DFS (UTS with L1 in Table 1). Children except the first child can omit part of the initialization (child->type = childType; child->height = parent->height + 1;). This small change does not impact the performance as shown in Table 1, but it has a potential impact if siblings of DFS have many common points.

Nq(n) with L2 in Table 1 refers to nqeeens2 shown in Fig. 3 that performs a backtracking search for the n-queens problem using a single workspace for sequential in-place updates of a single partial solution. Nq(n) with L1 in Table 1 refers to nqeeens1 shown in Fig. 3 that performs a backtracking search for the n-queens problem by reusing a workspace (for *nws) among siblings of DFS. Nq(n) with L0 in Table 1 refers to nqeeens0 without long-term workspace (re)use. Pen(n) with L0–L2 in Table 1 refer to C programs that perform a backtracking search for the Pentomino puzzle with n pieces with (re)use levels like Nq(n). Unlike UTS, the (re)use levels of Nq(n) and Pen(n) impact the performance significantly as shown in Table 1.

```
int TreeSearch0(Node *parent, int numChildren, int childType) {
  int r = 1; int i, j;
  for (i = 0; i < numChildren; i++) { // Recurse on the children
    Node child;
    child.type = childType; child.height = parent->height + 1;
    child.numChildren = -1;    // not yet determined
    for (j = 0; j < computeGranularity; j++)
      rng_spawn(parent->state.state, child.state.state, i);
    int cnc = uts_numChildren(&child), cct = uts_childType(&child);
    child.numChildren = cnc;
    if (cnc == 0) r += 1; else r += TreeSearch0(&child, cnc, cct);
  }
  return r;
}

int TreeSearch1(Node *parent, int numChildren, int childType,
                Node *child, int is_reusable) { ...
  for (i = 0; i < numChildren; i++) { // Recurse on the children
    if (!is_reusable) {
      child->type = childType; child->height = parent->height + 1;
    }
    child->numChildren = -1;    // not yet determined
    for (j = 0; j < computeGranularity; j++)
      rng_spawn(parent->state.state, child->state.state, i);
    int cnc = uts_numChildren(child), cct = uts_childType(child);
    child->numChildren = cnc;
    if (cnc == 0) r += 1;
    else { Node cChild; r += TreeSearch1(child, cnc, cct, &cChild, 0); }
    is_reusable = 1;
  } ...
}
```

Fig. 2. C programs for UTS depth-first search (DFS): `TreeSearch0` without workspace (re)use (L0) and `TreeSearch1` reusing a workspace among siblings of DFS (L1).

Histogram(n) with L0 in Table 1 refers to `acc_gcd` shown in Fig. 4 that performs a simple irregular search for non-one greatest common dividers (GCDs) among d integers ($d = 7$) between $[2, 2 + n)$ (n^d combinations in total) generating a histogram of non-one solutions by recursively generating and merging sub-histograms in a divide-and-conquer style. Histogram(n) with L2 in Table 1 refers to `acc_gcd_one` shown in Fig. 4 that performs the simple non-one GCD search with direct merging on a commonly-given single histogram in a single workspace. Note that Histogram(n) with L1 is proposed in Sect. 4. The use levels impact the performance considerably as in Table 1.

In most parallel languages for irregular applications, parallelized programs cannot easily enjoy higher (re)use levels for search nodes or a total result. This is not always the case in Tascell and HOPE as shown in the following sections.

3   Conventional Language

OpenMP cannot enjoy workspace (re)use levels other than L0. For UTS with L0, we can simply add directives `#pragma omp task firstprivate(i) shared(r)` for the body of the `for` statement in `TreeSearch0`, `#pragma omp taskwait` just after the `for` statement, and `#pragma omp atomic` for statements `r += 1;`. and replace `r += TreeSearch0(&child, cnc, cct);` with `int r0 = TreeSearch0 (&child, cnc, cct);\n #pragma omp atomic\n r += r0;`.

```
struct nq_workspace { int a[20]; int lb[40]; int rb[40]; };

int nqueens2(int n, int k, struct nq_workspace *ws) {
  int s = 0; int ix = k, iy = n; int i;
  for (i = ix; i < iy; ++i) {
    int ai = ws->a[i];
    if (!(ws->lb[n-1+k-ai] || ws->rb[ai+k]))
      if (k == n - 1)
        s++;
      else
        {
          ws->lb[n-1-ai+k] = 1;  ws->rb[ai+k] = 1;
          ws->a[i] = ws->a[k];   ws->a[k] = ai;
          s += nqueens2(n, k+1, ws);
          ai = ws->a[k];
          ws->a[k] = ws->a[i];   ws->a[i] = ai;
          ws->rb[ai+k] = 0;      ws->lb[n-1-ai+k] = 0;
        }
  }
  return s;
}

int nqueens1(int n, int k, struct nq_workspace *ws,
             struct nq_workspace *nws, int is_reusable_nws) { ...
         {
           if (!is_reusable_nws) {*nws = *ws;}
           nws->lb[n-1-ai+k] = 1;  nws->rb[ai+k] = 1;
           nws->a[i] = nws->a[k];  nws->a[k] = ai;
           struct nq_workspace nnws[1];
           s += nqueens1(n, k+1, nws, nnws, 0);
           ai = nws->a[k];
           nws->a[k] = nws->a[i];  nws->a[i] = ai;
           nws->rb[ai+k] = 0;      nws->lb[n-1-ai+k] = 0;
           is_reusable_nws = 1;
         } ...
}

int nqueens0(int n, int k, struct nq_workspace *ws) { ...
         {
           struct nq_workspace nws[1];
           *nws = *ws;
           nws->lb[n-1-ai+k] = 1;  nws->rb[ai+k] = 1;
           nws->a[i] = nws->a[k];  nws->a[k] = ai;
           s += nqueens0(n, k+1, nws);
         } ...
}
```

Fig. 3. C programs for the n-queens problem: `nqueens2` using a single workspace for sequential in-place updates of a single partial solution in a backtracking search (L2), `nqueens1` reusing a workspace among siblings of DFS (L1), and `nqueens0` without long-term workspace (re)use (L0).

For UTS with L0, Cilk Plus can simply use `cilk_for` (hereafter, "Cilk-for") or a combination of `cilk_spawn` and `cilk_sync` (hereafter, "Cilk-spawn"). For the total result, Cilk Plus can use `cilk::reducer_opadd<int>` as a reducer. For Histogram(n) with L2, we can write a Cilk-spawn program using a customized "reducers" [2].

For UTS with L1, we can write a Cilk-spawn program in which `cilk::holder<int>` is used to emulate Cilk-5 [3,6]'s SYNCHED pseudovariable for long-term (re)use of workspaces by comparing two views (since two views are different after work stealing). This technique can also be applied to Nq(n) and Pen(n) with L1.

```
void acc_gcd(int d, hist *h, long i, long left, long right, long n) {
  if (d == 0 && right - left < 1000) /* a threshold */
    {
      new_hist_array(h, nranks);
      long j;
      for (j = left; j < right; j++) {
        long point = gcd2(i, j) - 2; /* non-ones */
        if (0 <= point && point < nranks)
          add_point_to_hist(0, h, point);
      }
    }
  else if (d > 0 && left + 1 == right)
    {
      long i1 = gcd2(i, left);
      if (i1 > 1) /* non-ones */
        acc_gcd(d - 1, h, i1, 2, n + 2, n);
      else
        temp_init(h);
    }
  else
    {
      long m = (left + right) / 2;
      hist h1; hist h2;
      acc_gcd(d, &h1, i, left, m, n);
      acc_gcd(d, &h2, i, m, right, n);
      merge_hist2(0, h, &h1, &h2);
    }
}

void acc_gcd_one(int d, hist *h, long i, long left, long right, long n) {
  if (d == 0 && right - left < 1000) /* a threshold */
    {
      long j;
      for (j = left; j < right; j++)  ...
    }
  else if (d > 0 && left + 1 == right)
    {
      long i1 = gcd2(i, left);
      if (i1 > 1) /* non-ones */
        acc_gcd_one(d - 1, h, i1, 2, n + 2, n);
    }
  else
    {
      long m = (left + right) / 2;
      acc_gcd_one(d, h, i, left, m, n);
      acc_gcd_one(d, h, i, m, right, n);
    }
}
```

Fig. 4. C programs for simple irregular search: acc_gcd generating a histogram by recursively generating and merging sub-histograms in a divide-and-conquer style (L0) and acc_gcd_one with direct merging on a commonly-given single histogram in a single workspace (L2).

4   Tascell and HOPE Languages

Tascell [4] is a task-parallel language that uses the *backtracking-based work-stealing strategy*. A Tascell worker always chooses not to spawn a task first and performs sequential computations. When a worker is chosen as a victim and receives a task request, it temporarily rewinds the execution of its task to back-track to the oldest point of potential task spawning, and then spawns the task.

```
hist_list_buf *g_lbuf; /* a globally shared buffer */

void acc_gcd_adapt(int d, hist *h, long i, long left, long right, long n) {
  if (d == 0 && right - left < 1000) /* a threshold */
    {
      new_hist_list(g_lbuf, h);  ...
    }
  ...
    {
      long m = (left + right) / 2;
      hist h1; hist h2;
      acc_gcd_adapt(d, &h1, i, left, m, n);
      acc_gcd_adapt(d, &h2, i, m, right, n);
      merge_hist2(g_lbuf, h, &h1, &h2);
      if (num_of_points(h) > nranks * 100) /* enough long */
        convert_to_hist_array(g_lbuf, h, nranks);
    }
}
```

Fig. 5. C program for simple irregular search with an adaptive workspace-sharing technique for unmerged distinct search results (L1).

Subsequently, the victim returns from the backtracking and resumes its own task. Tascell provides the `do_two` (for potential parallel execution of the following two statements) and `do_many` (for parallel loops) constructs.

Writing a UTS program with L1 and Pen(n), Nq(n) and Hisgtoram(n) programs with L2 in Tascell is easy, and lower-levels are easier. For Pen(n) and Nq(n) programs with L2, Tascell provides the `dynamic_wind` so that the victim can undo the in-place update temporarily before spawning and redo the in-place update after spawning.

In the HOPE fault-tolerant language [7], every HOPE worker executes the entire computation redundantly and sequentially in its own planned order and exchanges partial results sophisticatedly at runtime to omit redundant subcomputations. For HOPE, we cannot directly merge partial results to be exchanged. Thus, we propose an adaptive workspace-sharing technique for unmerged distinct search results.

For this technique, Histogram(n) with L1 in Table 1 refers to a C program shown in Fig. 5 that performs the simple non-one GCD search generating a histogram of non-one solutions by recursively generating and merging sub-histograms in a divide-and-conquer style. Unlike L0, sub-histograms globally share a single buffer in which lists of solutions are appended dynamically. Since only a single sub-histogram grows in sequential execution, a single large buffer can be used. Complete intervals in the buffer can be merged as an interval recursively. If the list length (the number of solutions) is sufficiently long, the list can be converted into a single array representing a sub-histogram. This use level impacts the performance considerably as shown in Table 1.

Writing UTS and Histogram(n) programs with L1 and Pen(n) and Nq(n) programs with L2 in HOPE is easy, and lower-levels are easier.

Table 3. Evaluation environment.

Host processor(s)	Intel Xeon E5-2697 v2 12-core × 2
Host memory	64 GB (shared)
Co-processor(s)	Intel Xeon Phi 3120P 57-core × 4 (four hardware threads per core)
Co-processor Memory	6 GB (for each co-processor)
Network	Each co-processor is connected to the host
	via PCIe 3.0 × 16 (Bandwidth = 15.6 GB/s)
OS	CentOS 6.5 (64bit)
Compiler	Intel Compiler 13.1.3 with -O3 optimizers
Closure	Trampoline-based implementation (compatible with the GCC extension [1])
MPI library	Intel MPI 4.1 Update 3 Build 20140124
Tascell server	Steel Bank Common Lisp 1.2.7 (runs on the host processors)

5 Evaluations

We evaluate the workspace-reuse techniques (L0, L1, and L2) using benchmark programs written in OpenMP, Cilk Plus, Tascell, and HOPE. The evaluation environment is summarized in Table 3. We used a single Xeon Phi coprocessor as a shared memory environment and up to four coprocessors distributed memory environments.

We used the following benchmark programs: $Nq(n)$ finds all solutions to the n-queens problem on the basis of a backtrack search, $Pen(n)$ finds all solutions to the Pentomino problem with n pieces (using additional pieces and an expanded board for $n > 12$) on the basis of a backtrack search, $Histogram(n)$ performs a simple irregular search for non-one GCDs among d integers ($d = 7$) between $[2, 2 + n)$ generating a histogram, and $UTSg(n)$ and $UTSb(n)$ perform a depth-first search for a UTS tree ($g(n)$ and $b(n)$ in Sect. 2, respectively). The performance of the sequential implementations using C is shown in Table 1.

Figure 6(a) shows the evaluation results in the shared memory environment when the number of workers is changed from 1 to 64. We attempted all the available workspace-reuse techniques in each implementation and showed the best performance in this figure. Tascell achieved the best performance for all benchmark programs. HOPE achieved the second best performance with the smaller number of workers but the performance drops rapidly when the number of workers increases, possibly because of the cost for the exchange of partial results. Comparing Cilk-for and Cilk-spawn in Cilk Plus, Cilk-spawn performed better because both the current spawned procedure and its continuation are often large in an irregular search tree.

Figure 6(b) compares the performance among the L0, L1, and L2 workspace-reuse techniques in 4-worker executions in the shared memory environment. In Tascell and HOPE, L2 is the most effective, followed by L1 and L0. Similar to

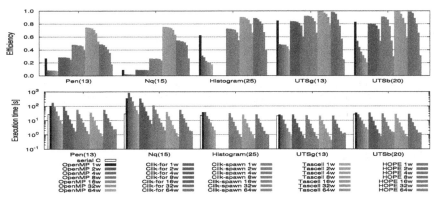

(a) in the shared memory environment using the best workspace-reuse technique.

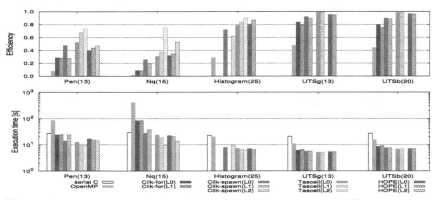

(b) 4-worker executions in the shared memory environment using different workspace-reuse techniques.

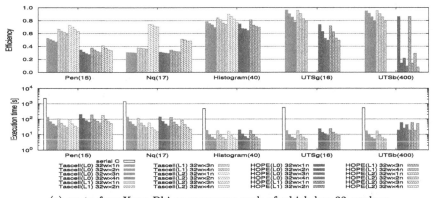

(c) up to four Xeon Phi coprocessors each of which has 32 workers.

Fig. 6. Efficiency (upper half) and execution times (lower half). Efficiency is defined as S/n_w where S is a speedup to a sequential C program and n_w is the number of workers ($S/n_\mathrm{w} = 1$ means an ideal speedup).

the results shown in Table 1, L2 improves the performance considerably for Nq. In contrast, L1 (emulation of SYNCHED) and L2 (a customized "reducer") cannot improve the performance in Cilk Plus.

Figure 6(c) shows the evaluation results of Tascell and HOPE in the distributed memory environment. As in the shared memory environment, the implementations using L2 showed the best performance, followed by L1 and L0. The effect of L2 is considerable especially for Nq. Comparing Tascell and HOPE, Tascell the showed better performance.

6   Conclusion

In this study, we evaluated techniques for long-term (re)use of workspaces by using the UTS benchmark and multiple backtracking search algorithms optionally combined with histogram generation. In Tascell and HOPE, these techniques were generally effective.

In a distributed memory environment, Tascell and HOPE showed good scalability except Binomial UTS in HOPE. For shared memory environments, Cilk Plus and OpenMP were also examined. In most cases, Tascell and HOPE showed better performance than Cilk Plus and OpenMP. In Cilk Plus, a customized "reducer" and Cilk-5 [3,6]'s SYNCHED pseudovariable emulation for long-term (re)use of workspaces did not show their effectiveness.

References

1. Breuel, T.: Lexical closures for C++. In: Usenix Proceedings, C++ Conference (1998)
2. Frigo, M., Halpern, P., Leiserson, C.E., Lewin-Berlin, S.: Reducers and other Cilk++ hyperobjects. In: Proceedings of the Twenty-first Annual Symposium on Parallelism in Algorithms and Architectures, pp. 79–90. SPAA (2009)
3. Frigo, M., Leiserson, C.E., Randall, K.H.: The implementation of the Cilk-5 multithreaded language. In: ACM SIGPLAN Notices (PLDI 1998), vol. 33, no. 5, pp. 212–223 (1998)
4. Hiraishi, T., Yasugi, M., Umatani, S., Yuasa, T.: Backtracking-based load balancing. In: Proceedings of the 14th ACM SIGPLAN Symposium on Principles and Practice of Parallel Programming (PPoPP 2009), pp. 55–64 (2009)
5. Olivier, S., et al.: UTS: an unbalanced tree search benchmark. In: Proceedings of the 19th International Conference on Languages and Compilers for Parallel Computing, pp. 235–250. LCPC (2006)
6. Supercomputing Technologies Group: Cilk 5.4.6 Reference Manual. Massachusetts Institute of Technology, Laboratory for Computer Science, Cambridge, Massachusetts, USA
7. Yasugi, M., Muraoka, D., Hiraishi, T., Umatani, S., Emoto, K.: HOPE: a parallel execution model based on hierarchical omission. In: Proceedings of the 48th International Conference on Parallel Processing (ICPP 2019), pp. 77:1–77:11 (2019). https://doi.org/10.1145/3337821.3337899

Best Papers

Distributed Parallel Tall-Skinny QR Factorization: Performance Evaluation of Various Algorithms on Various Systems

Takeshi Fukaya[1,2]([envelope])

[1] Information Initiative Center, Hokkaido University, Sapporo, Japan
fukaya@iic.hokudai.ac.jp
[2] JST Presto, Tokyo, Japan

Abstract. In this paper, we focus on the distributed parallel computation of tall-skinny QR factorization. Among various numerical algorithms, we evaluate the performance of four typical algorithms that have different characteristics on four different supercomputer systems. Together with a brief summary of each algorithm, this paper presents the current situation of the distributed parallel tall-skinny QR factorization, which will help applications to select an appropriate numerical algorithm for tall-skinny QR factorization.

Keywords: Distributed parallel computing · Dense matrix computation · Tall-skinny QR factorization · Communication-Avoiding algorithm

1 Introduction

Dense matrix factorizations such as LU, Cholesky, and QR factorizations are important building blocks in scientific computations, and development of efficient numerical algorithms for them has been continuously conducted. In this paper, we focus on the distributed parallel computation of tall-skinny QR factorization, which has various applications such as least square problem and singular value decomposition. In addition, it is worth noting that tall-skinny QR factorization is one of basic components in various numerical algorithms; for example, it is used for orthogonalizing vectors in iterative methods (e.g., Krylov subspace methods) for linear systems and eigenvalue problems.

As a numerical algorithm for computing QR factorization, the Gram-Schmidt and Householder QR algorithms have been widely known. On the other hand, in this decade, it was pointed out that Communication-Avoiding (CA) is important in the strong scaling regime on large scale distributed parallel systems [1,3]. Under this direction, the TSQR algorithm was proposed [3] for tall-skinny QR factorization. In addition, Cholesky QR type algorithms have attracted much attention, and several progresses were reported [7,8,15,17,18].

As a result of the above progresses, now we have various algorithms for distributed parallel tall-skinny QR factorization. This situation motivates us to conduct comprehensive performance evaluation; we evaluate the performance

© The Author(s), under exclusive license to Springer Nature Switzerland AG 2023
H. Takizawa et al. (Eds.): PDCAT 2022, LNCS 13798, pp. 275–287, 2023.
https://doi.org/10.1007/978-3-031-29927-8_22

of four typical algorithms that have different characteristics on four different supercomputer systems. We aim at providing insights that are helpful for better understanding the algorithms.

The rest of this paper is organized as follows: in Sect. 2, we show the problem setting and provide an overview of algorithms for QR factorization. In Sect. 3, we summarize the target algorithms that we evaluate in this paper. In Sect. 4, we give the results of the performance evaluation and discuss them. In Sect. 5, we remark related works. Finally, in Sect. 6, we conclude this paper.

2   Problem Setting and Overview of Algorithms

2.1   Problem Setting

For a tall and skinny matrix $A \in \mathbb{R}^{m \times n}$ ($m \gg n$), we consider its thin (reduced) QR factorization [16]

$$A = QR, \tag{1}$$

where $Q \in \mathbb{R}^{m \times n}$ is an orthogonal matrix; $Q^\top Q = I_n$ (I_n: n-dimensional identity matrix), and $R \in \mathbb{R}^{n \times n}$ is an upper triangular matrix. In this paper, we consider the case of explicitly computing the matrix Q. The 2-norm condition number of matrix is defined as

$$\kappa_2(A) = \frac{\sigma_{\max}(A)}{\sigma_{\min}(A)}, \tag{2}$$

where $\sigma_{\max}(A)$ and $\sigma_{\min}(A)$ are the maximum and minimum singular values of A, respectively. We assume that A is numerically column full rank, which means that $\kappa_2(A) \leq 10^{16}$ when using the double-precision floating-point (FP64) format.

In this paper, we consider distributed parallel computing (MPI parallelization), and we assume that A is distributed in one-dimensional block row layout:

$$A = \begin{pmatrix} A_1 \\ \vdots \\ A_P \end{pmatrix}, \tag{3}$$

where P is the number of processes. For the simplicity, we assume that m can be divided by P. For the distribution of Q, we assume the same layout as for A, while we require that at least one process has the whole of R; no further requirements on the data distribution of R.

2.2   Overview of Algorithms

The textbook [16] provides a clear viewpoint for numerical algorithms that compute QR factorization; algorithms can be classified into two types: Orthogonal Triangularization type and Triangular Orthogonalization type.

An algorithm in Orthogonal Triangularization type transforms A into an upper triangular matrix:

$$\hat{Q}_k \cdots \hat{Q}_2 \hat{Q}_1 A \to \begin{pmatrix} R \\ O \end{pmatrix}, \tag{4}$$

where $\hat{Q}_1, \ldots, \hat{Q}_k \in \mathbb{R}^{m \times m}$ are orthogonal matrices. The explicit form of Q is obtained via

$$\left(\hat{Q}_k \cdots \hat{Q}_2 \hat{Q}_1\right)^{-1} \begin{pmatrix} I_n \\ O \end{pmatrix} \to Q. \tag{5}$$

One of the well-known algorithms that belong to this type is the Householder QR algorithm [4,9,16].

On the other hand, an algorithm in Triangular Orthogonalization type computes a column-orthonormal matrix as

$$A \hat{R}_1 \hat{R}_2 \cdots \hat{R}_k \to Q, \tag{6}$$

where $\hat{R}_1, \ldots, \hat{R}_k$ are upper triangular matrices. The R factor in QR factorization is obtained by

$$\left(\hat{R}_1 \hat{R}_2 \cdots \hat{R}_k\right)^{-1} \to R. \tag{7}$$

The algorithms based on Gram-Schmidt orthogonalization [4,9,16] belong to this type.

Another important viewpoint for algorithms is Communication-Avoiding (CA) [1,3]. In this paper, if an algorithm requires only constant number of collective communications among all processes, then we regard it as CA; for example, if the number of the communications is $O(n)$, we regard it as Not CA.

3   Summary of the Target Algorithms

Among various numerical algorithms, we select four typical algorithms that have different characteristics; the selected algorithms are listed in Table 1. All of the four algorithms can compute an accurate QR factorization even if the target matrix is ill-conditioned (e.g., $\kappa_2(A) \simeq 10^{14}$).

In this paper, we aim for evaluating the performance of each algorithm in the storing scaling regime. The cost model of each algorithm is provided in Table 2. In this table, #flops means the number of floating-point operations, #issues means the number of issuing collective communication routines (e.g., MPI_Allreduce), and #words means the amount of data communicated. All costs are calculated along the critical path in parallel computation. P means the number of processes. It is assumed that collective communication is done based on the binary tree. For #flops, only dominant terms are shown. The term with $\log_2 P$ represents the computational cost in collective communication, and it is generally implicitly done in MPI routines excepting TSQR. For the details of constructing the cost model of TSQR, see the paper [6].

3.1   HQR: Householder QR

This algorithm is based on the Householder transformation [16], which is one of the famous orthogonal transformation in numerical linear algebra. This algorithm has been well-used because it can unconditionally provide an accurate

Table 1. Target algorithms.

	Orthogonal Triangularization	Triangular Orthogonalization
Not CA	Householder QR (HQR)	Classical Gram-Schmidt with reorthogonalization (CGS2)
CA	TSQR	Shifted CholeskyQR3 (S-CholQR3)

Table 2. Cost model for each algorithm: P means the number of processes.

Algorithm	#flops	#issues	#words
HQR	$\dfrac{4mn^2}{P} + O(n^2 \log_2 P)$	$O(n)$	$O(n^2)$
CGS2	$\dfrac{4mn^2}{P} + O(n^2 \log_2 P)$	$O(n)$	$O(n^2)$
TSQR	$\dfrac{4mn^2}{P} + O(n^3 \log_2 P)$	$O(1)$	$O(n^2)$
S-CholQR3	$\dfrac{6mn^2}{P} + O(n^2 \log_2 P)$	$O(1)$	$O(n^2)$

solution. For the use of the Level-3 BLAS routines (e.g., matrix-matrix multiplication), blocking techniques based on the compact-WY representation [12] have been proposed. The computation pattern in this algorithm is column by column, which requires $O(n)$ times collective communications.

3.2 CGS2: Classical Gram-Schmidt with Reorthogonalization

The Gram-Schmidt orthogonalization is more than 100 years old [10] and consists of vector scaling and projection onto orthogonal complement. There are several variants such as classical one (CGS) and modified one (MGS). Generally, the accuracy of the computed Q matrix (i.e., orthogonality) depends on the condition number of the target matrix. As a way of improving the accuracy of Q, reorthogonalization is known. Gram-Schmidt type algorithms are based on column by column computations, and $O(n)$ times collective communications are needed. For using the Level-3 BLAS routines, blocking techniques have been proposed [2,14], however no standard implementation for algorithms with reorthogonalization exits as far as the author knows. Thus, we do not employ blocking techniques in this paper. Since blocking techniques are employed to reduce the computational time by using Level-3 BLAS routines, with or without them will basically make almost no differences in the total execution time when the number of processes is large, in which the communication time is dominant. On the other hand, when the number of processes is small, there will be the possibility that blocking techniques will reduce the total execution time. However, in the case of tall-skinny QR factorization with sufficiently small n, the advantage of using Level-3 BLAS routines is often limited; the shape (size) of matrices computed by Level-3 BLAS routines is not suitable for them.

3.3 TSQR

This algorithm was developed under the purpose of Communication-Avoiding [3]. In this algorithm, each process first computes local QR factorization, and then the obtained R matrices are reduced into the final R factor, in which the data of the triangular matrices is transferred by point-to-point communication (Fig. 1). Similar to Householder QR, TSQR also provides an accurate solution [11]. The whole pattern of communication in TSQR can be regarded as a single collective communication with the specific reduction operation (i.e., so-called structured QR factorization) [6], and we can regard it as CA. It is worth noting that the computation of structured QR sometimes becomes a performance bottleneck, especially when n is large [5,6].

3.4 S-CholQR3: Shifted CholekyQR3

Let W be the Gram matrix of A: $W = A^\top A$, by using its Cholesky factorization: $W \to R^\top R$, mathematically we can obtain the QR factorization of A: $Q = AR^{-1}$ [9,13]. This is called the Cholesky QR algorithm. When A is tall and skinny, the dominant computational parts in Cholesky QR can be done only by the Level-3 BLAS routines. Thus, Cholesky QR is suitable for recent computer architectures, and high effective performance is expected. However, it has serious issues in stability and accuracy; similar to CGS and MGS, the accuracy of the computed Q matrix becomes worse as the condition number increases. In addition, if $\kappa_2(A) \gtrsim 10^8$, the algorithm often breaks down. To improve the stability and accuracy, first an algorithm of Cholesky QR with reorthogonalization was proposed [8,17], which is called CholeskyQR2. Then, for the further improvement, an approach of employing the preconditioning based on Cholesky QR with shift was proposed (Fig. 2), and the resulting algorithm is called Shifted CholeskyQR3 [7]. Although the computational and communication costs increase compared with the original Cholesky QR, Shifted CholeskyQR3 still preserves the suitability for high-performance computing and requires only a few collective communications.

4 Performance Evaluation

4.1 Overview of the Implementation of the Algorithms

We give the overview of the implementation of the target algorithms. All of the program code is written in Fortran90, and routines provided in the BLAS and LAPACK libraries are actively used. Distributed parallelization is manually done with the MPI library, while thread parallelization relies on the BLAS and LAPACK libraries; manual thread parallelization (e.g., that with OpenMP) is not done. It is worth mentioning the name of collective communication routines in each algorithm; HQR, CGS2, and S-CholQR3 use `MPI_Allreduce`, while TSQR repeats `MPI_Send`/`MPI_Recv`.

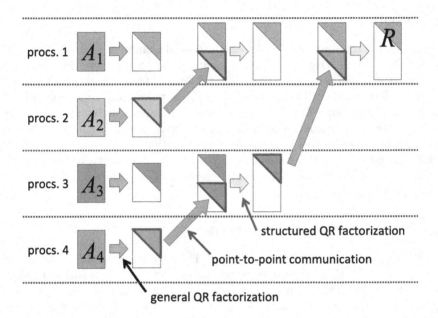

Fig. 1. Outline of the TSQR algorithm: an example when $P = 4$.

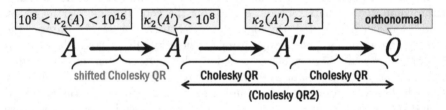

Fig. 2. Outline of the Shifted CholeskyQR3 algorithm: mechanism of the improvement of the stability.

Individual points for each algorithm are as follows:

- HQR: fixed size blocking technique is employed. Candidates for the block width are $l = 4, 8, 16, 32, 64, 128, 256$ ($l \leq n$).
- CGS2: the algorithm described in the paper [10] (Sect. 4.2) is implemented. Blocking techniques are not employed as mentioned in Sect. 3.2.
- TSQR: local QR factorization on each process is done by the `dgeqr` routine in LAPACK (when not available, `dgeqrf` is used). For the structured QR factorization an in-house code with the manual blocking technique is used [5], which is not thread parallelized.
- S-CholQR3: two variants (computing the Gram matrix with `dgemm` or `dsyrk` in BLAS) are implemented. Matrix multiplications with two triangular matrices are done by `dtrmm` in BLAS, in which one of the two matrices is dealt with as a general matrix after zero padding. The same shift value as in the previous work [7] (that based on $\|A\|_F$) is employed.

4.2   Computational Environments and Evaluation Settings

Performance evaluation is conducted on the four supercomputer systems. Specifications and settings of the systems are listed in Table 3. Compile options and settings are basically follow those recommended in the manual of the system. In this paper, we evaluate the execution time in the strong scaling regime; we fix the matrix size and change the number of computational nodes. In OFP and BDEC, we conduct evaluation with 8, 16, 32, 64, 128, 256, 512, 1024, 2048 nodes, while in OBCX and Grand, with 8, 16, 32, 64, 128, 256 nodes. The assignment of MPI processes and threads on single node in each environment is also listed in Table 3. The assignment of MPI processes is determined by taking the number of CPUs (in OFP, OBCX, and Grand) or CMG (Core Memory Group in BDEC) in account.

Test matrices are generated with randomly generated orthogonal matrices, which is the same way as in the previous work [8]. We set $\kappa_2(A) = 10^{14}$, however it has no effect on execution time in this evaluation. We fix $m = 16777216 \ (= 2^{24})$ and test three cases of $n = 16, 64, 256$. For each algorithm, we measure execution time five times (in a single job) and evaluate the shortest one. For HQR and S-CholQR3, we select the best time among all candidates of the block width or BLAS routines.

4.3   Results

Figure 3 provides the execution time of each algorithm on each system. In each graph, x-axis represents the number of nodes. Observations from the results are as follows:

- In almost all cases (system and number of nodes), S-CholQR3 is fastest. It also shows the good strong scalability excepting the case of $n = 256$ on BDEC. We guess that the slow down will be due to the characteristics of the MPI library (or setting), however it is currently not clear.
- When n is not large (e.g., $n = 16, 64$) and the number of nodes is sufficiently large, TSQR is the second fastest algorithm. Together with the results of S-CholQR3, this clearly demonstrates the importance of Communication-Avoiding; for example, in the results of $n = 16$ on OFP, we can find the difference in the scalability between CA algorithms (S-CholQR3 and TSQR) and not CA ones (HQR and CGS2) when the number of nodes is larger than 256. It is interesting that the behavior of TSQR on BDEC is different from those on other three systems, however its detail is under investigation.
- On BDEC, when $n = 16, 64$ and the number of nodes is not large, HQR and CGS2 are as fast as S-CholQR3. On Xeon cluster systems (OBCX and Grand), HQR and CGS2 show good scalability, however their execution time is much larger than that of S-CholQR3.

Figure 4 gives the breakdown of the execution time when the number of nodes is 256. From the graphs, we have the following observations:

- Excepting BDEC, both the cost for communication ("comm.") and computation ("other") are small in S-CholQR3. This is the main reason why S-CHolQR3 is the fastest algorithm. On BDEC, the computation cost of S-CholQR3 is not small when $n = 16, 64$, and we guess that it will be due to

Table 3. Specifications and settings of the systems used in the performance evaluation.

(a) OFP: Oakforest-PACS

Site	Joint Center for Advanced High Performance Computing
Overall configuration	8208 nodes, Intel Omni-Path (Full-bisection Fat Tree)
Node configuration	1 CPU, 96 GiB DDR4, 16 GiB MCDRAM
CPU	Intel Xeon Phi 7250 (KNL, 1.4 GHz, 68 cores)
Compiler	Intel mpiifort (ver. 19.0.5.281)
Options	`-O3 -ipo -qopenmp -align array64byte -xMIC-AVX512`
BLAS/LAPACK	Intel MKL (ver. 2019.0.5), `-mkl=parallel`
Settings in evaluation	1 process/node, 64 threads/process (excepting core #0 and core #1) using only MCDRAM (flat mode)

(b) BDEC: Wisteria/BDEC-01 (Odyssey)

Site	Information Technology Center, The University of Tokyo
Overall configuration	7680 nodes, Tofu Interconnect D (6D mesh/torus)
Node configuration	1 CPU, 32 GiB HBM2
CPU	Fujitsu A64FX (2.2 GHz, 48 cores, 2 or 4 assistant cores)
Compiler	Fujitsu mpifrtpx (ver. 4.7.0)
Options	`-Kfast -Kopenmp`
BLAS/LAPACK	Fujitsu BLAS/LAPACK (ver. 1.2.34), `-SSLBLAMP`
Settings in evaluation	4 processes/node, 12 threads/process, using libomp (default setting)

(c) OBCX: Oakbridge-CX

Site	Information Technology Center, The University of Tokyo
Overall configuration	1368 nodes, Intel Omni-Path (Full-bisection Fat Tree)
Node configuration	2 CPUs, 128 GiB DDR4
CPU	Intel Xeon Platinum 8280 (Cascade Lake, 2.7 GHz, 28 cores)
Compiler	Intel mpiifort (ver. 19.1.3.304)
Options	`-O3 -qopenmp -axCORE-AVX512`
BLAS/LAPACK	Intel MKL (ver. 2020.0.4), `-mkl=parallel`
Settings in evaluation	2 processes/node, 28 threads/process

(d) Grand: Grand Chariot

Site	Information initiative Center, Hokkaido University
Overall configuration	1004 nodes, Intel Omni-Path (Full-bisection Fat Tree), 2 ports/node
Node configuration	2 CPUs, 384 GiB DDR4
CPU	Intel Xeon Gold 6148 (Skylake, 2.4 GHz, 20 cores)
Compiler	Intel mpiifort (ver. 19.1.3.304)
Options	`-O3 -qopenmp -xCORE-AVX512`
BLAS/LAPACK	Intel MKL (ver. 2020.0.4), `-mkl=parallel`
Settings in evaluation	2 processes/node, 20 threads/process

the characteristics of the BLAS libraries; Intel MKL is used on other three systems, while Fujitsu BLAS is used on BDEC.

- It is clear that the communication cost in HQR and CGS2 is much larger than that in TSQR and S-CholQR3, which clearly shows the impact of Communication-Avoiding. Since the computational cost is still large, HQR and CGS2 show the good scalability when the number of nodes is 256.
- As reported in the previous work [5,6], we can observe that the cost of computing structured QR factorizations ("st-qr") in TSQR becomes a bottleneck when n is large.

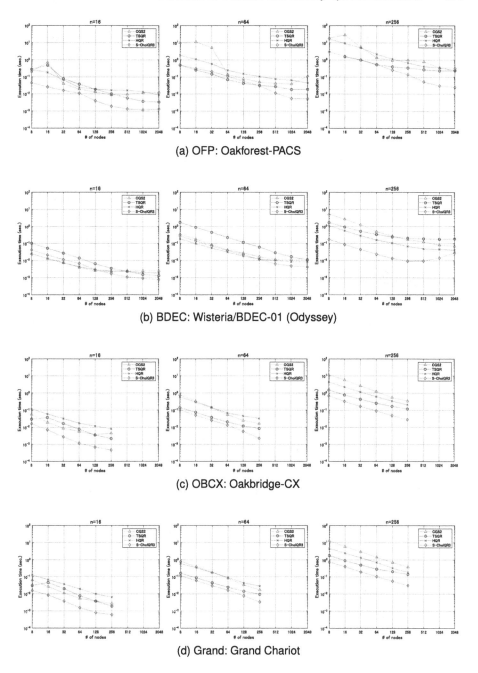

(a) OFP: Oakforest-PACS

(b) BDEC: Wisteria/BDEC-01 (Odyssey)

(c) OBCX: Oakbridge-CX

(d) Grand: Grand Chariot

Fig. 3. Execution time of each algorithm on each system (strong scaling): $m = 16777216$.

284   T. Fukaya

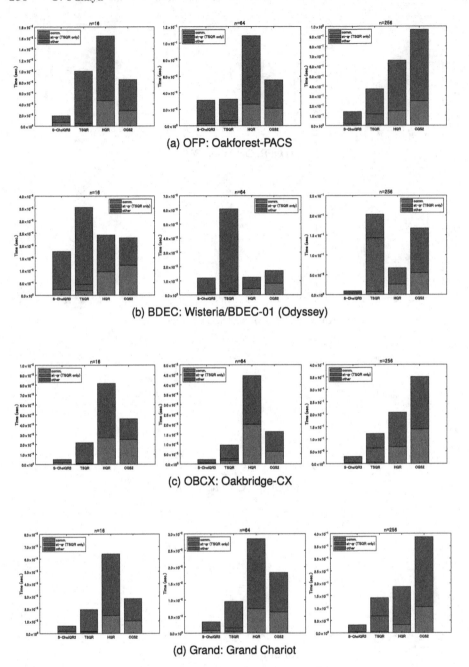

Fig. 4. Breakdown of the execution time when the number of nodes is 256: $m = 16777216$.

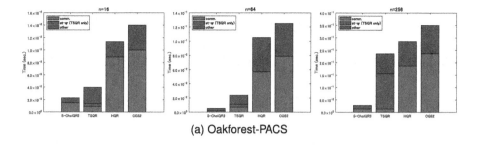

(a) Oakforest-PACS

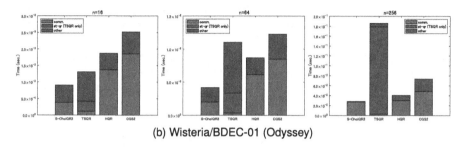

(b) Wisteria/BDEC-01 (Odyssey)

Fig. 5. Breakdown of the execution time when the number of nodes is 2048: $m = 16777216$.

Finally, Fig. 5 presents the breakdown of the execution time when the number of nodes is 2048 (only OFP and BDEC). Following observations are obtained from the graphs:

- Even in S-CholQR3 and TSQR, the communication cost is dominant, which limits the strong scalability.
- Communication-Avoiding has a larger impact compared with the case when the number of nodes is 256.

5 Related Work

In the paper [8], the results of performance evaluation for Householder QR, TSQR, and CholeskyQR2 on the supercomputer K were presented. Shifted CholeskyQR3 was proposed in the paper [7], however only the estimation for a distributed parallel case was provided. Thus, as far as the author knows, this paper first presents the actual performance comparison including Shifted CholeskyQR3 on distributed parallel systems.

There are some variants of Cholesky QR type algorithms whose stability and accuracy are improved. For example, LU-CholeskyQR2 [15], which employs LU factorization as preconditioning, was proposed, however LU factorization requires $O(n)$ times collective communication for the partial pivoting, and it is thus regarded as Not CA. Another example is mixed precision Cholesky QR [18], in which partial computations are done in higher precision (e.g., double-double precision). However, in current standard environments, such higher precision arithmetic requires much higher cost than the standard arithmetic supported by hardware. Thus, it is difficult to outperform Shifted CholeskyQR3 in execution time.

6 Conclusion

In this paper, we considered the distributed parallel computation of tall-skinny QR factorization. For the four numerical algorithms that have different characteristics, we evaluated their performance on the four different supercomputer systems in the strong scaling regime. From the presented results, it is shown that the Shifted CholeskyQR3 algorithm has a remarkable advantage. In addition, the importance of Communication-Avoiding (CA) is also confirmed. The obtained results help to understand the current situation of the numerical algorithms; for example, they will be helpful when selecting an appropriate algorithm in applications.

One of important future works is further investigation of the obtained performance results; for example, it will be vital to investigate into the relation to the benchmark results of BLAS and MPI routines. In addition, it will be interesting to conduct performance evaluation on a system with GPUs.

Acknowledgments. The author thanks the anonymous reviewers for their valuable comments. This research was supported by JSPS KAKENHI (Grant Number: JPJP21K11909), JST, PRESTO (Grant Number: JPMJPR20M8), and "Joint Usage/Research Center for Interdisciplinary Large-scale Information Infrastructures" and "High Performance Computing Infrastructure" in Japan (Project ID: jh210044-NAH).

References

1. Ballard, G., Demmel, J., Holtz, O., Schwartz, O.: Minimizing communication in numerical linear algebra. SIAM J. Matrix Anal. Appl. **32**(3), 866–901 (2011)
2. Carson, E., Lund, K., Rozložník, M., Thomas, S.: Block Gram-Schmidt algorithms and their stability properties. Linear Algebra Appl. **638**, 150–195 (2022)
3. Demmel, J., Grigori, L., Hoemmen, M., Langou, J.: Communication-optimal parallel and sequential QR and LU factorizations. SIAM J. Sci. Comput. **34**(1), A206–A239 (2012)
4. Demmel, J.W.: Applied numerical linear algebra. SIAM (1997)
5. Fukaya, T.: An investigation into the impact of the structured QR kernel on the overall performance of the TSQR algorithm. In: Proceedings of the International Conference on High Performance Computing in Asia-Pacific Region (HPC Asia 2019), pp. 81–90 (2019)
6. Fukaya, T., Imamura, T., Yamamoto, Y.: Performance analysis of the householder-type parallel tall-skinny QR factorizations toward automatic algorithm selection. In: Daydé, M., Marques, O., Nakajima, K. (eds.) VECPAR 2014. LNCS, vol. 8969, pp. 269–283. Springer, Cham (2015). https://doi.org/10.1007/978-3-319-17353-5_23

7. Fukaya, T., Kannan, R., Nakatsukasa, Y., Yamamoto, Y., Yanagisawa, Y.: Shifted Cholesky QR for computing the QR factorization of ill-conditioned matrices. SIAM J. Sci. Comput. **42**(1), A477–A503 (2020)
8. Fukaya, T., Nakatsukasa, Y., Yanagisawa, Y., Yamamoto, Y.: CholeskyQR2: a simple and communication-avoiding algorithm for computing a tall-skinny QR factorization on a large-scale parallel system. In: Proceedings of the 5th Workshop on Latest Advances in Scalable Algorithms for Large-Scale Systems (ScalA 2014), pp. 31–38 (2014)
9. Golub, G., Van Loan, C.: Matrix Computations, 4th edn. Johns Hopkins University Press, Baltimore (2013)
10. Leon, S.J., Björck, Å., Gander, W.: Gram-Schmidt orthogonalization: 100 years and more. Numer. Linear Algebra Appl. **20**(3), 492–532 (2013)
11. Mori, D., Yamamoto, Y., Zhang, S.L.: Backward error analysis of the AllReduce algorithm for householder QR decomposition. Jpn. J. Ind. Appl. Math. **29**(1), 111–130 (2012). https://doi.org/10.1007/s13160-011-0053-x
12. Schreiber, R., Van Loan, C.: A storage-efficient WY representation for products of householder transformations. SIAM J. Sci. Stat. Comput. **10**(1), 53–57 (1989)
13. Stathopoulos, A., Wu, K.: A block orthogonalization procedure with constant synchronization requirements. SIAM J. Sci. Comput. **23**(6), 2165–2182 (2002)
14. Stewart, G.W.: Block Gram-Schmidt orthogonalization. SIAM J. Sci. Comput. **31**(1), 761–775 (2008)
15. Terao, T., Ozaki, K., Ogita, T.: LU-Cholesky QR algorithms for thin QR decomposition. Parallel Comput. **92**, 102571 (2020)
16. Trefethen, L.N., Bau, D.: Numerical Linear Algebra. SIAM (1997)
17. Yamamoto, Y., Nakatsukasa, Y., Yanagisawa, Y., Fukaya, T.: Roundoff error analysis of the CholeskyQR2 algorithm. Electron. Trans. Numer. Anal. **44**, 306–326 (2015)
18. Yamazaki, I., Tomov, S., Dongarra, J.: Mixed-precision Cholesky QR factorization and its case studies on multicore CPU with multiple GPUs. SIAM J. Sci. Comput. **37**(3), C307–C330 (2015)

A Partitioned Memory Architecture with Prefetching for Efficient Video Encoders

Masayuki Sato[1]([✉])[iD], Yuya Omori[2], Ryusuke Egawa[1,3][iD], Ken Nakamura[1,2], Daisuke Kobayashi[2], Hiroe Iwasaki[1,4], Kazuhiko Komatsu[1][iD], and Hiroaki Kobayashi[1][iD]

[1] Tohoku University, Sendai, Miyagi 980-8579, Japan
{masa,komatsu,koba}@tohoku.ac.jp
[2] NTT Device Innovation Center, Nippon Telegraph and Telephone Corporation, Atsugi, Kanagawa 243-0124, Japan
{yuya.omori.hg,ken.nakamura.wt,daisuke.kobayashi.hv}@hco.ntt.co.jp
[3] Tokyo Denki University, Adachi, Tokyo 120-8551, Japan
egawa@mail.dendai.ac.jp
[4] Tokyo University of Agriculture and Technology, Fuchu, Tokyo 183-8538, Japan
hiroe@go.tuat.ac.jp

Abstract. A hardware video encoder based on recent video coding standards such as HEVC and VVC needs to efficiently handle a massive number of memory accesses to search motion vectors. To this end, first, this paper preliminarily evaluates the memory access behavior of a hardware video encoding pipeline. The preliminary evaluation suggests that the behavior of the early stages of the pipeline, accessing the wide areas of reference frames for the rough search, is quite different from those of the subsequent ones, accessing the small areas of them for the precise search. Therefore, this paper proposes a partitioned memory architecture for the hardware video encoding pipeline. This architecture adopts a *split cache structure* that consists of *a front-end cache* and *a back-end cache*. The front-end cache stores shrunk reference frames and provides them for the rough search in the early stages. Normal reference frames for the precise search are provided only to the subsequent stages through the back-end cache. As a result, this structure can reduce the memory bandwidth requirement. On the other hand, the split cache structure cannot reuse the data loaded by the early stages. It increases cache misses in the subsequent stages and may violate the deadline of memory accesses for real-time encoding. To solve this problem, this paper also designs and implements a *coding tree unit (CTU) prefetcher* to the back-end cache. The CTU prefetcher loads the data used by the subsequent stages without waiting for the results of the early stages. The evaluation results show that the proposed memory system can successfully reduce the cache miss rate and the deadline miss rate in the subsequent stages. As a result, the proposed memory architecture can contribute to satisfying the demands for real-time encoding while reducing energy consumption.

Keywords: Video Encoder · Cache Memory · Prefetcher

H. Takizawa et al. (Eds.): PDCAT 2022, LNCS 13798, pp. 288–300, 2023.
https://doi.org/10.1007/978-3-031-29927-8_23

1   Introduction

HEVC [11] is a successful video coding standard, which increases the coding efficiency compared with the predecessor standard H.264/Advanced Video Coding (AVC) [14]. Even the successor VVC [2] becomes already available, HEVC is still important and most widely used, as shown in the HEVC inclusion in ATSC3.0 [12]. Hence, these advanced codecs are used by 4K/8K digital broadcast and video casting on the broadband internet. One of the major challenges in video encoding is to handle a lot of memory accesses for the motion vector search [3,6,10].

Under this situation, various encoder LSIs have been developed. Among these LSIs, *NARA* [8,9] can encode movies with multiple frame sizes and rates, and can act as the first real-time 8K/60 fps encoder. NARA has an SRAM buffer to store forward and backward reference frames needed for the pipeline stages. The capacity reaches 26 MB. The area and energy costs of the SRAM buffer are very expensive. Therefore, its successor LSI should decrease the size of the on-chip SRAM buffer.

Toward the smaller on-chip cache, this paper preliminarily evaluates the memory access characteristics of the encoding pipeline. In the encoding pipeline, the early stages roughly search candidate motion vectors for wide areas of reference images, and the subsequent stages narrow down the candidates by precisely accessing small areas of reference frames. The preliminary evaluation results give us two important observations. First, the early stages that roughly estimate candidate motion vectors require a large bandwidth of the external DDR memory. In the early stages, the wide areas of the referenced frames are exhaustively accessed for estimating candidate motion vectors. Next, the subsequent stages access only the limited area of the reference frames because the number of candidate motion vectors are very limited based on the results of the early stages. These results indicate that the early stages do not require precise data of reference frames, while the subsequent stages only require the small areas of the reference frames.

Based on the above discussions, this paper proposes a partitioned memory architecture with prefetching for efficient video encoders. The proposed memory architecture adopts a split cache structure, in which an on-chip cache is divided into a front-end cache for the first two stages and a back-end cache for the subsequent stages. The front-end cache stores reference frames shrunk in advance used in the early stages, and the back-end cache stores the precise data of the small area of reference frames. Hence, this architecture can contribute to reductions in both the total cache capacity and the bandwidth required for the external DDR memory and the total capacity of the caches. On the other hand, because of the split cache structure, the subsequent stages cannot reuse the data in the front-end cache. Hence, these stages suffer from deadlines of memory accesses for real-time encoding, in which the stages cannot wait for the pixel data of reference frames from the external memory. Therefore, this paper also proposes a CTU prefetcher that preloads the data of the referenced frames from the external DDR memory to the back-end cache.

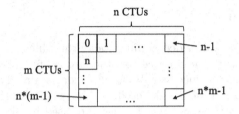

Fig. 1. The concept of the coding tree units (CTUs).

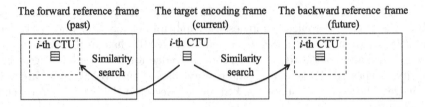

Fig. 2. The concept of inter prediction (motion vector search).

The rest of this paper is organized as follows. Section 2 describes the details of the HEVC encoding and its pipeline, and discusses the memory access characteristics. Section 3 proposes an effective memory subsystem for HEVC encoders, which includes the split cache structure and the CTU prefetcher. Section 4 evaluates the proposed memory architecture in terms of cache miss rates, deadline miss rates, and energy consumption. Section 5 describes related work. Section 6 concludes this paper.

2   Memory Subsystems for Video Encoding

2.1   Video Encoding

In the video-coding standards, it is important to understand the concept of the coding tree units (CTUs), which is shown in Fig. 1. A CTU is a maximum 64×64-pixel area in a frame. In the case of the HEVC coding of a 4K (3840×2160) movie, one frame includes 2040 CTUs (60×34 CTUs). When encoding a frame, the encoding process is done in a unit of CTU.

When encoding one CTU, the encoding algorithm converts CTUs to an encoded stream one by one, using two main coding tools; *intra* prediction and *inter* prediction. The intra prediction is to predict whether the neighboring pixels around the encoding CTU can compensate for the pixels of the CTU. A decoder can regenerate the picture of the encoded CTU from the already-decoded pixels within the frame itself. The computation cost of the intra prediction is not very high compared with the total computation of the encoding.

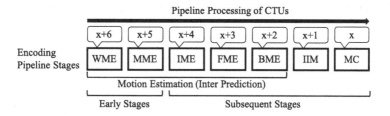

Fig. 3. The hardware encoding pipeline.

The inter prediction is to search for an area that can be copied from the referenced frames to the target frame. The encoding cost of the video coding standards highly depends on the inter prediction. Figure 2 shows the concept of the inter prediction. Let us assume that the encoder tries to encode the i-th CTU in the encoded frame. The encoder searches an area that has pixels very similar to the encoded CTU from the shaded areas of the forward and backward reference frames. The encoder searches the wide areas surrounded by dashed lines in Fig. 2. If the encoder can discover a similar area from the reference frame, the picture of the encoded CTU is replaced to a *motion vector* that represents the positional differences between the discovered area in the reference frame and the encoded CTU in the encoded frame. By using the motion vector, a decoder can regenerate the picture of the CTU from the pixels of the already-decoded reference frame without that of the target frame. However, the inter prediction needs a lot of comparisons between the encoded CTU and the reference frames, which induces a large number of memory accesses. Hence, it is important to reduce the number of memory accesses for making efficient video encoders.

2.2 Hardware Encoding Pipeline

The encoder LSI on which this paper focuses, NARA, makes the inter prediction and the final decision of encoding by pipeline processing. Figure 3 shows an overview of the pipeline stages and their roles. The process of the inter prediction is divided into five stages, Wide-range Motion Estimation (WME), Multi-block-size Motion Estimation (MME), Integer Motion Estimation (IME), Fractional Motion Estimation (FME), and Bipred Motion Estimation (BME). To satisfy the requirement for real-time encoding, each stage must finish its processing within a certain time. Therefore, real-time encoding forces each memory access to keep the strict deadline.

To alleviate the memory pressure on the external DDR memory, NARA has on-chip SRAM buffers. These buffers can store 10 horizontal CTU lines of two 8K reference frames, and the capacity of this SRAM buffer reaches 26 MB. As the SRAM buffers occupy a large area of the chip, it consumes a large amount of energy. Therefore, in the future encoder LSI, the capacity of the buffer should be reduced from the viewpoint of the production cost and energy consumption.

Table 1. Required memory bandwidth by each stage in GB/s.

Stages	WME	MME	IME	FME	BME	IIM	Total
Results	5.59	0.006	0.51	0.09	0	0	6.19

2.3   Analysis of Memory Access Pattern

Toward the memory system of the future encoder LSI, this paper preliminarily evaluates and analyzes the memory accesses in the encoding pipeline stages
by using an in-house memory access tracer of the HEVC encoder based on the
HEVC reference software, HM [4]. The detailed evaluation conditions are as
follows. The simulator outputs the stream of pixels accessed by encoding the
movie called *churaumi*, whose picture is later shown in Sect. 4.1. The format of
this movie is 4K/60 fps/10b/4:2:2, and the quantization parameter is 37. This
evaluation supposes that the stages access the data of the reference frames in a
unit of an 8×8-pixel block. Hence, one CTU consists of 64 blocks. In this evaluation, the on-chip memory is organized as a cache. The capacity is tentatively
set to 10 MB, which is equivalent to the size of a 2048×2048-pixel area. The
data blocks in the cache are managed by the LRU replacement policy.

Table 1 shows the required memory bandwidth of each pipeline unit. The
bandwidth is calculated by a memory access trace of each unit and required
deadlines for the data, which should be kept for the real-time 4K/60 fps encoding.
These results indicate that WME occupies 90% of the total memory traffic. This
is because WME roughly estimates candidate motion vectors from the wide-
range areas in the reference frames. These data are first accessed by WME
because WME is the first stage of the pipeline. Hence, WME causes compulsory
cache misses to the data and increases the amount of memory traffic.

In this evaluation, the access patterns of the pipeline stages are also investigated. Figure 4 shows heat maps of the accesses to the pixels of the backward
reference frame in terms of encoding one frame. The horizontal and vertical axes
are those of directions in the reference frame, respectively. The x-y coordinates
are relative to those of the left bottom of the encoded CTU. Note that the results
in Fig. 4 are obtained by encoding one frame of a movie. However, this trend is
the same in encoding the entire movies examined in this paper.

Figure 4(a) is the heat map of WME. Since WME exhaustively searches candidate motion vectors from the wide area in the reference frame, the accesses
are widely spread, and the number of accesses per pixel does not change.
Figure 4(b) shows the heat map of MME. The number of accessed pixels significantly decreases compared with that in the case of WME. However, to precisely
check the candidate motion vectors obtained by WME, it still needs the pixels
across the area where WME has accessed. As a result, these stages need to access
the many pixels spread over the wide area searched by WME.

Figures 4(c), 4(d), 4(e), and 4(f) show the heat maps of the subsequent
stages; IME, FME, BME, and IIM, respectively. The regions where these stages
access become smaller than those of the early stages, WME and MME. Since the

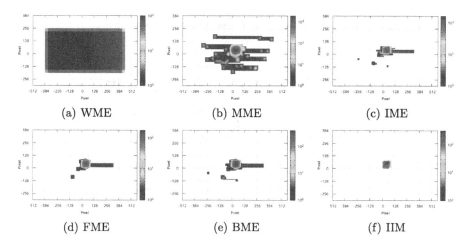

Fig. 4. Access maps of all the stages to the backward (future) reference frame of Churaumi.

number of candidate motion vectors for an encoded CTU is limited by MME, the number of candidate vectors checked in these stages is further limited. In addition, the frequently accessed pixels are in the central CTU and its surrounding eight CTUs. From these observations, we figure out that accesses in the subsequent stages concentrate on the nine CTUs, which are at the center of the areas where the stages search for motion vectors.

3 A Partitioned Memory System for CTU-Pipelined Video Encoders

From the discussions in Sect. 2, this paper proposes an effective memory system for CTU-pipelined video encoders. Figure 5 shows an overview of an encoder architecture. The memory system adopts a split cache structure, which consists of a front-end cache and a back-end cache. Moreover, a CTU prefetcher is introduced to the back-end cache to hide the access latency to the external DDR memory.

3.1 Split Cache Structure

As the early pipeline stages, especially WME, require a large amount of memory bandwidth, it should be reduced. To this end, this paper focuses on the fact that the early stages shrink the size of the image taken from the forward/backward reference frames after loading them. This is because the computation cost of motion vector search decreases by shrinking the reference frames. Since the function of these stages is to roughly search the reference frames for candidate motion vectors, the pixel-wise images of the reference frames are not needed.

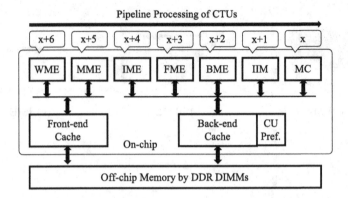

Fig. 5. Architecture overview.

Based on this fact, the shrunk reference frames used for the early stages are prepared in the external DDR memory in advance. The early stages access these shrunk frames rather than shrinking the size of frames after loading them in cache memories. Loading the shrunk frames can reduce the required bandwidth for the external DDR memory. Since WME and MME need 1/8-sized images and 1/2-sized images, respectively, the 1/2-sized images are prepared in the external DDR memory, in addition to the pixel-wise pictures of reference frames. The 1/8-sized images for WME are generated from the 1/2-sized images for MME. As a result, the bandwidth of the early stages can be reduced to one-fourth.

Since the early stages and the subsequent stages require different data, the split cache structure is employed. The cache for the early stages and that for the subsequent stages are called the front-end cache and the back-end cache, respectively. This structure is reasonable from the viewpoint of the effective usage of the caches.

3.2   Coding Tree Unit Prefetcher

In the split cache structure mentioned before, the subsequent stages cannot reuse the data stored in the front-end cache. The subsequent stages need to load the pixel-wise data from the external DDR memory. However, the access latency of the subsequent stages increases because all the accesses go to the external memory, compared with the case where all the stages access the same pixel-wise data in the unified cache. As a result, the data used in the subsequent stages cannot keep the deadline to maintain the rate of the real-time 4K 60 fps HEVC encoding.

To solve this problem, a CTU prefetcher is introduced into the back-end cache. This prefetcher loads the pixel-wise reference frames used in IME into the back-end cache before MME determines the candidate motion vectors that will be informed to IME. In Sect. 2.3, we observed that the accesses to the reference frames from the back-end stages are concentrated on the CTU at the same

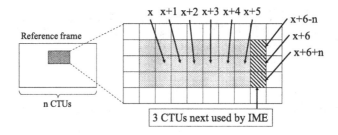

Fig. 6. Concept of the CTU Prefetcher.

position as the encoded one and its surrounding eight CTUs. Based on this observation, Fig. 6 shows how CTUs in the reference frames are accessed when the CTUs of the target frame are encoded in a pipelined fashion, as shown in Fig. 5. Figure 5 assumes that the five subsequent stages currently process the x-th to $(x+4)$-th CTUs. In this case, Fig. 6 shows the accessed CTUs in the reference frames. Since each stage uses the nine CTUs, the left three CTUs and the right three CTUs accessed by one stage are overlapped with those of the previous and next stages, respectively. Therefore, the light-shaded area including 21 CTUs is mainly accessed. From Figs. 5 and 6, it is very clear that, when IME starts the processing of the $(x+5)$-th CTU, IME requires the 9-CTU areas whose center is the $(x+5)$-th CTUs in the reference frames. Therefore, the prefetcher covers this area and reduces the access latency to the areas by prefetching three CTUs, $(x+6)$-th, $(x+6-n)$-th, and $(x+6+n)$-th, when IME processes the $(x+4)$-th CTU. Thanks to this prefetcher, when IME tries to obtain the data, the data are already on the back-end cache. Therefore, IME can receive the data before the deadlines of the real-time HEVC encoding.

4 Evaluations and Discussions

4.1 Experimental Methodology

This section evaluates the proposed memory system using benchmark movies. For this evaluation, a simulator for the HEVC hardware encoder is developed based on the gem5 architecture simulator [1] and the tracer used in Sect. 2.3. It simulates an encoder chip of the HEVC encoding pipeline at a 600 MHz clock frequency. The encoder chip is connected to one DDR4-2400 DIMM as an external DDR memory. The maximum bandwidth of the external memory reaches 19.2 GB/s. The energy consumption of the external DDR memory is estimated by the DRAM models included in the gem5 simulator.

Figure 7 shows the movies examined in this paper, which are taken from the various scenes; *churaumi*, *sl*, *fire*, *flower*, *pool* and *balls*. The formats of the movies are the same as the preliminary evaluations in Sect. 2.3, but their quantization parameters are 22.

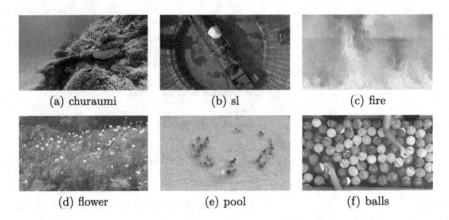

(a) churaumi   (b) sl   (c) fire

(d) flower   (e) pool   (f) balls

Fig. 7. Benchmark movies.

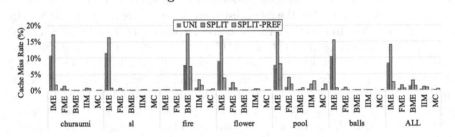

Fig. 8. Evaluation results of cache miss rate.

In this evaluation, three configurations of the cache memories for the encoder are examined. The first configuration is that the cache is *UNI* and shared by all the stages. This configuration is corresponding to NARA, which has a 26 MB on-chip buffer. The reason for the 32 MB capacity while the actual chip has the 26 MB capacity is that the gem5 simulator can model only 2^n-byte cache memories. The second configuration is *SPLIT*. As same as the proposed memory system, this configuration is with the 2 MB front-end and 256 kB back-end caches but excludes the proposed prefetcher to know its effectiveness. This evaluation compares these configurations with the third configuration that is the proposed memory system including the prefetcher, *SPLIT-PREF*. The parameters of all the caches are 16 banks, each of which is a direct map cache. The energy consumption of the cache is estimated by using the cache modeling tool CACTI [7], supposing a 22 nm process node with ITRS-HP for tag arrays and ITRS-LSTP for data arrays.

4.2 Evaluation Results

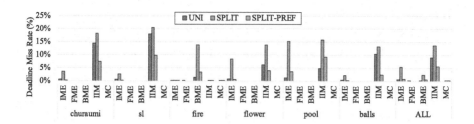

Fig. 9. Evaluation results of deadline miss rate.

Cache Miss and Deadline Miss Rate. Figure 8 shows the evaluation results in terms of the cache miss rates. These results show which subsequent stage issues each cache request and whether the request results in a miss for each configuration or not. From this figure, it is observed that *SPLIT-PREF* achieves better cache miss rates than *UNI* and *SPLIT* on average. Especially, the cache miss rate in IME is significantly reduced from around 10% and 14% in *UNI* and *SPLIT* to 2% in *SPLIT-PREF* on average. Therefore, the split cache structure with the CTU prefetcher is effective to reduce the number of cache misses with the smaller cache capacity.

Figure 8 indicates that *SPLIT* increases the cache miss rates. These results are natural because *SPLIT* reduces the total cache capacity compared with *UNI*. Although *UNI* has the largest cache capacity, *UNI* cannot achieve the smallest cache miss rate. This fact indicates that the CTU prefetcher is important for decreasing cache miss rates compared with increasing the cache capacity.

In the case of the *pool* movie data, the cache miss rates of *SPLIT-PREF* are slightly larger than those of *UNI*. The movie requires accesses to wider areas of reference images compared with the other movie data. Hence, prefetching for the 3-CTU area cannot cover those areas in this movie data, resulting in increases in the cache miss rates. However, for most of the movie data, the CTU prefetcher works well.

Figure 9 also shows the evaluation results of the deadline miss rates. Here, a deadline miss rate is a ratio of the number of overdue cache requests to that of the total requests. The deadline miss rates are around 1%, 5%, and 1% in IME of *UNI*, *SPLIT*, and *SPLIT-PREF* on average, respectively. Therefore, the split cache structure with the CTU prefetcher can successfully suppress the deadline miss rate with the smaller cache size.

In the case of the *pool* movie data, the deadline miss rates of *SPLIT-PREF* is larger than those of *UNI*. This is due to the increases in the cache miss rates. However, such movie data are not the majority among the examined data. Note that the deadline miss rates are also large in the IIM stage for all the configurations. In this stage, it is often difficult to satisfy the deadline due to the characteristics of the process.

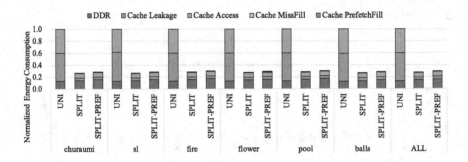

Fig. 10. Evaluation results of energy consumption.

From these observations, the combination of the split cache structure and the CTU prefetcher can contribute to the reduction in the cache miss rates and the deadline miss rates despite the small total cache capacity.

Energy Consumption. Figure 10 shows the evaluation results of the energy consumption of the memory system. From Fig. 10, it is observed that the energy consumption of *UNI* is enormously large compared with the other two configurations. This is because the total capacity of the caches decreases from 32 MB to 2.25 MB. Therefore, the split cache structure can successfully reduce the energy consumption of the memory system.

On the other hand, though the difference is small, the energy consumption of *SPLIT-PREF* slightly increases compared with those of *SPLIT*. The energy reduction rates from *UNI* are 74% in *SPLIT* but 72% in *SPLIT-PREF* on average. This is because of an increase in the energy consumption of DDR. The CTU prefetcher proposed in this paper always loads the data of 3 CTUs. However, not all the pixels of the 3 CTUs are required, and such data are loaded excessively by the CTU prefetcher. As a result, the energy consumption of DRAM becomes large. Note that the CTU prefetcher also decreases the MissFill energy and increases the PrefetchFill energy. However, the ratio of these energies to the total energy is not significant.

5   Related Work

Tsai et al. [13] have developed the HEVC encoder LSI to realize 8K real-time encoding. This LSI has a three-level on-chip memory hierarchy, and the search area in the early stages is stored by prefetching. On the other hand, in this paper, the detailed access patterns are precisely analyzed for each stage. The analysis suggests splitting the cache for more effective data handling.

Kondo et al. [5] have investigated the memory access behavior of the latest video coding standard, VVC. Their work focuses on the behavior of generic shared cache architecture. Since VVC inherits the major coding tools of HEVC, the outcomes of this paper, considering HEVC, will be able to apply to the future VVC encoder LSI.

6   Conclusions

This paper has proposed a partitioned memory architecture for CTU-pipelined hardware encoders. This memory system adopts the split cache structure. Moreover, since the subsequent stages cannot reuse the data loaded in the front-end cache, the data used in the back-end stages cannot arrive at the stages until the deadline for the real-time HEVC encoding. Hence, this paper proposes the CTU prefetcher and applies it to the back-end cache. This prefetcher loads the data of the CTUs to be used in the subsequent stages to the back-end cache before the early stages give the information for loading the pixels to the subsequent stages. The evaluation results show that the split cache structure can significantly reduce the energy consumption by 72% on average. Moreover, despite the reduction in the total cache capacity, the CTU prefetcher can successfully suppress the cache miss rates and the deadline miss rates.

In future work, detailed evaluations should be performed by using more benchmark movie data. It will result in a more sophisticated prefetcher that may further reduce the memory bandwidth.

Acknowledgements. This work was partially supported by Grant-in-Aid for Scientific Research (B) No. 22H03571 and the joint research between Tohoku University and NTT Device Innovation Center, NTT Corporation.

References

1. Binkert, N., et al.: The gem5 simulator. ACM SIGARCH Comput. Architect. News **39**(2), 1–7 (2011). https://doi.org/10.1145/2024716.2024718
2. Bross, B., et al.: Overview of the versatile video coding (VVC) standard and its applications. IEEE Trans. Circuits Syst. Video Technol. **31**(10), 3736–3764 (2021). https://doi.org/10.1109/TCSVT.2021.3101953
3. Cerveira, A., Agostini, L., Zatt, B., Sampaio, F.: Memory assessment of versatile video coding. In: International Conference on Image Processing, vol. 2020, pp. 1186–1190. IEEE Computer Society (2020). https://doi.org/10.1109/ICIP40778.2020.9191358
4. JCT-VC: HEVC test model (2022). https://hevc.hhi.fraunhofer.de/
5. Kondo, Y., et al.: A shared cache architecture for VVC coding. In: COOL Chips 25 Poster (2022)
6. Mativi, A., Monteiro, E., Bampi, S.: Memory access profiling for HEVC encoders. In: IEEE 7th Latin American Symposium on Circuits and Systems (LASCAS), pp. 243–246 (2016). https://doi.org/10.1109/LASCAS.2016.7451055
7. Muralimanohar, N., Balasubramonian, R., Jouppi, N.P.: CACTI 6.0: a tool to model large caches. Technical report. HPL-2009-85, HP Labs (2009)

8. Omori, Y., Onishi, T., Iwasaki, H., Shimizu, A.: A 120 fps high frame rate real-time HEVC video encoder with parallel configuration scalable to 4K. IEEE Trans. Multi-Scale Comput. Syst. **4**(4), 491–499 (2018). https://doi.org/10.1109/TMSCS. 2018.2825320

9. Onishi, T., et al.: A single-chip 4K 60-fps 4:2:2 HEVC video encoder LSI employing efficient motion estimation and mode decision framework with scalability to 8K. IEEE Trans. Very Large Scale Integr. (VLSI) Syst. **26**(10), 1930–1938 (2018). https://doi.org/10.1109/TVLSI.2018.2842179

10. Sinangil, M.E., Chandrakasan, A.P., Sze, V., Zhou, M.: Memory cost vs. coding efficiency trade-offs for HEVC motion estimation engine. In: International Conference on Image Processing, pp. 1533–1536 (2012). https://doi.org/10.1109/ICIP. 2012.6467164

11. Sullivan, G.J., Ohm, J.R., Han, W.J., Wiegand, T.: Overview of the high efficiency video coding (HEVC) standard. IEEE Trans. Circuits Syst. Video Technol. **22**(12), 1649–1668 (2012). https://doi.org/10.1109/TCSVT.2012.2221191

12. The Advanced Television Systems Committee Inc: ATSC3.0 standards (2022). https://www.atsc.org/atsc-documents/type/3-0-standards/

13. Tsai, S.F., Li, C.T., Chen, H.H., Tsung, P.K., Chen, K.Y., Chen, L.G.: A 1062Mpixels/s 8192×4320p high efficiency video coding (H.265) encoder chip. In: IEEE Symposium on VLSI Circuits, Digest of Technical Papers, pp. C146–C147. IEEE (2013). https://ieeexplore.ieee.org/abstract/document/6578657

14. Wiegand, T., Sullivan, G.J., Bjøntegaard, G., Luthra, A.: overview of the H.264/AVC video coding standard. IEEE Trans. Circuits Syst. Video Technol. **13**(7), 560–576 (2003). https://doi.org/10.1109/TCSVT.2003.815165

A Hardware Trojan Exploiting Coherence Protocol on NoCs

Yoshiya Shikama[1], Michihiro Koibuchi[2(✉)], and Hideharu Amano[1]

[1] Keio University, Yokohama, Kanagawa 223-8522, Japan
{shikama,hunga}@am.ics.keio.ac.jp
[2] National Institute of Informatics, Chiyoda-ku, Tokyo 101-8430, Japan
koibuchi@nii.ac.jp

Abstract. Intellectual property (IP) has been used in Network on chips (NoCs) for reducing costs and shortening the time to market. However, there is a probability that a third-party vendor injects hardware that behaves maliciously. This study firstly illustrates the security risk of a hardware Trojan for eavesdropping and reducing the system performance by malicious coherent messages. It only increases the amounts of communications and calculations obeying a coherence protocol, allowing applications to perform correctly. This study secondly presents its countermeasure at network interfaces. It compares the number of output messages to input messages at network interfaces to detect malicious coherent messages. This risk causes, on a chip-multiprocessor, execution time to increase by up to 24%, the amount of traffic to increase by up to 18%, and the energy consumption to increase by up to 8.9%. Since the benchmarks in the evaluation are small, we expect that real-life applications would be highly affected by the hardware Trojan. Our countermeasure avoids these performance degradation, and it can be implemented with a significantly low overhead of only 1.3% in a network interface on a chip.

Keywords: Interconnection networks · Hardware Trojan · Network interface · Network on chip (NoC)

1 Introduction

Network-on-chip (NoC) technology has attracted attention as a communication infrastructure on not only chip multiprocessors (CMPs) but also internet-of-things (IoT) embedded devices. The use of intellectual property (IP) is promoted to reduce manufacturing costs and shorten the time-to-market for NoCs [1,3]. However, there is a security risk; malicious third-party vendors may incorporate circuitry that behaves in a suspiciously manner into such IPs [3,4,7,9]. Such circuits with malicious behavior are called Hardware Trojans (HTs). Many countermeasures have been proposed to uncover HTs in the manufacturing process. However, SoC designs have become more highly sophisticated, making HT detection increasingly difficult. The security risk noted in many existing studies

© The Author(s), under exclusive license to Springer Nature Switzerland AG 2023
H. Takizawa et al. (Eds.): PDCAT 2022, LNCS 13798, pp. 301–313, 2023.
https://doi.org/10.1007/978-3-031-29927-8_24

assumes that an HT is embedded in the NoC router. Effective countermeasures include message encryption and authentication functions [3]. By contrast, a limited number of security technologies can counter the security risk of HTs being embedded in network interfaces.

Firstly in this work, we present a new security risk, an HT attack targeting the coherence management mechanism for coherence directories in CMPs, with the aim of alerting people to the system's danger. This HT can execute two separate types of attacks, the eavesdropping attack and the denial-of-service attack. These two types of attacks are characterized by the fact that the malicious messages are properly processed according to the MOESI coherence protocol on a CMP, and do not cause any system errors; thus, they are difficult to detect and counteract. Notice that most CMP systems provide programmers with shared-memory model. It requires a support for cache coherence to maintain the consistency of data. MOESI uses the five data states, Modified, Owned, Exclusive, Shared, and Invalid, is a high-performance cache coherence protocol.

This HT can be embedded in a network interface. It abuses the fact that in the MOESI coherence protocol, reads of dirty data are processed by forwarding data from the owner. The HT in the network interface can generate coherent request messages by entering malicious commands into the coherence directory. It generates redundant memory copies by faking the mark of dirty for non-dirty cache data in the MOESI coherence protocol. Therefore, it will significantly degrade the performance and energy consumption due to the coherent processing and increased communication volume. The HT operation follows the MOESI coherence protocol. Thus, the HT cannot be protected by typical countermeasures, such as encryption at a network interface.

Secondly, we propose a countermeasure against this new security risk. Our method monitors and compares the number of output messages to the number of input messages at network interfaces to detect malicious coherent messages on CMPs. When an HT attacks to increase the traffics using a cache coherent protocol, an additional multicast, such as announcing "invalid", occurs. Our countermeasure detects and removes it at a network interface. Our contribution is listed as follows.

- We illustrate a new security risk, an HT attack targeting the coherence management mechanism for coherence directories in CMPs.
- Full-system simulation results illustrate that the HT causes execution time to increase by up to 24%, the amount of traffic to increase by up to 18%, and the power consumption to increase by up to 8.9%.
- The countermeasure can be implemented with a significantly low overhead of only 1.3% in a network interface.

The remainder of the paper is organized as follows. Section 2 discusses the related works. Section 3 illustrates the new security risk using a coherence protocol on CMPs. Section 4 presents the countermeasure at a network interface. Section 5 presents the comprehensive performance evaluation of the countermeasure. Section 6 concludes with a summary of our findings.

2   Related Work

Hardware Trojans can be classified into eavesdropping attack, spoofing/data integrity attack, denial-of-service attack, buffer overflow/memory extraction attack, and side channel attack [3]. In this study, we focus on eavesdropping attack and denial-of-service attack on NoCs.

2.1   Hardware Trojan Embedded in Network Interfaces

Many previous studies did not address re-attacks by software tasks that initiated eavesdropping attacks. The cost of preventing attacks leads to performance degradation and increased power consumption [8]. Therefore, as a countermeasure with less overhead, they proposed a snooping invalidation module (SIM). SIM can detect illegal messages using a key with a buffer column ID in the AXI handshake protocol. They also proposed a module for detecting snooping using a threshold value. The ratio of the number of packets to the number of received packets would implicit an anomaly in a processing element (PE) where the malware is running to obtain the snooped packets. However, in this threat model, malicious attack packets are not detected because they pass through the network interface in a regular coherent processing procedure. Therefore, in this threat model, the attack cannot be prevented by the countermeasure proposed by Raparti et al.

2.2   Hardware Trojan Colluding with Malware

Tehranipoor et al. provided a detailed categorization of how HTs are launched under specific circumstances [10]. First, HTs can be categorized into external-kicked and internal-kicked starts. An HT is activated by satisfying the threshold value of temperature, voltage, humidity, altitude, etc., which are acquired by sensors on a chip. Another HT is activated as long as the power is supplied on a chip, or it is activated when specific input patterns or counter values are met in the internal logic. Wolff et al. note that, from the attacker's point of view, HTs should not always attack; rather, they should devise their startup conditions to avoid an attack detection [11].

2.3   Attack by Hardware Trojan Using Messages Controlling Data Coherence

Attacks by HTs using coherent control messages have been discussed by Kim et al. [5]. Cache-coherent interfaces for hardware accelerators have been provided by CPU manufacturers that provide significant advantages in terms of performance improvement and power consumption in the system. However, it has been noted that they are subject to attacks by HTs. Kim et al. proposed two Trojan models, which assume that an HT is embedded in a hardware accelerator and attacks the accelerator using coherent control messages. A Trojan model sends continuous read request messages to an inclusive last-level cache (LLC) shared by the CPU and hardware accelerator. Inclusive caches must invalidate copies of cache lines evicted by replacement in the LLC if they are held in higher-level caches. Inclusive caches must invalidate the copy of the cache line evicted by replacement in the LLC if it is held in a higher-level cache. In the case of an inclusive cache, if a copy of a cache line evicted by a replacement in the LLC is held in a higher-level cache, it must be invalidated. This causes frequent invalidations of cache lines in higher-level caches due to replacements, significantly reducing system performance.

Another Trojan model causes performance degradation of higher-level cache lines differently. An HT in the accelerator sends a write invalidation message to the LLC; if the CPU has a copy of the memory block corresponding to the address, the LLC requests the CPU to invalidate the cache line.

However, the write invalidation attack is unstable because the coherent status of the LLC is updated. Therefore, there is a high possibility that the attack can be easily detected. In fact, in a previous study, they exploited a vulnerability in the ACP interface that provides the coherence function to the accelerator. Therefore, it is generally considered unlikely that this attack will succeed.

2.4 Packet Tampering Attack

In [2], a threat model is presented in which packets are tampered with by HTs on an NoC equipped with cryptographic and authentication functions. Since the arriving packets are decrypted and then authenticated, if the packets are tampered with, unnecessary decryption operations and performance degradation due to retransmissions will occur. To address this problem, Charles et al. proposed a routing method that defines and quantifies the trustworthiness of network nodes and judges whether a node is trustworthy or not under a certain threshold, thereby avoiding nodes that may harbor HTs. Another prior work proposed adding a bit shuffling function to the router pipeline as a countermeasure against DoS attacks that aim to degrade performance by tampering with critical fields (number of flits, addresses, and head/tail indication bits) in the packet header and generating retransmission requests. They proposed adding a bit shuffling function to the router pipeline. This protects the critical field and performs 1-bit error correction using a Hamming code on each router.

3 New Security Risk

3.1 Prerequisite

Each node consists of a processing element (core and private cache), a coherence directory, and/or a distributed shared cache. Each of which is connected to the NoC through a separate network interface to send and receive messages. Of these, the HT is embedded in the network interface connected to the directory that maintains coherence between the private and shared caches, as shown in Fig. 1.

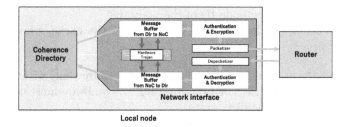

Fig. 1. Network interface of NoC.

We assume MOESI coherence protocol that defines the behavior of this directory in target NoCs. In MOESI, a read request for an address with a coherent status of "dirty" is handled by sending a forwarding request for the corresponding data to the core that requested the read instead of a write-back request for the dirty data to the owner core[1]. This is done by sending a forwarding request to the core that requested the read. The proposed threat model exploits this method of processing MOESI read requests for dirty data and attacks the application with fake coherent control messages in a way that does not affect the computation process of the application, thus making it difficult to notice the attack.

We also assume that the HT has the following prerequisite information.

– The format of a message exchanged with the directory.
– Message types of coherent control (e.g., read/write requests and forward requests).

Based on this prerequisite information, the HT can duplicate any bit of information in the snoop message and use it to forge a coherent control message, while it successfully avoids failing the application execution.

3.2   New Eavesdropping Attack

Attack Preparation Process. The HT monitors the message buffers in the network interface. The HT is embedded and can replicate coherent control messages to the target address in different parts of the format (Fig. 1). The preparation process for the attack is initiated by sending a specific sequence of activation messages from the processing element (PE) to which the malware is assigned to the network interface in which the HT is embedded. The following two conditions have to be met in the preparation process:

---

[1] The word "owner" appears frequently in this study. This is not the owner of the owned status in the coherent status, but it is used in the sense of "having the final write back responsibility to the lower cache hierarchy". Therefore, "the owner core of the data corresponding to a specific address" refers to both the owner of the data corresponding to the address in the owner status and the only core that caches the data corresponding to the address in the modified status in the coherent status.

Condition I-1 Obtain the node ID of the malware.
Condition I-2 Obtain the address information of the cache, whose coherent status is "dirty".

Condition I-1 is assumed to be notified by the malware along with the startup message sequence of the HT. For Condition I-2, the malware must confirm that the target address is in the dirty state.

The HT identifies the above two conditions by either of the following actions:

- Snoop the message buffer from the directory to the NoC and capture the forwarding message.
- Snoop the message buffer from NoC to the directory and catch the write message.

Attack Process. Once the two conditions of the preparation process are met, the HT immediately launches its attack. Using the duplicate node ID obtained by Condition I-1 and the duplicate address obtained by Condition I-2, it forges a read request message from the node on which the malware is running and writes it into the message buffer of the coherence directory. This message causes the coherence directory to send a forwarding request message to the owner core. Based on the forwarding request message, the owner core reads the corresponding dirty data from the private cache and forwards it to the node where the malware is located. The forwarded dirty data are leaked to the outside by the malware.

3.3   Denial-of-Service Attack

Attack Preparation Process. As in the case of Sect. 3.2, the HT monitors the message buffer of the network interface and performs partial replication of the messages (Fig. 1). Similarly, for the activation sequence, the preparation process of the attack is initiated by sending a specific message sequence. The following three conditions have to be met in the preparation process:

Condition II-1 Obtain the node ID of the malware.
Condition II-2 Obtain the owner node ID of the data at the target address.
Condition II-3 Verify that the coherent status of the target address is owned.

As in the case of an eavesdropping attack, Condition II-1 is assumed to be notified by the malware along with the startup message sequence of the HT. For Conditions II-2 and II-3, since the malware must confirm that the target address is owned, the HT snoops the message buffer from the directory to the NoC and sends it to the NoC. Therefore, the HT snoops the message buffer from the directory to the NoC and supplements the forwarding message to ensure that the coherent status of the address is owned and simultaneously achieves Condition II-3.

Attack Process. As soon as the three conditions in the preparation process are met, the HT starts its attack. Using the duplicate owner node ID obtained by Condition II-2 and the duplicate address obtained by Condition II-3, it forges a write request message from the owner core and writes it into the message buffer of the coherence directory. By this message, the coherence directory sends an invalidation message to the shared core that caches the data of the corresponding address. Each shared core invalidates the cache line corresponding to the address in its private cache and returns an ack to the coherence directory. Upon receiving the ack, the coherence directory sends a write permission message to the owner core. Since this write permission message is an invalid message and triggers an abnormal operation at the destination, the HT deletes this message from the message buffer flowing toward the NoC. Then, the HT forges a write ack message using the duplicate owner node ID obtained by Condition II-2 and the duplicate address obtained by Condition II-3 and writes it in the message buffer to the coherence directory.

4   Countermeasure

In this section, we propose effective countermeasures against the security risk pointed out in the previous section. Many existing studies have adopted the case of HTs embedded in router IPs and authentication, encryption, bit shuffling, etc., have been proposed as countermeasures (see Sect. 2.4). However, the security risk noted in this study is the incorporation of HTs into the network interface, which makes it difficult to apply existing methods as a countermeasure. In this security risk, the HT adds illegal messages to the message buffer in the network interface and malformed messages to the message buffer in the network interface and exploits the coherence control mechanism, which adversely affects the system. Therefore, we propose a set of simple detection methods and countermeasures.

4.1   Detection Method

Communication between the coherence directory and the router is always performed through the network interface. Our detection method inserts the inter-link countermeasure logic, as shown in Fig. 2. It counts the number of messages between a router and a coherence directory. Then, it compares the output number of messages to the input numbers of messages.

More precisely, the following equations hold for each router-to-directory and directory-to-router communication direction if no illegal messages are added, as shown in Fig. 2.

$$IN1 = OUT1 + STAY1, \tag{1}$$

$$IN2 = OUT2 + STAY2, \tag{2}$$

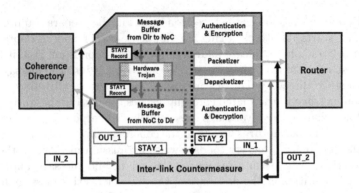

Fig. 2. Overview of the countermeasure in network interface.

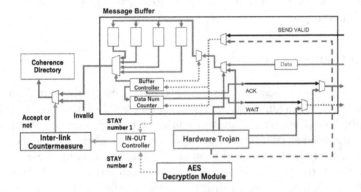

Fig. 3. Block diagram of the countermeasure in network interface.

where IN# is the number of flits entering the network interface, OUT# is the number of flits exiting the network interface, and STAY# is the number of flits remaining in the message buffer in the network interface.

The target HT completes the addition of the malicious message without causing the loss of the legitimate message. Therefore, due to the addition of malformed messages by the Trojan, the sum of the right-hand sides of the equations becomes larger than the left-hand side, and the equality does not hold. In general, network interfaces do not have the ability to create messages from scratch, so the equations will only fail if there is a message loss due to a module failure. However, since the sum of the right-hand sides of each equation becomes less than the left-hand side when packet loss occurs, it is possible to distinguish them from the addition of illegal messages by a Trojan. The above makes it possible to detect an attack by a Trojan.

4.2 Countermeasure

The message buffer of the network interface is assumed to be first in, first out (FIFO). Therefore, the timing at which a malformed message is output from the network interface can be predicted by the number of messages in the message buffer when the malformed message is detected. This is independent from the network congestion, and the operation time to a message within the network interface is predictable. At this predicted time, as shown in Fig. 3, the attack can be stopped by blocking the transmission of the malicious message with a simple multiplexer.

Our concern is a hard-to-detect security risk in this study. Notice that, if an HT modifies a coherent-control message and does not increase the number of messages at a network interface, it cannot detect the modification of a message. However, such a modification leads to fail a program execution by making the shared cache inconsistent, and a system can easily find out the HT.

5 Evaluation

5.1 Execution Time and Traffic Amount

Using a full-system simulator called gem5 [6], we executed six applications (BT, CG, FT, EP, IS, and LU) of NAS Parallel Benchmarks (NPB), OpenMP version, as well as a summation application leading to the largest performance degradation by the HT. We developed an OpenMP summation application that increments the values of an array, then calculates the sum of the array. It has a large number of opportunities to be attacked. Table 1 is parameters used in the simulation, and we assumed a conventional 4 × 4-mesh NoC. We obtained the execution time and the amount of traffic for each.s In addition, to evaluate the network latency, we obtained the traffic trace on the NoC when each application was executed.

Table 1. Simulation parameters.

Processor	X86_64	Memory size	512 MB
L1 I/D cache size	32 KB (line:64B)	Protocol	MOESI directory
L1 cache latency	2 cycle	Control/data packet size	1 flit/5 flits
L2 cache bank size	16 MB (assoc:8)	Topology	4 × 4 Mesh
L2 cache latency	20 cycles	# of Cores	16
# of shared L2 cache	16	# of Directories	16

In this study, we propose an HT attack using coherence directories as a new security risk. To simulate the HT attack, the conventional gem5 simulator was used as a baseline, Then, we modified gem5 to introduce the HT attack on the coherence control mechanism between the L1 and L2 caches. When the conditions are met, the corresponding HT attacks automatically starts on a running application. Thus, we conducted a comparative evaluation of the impact of this security risk on the execution of applications.

Figure 4(a) shows the execution time for each application of NPB, and a home-built application assuming the worst-case scenario. For each of the NPB applications, the increase in execution time due to hardware Trojan attacks is small, ranging from 0.00% to 0.88%, while the increase is 24.26% for the execution of home-built applications. The impact of attacks on execution time is so different between the real application and the worst case is the difference in the number of attacks. In the worst case, 2,014 attacks were made, whereas in the NPB case, the maximum number of attacks was only 369 for CG. This is because our application, which uses OpenMP for parallel processing as well as NPB, was programmed to artificially increase the degree of parallelism to maximize the impact of the attacks in order to achieve the worst case, which has the most negative impact on the execution time. On the other hand, the number of messages increases from 0.00% to 18.32% for NPB, and 16.06% for the worst case. (The worst case for EP is 0.00% since no attack occurs.) While the execution time and the dirty data-sharing rate are expected to affect the impact of a single attack, it is the number of attacks that has a more significant impact. The number of attacks depends on the characteristics of each NPB application. It is predicted that the attacks presented in this study will be effective for those applications in which communication performance is the dominant factor.

We analyzed the behaviour of the HT attacks during the execution of each application. Figure 4(b) represents the traffic amount when executing each application, whereas Fig. 4(c) represents the number of attacks. We found that each application has different impact of the HT attacks on the traffic amount. For example, EP application generates almost zero attacks, due to its almost zero communication between processor cores. This situation does not introduce the data sharing. By contrast, CG application 369 attacks, which increases by 12% the amount of traffic for the coherence protocol. Interestingly, NPB applications have different occurrence frequencies of shared data.

5.2   Energy Consumption

We implemented a network interface and a router using Verilog-HDL and obtained the end-to-end energy consumption for the transmission of 1-flit and 5-flit packets on a chip. We simulated the router with a bit width of 67 bits and an operating frequency of 588 MHz under the condition of a Nangate 45 nm open cell library. Other parameters are the same as the evaluation in the previous section. We completed its synthesis using Synopsys Synopsys Design CompilerQ-2019.12-SP1. The quantity of each packet was extracted from the traffic trace, and based on the results of the latency evaluation, we calculated the energy consumption of the network required to run each application.

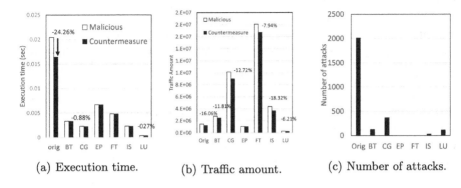

(a) Execution time.   (b) Traffic amount.   (c) Number of attacks.

Fig. 4. Simulation results of each parallel application.

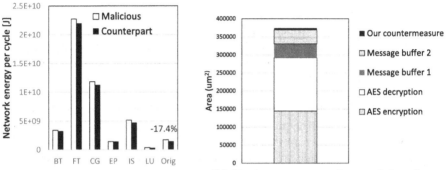

(a) Network energy consumption per cycle of each parallel application.

(b) Hardware amount of network interface.

Fig. 5. Energy and hardware evaluation.

The energy consumption per cycle is shown in Fig. 5(a). The maximum rate of increase or decrease in consumption due to attacks is 8.93%, while the average for NPB only is 3.95%. This energy consumption is evaluated only for the network portion, and in an actual system, the energy consumption is expected to worsen due to memory reads during deactivation, waiting time in the network interface, and other factors. In addition, the existing encryption and authentication functions to enhance security on the network will further deteriorate the energy consumption of this threat model. Figure 4(b) illustrates original, BT, CG and IS increases by at least 10% the traffic amount by the HT. As expected, they increase the network energy in Fig. 5(a).

5.3 Hardware Amount

Using Verilog-HDL, we implemented a network interface including an AES cryptographic function to protect the end-to-end communication on the NoC router network. An HT was embedded in the message buffer, and the above detection method and countermeasure were confirmed to work by logical simulation. We generated a network interface design with a Nangate 45 nm open cell library, and we completed its synthesis using Synopsys Synopsys Design CompilerQ-2019.12-SP1. We used a waveform display tool to verify that both the detection method and countermeasure were functioning properly. The area of the hardware was obtained by logic synthesis.

Figure 5(b) illustrates the area of each component module of the network interface. The overhead of the detection method and countermeasure for the network interface is 1.25%, indicating that it can be implemented with a small overhead. The AES cryptographic function accounts for 79% of the area of the network interface.

6   Conclusions

In this study, we noted a new security risk, which is the exploitation of the coherence control mechanism to perform eavesdropping and denial-of-service attacks on CMPs. In the eavesdropping attack, the forwarding process of dirty data in the MOESI coherence protocol is exploited to eavesdrop on the data. In denial-of-service attacks, the owner node disguises its writes to one dirty cache line and invalidates the cache lines of other nodes, resulting in poor system performance and increased energy consumption. These attacks are difficult to detect and counteract because the malicious messages are properly handled according to the MOESI coherence protocol and do not cause any system errors. This risk causes execution time to increase by up to 24%, the amount of traffic to increase by up to 18%, and the energy consumption to increase by up to 8.9% in CMPs. Since the benchmarks in the evaluation are small, we expect that real-life applications would be highly affected by the HT.

In this study, we assume that a HT adds malformed messages to the message buffer to exploit the coherence control mechanism. Therefore, we proposed a detection method to detect the addition of this malicious message by measuring the number of messages flowing into, out of, and parked in the network interface and a countermeasure to prevent the transfer of messages to the coherence directory. We performed a hardware implementation of the network interface using Verilog-HDL and added an HT, a detection method, and a countermeasure. We found that our countermeasure can be implemented with a small area overhead of 1.3% of the hardware area of the network interface.

Acknowledgments. This work was partly supported by JSPS KAKENHI Grant Number 19H01106.

References

1. Ancajas, D.M., Chakraborty, K., Roy, S.: Fort-NoCs: mitigating the threat of a compromised NoC. In: Design Automation Conference (DAC), pp. 1–6 (2014)
2. Charles, S., Mishra, P.: Securing network-on-chip using incremental cryptography. In: Symposium on VLSI (ISVLSI), pp. 168–175 (2020)

3. Charles, S., Mishra, P.: A survey of network-on-chip security attacks and counter-measures. ACM Comput. Surv. (CSUR) **54**(5), 1–36 (2021)
4. Hussain, M., Malekpour, A., Guo, H., Parameswaran, S.: EETD: an energy efficient design for runtime hardware trojan detection in untrusted network-on-chip. In: Symposium on VLSI (ISVLSI), pp. 345–350 (2018)
5. Kim, M., Kong, S., Hong, B., Xu, L., Shi, W., Suh, T.: Evaluating coherence-exploiting hardware trojan. In: Design, Automation Test in Europe Conference Exhibition (DATE), pp. 157–162 (2017)
6. Binkert, N., et al.: The gem5 Simulator. ACM SIGARCH Comput. Archit. News **39**(2), 1–7 (2011)
7. Rajesh, J., Ancajas, D.M., Chakraborty, K., Roy, S.: Runtime detection of a band-width denial attack from a rogue network-on-chip. In: International Symposium on Networks-on-Chip, pp. 1–8 (2015)
8. Raparti, V.Y., Pasricha, S.: Lightweight mitigation of hardware trojan attacks in NoC-based manycore computing. In: Design Automation Conference (DAC), pp. 1–6 (2019)
9. Ro, Y., Jin, S., Huh, J., Kim, J.: Ghost routing to enable oblivious computation on memory-centric networks. In: International Symposium on Computer Architecture (ISCA), pp. 930–943 (2021)
10. Tehranipoor, M., Koushanfar, F.: A survey of hardware trojan taxonomy and detection. IEEE Des. Test Comput. **27**(1), 10–25 (2010)
11. Wolff, F., Papachristou, C., Bhunia, S., Chakraborty, R.S.: Towards trojan-free trusted ICs: problem analysis and detection scheme. In: Design, Automation and Test in Europe (DATE), pp. 1362–1365 (2008)

A System-Wide Communication to Couple Multiple MPI Programs for Heterogeneous Computing

Shinji Sumimoto[1]([✉]), Takashi Arakawa[2], Yoshio Sakaguchi[3], Hiroya Matsuba[4], Hisashi Yashiro[5], Toshihiro Hanawa[1], and Kengo Nakajima[1,6]

[1] The University of Tokyo, Kashiwa, Japan
sumimoto@cc.u-tokyo.ac.jp
[2] CliMTech Inc., Funabashi, Japan
[3] Fujitsu Ltd., Tokyo, Japan
[4] Hitachi Ltd., Tokyo, Japan
[5] National Institute for Environmental Studies, Tsukuba, Japan
[6] RIKEN CCS, Kobe, Japan

Abstract. This paper proposes a system-wide communication library to couple multiple MPI programs for heterogeneous coupling computing called h3-Open-SYS/WaitIO-Socket (WaitIO-Socket for short). WaitIO-Socket provides an inter-program communication environment among MPI programs and supports different MPI libraries with various interconnects and processor types. We have developed the WaitIO-Socket communication library and tested it on the Wisteria/BDEC-01 supercomputing system, including Odyssey (Fujitsu A64FX-aarch64/Fujitsu-MPI/Tofu) and Aquarius (Intel Xeon-x86_64+NVIDIA-A100/Intel MPI/InfiniBand). As a result of the evaluation, WaitIO-Socket can execute large-scale programs on the Wisteria system, our first target system. The Odyssey and Aquarius MPI programs are able to communicate using WaitIO-Socket and achieve 53.2 GB/s using multiple streams throughout the system. We also show that the application NICAM/ADA is able to run with the h3-Open-UTIL/MP coupler 35% faster on the combination of Odyssey with Arm CPU and Aquarius with NVIDIA GPU than Odyssey with Arm CPU.

Keywords: Heterogeneous Computing · System Wide Communication · Simulation and Deep Learning

1 Introduction

The world has entered the era of Exa-scale class systems, and now discussions of the Post Exa-scale systems have begun.

With the spread of higher-scale computing systems, HPC applications have become able to solve more practical problems. They can solve not only simple problems but also more complex problems. For example: 1) Some applications

H. Matsuba—Achievements as a visiting professor at the University of Tokyo, 2021.

H. Takizawa et al. (Eds.): PDCAT 2022, LNCS 13798, pp. 314–327, 2023.
https://doi.org/10.1007/978-3-031-29927-8_25

make it possible to realize real-time simulation with various kind of sensor data and estimate the future. 2) Some applications improve calculation accuracy by assimilating calculation results and real-time data. 3) Some applications use computer simulation results as machine learning data and do simulation using inference computation.

Demanding needs for higher computing power have faced electricity issues. So, the next flagship-level supercomputer will be heterogeneous computing systems which consist of several different hardware configurations for each target application area optimized.

In these cases, to solve complicated problems by using multiple applications in next-generation supercomputers, using heterogeneous systems will be an optimized way. This computing technique is called heterogeneous coupling computing. In this computing technique, a cooperative way among multiple systems is a key to integrating heterogeneous systems.

We are developing h3-Open-SYS, which is a group of system software that can realize collaborative calculation between different types of systems. The goal of h3-Open-SYS is to enable cooperative operation in multiple systems to integrate simulation processing, data processing, and learning processing at a higher level. The h3 in the h3-OpenSYS means Hierarchical, Hybrid, and Heterogeneous.

Our first target system of h3-Open-SYS is the Wisteria/BDEC-01 system which is a heterogeneous cluster system. It connects a large-scale Arm-based simulation node group and a data/learning node group consisting of x86_64+GPU with a high-performance network. In this system, we plan to research and develop innovative simulation methods in the exascale era by calculation+data+learning integration.

This paper discusses an execution environment of heterogeneous coupling computing and its critical components to realize communication among heterogeneous systems. We have developed the communication library named h3-Open-SYS/WaitIO-Socket (WaitIO-Socket for short) and evaluated it on the Wisteria/BDEC-01 system.

The structure of this paper is as follows. Section 2 outlines heterogeneous coupling computing we should realize. Section 3 describes the requirements of heterogeneous coupling communication, and Sect. 4 describes the design of WaitIO-Socket, which is the subject of this paper, Sect. 5 describes its implementation Sect. 6 describes the evaluation of target systems, Sect. 7 describes related research, and Sect. 8 summarizes the results.

2   Heterogeneous Coupling Computing as a Next Computing Environment

The paper [12] shows that the limitation of exponential clock frequency scaling and lithographic scaling lead to the end of Moore's law, and the computing system will be more dedicated hardware configuration for each application target. This fact shows that heterogeneous computing is the key to solving complex problems. The report concludes that post-Exascale computing will be extreme heterogeneity.

With the spread of higher-scale computing systems, HPC applications have become able to solve more practical problems. To efficiently solve the coupled computing of multiple problems with different characteristics, it is better to process the system with the calculation mechanism with the processing unit suitable for each calculation in an integrated manner. It means heterogeneous coupling computing is the way to realize.

However, the problem is that there is currently no standard for communication protocols for coupled computation between systems and computer centers. A communication mechanism that realizes this communication is required. Therefore, we have started the development of a communication mechanism capable of coupled calculation between systems and computer centers.

3   Heterogeneous Coupling Communication Requirements

This section discusses the requirements of the heterogeneous coupling communication described in Sect. 2.

The WaitIO is one of the h3-Open-BDEC [1] software systems which aims to realize heterogeneous communication between system areas and computer centers. We have developed the WaitIO for the heterogeneous coupling communication among systems and computer centers.

The WaitIO should be applicable to the following requirements:

- Operating on Heterogeneous Hardware and Software:
  - WaitIO requires multiple applications on different kinds of nodes to be combined to enable mutual data exchange.
  - Applicable to Heterogeneous Hardware Environments: CPUs, Accelerators, Interconnects, Network configuration.
  - Applicable to Heterogeneous Software Environments: Operating systems, Low level communication libraries(MPI etc.).
- Combining multiple application groups with less effort:
  - Existing software modification can be achieved by minimal change and only the combined part.
  - Needed a programming style close to the standard to have a to facilitate programming easily.
  - Needed to be coexistent with other system software

To realize the requirements described above, we have developed the WaitIO using the POSIX Socket interface. We called this WaitIO the WaitIO-Socket.

4   WaitIO-Socket Design

This section describes our first target system and the design policy for realizing WaitIO-Socket requirements described in Sect. 3.

Our first target system of WaitIO-Socket is Wisteria/BDEC-01 system. Figure 1 shows the overview of the Wisteria/BDEC-01 system (hereafter

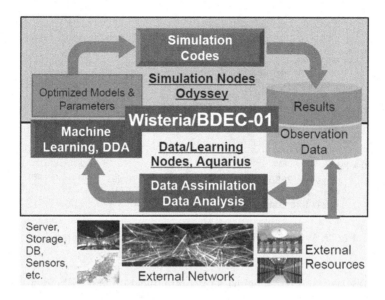

Fig. 1. The configuration of the Wisteria/BDEC-01 system

Wisteria). It connects a large-scale Arm-based simulation node group and a data/learning node group consisting of x86_64+GPU. The two node groups are connected a high-speed file system and a shared file system. It also connected to each other by InfiniBand EDR/HDR interconnects in a Fat tree configuration with a total full-bisection bandwidth of 2 TB/s.

The Odyssey system consists of 20 racks of 7,680 A64FX compute nodes. Each computing rack has eight InfiniBand EDR links (100 Gbps) via each GIO (Global I/O) node, as shown in Fig. 2. Each node of the Aquarius system, which consists of 45 compute nodes, is equipped with four InfiniBand HDR (200 Gbps), a total of 800 Gbps per node.

We plan to research and develop innovative simulation methods in the exascale era by calculation+data+learning integration on the system.

The design policy of WaitIO-Socket is described below.

- **Adoption of Socket dedicated interface:** The socket interface is adopted as a communication protocol to connect programs composed of different types of processors, different types of interconnects, and different kinds of MPIs. Odyssey's interconnect, Tofu-D Interconnect, also supports TCP/IP communication over the interconnect, and communication between compute nodes and systems outside the system is feasible via Global I/O (GIO) nodes. Also, implementing the communication library directly on the socket interface makes it possible to coexist with MPI and other system software.
- **Providing APIs that conform to the MPI specifications:** The provided APIs and communication semantics should be as much as possible the same as the communication libraries that are usually used. Therefore, the API of

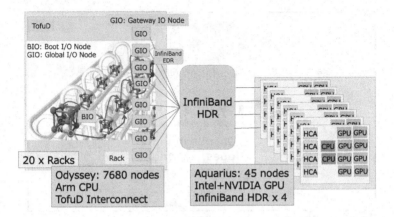

Fig. 2. Wisteria(Odyssey+Aquarius) Network Configuration

WaitIO-Socket and the semantics of communication should be defined based on MPI.

- **Operating with minimal computer resources:** To operate stably on a scale of tens of thousands of processes, it is necessary to minimize the number of processes that each process directly communicates with and the number of computer resources such as memory and CPU. This is because computer resources are required in proportion to the number of communication processes. Therefore, in the design of WaitIO, the application user can select processes needed to communicate. And all communication resources are allocated on demand. In addition, synchronization between the entire process should be minimized to minimize communication overhead.

We implement WaitIO-Socket based on the above design policy. In the design of WaitIO-Socket, we can not use existing related works, such as MPI [2–4,11] and low-level communication libraries [5,6], etc. Because they require the same libraries and versions, and some existing commercial systems do not support the libraries. This limits the system-wide portability.

5   WaitIO-Socket Implemanetation

This section outlines the implementation of WaitIO-Socket. After describing the operation specifications and implementation API of WaitIO-Socket, we explain the implementation outline.

5.1   WaitIO Overview and Application Program Interface

Figure 3 demonstrates an operation image of WaitIO-Socket. WaitIO-Socket can combine multiple applications. The outline of WaitIO specifications is shown below.

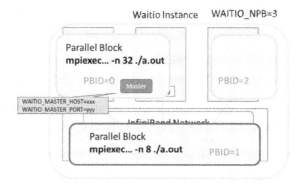

Fig. 3. WaitIO-Socket Operational Image

- Each application is managed by multiple process groups called Parallel Blocks (PBs).
- The entire WaitIO configuration consisting of multiple PBs is called WaitIO Instance, and each PB is managed by an identifier called PBID.
- A PB with PBID = 0 is called a MASTER, which is initialized at program startup and synchronizes between the configured PBs to exchange process information.
- The information required for initialization is defined in the shell environment variables.

5.2   Implementation Overview

Table 1 shows the WaitIO-Socket API. Except for the initialization and support functions, there are only three basic communication functions, "Non Blocking

Table 1. WaitIO Functions

Functions	Descriptions
waitio_isend	Non-Blocking Send
waitio_irecv	Non-Blocking Receive
waitio_wait	Senc/Recv Wait Completion
waitio_init	WaitIO Initialization
waitio_get_nprocs	Get # of PB member
waitio_create_group	Create a PB group by function
waitio_create_group_wranks	Create a PB group by member list
waitio_group_rank	Get my group rank
waitio_group_size	Get my group size
waitio_pb_size	Get PB size
waitio_pb_rank	Get PB rank

Send/Recv" and "Wait" function. This section outlines the implementation of
WaitIO-Socket.

- **WaitIO initialization:** When calling "waitio_init," a set of IP addresses and
  port numbers created by processes on all PBs is shared among all processes
  on PBs. Then, a group is created with the process information selected at the
  time of calling waitio_create_group. Since all of this group creation process
  is completed within the process, total synchronization is not required as in
  the case of communicator generation such as MPI_Comm_split of MPI. When
  creating a group, only the table is created, and the communication between
  each process is established from the receiving side at the time of the first
  communication.
- **Communication protocol:** The communication protocol between each process uses the Eager protocol, which integrates control and data up to 128
  bytes, and the Rendezvous protocol when it exceeds 128 bytes.
- **Communication progress processing:** Communication progress processing is executed when the waitio_wait function is called, except for the Eager
  protocol for which communication has been established.
- **Receive message processing:** All receive message processing is implemented using the "Linux epoll" (event polling) functions.
- **Send message processing:** Send message processing is implemented by the
  basic "write" system-call directly and shifts to the processing by the "Linux
  epoll" when the write processing to the socket causes an error such as an
  EINTR factor.
- **Ensuring communication reliability:** Magic numbers and sequence numbers are introduced in control packets to detect data loss due to software and
  hardware errors. When receiving control packets, it is confirmed that the correct control packets are received in the correct order to ensure the reliability
  of communication.
- **Implementation code size:** Library is 5.7K steps in C.

6   WaitIO-Socket Evaluation

This section describes the results of basic communication performance evaluation for verifying how much communication performance the WaitIO-Socket
communication library can bring out on the Wisteria system and the others.

6.1   Evaluation Environment

In the evaluation of WaitIO-Socket, Wisteria (Odyssey+Aquarius), Oakbridge-
CX (OBCX) and Oakforest-PACS (OFP) shown in Table 2 were used to confirm
that it can be operated even on broader in many systems.

We created an evaluation program for PingPong communication in multiple streams to evaluate the data communication performance between systems.
This is to make a two-process pair for all processes among PBs and perform

Table 2. Evaluation System Specification

	Oakbridge-CX (OBCX)	Oakforest-PACS (OFP)	Wisteria-Odyssey (Odyssey)	Wisteria-Aquarius (Aquarius)
Peak FLOPS	6.61 PFLOPS	25 PFLOPS	25.9 PFLOPS	7.2 PFLOPS
Total # of Nodes	1,368	8,208	7,680	45
CPU	Intel Xeon Platinum 8280 x2, 2.7GHz (28+28 Core)	Intel Xeon Phi 7250 x1, 1.4GHz (68 Core)	A64FX(Arm+SVE) x1, 2.2GHz (48+2or4 Core)	Intel Xeon Platinum 8360Y x2, 2.4GHz (36+36 Core)
Interconnect	Omni-Path (100Gbps x1)	Omni-Path (100Gbps x1)	Tofu-D (54.4Gbps x6)	InfiniBand HDR (200Gbps x4)
Memory/Node	192 GB	96GB(DDR4)+ 16GB(MCDRAM)	32 GiB	512GiB
Memory BW	281.6GB/s	115+490 GB/s	1024GB/s	409.6GB/s
GPU/Node	-	-	-	NVIDIA A100 x8
Compiler	Intel Compiler	Intel Compiler	Fujitsu Compiler	Intel Compiler
MPI	IntelMPI	IntelMPI	Fujitsu MPI	IntelMPI
Operating System	Red Hat EL7	Red Hat EL7	Red Hat EL8	Red Hat EL8

PingPong communication. MPI_Barrier is waiting for and measuring the end of PingPong communication for all pairs. When we evaluated the intra-node communication benchmark, we allocated pair processes and socket connections in a node. And, when we evaluated inter-node communication, we allocated pair processes between the different nodes in a PB or between the other PBs.

The performance evaluation program was executed using the vendor compiler installed in each system and the vendor MPI. We also confirmed with the combination of Open MPI+GCC on the system equipped with the Xeon processor.

Wisteria system is currently operated as two separate subsystems from Odyssey and Aquarius. However, both subsystems are managed by a single job scheduling system and can be used from a common front-end system from the users' perspective.

6.2 Multiple Stream Performance

Multiple Stream Performance on Single PB. In this section, the Ping-Pong Multi-Stream performance in 1PB (Parallel Block) is evaluated using each system in Table 2. In this evaluation, 16 nodes were used and the number of processes on each node was changed for evaluation from 1 process to the upper limit. The upper limit of the number of processes in each system is Odyssey = 48, Aquarius = 72, Oakbridge-CS = 56, Oakforest-PACS = 68, respectively. The 1 process per node (total 16 processes) means simple PingPpong performance.

Table 3 shows the results of the minimum value of half of Round Trip Time (RTT) of each system. Among the Intra-Node measurements, the time of Aquarius had the shortest delay, and that of OFP had the longest. The time of OBCX had the shortest one on Inter-node, and that of OFP had the longest one.

Table 3. 1/2 RTT Evaluation

usec	Odyssey	Aquarius	OBCX	OFP
Intra-Node	26.8	6.57	6.85	49.7
Inter-Node	37.1	21.1	14.5	83.7

We can see that the CPU with relatively high CPU performance is faster. The time of OBCX using Intel Omni-Path (Omni-Path) has a shorter Inter-node delay than that of Aquarius using InfiniBand-HDR because Omni-Path communication processing is executed in the CPU, while InfiniBand communication processing within InfiniBand HCA.

Table 4 shows the maximum per-node PingPong bandwidth performance of Multi-Stream for each system.

Table 4. Bandwidth Evaluation

GB/s per Node	Odyssey	Aquarius	OBCX	OFP
Intra-Node	21.3	259.7	45.7	8.2
Inter-Node	0.35	27.1	9.3	1.12

Among the Intra-node measurements, Aquarius had the highest bandwidth, and OFP had the lowest bandwidth. Aquarius has the highest bandwidth performance on Inter-node, and Odyssey is the lowest bandwidth performance. It was because the high performance of Aquarius comes from high CPU performance with InfiniBand HDR for both 1/2 RTT and bandwidth performance.

Now, let's take a closer look at the communication performance of Odyssey. Figure 4 show the PingPong bandwidth performance of Odyssey when the message size and the number of processes per node are changed, respectively. These results are the total performance with 16 nodes (8 pairs).

From the results shown in Fig. 4, the bandwidth of the intra-node communication on the Odyssey node is higher as the number of processes in the node is increased. These are because intra-node socket communications run in parallel, including in-kernel processing.

However, the total performance of 8 pairs is about 170 GB/s, which is 2% of the 1TB/s memory bandwidth of A64FX (means 8TB/s using eight streams) because A64FX CPU copy performance is not higher than that of Intel Xeon CPU.

On the other hand, the bandwidth of the inter-node communication on the Odyssey node peaks at around 200K bytes of message length and is not proportional to the increase in the number of processes per node. These are because TCP/IP protocol receive-processing between nodes is processed by 2 to 4 assistant cores per node. This assistant core processing becomes a bottleneck and has no performance improvement.

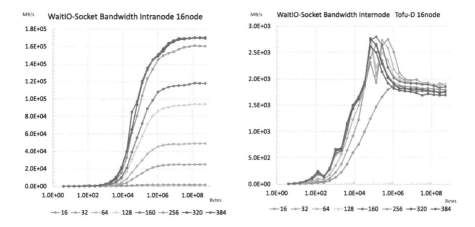

Fig. 4. PingPong Stream Bandwidth on Odyssey

6.3 Wisteria System Performance

This section shows the evaluation of WaitIO-Socket using the entire Wisteria system. The evaluation items are "Programs run on the entire system" and "Evaluate communication performance".

Programs Run on the Entire System: We evaluated using all nodes of Odyssey and Aquarius and found that the Odyssey nodes (7,680 nodes, 24 process/node) + the Aquarius nodes(45 nodes, 64 process/node) were executed and operated with a total of 187,200 processes.

Evaluate Communication Performance: Communication between Odyssey and Aquarius consists of two types. One is direct communication using Infini-Band with GIO nodes and the other via GIO routing. Figure 5 shows the results of a communication performance evaluation using Odyssey and Aquarius. This evaluation result used Odyssey BIO 480 node and Aquarius 8 node due to the maintenance environment. From Fig. 5, communication bandwidth when GIO used achieved 53.2 GB/s, and the results of BIO used due to limited evaluation time achieved 22.1 GB/s. We found that the introduction of GIO routing reduced by 58%.

These results show that WaitIO-Socket works on an ultra-large-scale system.

6.4 Application Performance

This section evaluates real application performance using WaitIO communication libraries on Wisteria/BDEC-01 system. The target application programs are NICAM and ADA. To couple two different applications, a coupler library h3-Open-UTIL/MP is used. In this section, we describe an overview of h3-Open-UTIL/MP and evaluate its application performance.

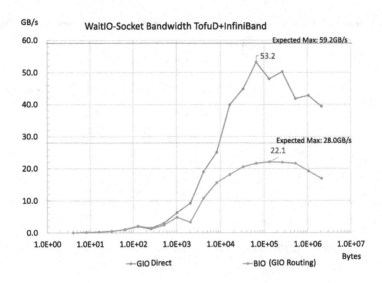

Fig. 5. PingPong Stream Bandwidth on Wisteria(Odyssey+Aquarius)

The H3-Open-UTL/MP Coupler Library: The h3-Open-UTIL/MP is a higher level coupler library and exchanges data at set time intervals for multiple model components with different grid systems and performs grid transformation. Furthermore, in addition to these functions, it is equipped with a combined ensemble function that executes combined models in parallel for statistical processing and a Python interface for coupling Python applications.

There are many advantages to coupling simulation models. For example, when machine learning processes usually use a low-resolution picture, and simulation results output a high-resolution one, in this case, the coupling process can convert the high-resolution ones to lower resolution ones.

Against this background, a project to couple the atmospheric model NICAM [7] with the machine learning library PyTorch is underway, and preliminary results evaluated. However, learning with PyTorch is computationally expensive and is a bottleneck for execution.

To improve this situation, the simulation model can be executed in the Odyssey while the machine learning library is executed in the Aquarius. Both models are combined to simulation using the h3-Open-UTIL/MP coupler. Figure 6 shows the h3-Open-UTIL/MP architecture for realizing this function.

In Fig. 6, the NICAM-ADA coupling uses h3-Open-UTIL/MP to convert NICAM data in a high-resolution grid to a low-resolution grid for machine learning. Deep learning is performed using GPU on Aquarius using this low-resolution grid. Conventionally, the application was executed by the MPI library on a single system, but using the h3-Open-UTIL/MP coupler compatible with WaitIO, the computer simulation result by the NICAM application on Odyssey can be displayed on Aquarius. It supplies data to GPU and enables deep learning.

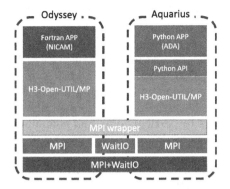 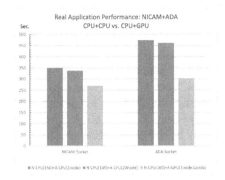

Fig. 6. H3-Open-UTIL/MP Architecture

Fig. 7. NICAM+ADA Real Application Performance on Wisteria/BDEC-01

Real Application Performance Evaluation: We evaluated NICAM+ADA with h3-Open-UTIL/MP coupler library on WaitIO libraries. In this evaluation, we compare ADA on Odyssey by CPU processing with ADA on Aquarius by GPU processing. The PyTorch environment for Aquarius uses torch version 1.9.0+cu111, PyTorch version 1.10.0, and cuda112py93 with miniconda 11.2.

Figure 7 shows the NICAM+ADA application results, it simulates 6 h of the earth's climate situation and puts simulation results to ADA, and ADA does 100 epoch machine learning. The number of application processes was the same. We changed the execution environment, such as ADA execution on CPU or GPU, using WaitIO libraries, and the number of nodes on Odyssey.

In Fig. 7, the blue bar means NICAM 160 node 160 processes on Odyssey and ADA 1 node 20 processes on Odyssey, the orange bar means NICAM 160 node 160 processes on Odyssey and ADA 20 node 20 processes on Odyssey, and the gray bar means NICAM 160 node 160 processes on Odyssey and ADA 1 node 20 processes on Aquarius with GPU.

From the results of Fig. 7, the yellow bar is the fastest for each NICAM by CPU and ADA by GPU processing. About 20% of the execution time of NICAM was reduced, and 35% of the time of ADA by using GPU. The results mean that h3-Open-SYS/WaitIO and h3-Open-UTIL/MP realize heterogeneous coupling computing effectively.

7 Related Work

This section describes related research for dynamically combining multiple running applications implemented in WaitIO-Socket.

IMPI [4] is a communication library designed to integrate systems on the Grid. It implements a token-based protocol that connects systems called IMPI servers and determines the connection and communication specifications between systems. IMPI also supports secure systems such as firewalls. On the other hand,

WaitIO-Socket is different in that it realizes simple application-to-application communication by assuming secure communication such as VPN for the use of the same communication protocol and communication between centers.

PACX-MPI [10,11] uses the Global view and Local view to which all MPI processes belong to integrate multiple application programs. In addition, it is relayed between applications by a special transmission/reception process. Therefore, the relay process becomes a performance bottleneck. WaitIO-Socket allows the application user to select the MPI process to participate in, and communication using WaitIO-Socket directly communicates between MPI processes, so scalable communication can be executed.

GridMPI [8] supports Grid and Cluster environment in single MPI library. It supports multiple MPI libraries with vendor MPI and others including IMPI protocol, however, it needs to integrate in MPI level.

Method using MPI standard [9]: As a method using Open MPI [3] and MPICH [2]. Open MPI can execute applications on different networks and different processors in the same MPI library, but it required to install same MPI library among all systems. It limits the system-wide portability.

UCX [6], OFED [5]: Both UCX and OFED have a track record of operating on TCP/IP, heterogeneous networks, and heterogeneous processors. However, it is unclear whether multiple systems with different environments have the same communication library. Odyssey does not support them in user applications.

As mentioned above, each of the existing methods has its restrictions, and especially, execution portability is limited. For this reason, we have realized WaitIO-Socket using TCP/IP, which almost all existing systems have as the POSIX Socket function.

8   Summary

In this paper, we proposed the WaitIO-Socket communication library. The WaitIO-Socket enables to couple multiple MPI programs for system-wide heterogeneous coupling computing.

The WaitIO-Socket uses POSIX Socket to operate on various systems. In addition, an API similar to MPI is used to implement multiple applications with less effort, and the implementation can operate with the minimum computer resources to execute applications on the full scale of the system.

As a result of the evaluation, WaitIO-Socket could execute large-scale programs on the Wisteria system, our first target system. The Odyssey and Aquarius MPI programs were able to communicate using WaitIO-Socket and achieved 53.2 GB/s using multiple streams throughout the system. We also showed that the application NICAM/ADA was able to run with the h3-Open-UTIL/MP coupler 35% faster on the combination of Odyssey with Arm CPU and Aquarius with NVIDIA GPU (heterogeneous coupling computing) than Odyssey with Arm CPU (homogeneous coupling computing). These results show that WaitIO-Socket is effective to realize heterogeneous coupling computing with Arm CPU, Intel CPU, and NVIDIA GPU.

In the future, we will try to improve WaitIO-Socket communication performance and apply WaitIO-Socket to real-time earthquake prediction applications.

Acknowledgments. This work is supported by "JSPS Grant-in-Aid for Scientific Research (S) (19H05662)", and by "Joint Usage/Research Center for Interdisciplinary Large-scale Information Infrastructures (jh210022-MDH)".

References

1. H3-Open-BDEC. http://nkl.cc.u-tokyo.ac.jp/h3-Open-BDEC/
2. MPICH. https://www.mpich.org/
3. Graham, R.L., Woodall, T.S., Squyres, J.M.: Open MPI: a flexible high performance MPI. In: Wyrzykowski, R., Dongarra, J., Meyer, N., Waśniewski, J. (eds.) PPAM 2005. LNCS, vol. 3911, pp. 228–239. Springer, Heidelberg (2006). https://doi.org/10.1007/11752578_29
4. George, W.L., et al.: IMPI: making MPI interoperable. J. Res. Natl. Inst. Standards Technol. **105**(3), 343–348 (2000). https://doi.org/10.6028/jres.105.035
5. OFED. https://www.openfabrics.org/
6. Shamis, P., et al.: UCX: an open source framework for HPC network APIs and beyond. In: 2015 IEEE 23rd Annual Symposium on High-Performance Interconnects, pp. 40–43 (2015). https://doi.org/10.1109/HOTI.2015.13
7. Satoh, M., et al.: The non-hydrostatic icosahedral atmospheric model: description and development. Prog. Earth Planet. Sci. **1**(1), 1–32 (2014). https://doi.org/10.1186/s40645-014-0018-1
8. GridMPI. http://aist-itri.github.io/gridmpi/
9. MPI: A Message-Passing Interface Standard Version 4.0. https://www.mpi-forum.org/docs/mpi-4.0/mpi40-report.pdf
10. Beisel, T., Gabriel, E., Resch, M.: An extension to MPI for distributed computing on MPPs. In: Bubak, M., Dongarra, J., Waśniewski, J. (eds.) EuroPVM/MPI 1997. LNCS, vol. 1332, pp. 75–82. Springer, Heidelberg (1997). https://doi.org/10.1007/3-540-63697-8_72
11. Klimach, H., Roller, S.P., Munz, C.D.: Heterogeneous parallelism of aero-acoustic applications using PACX-MPI. Interdiscip. Inf. Sci. **15**(1), 79–83 (2009)
12. Vetter, J.S., Brightwell, R., et al.: Extreme heterogeneity 2018 - productive computational science in the era of extreme heterogeneity: report for doe ASCR workshop on extreme heterogeneity. https://doi.org/10.2172/1473756

Heterogeneous System (2)

A Task-Parallel Runtime
for Heterogeneous Multi-node Vector
Systems

Kazuki Ide[1]([✉]) [ID], Keichi Takahashi[1] [ID], Yoichi Shimomura[2],
and Hiroyuki Takizawa[1] [ID]

[1] Graduate School of Information Sciences, Tohoku University,
Sendai, Miyagi 980-8578, Japan
`ide@hpc.is.tohoku.ac.jp`, `{keichi,takizawa}@tohoku.ac.jp`
[2] Cyberscience Center, Tohoku University, Sendai, Miyagi 980-8578, Japan
`shimomura32@tohoku.ac.jp`

Abstract. In recent years, high-performance computing systems are
equipped with not only host processors but also accelerators, and becoming more heterogeneous as well as becoming larger in scale. The task parallel execution model is promising to efficiently utilize such a large-scale
system by minimizing synchronizations in comparison with traditional
models. In this paper, we propose a task-parallel runtime system that
individually considers the processors for task management and task execution; those two roles could be assigned to different processors. This
paper focuses on NEC SX-Aurora TSUBASA as an example of heterogeneous multi-node systems, which are equipped with two kinds of
general-purpose processors, to exploit the system heterogeneity for efficient task-parallel execution. Specifically, the proposed runtime system
is used to select an appropriate processor for task management, depending on several execution conditions. The performance of the proposed
runtime is discussed by running a Cholesky factorization implementation. The evaluation results show that the proposed runtime system can
improve performance by more than 25% in comparison with a conventional a conventional implementation.

Keywords: runtime system · task-parallel programming · distributed
computing · heterogeneous computing · Cholesky factorization

1 Introduction

High-performance computing (HPC) systems are equipped with not only host
processors (CPUs) but also accelerators, and becoming more heterogeneous as
well as larger in scale. As a result, we are facing a variety of challenges.

First, the overhead of synchronization among tasks increases with the system scale. In many HPC application codes, MPI processes and threads frequently
need to synchronize, and load imbalance among them could result in long waiting time. In addition, for global synchronous collective communications, only a

H. Takizawa et al. (Eds.): PDCAT 2022, LNCS 13798, pp. 331–343, 2023.
https://doi.org/10.1007/978-3-031-29927-8_26

small number of nodes may work and the others could be idle, degrading parallelization efficiency. As the system scales, such overheads could become non-negligibly large. To achieve high performance with large-scale systems, global synchronizations must be avoided whenever possible. A *task-parallel* model, a parallel programming model that does not involve expensive synchronization unless task dependencies are violated, is a promising approach for minimizing global synchronizations [3,13,14]. A task-parallel model divides an application into tasks and then assigns each task to a process/thread for execution. Each process may have to communicate with other processes to complete the overall application execution. A task-parallel model has demonstrated to perform better than the conventional *Bulk Synchronous Parallel (BSP)* model in some cases such as ScaLAPACK [3,13].

Second, an HPC system could be equipped with different kinds of processors such as CPUs and Graphics Processing Units (GPUs), and should properly be coordinated. Modern multi-core CPUs use dozens of cores that issue multiple instructions out-of-order, making them suitable for latency-critical applications. GPUs have a very large number of in-order cores that share control units, making them suitable for throughput-critical applications. Thus, rather than using either CPUs or GPUs alone, they can be combined and used appropriately to provide higher performance for a much wider variety of applications and usage scenarios [18].

In this paper, we propose and evaluate a task-parallel runtime that coordinates heterogeneous resources in *SX-Aurora TSUBASA (SX-AT)* [15], one of heterogeneous systems. SX-AT consists of Vector Hosts (VHs) equipped with x86 processors to execute Linux OS, and Vector Engines (VEs) equipped with vector processors to execute applications. On an SX-AT system, applications running on VEs are executed as user processes on the Linux OS environment managed by VHs. A VE has multiple vector cores and High Bandwidth Memory (HBM), making it possible to achieve high sustained performance on executing memory-intensive HPC applications such as computational fluid dynamics simulations [20]. Unlike CPU-GPU systems, both a VH and a VE can fully execute applications written in standard programming languages such as C/C++ and Fortran, and thus are both general-purpose processors to some extent. Task assignment to VHs and VEs is more flexible than that in CPU-GPU systems. Therefore, to develop a multi-node task-parallel runtime on SX-AT, we need to consider task assignment to make efficient use of heterogeneous computing resources. We propose a multi-node task-parallel runtime that makes efficient use of heterogeneous resources by having VE execute tasks and VH or VE manage tasks depending on the situation. The proposed runtime allows for efficient execution with minimal synchronization of large systems based on task dependencies, while further improving performance by using different types of processors.

The performance of the proposed runtime is discussed by comparing it with the BSP model on running Cholesky factorization implementations such as ScaLAPACK. The evaluation results indicate that the proposed task-parallel runtime can achieve higher performance than the original ScaLAPACK implementation by reducing synchronization. Further performance improvement can be expected by good use of both VHs and VEs, and we demonstrate the importance of considering their performance characteristics at the task-parallel runtime design.

The rest of this paper is organized as follows. In Sect. 2, we briefly review related work: a task-parallel runtime system (Sect. 2.1), and SX-Aurora TSUBASA (Sect. 2.2). Section 3 describes the proposed runtime that appropriately uses VHs and VEs. Section 4 discusses the performance gain by the proposed runtime through comparison with the BSP model, and the performance change with the use of VH and VE. Finally, Sect. 5 gives concluding remarks.

2 Related Work

2.1 Task-Parallel Runtime System

Various task-parallel runtimes have been developed and evolved to cope with hardware changes. The proliferation of accelerator-equipped heterogeneous and multicore systems has led to the popularization of task-parallel approaches to reduce the programming burden and to make more efficient use of intra-node parallelism [12,14]. The task-parallel programming model has been implemented as language extensions such as OpenMP 3 [1,2], and as libraries such as StarPU [5] and PaRSEC [7,8]. Furthermore, some of them have also evolved to support multi-node systems as mentioned later.

Although OpenMP version 3 and later introduced task parallelism, it could only exploit intra-node parallelism. OpenMP defines the code associated with a task and its data environment by means of a task directive. A thread creates a task defined by a task construct. The thread either executes the task immediately or places it in a task pool to defer its execution. Afterwards, the thread repeats retrieving and executing tasks until its pool becomes empty. OpenMP has evolved to support offloading tasks to accelerators, but not multi-node systems.

StarPU and PaRSEC support multi-node systems, where each process plays not only a role of executing tasks but also managing tasks, such as task scheduling and data transfers among tasks. StarPU handles a node equipped with CPUs and GPUs as a StarPU instance, and performs task execution and management on each instance. In a multi-node system, task scheduling is considered for each node, and data movement is for each processor. Given a task graph, each instance saves only the necessary part of the whole graph, and manages and executes its own subset of the tasks while considering their data dependencies. Similarly in PaRSEC, each process executing tasks is responsible also for task scheduling and data movement. A domain-specific language is used to express dependencies among tasks, and the runtime compiles them into a compact, parametric representation of the dependency graph. This allows each process to make individual decisions to manage tasks. Unlike these prior studies, the proposed runtime in this paper executes different processes for task execution and task management.

As a result, each kind of processes can potentially be executed on a different processor, and the proposed runtime can exploit the processor heterogeneity of an HPC system.

2.2 SX-Aurora TSUBASA

SX-Aurora TSUBASA is a new type of supercomputer that began shipping in 2018, as the successor of NEC SX-series vector supercomputers. A VE has a vector processor of eight vector cores and high bandwidth memory, making it possible to achieve high sustained performance on executing memory-intensive applications. A VH can host multiple VEs. VEs are hosted by VHs connected to the VEs via PCI-express links. A combination of VHs and VEs hosted by the VHs is called a Vector Island (VI). Typically, execution of an application running on the host is partially offloaded to accelerators such as GPUs and FPGAs to reduce the overall execution time, *i.e.*, an accelerator executes only a portion of an application as shown in Fig. 1(a). SX-AT, on the other hand, uses the Aurora architecture, which executes the entire application on a VE as shown in Fig. 1(b). SX-AT also supports an execution model where both VHs and VEs collaborate to run one application via MPI communication. This execution model is called NEC MPI Scalar-Vector Hybrid *(VH-VE hybrid MPI)*, and launches MPI processes on both VHs and the VEs.

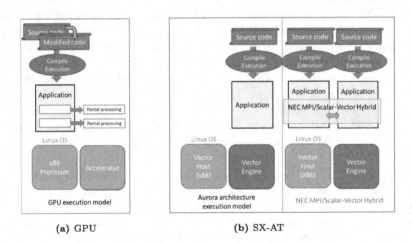

(a) GPU   (b) SX-AT

Fig. 1. How to run an application on heterogeneous systems.

3   A Task-Parallel Runtime for SX-AT

3.1   An Overview of the Proposed Runtime

This paper proposes a multi-node task-parallel runtime that makes efficient use of heterogeneous resources by using VEs for task execution while using either

VEs or VHs for task management. A VE is able to achieve high performance in executing vectorizable loops, while a VH is likely to achieve much higher performance in executing non-vectorizable codes. Vectorizable loops are very frequently involved in many numerical simulation codes and usually constitute the most time-consuming portions of the codes, so-called kernels. Hence, the VE is promising for executing numerical simulation tasks. On the other hand, task management is generally non-vectorizable and thus the VH is more promising for task management in terms of computational efficiency. One problem is that, if task execution and task management are executed by different processors running on distinct processors, the amount of data transferred between them increases, and the data transfer overhead could be a performance bottleneck and degrade the overall performance. Therefore, even if we can assume that tasks are executed on VEs, we need to decide whether the VE or the VH should be responsible for task management, considering the trade-off between computational efficiency and data transfer overhead.

3.2   Hybrid MPI for SX-Aurora TSUBASA

The proposed runtime is built on top of *Asynchronous Dynamic Load Balancing (ADLB)* [17]. ADLB provides a high-level and easy-to-use programming model and a portable library for multi-node task parallelism. In ADLB, an MPI application is executed with using some of the MPI processes as *ADLB servers* for task management, and the other MPI processes called *application processes* execute the tasks being managed by the ADLB servers. Each application process is associated with one of the available ADLB servers. When an application submits a task to an ADLB server, one of the application processes associated with the ADLB server is selected to execute the task. In the current implementation of ADLB, MPI communication is internally used behind the data transfer between ADLB servers and application processes. Therefore, VH-VE hybrid MPI enables to execute ADLB servers on either of VHs and VEs, and allows ADLB servers to communicate with tasks running on VEs via MPI communication.

Figure 2 shows an overview of the proposed runtime built on top of ADLB. When ADLB servers as well as application processes are running on VEs, an application just uses MPI for communication between ADLB servers and application processes in a standard way. ADLB does not allow application processes to directly communicate with each other for task execution, and thus application processes transfer data via ADLB servers for data exchange among tasks. On the other hand, when ADLB servers are executed on VHs, VH-VE hybrid MPI is used for the communication between ADLB servers and application processes. The data transfer between VHs and VEs could be a performance bottleneck especially if they are located in different VIs. Therefore, in the proposed runtime, each application process running on a VE is associated with an ADLB server running on a VH within the same VI as shown in Fig. 2.

If ADLB servers are executed on VHs, task management is performed more efficiently in comparison to executing them on VEs because task management is non-vectorizable. However, if the amount of data communicated between tasks

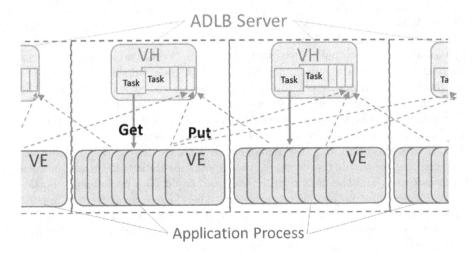

Fig. 2. Task-parallel runtime for VH-VE.

is large, processing on that data may dominate. Therefore, if the amount of communication data is large, it could be more performant to execute ADLB servers also on VEs with high memory bandwidth. This will experimentally be discussed in Sect. 4.

4   Evaluation and Discussions

We discuss the performance of the proposed runtime with changing various parameters and execution conditions.

4.1   Evaluation Setup

In this paper, the performance gain of the proposed runtime is discussed using the Cholesky factorization algorithm shown in Algorithm 1.1. The Cholesky factorization code used in this paper consists of three nested loops, and is developed with reference to its implementations in some numerical libraries [4,6,9,11]. In Cholesky factorization, the number of parallelizable tasks is different for the BLAS function [16] to be called. For example, the POTRF function is called at the beginning of the outermost loop body, and executable by only one node. This means that, in the BSP model, all the other processes need to wait for the completion of POTRF execution by the particular node, leading to a severe synchronization overhead. In contrast, in task-parallel model, POTRF is executed as soon as its dependencies are resolved, so it can be executed in parallel with other functions such as GEMM, SYRK.

Algorithm 1.1. Baseline tile Choledsky algorithm.

```
for (k = 0; k < NT; k++){
    potrf(A[k][k]);
    for (m = k+1; m < NT; m++)
            trsm(A[k][k], A[m][k]);
    for (n = k+1; n < NT; n++){
        syrk(A[n][k], A[n][n]);
        for(m = n+1; m < NT; m++)
            gemm(A[m][k], A[n][k], A[m][n]);
    }
}
```

We implemented the Cholesky factorization in a task-parallel fashion by using the tile-based algorithm employed in PLASMA [9] and DPALSMA [6]. In the tile-based algorithm of Cholesky factorization, the matrix is divided into tiles, and four BLAS functions, POTRF, TRSM, SYRK, and GEMM, are executed as tasks on each tile as shown in Fig. 3. In the multi-node task-parallel implementation, partitioned tiles are allocated to multiple nodes in advance by 2D block cyclic distribution. Tasks are statically scheduled so that they are assigned on the node that has the data written by the task. Tasks assigned to a node are executed in intra-node parallel at a finer granularity using OpenMP. In ADLB, task dependencies need to be explicitly described. After each task is executed, the resultant matrix is sent to the ADLB server. Each application process executing a task that needs the result receives the data as soon as it is ready.

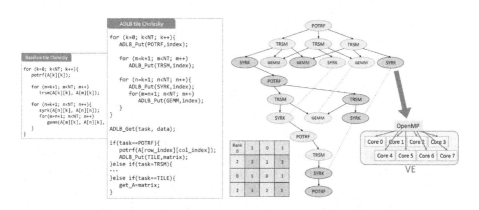

Fig. 3. Implementation of Cholesky Factorization with ADLB.

The following evaluation was conducted with two systems, AOBA-A and AOBA-B, installed at the Cyberscience Center, Tohoku University [10]. The system specifications are summarized in Table 1.

Table 1. Performance per socket.

System	Name	cores	sockets	Number of VEs	Performance	Memory BW
AOBA-A	VE Type 20B	8	-	-	2.45 TFLOPS	1.5 TB/s
	AMD EPYC 7402P	24	1	8	1.08 TFLOPS	0.2 TB/s
AOBA-B	AMD EPYC 7702	128	2	-	4.00 TFLOPS	0.4 TB/s

4.2 Performance Gain by Proposed Runtime

Comparison with the BSP Model. The proposed and ScaLAPACK implementations of Cholesky factorization are executed on AOBA-A, changing the
number of VEs from 4 to 256. ADLB servers are executed always with four VH
cores for each VI, and the number of ADLB servers is not changed to discuss
the effect of changing only the number of VEs, *i.e.*, the number of tasks. The
tile size is set to 4096 × 4096, and the overall matrix size is determined so that
each node has 3 × 3 tiles.

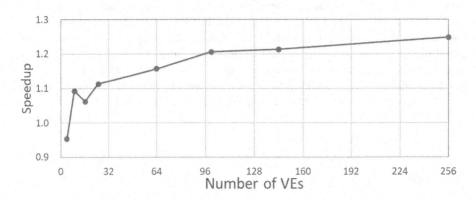

Fig. 4. The speedup ratio of task-parallel execution against ScaLAPACK.

Figure 4 shows the speedup ratio of the proposed implementation against the
original ScaLAPACK implementation. When the number of VEs is 4, the proposed runtime is 0.95 times faster than the ScaLAPACK implementation. When
the number of VEs is extremely small, the ScaLAPACK implementation could
outperform the proposed one because the overhead for inter-task communication
on ADLB is non-negligible. Remember that VEs communicate via VHs in the
ADLB environment. On the other hand, the proposed runtime was faster for 9
or more VEs, with a maximum speedup of about 1.25 times faster at 256 VEs.
The speedup ratio increases with the number of VEs, because the performance
gain by avoiding synchronizations exceeds the communication overhead. While
related studies have shown 15–20% [13] or about 30% [3] speedup by reducing the
synchronizations, the performance gain by the proposed runtime is comparable
with theirs in spite of the relatively large communication overheads induced by

the ADLB runtime. Therefore, these results clearly show the performance benefit of using task-parallel execution for a large-scale system, even though the proposed runtime could require a larger communication overhead. In addition, the proposed runtime can further improve performance by appropriately selecting a processor as the ADLB server.

(a) ScaLAPACK   (b) Task-Parallel

Fig. 5. MPI communication trace obtained with TAU.

To discuss the source of the performance gain, we use a performance analysis tool, TAU [19], to visualize the execution. Figure 5 shows the MPI communication trace obtained with TAU. Figure 5(a) shows the trace data of the ScaLA-PACK implementation with 16 MPI processes on AOBA-B. In the figure, the light blue areas indicate that MPI_Recv is called and thus execution is blocked until the destination MPI process finishes to receive data. On the other hand, Fig. 5(b) shows the MPI profile data at using 16 application processes and eight ADLB servers on AOBA-B. Pink areas in Fig. 5(b) indicate that MPI_Wait is called by the application process to synchronize with an ADLB server. The light blue areas in Fig. 5(a) are smaller than pink ares in Fig. 5(b). Quantitatively, when measured with AOBA-A's 64 VEs, the ScaLAPACK implementation spends about 72% of the communication time and idle time, while the proposed implementation spends only 67%. Therefore, for larger-scale practical Cholesky factorization, the proposed runtime will be faster than the standard implementation.

Number of ADLB Servers. We investigate how much the execution time changes by varying the number of ADLB servers. We measure the execution time of Cholesky factorization by varying the number of ADLB servers (VH cores) with fixing the number of application processes to be 64.

Figure 6 shows the execution time for each number of ADLB servers. It also shows the breakdown of execution time as computation, communication, and idle in the application process. When the number of ADLB servers is reduced, the performance of the proposed runtime drastically decreases. The execution time of the proposed runtime with a single ADLB server per eight VEs of application processes is 1.37× longer than that with four ADLB servers. This is because the idle time of waiting for the communication with ADLB servers decreases as

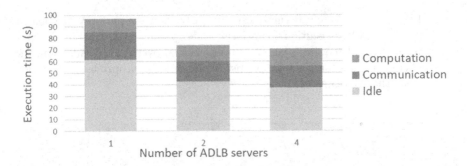

Fig. 6. Performance with different number of ADLB servers.

the number of ADLB servers increases. Therefore, these results indicate a sufficient number of ADLB servers are needed for the proposed runtime to achieve high performance. Note that the computation time is short when the number of ADLB servers is one. This is because the application processes that are not busy continue communication and related processing to receive data for the next task from the ADLB server until the task dependency is resolved. When the performance of the ADLB server is low and the response is slow, such communication processing is reduced in the application process compared to when there are many ADLB servers.

Use of VH and VE. We finally investigate the performance gain by using system heterogeneity, by assigning ADLB servers properly to either VHs or VEs. 64 VEs were used as a fixed number of application processes, and the number of ADLB servers was changed as 8, 16, 32, and 64 cores. In the experiments above, VEs and VHs within the same VI are used for execution of both ADLB servers and application processes. However, in the following experiment, application processes and ADLB servers are executed on different VIs so that the change in the number of ADLB servers does not affect the core count available for application processes. The tile size was changed from 64 × 64 to 4096 × 4096, and 3 × 3 tiles were assigned to each VE at the experiment.

Figure 7 shows the speedup ratio by using VH cores in a different VI for executing ADLB servers. The baseline is the performance at executing ADLB servers on 1, 2, 4, 8 VEs in a different VI. The results show that when the number of servers is small of only one VH core for eight VEs, the VH server is considerably faster, with a maximum speedup ratio of 3.9 when the tile size is 64. However, as the tile size increases, the VH speedup ratio decreases. For a tile size of 4096, the speedup ratio is 0.88. In other words, when the tile size is large, the performance becomes higher by executing both ADLB servers and application processes on VEs. When the tile size is small, VH can execute task management more efficiently because non-vectorization processes of task management, such as scheduling, are dominant in the execution time. However, when the tile size becomes larger, VE with a larger memory bandwidth can

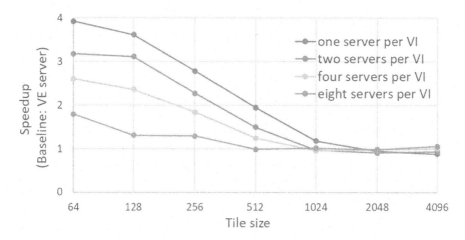

Fig. 7. How much higher the performance is with VH as the ADLB servers than with VE as the ADLB servers.

execute also the task management more efficiently because the execution time is spent more for accessing data.

As the number of ADLB servers increases, the performance difference between VHs and VEs becomes smaller. For the tile size of 64, the speedup ratio with eight VH cores over one VE code is about 1.8, which is less than 50% of that with one VH core, about 3.9. Furthermore, when the number of ADLB servers is 8, the speedup ratio of VH cores over VE cores decreases as the tile size increases, and becomes almost the same for the tile size of 512 or larger. This is because use of more servers leads to a longer idle time and thus the server performance becomes less significant.

These results clearly indicate that the processor to run the ADLB server must be selected according to the characteristics of the system and application. In the application used in this paper, the tile size is the most important factor in determining the appropriate processor for executing ADLB servers. When teh tile size is small, a VH is more suitable for executing ADLB servers because the computational efficiency of task management that is non-vectorizable is more significant. On the other hand, when the tile size is large and the ADLB server count is small, a VE can work better because the memory bandwidth is more significant.

5   Conclusion

As HPC system architectures are becoming larger in scale and more heterogeneous, we need to use the system heterogeneity efficiently with avoiding global synchronizations as much as possible. This paper has proposed a task-parallel runtime that can execute task execution and task management on different types of processors based on ADLB and VH-VE Hybrid MPI. Then, the performance is discussed by implementing a task-parallel implementation of Cholesky factorization.

The evaluation results show that the proposed runtime can improve the performance by up to 25% when the system size is large, even though the overhead of data exchange among tasks becomes large by using ADLB servers. Since task management by ADLB servers is likely to be a performance bottleneck, a key parameter is the number of ADLB servers. If the number of ADLB server is not enough, the performance drops drastically. Moreover, when the tile size is small, since non-vectorizable operations in managing tasks is important, VHs can execute it more efficiently than VEs. However, when the tile size is large, since handling tile data in managing tasks is important, ADLB servers should be executed on VEs. Consequently, a task-parallel runtime needs to properly select the computing resources for task management to exploit the system heterogeneity and attain high performance.

In our future work, we will evaluate the performance with other applications as well as Cholesky factorization. We will also discuss automatic processor selection for both task management and task execution, considering the performance characteristics of each processor type and tasks.

Acknowledgements. This work was partially supported by MEXT Next Generation High-Performance Computing Infrastructures and Applications R&D Program "R&D of A Quantum-Annealing-Assisted Next Generation HPC Infrastructure and its Applications," Grant-in-Aid for Scientific Research(B) #21H03449, Grant-in-Aid for Challenging Research (Exploratory) #22K19764, and Joint Usage/Research Center for Interdisciplinary Large-scale Information Infrastructures jh220025.

References

1. OpenMP Architecture Review Board. OpenMP application program interface version 4.0, July 2013. http://www.openmp.org/mp-documents/OpenMP4.0.0.pdf
2. Board, O.M.P.A.R.: OpenMP application program interface version 4.5 (2015)
3. Agullo, E., et al.: Achieving high performance on supercomputers with a sequential task-based programming model. IEEE Trans. Parallel Distrib. Syst., 1–14 (2017)
4. Anderson, E., et al.: LAPACK Users' Guide. SIAM (1999)
5. Augonnet, C., Thibault, S., Namyst, R., Wacrenier, P.-A.: STARPU: a unified platform for task scheduling on heterogeneous multicore architectures. In: Sips, H., Epema, D., Lin, H.-X. (eds.) Euro-Par 2009. LNCS, vol. 5704, pp. 863–874. Springer, Heidelberg (2009). https://doi.org/10.1007/978-3-642-03869-3_80
6. Bosilca, G., et al.: Flexible development of dense linear algebra algorithms on massively parallel architectures with DPLASMA. In: 2011 IEEE International Symposium on Parallel and Distributed Processing Workshops and PhD Forum, pp. 1432–1441. IEEE (2011)
7. Bosilca, G., et al.: Scalable dense linear algebra on heterogeneous hardware (2013)
8. Yoichi, S., Akihiro, M., Konja, S., Cui, A., Takahashi, T.: A real-time flood inundation prediction on SX-Aurora TSUBASA. In: HiPC2022: Conference on High Performance Computing, Data, and Analytics. IEEE (2022)
9. Buttari, A., Langou, J., Kurzak, J., Dongarra, J.: A class of parallel tiled linear algebra algorithms for multicore architectures. Parallel Comput. **35**(1), 38–53 (2009)
10. Center: Tohoku university cyberscience center. https://www.cc.tohoku.ac.jp/

11. Choi, J., et al.: ScaLAPACK: a portable linear algebra library for distributed memory computers-design issues and performance. Comput. Phys. Commun. **97**(1–2), 1–15 (1996)
12. Dongarra, J., et al.: Parallel programming models for dense linear algebra on heterogeneous systems. Supercomput. Front. Innov. **2**(4), 67–86 (2015)
13. Haidar, A., YarKhan, A., Cao, C., Luszczek, P., Tomov, S., Dongarra, J.: Flexible linear algebra development and scheduling with Cholesky factorization. In: 2015 IEEE 17th International Conference on High Performance Computing and Communications, 2015 IEEE 7th International Symposium on Cyberspace Safety and Security, and 2015 IEEE 12th International Conference on Embedded Software and Systems, pp. 861–864. IEEE (2015)
14. Kaiser, H., Heller, T., Adelstein-Lelbach, B., Serio, A., Fey, D.: HPX: a task based programming model in a global address space. In: Proceedings of the 8th International Conference on Partitioned Global Address Space Programming Models, pp. 1–11 (2014)
15. Komatsu, K., et al.: Performance evaluation of a vector supercomputer SX-aurora TSUBASA. In: SC18: International Conference for High Performance Computing, Networking, Storage and Analysis, pp. 685–696. IEEE (2018)
16. Lawson, C.L., Hanson, R.J., Kincaid, D.R., Krogh, F.T.: Basic linear algebra subprograms for Fortran usage. ACM Trans. Math. Softw. (TOMS) **5**(3), 308–323 (1979)
17. Lusk, E.L., Pieper, S.C., Butler, R.M., et al.: More scalability, less pain: a simple programming model and its implementation for extreme computing. SciDAC Rev. **17**(1), 30–37 (2010)
18. Mittal, S., Vetter, J.S.: A survey of CPU-GPU heterogeneous computing techniques. ACM Comput. Surv. (CSUR) **47**(4), 1–35 (2015)
19. Shende, S.S., Malony, A.D.: The tau parallel performance system. Int. J. High Perform. Comput. Appl. **20**(2), 287–311 (2006)
20. Shimomura, Y., Musa, A., Konja, S., Aoyagi, C., Takizawa, T.: A real-time flood inundation prediction on SX-aurora TSUBASA. In: HiPC2022: Conference on High Performance Computing, Data, and Analytics. IEEE (2022)

Accelerating Radiative Transfer Simulation on NVIDIA GPUs with OpenACC

Ryohei Kobayashi[1,2]($\boxtimes$), Norihisa Fujita[1,2], Yoshiki Yamaguchi[1,2], Taisuke Boku[1,2], Kohji Yoshikawa[1,3], Makito Abe[1], and Masayuki Umemura[1,3]

[1] Center for Computational Sciences, University of Tsukuba, Tsukuba, Japan
{kobayashi,yoshiki}@cs.tsukuba.ac.jp,
{fujita,taisuke,kohji,mabe,umemura}@ccs.tsukuba.ac.jp
[2] Degree Programs in Systems and Information Engineering, University of Tsukuba, Tsukuba, Japan
[3] Degree Programs in Pure and Applied Sciences, University of Tsukuba, Tsukuba, Japan

Abstract. To accelerate multiphysics applications, making use of not only GPUs but also FPGAs has been emerging. Multiphysics applications are simulations involving multiple physical models and multiple simultaneous physical phenomena. Operations with different performance characteristics appear in the simulation, making the acceleration of simulation speed using only GPUs difficult. Therefore, we aim to improve the overall performance of the application by using FPGAs to accelerate operations with characteristics which cause lower GPU efficiency. However, the application is currently implemented through multilingual programming, where the computation kernel running on the GPU is written in CUDA and the computation kernel running on the FPGA is written in OpenCL. This method imposes a heavy burden on programmers; therefore, we are currently working on a programming environment that enables to use both accelerators in a GPU–FPGA equipped high-performance computing (HPC) cluster system with OpenACC. To this end, we port the entire code only with OpenACC from the CUDA-OpenCL mixture. On this basis, this study quantitatively investigates the performance of the OpenACC GPU implementation compared to the CUDA implementation for ARGOT, a radiative transfer simulation code for fundamental astrophysics which is a multiphysics application. We observe that the OpenACC implementation achieves performance and scalability comparable to the CUDA implementation on the Cygnus supercomputer equipped with NVIDIA V100 GPUs.

Keywords: GPU · OpenACC · MPI · Astrophysics

1 Introduction

Graphics processing units (GPUs) offer good peak performance and high memory bandwidth. They have been widely used in high-performance computing

H. Takizawa et al. (Eds.): PDCAT 2022, LNCS 13798, pp. 344–358, 2023.
https://doi.org/10.1007/978-3-031-29927-8_27

(HPC) systems as accelerators; however, they are not suitable for all applications. Multiphysics applications are a typical example. Multiphysics is the coupled processes or systems involving more than one simultaneously occurring physical phenomenon and the studies of and knowledge about these processes and systems. Therefore, multiphysics applications perform simulations with multiple interacting physical properties and there are various computations within a simulation, which may include calculations not suited to GPUs; because of this, accelerating simulation speed using GPU only is difficult. We thus attempt to combine GPUs and field-programmable gate arrays (FPGAs) and use the FPGA to carry out the computations not suited to the GPU. We call this concept Cooperative Heterogeneous Acceleration with Reconfigurable Multidevices (CHARM) and have been working on GPU–FPGA-accelerated computation for radiative transfer simulation in astrophysics as a proof of concept [5].

One possible approach to implement GPU–FPGA-accelerated computing is to control both devices using OpenCL, but because the majority of existing HPC applications are implemented with CUDA, rewriting them places a significant burden on application developers. Therefore, we currently employ a mixed programming approach, using CUDA for the GPU implementation and OpenCL for the FPGA implementation. However, such multilingual programming imposes a heavy burden on programmers, and therefore, we are currently working on a programming environment that enables the use of both accelerators in a GPU–FPGA equipped HPC cluster system using OpenACC [11]. Because this is a directive-based programming model, we can use directives to specify to the compiler which part of the application should be offloaded to which accelerator. In addition, Oak Ridge National Laboratory (ORNL) is developing a compiler that can write computation kernels for FPGAs as well as GPUs in OpenACC [6]. We are currently collaborating with ORNL with the goal of realizing cooperative computation of both accelerators in a GPU–FPGA equipped HPC cluster system. As part of this collaboration, we are using the compiler being developed by ORNL to realize the high-usability GPU-FPGA-accelerated computation. Towards this end, we have ported all code from mixed CUDA-OpenCL to OpenACC only, and we expect that writing all code in OpenACC will unify the program and smoothen the partial implementation on an FPGA.

In order to make the above scenario successful, it is mandatory to first quantitatively assess the practicality of OpenACC itself for real-world application implementations. In this study, as a first step toward realizing a usable GPU–FPGA-accelerated computing based on OpenACC, we implement the radiative transfer simulation code with OpenACC and evaluate the GPU performance by comparing it with that of CUDA-based implementation. The evaluation results quantitatively show that the performance of the OpenACC implementation achieves at least 80% of that of the CUDA implementation and that the OpenACC implementation is not a problematic replacement for the CUDA implementation.

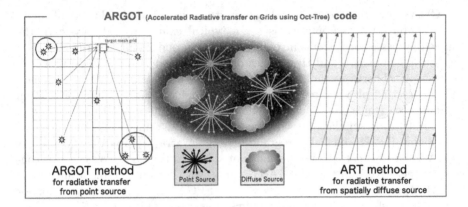

Fig. 1. Overview of the ARGOT code.

2 ARGOT: Radiative Transfer Simulation Code for Astrophysics

ARGOT is an astrophysics simulation code developed in our organization. As shown in Fig. 1, it combines two methods to solve radiative transfer problems: the ARGOT method [9], which computes the radiative transfer from point sources, and the ART method [10], which computes the radiative transfer from sources spread out in the target space. We have given a brief description of the two methods in the next section.

2.1 ARGOT Method

To deduce the radiative transfer from point radiation sources, computation of the optical depth between each pair of a point radiation source and a target mesh grid, i.e., an end point of each light-ray, is necessary. Assuming that the number of mesh grids is constant, the computational complexity is proportional to the number of point radiation sources. To address this, the ARGOT method builds an oct-tree data structure for the distribution of radiation sources [9]. A cubic computational domain is hierarchically subdivided into eight cubic cells until each cell contains only one radiation source, or the size of a cell becomes sufficiently small compared to that of the computational domain. In other words, all sources in a distant tree node can be treated as a single luminous source and the effective number of point radiation sources is reduced from N to $logN$. When targeting a mesh grid, such as a target mesh grid in Fig. 1, the photon flux coming from each radiation source at target mesh grids is given by

$$f(\nu) = \frac{L(\nu)e^{-\tau(\nu)}}{4\pi r^2} \qquad (1)$$

where $L(\nu)$ and $\tau(\nu)$ denote the intrinsic luminosity and the optical depth for a given frequency ν, respectively. $\tau(\nu)$ is given by

$$\tau(\nu) = \sigma(\nu) \int n(\boldsymbol{x}) dl \simeq \sigma(\nu) \sum_i n(\boldsymbol{x}_i) \Delta l \qquad (2)$$

where $n(x)$ is the number density of gas molecules that absorb light.

2.2 ART Method

The ART method is used to deduce radiative transfer from spatially diffuse sources. This method is based on a ray-tracing method in a 3D space split into meshes [10]. As shown in Fig. 1, multiple incident rays come from a boundary and move in a straight direction parallel to each other without any reflection or refraction. The ART method solves the radiative transfer equation along parallel light-rays starting from one edge of the computational volume to another, using the following equation.

$$I_\nu^{out}(\hat{\boldsymbol{n}}) = I_\nu^{in}(\hat{\boldsymbol{n}}) e^{-\Delta \tau_\nu} + S_\nu (1 - e^{-\Delta \tau_\nu}) \qquad (3)$$

This calculation is performed every time the ray is passed through a mesh grid. For a given incoming radiation intensity I_ν^{in} along a direction $\hat{\boldsymbol{n}}$, the outgoing radiation intensity I_ν^{out} after passing through a path length ΔL of a single mesh is computed by the above integrating equation, where $\Delta \tau$ is the optical depth of the path length ΔL (i.e. $\Delta \tau = \kappa_\nu \Delta \tau$), and S_ν and κ_ν are the source function and the absorption coefficient of the mesh grid, respectively. The direction (angle) of the ray is computed using the HEALPix algorithm [3]. The number of meshes depends on the configuration of the target problem; there are between 100^3 and 1000^3 meshes in our target problems. The number of ray angles also depends on the problem size. It will be at least 768, where resolution parameter $N_{side} = 8$ in the HEALPix algorithm.

3   GPU Implementation with OpenACC

3.1 OpenACC

OpenACC is a parallel programming language standard for easily writing programs for GPUs and many-core accelerators. By inserting OpenMP-like compiler directives (`#pragma`) into programs written in C/C++ or Fortran, it is possible to specify to the compiler the hot spots in the program that should be offloaded to the accelerator. Therefore, unlike CUDA and OpenCL, which require writing low-level code that is aware of the accelerator's architecture, this programming model enables the use of accelerators with only minor modifications to existing source code, and it is expected to be a method for porting previously developed computational science application code to accelerator environments.

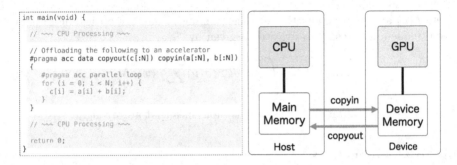

Fig. 2. Overview of OpenACC programming model.

Figure 2 shows the overview of the OpenACC programming model. In this figure, the part of the loop that performs vector addition, adding the elements of arrays a and b respectively and storing them in array c, is cut out and offloaded to the GPU, while the CPU performs the remaining processing. To offload to the GPU, the compiler directive `#pragma acc parallel loop` is added to the code. This directive (`#parallel`) belongs to the parallel area directive, one of the main directives of OpenACC, and specifies the parallel execution area to be offloaded to the accelerator.

As shown in Fig. 2, OpenACC has a hybrid configuration with two memory spaces (host and device memory), and the data required for offloaded operations must be copied to the accelerator (device) side. It is also necessary to write the data back to the host side after processing is complete. OpenACC achieves this by inserting the data transfer directive (`#pragma acc data`) into the code. Here, `copyin(a[:N],b[:N])` specifies the data transfer of arrays a and b of length N from the host to the device, while `copyout(c[:N])` specifies the data transfer of array c (the vector addition result) of length N from the device to the host. In this figure, the programmer explicitly specifies a directive for data transfer, but data transfer may also be left to the compiler. In the latter case, there is no need to specify the data transfer explicitly.

Thus, all parallel execution sections and data transfers can be specified by compiler directives without directly modifying the source code, which makes the programming model highly maintainable and portable.

3.2 OpenACC Implementation of the ARGOT Code

When implementing GPU-accelerated applications with OpenACC, the implementation steps are mainly as follows:

1. Utilize profiling tools to derive application hotspot sites.
2. Parallelize hotspot areas by adding **parallel** and **kernels** directives to the code.
3. Optimize data transfer using **data**, **enter/exit data**, **update** directives.
4. Optimization of parallel granularity with **gang, vector** clauses.
5. Repetition of (1)–(4)

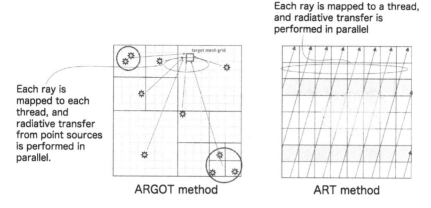

Fig. 3. Overview of the ARGOT and ART methods with loop optimization.

The hotspots in the ARGOT code have already been identified by previous studies [2,5] and it is obvious from existing OpenMP-based CPU implementation and CUDA-based GPU implementation which loops should be kernelized for OpenACC. Therefore, we start with the loop optimization in (2).

Loop Optimizations. In OpenACC programming, the parallel region or the kernels region is applied to generate the GPU kernel. In the former, the loop parallelization method is user-dependent, while in the latter, the compiler automatically analyzes and parallelizes the corresponding part. In this study, the OpenMP implementation (`#pragma omp parallel for`), which is equivalent to the CUDA implementation in the ARGOT code, is rewritten as `#pragma acc parallel loop`. When a function call is included in the specified parallel region, `#pragma acc routine seq` is added to the function. Figure 3 shows an overview of the ARGOT and ART methods with loop optimization. In the ARGOT method, rays from each point source are mapped to each thread and radiative transfer calculations are executed in parallel. However, in the ART method, rays are mapped to each thread and radiative transfer calculations based on ray tracing are executed in parallel.

Data Management. In GPU programming, it is extremely important to minimize the data transfer between CPU and GPU while parallelizing the loop structure. Figure 4 shows a simulation flow of the ARGOT code. In the CUDA implementation, all data necessary for execution of the ARGOT code is copied to the GPU memory at initialization; thereafter, data is written back from the GPU to the CPU as necessary. For this reason, the OpenACC implementation uses `#pragma acc enter data copyin()` to copy the main data into GPU memory during initialization, and uses `#pragma acc update host()` to write data from the GPU back to the CPU only for operations that must be performed on the host, such as writing log files.

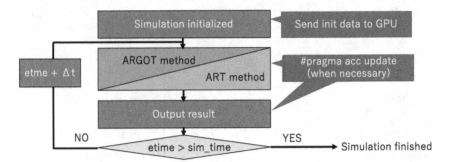

Fig. 4. Simulation flow of the ARGOT code.

Optimization of Parallel Granularity and Application of Asynchronous Execution. OpenACC defines three levels of granularity of parallelism: gang parallelism, worker parallelism, and vector parallelism. Gang parallelism corresponds to the coarsest granularity of parallelism, vector parallelism corresponds to the finest granularity of parallelism, and worker parallelism corresponds to medium granularity. Which of these three types of parallelism corresponds to a specific piece of hardware depends on the target accelerator. For GPUs, each iteration of a loop partitioned in fine-grain vector parallelism is assigned to a single GPU thread. In coarse-grain gang parallel, each iteration of a segmented loop is allocated to a single thread block (a group of up to 1024 GPU threads). Worker parallelism corresponds to warping (a group of 32 GPU threads) in CUDA. Worker parallelism is needed when warp-aware optimization is described in OpenACC; however, it is not used in this study because two levels of parallelism, i.e., gang and vector parallelism, are sufficient in many cases. In the ARGOT code with OpenACC, the parallel granularity is set to be equivalent to that of the CUDA implementation by setting the `num_gang` and `vector_length` with reference to the block size and number of threads of the CUDA implementation.

Programmers experienced with CUDA should be aware that the GPU kernel launch is asynchronous by default in CUDA, whereas it is synchronous in OpenACC. To realize the same behavior, the OpenACC implementation adds `async` clause is added to the parallel syntax corresponding to the parts of the CUDA kernel that are executing asynchronously. While `cudaDeviceSynchronize()` is used as a barrier to asynchronous execution of the CUDA kernel, the OpenACC implementation uses `wait` clauses to achieve the same behavior as the CUDA implementation.

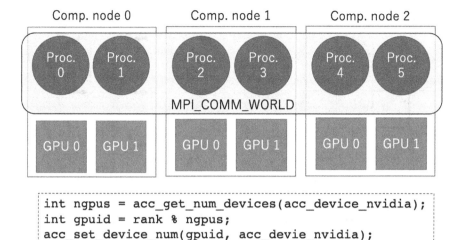

A code snippet to realize 1 GPU / process
(# of processes / node ≦ ngpus)

Fig. 5. Overview of the OpenACC implementation using multiple GPUs.

4 OpenACC Implementation Using Multiple GPUs

4.1 Overview

Since OpenACC does not provide a function for using multiple GPUs, it is necessary to parallelize the CPU-side process that calls the GPUs in order to use multiple GPUs. In this paper, we adopt the Message Passing Interface (MPI) + OpenACC approach, in which one GPU is allocated to one MPI process. An overview of the implementation is shown in Fig. 5.

Since this implementation is based on MPI, its greatest advantage is its scalability that allows GPUs to be used not only within a node but also across nodes. The code to realize this is shown in the lower part of Fig. 5. First, by passing acc_device_nvidia as an argument to the acc_get_num_devices() function in the first line, the number of NVIDIA GPUs available within the computation node is queried. Next, in line 2, the number of GPUs to be used is calculated according to the rank number of each MPI process. Then, by passing the GPU number obtained in the second line to the acc_set_device_num() function in the third line as the first argument, the allocation of the GPU to be used by each MPI process is completed. However, for the allocation of one GPU per MPI process to work correctly, the number of processes assigned to a computation node must be less than or equal to the number of GPUs available in the computation node. If this assignment is not made, all processes in a computation node use the GPU numbered 0.

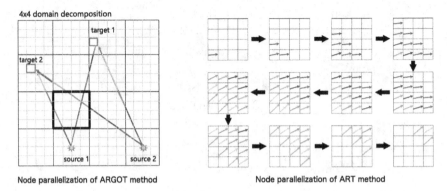

Fig. 6. Node parallelization for ARGOT code. An overview of node parallelization for the ARGOT and ART methods are cited from [9] and [10], respectively.

4.2 Node Parallelization for ARGOT Code

The ARGOT code initially has parallelization features with MPI programming model. The node parallelization of the ARGOT and ART methods are described below.

ARGOT Method. An overview of the node parallelization of the ARGOT method is shown in Fig. 6. In node parallelization, the simulation space is equally divided into dimensions (4 × 4 domain decomposition in the figure). Rays spanning multiple nodes are divided into "ray segments" at the boundaries between nodes (each segment has a different color as shown in the figure), and the computation of each segment is performed on each node in parallel. Because the segments for which each node is responsible are independent of each other, each segment is assigned to a thread and processed in parallel. The overall computation result is obtained by summing the optical thickness computation results for each segment. If only one MPI process is used, four ray segments, source 1 → target 1, source 1 → target 2, source 2 → target 1, and source 2 → target 2, are considered as "ray segments," and each ray is assigned to a thread and processed in parallel.

ART Method. The ART method divides the three-dimensional problem space into meshes and performs radiative transfer simulation by firing multiple rays from the boundary surfaces. When applying domain decomposition with multiple MPI processes, the problem space is divided and allocated along the x, y, and z directions according to the number of processes (e.g., the problem space was divided into two parts along the x direction for 2 processes, two parts along the x and y directions for 4 processes). Therefore, the ART method on multiple nodes is realized by receiving rays sent out from the problem space that one process handles by the process in charge of the next problem space located in the direction of the rays and executing the radiative transfer simulation.

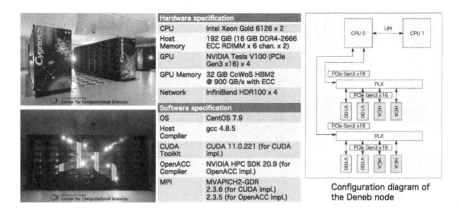

Fig. 7. Hardware and software specification of evaluation environment (the Cygnus supercomputer [1]).

A possible method to implement parallelization as part of the ART method for multiple nodes is the simultaneous computation of rays with different directions. However, because the order of processes responsible for each ray can be different for each ray (even if the direction is the same), GPU kernel startup control and MPI communication management become very complicated. For this reason, the current implementation employs the multiple wavefront method [10] to achieve pipelined node parallelization while restricting the firing order for each ray direction.

5   Evaluation

5.1   Experimental Settings

The Cygnus supercomputer [1], which is currently in operation at the Center for Computational Sciences, University of Tsukuba, was used as the platform for performance evaluation. Figure 7 shows the details of the evaluation environment. The Cygnus consists of two types of computation nodes: Deneb nodes with only GPUs as accelerators and Albireo nodes with GPUs and FPGAs. In this study, we used two Deneb nodes (8 GPUs) for performance evaluation.

We evaluated the performance of the OpenACC implementation of ARGOT by comparing it with the CUDA implementation under the strong scaling condition. The CUDA implementation was compiled with the option -O3 -ffast-math -funroll-loops -std=c99 -mcmodel=medium -fopenmp and the OpenACC implementation was compiled with the option -fast -acc -ta=tesla,cc70 -Minfo=accel -c99 -mcmodel=medium -mp. The number of processes (GPUs) was 1 to 8, and the problem space was divided into two parts along the x direction for 2 processes, two parts along the x and y directions for 4 processes, and two parts along the x, y, and z directions for 8 processes. The Cygnus supercomputer

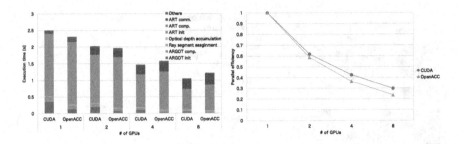

Fig. 8. Comparison result under the condition of strong scaling with problem size fixed at 64^3.

has four GPUs per node, and therefore, up to four processes were executed on a single node. For cross-node execution such as 8 processes, we specified -genv MV2_NUM_HCAS 4 to use 4 lanes of InfiniBand HDR100. In the CUDA implementation, one process was responsible for all GPUs in a node, but we used export CUDA_VISIBLE_DEVICES=${MV2_COMM_WORLD_LOCAL_RANK} to limit the number of GPUs visible to a process to one to ensure that only one GPU could be assigned to each MPI process.

5.2 Performance Comparison Between CUDA and OpenACC Implementations

Figure 8 shows the result of evaluation under the condition of strong scaling with the problem size fixed at 64^3. Thus, with 8 processes, each GPU is responsible for 32^3 problem spaces. The vertical axis of the bar graph on the left shows the execution time required for one iteration of the radiative transfer simulation, and the vertical axis of the line graph on the right shows the parallel efficiency normalized by the performance of a single GPU. In both graphs, the horizontal axis shows the number of GPUs used.

First, a comparison of the CUDA and OpenACC implementations on one GPU shows that the OpenACC implementation achieves 98% of the performance of the CUDA implementation, except for "ARGOT init", which denotes the initialization of the ARGOT method. The CUDA implementation uses cudaHostAlloc() to allocate pinned memory during the initialization of the ARGOT method. Although cudaHostAlloc() has a large overhead, this is not a significant concern if it is executed only once during initialization. However, in the CUDA implementation of the ARGOT method, cudaHostAlloc() must be repeatedly called to cope with dynamic changes in light sources, such as light source movement and light source increase/decrease, and this overhead becomes apparent. Since this overhead is proportional to the allocated problem size, the more GPUs are used, the shorter the time required for "ARGOT init" becomes.

As the number of GPUs used is increased, the execution time of the OpenACC implementation of the ART method becomes longer than the CUDA

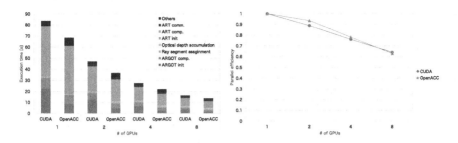

Fig. 9. Comparison result under the condition of strong scaling with the problem size fixed at 256^3.

implementation, and at 8 GPUs, the performance of the OpenACC implementation is 86% that of the CUDA implementation. In other words, the performance difference between the OpenACC implementation and the CUDA implementation is reversed, even if "ARGOT init" is included. To investigate why the performance of the OpenACC implementation of the ART method is not as good as that of the CUDA implementation of this method, we checked the compiler messages in the core arithmetic loop of the ART method. It was found that the compiler was not able to successfully analyze whether the compiler was data independent or not, displaying logs such as "`Complex loop carried dependence of...`". In addition to this, the problem size of 32^3/GPU is insufficiently parallel to fully utilize the 5,120 CUDA cores. This may be due to the fact that the impact of the compiler's analysis capability is more apparent. The fact that the problem size is too small for a single GPU is also evident from the fact that the communication overhead becomes more apparent as the number of GPUs used increases, resulting in a parallel efficiency of 30% when 8 GPUs are used, even with the CUDA implementation.

Therefore, we evaluated the performance of increasing the problem size allocated to a single GPU. Figure 9 shows the result of evaluation under the condition of strong scaling with the problem size fixed at 256^3. Thus, with 8 processes, each GPU is responsible for 128^3 problem spaces. As expected, the performance difference between the two ART methods was eliminated as the problem size allocated to one GPU was increased, and the communication overhead did not become apparent because the ratio of operations was larger than the communication ratio. As a result, the parallel efficiency of the two methods was almost the same, 63% even when 8 GPUs were used. In summary, this study shows that the OpenACC implementation of ARGOT achieves performance that is nearly equivalent to the CUDA implementation, provided that the problem size allocated to one GPU is set appropriately. Our previous study has shown that offloading the ART method to FPGAs achieves better performance than implementation using CUDA when the allocated problem size is small [2]. Incorporating this research outcome into the OpenACC implementation of the ARGOT code enables it to outperform the CUDA implementation while maintaining higher readability and maintainability than the CUDA implementation.

6   Related Work

Since the first version of the OpenACC model was introduced in 2012, the extent to which OpenACC's performance can match the performance of CUDA implementations has been a constant topic of interest in the HPC domain. As a result, researchers in various fields have conducted studies comparing the performance of CUDA and OpenACC implementations [4,7,8].

Hoshino et al. [4] investigated the performance impact of OpenACC on two microbenchmarks and one real-world CFD application, and found that OpenACC performance is typically approximately 50% lower than CUDA, but may reach up to 98% with careful manual optimization for some applications. Memeti et al. [8] conducted a comparative study of the SPEC Accel and Rodinia benchmark suites, evaluating not only OpenACC and CUDA implementations, but also OpenMP and OpenCL implementations in terms of productivity, performance, and energy. Li et al. [7] conducted a performance comparison of CUDA and OpenACC using 19 kernels on 10 benchmarks, focusing on the programming model, optimization techniques, and underlying compiler, and claimed that OpenACC is a highly reliable programming model and a good alternative to CUDA for accelerator devices.

However, these studies are limited to performance comparisons using a single GPU, and the performance differences and parallel efficiency when multiple nodes/multiple GPUs are used are not clear. In addition to this, performance comparisons are mainly based on benchmark applications, and few studies have been conducted targeting real-world applications. In contrast, this study compares the performance of OpenACC implementations based on these two criteria and quantitatively clarifies the practicality of OpenACC implementations targeting real applications. Furthermore, in order to overcome the limitation of accelerated computing using only GPUs, we are developing an OpenACC-based programming environment that also uses FPGAs [11].

7   Conclusion

In this study, as a first step toward realizing usable GPU–FPGA-accelerated computing based on OpenACC, we have quantitatively evaluated the practicality of the OpenACC implementation by comparing it with a CUDA implementation for the ARGOT code, a radiative transfer simulation code for astrophysics, which is a multiphysics application. As a result, we have clarified that the OpenACC implementation achieves performance that is nearly equivalent to the CUDA implementation as long as the problem size is not allocated such that the parallelism is insufficient to fully utilize the GPU's computation cores. Because our previous studies have shown that the advantage of FPGA offloading becomes significant when the allocated problem size is small, we may incorporate FPGA offloading into the OpenACC version of the ARGOT code implemented in this study. In other words, our future research priority is to quantitatively show that OpenACC can provide higher code readability and maintainability than CUDA, and can accelerate operations even when small problem sizes are allocated by using FPGAs together.

Acknowledgements. This work used computational resources of TSUBAME3.0 provided by Tokyo Institute of Technology through the HPCI System Research Project (Project ID: hp190099). This work was supported by JSPS KAKENHI (Grant Number 21H04869). The Cygnus utilization is supported by the MCRP 2022 Program by the Center for Computational Sciences, University of Tsukuba. We also thank Dr. Naruhiko Tan of NVIDIA for his advice on OpenACC optimization.

References

1. Boku, T., Fujita, N., Kobayashi, R., Tatebe, O.: Cygnus - world first multihybrid accelerated cluster with GPU and FPGA coupling. In: Workshop Proceedings of the 51st International Conference on Parallel Processing, ICPP Workshops '22. Association for Computing Machinery, New York (2023). https://doi.org/10.1145/3547276.3548629

2. Fujita, N., et al.: OpenCL-enabled parallel raytracing for astrophysical application on multiple FPGAs with optical links. In: 2020 IEEE/ACM International Workshop on Heterogeneous High-Performance Reconfigurable Computing (H2RC), pp. 48–55 (2020). https://doi.org/10.1109/H2RC51942.2020.00011

3. Gorski, K.M., et al.: HEALPix: a framework for high-resolution discretization and fast analysis of data distributed on the sphere. Astrophys. J. **622**(2), 759–771 (2005). https://doi.org/10.1086/427976

4. Hoshino, T., Maruyama, N., Matsuoka, S., Takaki, R.: CUDA vs OpenACC: performance case studies with kernel benchmarks and a memory-bound CFD application. In: 2013 13th IEEE/ACM International Symposium on Cluster, Cloud, and Grid Computing, pp. 136–143 (2013). https://doi.org/10.1109/CCGrid.2013.12

5. Kobayashi, R., et al.: Multi-hybrid accelerated simulation by GPU and FPGA on radiative transfer simulation in astrophysics. J. Inf. Process. **28**, 1073–1089 (2020). https://doi.org/10.2197/ipsjjip.28.1073

6. Lee, S., Kim, J., Vetter, J.S.: OpenACC to FPGA: a framework for directive-based high-performance reconfigurable computing. In: 2016 IEEE International Parallel and Distributed Processing Symposium (IPDPS), pp. 544–554 (2016). https://doi.org/10.1109/IPDPS.2016.28

7. Li, X., Shih, P.C.: Performance comparison of CUDA and OpenACC based on optimizations. In: Proceedings of the 2018 2nd High Performance Computing and Cluster Technologies Conference, HPCCT 2018, pp. 53–57. Association for Computing Machinery, New York (2018). https://doi.org/10.1145/3234664.3234681

8. Memeti, S., Li, L., Pllana, S., Kołodziej, J., Kessler, C.: Benchmarking OpenCL, OpenACC, OpenMP, and CUDA: programming productivity, performance, and energy consumption. In: Proceedings of the 2017 Workshop on Adaptive Resource Management and Scheduling for Cloud Computing, ARMS-CC 2017, pp. 1–6. Association for Computing Machinery, New York (2017). https://doi.org/10.1145/3110355.3110356

9. Okamoto, T., Yoshikawa, K., Umemura, M.: ARGOT: accelerated radiative transfer on grids using oct-tree. Monthly Not. R. Astron. Soc. **419**(4), 2855–2866 (2012). https://doi.org/10.1111/j.1365-2966.2011.19927.x

10. Tanaka, S., Yoshikawa, K., Okamoto, T., Hasegawa, K.: A new ray-tracing scheme for 3D diffuse radiation transfer on highly parallel architectures. Publ. Astron. Soc. Jpn. **67**(4), 62 (2015). https://doi.org/10.1093/pasj/psv027

11. Tsunashima, R., et al.: OpenACC unified programming environment for GPU and FPGA multi-hybrid acceleration. In: 13th International Symposium on High-level Parallel Programming and Applications (HLPP) (2020)

QR Factorization of Block Low-Rank Matrices on Multi-instance GPU

Satoshi Ohshima[1](✉), Akihiro Ida[2], Rio Yokota[3], and Ichitaro Yamazaki[4]

[1] Information Technology Center, Nagoya University, Aichi, Japan
`ohshima@cc.nagoya-u.ac.jp`
[2] Research Institute for Value-Added-Information Generation, Japan Agency
for Marine-Earth Science and Technology, Kanagawa, Japan
[3] Global Scientific Information and Computing Center, Tokyo Institute
of Technology, Tokyo, Japan
[4] Scalable Algorithms Department, Sandia National Laboratories, New Mexico, USA

Abstract. The QR factorization, which is a fundamental operation in linear algebra, is used extensively in scientific simulations. The acceleration and memory reduction of it are important research targets. QR factorization using block low-rank matrices (BLR-QR) has previously been proposed to address this issue. In this study, we consider its implementation on a GPU. Current CPUs and GPUs have numerous computational cores and the performance consists of the total performance of them. Therefore, the degree of parallelism of the target calculation is important for obtaining high performance. By contrast, many applications, including BLR-QR, do not have sufficient parallelism. Batched computation has attracted attention for achieving high performance in such calculations. However, the use of it requires major code rewriting and is extremely laborious. Thus, we propose the use of the multi-instance GPU (MIG) feature of current GPUs. Using MIG, we succeeded in obtaining a 53.3% time reduction over the CPU and 77.6% over the GPU without MIG. From the above result, we succeeded in demonstrating rapid implementation of BLR-QR on MIG and usefulness of MIG.

Keywords: Multi-Instance GPU · Low-Rank Matrices · QR Factorization

1 Introduction

Although the computational performance of processors is improving based on Moore's law, it is approaching the limit, with continued growth owing to various hardware and software efforts. An important issue is the degree of parallelism, that is, the length of the computational loop of target applications. Current high-performance computing processors have numerous cores, the summation of the performance of which yields the overall performance. This trend is remarkable in graphics processing units (GPUs). As current high-performance GPUs have thousands of computational cores, a very long computational loop is required

© The Author(s), under exclusive license to Springer Nature Switzerland AG 2023
H. Takizawa et al. (Eds.): PDCAT 2022, LNCS 13798, pp. 359–369, 2023.
https://doi.org/10.1007/978-3-031-29927-8_28

to fill all cores and to obtain high performance. Moreover, both the capacity and speed of memory are important. While computational performance is still increasing, memory performance remains lacking. The large demand for calculating large-scale problems in a short time is becoming increasingly difficult. Low-rank approximation methods and their rapid implementation have attracted attention as a solution to this issue.

In this study, we focus on the QR factorization of block low-rank matrices (BLR-QR) on a GPU. BLR-matrices [2] are regarded as special cases of $\mathcal{H}$-matrices [1] with simplified structures. Ida et al. [3] proposed BLR-QR for CPU clusters and demonstrated that it could achieve both large-scale computing and high speed. We consider the same calculation on a GPU. BLR-QR consists of basic matrix and vector calculations, most of which are provided by existing numerical libraries and are not very difficult to implement on GPUs. However, the BLR-QR calculations are not sufficiently large to achieve high performance on current GPUs. One solution for rapid calculation is "batched" calculation, whereby many of the same calculations are performed in parallel and high overall performance is achieved. However, it is not always easy to apply batched calculation because users must change the data structure to use batched libraries, which is extremely laborious. We consider the use of the multi-instance GPU (MIG) feature to address the above issues. We employ this feature to limit the GPU resources per process and to achieve high overall performance in BLR-QR.

The contributions of this study are summarized as follows: First, we investigate the implementation of BLR-QR on a GPU. Although this study only focuses on a GPU workstation with a single GPU, we believe that our approach can aid in improving large-scale hierarchical computation environments, such as GPU supercomputers. Second, we demonstrate that MIG can achieve high performance in applications that are considered unsuitable for GPUs. Several existing works have demonstrated the effectiveness of MIG in various applications, and we present a new effective case example.

The remainder of this paper is organized as follows. Section 2 summarizes the work relating to this study. In Sect. 3, we present the issue of small numerical calculations and a solution using MIG. In Sect. 4, we discuss the algorithm and the implementation of BLR-QR on CPU, GPU, and MIG. The performance evaluation is outlined in Sect. 5. Finally, the conclusions and suggestions for future work are provided in Sect. 6.

2   Related Work

The BLR-QR algorithm and implementation in this study are based on the work in [3], which is the first study of BLR-QR. In [3], the BLR-QR was implemented on a CPU cluster and the performance was evaluated. Subsequently, [4] proposed an improved implementation of [3]. Moreover, [5] proposed the QR decomposition of $\mathcal{H}$-matrices. As these works only investigated CPUs, our study contributes to the research by considering GPUs.

Many studies have focused on low-rank matrices or QR factorization, some of which used GPUs as the target hardware. For example, [6] studied low-rank matrices on a GPU. However, no existing works have used both low-rank matrices and QR factorization on GPUs. Various works have used MIG for simulations [7,8]. However, to the best of the authors' knowledge, no studies have applied MIG for low-rank structure matrices.

Batched calculation is a promising solution for improving performance, particularly in numerical calculations, on current processors. The fact that many well-known numerical libraries support such calculations provides definitive evidence thereof. However, from the perspectives of productivity and continuity, we believe that batched calculation is not always a suitable solution. Thus, an open discussion remains regarding the performance of batched calculation and multiple process calculations on GPUs.

3   Numerical Calculations on MIG

3.1   Small Numerical Calculations on GPU

As mentioned previously, a high degree of parallelism that is sufficient to fill the cores is required to achieve high performance on GPUs. In general, long loop structures are the targets of parallel calculations. However, many applications do not have very long loops and cannot fill the cores of the GPU. This issue is not limited to GPUs, but also occurs on current CPUs.

Furthermore, several applications perform many small calculations in parallel. For example, many blocking numerical calculation algorithms perform many similar small calculations. If the target data of their calculations are independent, then they can be calculated in parallel. Therefore, when many blocks are calculated in parallel on a partial GPU, many computational cores of the GPU are filled and high overall performance is expected, even if each calculation is small. This calculation style is known as batched calculation and has attracted significant research attention [9]. Moreover, various well-known numerical libraries already support batched calculations [10,11]. However, as these libraries require their own special data structure, users need to reconstruct their programs. Therefore, although batched calculations offer a promising solution, their widespread use remains challenging.

3.2   Small Numerical Calculations on MIG

We consider the use of the MIG feature to address the abovementioned issues. MIG is a new GPU feature that is supported by NVIDIA Ampere architecture and newer GPUs. It can securely partition one GPU into separate GPU instances. In general, the separated GPUs are used by multiple users concurrently. This feature is mainly expected to be applied in cloud computing services.

In NVIDIA GPUs, multiple host processes and threads can share hardware resources on one GPU for a long time. In particular, in the Volta architecture, the multiple process execution system is improved by the Multi-Process Service (MPS) feature. Figures 1 and 2 show the differences between MPS and MIG. In

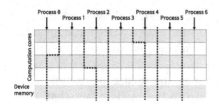

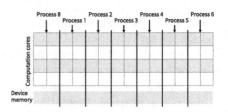

Fig. 1. MPS (and traditional multi-process) execution model. Each GPU kernel can access all GPU resources and use them freely under loose limitations.

Fig. 2. MIG execution model. The GPU is explicitly divided into up to seven partial GPUs. Each GPU kernel can recognize only limited GPU resources and cannot cross their borders.

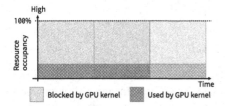

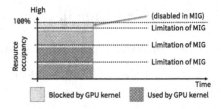

Fig. 3. Multiple GPU kernels with MPS.

Fig. 4. Multiple GPU kernels with MIG.

MPS, each GPU kernel can access all GPU resources and use them freely under loose limitations. In summary, if unused resources are available on the GPU, other GPU kernels that require a small amount of resources can be executed in parallel. By contrast, when MIG is enabled, the GPU is explicitly divided. Each GPU kernel can recognize limited resources and cannot cross their borders.

Let us assume that a GPU kernel that is provided by a numerical library is designed to use all GPU resources. In the case of MPS, even if the target data are small and cannot fill the entire GPU resource, the whole GPU will be blocked by one GPU kernel execution (Fig. 3). However, in the case of MIG, the GPU kernel can use only the separated GPU (Fig. 4). Therefore, in MIG, if the GPU kernels attempt to fill the whole GPU, multiple GPU kernels can be executed in parallel and the total execution time will be reduced. Many of GPU libraries require all GPU resources because their objective is to obtain the highest performance. However, no special technical efforts are required to use MIG, and the total amount of GPU resources (e.g., streaming multiprocessors) is dependent on the GPU product. Therefore, most GPU libraries can support split GPUs and are excepted to obtain reasonable performance in this manner.

MIG also exhibits several demerits.

First, MIG cannot use all GPU resources. In the case of the NVIDIA A100 (40 GB) GPU, the entire GPU has 108 streaming multiprocessors and 40 GB of memory. However, in MIG, 98 streaming multiprocessors and 35 GB (7×5 GB)

(A) $\mathcal{H}$-matrix   (B) BLR-matrix

Fig. 5. Examples of $\mathcal{H}$-matrix and BLR-matrix. (B) is converted from (A) with a weak admissibility condition.

of memory can be used. Therefore, the total theoretical peak performance and memory amount of MIG are lower than those of the entire GPU without MIG.

Second, the reduction of the GPU resources per process may be a critical issue. If the GPU is divided into seven partial GPUs, each of which is assigned to a host process, then each host process can use only 5 GB of device memory. This limitation may be a critical limit of execution. The use of unified virtual memory (UVM) could be a helpful solution, which remains for future work.

Finally, the maximum number of partial GPUs may be an important issue. The maximum number of divided GPUs of the flagship GPUs (NVIDIA A100 and H100) is seven, which is not suitable for applications that require a power-of-two number of processes. In such cases, the available maximum number is four out of seven and only 57% of the resources can be used. Several small GPUs with a smaller number of cores are also available. For example, the maximum number of partial GPUs of the A30 GPU is four. Therefore, from this perspective, the A30 GPU is more suitable for the use of MIG than the A100 and H100 GPUs.

4 BLR-QR on GPU and MIG

4.1 BLR-QR

Many large-scale simulations using massive matrices require both large memory and lengthy computations. Low-rank approximation methods are expected to reduce both memory amount and execution time of various matrix computations. Low-rank matrices replace parts of dense matrices with approximated matrices. The BLR matrix is a simple and nonhierarchical low-rank matrix based on the lattice structure as illustrated in Fig. 5. In this figure, the blocks in deep purple indicate dense submatrices, and the off-diagonal blocks in light purple indicate low-rank submatrices. Each low-rank submatrix consists of the multiplication of two small dense matrices. These low-rank matrices can be generated in several applications, including magnetic field analysis.

Several studies have focused on the QR factorization of low-rank approximation methods, as detailed in Sect. 2. We focus on the BLR-QR. One existing work [3] proposed BLR-QR on a CPU cluster. The BLR-QR algorithm is based on the modified block Gram-Schmidt (MBGS) algorithm [12] (Algorithm 1). In

---

Algorithm 1. MBGS algorithm, where N_b is the number of blocks in a column (or row) of matrices A, Q, and R. The subscripts of the matrices denote the row and column indices of the lattice. The symbol $*$ represents all blocks, e.g., $A_{*,j}$ is the j-th block column which is a tall-skinny matrix. The function $\text{TSQR}(A_{*,j})$ returns the QR factorization of the tall-skinny matrix $A_{*,j}$ such that $Q_{*,j}^T Q_{*,j} = I$ and $Q_{*,j}, R_{j,j} = A_{*,j}$, where $Q_{*,j} \in \mathbb{R}^{N \times l}$ and $R_{j,j} \in \mathbb{R}^{l \times l}$.

Input: A with $N_b \times N_a$ blocks
Output: Q, R with $N_b \times N_a$ blocks such that QR=A
  1: **for do**$j = 1, 2, \cdots, N_b$
  2:    $[Q_{*,j}, R_{j,j}] := \text{TSQR}(A_{*,j})$
  3:    **for do**$k = j+1, j+2, \cdots, N_b$
  4:       $R_{j,k} := Q_{*,j}^T A_{*,k}$
  5:       $A_{*,k} := A_{*,k} - Q_{*,j} R_{j,k}$
  6:    **end for**
  7: **end for**

---

[3], the algorithm was written using Fortran 90, and parallelized using MPI and OpenMP. Each MPI process takes charge of each block calculation. If the number of blocks is larger than the number of MPI processes, each MPI process takes charge of multiple blocks. As the construction of the BLR-matrix is simple, it is suitable for calculation in a distributed computing environment. Moreover, OpenMP is applied to each calculation process in lines 4 and 5. As with the QR factorization of a dense matrix, the operations in BLR-QR are performed block by block. The difference is that the submatrices in the off-diagonal blocks are formatted by the low-rank representation. Therefore, block calculations are performed in a low-rank manner. Tall skinny QR (TSQR) is applied for each block column $A_{*,j}$ in line 2 of Algorithm 1. In this case, many small dense TSQR decompositions and one large dense QR decomposition are performed. The detailed algorithm is presented in [5].

We focus on the processes from lines 3 to 6 in Algorithm 1, and consider the implementation thereof on a GPU. Matrix-matrix calculations are executed in line 4 of Algorithm 1. These calculations can be performed using the double-precision matrix-matrix multiplication and addition (DGEMM) function of BLAS libraries for dense matrices, whereas they are performed using combinations of DGEMM for low-rank submatrices. Moreover, the summation of a dense matrix and low-rank matrix, and two low-rank matrices increases the rank of the low-rank matrix. In such cases, rank reduction is required to perform the following calculations. This reduction process is known as "reducerank" and it mainly consists of QR factorization and singular value decomposition (SVD) (Algorithm 2). Similarly, DGEMM and reducerank are executed in line 5 of Algorithm 1.

4.2   BLR-QR on GPU

We investigate the implementation of BLR-QR on a GPU. We implement the GPU kernels using CUDA C and execute them using Fortran 90.

Algorithm 2. Rank reduction algorithm for matrices with low-rank representation, where $(Q^U \mu) \sigma (\nu Q^V)$ is the SVD of UV and the corresponding truncated SVD with the k' largest singular values gives the best rank k' approximation of UV.

Input: $U \in \mathbb{R}^{m \times k}, V \in \mathbb{R}^{k \times n}$ composing $A := UV$

Output: $U' \in \mathbb{R}^{m \times k'}, V' \in \mathbb{R}^{k' \times n}$ such that $U'V'$ approximates UV
1: $[Q^U, R^U] := \text{TSQR}(U)$, $[Q^V, R^V] := \text{TSQR}(V)$
2: $[\mu, \sigma, \nu] := \text{SVD}(R^U R^V)$
3: Truncate σ at $k' : \sigma \in \mathbb{R}^{k \times k} \to \sigma' \in \mathbb{R}^{k' \times k'}$
4: Set U' as the first k' columns of $Q^U \mu \sigma'$
5: Set V' as the first k' rows of νQ^V

In [3], most of these calculations were implemented using the BLAS and LAPACK libraries to obtain high performance. As several numerical libraries for GPUs already support BLAS and LAPACK functions, we implement BLR-QR on the GPU using these libraries. The DGEMM function provided by BLAS is executed in many cases for the target calculations. In the reducerank process, the double-precision QR factorization (DGEQRF and DORGQR) and double-precision SVD for general matrices (DGESVD) functions provided by LAPACK are executed. DGEMM is provided by the cuBLAS library, whereas DGEQRF, DORGQR, and DGESVD are provided by the cuSOLVER library in the GPU. Although these libraries are generally used by the C language, they can easily be called by Fortran 90 using wrapper functions. Furthermore, unnecessary data transfer between the CPU and GPU is suppressed because these functions expect that the target arrays are located on the device memory.

4.3   BLR-QR on MIG

When the above functions that are provided cuBLAS and cuSOLVER are implemented effectively, high performance is expected. These functions focus on high performance on an entire GPU or a multiple-GPU environment and their main target matrices are large matrices. However, the target matrices in this study are not sufficiently large to fill the entire computational cores on current high-performance GPUs. Therefore, it is expected that straight-forward GPU implementation using cuBLAS and cuSOLVER will result in low performance.

In such cases, the use of a batched library is a promising solution to obtain high performance on a GPU. In fact, batched DGEMM and DGESVD are provided by cuBLAS and cuSOLVER. However, the use of batched libraries requires major rewriting of the code. For this reason, we propose the use of MIG.

In many cases, MIG does not require major rewriting of the code. In this study, source codes of GPU and MIG are the same. If the target program supports MPI and each MPI process uses one GPU, users only need to assign a GPU using the CUDA_VISIBLE_DEVICES environment variable. Our program is parallelized using MPI and OpenMP. As described in Sect. 3, each block calculation is executed by one MPI process. Moreover, all calculation processes in

Table 1. Execution environment

Processor	AMD EPYC 7313	NVIDIA A100 (40 GB, PCIe)
Architecture	Milan	Ampere
# cores	16 physical cores (2 threads per physical core)	3,456 FP64 cores (32 cores × 108 SMs)
Clock speed	3.0 GHz (up to 3.7 GHz)	Up to 1,410 MHz
Peak performance (DP)	768 GFLOPS	9.7 TFLOPS
Memory	DDR4-3200, 512 GB, 205 GB/s	HBM2, 40 GB, 1,555 GB/s

lines 4 and 5 of Algorithm 1 are parallelized by OpenMP. In the case of BLR-QR on a GPU, all MPI processes share one entire GPU. By contrast, in the case of BLR-QR on MIG, each MPI process uses a different partial GPU. In both cases, each OpenMP thread executes the library functions concurrently in the execution of multiple OpenMP threads. In our implementation, each OpenMP thread uses a different CUDA Stream to reduce the overhead and to increase the GPU occupancy.

5 Performance Evaluation

We compared the execution times of BLR-QR on a CPU, BLR-QR on a GPU without MIG, and BLR-QR on MIG.

5.1 Execution Environment and Target Matrices

We used a GPU workstation as the evaluation environment. Table 1 presents the specifications. We used an Intel compiler and MPI (oneAPI Toolkits, 2021.5.0), and CUDA 11.6.2. We used the following main compiler options: `-Ofast -axCORE-AVX2 -fma -qopenmp -ip -qmkl` for the Intel compiler and `-O3 -arch=sm_80` for CUDA. All MPI processes and OpenMP threads were assigned to the physical cores while the SMT feature of the CPU was enabled.

Table 2 displays the target matrices for the evaluation. These matrices were generated from electric field analysis problems with single spherical objects. The number of blocks and rank size of the matrices can be controlled by parameters of the low-rank approximation method. It is expected that these parameters will have a non-negligible effect on the performance. An investigation into this relationship remains as future work.

5.2 Performance Evaluation

We measured the execution time of each implementation. In each graph, the Y-axis indicates the total execution time, which includes both line 4 and 5 of Algorithm 1, whereas the X-axis indicates the execution condition; "mαtβ" means that α MPI processes are launched and each process has β OpenMP threads.

Table 2. Target matrix

Matrix name	50 ts		70 ts	
Number of lines (= degree of freedom) and blocks	50,864	32	69,312	32
Maximum rank and average rank of matrices	273	45	304	39
Memory amount of low-rank matrix (MB)	1,777		2,625	

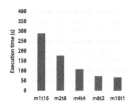

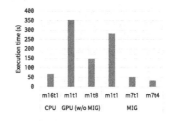

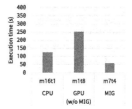

Fig. 6. Execution time of CPU (50 ts).

Fig. 7. Execution times of CPU and GPU (50 ts).

Fig. 8. Execution times of CPU and GPU (70 ts).

The CPU execution time is depicted in Fig. 6. Most of the numerical calculations were executed by MKL. As the CPU had 16 physical cores and the program supported MPI+OpenMP hybrid parallel execution, we measured several combinations of processes and threads. The use of a higher number of MPI processes resulted in shorter execution times. Therefore, in the following evaluation, the case of "m16t1" (pure MPI execution) was used as the CPU execution time.

Figures 7 and 8 present the execution times of the CPU, GPU, and MIG.

In the case of 50 ts in Fig. 7, the execution time of one MPI process, one OpenMP thread per MPI process, and only one thread to handle the entire GPU (m1t1) for the GPU without MIG was much slower than the fastest case of the CPU. By contrast, when the number of OpenMP threads per MPI process increased, the execution time was reduced. However, the fastest execution time of one MPI process, eight OpenMP threads per MPI process, and eight threads sharing one GPU (m1t8) was 218.9% longer than the fastest case of the CPU. Although we attempted to increase the number of MPI processes of the GPU, this did not outperform the execution time of m1t8 and the CPU.

We applied several variations in the number of MPI processes and OpenMP threads for MIG. The shortest execution time was achieved in the case of seven MPI processes, with each using a partial GPU, four OpenMP threads per MPI process, and four threads in one MPI process sharing one partial GPU (m7t4). The execution time was 49.1% of that of the CPU. When we used large number of OpenMP threads (e.g., m7t8), the execution time increased slightly. Moreover, the cases with four, five, six, and seven partial GPUs achieved almost the same execution times. This result was not unexpected because the execution time of BLR-QR on a CPU is short when a power-of-two number of processes is used.

The case of 70 ts in Fig. 8 was similar to that of 50 ts. The execution times of the GPU and MIG were 200.9% and 46.7% of that of the CPU, respectively.

The above results demonstrate that MIG is a reasonable method for achieving high performance.

6   Conclusions and Future Work

We have proposed the rapid implementation of BLR-QR on MIG. The main issue of BLR-QR on a GPU is the size of each calculation in BLR-QR, as a GPU is smaller than the suitable size of current GPUs, making it difficult to achieve high performance. The use of batched calculations has previously been proposed to address this issue. However, this requires major rewriting of the code and is extremely laborious. Therefore, we have investigated the use of the MIG feature on current GPUs.

We demonstrated that the execution time of MIG was faster than a CPU and a GPU without MIG. The maximum improvement was 53.3% (70 ts) over the CPU and 77.6% (50 ts) over the fastest case of the GPU without MIG. Thus, we have succeeded in demonstrating the rapid implementation of BLR-QR on a GPU and the effectiveness of MIG on low-rank matrices.

This study can be improved in several respects. First, we evaluated the performance in only one execution environment and using only one type of matrix. As our proposal of BLR-QR on MIG may be useful for various matrices and environments, the evaluation of additional cases will be valuable to enforce the effectiveness thereof. Moreover, in this study, we compared the execution time of part of the BLR-QR. We also used only one MIG-enabled GPU. A comparison of the execution time of entire BLR-QR and multiple GPUs will be important future work. The communication times between MPI processes will be affected, which has not been sufficiently evaluated in MIG. As MIG is not often used on research supercomputers, it could be applied effectively depending on the results. The use of UVM with MIG is another interesting consideration, which may aid in the calculation of large matrices. Finally, eigenvalue calculations use similar calculations to those of QR factorization. In fact, [13] focused on eigenvalue problems of BLR on a CPU. Therefore, the implementation and evaluation of these calculations on MIG will be investigated in future work.

Acknowledgments. This work was partially supported by JSPS KAKENHI Grant Numbers 21H03447 and 21K19763, and Joint Usage/Research Center for Interdisciplinary Large-scale Information Infrastructures (JHPCN)" in Japan (Project ID: jh220009). We would like to thank Dr. Tasuku Hiraishi for providing a support script program. We would like to thank Editage (https://www.editage.com/) for English language editing. Sandia National Laboratories is a multimission laboratory managed and operated by National Technology and Engineering Solutions of Sandia, LLC, a wholly owned subsidiary of Honeywell International, Inc., for the U.S. Department of Energy's National Nuclear Security Administration under contract DE-NA-0003525. This paper describes objective technical results and analysis. Any subjective views or opinions that might be expressed in the paper do not necessarily represent the views of the U.S. Department of Energy or the United States Government.

References

1. Hackbusch, W.: A sparse matrix arithmetic based on H-matrices. Part I: introduction to H-matrices. Computing **62**, 89–108 (1999). https://doi.org/10.1007/s006070050015

2. Amestoy, P., Ashcraft, C., Boiteau, O., Buttari, A., L'Excellent, J.-Y., Weisbecker, C.: Improving multifrontal methods by means of block low-rank representations. SIAM J. Sci. Comput. **37**(3), A1451–A1474 (2015)

3. Ida, A., Nakashima, H., Hiraishi, T., Yamazaki, I., Yokota, R., Iwashita, T.: QR factorization of block low-rank matrices with weak admissibility condition. J. Inf. Process. **27**, 831–839 (2019). https://doi.org/10.2197/ipsjjip.27.831

4. Apriansyah, M.R., Yokota, R.: Parallel QR factorization of block low-rank matrices. ACM Trans. Math. Softw. (2022). https://doi.org/10.1145/3538647

5. Benner, P., Mach, T.: On the QR decomposition of H-matrices. Computing **88**(3–4), 111–129 (2010). https://doi.org/10.1007/s00607-010-0087-y

6. Ohshima, S., Yamazaki, I., Ida, A., Yokota, R.: Optimization of numerous small dense-matrix-vector multiplications in H-matrix arithmetic on GPU. In: 2019 IEEE 13th International Symposium on Embedded Multicore/Many-core Systems-on-Chip (MCSoC), pp. 9–16 (2019). https://doi.org/10.1109/MCSoC.2019.00009

7. Gandham, R., Zhang, Y., Esler, K., Natoli, V.: Improving GPU throughput of reservoir simulations using NVIDIA MPS and MIG. In: Fifth EAGE Workshop on High Performance Computing for Upstream, vol. 2021, pp. 1–5 (2021). https://doi.org/10.3997/2214-4609.2021612025

8. Agrawal, N., Das, A., Pathak, R., Dorlikar, P., Modani, M.: Molecular dynamics simulations accelerate on elastic multi-GPU architecture build with FP64/TF32 latest streaming multiprocessor ampere architecture. In: Kaiser, M.S., Xie, J., Rathore, V.S. (eds.) Information and Communication Technology for Competitive Strategies (ICTCS 2021). LNNS, vol. 401, pp. 109–120. Springer, Singapore (2023). https://doi.org/10.1007/978-981-19-0098-3_12

9. Batched BLAS: https://icl.utk.edu/bblas/. Accessed 19 Aug 2022

10. BLAS-like   Extensions: https://www.intel.com/content/www/us/en/develop/documentation/onemkl-developer-reference-c/top/blas-and-sparse-blas-routines/blas-like-extensions.html. Accessed 19 Aug 2022

11. Tomov, S., Dongarra, J., Baboulin, M.: Towards dense linear algebra for hybrid GPU accelerated manycore systems. Parallel Comput. **36**(5–6), 232–240 (2010). https://doi.org/10.1016/j.parco.2009.12.005

12. Jalby, W., Philippe, B.: Stability analysis and improvement of the block Gram-Schmidt algorithm. SIAM J. Sci. Stat. Comput. **12**(5), 1058–1073 (1991)

13. Ida, A.: Solving block low-rank matrix eigenvalue problems. J. Inf. Process. **30**, 538–551 (2022). https://doi.org/10.2197/ipsjjip.30.538

Equivalence Checking and Model Checking

Equivalence Checking of Code Transformation by Numerical and Symbolic Approaches

Shunpei Sugawara[1]([✉]), Keichi Takahashi[1,2][iD], Yoichi Shimomura[2],
Ryusuke Egawa[2,3][iD], and Hiroyuki Takizawa[1,2][iD]

[1] Graduate School of Information Sciences, Tohoku University, Sendai, Japan
`shunpei@hpc.is.tohoku.ac.jp`
[2] Cyberscience Center, Tohoku University, Sendai, Japan
`{keichi,shimomura32,takizawa}@tohoku.ac.jp`
[3] Tokyo Denki University, Adachi City, Japan
`egawa@mail.dendai.ac.jp`

Abstract. Due to the increasing diversity and complexity of high-performance systems, system-specific optimization is vital to extract the system performance. To ensure that optimization does not degrade code readability and maintainability, user-defined code transformation tools are used. However, such transformation tools may change the behavior of a program. This paper focuses on Xevolver, a code transformation tool where code patterns before and after transformation are used to define transformation rules, and proposes a method to check the equivalence of transformation rules based on symbolic execution. Since equivalence checking by symbolic execution has limitations such as long runtime and inability to detect numerical errors, we also propose an equivalence checking method by numerical comparison to assist the equivalence checking by symbolic execution. In the evaluation, various optimization methods described as Xevolver transformation rules are checked for equivalence using the proposed method. The evaluation results demonstrate that the proposed equivalence checking method can cover a wider range of application codes.

Keywords: Equivalence Checking · Code Optimization · Symbolic Execution

1 Introduction

Recent years, high-performance computing (HPC) systems have become increasingly complex and diverse. In order to extract performance from such an HPC systems, application codes need to be specialized to the system. However, such system-specific application codes that include system-dependent parts have various drawbacks, such as loss of code readability, difficulty in maintenance, and low performance portability.

H. Takizawa et al. (Eds.): PDCAT 2022, LNCS 13798, pp. 373–386, 2023.
https://doi.org/10.1007/978-3-031-29927-8_29

One way to solve this problem is the use of code transformation tools. For example, by using a code transformation tool, *Xevolver* [3,7], users can define their own code transformations. Such user-defined code transformation allows the users to optimize a code without writing system-dependent information into the original application code. This can greatly increase maintainability and reduce the code porting time and effort.

In general, program optimization is expected to reduce execution time without changing the program behaviors. However, in the case of a user-defined code transformation, users are responsible for making sure that the code transformation rule does not change the program behavior. Therefore, there is a need to establish a systematic means of checking if the behavior of a program does not change through the code transformation, *i.e.,* a means of verifying program equivalence.

This paper focuses on Xevolver's approach that defines a code transformation by writing two versions of a code, the original and transformed codes. Its approach is highly compatible with equivalence checking by symbolic execution, in which two codes are compared to check if they have the same behavior for any input. Hence, this paper proposes an equivalence checking method for such a user-defined code transformation rule. While symbolic execution can encompass any behavior of a program, it has drawbacks such as time-consuming analysis for large scale code and the inability to detect floating-point errors. In such cases, it is difficult to check equivalence by symbolic execution, and hence the proposed method also employs numerical comparison of outputs as well as symbolic execution to check if the two versions produce the same output for given inputs. Although the use of numerical comparison can further increase the possibility of detecting non-equivalent codes, the time for equivalence checking becomes longer to actually execute the codes to be checked. To reduce the checking time, a checkpoint is taken right before calling the function being transformed and thus equivalence-checked by the proposed method. We first execute the original function to get the output. Then, the program is restarted from the checkpoint and obtains the output of the transformed function. As a result, the outputs of the original and transformed functions can be compared for equivalence checking.

We also express various optimization methods as transformation rules of Xevolver, perform equivalence checking using the proposed method on them, and evaluate whether equivalence checking by numerical comparison can assist checking by symbolic execution prior to implementing the checking time reduction techniques.

The rest of this paper is organized as follows. Section 2 briefly reviews the related work of this paper. Section 3 describes how the proposed equivalence checking method works. Section 4 presents the results of equivalence checking using the proposed method for various optimizations and clarifies the accuracy of equivalence checking. Finally, Sect. 5 gives concluding remarks and describes our future work.

```
zwzwzw
1zw#include "xev_defs.h"
2zw
3zwint i,j;
4zwxev_expr n;
5zwxev_stmt* stmt;
6zw
7zwint main(){
8zw     xev_expr_replace(pow(n,2),(n)*(n));
9zw     xev_stmt_src("label1");{
10zw        for(i=0;i<10;i++)
11zw            for(j=0;j<10;j++)
12zw                stmt;
13zw    }
14zw     xev_stmt_dst("label1");{
15zw        for(j=0;j<10;j++)
16zw            for(i=0;i<10;i++)
17zw                stmt;
18zw    }
19zw}
```

Fig. 1. An example of transformation rules.

2 Related Work

2.1 Xevolver for C

Xevolver is a framework that allows users to perform code transformation on arbitrary code by defining their own transformation rules [3,7]. A code transformation rule in Xevolver is expressed by simply presenting two Fortran code patterns that represent code patterns before and after transformation, thus eliminating the need for programmers to be familiar with compiler implementation. As described later in this paper, we propose to apply CIVL [5], an equivalence checking tool based on symbolic execution, to Xevolver's transformation rules to ensure that the transformation does not change the program behavior. For Xevolver users to use external programming tools supporting only the C language, such as CIVL, we have been developing Xevolver for C (Xev-C), which is a high-level interface for Xevolver to optimize C/C++ application codes [6,8].

Figure 1 is an example of transformation rules for Xev-C. The function xev_expr_replace in Line 8 will replace an expression given as its first argument with the second argument. In addition, when the code pattern in Lines 10 to 14 matches a loop in the target application being transformed, this rule transforms the loop to another code pattern defined in Lines 17 to 21. As shown in this rule, the code pattern before transformation follows a function call of xev_stmt_src, while the code after transformation follows a function call of xev_stmt_dst. This code transformation rule represents loop interchange. In this example, a special variable called an *Xev variable* is defined in Line 4 to represent any expression, and used for the rule defined with xev_expr_replace. The Xev variable defined in Line 5 can be used to express statements. As shown in this example, a pointer of xev_stmt type variable matches any number of

```
zwzwzw                                    zwzwzw
1 zw #include <math.h>                    1 zw #include <math.h>
2 zw                                      2 zw
3 zw int main(){                          3 zw int main(){
4 zw     int a,b,c,d,i,j,n,m;             4 zw     int a,b,c,d,i,j,n,m;
5 zw                                      5 zw
6 zw     for(i=0;i<10;i++)                6 zw     for(j=0;j<10;j++)
7 zw         for(j=0;j<10;j++)            7 zw         for(i=0;i<10;i++)
8 zw             a = b * j + c * i;       8 zw             a = b * j + c * i;
9 zw                                      9 zw
10 zw    d = pow(n+m,2);                  10 zw    d = (n + m) * (n + m);
11 zw                                     11 zw
12 zw    return 0;                        12 zw    return 0;
13 zw }                                   13 zw }
```

(a) Before   (b) After

Fig. 2. Codes before and after transformation.

statements. Accordingly, in this particular example, any number of statements in the loop body remain unchanged even after transforming the loop structure.

An example of actual code transformation results using the transformation rule in Fig. 1 is shown in Fig. 2. Here, Fig. 2 shows the codes before and after the transformation. Since the loop in Lines 6 to 10 of Fig. 2(a) matches the code pattern in Lines 10 to 14 of the transformation rule in Fig. 1, the loop is translated to the code pattern in Lines 17 to 21 of Fig. 1, which is the loop in Lines 6 to 10 of Fig. 2(b). In addition, the function call in Line 12 of Fig. 2(a) is replaced with the expression as shown in Line 12 of Fig. 2(b). In this way, by writing the code patterns before and after the transformation as shown in Fig. 1, Xev-C can transform the parts of the former code pattern to those of the latter pattern without requiring any knowledge about compiler implementation.

2.2   CIVL

CIVL is a program checking tool that supports multiple parallel execution environments such as OpenMP [4]. It can identify various bugs such as deadlocks, memory leaks, and division by zero. In this paper, we use it to verify the equivalence of programs written in the C language.

In CIVL, equivalence checking is performed based on symbolic execution. Symbolic execution is a method that treats the input as a symbol, which is a variable without a concrete value. When a conditional branch involving a symbol in a program is executed, it is divided into false and true cases, and each case is executed while maintaining the condition at that time. At this time, a Satisfiable Modulo Theories (SMT) solver is used to determine the possibility of such a case with reference to the conditions that have been maintained up to this point. By repeating this operation, all possible behaviors of the program can be covered.

```
ZWZWZW                                    ZWZWZW
1zw#define N 16                           1zw#define N 16
2zw                                       2zw
3zw$output int c[N][N];                   3zw$output int c[N][N];
4zw$input int a[N][N];                    4zw$input int a[N][N];
5zw$input int b[N][N];                    5zw$input int b[N][N];
6zw                                       6zw
7zwint main(){                            7zwint main(){
8zw    int i,j;                           8zw    int i,j;
9zw    for(i=0;i<N;i++)                   9zw    for(j=0;j<N;j++)
10zw        for(j=0;j<N;j++)              10zw        for(i=0;i<N;i++)
11zw            c[j][i] = a[j][i]  + b[jw             c[j][i] = a[j][i]  + b[j
             ][i];                                        ][i];
12zw}                                     12zw}
```

(a) civl_test_orig.c   (b) civl_test_trans.c

Fig. 3. Codes to be checked by CIVL.

An example of equivalence checking by CIVL is shown in the source codes of Fig. 3, which are expected to have the same behavior. In those codes, arrays a and b are specified as inputs using the $input keyword in Lines 4 and 5. This causes a and b to be treated as symbolic values by CIVL. Also, array c is specified as an output using the $output keyword in Line 3. This keyword directs CIVL to check if the two codes generate the same value for variable c. Then, the command "civl compare" verifies if both the two codes generate the same output value for c. Figure 4 shows the results of checking program equivalence. In this example, the value of c generated by the original code is the same as that by the transformed code, indicated by "The standard properties hold for all executions."

3 Equivalence Checking Method

Figure 5 shows the equivalence checking flow proposed in this paper. As described in Sect. 2.1, Xev-C's transformation rules are defined by describing the code patterns before and after the transformation. This approach of presenting some concrete codes has a high affinity with equivalence checking by symbolic execution. This is because symbolic execution encompasses program behavior by actually executing the code with the inputs as variables that have no concrete values. Therefore, this paper applies CIVL, a program checking tool using symbolic execution, to Xev-C's transformation rules, as shown in the left half of Fig. 5. Since a single transformation rule is often applied to multiple locations in the original code, the checking time can be reduced by performing checking on the transformation rules rather than on the output codes.

Since not all transformation rules can be checked correctly using only CIVL, this paper assists equivalence checking by comparing the outputs of functions before and after the transformations as shown in the lower right of Fig. 5. One limitation of this approach, numerical comparison, is that it can only check the equivalence for specific inputs. In addition, it could be time-consuming because

```
ZWZWZW
 1zw    === Source files ===
 2zw    civl_test_trans.c  (civl_test_trans.c)
 3zw    civl_test_orig.c  (civl_test_orig.c)
 4zw
 5zw    === Command ===
 6zw    civl compare -impl civl_test_orig.c -spec civl_test_trans.c
 7zw
 8zw    === Stats ===
 9zw        time (s)              : 0.55
10zw        memory (bytes)        : 1061158912
11zw        max process count     : 1
12zw        states                : 1683
13zw        states saved          : 1097
14zw        state matches         : 0
15zw        transitions           : 1682
16zw        trace steps           : 1092
17zw        valid calls           : 5192
18zw        provers               : cvc4, z3
19zw        prover calls          : 0
20zw
21zw    === Result ===
22zw    The standard properties hold for all executions.
```

Fig. 4. Result of equivalence checking by using CIVL.

it actually executes the code several times. To reduce the runtime required for checking, a checkpoint is taken just before calling the function to be transformed, and the program is restarted from the checkpoint to execute the transformed version of the same function, instead of executing the entire code several times.

3.1 Extension of Xev-C Notation for Symbolic Execution

As explained in Sect. 2.2, equivalence checking using CIVL requires the user to specify the inputs and outputs to be compared. However, since the original Xev-C is designed to express code transformation rules, which do not need to specify inputs nor outputs, it cannot directly be applied to equivalence checking with CIVL. Therefore, this paper extends Xev-C and provides notations for programmers to specify the inputs and outputs of a code pattern to be transformed.

Figure 6 shows an example of the extended rule notation. In Lines 8 and 16, the inputs are specified as in(a,b) and the output as out(c) with the pragma directive indicating the code patterns before and after the transformation. Furthermore, this paper improves Xev-C to automatically transform and divide transformation rules such as Fig. 6 into CIVL-applicable codes such as Fig. 7.

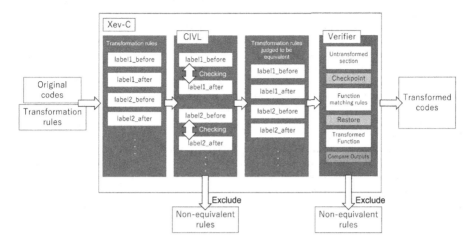

Fig. 5. Flow of equivalence checking by the proposed method.

3.2 Checking by Numerical Comparison

There are several cases where CIVL cannot simply be applied to equivalence checking of Xevolver's code transformation rules in a straightforward way. First, CIVL is unable to detect numerical errors caused by changing the order of arithmetic operations on floating-point numbers. Moreover, CIVL suffers from long runtime when checking the equivalence of codes that have long loops or many branches. For these reasons, it is difficult to ensure the equivalence only by applying CIVL to an Xev-C transformation rule.

The proposed method also performs numerical comparison of outputs to cover a wider range of code transformation rules. The lower right of Fig. 5 shows the flow of numerical comparison. Similar to the mechanism proposed in [2], a checkpoint is first taken just before calling the function to be transformed, yielding the output of the original function. Next, the program is resumed from the checkpoint just created, yielding the output of the transformed function. Finally, the outputs are compared to verify that the transformations do not change the program behavior.

4 Evaluation

To evaluate the effectiveness of the proposed method for common optimization, we first describe the code optimization patterns in the HPC refactoring catalog [1] as equivalent transformation rules for Xev-C. These patterns in the original catalog are written in Fortran, while CIVL does not support Fortran codes. In our previous work [6], hence, we have rewritten the patterns in C. In this paper, we also write a non-equivalent transformation rule to evaluate whether the proposed method can correctly detect non-equivalent ones. Equivalence checking is first done based on symbolic execution with CIVL, and then

```
 zwzwzw
1 zw      #include "xev_defs.h"
2 zw
3 zw      int i,j,k;
4 zw      xev_expr a,b,c;
5 zw
6 zw      int main(){
7 zw          #pragma xev src("label1") in(a,b) out(c){
8 zw              for(i=0;i<10;i++)
9 zw                  for(j=0;j<10;j++)
10 zw                     c = a * i + b * j;
11 zw         }
12 zw          #pragma xev dst("label1") in(a,b) out(c){
13 zw              for(j=0;j<10;j++)
14 zw                  for(i=0;i<10;i++)
15 zw                     c = a * i + b * j;
16 zw         }
17 zw     }
```

Fig. 6. Notation extensions for Xev-C.

numerical comparison of the original and transformed codes is performed to check if their outputs are identical.

4.1 Evaluation Setup

We have implemented the proposed method with Xev-C built on top of Clang/LLVM version 12.0.0, and CIVL version 1.2. In the following evaluation, SX-Aurora TSUBASA (SX-AT) [9] with vector engine Type 20B is used to execute the code. NEC C compiler for SX-AT, ncc, version 3.2.0 with -O2 (default) or -O4 option flags are used to compile the code.

4.2 Evaluation Results

Table 1 shows the results of equivalence checking by symbolic execution and numerical comparison for transformation rules that represent optimization cases in the HPC refactoring catalog. Also, Table 2 shows equivalence checking results for non-equivalent transformation rules. The first column of Table 1 shows the catalog number of the optimization case in the catalog. In Table 2, the first column shows the type of the transformation. The second column shows the results of equivalence checking by symbolic execution. In this column, "E" indicates that the case is judged to be equivalent, "TO" indicates that CIVL timed out (300s), "-" indicates that checking failed, and "NE" indicates that the case is judged to be non-equivalent. Also, the third and fourth columns show the relative errors before and after transformation detected by numerical comparison. The relative error, RE, is defined by

$$RE = \frac{|O_b - O_a|}{O_b}, \tag{1}$$

```
ZWZWZW                                    ZWZWZW
1zw#include "xev_defs.h"                   1zw#include "xev_defs.h"
2zw                                        2zw
3zwint i;                                  3zwint i;
4zwint j;                                  4zwint j;
5zw$input xev_expr a;                      5zw$input xev_expr a;
6zw$input xev_expr b;                      6zw$input xev_expr b;
7zw$output xev_expr c;                     7zw$output xev_expr c;
8zw                                        8zw
9zwint main(){                             9zwint main(){
10zw    for(i=0;i<10;i++)                  10zw    for(j=0;j<10;j++)
11zw        for(j=0;j<10;j++)              11zw        for(i=0;i<10;i++)
12zw            c = a * i + b * j;         12zw            c = a * i + b * j;
13zw}                                      13zw}
```

(a) Code pattern before transformation di-   (b) Code pattern after transformation divided in Xev-C   vided in Xev-C

Fig. 7. Codes divided in Xev-C.

where O_b and O_a are the outputs before and after the transformation, respectively. If the output was an array, the largest relative error within the array was used.

The fifth column of Table 1 shows the reason why equivalence checking by CIVL failed in Table 1. In Table 2, it shows details of transformations.

First, in Table 1, symbolic execution with CIVL could verify the equivalence of 10 cases out of 26. This indicates that the proposed method can ensure the equivalence of those 10 transformations without regard to their inputs. This information is helpful in practice for Xevolver users to use the rules. Our evaluation also clarifies that, in addition to time out, symbolic execution with CIVL could fail for the following reasons:

1. One transformation using multiple different rules.
2. Array-type outputs with different sizes.
3. Array elements with different indexes to be compared.
4. Libraries or directives used but not supported by CIVL.

The first one indicates that equivalent checking could fail if an equivalent transformation is expressed by a sequence of multiple transformation rules. This is because the proposed method is considered to check the equivalence of each rule, not the transformation sequence. For example, if a code transformation is expressed by two transformation rules, the first rule is applied to improve performance with changing the program behavior, and the second rule is used to recover the original behavior without changing the performance. In such a case, the transformation sequence does not change the program behavior, but each rule does. The current implementation of the proposed method does not support such cases. The second and third reasons indicate that the array size and dimensionality of outputs or indexes of elements to be compared are different. In CIVL, it is difficult to compare elements unless they are in arrays of the same size and dimensionality and have the same index. We might reduce the failures

Table 1. Equivalence checking results of equivalent transformations.

No.	Checking Result			Remarks
	CIVL	Relative Error		
		-O2	-O4	
1	-	0	0	Multiple transformations
2	-	0	1.89e-27	Multiple transformations
3	-	0	0	Multiple transformations
4	-	0	0	Multiple transformations
5	TO	4.36e-09	4.36e-09	
7	E	6.19e-16	0	
8	E	9.61e-16	9.50e-16	
9	TO	5.67e-16	5.67e-16	
10	-	3.78e-16	3.78e-16	Multiple transformations
11	E	0	0	
12	E	0	0	
14	E	0	0	
15	TO	1.72e-15	1.72e-15	
17	E	4.12e-16	0	
19	E	0	0	
20	E	0	0	
21	TO	0	3.21e-15	
22	-	0	0	Arrays with different sizes
24	-	0	0	Elements with different indexes
25	E	0	0	
26	E	0	0	
27	TO	0	0	
29	TO	0	0	
30	TO	0	0	
31	-	0	0	Unsupported compiler directives
32	-	0	0	Unsupported library

Table 2. Equivalence checking results of non-equivalent transformations.

Type	Checking Results			Remarks
	CIVL	Relative Error		
		-O2	-O4	
Loop interchange	NE	2.50e-01	2.50e-01	Swap two loops
Non-deterministic behavior	NE	0	0	Rarely result in different outputs
Summation	E	1.09e-01	1.09e-01	Change the order of calculations

due to these two reasons by further extending Xevolver's rule notation to express additional information about a sequence of multiple rules and arrays. This will be further discussed in our future work.

Second, after equivalence checking with symbolic execution, numerical comparison of outputs is performed. As shown in Table 1, numerical comparison can be applied to all the cases. When the code was compiled with the -O2 compiler flag, comparison errors were detected in 7 out of 26 cases. When the -O4 compiler flag was used, comparison errors were detected in 7 cases as well, but the detected cases and relative errors were different. This may be due to compiler optimizations that change the program behavior, such as reordering of calculations. Since the acceptable error depends on the application, the user is required to specify the maximum acceptable error. Furthermore, it should be emphasized that numerical comparison can ensure the equivalence of output values only for given inputs. The output values may differ for other inputs. Yet, this numerical comparison approach is helpful for Xevolver users especially if potential input values are limited.

Finally, we discuss equivalence checking of non-equivalent transformations. As shown in Table 2, either the symbolic execution or the numerical comparison, or both correctly detects that they are non-equivalent for the three non-equivalent transformations. Figure 8 shows an example where the outputs differ after loop interchange. This transformation swaps the order of the i-loop and j-loop. Since the loop indices are iterated in a different order before and after the loop interchange, their outputs are not equal. In this case, both symbolic execution and numerical comparison can correctly detect that the two codes are non-equivalent. Also, Fig. 9 shows an example where the outputs rarely differ. The two codes produce the same output for almost all values of k, but the output is different only for certain values of k. In this case, numerical comparison fails to detect the non equivalence because it only covers a limited number values for k. On the other hand, the symbolic execution produces correct checking results because it checks if the outputs are correct for all inputs. Next, we show a typical example where the numerical error grows at accumulating floating-point numbers as shown in Fig. 10. In this particular example, arrays a and b are initialized so that the values of their array elements become larger with the array index, and elements of a and b have approximately the same value. Although both the two codes in Fig. 10 calculate the sum of the subtraction between a and b, the order of subtraction operations is different. Symbolic execution with CIVL judges that the two codes should produce the same output values, because it does not consider any concrete values nor rounding errors of the array elements. As expected easily, the numerical error becomes larger in Fig. 10(b) due to a cancellation of significant digits. To check if the error is acceptable, numerical comparison employed in the proposed method is effective. By defining a threshold to indicate the maximum acceptable error, we confirm that numerical comparison in our implementation can judge if the codes produce the same results. Therefore, even in the case where symbolic execution can check the equivalence, numerical comparison is still useful for numerical calculation with floating-point operations, although it can ensure the equivalence for only a finite set of inputs, not for any inputs.

ZWZWZW

```
1zw#define N 8
2zwint main(){
3zw    int i,j,k,m;
4zw    m = rand();
5zw    for(i=0;i<N;i++){
6zw        k = 0;
7zw        for(j=0;j<N;j++){
8zw            a += i+j*k+m;
9zw            k++;
10zw        }
11zw    }
12zw}
```

ZWZWZW

```
1zw#define N 8
2zwint main(){
3zw    int i,j,k,m;
4zw    m = rand();
5zw    for(j=0;j<N;j++){
6zw        k = 0;
7zw        for(i=0;i<N;i++){
8zw            a += i+j*k+m;
9zw            k++;
10zw        }
11zw    }
12zw}
```

(a) Before transformation   (b) After transformation

Fig. 8. Loop interchange.

ZWZWZW

```
1zwint main(){
2zw    int a,k;
3zw    k = rand();
4zw    if(k == 1)
5zw        a = 0;
6zw    else
7zw        a = 1;
8zw}
```

ZWZWZW

```
1zwint main(){
2zw    int a,k;
3zw    k = rand();
4zw    if(k == 2)
5zw        a = 0;
6zw    else
7zw        a = 1;
8zw}
```

(a) Before transformation   (b) After transformation

Fig. 9. Non-deterministic behavior.

ZWZWZW

```
1zw#define N 128
2zw#define K 1000
3zw
4zwvoid init(float *a, float *b){
5zw    a[0] = 0.0;
6zw    b[0] = 0.0;
7zw    for(int i=1;i<n;i++){
8zw        a[i] = a[i-1] + 1.0f/k;
9zw        b[i] = (float)i/k;
10zw    }
11zw}
12zw
13zwint main(){
14zw    float a[n],b[n];
15zw    float sum=0;
16zw    init(a,b);
17zw    for(i=0;i<n;i++)
18zw        sum += a[i] - b[n-1-i];
19zw}
```

ZWZWZW

```
1zw#define N 128
2zw#define K 1000
3zw
4zwvoid init(float *a, float *b){
5zw    a[0] = 0.0;
6zw    b[0] = 0.0;
7zw    for(int i=1;i<n;i++){
8zw        a[i] = a[i-1] + 1.0f/k;
9zw        b[i] = (float)i/k;
10zw    }
11zw}
12zw
13zwint main(){
14zw    float a[n];
15zw    float sum=0;
16zw    init(a,b);
17zw    for(i=0;i<n;i++)
18zw        sum += a[i] - b[i];
19zw}
```

(a) Before transformation   (b) After transformation

Fig. 10. A code that performs a summation.

5   Concluding Remarks and Future Work

In this paper, we have discussed equivalence checking to ensure that a code transformation does not change behaviors of the transformed program. We focus on a user-defined code transformation tool named Xevolver, because it allows users to define a code transformation by writing the original and transformed code patterns. By checking the two patterns with symbolic execution, we can check the equivalence of the original and transformed codes for any inputs in some cases. For several reasons, however, symbolic execution is not applicable nor correct in other cases. Therefore, this paper has proposed to combine symbolic execution and numerical comparison of outputs to cover a wider range of code transformation rules.

The evaluation results suggest that the proposed method of symbolic execution and numerical comparison is helpful for equivalence checking of Xevolver's transformation rules in a catalog of code optimization rules. Although both symbolic execution and numerical comparison have pros and cons, their combination can achieve accurate equivalence checking in more cases.

As discussed in Sect. 3.2, the proposed method still has several limitations. In particular, more additional information needs to be provided by users to achieve symbolic execution in more cases. In addition, since checking by numerical comparison is time-consuming, reducing checking time by taking checkpoints is also needed. Therefore, we will discuss further extensions of Xevolver's rule description to realize more robust equivalence checking in our future work.

Acknowledgement. This work was partially supported by MEXT Next Generation High-Performance Computing Infrastructures and Applications R&D Program "R&D of A Quantum-Annealing-Assisted Next Generation HPC Infrastructure and its Applications," Grant-in-Aid for Scientific Research(A) #20H00593, Grant-in-Aid for Scientific Research (B) #21H03449, and Grant-in-Aid for Challenging Research (Exploratory) #22K19764.

References

1. Egawa, R., Komatsu, K., Takizawa, H.: Designing an open database of system-aware code optimizations. In: The Fifth International Symposium on Computing and Networking (CANDAR), pp. 369–374 (2017)
2. Hirasawa, S., Takizawa, H., Kobayashi, H.: A light-weight rollback mechanism for testing kernel variants in auto-tuning. IEICE Trans. Inf. Syst. **98**(12), 2178–2186 (2015)
3. Komatsu, K., Gomi, A., Egawa, R., Takahashi, D., Suda, R., Takizawa, H.: Xevolver: a code transformation framework for separation of system-awareness from application codes. Concurr. Comput.: Pract. Experience **32**(7), 1–20 (2019)
4. OpenMP Architecture Review Board: OpenMP 5.2 Reference Guide (2021). https://www.openmp.org/wp-content/uploads/OpenMPRefCard-5-2-web.pdf
5. Siegel, S.F., et al.: CIVL: the concurrency intermediate verification language. In: Storage and Analysis (SC 2015): The International Conference for High Performance Computing, Networking, Storage and Analysis, pp. 1–12. IEEE (2015)

6. Sugawara, S., Shimomura, Y., Egawa, R., Takizawa, H.: Portability of vectorization-aware performance tuning expertise across system generations. In: 2021 IEEE 14th International Symposium on Embedded Multicore/Many-core Systems-on-Chip (MCSoC), pp. 242–248. IEEE (2021)
7. Takizawa, H., Hirasawa, S., Hayashi, Y., Egawa, R., Kobayashi, H.: Xevolver: an XML-based code translation framework for supporting HPC application migration. In: The 21st Annual IEEE International Conference on High Performance Computing (HiPC 2014) (2014)
8. Takizawa, H., Sugawara, S., Shimomura, Y., Takahashi, K., Egawa, R.: Xevolver for performance tuning of C programs. In: Resch, M.M., Gebert, J., Kobayashi, H., Bez, W. (eds.) WSSP 2021, pp. 85–93. Springer, Cham (2023)
9. Yamada, Y., Momose, S.: Vector engine processor of NEC's brand-new supercomputer SX-Aurora TSUBASA. In: Proceedings of A Symposium on High Performance Chips (Hot Chips), vol. 30, pp. 19–21 (2018)

MEA: A Framework for Model Checking of Mutual Exclusion Algorithms Focusing on Atomicity

Junfu Luo[1], Jiaqi Yin[2(✉)], and Huibiao Zhu[1(✉)]

[1] Shanghai Key Laboratory of Trustworthy Computing,
East China Normal University, Shanghai, China
hbzhu@sei.ecnu.edu.cn
[2] Northwestern Polytechnical University, Xi'an, China
jqyin@nwpu.edu.cn

Abstract. The mutual exclusion problem is a classic and essential problem in computer science. Since its inception, many related algorithms and variants have been proposed. However, finding the atomicity requirement of mutual exclusion algorithms remains challenging. In this paper, we proposed a model-checking framework called MEA to solve this issue, which is implemented in Maude. MEA provides a workflow to model a mutual exclusion algorithm and can easily perform verification. We use two classic mutual exclusion algorithms as examples to elaborate on how it works. Both two cases denote that MEA is capable of basic modeling of mutual exclusion algorithms focusing on atomicity.

Keywords: MEA · Mutual exclusion algorithm · Model checking · Maude · Atomicity

1 Introduction

The mutual exclusion problem is a classical problem in computer science, first introduced by Dijkstra in [9]. The core of this problem is how to ensure that only one process of many can access a shared resource at a time. Since the problem was first introduced, it is always a highly focused area, especially in distributed computing, for its essence of maintaining data consistency [3].

Many efforts have been made to advance the research, and multiple algorithms are proposed to achieve mutual exclusion. For distributed computing, there are two major groups of algorithms [4], one is permission-based, and the other is token-based. Moreover, many variants of this problem are proposed to suit more scenarios. For example, in [2], the *local mutual exclusion* problem is proposed as an extension of the dining philosophers problem, which was first introduced in [10]; in this variant, each node has to enter the critical section in exclusion with respect to the neighbors, usually the physically adjacent nodes. In [11], a generalized mutual exclusion problem was defined as *group mutual exclusion* in which every critical section is associated with a *session*. Critical sections

© The Author(s), under exclusive license to Springer Nature Switzerland AG 2023
H. Takizawa et al. (Eds.): PDCAT 2022, LNCS 13798, pp. 387–398, 2023.
https://doi.org/10.1007/978-3-031-29927-8_30

in the same session can be executed, but the execution of those in different sessions must be serialized.

Though it seems easy to give a proper algorithm for mutual exclusion, and the advancement in this area is tremendous, some challenges remain to be solved, one of which is how to find the least atomicity to implement those algorithms. While a mutual exclusion algorithm is being designed, the atomicity requirement is usually not known and not concerned with, but when it comes to actual implementation at the assembly level or even hardware level, the atomicity requirement becomes a crucial issue in maintaining its correctness.

Thus, we propose a framework **MEA** which is a model-checking framework for mutual exclusion algorithms focusing on atomicity. Its goal is to determine the least atomicity requirement for a given mutual exclusion algorithm, which can assist in the designation and verification of such algorithms.

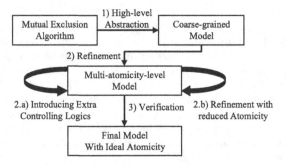

Fig. 1. The workflow of the MEA

As shown in Fig. 1, the workflow consists of the following steps:

1. **High-level abstraction**: for a given mutual exclusion algorithm, the most urgent task is to verify its correctness. Hence, the first step is to capture the algorithm's basic behavior with very high-level abstraction and little heed to its implementation details.
2. **Refinement**: refinement on the coarse model consists of two parts of work:
   (a) **Introducing extra controlling logic**: some algorithms' specifications may incur some urgent problems. For example, we can see later in this paper how the modeling bakery algorithm runs into trouble. When this happens, we need to introduce extra controlling logic.
   (b) **Refinement with reduced atomicity**: after the algorithm's correctness has been proved with the coarse-grained model, the model should be continually refined with gradually reduced atomicity until the correctness is not held, or the atomicity level is well accepted.
3. **Verification**: the final model should be verified. Though the verification is listed as the third, it should be done after every refinement(including the coarse-grained model) to assure correctness. There are four major properties to be verified: deadlock-free, livelock-free, mutual exclusion, and fairness. They are further discussed later.

We begin in Sect. 2 by briefly introducing the background, mainly about those algorithms used for the illustration and the tool Maude for modeling. In Sect. 3, we give a detailed introduction to the basic infrastructure of the framework with Peterson's algorithm as an example. In Sect. 4, we use the bakery algorithm as a case study to show how to refine a model with reduced atomicity and how the infinite-states problem can be dealt with by introducing extra controlling logic. We conclude the work in Sect. 5. For conciseness, we do not show all codes in detail. Please refer to this GitHub repository for the complete codes[1].

2   Background

In this section, we first introduce the two algorithms used as examples. They are Peterson's algorithm and the bakery algorithm. Then, we give a brief introduction to Maude.

2.1   The Mutual Exclusion Algorithms

One algorithm used in this paper is the famous and classic *Peterson's algorithm* introduced in [13]. For brevity, we only present the n-processes version as below.

Peterson's algorithm

1: **for** j=1 to N-1 **do**
2:      Q[i]:= j;
3:      TURN[j] := i;
4:      wait until ($\forall$k$\neq$i Q[k]<j) or TURN[j]$\neq$ i;
5: < Critical Section >
6: Q[i] := 0;

The array Q and $TURN$ are global, and they are used to record the statuses of the processes. Each process has a local variable i to represent its own index. In every iteration of the for-loop, all the unblocked processes vie to modify the location $TURN[j]$; those who succeeded in the modification are blocked. Hence, theoretically, the algorithm filters out one process each iteration. All processes also record which iteration they are in by modification of $Q[i]$. A process can be unblocked if all other processes's progress are behind it to prevent the deadlock.

The other algorithm used in this paper is the *bakery algorithm* proposed by Lamport in [12]. Every process takes a number when requests entering the critical section. The process holding the least number and least process index is granted to enter the critical section. The algorithm is as follows.

$(a, b) < (c, d)$ means that $a < c$ or $a = c \wedge c < d$.

---

[1] https://github.com/harveylo/MEA-RAWCODE/.

The bakery algorithm

1: choosing[i] := 1;
2: number[i] := 1 + maximum(number[l],..., number[N]);
3: choosing[i] := 0;
4: **for** j = 1 to N **do**
5:     L2:
6:     **if** choosing[j] ≠ 0 **then**
7:         goto L2;
8:     L3:
9:     **if** number[j]≠0 and (number[j], j)<(number[i],i) **then**
10:         goto L3;
11: < Critical Section >
12: number[i] := 0;

2.2   Maude

First introduced in [8] and extended in [6], Maude is a high-level language and a high-performance system supporting executable specification and declarative programming in rewriting logic. In [7], the work was concluded into a book, which is still the most cited reference on Maude. For more information about Maude and its syntax, please refer to Maude manual [5].

3   The Methodology

In this section, we introduce the framework MEA in detail and explain its workflow based on the example of Peterson's algorithm. First, we explain the ideas about *Snapshot* and how to utilize transition rules in modeling. Then we briefly explain how to verify four basic properties in MEA.

3.1   The *Snapshot* and Transition Rules

The *Snapshot*. We use a structure called *Snapshot* to record the necessary information while the model is being executed. Therefore, we suggest defining the *Snapshot* structure first and then giving the transition rules, but the two steps' order is not strictly restrained. When confusing whether the *Snapshot* is well-defined, it is recommended to continue to the transition rules, then refine the *Snapshot* structure (usually adding more gadgets) if needed. A *Snapshot* contains multiple gadgets, and the structure of *Snapshot* is shown in Fig. 2.

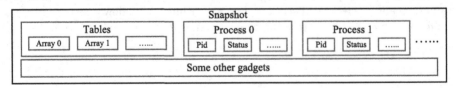

Fig. 2. The structure of Snapshot

The substructure *Process* keeps the process's information. A *Process* records its own *Pid* and *Status*. *Status* specifies which state the *Process* is in; it is essential for designing the model's transitions. Different models or even different refinement stages of the same model require specific *Statuses* to simulate the algorithm in specific atomicity correctly. The *Process* can also have other fields to assist modeling, which is illustrated in the later examples. Besides, many mutual exclusion algorithms require some global variables to function. The gadget called *Tables* contains multiple arrays functioning as the global variables.

Snapshot may contain some extra gadgets, which are highly specialized according to different algorithms. We explain when and how to introduce those extra gadgets in modeling different algorithms later by examples.

Now we utilize Peterson's algorithm to illustrate how to define a snapshot. First, we declare the necessary types: Snapshot, Process, and Tables.

```
sorts Snapshot Process Tables .
```

Since every process must go through a loop to enter the critical section, the *Process* must have a natural number property to record its iteration. The three *Statuses wait, ready, in* are enough for this example, and their meanings are obvious. The two fields and their detailed definition are given.

```
sort Pid Statuses .
op p[_] : Nat -> Pid [ctor] .
ops wait ready in : -> Status [ctor] .
op [_:_:_] : Pid Status Nat -> Procc [ctor] .
```

The algorithm requires two global arrays, so we define an operator to construct *Tables* from two natural number lists as below. The ListNat is the nature number list implemented in our predefined module, containing some other functions. For brevity, this part of the code is not shown.

```
op _||_ : ListNat ListNat -> Tables [ctor] .
```

An extra gadget is needed to record the number of processes in the system. This gadget can be a simple natural number. All the two gadgets, *Process*, *Tables*, and natural numbers are *Snapshot*'s subtypes. The meta unit of *Snapshot* is *none*; two *Snapshots* can compose a bigger *Snapshot* associatively and commutatively. We give the definition below.

```
subsorts Process Tables Nat < Snapshot .
p none : -> Snapshot [ctor] .
op __ Snapshot Snapshot -> Snapshot [assoc comm ctor id: none] .
```

3.2   Transition Rules

In Maude, we can use the rule to simulate the unconditional transition and the conditional rule for the conditional one.

To begin with, we declare these variables used in the transition rules below.

```
vars i t j k n : Nat .
var turn q : ListNat .
```

A process can request entering the critical section whenever they want, so here comes the following unconditional rule.

```
rl [getready] : [p[i] : wait] c => [p[i] : ready] set[c : i , 1] .
```

This rule implies that only a Process in *wait* can practice this transition. The $set[c : i , n]$ is an operation that sets the value at index i of array c to n.

Then we use a conditional rule to simulate the loop check. Only those processes that satisfy the condition $(\forall k \neq i, Q[k] < j)$ or $\text{TURN}[j] \neq i$ can pass the check and enter the next iteration. We introduce a function *checkTurn* to help check whether the condition $\forall k \neq i, Q[k] < j$ is true for the current process. The function $get[c : i]$ returns the value of index i of array c.

```
crl [nextstep] : n [p[i] : ready : j] (q || turn) =>
    n [p[i] : ready : j + 1]
    (set[q : i , j + 1] || set[turn : j + 1 , i])
  if j < n
    and (checkTurn[q : i : get[q : i]] or get[turn : j] =/= i) .
```

A process can enter the critical section if it has finished the loop and leave at any time.

```
crl [getin] : n [p[i] : ready : j] (q || turn) =>
    n [p[i] : in : j] (q || turn)
  if j == n and
    (checkTurn[q : i : get[q : i]] or get[turn : j] =/= i) .
rl [leave] : [p[i] : in : j] (q || turn) =>
    [p[i] : wait : 0] (set[q : i , 0] || turn) .
```

3.3 Verification

Generally, a mutual exclusion algorithm is considered correct if it satisfies deadlock-free, livelock-free, fairness, and mutual exclusion. We use the LTL-SIMPLIFIER and MODEL-CHECKER modules of Maude (included in the model-checker.maude file) to verify the correctness of the model.

In Maude, *State* and type *Prop* represent the system states and property, respectively. Those two types are defined in the SATISFACTION module. We should explicitly tell Maude which state satisfies what properties using equations in the following formality; the s is of type State, and p is of type Prop.

```
eq s |= p = true .
```

Snapshot functions as system states, so we make *Snapshot* a subtype of *State*. Then we give two functions that map a Pid to a *Prop* denoting that the *Process* with a given Pid is requesting to enter the critical section or already in. And we should specify which state satisfies those two properties and give the initial state. The definition of variables is not presented.

```
eq [pi : in] s |= in(pi) = true .
eq [pi : ready] s |= want(pi) = true .
eq s |= p = false [owise] .
op ini : -> Snap .
eq ini = 3 [p[0] : wait : 0] [p[1] : wait : 0] [p[2] : wait : 0]
        (0,0,0 || 0,0,0,0) .
```

Firstly, we use the search command of Maude to find whether the model has a deadlock state.

```
search ini =>! s:State .
```

This command tells Maude to search from *State ini*, and find whether there is a *State* that no more rewrite can be done on. Such *State* definitely incurs a deadlock. Maude gives the output below, denoting that such state will not occur.

```
No solution.
states:81 rewrites:12164 in 4ms cpu(5ms real)(3041000 rewrites/second)
```

The livelock should also be avoided, which means we expect at least one process can ultimately enter the critical section. This property can be verified in the following command using LTL logic, and the model passes this verification.

```
red modelCheck(ini, <> (in(p[0]) \/ in(p[1]))).
--- Maude output:
rewrites: 5736 in 4ms cpu (3ms real) (1434000 rewrites/second)
result Bool: true
```

Then we verify whether the most crucial property that is mutual exclusion. An algorithm satisfies mutual exclusion if only one process can be in the critical section at a time. This property can be described in LTL logic, and the output shows that the model satisfies this property.

```
red modelCheck(ini, []~ ((in(p[0]) /\ in(p[1]))
                    \/ (in(p[0]) /\ in(p[1]))
                    \/ (in(p[0]) /\ in(p[1])))) .
--- Maude output:
rewrites: 12268 in 0ms cpu (16ms real) (~ rewrites/second)
result Bool: true
```

Also, a proper mutual exclusion algorithm should satisfy fairness: if a process infinitely often requests entering the critical section, then it can infinitely often enter the critical section. We verify this property as follows:

```
red modelCheck(ini, (([](want(p[0]) -> <> in(p[0])))
              /\ ([](want(p[1]) -> <> in(p[1])))
              /\ ([](want(p[2]) -> <> in(p[]))))) .
```

The verification suggests that Peterson's algorithm does not satisfy fairness. Maude gives us an unfair pass, which is too lengthy to present. We use a case to describe how an unfair path may happen.

The condition '∀k ≠ i, Q[k] < j' is introduced to eliminate the deadlock, but when a process executes too fast, it can utilize this condition to bypass the block. For example, if the process *p[1]* is the first process enter iteration 2, *p[2]* is blocked in iteration one, *p[3]* has not entered iteration two yet, then *p[1]* should be blocked for the *TURN[2]* is 1. However, since *Q[0]*, *Q[2]* are both less than *Q[1]*, so *p[1]* can pass the 'wait until (∀k ≠ i, Q[k] < j) or TURN[j] ≠ i' examination, entering the critical section. This problem also has been discussed in [1], and the same conclusion is given.

We can enhance the block condition by checking whether all the non-zero elements are distinct to fix this problem. Because if this holds, it means that all unblocked processes have entered the next iteration and are blocked for their success in modification of *TURN*.

```
wait until ((∀k ≠ i, Q[k] < j) and ∀ m≠ 0 ∈ Q,¬(∃ n, n=m)) or TURN[j] ≠ i
```

We modified transition rules *nextstep* and *getin* by changing their conditions as described. After the modification, the model passes the verification.

```
rewrites: 12807 in 4ms cpu (7ms real) (3201750 rewrites/second)
result Bool: true
```

4   Case Study

In this section, we use the bakery algorithm as an example to show how MEA succeeds in reducing the atomicity of a mutual exclusion model to an ideal level.

4.1   High-Level Abstraction

The type definition has no difference with those in Sect. 3, we only show the transition rules of the coarse-grained bakery algorithm model here:

```
rl [getready] : [p[i] : wait] (flag || number) =>
  [p[i] : ready]
  (set[flag : i , 1] || set[number : i , (max[number : 0] + 1)]) .
crl [getin] : [p[i] : ready] (flag || number) =>
  [p[i] : in] (flag || number)
  if checkReady[flag : number : i : get[number : i]] .
rl [leave] : [p[i] : in] (flag || number) =>
  [p[i] : wait] (set[flag : i , 0] || number) .
```

The function *checkReady* is to check whether a *Process* holds the minimum number and *Pid*; function *max* returns the maximum element of an array.

Although the modeling is easy, the verification runs into trouble. None of the properties can be verified, and there is part of the output by Maude:

```
Fatal error: stack overflow.
This can happen because you have an infinite computation,
say a runaway recursion, or model checking an infinite model.
```

The model has infinite states, for we do not restrict the number a process can get. It increases infinitely. So we need to refine the coarse-grained model to solve this problem first.

4.2   Refinement

First Refinement. We can add extra controlling logic to solve the infinite-states issue. Consider introducing an upper bound for the number a process can get. When the upper bound is reached, no processes are allowed to request for the critical section until all the processes that are holding a number leave the critical section. To implement this refinement, the *Snapshot* needs more gadgets. We first define a new type, *Ctrls*; this type records the upper bound and the number of processes that have made their requests.

```
sort Ctrls .
subsort Ctrls < Snapshot .
op _-_ : Nat Nat -> Ctrls [ctor] .
```

Then we modify rules to support the refinement. The definition of variables is left out. We only show *getready* rule here as an example.

```
crl [getready] : (n - m) [p[i] : wait] (flag || number) =>
    (n - (m + 1)) [p[i] : ready]
    (set[flag : i , 1] || set[number : i , (max[number : 0] + 1)])
    if max[number : 0] < n .
```

All the aforementioned four properties can be verified now, with the upper bound chosen to be four, and the model passes them all.

Second Refinement. In the previous model, the selection of the maximum number and assigning the value to the number array are finished atomically. So it can not simulate the situation where two or more processes get the same number. We reduce this atomicity in the second refinement.

The *Process* now needs a new property as a buffer to store the number it has got. Moreover, the gadget *Ctrls* is modified to only record the upper bound because the number of ready *Processes* is redundant now.

```
op [_:_:(_)] : Pid Status Nat -> Proc [ctor] .
subsort Nat < Ctrls .
```

The refinement requires more states in the system, so we add more *Statuses*:

```
ops wait ready finishget getnum setnum in : -> Status [ctor] .
```

As for the transition rules, the *getready* rule now only sets the flag to 1, and we add three new rules to simulate the number selection and setting value procedure. The *leave* rule now also resets the number, so the redundant *reset* rule is removed. All four properties still hold for this model.

396   J. Luo et al.

Third Refinement. We notice that the number selection is still atomic. Introducing a number selection loop can eliminate this atomicity. The *Process* needs a new property to record which selection iteration it is in. For better readability, we now attach labels to the properties:

```
op [_:_:num(_):selecting(_):checking(_)] :
        Pid Status Nat Nat Nat -> Process [ctor] .
```

Process now needs to go through the number selection procedure first and get ready only when the number they get is valid (less than the upper bound). After this refinement, the upper bond is fixed to be the number of *Processes* in the system. If a process gets an invalid number, it enters *concede* status and restarts until all other processes have left the critical section. We attach a counter gadget to the *Snapshot* to record the number of *Processes* holding a valid number.

```
op concede : -> Status [ctor] .
sort Counter .
subsort Counter < Snapshot .
subsort Nat < Counter .
```

New transition rules are added to simulate the selection and concession procedure. For brevity, new rules are not presented. All four properties still hold after this refinement.

Fourth Refinement. Although the atomicity has been reduced significantly, the check procedure remains atomic. Now we should refine to expose more details.

The check contains two parts in each iteration: checking the flag array and the number array. We add two new *Statuses* and update the *Process* structure.

```
ops checkf checkn : -> Status [ctor] .
op [_:_:num(_):selecting(_):checking(_)] :
    Pid Status Nat Nat Nat -> Process [ctor] .
```

Then two new transition rules representing each checking stage can be added to replace the atomic check function. Till now, we have finished four rounds of refinement on the model. Figure 3 shows the state transition diagram of the model after four rounds of refinement. Different color indicates in which refinement it is introduced.

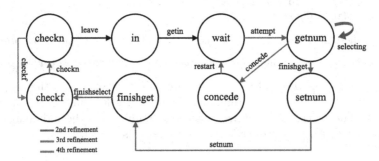

Fig. 3. The state transition diagram of the bakery algorithm.

We have almost eliminated all the atomicity requirements except the assignment action, which is acceptable for implementation using some high-level programming language. Hence, we can say that the model is fine-grained with desired atomicity. Most importantly, even at this atomicity level, the model still satisfies the four properties, which leads to the conclusion that the bakery algorithm is a classic and robust algorithm and MEA is capable of modeling different mutual exclusion algorithms with variable atomicity.

5   Conclusion

In this paper, we proposed a model-checking framework called MEA for mutual exclusion algorithms with the scope of atomicity. We used Peterson's algorithm as an example to explain the methodology. Specifically, we adopted the bakery algorithm as a case study to explain how the framework MEA can model, verify, and refine a model in detail. Further, the refinement can deal with the infinite-states issue and find the least atomicity or check whether the algorithm can maintain correctness at the desired atomicity level, proving MEA can be helpful when modeling mutual exclusion algorithms focussing on different atomicity.

Acknowledgement. This work was partially supported by the National Natural Science Foundation of China (Grant Nos. 62032024, 61872145), the "Digital Silk Road" Shanghai International Joint Lab of Trustworthy Intelligent Software (Grant No. 22510750100), Shanghai Trusted Industry Internet Software Collaborative Innovation Center, and the Dean's Fund of Shanghai Key Laboratory of Trustworthy Computing (East China Normal University).

References

1. Alagarsamy, K.: Some myths about famous mutual exclusion algorithms. SIGACT News **34**(3), 94–103 (2003)
2. Attiya, H., Kogan, A., Welch, J.L.: Efficient and robust local mutual exclusion in mobile ad hoc networks. IEEE Trans. Mob. Comput. **9**(3), 361–375 (2010)
3. Bagchi, S.: Design and topological analysis of probabilistic distributed mutual exclusion algorithm with unbiased refined ordering. Futur. Gener. Comput. Syst. **95**, 175–186 (2019)
4. Bertier, M., Arantes, L., Sens, P.: Hierarchical token based mutual exclusion algorithms. In: CCGrid, vol. 2004, pp. 539–546 (2004)
5. Clavel, M., et al.: Maude manual (version 3.0). SRI International (2020)
6. Clavel, M., et al.: Maude: specification and programming in rewriting logic. Theoret. Comput. Sci. **285**(2), 187–243 (2002)
7. Clavel, M., et al.: All About Maude - A High-Performance Logical Framework. LNCS, vol. 4350. Springer, Heidelberg (2007). https://doi.org/10.1007/978-3-540-71999-1
8. Clavel, M., Eker, S., Lincoln, P., Meseguer, J.: Principles of Maude. Electron. Notes Theor. Comput. Sci. **4**, 65–89 (1996)
9. Dijkstra, E.W.: Solution of a problem in concurrent programming control. Commun. ACM **8**(9), 569 (1965)

10. Dijkstra, E.W.: Hierarchical ordering of sequential processes. Acta Informatica **1**, 115–138 (1971). https://doi.org/10.1007/BF00289519
11. Joung, Y.: Asynchronous group mutual exclusion. Distrib. Comput. **13**(4), 189–206 (2000)
12. Lamport, L.: A new solution of Dijkstra's concurrent programming problem. Commun. ACM **17**(8), 453–455 (1974)
13. Peterson, G.: Myths about the mutual exclusion problem. Inf. Process. Lett. **12**(3), 115–116 (1981)

Interconnect

A High-Radix Circulant Network Topology for Efficient Collective Communication

Ke Cui[1,2] and Michihiro Koibuchi[1,2(✉)]

[1] The Graduate University for Advanced Studies, Hayama, Kanagawa 240-0193,
Japan
[2] National Institute of Informatics, Chiyoda-ku, Tokyo 101-8430, Japan
{cuike,koibuchi}@nii.ac.jp

Abstract. Collective communication is widely used in parallel applications. Collective-communication operations, such as Broadcast, Allreduce, and Alltoall, are frequently formed by a large number of peer-to-peer (P2P) communications. The latency of P2P communication affects the overall performance of collective communication. This paper proposes using circulant network topologies for a high-radix interconnection network to improve the performance of collective communications. The circulant network topology takes advantage of an algorithmic feature that reduces the total hop counts of collective communications. The SimGrid discrete-event simulation results showed that the execution time of the collective communication on a circulant network topology improved by 25.7% and 43.1% compared with random and dragonfly network topologies with the same degree, respectively. It also enhances 40.6% and 19.5% on average compared with 3-D torus and hypercube topologies, respectively.

Keywords: Interconnection networks · circulant network topology · collective communication · Message Passing Interface (MPI) · parallel computers

1 Introduction

Current parallel computers consist of hundreds of thousands of compute nodes, and the number of compute nodes continues to increase. In parallel computers, collective communication significantly affects the execution time of parallel applications. Collective communication in parallel computers is usually implemented through message-passing interface (MPI). MPI defines many collective communication operations, such as MPI_Bcast, MPI_Allreduce, MPI_Alltoall, etc.

Hardware-, path-, and unicast-based techniques are typical methods for multicast in interconnection networks. Hardware multicasts proceed collective operations at a switch, such as NVIDIA Scalable Hierarchical Aggregation and Reduction Protocol (SHARP). It reduces the total hop counts and the number of packets in multicast. However, current conventional network products,

H. Takizawa et al. (Eds.): PDCAT 2022, LNCS 13798, pp. 401–412, 2023.
https://doi.org/10.1007/978-3-031-29927-8_31

such as Ethernet, do not always support hardware- and path-based multicast techniques. These collective communication operations are usually implemented in MPI through a series of point-to-point (P2P) communication. In this study, we consider unicast-based collective communication.

Large-scale parallel applications suffer from communication delays. Switches in massively parallel systems typically have tens to hundreds of nanoseconds latencies. For example, the 36-port 200Gb/s EDR InfiniBand switch in super-computer Summit has a latency of 90 nanoseconds [1]. To reduce the delay of messages through the switches, some low-diameter and average shortest path length (ASPL) topologies have been proposed to design interconnection networks for parallel computers. Messages pass through as few intermediate switches as possible from source to destination, i.e., fewer hop counts. The low diameter topologies, Dragonfly and Slim Fly, have a maximum of three and two hops, respectively [2,3]. Due to the low diameter and ASPL, random shortcut network topologies [4] are also proposed, and the corresponding heuristic method to reduce the number of hops of collective communications [5].

The ideal situation to reduce the latency of collection communication is that each a P2P communication takes one hop with no contention. However, a network topology that meets this condition would be extremely expensive, such as a fully connected topology. The fully connected topology ensures that any two nodes are adjacent. Messages in an arbitrary P2P communication will not pass through any intermediate nodes. Fully-connected topologies could be applied to a small interconnection network for efficient collective communication [6]. However, as the size of fully connected topology increases, the explosion in the number of links is unacceptable.

In this paper, we take another network topological approach to obtain the ideal hops in the typical collective-communication operations, i.e., broadcast, allreduce, and alltoall. Their number of links is much smaller than that in a fully connected topology with the same nodes. The circulant network topology is introduced. The circulant network topology takes a higher diameter and ASPL than the counterpart random shortcut network topology with the same degree. However, we find out that the circulant network topology interestingly enables the collective-communication operations with lower aggregate path hops than the random shortcut network topology. More precisely, for MPI_Bcast, MPI_Allreduce, and MPI_Alltoall operations with a specific algorithm, such as binomial tree broadcast, recursive-doubling allreduce, Bruck's alltoall [7], the aggregate path hops can reach a theoretical minimum. The theoretical minimum hop counts mean that all the unicasts, that form a collective-communication operation, take only one hop.

Our main contributions are listed as follows.

- We propose using circulant network topologies. A class of particular circulant network topologies achieves the theoretical minimum hop counts for some collective operations, such as Broadcast, Allreduce, and Alltoall.
- SimGrid's discrete event simulation results show that Broadcast, Allreduce, and Alltoall collective operations on circulant network topologies outperform those on random and dragonfly network topologies.

The rest of this paper is organized as follows. The related work is introduced in Sect. 2. Section 3 describes the definition of circulant network topologies, and the collective communication operations on target circulant network topologies. Section 4 presents the results of SimGrid computer simulation evaluation. Section 5 discusses why to use a circulant network topology as the interconnection of parallel computers. Section 6 concludes with a summary of our findings.

2   Background

2.1   Circulant Network Topology

Circulant network topology is widely used in various network designs. They are used as a ring extension to design and implement local area networks. The networks are also called distributed loop computer-networks [8,9]. A variant of circulant network topology called Multi-Ring topology is used to achieve high-performance group communication in peer-to-peer networks [10]. The paper [11] proposed recursive circulant network topology for multicomputer systems. The recursive circulant network topology is also circulant network topology. [12] proposed generalized recursive circulant graphs, which are the extension of recursive circulant graphs. Recently, [13] proposed the optimal circulant network topologies as low latency network topologies.

2.2   Target Collective Communication

We mainly consider three types of collective communication operations, which are Broadcast, Allreduce, and Alltoall. Statistics showed that these three operations were most frequently used on real supercomputers [14]. Broadcast is a one-to-all communication pattern, a source process broadcasts a message to all processes in the same group. Allreduce is a variant of Reduce operation where the same result is returned to all processes in a group. Alltoall is an operation in which a process sends distinct data to each of the receivers in the same group. In this paper, Broadcast, Allreduce, and Alltoall use the binomial tree, recursive doubling, and Bruck algorithms, respectively.

Binomial Tree Algorithm. Binomial tree-based broadcast is widely used in many MPI libraries due to its lower communication steps [15–17]. Assuming that there are N processes performing broadcast operations, if the binomial tree algorithm is employed, the entire operation will be completed in $\lceil \log_2 N \rceil$ steps.

Recursive Doubling Algorithm. Recursive doubling algorithm is often used to implement Allreduce operation, and it is easy to implement when the number of processes N is a power of two. The recursive doubling algorithm takes $\log_2 N$ steps to complete the Allreduce operation. In the first step, processes that distance one apart exchanges their data. In the second step, processes that distance two apart exchange their data. Until the $\log_2 N$th step, processes that are a distance $2^{(\log_2 N - 1)}$ apart exchange their data [18].

Bruck's Algorithm. Bruck's algorithm is an efficient algorithm for Alltoall operations [7]. Bruck's algorithm consists of three phases. In the first and the third phases, each process only needs to rearrange the data locally. The second phase performs inter-process communication. Bruck's algorithm takes $\lceil \log_2 N \rceil$ steps to complete the Alltoall operations.

3   Using Circulant Network Topology

First, we introduce the definition of the circulant network topology. Second, we state the behavior of the collective-communication operations on the circulant network topology.

3.1   Definition of Circulant

A circulant graph $C(n; c_1, c_2, ..., c_k)$ has n vertices $v_0, v_1, ...v_{n-1}$, in which $c_1 = 1$ and $c_i < c_{i+1}$, v_a is connected to v_b if and only if $a \equiv b \pm c_i \mod n$. The sequence $< c_1, c_2, ..., c_k >$ is called jump sequence, $c_1, c_2, ..., c_k$ are called jumps, the maximum jump $c_k \leq \lfloor n/2 \rfloor$ [12,19]. Figure 1 illustrates the examples of circulant graphs with 16 vertices.

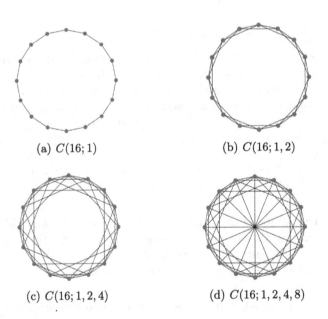

(a) $C(16; 1)$ (b) $C(16; 1, 2)$

(c) $C(16; 1, 2, 4)$ (d) $C(16; 1, 2, 4, 8)$

Fig. 1. Circulant graphs with 16 vertices.

In this work, we focus on the circulant graphs $C(n; c_1, c_2, ..., c_k)$ with the following properties:

- The number of vertices n is powers of 2.
- The jump $c_i = 2^{i-1}$, c_i is in jump sequence $< c_1, c_2, ..., c_k >$, $1 \leq k \leq \log_2 n$.

We can use $G(n, k)$ to represent this class of circulant graphs. n is the number of vertices, k is the number of elements of sequence $< c_1, c_2, ..., c_k >$, $n = 2^k$ and the degree of each vertex is $2k - 1$. The circulant graphs in Fig. 1 can be represented as $G(16; 1), G(16; 2), G(16; 3), G(16; 4)$, respectively.

3.2   Collective-Communication Operations on Circulant Network Topology

We apply the circulant graphs $G(n, \log_2 n)$ to the network topology of parallel systems, assuming that each vertex represents a compute node. Then we detail the behavior of Broadcast, Allreduce, and Alltoall on the circulant network topology $G(16, 4)$. We find that the binomial tree Broadcast, recursive doubling Allreduce and Bruck's Alltoall on circulant $G(n, \log_2 n)$can achieve the minimum number of total hop counts.

Broadcast. Figure 2(a) shows an example Broadcast operation by binomial tree algorithm on $G(16, 4)$ network topology. It takes four steps to finish the broadcast operation. In the first step, we perform the P2P communicaton $v_0 \rightarrow v_8$. Fortunately, there is a link between v_0 and v_8. In the second step, we can get the P2P communicaton $v_0 \rightarrow v_4$ and $v_8 \rightarrow v_{12}$, there are also links between nodes v_0, v_4 and v_8, v_{12}. In the last two steps, each P2P communicaton has one hop as the previous two steps. As the Fig. 2(a) shows each P2P communication of Broadcast operation on circulant network topology has one hop, so the total hops reach the ideally minimum hops.

Allreduce. Figure 2(b) shows an example Allreduce operation with recursive doubling algorithm on $G(16, 4)$ circulant network topology. It takes four steps to finish the Allreduce operation. In the first step, eight pairs nodes exchange there messages $v_0 \leftrightarrow v_1$, $v_2 \leftrightarrow v_3$, $v_4 \leftrightarrow v_5$, $v_6 \leftrightarrow v_7$, $v_8 \leftrightarrow v_9$, $v_{10} \leftrightarrow v_{11}$, $v_{12} \leftrightarrow v_{13}$, $v_{14} \leftrightarrow v_{15}$, we can clearly see that each pair of nodes are connected. In the last three steps, each step also has eight pairs of nodes exchanging their messages, and each pair of nodes are connected. The total hops of Allreduce operation also can reach the ideally minimum hops.

Alltoall. Figure 2(c) shows an example of Alltoall operations with Bruck's algorithm on $G(16, 4)$ network topology. All the links of topology are used in the Altoall operation. Since each hop of the node pair is one, the total hop counts of Alltoall operation can also reach the ideal hop counts.

We explained the collective operations on $G(16, 4)$ circulant network topology in the above. It can be generalized as follows.

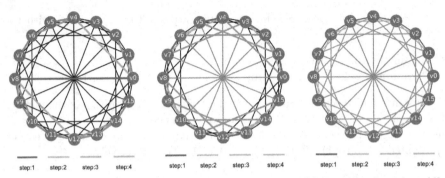

(a) Binomial tree Broadcast.   (b) Recursive doubling Allreduce.   (c) Bruck's algorithm Alltoall.

Fig. 2. Behaviour of collective communication on circulant network topology $G(16, 4)$.

For any node v_a in the $G(n, \log_2 n)$ network topology, it has $2k-1$ neighboring nodes $\{v_b | b \equiv a \pm 2^{i-1} \mod n, 1 \le i \le k\}$. For the sake of convenience, in the broadcast operation, we select v_0 as the root node. Due to the symmetry of the above ring topology, choosing any node as the root node has the same effect. In the first step, v_0 as the source node, there is P2P communication $v_0 \to v_{\frac{n}{2}}$. In the second step, nodes v_0 and $v_{\frac{n}{2}}$ are the source nodes, there are P2P communications $v_0 \to v_{\frac{n}{4}}$ and $v_{\frac{n}{2}} \to v_{\frac{3n}{4}}$. More generally, in the ith step, there are 2^{i-1} source nodes $\{v_{\frac{jn}{2^{i-1}}} | 0 \le j \le 2^{i-1} - 1\}$, the P2P communication from source node $v_{\frac{jn}{2^{i-1}}}$ is $v_{\frac{jn}{2^{i-1}}} \to v_{\frac{(2j+1)n}{2^i}}$. Let $a = \frac{jn}{2^{i-1}}$, the P2P communication $v_{\frac{jn}{2^{i-1}}} \to v_{\frac{(2j+1)n}{2^i}}$ can be converted to $v_a \to v_{a+\frac{n}{2^i}}$. Since $n = 2^k$, $\frac{n}{2^i}$ can be represented as 2^{k-i}. It's obvious that the destination node of P2P communication $v_{a+2^{k-i}}$ is the neighboring node of source node v_a. For any P2P communication of broadcast operation, the source node and destination node are connected, and the hop counts of the P2P communication is one, so the Broadcast operation on the $G(n, \log_2 n)$ circulant network topology can reach the ideally minimum hops.

In the Allreduce operation using recursive doubling algorithm, at the ith step, the two nodes have a distance 2^{i-1} to exchange their data. Assume that nodes v_a and $v_b (b > a)$ exchange their data at ith step, the equation $b = a + 2^{i-1}$ holds. It's obvious that v_a and v_b are connected, the total hops of two P2P communication $v_a \to v_b$ and $v_b \to v_a$ are two.

Therefore, the Allreduce operation on $G(n, \log_2 n)$ network topology can reach the ideally minimum hops.

In the Alltoall operation using Bruck's algorithm, at the ith step, node v_a sends message to node $v_b, b = a - 2^i + n \mod n$, so the node v_b is the neighboring node of v_a, the hop count of P2P communication $v_a \to v_b$ is one. Thus, the Alltoall operation on $G(n, \log_2 n)$ network topology can also reach the ideal minimum hops.

4   Evaluation

In this section, we evaluate the diameter/ASPL, hop counts, and execution time of collective operations.

4.1   Methodology

We use the discrete-event simulator SimGrid (v3.28) [20] to evaluate the performance of collective operations. We compare circulant network topology to 3D-torus, hypercube, dragonfly, and random network topologies. In this evaluation, we focus on the impact of latency on performance, assuming that there is one compute node on each switch and only one processor per compute node. The parameters of the interconnection network are illustrated in Table 1.

Table 1. Parameters of the interconnection network.

Power of compute node	100GFLOPS
Switch latency	100ns
Link bandwidth	100Gbps
Switch bandwidth	3.2Tbps
Routing algorithm	Floyd

Diameter and ASPL are essential properties to measure the performance of network topology. Firstly, we compared the diameter and ASPL of the five network topologies. Secondly, we compared the variation of hop counts of the five network topologies. Finally, we evaluated the execution time of collective communication on the five network topologies, such as Broadcast, Allreduce, and Alltoall. We used the binomial tree algorithm on broadcast, recursive doubling algorithm on allreduce, and Bruck's algorithm on alltoall, as introduced in Sect. 2.

4.2   Diameter and ASPL

Figures 3(a) and 3(b) illustrated that the diameter and average shortest path length (ASPL) for circulant, random, 3D- torus, hypercube and dragonfly network topologies, respectively. The x-axis in both graphs represents the network size, i.e., the number of switches and compute nodes. The y-axis in Fig. 3(a) is diameter and that in Fig. 3(b) represents their ASPL. As the figures show, we confirm that the random shortcut network topology always has the lowest diameter and ASPL. Thus, the circulant network topology is inferior to the random shortcut network topology. However, it is better than hypercube and 3D-torus network topology. As shown in the figures, we confirm that the random shortcut network topology always has the lowest ASPL, while the dragonfly topology has the lowest diameter since its diameter is always 3. On the other hand, the circulant network topology with the same network size and degree as random and dragonfly, the diameter, and ASPL are larger.

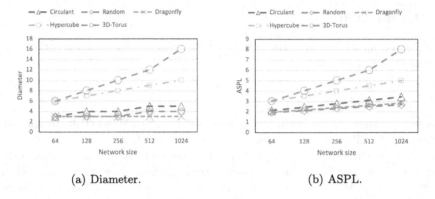

(a) Diameter.   (b) ASPL.

Fig. 3. Diameter and ASPL of five network topologies.

4.3 Hop Counts of Collective-Communication Operations

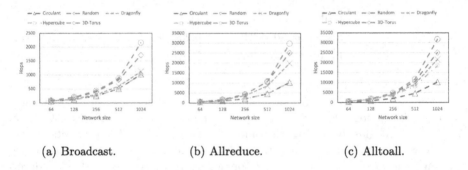

(a) Broadcast.   (b) Allreduce.   (c) Alltoall.

Fig. 4. Total hop counts of Broadcast in five network topologies.

Figure 4 illustrated the hop counts of Broadcast, Allreduce, and Alltoall for circulant, random, dragonfly, hypercube, and 3D-torus network topologies. Figures 4(a), 4(b) and 4(c) represent the hop counts of broadcast, allreduce and alltoall, respectively.

In Sect. 3.2, we illustrated that the binomial tree broadcast, recursive doubling, and Bruck's Alltoall operations on the circulant network topologies can achieve the minimum total hop counts. The figures show that the hop counts on circulant network topology are the lowest. The hop counts of Broadcast and Allreduce on hypercube topology also achieve the minimum number [21,22]. In Sect. 4.2, Figs. 3(a) and 3(a) show that the random and dragonfly topology have a small diameter and ASPL than circulant network topology. However, their hop counts of collective operations are more significant than circulant network topology. When the network size is 1,024, for the binomial tree broadcast operation, the hop counts on circulant are 9% and 40% less than dragonfly and random network topology. For the recursive doubling Allreduce operation, the hop counts on circulant network topology are 48% and 59% less than dragonfly and random network topologies. For the Bruck's Alltoall operation, the hop counts on circulant network topologies are 52% and 59% less than dragonfly and random network topologies.

4.4   Execution Time of Collective-Communication Operations

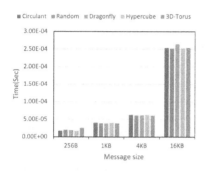

(a) Small message size.

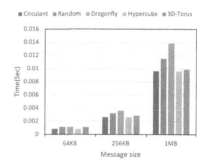

(b) Large message size.

Fig. 5. Execution time of Broadcast in five network topologies.

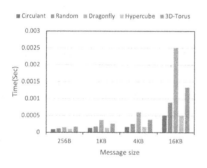

(a) Small message size.

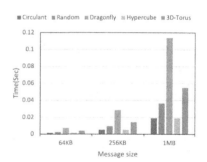

(b) Large message size.

Fig. 6. Execution time of Allreduce in five network topologies.

In this section, we evaluate the execution time of Broadcast, Allreduce, and Alltoall with different message sizes. The network size is set to 1,024, which means the number of switches and compute nodes are both 1024. Then, we divide the message size into small and large groups. The small size includes 256B, 1 KB, 4 KB, and 16 KB. The large size has 64 KB, 256 KB, and 1 MB.

Figure 5 illustrated the execution time of broadcast operation with small and large message sizes. The circulant network topology and hypercube for the broadcast operation can reach the lower bound of hop counts. The evaluation results show that the circulant and hypercube topologies perform best. The performance of broadcast on circulant network topology outperforms by 9.9%, 13.2%, and 8.9% than random, dragonfly 3D-torus topologies, respectively.

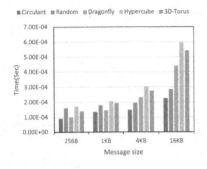 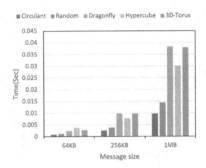

(a) Small message size.   (b) Large message size.

Fig. 7. Execution time of Alltoall in five network topologies.

Figure 6 illustrated the execution time of broadcast operation with small and large message sizes. The circulant network topology and hypercube can reach the lower bound of hop counts. The results also show that the circulant and hypercube topologies have the best performance. The performance of Allreduce on circulant network topology outperforms by 38.0%, 71.8%, and 58.2% than random, dragonfly, and 3D-torus topologies, respectively.

Figure 7 illustrates the execution time of Alltoall operation with different message sizes. For Alltoall operation, the message size means the gathered message size of each node. In this case, only circulant network topology can achieve the minimum hop counts. Therefore, the Alltoall operation on circulant has the best performance. The performance of Alltoall on circulant network topology outperforms by 29.1%, 44.4%, 57.6%, and 54.6% than random, dragonfly, 3D-torus, and hypercube topologies, respectively.

5   Discussions

Our simulation results interestingly unveiled that the circulant network topology provided high-performance collective communications at the cost of relatively high ASPL and high diameter, both of which would degrade P2P performance. Prior works focused on only P2P communication performance when considering the network topology of the parallel computers. In this context, the circulant network topology introduces a new design space for interconnection networks.

Indeed, it was reported that 15 main applications out of 64 consume 60% or more execution time by MPI communication in a production supercomputer [14].

Then, it was reported that Allreduce, Alltoall, Barrier operations were most frequently used MPI. In a realistic scenario, we expected that the performance improvement of collective communication would be more critical than P2P communication. In this context, we can recommend the circulant network topology on parallel computers.

6 Conclusions

In this study, we proposed using the high-radix circulant network topology for improving the performance of collective communications. We found that a particular class of circulant network topologies provides ideal lower hop counts of binomial-tree broadcast, recursive-doubling Allreduce, and Bruck's Alltoall.

The circulant network topology is inferior to the random and dragonfly network topologies in terms of diameter and ASPL. However, the circulant network topology achieved the lowest aggregate path hop counts of Broadcast, Allreduce, and Alltoall. It reached the theoretical lower bounds. This interesting fact leads to the lower execution time of collective communications on the circulant network topologies. Compared with the hypercube network topology, the circulant network topology has a much lower diameter and ASPL.

The SimGrid discrete-event simulation results showed that the execution time of the collective communication on a circulant network topology improved by 25.7% and 43.1% compared with random and dragonfly network topologies with the same degree. It also enhances 40.6% and 19.5% on average compared with 3-D torus and hypercube topologies.

Through this study, we recommend using the high-radix circulant network topologies when target applications heavily rely on collective communications.

Acknowledgment. This work was partly supported by JSPS KAKENHI Grant Number 19H01106.

References

1. Stunkel, C.B., et al.: The high-speed networks of the summit and sierra supercomputers. IBM J. Res. Dev. **64**(3/4), 3–1 (2020)
2. Kim, J., Dally, W. J., Scott, S., Abts, D.: Technology-driven, highly-scalable dragonfly topology. In: ISCA, 2008, pp. 77–88 (2008)
3. Besta, M., Hoefler, T.: Slim fly: a cost effective low-diameter network topology. In: SC: Proceedings of the International Conference for High Performance Computing, Networking, Storage and Analysis, pp. 348–359. IEEE (2014)
4. Koibuchi, M., Matsutani, H., Amano, H., Hsu, D.F., Casanova, H.: A case for random shortcut topologies for HPC interconnects. ISCA **40**(3), 177–188 (2012)
5. Cui, K., Koibuchi, M.: Efficient two-opt collective-communication operations on low-latency random network topologies. IEICE Trans. Inf. Syst. **103**(12), 2435–2443 (2020)
6. Mizutani, K., Yamaguchi, H., Urino, Y., Koibuchi, M.: OPTWEB: a lightweight fully connected inter-FPGA network for efficient collectives. IEEE Trans. Comput. **70**(6), 849–862 (2021)

7. Bruck, J., Ho, C.-T., Kipnis, S., Upfal, E., Weathersby, D.: Efficient algorithms for all-to-all communications in multiport message-passing systems. IEEE Trans. Parallel Distrib. Syst. **8**(11), 1143–1156 (1997)

8. Liu, M.T.: Distributed loop computer networks. Adv. Comput. **17**, 163–221. Elsevier (1978)

9. Bermond, J.-C., Comellas, F., Hsu, D.F.: Distributed loop computer-networks: a survey. J. Parallel Distrib. Comput. **24**(1), 2–10 (1995)

10. Junginger, M., Lee, Y.: The multi-ring topology-high-performance group communication in peer-to-peer networks. In: Second International Conference on Peer-to-Peer Computing, 2002, pp. 49–56 (2002)

11. Park, J.-H., Chwa, K.-Y.: Recursive circulant: a new topology for multicomputer networks. In: International Symposium on Parallel Architectures, Algorithms and Networks (ISPAN), 1994, pp. 73–80 (1994)

12. Tang, S.-M., Wang, Y.-L., Li, C.-Y.: Generalized recursive circulant graphs. IEEE Trans. Parallel Distrib. Syst. **23**(1), 87–93 (2011)

13. Huang, X., Ramos, A.F., Deng, Y.: Optimal circulant graphs as low-latency network topologies, arXiv preprint arXiv:2201.01342 (2022)

14. Chunduri, S., Parker, S., Balaji, P., Harms, K., Kumaran, K.: Characterization of MPI usage on a production supercomputer. In: SC: International Conference for High Performance Computing, pp. 386–400. Storage and Analysis, Networking (2018)

15. Open MPI: Open Source High Performance Computing. http://www.open-mpi.org/

16. MPICH — High-Performance Portable MPI. http://www.mpich.org/

17. MVAPICH. http://mvapich.cse.ohio-state.edu/

18. Thakur, R., Rabenseifner, R., Gropp, W.: Optimization of collective communication operations in MPICH. Int. J. High Perform. Comput. Appl. **19**(1), 49–66 (2005)

19. Boesch, F., Tindell, R.: Circulants and their connectivities. J. Gr. Theory **8**(4), 487–499 (1984)

20. Casanova, H., Giersch, A., Legrand, A., Quinson, M., Suter, F.: Versatile, scalable, and accurate simulation of distributed applications and platforms. J. Parallel Distrib. Comput. **74**(10), 2899–2917 (2014)

21. Bertsekas, D.P., Özveren, C., Stamoulis, G.D., Tseng, P., Tsitsiklis, J.N.: Optimal communication algorithms for hypercubes. J. Parallel Distrib. Comput. **11**(4), 263–275 (1991)

22. Ho, C.-T., Kao, M.-Y.: Optimal broadcast in all-port wormhole-routed hypercubes. IEEE Trans. Parallel Distrib. Syst. **6**(2), 200–204 (1995)

Fault Tolerance and Packet Latency of Peer Fat-Trees

Yamin Li[1][✉] and Wanming Chu[2]

[1] Department of Computer Science, Hosei University, Tokyo 184-8584, Japan
yamin@hosei.ac.jp
[2] Division of Information Systems, University of Aizu,
Aizu-Wakamatsu 965-8580, Japan

Abstract. Clos- or fat-tree-based interconnection networks are widely used in data center and supercomputer designs. Both Clos and fat-tree are non-blocking multistage switch networks. The non-blocking property improves path diversity but meanwhile increases both hardware cost and packet latency. Some applications may not require non-blocking routing but prefer low packet latency. To cope with it, this paper proposes a *peer k-ary n-tree* or *peer fat-tree* network that takes the factors of path diversity, hardware cost, and packet latency into consideration. A peer k-ary n-tree network connects compute nodes with about half as many switches and links compared to Clos and fat-tree networks. It has two groups of compute nodes and provides short routing paths between the nodes in distinct groups and non-blocking routing between the nodes in the same group. We describe the peer k-ary n-tree network structure, investigate the topological properties, give a minimal per-hop deterministic routing algorithm, and evaluate the fault tolerance and packet latency of the peer k-ary n-tree network and compare the performance to that of Clos and fat-tree networks.

Keywords: multistage interconnection network · fat-tree · k-ary n-tree · routing · path diversity · fault tolerance · packet latency

1 Introduction

The fat-tree [5] is one of the most commonly used interconnection network topologies in today's data centers and supercomputers [10]. A fat-tree is a folded version of the Clos network [3,9]. Both Clos and fat-tree are non-blocking networks. Non-blocking means that the network is always capable of routing a packet to any free destination node without interfering with other traffic. To implement the non-blocking routing, the network must provide a high path diversity so that a packet can be routed to an arbitrary middle stage switch in a Clos network or an arbitrary root switch in a fat-tree network and then to their ultimate destination. This approximately doubles the number of switches and links, resulting in a high hardware cost and a high packet latency [1].

To solve these problems, this paper proposes an alternative to the fat-tree network, called *peer k-ary n-tree* or *peer fat-tree* network, that reduces both

© The Author(s), under exclusive license to Springer Nature Switzerland AG 2023
H. Takizawa et al. (Eds.): PDCAT 2022, LNCS 13798, pp. 413–425, 2023.
https://doi.org/10.1007/978-3-031-29927-8_32

hardware cost and packet latency and meanwhile provides the ability of non-blocking routing for half source-destination node pairs. The advantages and disadvantages of the proposed peer fat-trees are summarized below.

– Pros: The hardware cost and packet routing latency are reduced.
– Cons: The path diversity is also reduced, resulting in worse fault tolerance.

The rest of the paper is organized as follows. Section 2 reviews some multistage interconnection networks that are related to the peer k-ary n-tree network. Section 3 describes the peer k-ary n-tree network structure and its topological properties. Section 4 gives a minimal per-hop deterministic routing algorithm. Section 5 evaluates the fault tolerance and Sect. 6 evaluates the packet latency of the fat-tree networks. And Sect. 7 concludes the paper.

2   Related Fat-Tree Networks

There are many different structures of fat-trees. This section reviews six multistage interconnection networks that are related to the proposed network.

2.1   k-ary n-fly Butterfly Network

A k-ary n-fly butterfly network [4] has $N = k^n$ compute nodes; it has n stages; each stage has N/k switches; and each switch has k input ports and k output ports ($2k$ is the radix of the switch). From the point of view of a compute node, the butterfly looks like a k-ary tree. Butterfly minimizes the network diameter and reduces the network cost. However, there is a lack of path diversity because there is only one path between the source node and the destination node. In addition, butterfly networks cannot exploit the locality of traffic because all packets must traverse the diameter of the network [1].

2.2   k-ary n-tree Clos Network

A k-ary n-tree Clos network is a non-blocking network that has $N = k^n$ compute nodes and $2n - 1$ stages [3]. Each stage has N/k switches and each switch has k input ports and k output ports. It can be created by combining two k-ary n-fly butterfly networks back-to-back where the two back stages are fused [1]. The k-ary n-tree Clos network provides many paths. The input network can route from any source compute node to any middle-stage switch. The output network can route from any middle-stage switch to any destination compute node. Like a k-ary n-fly butterfly network, the links in a k-ary n-tree Clos network are also unidirectional.

2.3   k-ary n-tree Fat-Tree Network

Because in a k-ary n-tree Clos network, the nodes in the input side and the nodes in the output side are the same compute nodes, and the ports of a switch are unidirectional, we can fold the k-ary n-tree Clos network and combine two unidirectional switches to a bidirectional switch. And we use bidirectional links[1] to connect switch ports. We call it a k-ary n-tree folded Clos network, or a k-ary n-tree fat-tree [8]. It has n stages and k^n compute nodes. A k-ary n-tree Clos network, or its folded version, a k-ary n-tree fat-tree network, has a cost that is nearly double that of a k-ary n-fly butterfly network with equal capacity and has greater latency than a k-ary n-fly butterfly network. The increased cost and latency both stem from the need to route packets first to an arbitrary middle stage switch and then to their ultimate destination. This doubles the number of long cables in the network, which approximately doubles cost, and doubles the number of inter-router channels traversed, which drives up latency [1].

2.4   Bidirectional k-ary n-tree Clos Network

We can re-design the switches in a k-ary n-tree Clos network so that the switches have bidirectional ports. Also, we use the bidirectional links and double the number of compute node (the top nodes and bottom nodes are distinct compute nodes). Thus, we get a *bidirectional k-ary n-tree Clos network*. It has $2n - 1$ stages and $2k^n$ compute nodes. All the switches in a bidirectional k-ary n-tree Clos network have a same radix which is $2k$.

2.5   k-ary Fat-Tree Network

A k-ary fat-tree network [2] can be created as follows. It has three layers (stages). The top layer is called *core* layer. There are k pods below the core layer. Each pod contains two layers: The *aggregation* layer in the middle and the *edge* layer in the bottom. There are $k/2$ switches in each of these two layers and each switch has k ports. The $k/2$ ports in a switch of the edge layer connects $k/2$ compute nodes, and each of the other $k/2$ ports connects one port of a distinct switch in the aggregation layer inside the same pod. Thus $k/2$ ports of a switch in aggregation layer connect ports of switches in the edge layer. The other $k/2$ ports of a switch in aggregation layer connect ports of switches in core layer. In each pod, there are $(k/2) \times (k/2) = (k/2)^2$ such ports. In the core layer, there are $(k/2)^2$ switches and each switch has also k ports. Each core switch has one port connected to each of k pods. A k-ary fat-tree has $k^3/4$ compute nodes. Note that a k-ary fat-tree network is not a k-ary n-tree fat-tree network. A k-ary n-tree fat-tree network has k^n compute nodes. The definition above is difficult to understand. Actually, a $2k$-ary fat-tree network is exactly a bidirectional k-ary n-tree Clos network with a fixed $n = 3$. Therefore, we say that a k-ary fat-tree network is a special case of a bidirectional k-ary n-tree Clos network.

2.6   Mirrored k-ary n-tree Network

A k-ary n-tree fat-tree has n stages. We use the number 0 to denote the leaf stage; then the root stage number is $n - 1$. A mirrored k-ary n-tree (MiKANT) network [6] consists of two k-ary n-tree fat-trees combined back-to-back where

---

[1] A bidirectional link consists of a unidirectional input link and a unidirectional output link.

the switches in the $(n-2)$th stage of a fat-tree serve as the root switches of the other fat-tree. That is, a mirrored k-ary n-tree network has $2n-2$ stages. We use *group 0* and *group 1* to distinguish the two fat-tree. Compared to the k-ary n-tree fat-tree network, MiKANT doubles the number of compute nodes. Compared to the k-ary n-tree Clos network, MiKANT uses fewer switches with equal capacity. If the source node and destination node belong to the same group, the MiKANT acts the same as the k-ary n-tree fat-tree network. If the source node and destination node belong to different groups, the MiKANT reduces path length and path diversity. Reducing path diversity will lose the non-blocking property but there are still multiple paths between the source node and destination node.

3   Peer k-ary n-tree Network

In a k-ary n-tree fat-tree network, the radix of the root switches is k and the radix of other switches is $2k$. Then we can use the radix-$2k$ switches at the root stage and attach k compute nodes to each of the root switches. Thus, the root switches become the same as the leaf switches. We call such a network a *peer k-ary n-tree* or *peer fat-tree*. Figure 1 shows a peer 3-ary 3-tree network. It has 3 stages and 54 compute nodes.

We define switch and compute node labels and connection rules as follows. A peer k-ary n-tree network has n stages. A switch is labeled as $\langle L, D_{n-2}, \ldots, D_0 \rangle$, where L (level) indicates the *stage* with $L \in \{0, \ldots, n-1\}$, and $D_{n-2}, \ldots, D_0$ identifies the switches inside stage L, with $D_i \in \{0, \ldots, k-1\}$ for $0 \leq i \leq n-2$. In stage L for $0 \leq L \leq n-2$, a switch

$$\langle L, D_{n-2}, \ldots, D_{L+1}, D_L, D_{L-1}, \ldots, D_0 \rangle$$

will connect to switches

$$\langle L+1, D_{n-2}, \ldots, D_{L+1}, *, D_{L-1}, \ldots, D_0 \rangle$$

where $* \in \{0, \ldots, k-1\}$. For example, in a peer 3-ary 3-tree shown in Fig. 1, switch $\langle 0, 0, 0 \rangle$ in stage 0 connects to switches $\langle 1, 0, 0 \rangle$, $\langle 1, 0, 1 \rangle$, and $\langle 1, 0, 2 \rangle$ in stage 1. And switch $\langle 1, 0, 0 \rangle$ in stage 1 connects to switches $\langle 2, 0, 0 \rangle$, $\langle 2, 1, 0 \rangle$, and $\langle 2, 2, 0 \rangle$ in stage 2. The connection links are bidirectional.

A peer k-ary n-tree network has $2k^n$ compute nodes. A compute node is labeled as $\langle G, C_{n-1}, C_{n-2}, \ldots, C_0 \rangle$, where G indicates the *group* with $G \in \{0, 1\}$, and $C_{n-1}, C_{n-2}, \ldots, C_0$ identifies the switches in group G, with $C_i \in \{0, \ldots, k-1\}$ for $0 \leq i \leq n-1$. In group 0, a compute node

$$\langle 0, C_{n-1}, C_{n-2}, \ldots, C_0 \rangle$$

will connect to the switch

$$\langle 0, D_{n-2}, \ldots, D_0 \rangle = \langle 0, C_{n-2}, \ldots, C_0 \rangle$$

in stage 0. And in group 1, a compute node

$$\langle 1, C_{n-1}, C_{n-2}, \ldots, C_0 \rangle$$

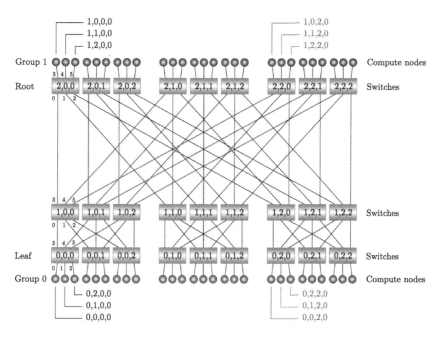

Fig. 1. A peer 3-ary 3-tree network (bidirectional links)

will connect to the switch

$$\langle n-1, D_{n-2}, \ldots, D_0 \rangle = \langle n-1, C_{n-2}, \ldots, C_0 \rangle$$

in stage $n-1$. For example, in a peer 3-ary 3-tree shown in Fig. 1, compute nodes $\langle 0,0,0,0 \rangle$, $\langle 0,1,0,0 \rangle$, and $\langle 0,2,0,0 \rangle$ in group 0 connect to the switch $\langle 0,0,0 \rangle$ in stage 0. And compute nodes $\langle 1,0,2,0 \rangle$, $\langle 1,1,2,0 \rangle$, and $\langle 1,2,2,0 \rangle$ in group 1 connect to the switch $\langle 2,2,0 \rangle$ in stage 2.

Different from the traditional k-ary n-fly butterfly network where there is only one path from the source node to the destination node, in a peer k-ary n-tree network, if the source node and destination node are of the same group, the peer k-ary n-tree network acts as the same of the k-ary n-tree fat-tree non-blocking network. If the source and destination nodes belong to different groups, there is only one shortest path. However, there are many *Z-paths* between the source node and destination node. For example, if the source node is of group 0 and the destination node is of group 1, we can route from the source to any intermediate switch of the stage 0, just like the routing in a k-ary n-tree fat-tree network, and then we route from that intermediate switch to the destination node through the shortest path. The shape of the path is something like the shape of character "Z". Note that a switch other than stage 0 can also be such an intermediate switch.

Table 1 summarizes the topological properties of classical k-ary n-tree, bidirectional Clos k-ary n-tree, mirrored k-ary n-tree, and peer k-ary n-tree net-

Table 1. Comparison of topological properties

	d	D	N	S	L	B	A
Classical	$2k$	$2n$	k^n	nk^{n-1}	nk^n	$k^n/2$	$2n - \dfrac{2}{k-1} + \dfrac{2}{(k-1)k^n}$
Bi. Clos	$2k$	$2n$	$2k^n$	$(2n-1)k^{n-1}$	$2nk^n$	$k^n/2$	$2n - \dfrac{1}{k-1} + \dfrac{1}{(k-1)k^n}$
Mirrored	$2k$	$2n$	$2k^n$	$(2n-2)k^{n-1}$	$(2n-1)k^n$	$k^n/2$	$2n - \dfrac{1}{k-1} + \dfrac{1}{(k-1)k^n} - \dfrac{1}{2}$
Peer	$2k$	$2n$	$2k^n$	nk^{n-1}	$(n+1)k^n$	$k^n/2$	$\dfrac{3}{2}n - \dfrac{1}{k-1} + \dfrac{1}{(k-1)k^n} + \dfrac{1}{2}$

works. Columns d shows radix; D is diameter; N is number of nodes; S is number of switches; L is number of links; B is bisection width; and A is average distance. The number of switches, the number of links, and the average distance of the peer k-ary n-tree network are reduced greatly compared to other k-ary n-tree networks. We can see this from Fig. 2 and Fig. 3.

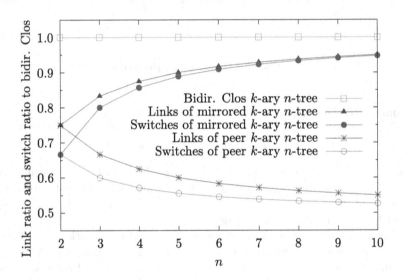

Fig. 2. Cost ratios of links and switches to bidirectional Clos network

Figure 2 shows the link ratios and switch ratios of the mirrored and peer k-ary n-tree networks to that of the bidirectional Clos k-ary n-tree network. Figure 3 shows the relative average distance ratios of the mirrored and peer k-ary n-tree networks to that of the bidirectional Clos k-ary n-tree network. Note that for $n = 2$, the curve of the mirrored k-ary 2-tree network and the curve of the peer k-ary 2-tree network are the same, because the average distance of the mirrored k-ary 2-tree network is $4 - 1/(k-1) + 1/((k-1)k^2) - 1/2 = 3.5 - 1/(k-1) + 1/((k-1)k^2)$ and the average distance of the peer k-ary 2-tree network is $3 - 1/(k-1) + 1/((k-1)k^2) + 1/2 = 3.5 - 1/(k-1) + 1/((k-1)k^2)$.

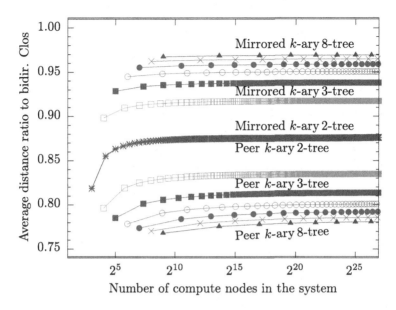

Fig. 3. Average distance ratios to bidirectional Clos network

A peer k-ary n-tree can connect $2k^n$ compute nodes. To determine k and n for a given scale of the peer fat-tree, we define a *relative cost performance* (RCP) to the hypercube with equal capacity as following.

$$\text{RCP} = \frac{d_p \times D_p}{d_q \times D_q} \tag{1}$$

where d_p and D_p are the switch radix and network diameter of the peer k-ary n-tree, respectively, and d_q and D_q are the router degree and network diameter of the hypercube, respectively. The switch radix or router degree affects the hardware cost, and the network diameter affects the communication performance. For a given number of compute nodes N, we can design a hypercube as follows. There are N/p routers; each router connects p compute nodes. Then we can build an m-cube with $m = \log_2(N/p)$. The router degree is $d_q = m + p$; and the network diameter $D_q = m + 2$, where 2 is the distance for a compute node from and to its router. To calculate the RCP, we let both networks have a same number of compute nodes N, which is $2k^n$.

Figure 4 plots the RCP of the peer k-ary n-tree networks with different n. For a given N, we can find an n so that the RCP has the minimum value. Note that the RCP of the hypercube is always a 1. For a given n, there is a k at which the RCP has the minimum value.

4   Routing in Peer k-ary n-tree Network

Routing is defined as that a source node in a network sends a packet to a destination node through a path. In this section, we describe a minimal per-hop deterministic routing algorithm.

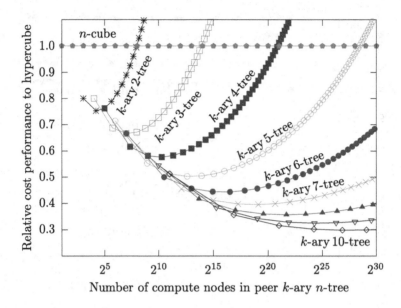

Fig. 4. RCP comparison of peer k-ary n-tree

We use examples to show how to find a shortest path from a source node S to a destination node T in a peer 3-ary 4-tree network. Let $S = 02002$ and $T = 02210$. First, S sends a packet to the switch $u = 0002$; and finally, T receives the packet from the switch $v = 0210$. The routing consists of two phases. The first phase routes the packet to an NCA switch of S and T; and the second phase routes the packet from the NCA switch to v and then to T. The path from u to v is: $0002 \rightarrow 1000 \rightarrow 2010 \rightarrow 3210 \rightarrow 2210 \rightarrow 1210 \rightarrow 0210$. The path from 0002 to 3210 is an upward path to an NCA and the path from 3210 to 0210 is a downward path to the destination node. If $S = 12002$, then $u = 3002$. The path from u to v is as below. $3002 \rightarrow 2202 \rightarrow 1212 \rightarrow 0210$.

The two examples above have a destination node of group 0. If the destination node is of group 1, we can use a similar routing method in the opposite direction. The routing algorithm for a peer k-ary n-tree network is formally given in **Algorithm** 1. We use the current switch port label to send the packet to the next switch. The value of port label T_{Lw}^{+} equals $T_{Lw} + k$ and the value of port label T_{Lw}^{-} equals $T_{Lw} + 0$.

5   Fault Tolerance of Peer k-ary n-tree Network

Fault tolerance is the ability of the network to continue operating properly in the presence of switch or link faults. It is affected by the path diversity of the network. Path diversity is defined as the number of minimal paths between two compute nodes. For the peer k-ary n-tree, if the source and destination compute

Algorithm 1. Peer_Fat_Tree_Routing (*packet*)

Input: *packet* = $\langle T, data \rangle$;   /* received packet */

$T = \langle G_T, T_{n-1}, T_{n-2}, ..., T_1, T_0 \rangle$;   /* destination node ID */

$W = \langle L_W, W_{n-2}, ..., W_1, W_0 \rangle$;   /* my switch ID */

if $G_T = 0$ /* group 0 destination node */

  if $L_W \leq n - 2$ and $W_{n-2}...W_{L_W} \neq T_{n-2}...T_{L_W}$

    send *packet* to $T_{L_W}^+$ port;   /* upward to NCA */

  else   /* downward to destination */

    if $(L_W > 0)$ /* not a level 0 switch */

      send *packet* to $T_{L_W-1}^-$ port;   /* downward to switch */

    else   /* a level 0 switch */

      send *packet* to T_{n-1}^- port;   /* to destination node */

    endif

  endif

else   /* group 1 destination node */

  if $L_W \geq 1$ and $W_{L_W-1}...W_0 \neq T_{L_W-1}...T_0$

    send *packet* to $T_{L_W-1}^-$ port;   /* downward to NCA */

  else   /* upward to destination */

    if $(L_W < n - 1)$ /* not a level $n - 1$ switch */

      send *packet* to $T_{L_W}^+$ port;   /* upward to switch */

    else   /* a level $n - 1$ switch */

      send *packet* to T_{n-1}^+ port;   /* to destination node */

    endif

  endif

endif

---

nodes are of the same group, the network acts exactly the same as the k-ary n-tree fat-tree. There are multiple minimal paths between the two compute nodes. If the two compute nodes are of different groups, there is only one minimal path between the two compute nodes. However, there are multiple non-minimal paths between the two compute nodes, Z-paths for example. This section presents the fault tolerance of the peer k-ary n-tree network and compares it to other fat-tree networks.

Reference [7] proposed three deadlock-free switch fault-tolerant routing algorithms for the MiKANT network. The one-port algorithm checks another port if the current port determined by the shortest-path routing algorithm cannot be used for sending packet because the switch connected to that port is faulty. There are k such ports. All-port algorithm tries to use k ports to send packet. One-port and all-port algorithms can be used only in the upward routing phase. If there is a faulty switch in the downward routing phase, these algorithms cannot be used because in the downward routing phase the path is deterministic. Go-back algorithm goes back to the upward routing phase to change port. Corresponding to the depth of going back, [7] examined the performance of "go-back one", "go-back two", and "go-back three" algorithms. The shortest-path routing algorithm for fat-trees is deadlock-free because the routing consists of only an upward phase and a downward phase. The go-back algorithm is also deadlock-free if we do not choose a path that has already been checked.

Here we evaluate the performance of the "go-back three" algorithm for the peer 4-ary 5-tree network. The network has 1,280 switches and 2,048 compute nodes. The faulty switches are randomly placed. For a certain number of faulty nodes, we simulate 100,000 times, and each time, we assign the source node and destination node randomly. Note that if the switch to which the source node or destination node connects is faulty, there is no way to route packets from the source node to the destination node.

The simulation results are shown in Fig. 5. The successful routing ratio of the "go-back three" algorithm for peer k-ary n-tree network is located in between that of its shortest-path routing algorithm and the "go-back three" algorithm for MiKANT network. Note that Go-back algorithms do not find Z-paths in the peer k-ary n-tree network.

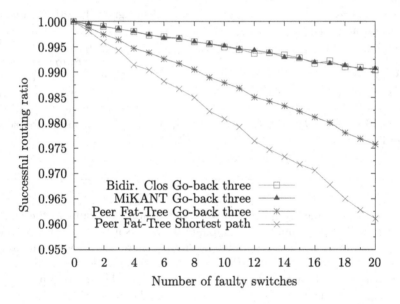

Fig. 5. Successful routing ratio on switch faulty

6   Packet Latency of Peer k-ary n-tree Network

Packet latency is the time required for a packet to traverse the network from source to destination. We have evaluated the packet latency through simulation. The network we simulated is a peer 4-ary 5-tree network with 1,280 switches and 2,048 compute nodes. Because it is a bidirectional network, a switch must have an 8×8 crossbar. We use a FIFO buffer of depth two in each of the input ports. We simulate two patterns of the traffic loads: random traffic and inversion traffic. Under the random traffic, each compute node is equally likely to send a packet to *any* other compute node. Under the inversion traffic, each compute node is equally likely to send a packet to a destination node whose address is the bit-inversion of the source node address. We perform the simulation cycle-by-cycle and terminate the simulation when at least 200 packets of each source node reached their destinations.

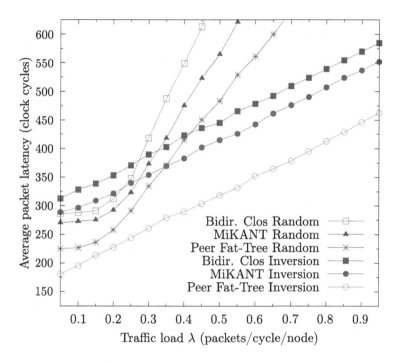

Fig. 6. Average packet latencies of 4-ary 5-tree networks

Figure 6 plots the average packet latencies for the bidirectional Clos network, MiKANT network, and peer fat-tree network. When the traffic load is low, the random pattern has a lower packet latency because there may exist some shorter paths. As traffic increases, the inversion pattern has a lower packet latency because the contention on the output ports is lower than random pattern. Also, we can understand that the peer fat-tree has the lowest packet latency.

7 Conclusions

In this paper, we proposed the peer fat-tree network that connects compute nodes with about half switches and links compared to Clos and fat-tree networks. It consists of two groups of compute nodes. The communications between the compute nodes in the same group are the same as the non-blocking Clos and fat-tree networks that provide high path diversity and have good fault tolerance performance. The communications between the compute nodes in the distinct groups can be performed fast because the peer fat-tree network has a short distance in this case.

We examined the fault tolerance and packet latency of the bidirectional Clos network, MiKANT network, and peer fat-tree network. The MiKANT network has almost the same fault tolerance performance as the bidirectional Clos network. Although the fault tolerance performance of the peer fat-tree is worse than the other two networks, the average packet latency of the peer fat-tree is shorter than the other two networks. For those systems where the fault probability is low, or the systems with high availability are actively maintained, the peer fat-tree is a better candidate network because it provides high performance for communications at low hardware cost.

To increase the fault tolerance performance when the source and destination are in different groups, we can route from the source to any switch that connects a node of the other group through a fault-free path. Then the routing can be done in a non-blocking fat-tree because the new source and destination are in the same group (Z-path). Future work may include developing a Z-path fault-tolerant routing algorithm for the peer fat-tree network so that it also has a good fault tolerance performance for the communications between the compute nodes in the distinct groups and evaluating its performance. Also, it seems to be needed to develop a job scheduling algorithm specific to the groups of the peer fat-tree network. Implementing a peer fat-tree using switches and cables is easy, but the challenging work is to implement a peer fat-tree network on a chip.

References

1. Abts, D., Kim, J.: High Performance Datacenter Networks: Architectures, Algorithms, and Opportunities. Morgan and Claypool, San Rafael, March 2011
2. Al-Fares, M., Loukissas, A., Vahdat, A.: A scalable, commodity data center network architecture. In: Proceedings of the ACM SIGCOMM 2008 Conference on Data Communication, pp. 63–74. Seattle, WA, USA, August 2008
3. Clos, C.: A study of non-blocking switching networks. Bell Syst. Tech. J. **32**(2), 406–424 (1953)
4. Dally, W., Towles, B.: Principles and Practices of Interconnection Networks. Morgan Kaufmann, Burlington (2003)
5. Leiserson, C.E.: Fat-trees: universal networks for hardware-efficient supercomputing. IEEE Trans. Comput. **C-34**(10), 892–901 (1985)
6. Li, Y., Chu, W.: MiKANT: a mirrored k-ary n-tree for reducing hardware cost and packet latency of fat-tree and clos networks. In: Proceedings of the 18th IEEE International Conference on Scalable Computing and Communications, pp. 1643–1650, October 2018
7. Li, Y., Chu, W.: Switch fault tolerance in a mirrored k-ary n-tree. In: Proceedings of the 2019 International Conference on Computer, Information and Telecommunication Systems, pp. 25–29, August 2019
8. Petrini, F., Vanneschi, M.: K-ary n-trees: high performance networks for massively parallel architectures. In: Proceedings of the 11th International Parallel Processing Symposium, pp. 87–93, April 1997

9. Singh, A., et al.: Jupiter rising: a decade of clos topologies and centralized control in Google's datacenter network. In: 2015 ACM Conference on Special Interest Group on Data Communication, pp. 183–197, August 2015
10. TOP500: Supercomputer Sites, June 2022. http://top500.org/

Accelerating Imbalanced Many-to-Many Communication with Systematic Delay Insertion

Hirotoshi Yamada, Masao Okita, and Fumihiko Ino[✉]

Graduate School of Information Science and Technology, Osaka University,
1-5 Yamadaoka, Suita, Osaka 565-0871, Japan
{h-yamada,okita,ino}@ist.osaka-u.ac.jp

Abstract. In this paper, we propose a runtime method for determining optimal delay insertion to avoid network contention in any communication pattern on a switching topology. The idea for finding an optimum solution is to deploy an arrival-consumption model that is able to independently estimate the occurrence of contention on sender processes. This independent estimation allows processes to calculate the optimal delay for each destination when processing send operations. The proposed method assumes that messages are transferred through a single network switch by an eager protocol. The experimental results on a 64-node cluster show that the maximum speedup over existing methods reached 10 times for an imbalanced case where the numbers of send operations and message sizes differ among processes.

Keywords: Intentional delay · Message Passing Interface · switching topology · one-sided communication

1 Introduction

Accelerating many-to-many (m2m) communication, which is sometimes called gossiping in the context of interconnection topologies, plays a key role in increasing the parallelization efficiency of large-scale parallel programs using Message Passing Interface (MPI) [7]. We classify m2m communication patterns into two types: (1) balanced and (2) imbalanced m2m communication. In the first type, all processor elements (PEs) issue the same number of *send/receive* operations for the same message size. This type, which frequently appears in dense matrix multiplication and stencil computation [9,11], can be efficiently processed by collective operations available with most of MPI implementations. On the other hand, the second type has a different number or message size of *send/receive* operations among PEs. This type frequently appears in sparse matrix multiplication [2] and graph-based processing [8].

MPI collective operations considerably increase the processing time for extremely imbalanced m2m communication. This increase is due to the limitation of general designs adopted by MPI implementations, which suffer from

H. Takizawa et al. (Eds.): PDCAT 2022, LNCS 13798, pp. 426–437, 2023.
https://doi.org/10.1007/978-3-031-29927-8_33

irregular network contention. This limitation motivates researchers to implement imbalanced m2m communication through a series of MPI point-to-point (p2p) operations. There have been several studies on contention avoidance in m2m communication [5]. However, these studies involve manual interactions to deal with network contention by appropriate scheduling of p2p operations.

An interesting approach for avoiding contention on communication channels is to insert intentional delays in a series of *send* operations [6]. Since excessive delay insertion increases the overall processing time of m2m communication, it is necessary to discover appropriate delays that reduce network contention while incurring the least amount of overhead. However, optimizing the delay insertion for imbalanced m2m communication is a burden because the occurrence of contention depends on the network topology and communication pattern; the bottleneck of message transfer and its maximal throughput vary based on network topology and transmission schedule. Furthermore, avoiding contention requires examining all receiving message combinations for each PE, because contention depends on the message size of the two *send* operations.

In this paper, we propose a method to find optimal delay insertion for arbitrary imbalanced m2m communication in a single-switching topology. The key idea of the proposed method is decomposing collective communication into gather patterns. The proposed method deploys a novel arrival-communication model that separately evaluates the occurrence of contention in each gather pattern. Under the following assumptions, the arrival-consumption model calculates the minimal delay required to avoid contention: (1) messages are transferred through a single network switch by an eager protocol and (2) all PEs synchronize at the beginning.

The key contributions of this paper are as follows.

1. We present an arrival-consumption model that evaluates the occurrence of contention based on a race between data arrival and consumption at the message transfer bottleneck.
2. We reveal the optimal delays required for avoiding network contention in a single-switching topology.

Note that the proposed method can be used without modifying the system configuration in high-performance computing (HPC) systems because the method relies on user-level APIs only. Consequently, the proposed method is useful for environments where a large number of users share the HPC Systems.

2 Related Work

The method proposed by Karwande et al. [5] aims to avoid contention for imbalanced m2m communications. The scheduling method avoids contention by inserting barrier synchronization so that the contending communications are sequential. Furthermore, they reduce the number of barrier synchronizations greedily. However, in the case of a communication structure where receptions are concentrated in one PE, the overhead of the barrier becomes significant since their scheduling inserts a barrier based on the maximum number of *receive* operations in all the PEs. Our proposed method avoids all contention without barrier synchronization with delay insertion for imbalanced m2m communication.

On the other hand, algorithms for all-to-all communication apply to imbalanced m2m communication because all-to-all communication encompasses m2m communication. Thakur et al. [10] proposed a scheduling method to avoid contention for all-to-all communication in a topology with equal distance between any pair of PEs. Their method of scheduling repeats step the *mod* pattern that PE i sends to PE $((r + i) \mod n)$ at step r, where n is the total number of PEs. The *mod* pattern avoids contention. This scheduling method avoids contention in a structure where the message size and the number of *send/receive* operations are equal between PEs. However, their algorithm causes contention for imbalanced m2m communication because it cannot generate a *mod* pattern. Our proposed method completely avoids contention using delay insertion for imbalanced m2m communication with arbitrary structure.

3   Preliminaries

In this paper, we focus on the m2m communication in which all PEs send a message at most once to every PE except themselves. Typical MPI collective operations are classified into the m2m communication, *e.g.*, `MPI_Alltoall`, `MPI_Gather` and, `MPI_Scatter`. We separate the communication structure, which is the source-destination relationship between PEs, from the communication schedule, which is the order in which *send/receive* operations are issued.

3.1   Communication Structure

We define the communication structure of an m2m communication as a simple directed weighted graph $G = (P, A, w : A \to \mathbb{N})$ with PEs as vertices, where $P = \{1, \ldots, n\}$ denotes the vertex set. A directed edge $(p, q) \in A$ denotes the communication from PE p to PE q. The weight $w((p, q))$ represents the amount of data sent from the sender PE p to the receiver PE q. Since G is a simple graph, the source and destination PEs are always different and the sender and receiver PEs pairs are separate. For the sake of simplicity, we assume that G is a connected graph. In the case of an unconnected graph, the schedule for each connected component is determined independently.

We also denote the communication structure A_i on PE $i \in P$ with the set of outgoing edges N_i^+ at vertex i, as in Eq. (1).

$$A_i = N_i^+ = \{(p, q) \in A \mid p = i\} \tag{1}$$

Since G is a simple graph, we have $|A_i| \leq n - 1$ and $A = \bigcap_i^n A_i$.

We define balanced m2m communication as m2m communication in which the communication structure is symmetric for all PEs. That is, the communication structure G of a balanced m2m communication meets the requirements of Eqs. (2) and (3).

$$\exists k \in \mathbb{N}, \forall i \in P, \ |N_i^+| = |N_i^-| = k \tag{2}$$

$$\exists l \in \mathbb{N}, \forall a_1, a_2 \in A, \ w(a_1) = w(a_2) = l \tag{3}$$

Note that $|N_i^-|$ denotes the set of input edges of vertex $i \in P$. For example, MPI_Alltoall is a balanced m2m communication.

On the other hand, we define imbalanced m2m communication as m2m communication that does not meet the requirements of Eqs. (2) and (3). For example, MPI_Gather and MPI_Scatter are imbalanced m2m communications.

3.2   Communication Schedule

First, we define the communication schedule s_i for a PE $i \in P$ as a sending order of the elements of A_i. In typical MPI programming, programmers specify the schedule simply by listing the call of *send* operations. As a result, s_i can be represented by an injective function shown in Eq. (4).

$$s_i : \{1, 2, \ldots, |A_i|\} \to A_i \tag{4}$$

Next, we extend s_i to a delayed communication schedule s_i'. Let delay $d(a) \in \mathbb{R}$ $(d(a) \geq 0)$ denote an idle time (*e.g.*, sleep(2)) before PE i issues a *send* operation $a \in A_i$. A delayed communication schedule s_i' defines an order of pairs of the delay and *send* operation as follows.

$$s_i' : \{1, 2, \ldots, |A_i|\} \to \{(d(a), a) \mid a \in A_i\} \tag{5}$$

Here $d(a) = 0$ means that there exists no delay before a.

Finally, we define the overall schedule S of m2m communication as a series of delayed communication schedules denoted by Eq. (6).

$$S = (s_1', s_2', \ldots, s_n') \tag{6}$$

The schedule of *receive* operations, on the other hand, is uniquely determined by the sending schedule S. Due to space limitation, we omit its details.

4   Proposed Method

The key idea of the proposed method is to decompose m2m communication into gather structures. In other words, we concentrate on message conflict at each destination. In the case of a single-switching network, there is no conflict between communications with different destinations. Therefore, we can estimate the occurrence of contention separately on different destinations and determine sending schedules for gather structures independently of each other.

Contention occurs depending on the environment, *i.e.*, hardware specification, network topology, message protocol, and transmission timing. The proposed method makes the following assumptions to clarify the target environment.

1. Network topology with a single switch connection.
2. Bidirectional communication.

3. Message passing based on MPI eager protocol [7].
4. Synchronization of all PEs at the beginning of execution.

Since an MPI program typically runs on an asynchronous distributed system, it is hard to achieve assumption 4. even if it starts with software synchronization, *i.e.*, MPI_Barrier. Therefore, the proposed method adds an extra delay to the statistically calculated delay for covering the error between theoretical and actual time.

4.1   Arrival-Consumption Model

We model a balance of message arrival and consumption at the receiver bottleneck in a gather structure. A gather structure $G_q = \{P_q \subseteq P, B_q \subseteq A, w\}$ is a subgraph of G that satisfies $\exists q \in P_q, \forall (i,j) \in B_q, j = q$. A receiver bottleneck means the network element which is the most congested point of the communication in a gather structure. In the case of a single-switching network, for example, the receiver bottleneck is the first-in, first-out (FIFO) buffer or bus for the receiver PE q inside the switch; message consumption corresponds to the message transfer from the switch to q, which includes a buffer copy and routing.

Given a sequence of incoming messages $(m_1, m_2, \ldots, m_k)$ $(m_i \in B_q)$, the arrival-consumption model decides the occurrence of contention. The following three parameters characterize the arrival-consumption model.

- L: latency from a sender PE to the receiver bottleneck.
- $\gamma(w)$: the time required to consume a message of size w.
- δ_i: a gap between the arrivals of m_i and m_{i+1}.

While L and γ are determined by the environment, δ_i is determined by schedule S.

The occurrence of contention is determined by the balance of message arrival and consumption. Figure 1(a) illustrates a point of contention. When a message arrives before the receiver bottleneck has completely consumed the previous messages, it causes contention; contention results in re-transmission and a significant increase in overall processing time. On the other hand, as shown in Figs. 1(b) and 1(c), no contention occurs if every gap is larger than the consumption time. Here we define predicate $C(m_i, m_{i+1})$ as Eq. (7), considering the assumptions 1. and 4.

$$C(m_i, m_{i+1}) = \begin{cases} \text{true,} & \text{if } \delta_i < \gamma(w(m_i)), \\ \text{false,} & \text{otherwise.} \end{cases} \tag{7}$$

Consequently, no contention occurs at the receiver bottleneck if Eq. (8) is true.

$$\forall i \in \{1, \ldots, k-1\}, \delta_i \geq \gamma(w(m_i)) \tag{8}$$

To cover the time error with respect to assumption 4., the proposed method adds an extra delay to δ. Let $E_i \in \mathbb{R}$ be the displacement of time from the

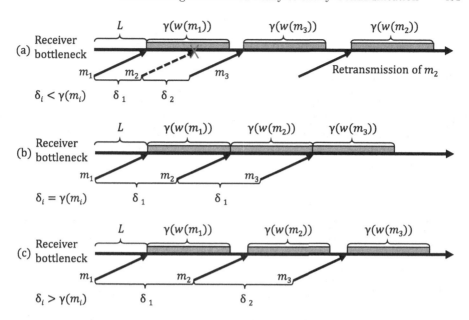

Fig. 1. Examples of message arrival and consumption races. The horizontal axis represents the time elapsed. An arrow and a box connected to the arrow represent the arrival of a message and the consumption of the message, respectively. A red cross denotes a point of contention. (Color figure online)

beginning of the theoretical schedule for each PE i. The complete avoidance of contention in the practical environment requires adding delays of $(\delta + \epsilon)$; where ϵ is $\max\{E_i\}$. Therefore, no contention occurs at the receiver bottleneck in the practical environment if Eq. (9) is true.

$$\forall i \in \{1, \ldots, k-1\}, \delta_i + \epsilon \geq \gamma(w(m_i)) \tag{9}$$

4.2 Model Parameter Estimation

We present a statistical approach for estimating $\gamma(w)$ for a given message size w depending on the environment. By measuring the processing time of a uniform gather structure with varying message size and gap, we derive an estimation model of $\gamma(w)$. In a uniform gather structure, where every communication sends a message of equal size w, the gap should be uniform in all arrivals.

According to the arrival-consumption model, the uniform gap $\delta^+ = (\delta + \epsilon)$ equals to $\gamma(w)$ if the processing time is minimal. Let $T_g(w)$ denotes the processing time of a uniform gather structure with message size w. The arrival-consumption model is used to derive the following expressions.

1. if $\delta^+ < \gamma(w)$ then $T_g(w) > L + (n-1) \times \gamma(w)$
   (increased processing time due to contention)

Algorithm 1. Determining the optimal time to issue *send* operations

---

Input: Communication structure $G = (P, A, w)$ and function of message consumption γ.

Output: Issue time of *send* operation $t : A \to \mathbb{R}$.

1: **for** $i = 1$ **to** n **do**   ▷ for each destination i
2:      $B_i \leftarrow \{(j, k) \in A \mid k = i\}$ ▷ extract gather structure
3:      $m \leftarrow$ sorting $\forall (j, i) \in B_i$ in ascending order of $((n + j - i) \mod n)$ ▷ get the list of arrival messages
4:      $t(m_1) \leftarrow 0$ ▷ m_l is the l-th element in list m
5:      **for** $l = 2$ **to** $|B_i|$ **do**
6:          $t(m_l) \leftarrow t(m_{l-1}) + \gamma(w(m_{l-1}))$
7: **return** t

Algorithm 2. Optimal delay derivation

Input: Communication structure $G = (P, A, w)$ and Issue time of *send* operation $t : A \to \mathbb{R}$.

Output: Map of inserted delays $d : A \to \mathbb{R}$.

1: **for** $i = 1$ **to** n **do**   ▷ for each destination i
2:      $A_i \leftarrow \{(k, j) \in A \mid k = i\}$ ▷ extract scatter structure
3:      $\mu \leftarrow$ sorting $\forall (i, j) \in A_i$ in ascending order of $t(\mu)$ ▷ get the list of sending messages
4:      $d(\mu_1) \leftarrow t(\mu_1)$ ▷ μ_i is the i-th element in list μ
5:      **for** $i = 2$ **to** $|A_i|$ **do**   ▷ for each message μ_i
6:          $d(m_i) \leftarrow t(\mu_i) - t(\mu_{i-1})$
7: **return** d

---

2. if $\delta^+ = \gamma(w)$ then $T_g(w) = L + (n - 1) \times \gamma(w)$
3. if $\delta^+ > \gamma(w)$ then $T_g(w) = L + (n - 2) \times \delta + \gamma(w)$

As a result, by determining the optimal value of δ^+, we can experimentally estimate $\gamma(w)$ for a given value of w.

4.3   Scheduling Algorithm

The proposed method indirectly controls the gaps in message arrival at receivers by adjusting delays inserted into the schedule S. The proposed method determines the optimal delays in two steps. The first step determines the issuing time for each *send* operation independently, focusing on each gather structure. The second step determines the delays for each *send* operation independently, focusing on the scatter structure. Algorithm 1 describes the algorithm of the first step and Algorithm 2 describes the pseudo-algorithm of the second step.

The proposed method determines the order of *send* operations based on the *mod* pattern algorithm [10], aiming to reduce the conflict of the issues of *send* operations. Since the proposed method determines delays independently of each gather structure, as for balanced communication structure, the proposed method generates an unfeasible schedule in which a PE is supposed to send two or more

Order of send operations (i,j)

	$i=1$	$i=2$	$i=3$	$i=4$
	(1,2)	(2,3)	(3,4)	(4,1)
	(1,3)	(2,4)		(4,2)
		(2,1)		(4,3)

Order of receive operations (j,i)

	$i=1$	$i=2$	$i=3$	$i=4$
	(4,1)	(1,2)	(2,3)	(3,4)
	(2,1)	(4,2)	(1,3)	(2,4)
			(4,3)	

(a) Sending schedule.   (b) Receiving schedule.

Fig. 2. Example of a schedule based on the *mod* pattern algorithm with 4 PEs ($n = 4$). As a sender, PE i calls *send* operations in a cyclic ascending order starting with $(i, i+1)$. As a receiver, PE i calls *receive* operations in a cyclic descending order starting with $(i-1, i)$.

messages at the same time. The *mod* pattern is useful to avoid the simultaneous issues of *send* operations. Inspired by the *mod* pattern, the proposed method determines s_i' by sorting $A_i = \{(i, j)\}$ in ascending order of $((n + j - i) \mod n)$, where n denotes the number of PEs. Consequently, the order of *receive* operations of PE i is determined by sorting $B_i = \{(j, i)\}$ in ascending order of $((n + j - i) \mod n)$, as shown in line 3 of Algorithm 1. Figure 2 illustrates an example of a *mod* pattern based schedule with $n = 4$. The PEs form a ring communication pattern in each row, which avoids conflict of *send* operation issues.

Algorithm 1 determines the time to issue the *send* operations so that messages arrive at the optimal gap required for contention avoidance based on the arrival-consumption model. According to the assumptions 1. and 4., the gap δ_l for message m_l is equivalent to the delay $d(m_{l+1})$ since δ_l includes the time required to issue the *send* operation. In addition, the processing time is minimal when $\delta_l = \gamma(w(m_l))$ for all $m_l \in A$ as described in Sect. 4.2. Let $t(m)$ denote the time when *send* operation m is issued. As a result, the issue time $t(m_l)$ of the *send* operation m_{l+1} is equivalent to $t(m_i) + \gamma(w(m_i))$ (see line 6 in Algorithm 1).

The proposed method requires sender PEs to insert delays such that messages arrive at an optimal gap. Therefore, to calculate delays for each *send* operation, Algorithm 2 decomposes the m2m communication into a scatter structure. A_p is the set of communications that the scatter structure of PE p contains. Given a sequence of outgoing messages $(\mu_1, \mu_2, \ldots, \mu_x)$ $(m_i \in A_p)$. The ascending order of $t(\mu)$ automatically determines the order in which the *send* operations are issued (see line 3 in Algorithm 2). As a result, a delay $d(\mu_{l+1})$ is equivalent to $t(\mu_{l+1}) - t(\mu_l)$ (see line 6 in Alg. 2).

5   Evaluation

We conducted experiments on a cluster system consisting of 64 computers. Table 1 presents the system configuration. The processing time of the measurement means the average of $1,000$ runs. The message consumption is modeled in $\gamma(w) = 0.0073 \times w - 60$ as described in Sect. 4.2.

Table 1. Experimental environment.

Item	Specification
Number of nodes	64
CPU/node	Intel Xeon E3-1230 3.2 GHz (4 cores)
Main memory/node	8 GB
Topology	Single crossbar switch
Switch	hp ProCurve Switch 5400zl
Interconnect	Gigabit Ethernet
OS	CentOS 7.6
Compiler	gcc 7.3.0
MPI	OpenMPI 3.1.0 [3]

We compared the proposed method, *delay*, with the following two scheduling methods in terms of the performance of m2m communication.

- *mod*. This scheduling method, proposed by Thakur *et al.* [10], does not insert delay. The method determines s'_i by sorting $A_i = \{(i,j)\}$ in ascending order of $((n + j - i) \mod n)$, where n denotes the number of PEs. `MPI_Gatherv` and `MPI_Scatterv` in OpenMPI generate the same schedule as *mod*.
- *pairwise*. The method provided as an algorithm for `MPI_Alltoallv` in Open-MPI. We implement *pairwise* with `MPI_Alltoallv`.

By using the scheduling methods mentioned above, we measured the processing time for typical m2m communication structures as follows.

- *scatterv*: PE#1 sends a message of different sizes to all the PEs other than itself.
- *gatherv*: all PEs except PE#1 send a message of different sizes to PE#1.
- *alltoallv*: each PE sends a message of different sizes to every PE except itself.

The imbalanced m2m communication consists of multiple *gatherv* structures or multiple *scatterv* structures. Therefore, the performance of these two structures is critical in determining the generality of the proposed method in any m2m communication. We also concentrate on *alltoallv* structure to evaluate the performance of the proposed method for relatively balanced communication structures. In all the communication structures, the size of a message follows a uniform random distribution between 1–63 KiB. The 63 KiB is the threshold value where the eager protocol works in the experimental environment.

Compared with the existing methods, proposed shows equal or higher performance for arbitrary structures; because proposed avoids contention and reduces waiting time for completion of communication. Figures 3, 4, and 5 illustrates the m2m communication processing time for the three scheduling methods in *gatherv*, *scatterv*, and *alltoallv* structures, respectively.

Compared with *mod*, *delay* avoids the contention that occurs in *gatherv*. *delay* was up to 10 times faster for *gatherv* compared with *mod*. The throughput

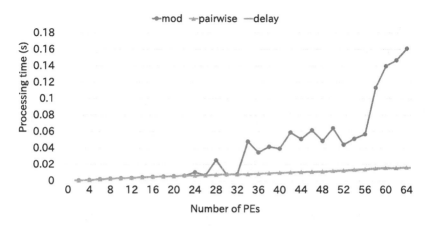

Fig. 3. Comparison of processing times in the *gatherv* communication structures. The horizontal axis represents the number of PEs and the vertical axis represents the average processing time for a m2m communication.

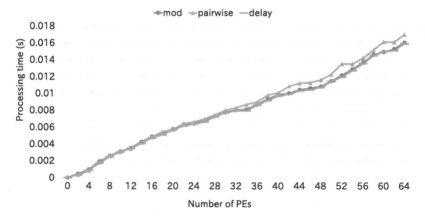

Fig. 4. Comparison of processing times in the *scatterv* communication structures. The horizontal axis represents the number of PEs and the vertical axis represents the average processing time for a m2m communication.

degradation of *gatherv* in *mod* may be due to the TCP incast [1]. For *scatterv*, the processing time in *delay* and *mod* was equivalent by less than 1%. Compared with *mod* for *alltoallv*, *delay* increased processing time by a factor of up to 1.2. This result implies that the delay time estimated with the arrival-consumption model may be greater than the optimal value.

Compared with *pairwise*, *delay* is useful in the case of *alltoallv*; results in *alltoallv* show that *delay* is up to 2.5 times faster than *pairwise*. The PE in *pairwise* issues a pair of *send* and *receive* operations at each step, and waits for the completion of both operations until the next step. Therefore, the larger the difference in the message sizes of the pairs, the more the unnecessary waiting time

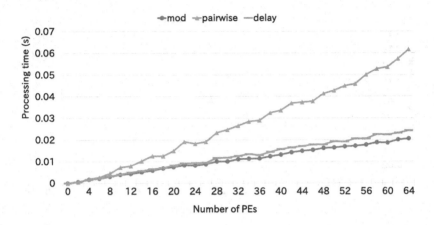

Fig. 5. Comparison of processing times in the *alltoallv* communication structures. The horizontal axis represents the number of PEs and the vertical axis represents the average processing time for a m2m communication.

increases. For *gatherv*, the processing time in *delay* and *pairwise* was equivalent by less than 5%. For scatter, *delay* reduced the processing time by up to 1.1 times compared with *pairwise*. This is because the root rank of *pairwise* waits for the completion of every *send* operation to make the communications sequential.

6   Conclusion

In this paper, we proposed a method to insert a minimum delay for imbalanced m2m communication under the condition of avoiding contention. The proposed method consists of two techniques: an estimate of contention using an arrival-consumption model, contention avoidance using systematic delay insertion. The first technique defines the occurrence of contention by the ability of message consumption at the receiver bottleneck for the gather structure. The second technique independently optimizes the delay in each gather structure of the m2m communication with a statistical approach. The schedule for each gather structure implicitly determines the communication schedule for the entire m2m communication.

The experimental results show that the proposed method performs comparable to or higher than the existing methods for arbitrary communication structures. For communication structures with a large variance in the number of *receive* operations, the proposed method achieved a speedup of up to 10 times compared with a simple extension of the algorithm for all-to-all to m2m communication. On the other hand, the proposed method achieves comparable performance for balanced m2m communication.

One of the future challenges will be to extend the proposed scheduling method for more practical environments where multiple switches are deployed with eager and rendezvous protocols [4].

Acknowledgment. This study was supported in part by the Japan Society for the Promotion of Science KAKENHI Grant Numbers JP22K11972 and JP20K21794. The authors would like to thank the anonymous reviewers for helpful comments to improve their paper.

References

1. Chen, Y., Griffith, R., Liu, J., Katz, R.H., Joseph, A.D.: Understanding TCP incast throughput collapse in datacenter networks. In: Proceedings of the 1st ACM Workshop Research on Enterprise Networking (WREN), pp. 73–82 (2009)
2. Demmel, J., Hoemmen, M., Mohiyuddin, M., Yelick, K.: Avoiding communication in sparse matrix computations. In: Proceedings of the 22nd IEEE International Parallel and Distributed Processing Symposium (IPDPS) (2008)
3. Gabriel, E., et al.: Open MPI: goals, concept, and design of a next generation MPI implementation. In: Kranzlmüller, D., Kacsuk, P., Dongarra, J. (eds.) EuroPVM/MPI 2004. LNCS, vol. 3241, pp. 97–104. Springer, Heidelberg (2004). https://doi.org/10.1007/978-3-540-30218-6_19
4. Ino, F., Fujimoto, N., Hagihara, K.: LogGPS: a parallel computational model for synchronization analysis. In: Proceedings of the 8th ACM SIGPLAN Symposium on Principles and Practice of Parallel Programming (PPoPP), pp. 133–142 (2001)
5. Karwande, A., Yuan, X., Lowenthal, D.K.: CC-MPI: a compiled communication capable MPI prototype for ethernet switched clusters. In: Proceedings of the 9th ACM SIGPLAN Symposium on Principles and Practice of Parallel Programming (PPoPP), pp. 95–106 (2003)
6. Kwak, B.J., Song, N.O., Miller, L.E.: Performance analysis of exponential backoff. IEEE/ACM Trans. Netw. **13**(2), 343–355 (2005)
7. Message Passing Interface Forum: MPI: A Message-Passing Interface Standard Version 4.0 (2021). https://www.mpi-forum.org/docs/mpi-4.0/mpi40-report.pdf
8. Okuyama, T., et al.: Accelerating ODE-based simulation of general and heterogeneous biophysical models using a GPU. IEEE Trans. Parallel Distrib. Syst. **25**(8), 1966–1975 (2014)
9. Shen, J., Ino, F., Farrés, A., Hanzich, M.: A data-centric directive-based framework to accelerate out-of-core stencil computation on a GPU. IEICE Trans. Inf. Syst. **E103-D**(12), 2421–2434 (2020)
10. Thakur, R., Rabenseifner, R., Gropp, W.: Optimization of collective communication operations in MPICH. Int. J. High Perform. Comput. Appl. **19**(1), 49–66 (2005)
11. Wonnacott, D.G., Strout, M.M.: On the scalability of loop tiling techniques. In: Proceedings of the 3rd International Workshop Polyhedral Compilation Techniques (IMPACT), pp. 3–11 (2013)

Optimization (1)

Optimizing Depthwise Convolutions on ARMv8 Architecture

Ruochen Hao[2], Qinglin Wang[1(✉)], Shangfei Yin[2], Tianyang Zhou[2], Qingyang Zhang[2], Songzhu Mei[1], Siqi Shen[3], and Jie Liu[2]

[1] Science and Technology on Parallel and Distributed Processing Laboratory, National University of Defense Technology, Changsha 410073, China
wangqinglin_thu@163.com
[2] College of Computer, National University of Defense Technology, Changsha 410073, China
[3] Xiamen University, Xiamen, China

Abstract. Depthwise convolutions are widely used in lightweight convolutional neural networks (CNNs). The performance of depthwise convolutions is mainly bounded by the memory access rather than the arithmetic operations for classic convolutions so that direct algorithms are often more efficient than indirect ones (matrix multiplication-, Winograd-, and FFT-based convolutions) with additional memory accesses. However, the existing direct implementations of depthwise convolutions on ARMv8 architectures feature a bad trade-off between register-level reuse of different tensors, which usually leads to sub-optimal performance. In this paper, we propose a new direct implementation of depthwise convolutions by means of implicit padding, register tiling, etc. Compared to the existing ones, our new implementations can incur much less communication overhead between registers and cache. Experimental results on two ARMv8 CPUs show that our implementation can averagely deliver 4.88× performance improvement over the existing direct ones in open-source libraries.

Keywords: CNNs · Depthwise Convolution · ARMv8 · Direct Convolution · Parallel Algorithm

1 Introduction

Convolution Neural Networks (CNNs), a class of artificial neural networks, have achieved amazing success in various machine learning tasks, such as image classification [5], object detection [9], and medical image diagnostics [19]. The building blocks of CNNs mainly involve convolutional, pooling, normalization, and fully connected layers. In general, the training and inference of CNNs require a large quantity of computation and memory resource, which are primarily consumed by convolutional layers. The optimization of convolutional layers plays a vital role in improving the performance of CNNs.

Supported by the National Natural Science Foundation of China under Grant No. 62002365.

H. Takizawa et al. (Eds.): PDCAT 2022, LNCS 13798, pp. 441–452, 2023.
https://doi.org/10.1007/978-3-031-29927-8_34

Now, many lightweight models have been proposed for mobile computing systems, such as MobileNetV1 [6], MobileNetV2 [18] and MnasNet-A1 [20]. These models often consist of a type of convolutions that adopt a single filter for each channel of input feature maps, named depthwise convolutions. In comparison with typical convolutions, depthwise convolutions have much less arithmetic operations and fewer parameters for filters. The sharp reduction of the arithmetic complexity makes the performance of depthwise convolutions is basically bounded by the hierarchical memory bandwidth rather than the peak performance on most platforms [28].

There are four common methods to perform convolutions, including matrix multiplication [8,25], Winograd [24], Fast Fourier Transform (FFT) [7,23] and direct algorithms [27]. All the three indirect algorithms introduce the additional transformations, which increase the total overhead of memory access. As a result, the direct algorithm has become a good choice for high-performance depthwise convolutions due to its relatively less memory access.

Although GPUs are the main hardware platforms in deep learning fields, there are many factors to motivate CNNs running on resource-constrained systems including mobile devices (computational and energy constraints) and CPU-based servers (computational constraints relative to popular GPUs) [12]. In mobile computing systems, CPUs maybe perform better than GPU in terms of performance and power consumption. Among all the mobile CPUs, the ones based on the ARMv8 architecture have got the largest market share. Moreover, ARMv8 CPUs are rapidly appearing in high performance computing systems, e.g. Mont-Blanc prototype [16], Tianhe-3 prototype [26], and Fugaku supercomputer [11]. Therefore, it's of great significance to optimize direct depthwise convolutions on ARMv8 CPUs.

In deep learning, the two most common data layouts on multi-core CPUs are NHWC (mini-batch, height, weight, channel) and NCHW (mini-batch, channel, height, weight). The latter exhibits better data locality for convolutions so that it is the default layout for Caffe, Mxnet, and Pytorch frameworks [2,8,14]. But the depthwise convolutions with NCHW layout feature much more irregular memory access under the vectorized optimization, which largely increase the difficulty of optimization. Existing open-source direct implementations with NCHW layout on ARMv8 architecture are not able to achieve a good balance between the register-level reuse of input and output feature maps tensors shown in Sect. 2, and often get sub-optimal performance.

This paper focuses on effective direct implementation of depthwise convolutions with NCHW layout. In order to optimize direct depthwise convolutions, many common techniques like register tiling [17], vectorization, and multithreading are collaboratively adopted in our work. The most critical part of our work is how register tiling and implicit padding are applied in the micro-kernel design because it greatly reduces the communication between register and cache under the vectorized optimization with complex access patterns. The main contributions of this paper can be concluded as follows.

- We analyze existing implementations of depthwise convolutions on ARMv8 architecture in detail. It's found that the existing direct implementations cannot achieve a good balance among the register-level reuse of all the tensors.

- We propose a new algorithm with good balanced register-level reuse for depth-wise convolutions by means of implicit padding, register tiling, etc., which has less communication overhead between registers and cache. And, the arithmetic intensities of the new algorithm and the existing ones are introduced to compare their theory performances.
- The new algorithm is benchmarked with all different depthwise convolutional layers from MobileNetV1 [6] and MobileNetV2 [18] on two ARMv8-based processors, Phytium FT1500A 16-core CPUs and Marvell ThunderX 48-core CPUs, and are compared with the direct implementations in open-source libraries Tengine, FeatherCNN, ncnn, and ARM Compute Library. The experimental results show that our new algorithm can achieve speedups of up to 2.73×, 6.15×, 7.61×, and 36.38× against Tengine, FeatherCNN, ncnn, and ARM Compute Library respectively. The optimizations are further confirmed by the inference speedup for MobileNetV1 and MobileNetV2, after the new algorithm is used to replace the corresponding kernel in Pytorch.

The structure of this paper is as follows. Section 2 describes the definition of depthwise convolutions, and discusses the relevant existing implementations in detail. Our new implementation is presented in Sect. 3, and the arithmetic intensities are also analyzed. Section 4 shows the benchmark results on two ARMv8-based CPUs. The conclusion of this paper and the future work can be found in the final section.

2   Analysis of Existing Implementations

The forward propagation of depthwise convolutions takes the input feature maps ($\mathcal{I}$) and filters ($\mathcal{F}$), and produces the output feature maps ($\mathcal{O}$). In NCHW layout, these tensors are expressed as $\mathcal{I}[N][C][H_i][W_i]$, $\mathcal{F}[C][H_f][W_f]$ and $\mathcal{O}[N][C][H_o][W_o]$. Thus, depthwise convolution is defined by

$$\mathcal{O}_{n,c,h_o,w_o} = \sum_{h_f=0}^{H_f-1} \sum_{w_f=0}^{W_f-1} (\mathcal{I}_{n,c,h_o \times s+h_f-p_t, w_o \times s+w_f-p_l} \\ \times \mathcal{F}_{c,h_f,w_f}),$$

(1)

where $0 \leq n < N$, $0 \leq c < C$, $0 \leq h_o < H_o$, $0 \leq w_o < W_o$, N is the mini-batch size, C is the number of channels, $H_{i/o/f}$ and $W_{i/o/f}$ denote the spatial height and width, $p_{t/l}$ refers to the padding size in the spatial dimension, and s is the stride size. In this paper, we mainly focus on depthwise convolutions with $H_f \times W_f = 3 \times 3$ and $s \in \{1, 2\}$, which are the most common cases in lightweight models. From the Eq. 1, it can be found that the forward propagation is actually performing N batched matrix-vetor multiplications. During the computation, the filters are the shared tensors and often small enough to be kept in the on-chip memory all the time. The input feature maps are streamed into the on-chip memory, and then the produced output feature maps are streamed back into the main memory. In other words, there is little space to optimize the access to the main memory, and we will mainly study the communication between cache

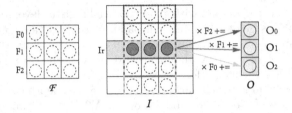

Fig. 1. Data reuse in Tengine where $H_f \times W_f = 3 \times 3$ and the stride size is 1.

and register in the following. We tested existing implementations of depthwise convolution in Tengine, FeatherCNN, ncnn and ARM Compute Library on two ARMv8 CPUs, and found that the best performance was achieved in most cases by Tengine. Tengine's implementation is illustrated in Fig. 1. In ARMv8 architecture, when the width of vector units is 128-bit, each vector unit can deal with 4 single precision numbers simultaneously. In Tengine, each row of $\mathcal{I}$ is only loaded one time from cache to vector registers while each row of $\mathcal{O}$ is repeatedly loaded from cache to vector registers. For each sample, the elements of $\mathcal{F}$ are also loaded into vector registers one time. In other words, in height direction, the elements of I in registers are reused H_f times while there is no reuse for the ones of $\mathcal{O}$. For example, I_r are reused three times to get O_{0-2} after loaded into registers, shown in Fig. 1. The elements of $\mathcal{O}_{0-2}$ are loaded into vector registers twice and stored back into cache three times. Therefore, we can find the philosophy in Tengine is reusing the elements of $\mathcal{I}$ in registers as much as possible so that the communication overhead of $\mathcal{O}$ between registers and cache are largely increased. The total communication between registers and cache is about
$$TC_{tg} = (N \times C \times H_i \times W_i + N \times C \times H_f \times W_f + 5 \times N \times C \times H_o \times W_o) \times 4$$
Bytes.

3   Our Approach

In this section, we will illustrate how the optimizing techniques are applied and analyze the arithmetic intensity.

3.1   Implementation

In depthwise convolutions, the elements of both $\mathcal{I}$ and $\mathcal{O}$ can be reused up to $H_f \times W_f$ times in registers. Each core in ARMv8 CPUs has only 32 vector registers so that we may need to load the same elements multiple times from cache to registers. As analyzed in Sect. 2, Tengine loads the elements of $\mathcal{O}$ multiple times while maximizing the reuse of the elements of $\mathcal{I}$. However, the repeated loading of $\mathcal{O}$ is always accompanied by the repeated reading and storing of $\mathcal{O}$ from registers to cache due to the accumulation. Therefore, our approach chooses to maximize the reuse of $\mathcal{O}$ in registers, and uses implicit padding, vectorization and register tiling techniques to maximize the reuse of $\mathcal{I}$ in registers, so that the total communication between registers and cache can be largely reduced. Our implementation is shown in Algorithm 1.

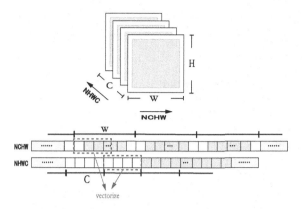

Fig. 2. The padded feature map in memory. The white and green blocks represent padded elements and input elements respectively. (Color figure online)

Implicit Padding. Compared to depthwise convolutions with NHWC layout, the ones with NCHW layout features irregular memory access, especially when dealing with padding. Figure 2 shows the way how the padding is carried out into the input feature maps with NCHW and NHWC layout. The vectorization is performed along width dimension and channel dimension in NCHW and NHWC data layout, respectively. The red blocks in Fig. 2 indicate that a vector may consist of input and padding elements simultaneously in NCHW layout, while a vector includes only padding elements or input elements from VL (vector length) channels in NHWC layout. Therefore, it's more difficult and expensive to deal with the padding under the vectorization optimization with NCHW layout. There are two common methods for padding. One method is explicitly padding input feature maps into a temporary space before computation, adopted by ncnn [22] and FeatherCNN [21]. The other is that the padding is implicitly done through data movement between registers during computation. In comparison with the former method, the latter brings the overhead of data movement in registers. However, the latter has only a half of the communication overhead between cache and registers in the former when only padding is considering. As the performance of depthwise convolution is mainly limited by memory access latency, our approach adopts the implicit padding to minimize the overhead of cache access in padding, shown in lines 13–14 of Algorithm 1.

Vectorization and Register Tiling. In convolutional operations, the filter firstly slides along the width dimension, so that the adjacent convolutions in the same row involve two overlapped regions from the input feature. To reduce the redundant loads, we vectorize the computations in width direction. Next, we divide the elements of $\mathcal{O}$ into blocks of $H_r \times W_r$ size in the height and width dimensions to fix the data used in the computation of a basic block in register. As the vectorization is carried out in the width dimension, W_r must be a multiple of VL. At the same time, H_r and W_r are also limited by the total number of vector registers in ARMv8 CPUs. The kernel function with $H_r \times W_r$ tiling is shown in

Algorithm 1: Our Implementation

input : Input feature maps $\mathcal{I}$, Filter $\mathcal{F}$
output: Output feature maps $\mathcal{O}$

1 **for** $n = 0: 1: N$ **do in parallel**
2   **for** $co = 0: C_b: C$ **do in parallel**
3   **for** $c = co: 1: co + C_b$ **do**
4       $vf_{0:H_f-1} = simd\_load(\mathcal{F}_{c,0:H_f-1,0})$
5   **for** $h_o = 0: H_r: H_o$ **do**
6   **for** $w_o = 0: W_r: W_o$ **do**
7   KernelHrxWr(n,c,h_o,w_o)
8 **Function** KernelHrxWr(n,c,h_o,w_o):
9   $W_n = W_r/VL$
10   $h_i = h_o \times s - p_t$
11   $w_i = w_o \times s - p_l$
12   **for** $r = 0: 1: H_f + (H_r - 1) \times s$ **do**
13   Step1: load $W_f + (W_r - 1) \times s$ elements from $\mathcal{I}_{n,c,h_i+r,w_i}$
14   Step2: extract padding/loaded elements into $vi_{0:W_n \times W_f-1}$
15   **for** $h = 0: 1: H_r$ **do**
16   **for** $h_f = 0: 1: H_f$ **do**
17   **if** $h \times s + h_f\, != r$ **then** break
18   **for** $w = 0: 1: W_n$ **do**
19   **for** $q = 0: 1: W_f$ **do**
20             $vo_{h \times W_n+w} = simd\_fma(vo_{h \times W_n+w}, vi_{w \times W_f+q}, vf_{h_f}[q])$
21   **for** $h = 0: 1: H_r$ **do**
22   Store $vo_{h \times W_n:(h+1) \times W_n-1}$ back into $\mathcal{O}_{n,c,h_o+h,w_o}$

lines 8–22 of Algorithm 1. The elements of $\mathcal{F}$ are loaded into registers $vf_{0:H_f-1}$ in advance in lines 4. There are $H_r \times W_r/VL$ registers for the $H_r \times W_r$ block of $\mathcal{O}$, namely, $vo_{0:H_r \times W_n-1}$. And $vo_{0:H_r \times W_n-1}$ are reused $H_f \times W_f$ times in the kernel function, and are only stored back into cache once. $H_f + (H_r - 1) \times s$ rows of $\mathcal{I}$ are involved to compute the $H_r \times W_r$ block of $\mathcal{O}$, and each row will be extracted into $W_f \times W_r/VL$ vectors, namely $vi_{0:W_f \times W_r/VL-1}$, through register manipulations, and the padding operation is performed implicitly in this step.

For a more intuitive description of the computation procedure, we will go through the examples depicted in Fig. 3 and Fig. 4. Figure 3 illustrates the case of unity stride. Without loss of generality, H_r and W_r are set to 2 and 8 in Fig. 3. We first load a row (r_1) of input and extract it into $vi_{0:5}$ along with padding elements. Then we multiply the corresponding elements of vf_0 and vf_1 to $vi_{0:5}$ as indicated by the red and blue arrows, and the generated results are accumulated to the output vectors $vo_{0:1}$ and $v0_{2:3}$. The elements in $vo_{0:3}$ are stored back until the final results of depthwise convolutions are acquired. Thus, when the stride is 1, the vectorization and register tiling strategy allow the elements of r_1 to be reused almost three times in width dimension and to be reused twice in height dimension, and the elements in $vo_{0:3}$ are reused 9 times. The case of stride 2 is shown in Fig. 4. The elements of the loaded row (r_1) are extracted into $vi_{0:2}$ with a stride of 2, as indicated by the different colors and numbers. The multiplication and accumulation operations follow the same process as the former case. The strategies play the same role in the case of stride 2, but exhibit much less reuse times on account of larger stride size. For example, in a kernel's computation, only the row r_2 is reused twice and the other rows $r_{0:1}$ and $r_{3:4}$ are used only once. In total, the register-level data locality is determined by the tiling size $H_r \times W_r$ and the stride size. The tiling size is mainly determined by maximizing attainable data locality in registers, and also limited by the total number of registers. As far as stride 1 is concerned, we adopt 4×4 tiling size in most cases. As the boundary part often requires additional logical judgement and can not be efficiently vectorized, the overhead of the boundary part increases

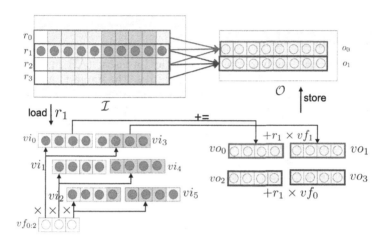

Fig. 3. A working example of our implementation of stride-1 depthwise convolutions on ARMv8 CPUs, where $VL = 4$, $H_f \times W_f = 3 \times 3$ and $H_r \times W_r = 2 \times 8$.

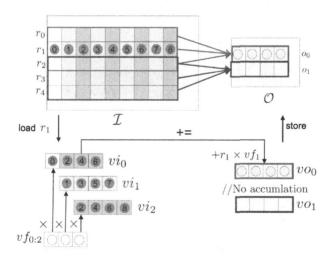

Fig. 4. A working example of our implementation of stride-2 depthwise convolutions on ARMv8 CPUs, where $H_f \times W_f = 3 \times 3$ and $H_r \times W_r = 2 \times 4$.

when the size $(H_i \times W_i)$ of feature maps become small. When the height of input size decreases to some threshold value, the implementation with 4×4 tiling size can only achieve suboptimal performance. Therefore, we lower the tiling size in height to 2 and increase the tiling size in width to 8 simultaneously to invoke the 2×8 kernel to handle the boundary. When it comes to stride-2 kernels, we get the best performance with 1×4 tiling size.

Additionally, register tiling also can increase the number of operations which can be processed in parallel and filled into the pipeline of ARMv8 CPUs, so that the latency of instructions can be efficiently hidden. It is worth noting that the function $KernelH_r \times W_r$ is implemented in assembly language, and all loops are unrolled.

3.2   Arithmetic Intensity

In this part, we will analyze the Arithmetic Intensity (AI) [4] of our optimized implementations and Tengine, which has the largest AI among the existing implementations. The total number of arithmetic operations is $TA = 2 \times N \times C \times H_o \times W_o \times H_f \times W_f$. When only the tiling size $H_r \times W_r$ is used, the total communication between registers and cache in our approach involves:

1. Loading $\mathcal{F}$ once for each batc h(Line 4). So the $\mathcal{F}$ incurs $TC_f = 4 \times N \times C \times H_f \times W_f$ bytes traffic.
2. Storing $\mathcal{O}$ once (Line 22). Thus the traffic of $\mathcal{O}$ is $TC_o = 4 \times N \times C \times H_o \times W_o$ bytes.
3. Loading $(W_r - 1) \times s + W_f$ elements of $\mathcal{I}$ in loop r (Line 13). So the traffic of $\mathcal{I}$ incurred by one complete execution of $KernelH_r \times W_r$ is $TC_{ik} = ((W_r - 1) \times s + W_f) \times ((H_r - 1) \times s + H_f)$. The $KernelH_r \times W_r$ is called $N \times C \times H_o/H_r \times W_o/W_r$ times. Hence the total traffic of $\mathcal{I}$ is $TC_i = 4 \times N \times C \times H_o/H_r \times W_o/W_r \times TC_{ik}$ bytes.

With the tiling size 4×4, the AI of our implementation is

$$AI_{ours} = \frac{TA}{TC_f + TC_o + TCi}$$
$$\approx \begin{cases} \frac{1}{(0.13 + 2/(H_o \times W_o))}(ops/Byte) \ s = 1 \\ \frac{1}{(0.31 + 2/(H_o \times W_o))}(ops/Byte) \ s = 2 \end{cases} \quad (2)$$

The AI of Tengine is:

$$AI_{tg} = \frac{TA}{TC_{tg}} \approx \begin{cases} \frac{1}{(1.33 + 2/(H_o \times W_o))}(ops/Byte) \ s = 1 \\ \frac{1}{(2 + 2/(H_o \times W_o))}(ops/Byte) \ s = 2 \end{cases} \quad (3)$$

Therefore, the AI of our implementation is larger than that of Tengine.

4   Experimental Evaluation

In this section, we firstly compare our algorithm to the existing ones in Tengine [13], FeatherCNN [21], ncnn [22] and ARM Compute Library (ACL) [1]. Secondly, we evaluate the full topology speedup of MobileNetV1 and MobileNetV2 based on our implementation.

4.1   Experimental Setup

We run our experiments on the following two ARMv8 processors:

Phytium FT1500A [3,15]: 1.5 GHz ARMv8 processor with 2 core groups each with 4 cores. Each core has 32 KB L1 instruction cache and 32 KB L1 data cache. 4 cores of a core group share 2 MB L2 cache.

Marvell ThunderX [10]: 2.0 GHz ARMv8 processor with 48 cores. Each core has 78 KB L1 instruction cache and 32 KB L1 data cache. All 48 cores share 16 MB L2 cache.

In the compilation of Pytorch, we use the OpenBLAS version 0.3.15 library to provide GEMM function. The depthwise convolutional layers from lightweight networks MobileNetV1 and MobileNetV2 are used in our tests. In the following tables and figures, MobileNetV1 and MobileNetV2 are labeled as v1 and v2. All the tests are iterated 10 times and the median runtime is reported as the result of each test.

4.2   Algorithm Performance

We compare our implementation against the existing ones in Tengine [13], FeatherCNN [21], ncnn [22] and ARM Compute Library (ACL) [1] using different cores. Tengine works best in most cases among four open implementations, so we normalize the performance to Tengine.

The relative single-core performance of five implementations on FT1500A and ThunderX is shown in Fig. 5(a) and Fig. 5(b), respectively. The x-axis indicates the different depthwise convolutional layers from MobileNetV1 and MobileNetV2, while the y-axis shows the speedup of five implementations over Tengine. In the test of the single-core performance, the mini-batch size of all layers is set to 1. The results show that our implementation is better than all four open implementations in all cases on these two ARMv8 platforms. Compared to Tengine, FeatherCNN, ncnn and ACL, our implementation obtains speedups up to 2.43×, 4.75×, 4.30×, 36.38× on FT1500A and 1.54×, 2.72×, 2.74×, 9.80× on ThunderX. When the same input size is adopted, the layers with stride 1 get much bigger speedup than the ones with stride 2. The main reason is that our approach reduces the access of output feature maps as much as possible and the larger output size let our implementation get higher performance improvements.

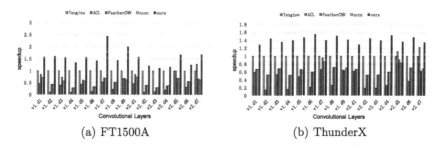

(a) FT1500A   (b) ThunderX

Fig. 5. Single-core performance of depthwise convolution implementations on FT1500A and ThunderX, where mini-batch size is 1 and performance is normalized to Tengine.

Figure 6(a) and Fig. 6(b) show the relative multi-core performances of our implementation on FT1500A and ThunderX. We set the mini-batch size to 256 since 256 is frequently used in network training. The results demonstrate that our approach surpasses FeatherCNN, ncnn, ACL on all tested layers and obtains speedups range from 1.36× to 5.67×, 1.23× to 5.70×, 3.83× to 14.66× on FT1500A and 1.86× to 6.15×, 2.48× to 7.53×, 9.1× to 28.62× on ThunderX. When compared to Tengine, our implementation exhibits higher performance in most tested layers and yields average speedups of 1.55× on FT1500A and 1.57× on ThunderX, respectively.

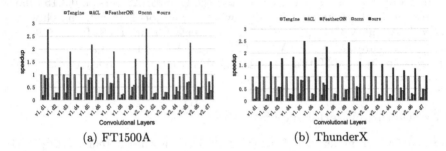

(a) FT1500A   (b) ThunderX

Fig. 6. Multi-core performance of depthwise convolution implementations on all 16 cores of FT1500A and 48 cores of ThunderX, where mini-batch size is 256 and performance is normalized to Tengine.

4.3 Full Topology Performance

Finally, we integrated our optimized implementation into Pytorch and evaluated the end-to-end inference speedup of MobileNetV1 and MobileNetV2 over original Pytorch. The experimental results under different number of threads and mini-batch sizes are provided in Table 1. For the inference of MobileNetV1 and MobileNetV2, our work achieves an average speedup of 4.23× and 3.67× against original Pytorch on FT1500A, and an average speedup of 9.24× and 7.36× against original pytorch on ThunderX.

Table 1. Inference speedup for MobileNetV1/MobileNetV2 of our work against original pytorch. tx denotes that x threads is used and tx/y means x threads is used on FT1500A and y threads is used on ThunderX. bx indicates that mini-batch size is x.

	FT1500A		ThunderX	
	MobileNetV1	MobileNetV2	MobileNetV1	MobileNetV2
$t1, b1$	3.04×	2.62×	4.26×	2.38×
$t16/48, b16$	7.00×	5.97×	19.76×	15.89×
$t16/48, b32$	5.28×	4.54×	13.21×	10.94×
$t16/48, b64$	3.74×	3.66×	8.39×	6.90×
$t16/48, b128$	2.85×	2.65×	5.81×	4.53×
$t16/48, b256$	3.44×	2.60×	4.03×	3.51×

5 Conclusion

In this paper, we propose a new direct implementation of depthwise convolutions on ARMv8 architectures. Our algorithm improve the register-level data locality through implicit padding, vectorization, register tiling and multi-threading techniques so that the communication between cache and registers is optimized. And the arithmetic intensities are analyzed as well. Through the experiments on two ARMv8 CPUs, we show that the new implementations can get better performance than existing implementations and reduce the overhead of end-to-end lightweight CNNs inference on ARMv8 CPUs.

References

1. ARM: Compute library (2021). https://github.com/ARM-software/ComputeLibrary. Accessed 3 Sept 2021
2. Chen, T., et al.: MXNet: a flexible and efficient machine learning library for heterogeneous distributed systems (2015)
3. Chen, X., Xie, P., Chi, L., Liu, J., Gong, C.: An efficient SIMD compression format for sparse matrix-vector multiplication. Concurr. Comput.: Pract. Exp. **30**(23), e4800 (2018)
4. Harris, M.: Mapping computational concepts to GPUs. In: ACM SIGGRAPH 2005 Courses, SIGGRAPH 2005, p. 50-es. Association for Computing Machinery, New York (2005). https://doi.org/10.1145/1198555.1198768
5. He, K., Zhang, X., Ren, S., Sun, J.: Delving deep into rectifiers: surpassing human-level performance on ImageNet classification. In: Proceedings of the IEEE International Conference on Computer Vision. pp. 1026–1034 (2015)
6. Howard, A.G., et al.: MobileNets: efficient convolutional neural networks for mobile vision applications. CoRR (2017)
7. Huang, X., Wang, Q., Lu, S., Hao, R., Mei, S., Liu, J.: Evaluating FFT-based algorithms for strided convolutions on ARMv8 architectures. Perform. Eval. 102248 (2021). https://doi.org/10.1016/j.peva.2021.102248
8. Jia, Y., et al.: Caffe: convolutional architecture for fast feature embedding. In: Proceedings of the 22nd ACM International Conference on Multimedia, MM 2014, pp. 675–678. Association for Computing Machinery, New York (2014). https://doi.org/10.1145/2647868.2654889
9. Li, S., Dou, Y., Niu, X., Lv, Q., Wang, Q.: A fast and memory saved GPU acceleration algorithm of convolutional neural networks for target detection. Neurocomputing **230**, 48–59 (2017)
10. Marvell: Thunderx_CP family (2022). https://www.marvell.com/server-processors/thunderx-arm-processors/thunderx-cp. Accessed 1 Jan 2022
11. Matsuoka, S.: Fugaku and A64FX: the first exascale supercomputer and its innovative arm CPU. In: 2021 Symposium on VLSI Circuits, pp. 1–3 (2021). 10.23919/VLSICircuits52068.2021.9492415
12. Mittal, S., Rajput, P., Subramoney, S.: A survey of deep learning on CPUs: opportunities and co-optimizations. IEEE Trans. Neural Netw. Learn. Syst. 1–21 (2021). https://doi.org/10.1109/TNNLS.2021.3071762
13. OPEN AI LAB: Tengine (2021). https://github.com/OAID/Tengine. Accessed 3 Sept 2021
14. Paszke, A., Gross, S., Massa, F., et al.: PyTorch: an imperative style, high-performance deep learning library (2019)

15. Phytium: FT-1500A/16 (2022). https://www.phytium.com.cn/Product/detail?language=1&product_id=9. Accessed 1 Jan 2022
16. Rajovic, N., et al.: The Mont-Blanc prototype: an alternative approach for high-performance computing systems (2016)
17. Renganarayana, L., Bondhugula, U., Derisavi, S., Eichenberger, A.E., O'Brien, K.: Compact multi-dimensional kernel extraction for register tiling. In: Proceedings of the Conference on High Performance Computing Networking, Storage and Analysis, SC 2009, Association for Computing Machinery, New York (2009). https://doi.org/10.1145/1654059.1654105
18. Sandler, M., Howard, A., Zhu, M., Zhmoginov, A., Chen, L.C.: MobileNetv 2: inverted residuals and linear bottlenecks. In: 2018 IEEE/CVF Conference on Computer Vision and Pattern Recognition, pp. 4510–4520 (2018). https://doi.org/10.1109/CVPR.2018.00474
19. Singh, R.K., Gorantla, R.: DMENet: diabetic macular edema diagnosis using hierarchical ensemble of CNNs. PLOS One **15**(2), e0220677 (2020)
20. Tan, M., et al.: MnasNet: platform-aware neural architecture search for mobile. In: 2019 IEEE/CVF Conference on Computer Vision and Pattern Recognition (CVPR), pp. 2815–2823 (2019). https://doi.org/10.1109/CVPR.2019.00293
21. Tencent: FeatherCNN (2021). https://github.com/Tencent/FeatherCNN. Accessed 3 Sept 2021
22. Tencent: nCNN (2021). https://github.com/Tencent/ncnn. Accessed 3 Sept 2021
23. Wang, Q., Li, D., Huang, X., Shen, S., Mei, S., Liu, J.: Optimizing FFT-based convolution on ARMv8 multi-core CPUs. In: Malawski, M., Rzadca, K. (eds.) Euro-Par 2020. LNCS, vol. 12247, pp. 248–262. Springer, Cham (2020). https://doi.org/10.1007/978-3-030-57675-2_16
24. Wang, Q., Li, D., Mei, S., Lai, Z., Dou, Y.: Optimizing winograd-based fast convolution algorithm on phytium multi-core CPUs (in Chinese). J. Comput. Res. Dev. **57**(6), 1140–1151 (2020). https://doi.org/10.7544/issn1000-1239.2020.20200107
25. Wang, Q., Songzhu, M., Liu, J., Gong, C.: Parallel convolution algorithm using implicit matrix multiplication on multi-core CPUs. In: 2019 International Joint Conference on Neural Networks (IJCNN), pp. 1–7 (2019). https://doi.org/10.1109/IJCNN.2019.8852012
26. You, X., Yang, H., Luan, Z., Liu, Y., Qian, D.: Performance evaluation and analysis of linear algebra kernels in the prototype Tianhe-3 cluster. In: Abramson, D., de Supinski, B.R. (eds.) SCFA 2019. LNCS, vol. 11416, pp. 86–105. Springer, Cham (2019). https://doi.org/10.1007/978-3-030-18645-6_6
27. Zhang, J., Franchetti, F., Low, T.M.: High performance zero-memory overhead direct convolutions. In: International Conference on Machine Learning, pp. 5771–5780 (2018)
28. Zhang, P., Lo, E., Lu, B.: High performance depthwise and pointwise convolutions on mobile devices. In: Proceedings of the AAAI Conference on Artificial Intelligence, pp. 6795–6802. AAAI Press (2020)

A Profiling-Based Approach to Cache Partitioning of Program Data

Sergej Breiter[1]([✉]), Josef Weidendorfer[2], Minh Thanh Chung[1],
and Karl Fürlinger[1]

[1] MNM Team, Ludwig-Maximilians-Universität München, Munich, Germany
{sergej.breiter,chungmi,karl.fuerlinger}@nm.ifi.lmu.de
[2] Leibniz Supercomputing Centre (LRZ), Garching, Germany
josef.weidendorfer@lrz.de

Abstract. Cache efficiency is important to avoid unnecessary data transfers and to keep processors active. Cache partitioning, a technique to virtually divide a cache into multiple partitions, has become available in recent hardware. Cache partitioning can improve efficiency by isolating data with high temporal locality to avoid its early eviction before reuse. However, deciding on the partitioning is challenging, because it depends on the locality of reference. To facilitate the decision-making, we propose a profiling-based approach that measures locality, providing knowledge for cache partitioning without requiring manual code analysis. We present a profiling tool and confirm its benefits through experiments on Fujitsu's A64FX processor, which supports the cache partitioning mechanism called *sector cache*. Our results show ways to optimize program codes to improve cache efficiency.

Keywords: Cache partitioning · Reuse distance · A64FX · Sector cache

1 Introduction

Caches are small but fast memory, bridging the gap between processor and main memory performance. Because of their low capacity, it is important to keep data that is likely reused in the near future (high temporal locality). In case of a cache miss, the replacement policy decides which data is evicted. The optimal policy [3] always replaces data that is not reused for the longest period of time. However, this is impossible to know in advance, and the replacement decision must be based on heuristics. A popular heuristic is the Least Recently Used (LRU) policy: replacing the cache line that was unused for the longest period of time. But LRU is not optimal and expensive to implement in hardware, and many alternative policies have been proposed [10].

A method to improve the implemented policy is *cache partitioning*. Cache partitioning divides a cache into multiple partitions, each managing its own policy. Typically, partitions are assigned to processes or threads [14]. Nevertheless, cache partitioning can also improve the performance of an application by dividing and allocating its data into partitions. However, deciding on a partitioning policy for data is difficult [16].

H. Takizawa et al. (Eds.): PDCAT 2022, LNCS 13798, pp. 453–463, 2023.
https://doi.org/10.1007/978-3-031-29927-8_35

In this paper, we want to solve how to decide on an optimized partitioning policy for application data. We present a profiling tool that identifies program functions where cache partitioning reduces cache misses. To this end, the program's locality of reference is profiled with the *reuse distance* metric. Our approach uses reuse distance analysis at function-granularity to choose an optimized cache partitioning policy. The tool is implemented using Intel PIN [7] and evaluated with the NAS parallel benchmarks [2]. Our experiments are performed using the A64FX processor's *sector cache*, a hardware cache partitioning mechanism. The experimental results confirm an optimized partitioning policy decided from the profiling results per function, reducing cache misses up to 30% in the NAS parallel benchmarks.

The rest is organized as follows: Sect. 2, 3 summarize the background and explain our methodology with implementation. In Sect. 4, we describe the experiments, and the improvement in cache behavior. Section 5 covers related work. Finally, we conclude and discuss further improvements in Sect. 6.

2   Background

2.1   Reuse Distance

Reuse distance (or *stack distance*) is a hardware-independent measure of program locality. The reuse distance $RD(x)$ of a reference to element x is the number of **distinct** data elements that have been referenced since the last reference to x, or ∞ if x has not been referenced before [20]. Reuse distance is used to assess whether a reference is a hit or miss in a fully associative LRU cache with n cache lines by using a reference granularity of the cache line size [4].

$$\text{miss}(x, n) = \begin{cases} 1 & RD(x) \geq n \\ 0 & \text{otherwise} \end{cases} \tag{1}$$

Reuse distances can be calculated by processing a program's *memory trace* (sequence of memory references) with a *stack processing algorithm*. However, stack processing is expensive and statistical methods [8] as well as sampling-based methods [19] have been developed. Traditionally, the memory trace is obtained by instrumentation of a program's memory instructions. Recently developed lightweight methods [18,21] use address sampling based on hardware events.

With reuse distance, the cache behavior of a program can be analyzed over multiple cache sizes with only a single pass [17]. Reference counts are accumulated into a reuse distance histogram (*reuse profile*) according to their reuse distance. Given any cache size n, the sum of references with $RD(x) \geq n$ is the sum of cache misses occurring during program execution.

Concurrent Reuse Distance. Reuse distance cannot be directly applied to multithreaded programs. The per-thread references must be interleaved to model the cache behavior of a shared cache [20]. *Concurrent reuse distance* counts the number of distinct references between two consecutive references at the same address of all threads sharing a cache. It is no longer hardware-independent, because its value depends on the order of the reference interleaving [8]. Instrumentation is problematic to obtain the trace for concurrent reuse distance, because it changes the relative execution speeds of threads, altering the order of references. However, concurrent reuse distance provides good accuracy for loop-based parallel programs [8,22].

2.2 Cache Partitioning

Cache partitioning allows dividing a cache into multiple partitions. Generally, one can differentiate between software-based cache partitioning and hardware-based cache partitioning, e.g., Intel's Cache Allocation Technology (CAT) [7] or Fujitsu's sector cache [6]. The granularity of cache partitioning can be categorized into way-based, set-based, and block-based. Typical goals of cache partitioning are performance, security, fairness, and quality-of-service improvements. Many partitioning techniques focus on the policies that assign partitions of a shared cache to co-running applications or threads [14]. The sector cache, on the other hand, is intended to assign data within a single application to partitions.

Sector Cache. The A64FX sector cache is a way-based hardware cache partitioning mechanism for the L1 and L2 caches. The technical name for the hardware implementation is *instruction-based way partitioning* [16]. It was first employed in the SPARC64VIIIfx processor [23], a predecessor of the A64FX. The partitioning policy (partition sizes and data assignment) can be changed dynamically at runtime without flushing the cache. Partition sizes are set by allocating a number of cache ways to partitions (*sectors*). The partition is specified on each memory instruction by *memory tagging* in the otherwise unused top byte of virtual addresses. More details can be found in the A64FX documentation [6].

Example 1. Listing 1.1 provides an example of using the sector cache with the Fujitsu C/C++ Compiler (FCC) directives in a Dense Matrix Transposed Vector Multiplication (DMTVM) code. The first directive specifies the number of cache ways allotted to Sector 1 in the L1 and L2 cache (N1 and N2). The remaining cache ways belong to Sector 0. The second directive specifies the data (m) assigned to Sector 1. Other data is assigned by default to Sector 0. Together, the procedure-directives specify the partitioning policy for the enclosing function. A more fine-grained policy can be specified using begin and end delimiters.

```
1  #pragma procedure scache_isolate_way L2=N2 L1=N1
2  #pragma procedure scache_isolate_assign m
3  #pragma omp for
4      for (int i = 0; i < nrow; ++i)
5          for (int j = 0; j < ncol; ++j)
6              x[j] += m[i * ncol + j] * b[i];
```

Listing 1.1. DMTVM using FCC sector cache compiler directives.

The DMTVM code is a simple example where performance can benefit from cache partitioning. The matrix data m is streamed while the vector x is used in each row. When the size of x is below the cache capacity, x can in principle be reused with LRU. However, if the size of x is above half the cache capacity, x is evicted from cache before it gets reused due to the accesses to m. Assigning m to a partition with minimal capacity increases the available cache space for x, potentially reducing cache misses.

3   Implementation and Experimental Methodology

Our tool consists of two phases shown in Fig. 1: (1) profiling and (2) reuse distance analysis. In phase 1, a binary executable compiled from the original code is automatically instrumented with the profiler to generate the reuse profile. The reuse profile contains profiling data for each *data object* (heap-allocated memory region) and each function. The reuse profile is analyzed in phase 2 to determine an optimized partitioning policy per function w.r.t. the target architecture's cache capacity. In the end, we (manually) apply the policy to the source code functions with the FCC sector cache directives.

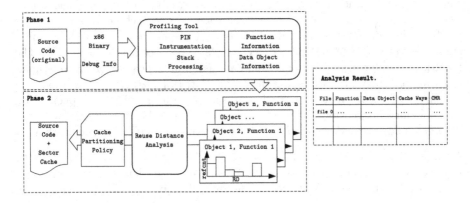

Fig. 1. Profiling tool and workflow

3.1   Profiler Components

The profiler instruments (1) memory instructions, (2) dynamic memory allocations, and (3) function calls. Additionally, debug information is read from the binary debug section to associate profiling data with symbols, file names, and line numbers of the source code. In detail, the three components are:

- **Memory Instructions**: are instrumented to retrieve their virtual address to calculate their reuse distance. We use the algorithm by Kim et al. [9] which uses a linked-list, representing a LRU stack, and a hash map to store positions within the stack. Since we consider concurrent reuse distance, multiple threads operate on shared data (hash map, linked-list). Therefore, the algorithm invocations are synchronized using a lock, and we choose the MCS lock [13]. The main reason is to provide fairness for the interleaving of thread's references in stack [19].

- **Memory Allocations**: the C standard dynamic memory allocation functions, i.e., `malloc`, are instrumented to retrieve the starting address, size, and code line of data objects. In the case of deallocation (`free`), the data object is invalidated. To identify whether a particular data object is referenced by a memory instruction, we can compare its address with the range [start, start + size) of the valid data objects. References without associated data objects, e.g., stack variables, are assigned to a special data object. Allocations with size < 10KB are also assigned to this data object.
- **Function Calls**: are instrumented to mark their entry and exit. We account for memory instructions inside a function in *per-function* reuse profiles. Based on the *per-function* profiles, we can decide a partitioning policy at function-granularity. However, data object accesses via aliasing pointers must be tagged explicitly with the aliasing pointer name instead of the data object variable name in the FCC directives. For example, Listing 1.2 shows a call to `Foo` where accesses via x must be tagged in the source code to assign a to a partition. Therefore, the variable name and position of function pointer parameters are retrieved in the first place using debug information. When a function is called, its pointer parameters can be associated with data objects by comparing the addresses. For this, function inlining and several interprocedural compiler optimizations must be disabled.

```
void Foo(double *x) { /* ... */ }
double *a = malloc(SIZE); Foo(a);
```

Listing 1.2. Function pointer-parameter problem

Binary Instrumentation. We use Intel PIN [7] to instrument the binary executable. PIN facilitates injecting arbitrary analysis code into a binary *just-in-time*, e.g., inspecting virtual addresses of memory instructions during execution. Another key aspect of choosing PIN is the ability to insert analysis code before and after a function is invoked. The input to the profiler is a compiled x86-binary and the output is profiling data used in the analysis phase.

3.2 Cache Partitioning Policy

We model the effect of assigning a data object D to a cache partition by maintaining two LRU stacks for D and calculating reuse distances in those stacks. Each of the stacks represents a cache partition. References to D are processed in the first stack, while the remaining references are processed in the second stack.

With Eq. (1), we can calculate the number of cache misses for arbitrary partition sizes n_0 and n_1 from the reuse distances of references in the two stacks:

$$\text{sum\_miss}(D, n_0, n_1) = \underbrace{\sum_{x \in D} \text{miss}(x, n_0)}_{\text{partition 0}} + \underbrace{\sum_{x \notin D} \text{miss}(x, n_1)}_{\text{partition 1}} \qquad (2)$$

The optimal cache partitioning policy P_{opt} for a cache with n cache lines minimizes the number of cache misses under the constraint $n = n_0 + n_1$:

$$P_{opt} = (D, n_0, n_1)_{opt} = \underset{(D, n_0, n_1)}{\arg\min}(\text{sum\_miss}(D, n_0, n_1)) \qquad (3)$$

The estimated cache miss reduction using this policy can be calculated by comparison to the policy without partitioning $P_{\emptyset} = (\emptyset, 0, n)$.

3.3 Limitations

The cache miss model from Eq. (2) assumes a fully associative true-LRU policy. It does not model conflict misses due to limited associativity in set-associative caches, and deviations from the true-LRU replacement policy. Also, cache misses caused by hardware prefetching or coherence traffic are not counted.

PIN does not support instrumenting ARM binaries. Therefore, we use an x86-binary for profiling. Since the reuse distance depends only on a program's memory access pattern, we can use the profiling results across other architectures. However, using a different compiler can alter the access pattern e.g. because of the optimization passes.

4   Experimental Results

4.1 Experimental Setup

We profile single- and multi-core benchmark runs with 12 threads (number of cores sharing a L2 cache on A64FX) using the x86-based AMD Epyc 7742 processor (64 cores). GCC v7.5.0 is used with the flags -O3 -g -march=native -fno-inline -fno-ipa-sra -fno-ipa-cp.

We evaluate our approach using the sector cache of a 48-core A64FX processor. Each core has a private L1 cache (64KiB, 4-way set-associative). The machine has four NUMA domains with 12 cores each, sharing a (last-level) L2 cache (8MiB, 16-way set-associative). The binaries for the A64FX are compiled by FCC 4.5.0 with the compiler flags -Kfast -Kopenmp -Kocl. We enforce thread pinning and placement on cores of a single NUMA domain using OpenMP.

We use the FCC sector cache directives to modify source code for cache partitioning policies when the profiling results indicate an advantage of using sector cache. Occurring cache misses (L1D_CACHE_REFILL and L2D_CACHE_REFILL performance events) in the original and modified version are measured with PAPI [15] to determine the measured cache miss reduction (CMR m.):

CMR m. $= 1 - $ sum_miss(modified)/sum_miss(original). Finally, for comparison, we calculate the predicted cache miss reduction (CMR p.) from the profiler results with Eq. (2), where CMR p. $= 1 - $ sum_miss(P_{opt}) / sum_miss$(P_\emptyset)$.

4.2 Workload

First, a proof of concept is shown using the DMTVM from Example 1. Second, we further evaluate our approach using the NAS parallel benchmarks [2] (BT, CG, EP, IS, LU, FT, MG, SP with recent C++ implementation [12]) in the working set sizes Class A, B, and C. Since the profiling involves a huge overhead ($>$ x100), we reduced the iteration count of the benchmarks to achieve shorter run times during profiling. This, however, does not change the locality of the program loops.

4.3 Dense Matrix Transposed Vector Multiplication

We expect the tool to decide on a policy for the DMTVM that assigns the matrix data m to a partition with a minimum size, when the size of the reusable vector x is above half the cache size, but fits into the remaining cache quota (36–48 KiB for the L1 and 4–7 MiB for the L2 cache). In this case, the CMR value is expected to be approximately 50%, because about half of the accesses are made to x which can be reused when it is isolated from the interfering accesses to m. We set the vector size to 40 KB (single-thread L1) and 6000 KB respectively.

Table 1 shows the measured and predicted L1 and L2 cache miss reduction (CMR m. and CMR p.) using the optimized partitioning policy. The values are approximately the same for vector size 6000 KB, even with parallel execution. However, the measured value of vector size 40 KB is lower than expected. The A64FX L1 cache has low associativity, and conflict misses are not modeled with reuse distance. This presumably explains the deviation from the prediction.

Table 1. Comparison of measured and predicted L1 and L2 CMR for DMTVM.

Function	Vec. Size [KB]	Cores	Object	Cache-level	Ways	CMR m. [%]	CMR p. [%]
dmtvm	40	1	m	1	1	42.96	50.12
dmtvm	6000	1	m	2	2	49.69	50.00
dmtvm	6000	12	m	2	2	49.07	50.01

4.4 NAS Parallel Benchmarks

The IS, EP, and FT profiling results indicated no advantage from using the A64FX sector cache. Therefore, we only discuss the results of CG, LU, and MG that profit from the sector cache in detail (see Table 2). We focus on the most significant functions in the benchmarks.

Table 2. Cache partitioning policy with measured and predicted L2 CMR.

Function	Benchmark	Cores	Object	L2 ways	CMR m. [%]	CMR p. [%]
conj_grad	CG C	1	a, colidx	2	0.92	1.37
conj_grad	CG C	12	a, colidx	2	1.25	1.23
ssor	LU B	1	u, b	2	18.18	45.37
ssor	LU B	12	u, b	2	17.88	38.24
ssor	LU C	1	rsd, b	13	8.94	14.29
ssor	LU C	12	rsd, a	13	-	16.84
resid	MG C	1	u	13	30.71	28.46
psinv			r	13	26.21	45.51

CG. CG is a conjugate gradient program, spending most of its time in the function `conj_grad` on a Sparse Matrix-Vector Multiplication (SpMV): $q = Ap$ (Listing 1.3). q and p are dense vectors and a is the sparse matrix stored in Compressed Row Storage (CRS) format. `rowstr` and `colidx` are the matrix row and column index arrays. Isolating `colidx` and a in a minimal cache space of the L2 cache is the suggested partitioning policy. This policy improves reuse of vector q and p by preventing them from being thrashed by the streaming access to `colidx` and a. Due to the irregular access pattern, cache blocking cannot be easily applied to SpMV, but cache partitioning can reduce cache misses.

```
for(j = 0; j < lastrow - firstrow + 1; j++) {
    q[j] = 0.0;
    for(k = rowstr[j]; k < rowstr[j+1]; k++)
        q[j] += a[k]*p[colidx[k]];
}
```

Listing 1.3. SpMV in the function `conj_grad` of the CG benchmark.

LU. LU is a Gauss-Seidel, spending most of the time in the function `ssor`. For LU class B, the suggested partitioning policy isolates data in a partition with minimal cache space. The policy is the same for 1 or 12 threads, but the measured CMR is lower than predicted. The indicated policy for class C with one thread is different, but a reduction in cache misses was achieved. With 12 threads, the suggested policy did not lead to an improvement.

MG. MG is a 3D multi-grid method, spending most of the time in a loop calling the functions `resid` and `psinv`. Both functions perform similar stencil operations, but on different data. A remarkable result is that the suggested partitioning policy differs in `resid` and `psinv`. This could be determined by using function-granularity profiles. Another interesting aspect is that the profiler indicates a cache miss reduction for class C using 1 thread, but not for 12 threads.

The 3D domain is decomposed due to the work-sharing using multiple threads, causing a shift in reuse distances. However, scaling the size of the 3D grid by the number of threads to compensate for the shift again leads to reductions in cache misses (36% CMR p. 14% CMR m.).

5   Related Work

The A64FX sector cache is a relatively understudied topic, with only a few works found. Alappat et al. [1] investigate the A64FX sector cache by applying it to DMTVM and SpMV. The authors report an extended high-performance level for larger vectors in DMTVM, and an improvement of 30% performance in SpMVs. Regarding cache partitioning policies based on profiling, many studies have been proposed [5,14]. Almost all of these works consider the cache partitioning problem for multiple co-running applications sharing a cache.

Lu et al. developed a profiling-based framework [11] that performs automatic cache partitioning of data objects for serial programs. The authors use multiple reuse profiles from varying training working set sizes and apply curve fitting to decide a partitioning policy for other inputs on the whole-program level. The most closely related work was introduced by Perarnau and Sato [16]. The authors develop profiling tool specifically for the SPARC64 VIIIfx processor. The user has to provide the symbol names of considered data objects in advance, and reuse profiles are generated on the whole-program level in serial. The work showed that a near-optimal partitioning policy could be predicted for their handcrafted 2D multigrid solver, reducing the number of cache misses up to 20%.

In contrast, our work differs in: (1) using concurrent reuse distance to optimize programs with multiple threads sharing a cache, and (2) allowing to decide a dynamic partitioning policy based on reuse profiles in function-granularity instead of whole-program granularity.

6   Discussion and Conclusions

In this paper, we have developed a profiling-based approach that enables deciding a cache partitioning policy in function-granularity. The policy improved cache efficiency, reducing cache misses up to 30% in the NAS benchmarks. The indicated policy did not always lead to the expected reduction in cache misses. Further investigation is required to determine the major factors limiting accuracy.

A partitioning policy placing data with a low temporal locality in a partition of minimal size (e.g. in CG class C, LU class B) was shown independent of the degree of parallelism. In contrast, the MG benchmark shows a relationship between the number of threads, working set size, and the resulting reuse distances. In this case, the policy must be adopted to those parameters.

Our profiling tool is not yet practical in its current state due to the profiling overhead. However, we argue that the approach is useful, because it helps deciding a partitioning policy for complex codes without requiring manual analysis.

Future Work. We plan to increase the prediction accuracy and reduce the profiling overhead. Another essential step will be training a model on profiling results for varying parameters to predict reuse distances across other input sizes and parallelizations. This was shown feasible for input parameters of the working set in prior work [11,24]. We want to extend those ideas to infer a pattern from multiple runs with a varied number of threads, including the effect of multithreading in the model.

Acknowledgement. This work has received funding from the European High-Performance Joint Undertaking under grant agreement no.956213 (SparCity), and the Federal Ministry of Education and Research of Germany (project number 16HPC045). Performance results have been obtained on systems in the test environment BEAST (Bavarian Energy Architecture & Software Testbed) (https://www.lrz.de/presse/ereignisse/2020-11-06_BEAST/) at the Leibniz Supercomputing Centre.

References

1. Alappat, C., et al.: Execution-Cache-Memory modeling and performance tuning of sparse matrix-vector multiplication and Lattice quantum chromodynamics on A64FX. Concurr. Comput.: Pract. Experience **34**(20), e6512 (2022). https://doi.org/10.1002/cpe.6512
2. Bailey, D.H., et al.: The NAS parallel benchmarks-summary and preliminary results. In: Proceedings of the 1991 ACM/IEEE Conference on Supercomputing, pp. 158–165. ACM (1991). https://doi.org/10.1145/125826.125925
3. Belady, L.A.: A study of replacement algorithms for a virtual-storage computer. IBM Syst. J. **5**(2), 78–101 (1966). https://doi.org/10.1147/sj.52.0078
4. Beyls, K., D'Hollander, E.: Reuse distance as a metric for cache behavior. In: Proceedings of the IASTED International Conference on Parallel and Distributed Computing and Systems, pp. 617–622 (2001)
5. El-Sayed, N., et al.: KPart: a hybrid cache partitioning-sharing technique for commodity multicores. In: 2018 IEEE International Symposium on High Performance Computer Architecture (HPCA), pp. 104–117 (2018). https://doi.org/10.1109/HPCA.2018.00019
6. Fujitsu Limited: A64FX Microarchitecture Manual, version 1.5 edn. (2021). https://github.com/fujitsu/A64FX/blob/master/doc/
7. Intel Corporation: Improving real-time performance by utilizing cache allocation technology. Intel Corporation (2015)
8. Jiang, Y., Zhang, E.Z., Tian, K., Shen, X.: Is reuse distance applicable to data locality analysis on chip multiprocessors? In: Gupta, R. (ed.) CC 2010. LNCS, vol. 6011, pp. 264–282. Springer, Heidelberg (2010). https://doi.org/10.1007/978-3-642-11970-5_15
9. Kim, Y.H., et al.: Implementing stack simulation for highly-associative memories. SIGMETRICS Perform. Eval. Rev. **19**(1), 212–213 (1991). https://doi.org/10.1145/107972.107995
10. Kumar, S., Singh, P.K.: An overview of modern cache memory and performance analysis of replacement policies. In: 2016 IEEE International Conference on Engineering and Technology, pp. 210–214 (2016). https://doi.org/10.1109/ICETECH.2016.7569243

11. Lu, Q., Lin, J., et al.: Soft-OLP: improving hardware cache performance through software-controlled object-level partitioning. In: 2009 18th International Conference on Parallel Architectures and Compilation Techniques, pp. 246–257 (2009). https://doi.org/10.1109/PACT.2009.35

12. Löff, J., et al.: The NAS parallel benchmarks for evaluating C++ parallel programming frameworks on shared-memory architectures. Future Gener. Comput. Syst. **125**(C), 743–757 (2021). https://doi.org/10.1016/j.future.2021.07.021

13. Mellor-Crummey, J.M., Scott, M.L.: Synchronization without contention. SIGPLAN Not. **26**(4), 269–278 (1991). https://doi.org/10.1145/106973.106999

14. Mittal, S.: A survey of techniques for cache partitioning in multicore processors. ACM Comput. Surv. **50**(2) (2017). https://doi.org/10.1145/3062394

15. Mucci, P.J., Browne, S., et al.: PAPI: a portable interface to hardware performance counters. In: Proceedings of the Department of Defense HPCMP Users Group Conference, vol. 710. Citeseer (1999)

16. Perarnau, S., Sato, M.: Toward automated cache partitioning for the K computer. IPSJ SIG-HPC (2012)

17. Sabarimuthu, J.M., Venkatesh, T.: Analytical miss rate calculation of L2 cache from the RD profile of L1 cache. IEEE Trans. Comput. **67**(1), 9–15 (2017). https://doi.org/10.1109/TC.2017.2723878

18. Sasongko, M.A., Chabbi, M., et al.: ReuseTracker: fast yet accurate multicore reuse distance analyzer. ACM Trans. Archit. Code Optim. **19**(1) (2021). https://doi.org/10.1145/3484199

19. Schuff, D.L., Kulkarni, M., Pai, V.S.: Accelerating multicore reuse distance analysis with sampling and parallelization. In: Proceedings of the 19th International Conference on Parallel Architectures and Compilation Techniques, pp. 53–64 (2010). https://doi.org/10.1145/1854273.1854286

20. Schuff, D.L., Parsons, B.S., Pai, V.S.: Multicore-aware reuse distance analysis. In: 2010 IEEE International Symposium on Parallel & Distributed Processing, Workshops and Phd Forum (IPDPSW), pp. 1–8 (2010). https://doi.org/10.1109/IPDPSW.2010.5470780

21. Wang, Q., Liu, X., Chabbi, M.: Featherlight reuse-distance measurement. In: 2019 IEEE International Symposium on High Performance Computer Architecture (HPCA), pp. 440–453. IEEE (2019). https://doi.org/10.1109/HPCA.2019.00056

22. Wu, M.J., Yeung, D.: Identifying optimal multicore cache hierarchies for loop-based parallel programs via reuse distance analysis. In: Proceedings of the 2012 ACM SIGPLAN Workshop on Memory Systems Performance and Correctness, pp. 2–11 (2012). https://doi.org/10.1145/2247684.2247687

23. Yoshida, T., Hondo, M., Kan, R., Sugizaki, G.: SPARC64 VIIIfx: CPU for the K computer. Fujitsu Sci. Tech. J **48**(3), 274–279 (2012)

24. Zhong, Y., Dropsho, S.G., et al.: Miss rate prediction across program inputs and cache configurations. IEEE Trans. Comput. **56**(3), 328–343 (2007). https://doi.org/10.1109/TC.2007.50

Optimization (2)

Memory Bandwidth Conservation for SpMV Kernels Through Adaptive Lossy Data Compression

Siyi Hu[1]([✉]), Makiko Ito[2], Takahide Yoshikawa[2], Yuan He[3],
and Masaaki Kondo[3,4]

[1] The University of Tokyo, Tokyo, Japan
hu@hal.ipc.i.u-tokyo.ac.jp
[2] Fujitsu Limited, Tokyo, Japan
[3] Keio University, Yokohama, Japan
[4] RIKEN Center for Computational Science, Kobe, Japan

Abstract. SpMV is a very common algorithm in linear algebra, which is widely adopted by machine learning applications nowadays. Especially, fully-connected MLP layers dominate many SpMV tasks that play a critical role in diverse services, and therefore a large fraction of data center cycles are spent. Despite exploiting sparse matrix storage techniques such as CSR/CSC, SpMV still suffers from limited memory bandwidth during data transferring because of the architecture of modern computing systems. However, we find that both integer type and floating-point type data used in matrix-vector multiplications are handled plainly without any necessary pre-processing. We added compression and decompression pre-processing between the main memory and Last Level Cache (LLC) which may dramatically reduce the memory bandwidth consumption. Furthermore, we also observed that convergence speed in some typical scientific computation benchmarks will not be degraded when adopting compressed floating-point data instead of the original double type. Based on these discoveries, in this paper, we propose a simple yet effective compression approach that can be implemented in general computing architectures and HPC systems preferably. When adopting this technique, a performance improvement of 1.92x is made in the best case.

Keywords: SpMV · Memory Bandwidth · Data Compression

1 Introduction

Sparse Matrix Vector Product (SpMV) is an important scientific computation kernel widely used in computational science computations as well as in graph processing and machine learning applications. Unlike ordinary matrices, sparse matrices store and compute information only on non-zero elements, making them highly efficient in terms of data volume and number of operations. Hence SpMV-based routines play an important role in many applications, such as Conjugate Gradients (CG) kernel, PageRank, and recommendation systems.

© The Author(s), under exclusive license to Springer Nature Switzerland AG 2023
H. Takizawa et al. (Eds.): PDCAT 2022, LNCS 13798, pp. 467–480, 2023.
https://doi.org/10.1007/978-3-031-29927-8_36

On the other hand, sparse matrices are known to cause processing bottlenecks, especially in memory accesses, because they are often too large to fit in the cache, the number of operations is small compared to the data accesses, and vector accesses are random. Therefore, the memory bandwidth almost always determines the performance, and the effective throughput is very small compared to the theoretical peak of a system. For example, the performance of the HPCG benchmark on the Fugaku supercomputer, which is dominated by SpMV processing, is about 16.0 PFLOPS, which is only about 3.0% of the peak state [1]. Therefore, the way to alleviate the memory bandwidth bottleneck is critical for overall improvement.

Several methods have been investigated to improve the data transfer bottleneck between the processor and the main memory. For example, lossless compression techniques can be used to reduce the data transfer volume [2]. However, sparse matrix data is usually floating-point data, and lossless compression has low compression efficiency and latency problems during decoding. Recently, the use of mixed-precision arithmetic, which actively uses low-precision data formats, has been considered [3,4]. On the other hand, the accuracy of the operation is reduced and convergence deteriorates, so double-precision floating-point operations must also be used in combination, resulting in overhead for switching data precision.

In this paper, we consider a method that reduces the amount of data transferred by automatically compressing, along with converting double-precision floating-point data to a lower precision format during memory accesses. With this scheme, it is possible to as well use mixed precision arithmetic easily whenever high precision is required to assure the accuracy of results.

We also evaluated the proposed method using sophisticated CG kernels and the results show that convergence speed was found to be not much different from that using double-precision floating-point numbers. Furthermore, the performance of the SpMV kernel in CG was evaluated using Onikiri2, a cycle-level processor simulator, and the result tells a 1.92x improvement at the best with our method.

The paper is organized as follows. Section 2 reviews the current status of SpMV processing and related work; Sect. 3 describes the data accuracy conversion mechanism for sparse matrix data structures used in SpMV; Sect. 4 illustrates evaluation experiments using the kernels of the CG method; Sect. 5 summarizes this work and discusses future issues.

2   Background

2.1   SpMV Kernel Overview

The Sparse Matrix-Vector Multiplication (SpMV) is one of the most important computational kernels today and is used in a wide range of applications, including structural analysis simulations and machine learning methods. The SpMV kernel is often used in iterative solvers for simultaneous linear equations

($Ax = b$), where the convergence of the solution requires many effective iterations. In particular, the larger the size of matrix A is, the larger the data and computational complexity are.

There are various data storage formats for sparse matrices, including compressed sparse row (CSR), compressed sparse column (CSC), and coordinate (COO). In this paper, the CSR format, which is the most common type, is used as a premise for the explanation. Unlike the conventional two-dimensional array, CSR format does not store values of zero elements in a matrix, while only non-zero elements are continuously stored in a contiguous space, known as the *Non-Zero List*. And, to indicate the position of each non-zero element in the original two-dimensional array, *Colidx*, an integer type array is used to hold the column index of each element in each row. Meanwhile, another integer array *Rowptr* indicates the index of the first non-zero element in each row of the *Non-Zero List*.

For sparse matrices with a high percentage of zero-valued elements, the CSR format can significantly reduce memory and storage usage. While, on the other hand, because of the indirect referencing caused by data structure, memory accesses are less efficient in the case of sparse matrix and vector products. References to vector data array are random and a single access to non-zero element in matrix also requires visiting both *Non-Zero List* and *Colidx* arrays at a time.

2.2   Performance Characteristics in SpMV Kernel

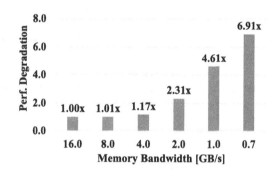

Fig. 1. Memory Bandwidth Bottleneck in SpMV Computation

As described in the previous subsection, the method of storing data in sparse matrix form reduces memory usage, but memory access is less efficient. For the SpMV kernel, which is a sparse matrix-vector product, if the non-zero elements are double-precision floating-point data, a total of 12B, one element (8B data) of *Non-Zero List*, and one element (4B data) of *Colidx*, must be accessed from memory for the power addition using one matrix element. In this case, the Byte/FLOP ratio of the SpMV kernel is 6. On the other hand, the hardware of the A64FX [5] processor used in the Fugaku supercomputer can provide a Byte/FLOP ratio of about 0.37, which is a large discrepancy from the

Byte/FLOP ratio required by the SpMV kernel. Therefore, the memory bandwidth is the most critical performance bottleneck for SpMV processing, and based on the Byte/FLOP ratio, A64FX can only provide about $0.37/6 = 6.17\%$ effective performance.

Specifically, we pre-evaluated the benchmark kernel described in Sect. 4.1 using a cycle-level processor simulator while changing the memory bandwidth. And, as shown in Fig. 1, there is no performance degradation up to about 4 GB/s. However, after that, as the memory bandwidth becoming lower, the performance degradation rate is almost as same as the bandwidth reduction rate, indicating that the SpMV kernel is the bottleneck for the overall throughput.

2.3   Related Work

Since SpMV is a very important kernel, many studies have been done to accelerate SpMV processing. For example, many SpMV kernel optimizations for GPUs and multi-core systems have been proposed [6–8]. Performance improvement techniques with efficient blocking for GPUs have also been proposed [9].

Grigoras et al. devised a compression algorithm for CSR-style non-zero element lists and implemented it in an FPGA-based accelerator [10]. The aim is to reduce the amount of data transferred from memory by using a hash table to compress and store the same non-zero element data in memory and reduce overhead and improve performance by using FPGAs to manage data compression while accelerating the computation process.

Sparse matrix data storage schemes have also been studied. Liu et al. proposed the CSR5 format as an improvement over the CSR format and reported a 3-fold performance improvement by using the SpMV algorithm for SIMD architectures [11]. Bian et al. proposed CSR2, an improved version of CSR5, which achieves a 1.5-fold performance improvement over CSR5 [12].

Although there have been many studies on SpMV for speeding up computations and storing data format, there have not been many studies on architectural methods to support mixed-precision computation. This research is considered novel in that it targets this point.

3   In-Memory Data Compression Architecture

In this section, we will first depict the target arrays, *Non-Zero List* and *Colidx*, which play essential roles in CSR data structure. And then, a corresponding data compression architecture, which may be implemented into the memory interface, is proposed in order to ease data transportation traffics between the main memory and LLC. To note that, *Rowptr* in CSR is also consuming data transportation bandwidth most of the time, however, this consumption is relatively tiny and could be blocked to fit on-chip memory hierarchies. Therefore, we will mainly focus on the two targets in later sections. Furthermore, we expect this technique to be suitable for other data structures such as CSC and COO with few changes.

3.1   Data Compression Memory Interface

As shown in Fig. 2, to ease memory bandwidth consumption during data transferring, we insert a simple yet efficient interface to the memory controller for data compression encoding and decoding functions.

In Fig. 2, the interface used to achieve data compression during runtime is appended to both the memory controller in the DRAM and processor side. This can help the processor decide the detailed parameters, such as precision adopted for floating-point data and memory address range that will be picked up for this procedure, and used to execute data compression. Therefore, when a read request is issued, dedicated raw data in the cache line is read from the main memory and will be encoded if the current cache line meets the standard of our schemes. After data is transferred through the bus, the processor will do the decoding operation. Meanwhile, when a write request has come in, the processor will do an encoding operation, and, on the contrary, the memory controller is to decode the data when it arrives at DRAM.

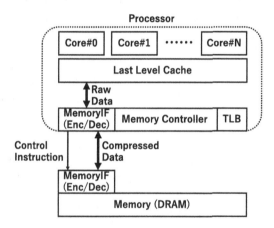

Fig. 2. Data Compression Interface Composed into Memory Controller I/F

Since this technique always targets the data in a whole cache line during data transfer, which is the same bit size as the one used for I/O operations on both the processor and memory, we may expect that it is feasible to perform this method without issuing extra CPU instructions or data formats to fit above compression/decompression procedures. Furthermore, since there is no change in addressing paradigms, extensions to CPU or cache architectures can be avoided and this also indicates that this approach could be effective yet lightweight.

Besides, we also expect this technique to handle specific data space, such as *Non-Zero List* and *Colidx*. In other words, data precision converting or data compression will be performed when the architecture detects dedicated ranges of address. In order to recognize the interesting address spaces, we suggest that extra parameter fields are needed to be added to page tables and TLBs. By setting up so, memory controllers are managed to differentiate target addresses from normal ones and perform our technique during physical/virtual address conversions. It is simply possible to clear these fields through system calls issued by the operating system. One limitation is, *Non-Zero List* and *Colidx* are required to be stored individually in pages, which may cause data fragmentation issues. However, since the size of the *Non-Zero List* and *Colidx* are expected to be huge, fragmentation will be a relatively tiny impact compared to actual data transferring overhead.

3.2   Data Compression Scheme

As stated in the previous section, to perform a data compression scheme during off-chip/on-chip across memory transferring, extra parameter fields and encoding/decoding principles are needed to be defined. For floating-point data type, it is considered to be more efficient to raise the compression ratio in return for sacrificing several significant bits, due to lacking considerable lossless compression schemes. While, when it comes to integer type *Colidx* which is in response to concisely point out the indices of each non-zero element, it is critical to remain the original value after decompression.

Therefore, we list the following data compression patterns based on common cache line size space (e.g. 64 Bytes), that will be discussed or verified in later sections: (1) **Double** type floating-point → 32-bit/16-bit **Float** type floating-point, (2) **Double** type floating-point → Custom scheme compressed floating-point, and (3) 32-bit **Integer** → Custom scheme compressed integer.

Specifically, pattern (1) is a common yet simple precision degradation converting scheme that has been adopted in various applications. However, despite its high compression ratio, since the *Exponent* part in a **Double** value is irreversibly converted from 11 bits to merely 5 bits or so, the impact is expected to be large on computation results where unacceptable errors may occur.

On the other hand, (2) and (3) using our proposed compression scheme aim to handle the balance between compression ratio and precision loss flexibly. In (2), we arrange the custom compression scheme as a combination of lossless compression and precision conversion methods for the *Exponent* part and *Significand* part respectively in one **Double** type value. For (3), we adopt a similar scheme used by the *Exponent* part in (2) since data in the same cache line tends to have the same characteristics as our compression scheme. By doing so, 32-bit integer values in *Colidx* can be decompressed without any precision loss. The rest of this section will discuss these custom schemes in detail.

Double Type Data Compression. As stated in previous sections, **Double** type floating-point data is mainly used in the *Non-Zero List*, a contiguous space, usually an array, storing the value of elements that is not 0 in a sparse matrix. *Non-Zero List* also possesses the largest memory usage in one CSR data structure. Currently, **Double** type floating-point data is commonly defined after the IEEE754 standard and has three parts within a 64-bit area: 1 bit of *Sign*, 11 bits of *Exponent*, and 52 bits of *Significand*. Our compression and precision conversion scheme for **Double** type floating-point data is shown in Fig. 3.

First of all, although depending on a specific dataset in each case, data in a contiguous address space tend to have similar values in SpMV based applications. In another word, for data values in the same cache line, their upper bits in *Exponent* have a considerable probability to be identical. We accordingly can pick up the upper n bits, which may be determined and configured flexibly, in each cache line and only store this part only once for all data. Then, for the rest $m = (11 - n)$ bits in *Exponent*, all data in the same cache line may have a unique value respectively and, therefore, need to be stored normally. Second, when it comes to the *Significand* part, most s bits are retained and the rest $52 - s$ bits will be discarded. Same as n, s could be as well defined and configured by user at an appropriate time. Furthermore, as *Non-Zero List* data is always read and treated as an operand in kernel computations, write-backs are not performed in most cases. This means that s can be adjusted dynamically to obtain various precision determined by need, and even original precision can be retrieved when necessary since original *Non-Zero List* values are still in the main memory.

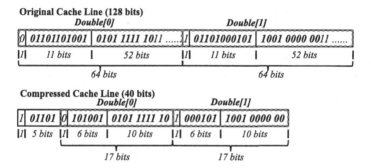

Fig. 3. Cache Line based **Double** Type Data Compression and Precision Conversion Scheme for *Non-Zero List*

Take the cache line shown in Fig. 3, a simple 16-Bytes space that may contain 2 **Doube** type floating-points, as an example. We set the parameter $n = 5$ here so that $m = 11 - 5 = 6$ accordingly, and meanwhile $s = 10$ to indicate only a 10-bit *Significand* will be maintained. As we can see, two **Double** values in this cache line both have the same upper $n = 5$ bits, so that it is recognized as available to our compression scheme. The first bit in this whole cache line will be set to indicate compression/decompression encoding is required during data transfers. And, following the flag bit, the common upper $n = 5$ bits in *Exponent* are aligned. Then, for each data, a sign bit followed by unique $m = 6$ bits lower part in *Exponent* and $s = 10$ bits of *Significand* are stored consecutively. More specifically, by performing the compression scheme to this sample 16-Byte cache line, the original size of 128 bits can be reduced to 40 bits during data transferring.

Table 1. Theoretical Compression Ratios for Different Patterns

(a) Theoretical **Double** Type Data Compression Ratio for a 64-Byte Cache Line using Different Patterns				
n	m	s	Total bits	Compression Ratio
4	7	10	149	3.43
5	6	10	142	3.61
6	5	10	135	3.79
7	4	10	128	4.00

(b) Theoretical **Signed Integer** Type Data Compression Ratio for a 64-Byte Cache Line using Different Patterns			
n	m	Total Bits	Compression Ratio
15	16	272	1.88
17	14	242	2.12
19	12	212	2.42
21	10	182	2.81

Table 1a lists the theoretically computed compression ratios for several patterns combined by different n, m, and s, some of which are also tested in later evaluations. As the result shows, reducing s to maintain fewer bits in the *Significand* part may raise the compression ratio, while precision is cut correspondingly. Meanwhile, setting a larger n to indicate using larger common upper bits in the *Exponent* part also gives a better compression ratio theoretically. However, as a trade-off, increasing n can also cause higher difficulties to have identical upper bits for all data within the cache line. This may decrease the number of cache lines that are able to be compressed in actual cases so that the overall compression ratio for *Non-Zero List* may be downgraded obviously.

Integer Type Data Compression. Besides the **Double** type value array *Non-Zero List*, *Colidx* is another memory bandwidth consuming element in SpMV-oriented data structures. *Colidx* is composed of a series of **Integer** type, usually 32-Bit, data and is responsible for precisely pointing out the column indices for *Non-Zero List* data that need to be accessed. Therefore, *Colidx* data is often accessed at the same rate as *Non-Zero List* data. Furthermore, it is difficult to exploit data locality during visiting *Colidx* data so that a large amount of memory bandwidth is occupied during computations, which makes compression among this data meaningful. As *Colidx* is storing the information for correctly accessing necessary *Non-Zero List* elements, it will be critical if any value loss has occurred. Hence, unlike **Double** type oriented schemes, a lossless compression scheme is required for **Integer** type data in *Colidx*.

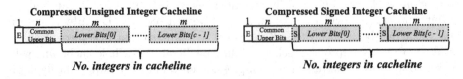

Fig. 4. Integer Data Compression Scheme for *Colidx*

In most SpMV based computation kernels, data stored in CSR structure is usually pre-processed and sorted finely. Although still depending on the exact dataset, column indices tend to have similar values and be incrementally stored in the contiguous memory space. This observation tells that the compression scheme used for the *Exponent* part in **Double** type data may as well be efficient to handle **Integer** type data in *Colidx*.

As Fig. 4 shows, parameter n is as well set to indicate the number of bits that the common upper part may contain. This is similar to the approach adopted in Sect. 3.2. For **Signed Integer** data, if all the values have identical upper bits, starting from b_{30} to b_{31-n} since b_{31}, the sign bit, is excluded, then the current cache line is recognized as compressible and the first bit in cache line data, marked as 'E', will be set. On the other hand, *Colidx* stores the column indices whose values are non-negative integers, so that, in this **Unsigned Integer** case, upper bits should start from b_{31} to b_{31-n}. In a compressed cache line, the n-bit common upper part will be stored only once adjacent to the first flag bit, and then follows the unique lower bits part for each data.

We also list a bunch of patterns combined by different n and m, accompanied by their corresponding theoretical compression ratios in Table 1b. The cache line size in these cases is 64 Bytes, which is a widely used cache line size in most computer architectures. As the result shows, enlarging n to set a larger common upper bits part may lead to a better theoretical compression ratio. However, the same trade-off stated in Sect. 3.2 also states that increasing n may at the same time prevent all cache line data to have identical upper bits. With a lower success rate on compressing cache lines, the total compression ratio for *Colidx* may also drop down in actual cases.

4 Evaluation

In this section, we show our simulations using the CG kernel benchmark among several widely adopted sparse matrix datasets and discuss the impacts caused by our compression schemes. Both performance improvement and effects brought by adopting lower precision floating-point data will be considered and evaluated.

4.1 Methodology

To estimate the exact compression ratio, as well as how compression data may influence the final calculation results in SpMV-based scientific kernel, we choose the widely used NAS Parallel Benchmarks (NPB) in its C++ version at branch 3.1 as the main benchmark software, and HPCG benchmark suite [13] as the supplementary benchmark. In complementary to CG benchmark generated datasets, matrix datasets with larger sizes picked up from the SuiteSparse Matrix Collection [14] are also adopted. The evaluation environment contains a normal Intel Xeon processor and 128 GB DRAM space.

Table 2. Specification of Simulating Environment in Onikiri2

CPU Core	RISC-V single core @ 2GHz
Memory	200 cycle latency, 2.0 GB/s Bandwidth
L1 Cache	32 KB, 4-way set associative, 64 Bytes cache line
L2 Cache	512 KB, shared, 8-way set associative, 64 Bytes cache line
L1 Prefetcher	Stream Prefetcher
L2 Prefetcher	Stream Prefetcher

Furthermore, to specifically evaluate the effect on the actual performance of the compression schemes, a cycle-accurate simulator is considered in our simulations. We adopted the cycle-level processor simulation tool, Onikiri 2, in this paper, and simulating architecture specifications are shown in Table 2. In order to focus on the execution time of CG kernel computations, we picked the internally generated sparse dataset, CLASS-S, in the NPB CG benchmark, and only 1 iteration was performed to check whether memory bandwidth matters the actual performance. To mention that, in this simulation, the L2 cache (LLC) size is set to 512 KB, which is lower than typical modern architectures. In most real cases, data in SpMV computations may not be contained by cache hierarchy, which will cause huge memory traffics, therefore L2 cache here is also adjusted not to fit the size of sparse matrix data.

Besides, our simulations are performed in 1 core 1 thread pattern environment, in this case, one float operation is performed per cycle. So that we defined memory bandwidth to be 2.0GB/s to have an actual B/F of 0.5. On the other hand, in the HPC system Fugaku, the main processor, A64FX, is offering a B/F at 0.37, which is approximate to our setup.

4.2   Empirical Compression Ratio

In Fig. 5a and Fig. 5b, we show the actual compression ratios using the compression schemes stated in Sect. 3.2 among various datasets, including CLASS-S sparse data generated by the NPB CG benchmark itself and larger size matrices in the SuiteSparse Matrix Collection that could be applied to CG kernel. Evaluated compression patterns are denoted as "n-m-s" in Fig. 5a for **Double** data and as "n-m" in Fig. 5b for **Unsigned Integer** data.

Figure 5a reveals the substantial compression ratio among the *Non-Zero List*. As stated in Sect. 3.2, parameters n and s are configurable so that, various patterns can be made to fit diverse cases. In this simulation, we simply change n to test different combinations of n and m in the *Exponent* part and fix s to 10. From the results, compression ratios among *Non-Zero List*, the **Double** type data, generously depend on specific structures of the dataset and distinguish from each other. However, patterns $5-6-10$ and $6-5-10$ are on average showing more stable effects among all datasets and the best score has reached 3.6, which indicates the effectiveness of these patterns.

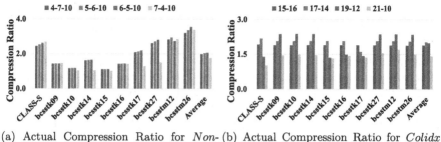

(a) Actual Compression Ratio for *Non-Zero List* Data

(b) Actual Compression Ratio for *Colidx* Data

Fig. 5. Actual Compression Ratio using Various Datasets

While on the other hand, the same tendency, where the final compression ratio is notably affected by value distribution within datasets, appeared as well. And, at the same time, patterns set in the compression scheme are also playing a remarkable role for *Colidx*, the **Unsigned Integer** data. Figure 5b indicates that pattern $17-14$ scored the best to reach 1.9 on average, which is approximate to the theoretical value calculated in Sect. 3.2.

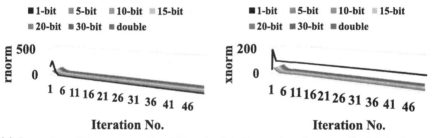

(a) Impact on Convergence Conditions by Lower Precision Floating-point Data

(b) Comparison between Real Solution and Actual Solutions

Fig. 6. Impacts caused by Lower Precision Floating-point Data

4.3   Impact on Convergence Conditions by Lower Precision Data

In this section, we state the impacts brought by lower precision values in the *Non-Zero List* data structure due to cutting off the length in *Significand* bits. Since the CG kernel in the NPB benchmark does not perform any pre-processing, we switch to a more sophisticated kernel provided by the HPCG benchmark in order to stably observe the effects introduced by lower precision floating-point values.

In HPCG kernel simulation, we choose the matrix data generated by the benchmark itself which has a similar size as CLASS-S in the NPB benchmark. Computations will be executed in 50 iterations to confirm that it reaches the convergence condition. Furthermore, in this simulation, we also added comparisons between theoretical solutions and actual solutions computed under different precisions respectively.

Figure 6a shows the final $||r||$, which is used to judge the convergence, computed in each case. 1-*bit* shows a relatively unstable curve and the final $||r||$ took 34 iterations to reach 3.54×10^{-11}, while **Double** precision only took 18 iterations before going down to less than 10^{-10}. However, precision higher than 5-*bit* appear at the same speed and accuracy as **Double**, which indicates that lower precision floating-point values adopting more than 5-bit $Significand$ barely affect the convergence in HPCG kernel computations.

On the other hand, comparing the solutions computed by the HPCG kernel to the theoretical one, we also yield the same tendency. $||x - x_{real}||$ values shown in Fig. 6b indicate that the solution norm yielded by the 1-*bit* precision method declined much slower than in other cases and finally stopped at the value of 104.82. While other methods with precision from 5-*bit* to **Double** managed to reduce fast and reach 1.66×10^{-14} from the 22nd iteration.

4.4   Cycle-Accurate Performance Evaluation

In Fig. 7, we show the exact total cycles that come from the experiments using cycle-level processor simulator, Onikiri2, and CG kernel in NPB among its CLASS-S dataset. In order to estimate the impact caused by our compression and precision converting scheme, we execute the CG kernel for only 1 iteration and record the total cycles consumed by 4 scenarios: original CG kernel denoted as *Base*, only *Non-Zero List* or *Colidx* scheme applied CG kernel denoted as *Non-Zero Only* and *Colidx Only* respectively, and *Both* that indicates all schemes are used.

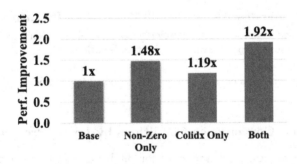

Fig. 7. Performance Improvement

Besides, in order to evaluate the maximum effect of the proposed approach, we only picked up the most effective compression patterns stated in Sect. 4.2, which are $6 - 5 - 10$ for *Non-Zero List* and $17 - 14$ for *Colidx*.

From Fig. 7, we can see that 1.48x improvement is achieved when only applying compression and precision converting scheme to the *Non-Zero List* since the amount of data that needs to be transferred is reduced by about 2.5x for 64-bit **Double** type values. While, in the case that only *Colidx* is compressed, 1.19x speedup is confirmed. Since the compression ratio for 32-bit **Unsigned Integer** is tested at about 2.1, the impact is less than the *Non-Zero Only* case. Finally, when both *Non-Zero List* and *Colidx* are handled by our scheme, 1.92x performance improvement is shown in the result, which can be expected as an obvious effect in the memory bandwidth-hungry SpMV-based kernel.

5 Conclusions

In this paper, we proposed a method to compress and convert the data precision in the memory interface for SpMV processing. With this approach, compression and conversion from a double-precision floating-point to a lower precision format during memory access are achieved. Further evaluations of the compression ratio and performance are also performed, and the results show that throughput could be increased by up to 1.92x when being evaluated with a cycle-level simulator.

Future work includes investigating architectures that reduce computation throughput and power consumption by computing data with low precision after conversion, even inside the processor core.

Acknowledgment. First and foremost, we would like to sincerely thank the anonymous reviewers for their valuable comments. This work was supported, in part, by JST CREST Grant Number JPMJCR18K1, Japan.

References

1. HPCG Ranking (2021). https://www.top500.org/lists/hpcg/2021/06/
2. Kourtis, K., Karakasis, V., Goumas, G., Koziris, N.: CSX: an extended compression format for SpMV on shared memory systems. SIGPLAN Not. **46**, 8 (2011)
3. Ahmad, K., Sundar, H., Hall, M.: Data-driven mixed precision sparse matrix vector multiplication for GPUs. ACM Trans. TACO **16**(4), 1–24 (2019)
4. Sakamoto, R., Kondo, M., Fujita, K., Ichimura, T., Nakajima, K.: The effectiveness of low-precision floating arithmetic on numerical codes: a case study on power consumption. In: Proceedings HPCAsia2020, pp. 199–206 (2020)
5. FUJITSU Processor A64FX Datasheet. https://www.fujitsu.com/downloads/SUPER/a64fx/a64fx_datasheet_en.pdf
6. Vazquez, F., Ortega, G., Fernandez, J.J., Garzon, E.M.: Improving the performance of the sparse matrix vector product with GPUs. In: Proceedings of the 10th IEEE ICCIT, ser. CIT, pp. 1146–1151 (2010)
7. Tang, W.T., et al.: Accelerating sparse matrix-vector multiplication on GPUs using bit-representation optimized schemes. In: Proceedings of the ICHPC (2013)
8. Yang, W., Li, K., Mo, Z., Li, K.: Performance optimization using partitioned SpMV on GPUs and multicore CPUs. IEEE Trans. Comput. **64**(9), 2623–2636 (2015)
9. Ashari, A., Sedaghati, N., Eisenlohr, J., Sadayappan, P.: An efficient two-dimensional blocking strategy for sparse matrix-vector multiplication on GPUs. In: Proceedings of the ICS 2014, pp. 273–282 (2014)

10. Grigoras, P., Burovskiy, P., Hung, E., Luk, W.: Accelerating SpMV on FPGAs by compressing nonzero values. In: 2015 IEEE 23rd Annual International Symposium on Field-Programmable Custom Computing Machines, pp. 64–67 (2015)
11. Liu, W., Vinter, B.: CSR5: an efficient storage format for cross-platform sparse matrix-vector multiplication. In: Proceedings of the ICS 2015, pp. 339–350 (2015)
12. Bian, B., Huang, J., Dong, R., Liu, L., Wang, X.: CSR2: a new format for SIMD-accelerated SpMV. In: CCGRID, pp. 350–359 (2020)
13. Dongarra, J., Heroux, M.A., Luszczek, P.: HPCG Benchmark: a new metric for ranking high performance computing systems. Knoxville, Tennessee (2015)
14. Davis, T.A., Hu, Y.: The University of Florida sparse matrix collection. ACM Trans. Math. Softw. **38**(1), Article no. 1 (2011)

SimdFSM: An Adaptive Vectorization of Finite State Machines for Speculative Execution

Le Li$^{(\boxtimes)}$ ⓘ and Kenjiro Taura ⓘ

The University of Tokyo, Bunkyo, Tokyo, Japan
lile@eidos.ic.i.u-tokyo.ac.jp

Abstract. Parallel execution of a Finite State Machine (FSM) is challenging due to strong data dependency. Previous work proposed speculative execution to distribute the workload to multiple threads. While without dependent data, threads working from the middle of the input speculate multiple states, possibly resulting in redundant computations. Advanced efforts have achieved significant performance improvements in each thread using SIMD gather/shuffle instructions.

This paper studies various SIMD-based strategies in depth, with the following factors considered: (1) FSM size, (2) processor microarchitectures, and (3) SIMD instructions used. We present SimdFSM incorporating various methods and profile their performances using a real-world FSM collection under different configurations of these factors. The results show that the performance differences among these methods can be significant, and the winner varies depending on these factors. Thus, a wrong choice can result in unexpectedly poor performance.

Therefore, we design an adaptive strategy using the profiling data to select the best method among the ones available under the current execution environment. The adaptive strategy further samples states' distribution in an input fragment to improve speculation success probability. The results show that it can always select the best method with an ignorable overhead.

Keywords: Finite State Machine · Parallelism · Single Instruction Multiple Data

1 Introduction

A Finite State Machine (FSM) is one of the most fundamental building blocks in computer algorithms. Many applications are powered by FSMs, including regular expression matching (regex) [12], tokenization [11], Hamming distance [13], and network intrusion detection [15]. The performance of FSM often determines the throughput of these applications. Figure 1 shows an example FSM that models the logic of Div7. Specifically, it is a Deterministic-FSM (D-FSM), whose transition function is a singleton, i.e., there is only one destination state

© The Author(s), under exclusive license to Springer Nature Switzerland AG 2023
H. Takizawa et al. (Eds.): PDCAT 2022, LNCS 13798, pp. 481–493, 2023.
https://doi.org/10.1007/978-3-031-29927-8_37

when given a particular input symbol c and current state q. This paper focuses on D-FSM which is the prerequisite of these vectorization methods, and any Nondeterministic-FSM can be converted into a deterministic equivalent via subset construction [12].

Definition 1. *A D-FSM can be represented by a quintuple* $(Q, \Sigma, \mathcal{T}, q_0, \mathcal{A})$, *where Q is a finite set of states; Σ is a finite set of input symbols; $\mathcal{T} : Q \times \Sigma \to Q$ is a transition function; $q_0 \in Q$ is an initial state; $\mathcal{A} \subseteq Q$ is a finite set of accepting states.*

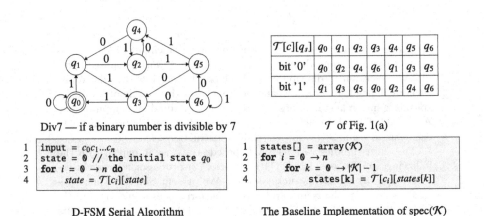

$\mathcal{T}[c][q_s]$	q_0	q_1	q_2	q_3	q_4	q_5	q_6
bit '0'	q_0	q_2	q_4	q_6	q_1	q_3	q_5
bit '1'	q_1	q_3	q_5	q_0	q_2	q_4	q_6

Div7 — if a binary number is divisible by 7 $\mathcal{T}$ of Fig. 1(a)

```
1   input = c_0c_1...c_n
2   state = 0 // the initial state q_0
3   for i = 0 → n do
4       state = T[c_i][state]
```

```
1   states[] = array(𝒦)
2   for i = 0 → n
3       for k = 0 → |𝒦| - 1
4           states[k] = T[c_i][states[k]]
```

D-FSM Serial Algorithm   The Baseline Implementation of spec(𝒦)

Fig. 1. Example FSM and Algorithm

We use a two-dimensional array $\mathcal{T}$ to represent the state transition function as in Fig. 1(b), such that $\mathcal{T}[c][s] = \mathcal{T}q_s c$. Note that the first index c is the next character, so a table row ($\mathcal{T}[c]$) is a one-dimensional array indexed by the current state, assuming the row-major ordering. As shown in Fig. 1(c), FSM computation is highly serial and irregular. Specifically, the main bottlenecks are the data dependency (state) between every two iterations and unpredictable memory access patterns. The importance of FSMs motivates much effort to design hardware-based [2] and multicore [14,16] parallel methods. When exploiting thread-level parallelism, speculative execution is necessary as threads working from the middle of the input do not know which state they should start from; specifically, each thread (except the thread that works on the beginning of the input) speculates k states as the possible initial state and performs k state transitions simultaneously, for which previous work [4,6,12] exploited SIMD instructions. However, these methods are either online unavailable or hard-coded for specific applications, regardless of their broad usability. In addition, we found that performance differences among them can be significant depending on circumstances, and therefore inappropriate use of them may result in unexpectedly poor performance. For these purposes, we propose SimdFSM, whose contributions are summarized as follows,

– **A Method Collection:** SimdFSM incorporates various FSMs vectorization methods, optimizations, and a new algorithm logic using permutation. It encapsulates low-level processor-specific details that are hard to maintain and error-prone.

– **A Performance Profiler:** We show through experiments that performances of various vectorizing methods depend on the size of an FSM, available SIMD instructions, and microarchitectures. We model the performance of each method based on the throughput of respective instructions.

– **An Adaptive Strategy:** Based on the profiling results, we propose an adaptive strategy to select the optimal method by trading off the throughput of the speculative phase and the success probability using state frequency sampling.

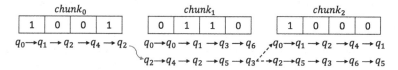

Fig. 2. An Example of The Speculative Execution — spec($[q_0q_2]$)

2 Background

This section begins by reviewing the multi-core parallelization of FSMs. Then, we introduce the factors that affect the efficiencies of the data-parallel techniques.

2.1 Speculative Execution — spec($\mathcal{K}$)

The basic idea of multi-thread FSM execution is to divide the input into chunks, each of which runs a speculating FSM $= (Q, \sum, \mathcal{T}, \mathcal{K}, \mathcal{A})$ that uses a set of states $\mathcal{K} \subseteq Q$ as possible initial states to obtain the end state corresponding to each initial state. In the rest of this paper, we call this scheme spec($\mathcal{K}$). Determining the $\mathcal{K}$ of each chunk relies on several factors, including convergence properties [6,16] and lookback technique [4,16]. After processing all chunks, it merges the sub-results by using the end state of a chunk as the correct initial state of the next chunk. Specifically, *enumerative execution*, which runs all states, is the term for spec(Q).

Figure 2 shows an example spec($\mathcal{K}$) with the input split into three chunks. **Speculating run:** speculate $[q_0q_2]$ as initial states and run them for $chunk_1$ and $chunk_2$; Fig. 1(d) is the baseline code without using SIMD. **Reduction:** chain the start and end states of neighboring chunks, like the state q_2 between $chunk_0$ and $chunk_1$. **Speculation failure & Re-execution:** when no end states of a chunk match any speculated state of the next chunk, re-execute the latter chunk with the now known initial state using the serial algorithm; for example, we need to re-execute $chunk_2$ with state q_3 after mismatching the correct end state q_3 of $chunk_1$ with the speculated states $[q_0q_2]$ of $chunk_2$.

2.2   Vector Extension and Processor Microarchitecture

spec($\mathcal{K}$) increases time complexity proportionally to the factor $|\mathcal{K}|$. To efficiently perform $|\mathcal{K}|$ state transitions, Todd et al. proposed a shuffle-based method [6], and Peng et al. designed a gather-based method that can simultaneously operate on multiple input parts [4]. In addition, this paper proposes another method using permute.

These operations rely on hardware-based instructions operating on vector registers. Vector length determines not only the number of packed data points but also the efficiency of instructions; for example, on Ice Lake, the CPI of the 8-bit indexing 128-bit shuffle (0.5 cycles) is lower than that of the 512-bit version (1.0 cycles). Besides, modern processors have a wide variety of microarchitectures, while the troublesome fact is that the efficiency of the same instruction may be different across different microarchitectures; for example, on SkyLake-X, the latency of the 16-bit indexing 512-bit shuffle (6 cycles) is higher than that on Ice Lake (4 cycles). Worse still, since parallel instructions may result in port contention, the above naive comparison lacks accuracy, and thus port usage information is also crucial [1]. These facts make it hard to carry out manual best method selection and motivate us to profile their performances. Note that, in this paper, the mentioned latencies and CPIs are all average values [8].

Table 1. State Encoding (#bits/state)

$|Q|$	$\sim 2^8$	$\sim 2^{16}$	$\sim 2^{31}$
gather		32	
shuffle / permute	8	16	32

Table 2. Vector Packing (#states/vector)

Vector (bits)	128	256	512
gather	4	8	16
shuffle / permute	16/8/4	32/16/8	64/32/16

2.3   FSM Size — The Number of States $|Q|$

FSM size affects the performance. First, it affects transition table size $|Q||\sum|$, and thus makes a difference in memory footprint [12]. Second, it dilutes speculation success rate $|\mathcal{K}|/|Q|$, and thus motivates the design of speculation strategies [16]. Besides, state encoding determines the number of data points packed in a vector, especially for vectorization. Table 1 classifies how to encode states when given a specific $|Q|$. Note that gather only supports 32-bit indexing, so it cannot encode a state with a smaller number of bits even if the number of states is smaller than, say, 2^{16}. Table 2 shows the maximum number of data points a single vector can pack under all types of state encoding.

3   Vectorized FSMs

This section illustrates the details of these methods, which vectorize the inner loop of the baseline code having independent iterations. We classify them into four categories (gather, shuffle, permute, and *interleaved-gather*). However, depending on available instructions, even methods of the same category may use a different set of instructions; for example, the 512-bit shuffle additionally calculates an intermediate mask to accomplish the same logic as the 128-bit version. This section introduces their basic logic. The low-level details are encapsulated in a higher-level interface of SimdFSM.

The following exposition assumes that a vector register can pack four states (*vector size*), though the actual number depends on instructions and FSM size (thus the required bits to represent a state). We use *vector length* to term the number of bits per vector.

3.1 Gather

The *gather* instruction takes a base address B on an integer register and a set of indices I on a vector register to access address $B + i$ (for each index $i \in I$). How to use it to implement simultaneous multiple state transitions of FSM is shown in Fig. 3(a). The figure depicts a situation where the next input character c is '1' and V_{index} are the four current states, each resulted from a speculated initial state of a given chunk. It looks up the table with each current state to get the next state using the gather instruction.

However, using gather has an obvious issue since it has relatively high latency and CPI, which can be 17–30 and 5–10 times larger than shuffle, respectively [3].

3.2 Shuffle

The drawbacks of gather motivate the use of shuffle, which takes a set of indices I on a vector register and accesses the ith data points in another vector for each $i \in$

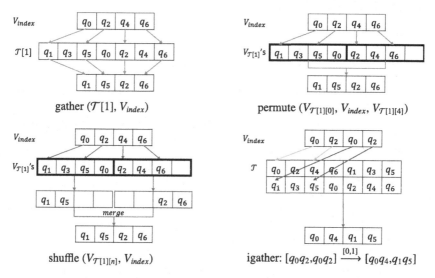

Fig. 3. Vectorizing Speculative Execution Using SIMD (V represents a vector)

$$1 \quad V_{\texttt{state}} = V_{T[\texttt{symbol}][\texttt{state}]} = V_{T[\texttt{symbol} \times |Q| + \texttt{state}]} = \mathbf{gather}(T, V_{\texttt{symbol}} \times V_{|Q|} + V_{\texttt{state}})$$

$$2 \quad V_{\texttt{symbol}} = V_{\texttt{input}[\texttt{chunk\_id} \times \texttt{chunk\_size} + \texttt{iteration}]} = \mathbf{gather}(\texttt{input}, V_{\texttt{id}} \times V_{\texttt{size}} + V_{\texttt{iteration}})$$

Listing 1.1. The Algorithm Logic of *igather*

I. A state transition using shuffle first loads an entire row of the transition table corresponding to the next character c, $T[c]$, into register(s) and then extracts values on these registers to obtain the next set of states, as illustrated in Fig. 3(b). However, suppose a single vector cannot pack an entire row, i.e., $T[c]$. In that case, we have to merge the results of several shuffle operations using SIMD blend instruction [6] or bitwise operations [5].

It can outperform the gather-based method thanks to the lower latency and CPI of shuffle; moreover, shuffle supports word sizes smaller than 32 bits (16 bits and 8 bits). However, the apparent overhead of the merging step indicates that a threshold of $|Q|$ exists beyond which shuffle becomes more expensive. Our profiling result tackles this issue by precisely capturing such thresholds under different microarchitectures.

3.3 Permute

SimdFSM additionally provides a method based on permutation [10], which is efficient in recent Intel microarchitectures. Similar to shuffle, permute instruction extracts values of specified vector lanes, but unlike shuffle, it can take *two* register operands to extract values from. A state transition using permute is similar to the one using shuffle, except a possibly fewer merge steps. However, merging steps are still inevitable if more than two vector registers are required to hold an entire row of the state transition matrix.

3.4 Interleaved-Gather (iGather)

The above methods only vectorize the inner loop of Fig. 1(d). Another usage of the gather primitive is parallelizing the outer and inner loops in an interleaved manner [4]. As shown in Fig. 3(d), $[q_0 q_2, q_0 q_2] \xrightarrow{[0,1]} [q_0 q_4, q_1 q_5]$ reads the first input symbols $chunk_1$('0') and $chunk_2$('1') of Fig. 2, simultaneously. We call this 2-way/spec($\mathcal{K}$) igather that processes two chunks (ways), each of which runs with two states ($|\mathcal{K}| = 2$). It advances the naive gather method by treating T as a 1D array; Listing 1.1 shows the algorithm which uses the gather instruction twice. It gathers $T[\texttt{symbol} \times |Q| + \texttt{state}]$, with the input symbols gathered from input array at indices starting from chunks' offset (chunk_id × chunk_size) and are incremented by 1 in each iteration.

However, to gather input symbols (Line 2), the ordinary implementation [7] needs to zero-extend each value in the input 8-bit char array into a 32-bit integer to have the same number of bits as state encoding, which introduces a conversion overhead and stresses the memory capacity four times. Instead of using gather, we directly form 32-bit data points from 8-bit chars using the SIMD set($input[i]$,$input[i]$,$input[o+i]$,$input[o+i]$) to accomplish the same logic, where i and o are the ith iteration and chunk offset, respectively. The throughput of the SIMD set instruction is worse than the gather's, but using it avoids input conversion with improved overall throughput. In Sect. 5.1, we only show the performance of the optimized implementation.

4   The Adaptive Strategy of SimdFSM

SimdFSM incorporates FSM vectorization methods described above with a profiling-based adaptive method selection. It considers not only the performance differences of these methods but also the set of speculated states $\mathcal{K}$. That is, when using different $\mathcal{K}$'s (e.g., different sizes or different elements but the same size), we may obtain different speculation success rates for the same input. We design the adaptive strategy to predict the best-performing method by modeling the performances of available ones (under current microarchitecture and vector extension) based on the profiling data.

As introduced in Sect. 2.1, the expected reciprocal throughput (cycles per byte) $T_{spec(\mathcal{K})}$ of spec($\mathcal{K}$), the algorithm speculating initial states as $\mathcal{K}$ and falling back to a serial algorithm upon speculation failure, can be modeled as follows,

$$T_{spec(\mathcal{K})} = T_{|\mathcal{K}|} + T_{redo} = T_{|\mathcal{K}|} + (1 - R_{\mathcal{K}}) \times T_{serial} \tag{1}$$

where $T_{|\mathcal{K}|}$ and T_{serial} are the reciprocal throughputs of a speculating run with $|\mathcal{K}|$ speculated states and serial execution, respectively, and $R_{\mathcal{K}}$ is speculation success probability. $T_{|\mathcal{K}|}$ depends only on $|\mathcal{K}|$ (the number of speculated states) and FSM (e.g., size, state encoding), and T_{serial} only on the latter; they do not depend on the input data, except that different inputs may induce different cache miss rates on the transition table, whose effect we do not consider in this paper. We obtain them by profiling with arbitrary inputs, as shown in Sect. 5.1. The success probability $R_{\mathcal{K}}$, on the other hand, depends on the chosen initial states ($\mathcal{K}$) and the actual input.

With randomly chosen initial states, the expected success probability $R_{\mathcal{K}} = |\mathcal{K}|/|Q|$ (with the average taken over all random choices of $|\mathcal{K}|$ states). However, state frequency is often highly skewed and input-sensitive, like the JSON tokenization case explained in Fig. 4. We want $\mathcal{K}$ to cover frequently occurring states. To that end, we estimate state frequency distribution using a part of the input data; in the JSON tokenization case, for example, we can achieve 82% success probability by just using the two most frequently occurring states, as shown in Fig. 7 (b) of Sect. 5.2.

Listing 1.2 shows the pseudocode. The outer loop builds the set of speculated states of size k, for $1 \le k \le |Q|$ (Line 3); each iteration sets $\mathcal{K}$ to the k most frequent states (Line 4) via the state sampling described in Line 1. The inner loop calculates the $T_{spec(\mathcal{K})}$ using the profiled $T_{|\mathcal{K}|}$ of each method (Line 6) and updates the optimal method and $\mathcal{K}$ if finding a better one (Line 7–8. In the end, the variable *optimal* will be updated to the best method with a set of speculated

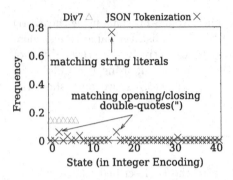

Div7 △   JSON Tokenization ×

0.8

0.6 matching string literals

Frequency

0.4

0.2   matching opening/closing
         double-quotes(")

0

0   10   20   30   40

State (in Integer Encoding)

Fig. 4. State Frequency Distribution

Table 3. Average Latency (Lat.)/CPI of SIMD Instructions (cycles) on SkyLake-X (SKX) and Ice Lake (ICL) [8]

Vector (bits)	OP	Indexing (bits)	SKX Lat. / CPI	ICL Lat. / CPI
128	shuffle	8	1 / 1.0	1 / 0.5
512	shuffle	8	NA	3 / 1.0
		16	6 / 2.0	4 / 1.0
	permute	8	NA	5 / 2.0
		16	7 / 2.0	7 / 2.0
	gather	32	25 / 9.25	25 / 9.0

```
1   sample = sampling state frequency using, for example, the first 1 KB of the input
2   optimal = {method = null, K = null}, T_optimal = +∞ // modeled T_spec(K) of optimal
3   for k = 1 → |Q| do
4       K = most frequent k states based on the estimated frequency using sample
5       R_K = the success probability for K
6       foreach method do
7           if method.T_spec(K) < T_optimal then
8               optimal = {method, K}, T_optimal = method.T_spec(K)
9   return optimal
```

Listing 1.2. Pseudocode of The Adaptive Strategy

states, and $T_{optimal}$ is the predicted minimum reciprocal throughput (Line 2). Then, the optimal method runs the corresponding $\mathcal{K}$ on the remaining input (except for the part used for state frequency sampling).

For example, on Ice Lake, an interesting trade-off arises between the 128- and 512-bit versions of shuffle; when $|Q| = 70$, each state can be encoded with 8 bits, so speculating 16 states with the 128-bit shuffle and speculating 64 states with the 512-bit shuffle are both favorable options. While the latter obviously has a higher speculation success probability, the former is still considered for having lower reciprocal throughput ($T_{16} = 7.89$ in our profiling result) than the latter ($T_{64} = 12.21$) in the speculation phase. Although the 128-bit version needs four ($\lfloor 70/16 \rfloor$) merge steps higher than that ($\lfloor 70/64 \rfloor$) of the 512-bit version; its higher throughput comes from the lower latency and CPI (1 and 0.5) compared to the advanced 512-bit version (3 and 1.0), as shown in Table 3. Thus, we can compare $7.89 + (1 - R_{16}) \times 5.00$ and $12.21 + (1 - R_{64}) \times 5.00$, where $T_{serial} = 5.00$, and predict that the 128-bit shuffle can outperform the 512-bit version if $R_{64} - R_{16} < 86.4\%$. Note that we assume $R_{|\mathcal{K}|}$ is the probability obtained using the top $|\mathcal{K}|$ frequent states. The adaptive strategy thus predicts the best-performing method by trading off the throughput of the speculative phase and the success probability.

Table 4. Processor Microarchitectures and Vector Extensions

Platinum 8176 (SkyLake-X)	SSE4.1, AVX512F, AVX512BW
Platinum 8360Y (Ice Lake)	SSE4.1, AVX512F, AVX512VBMI

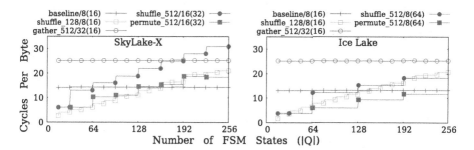

Fig. 5. Performance Profiling for gather, shuffle and permute

5   Evaluation

This section evaluates SimdFSM through the following two metrics; Sect. 5.1 looks at performance without considering the speculation failure and re-execution penalty; Sect. 5.2 illustrates the effect of the adaptive strategy in predicting the best method based on the profiling data, state sampling, and Eq. (1) in the presence of re-execution. We use GCC 9.2.0 with the -O3 optimization flag.

The profiler uses a real-world FSM collection, including Div7, HTML Tokenizer [4] and Brill, ClamAV, DotStar, PowerEN, Snort from ANMLZoo [13]. Each FSM is generated from a set of regex rules of these benchmarks to form a wide range of $|Q|$. Due to space constraints, this paper only shows the data collected from the microarchitectures shown in Table 4. Results on other microarchitectures (e.g., Haswell, Broadwell) with different parameters (e.g., $|Q|$ range, $|\mathcal{K}|$) are available on GitHub[1].

5.1   Performance Profiling of Speculating Phase

We first focus on the reciprocal throughput of shuffle and permute shown in Fig. 5. The x-axis is the size of the FSM only up to 256. Performance of shuffle and permute quickly degrade for larger FSMs due to the merging overhead and are outperformed by gather/baseline. Note that the data is the reciprocal throughput of the speculating run with $|\mathcal{K}|$ states without considering the speculation failure and re-execution procedure. Notation $M\_L/I(K)$ means using method M (L-bit vector with I-bit indexing) to speculate K states. In this paper, we only consider cases where $K = L/I$ holds (i.e., all states fit a single register), though it does not have to be the case in general.

---

[1] https://github.com/lile-riraku/simdfsm/blob/main/supplementary.pdf.

SkyLake-X supports the 512-bit shuffle and permute, but only with 16-bit indexing, which results in a wasteful state encoding; when $|Q| \leq 256$, they can manipulate up to $32 = 512/16$ states per execution, while the 128-bit shuffle can pack up to $16 = 128/8$ states for supporting 8-bit indexing. Not surprisingly, the 128-bit shuffle has much lower latency and CPI than the 512-bit version, as shown in Table 3. While the 512-bit version is advantageous when the benefit (success rate) of speculating 32 states outweighs the cost of the lower throughput and higher latency. The 512-bit permute has slightly higher latency and CPI than shuffle but is beneficial for requiring fewer merging steps when we need two or more vectors to pack a transition table row.

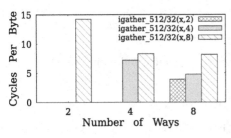

Fig. 6. Profiling 512-bit igather (Ice Lake)

Table 5. Intermediate Result of Listing 1.2 for Fig. 7 (c), where $T_{serial} = 5.00$

Method	$T_{|\mathcal{K}|}$	$R_{\mathcal{K}}$	$T_{spec(\mathcal{K})}$
gather_512/32(8,2)	3.92	0.47	6.57
gather_512/32(8,4)	4.79	0.52	7.19
gather_512/32(8,8)	8.16	0.61	10.11
shuffle_128/8(16)	7.89	0.81	8.84
shuffle_512/8(64)	12.21	1	12.21
permute_512/8(64)	5.98	1	**5.98**

Ice Lake supports shuffle and permute with 8-bit indexing, so we can encode states with 8-bit integers when $|Q| \leq 256$. Moreover, the latency and CPI of the 8-bit indexing shuffle_512 (4 and 1.0) are much lower than the 16-bit indexing version of SkyLake-X (6 and 2.0). Thus, we observed that the 512-bit shuffle outperforms the 128-bit version when $32 < |\mathcal{K}| \leq 64$, which was not the case in SkyLake-X. Besides, when $|Q| > 64$, the 512-bit permute outperforms others up to $|Q| = 256$ and has the largest number of speculation states (64). Therefore, it is the best choice up to $|Q| = 256$.

Note that, with high latency (25) and CPI (9.25 or 9.0), gather performs so poorly that it finds little use except for large $|Q|$'s; we can mitigate its high latency by scanning multiple chunks using a single thread. It can also scan multiple chunks with a single instruction (igather), with the result separately shown in Fig. 6; the x-axis is the number of chunks scanned. Notation igather_$L/I(C, K)$ means using igather (L-bit vector with I-bit indexing) to scan C chunks (ways) with K states per chunk. The gather in Fig. 5 is a special case of 1-way igather. In contrast to other methods whose performances degrade significantly with increased $|Q|$ due to the merging cost, igather has a constant throughput independent of $|Q|$ and thus is favorable for large $|Q|$'s. The igather is advantageous when a small $|\mathcal{K}|$, such as 2, 4, or 8, is sufficient to attain a speculation success rate comparable to the 1-way case when $|\mathcal{K}|$ is the number of 32-bit lanes (i.e., 16).

5.2 Evaluation of the Adaptive Vectorization Strategy

In addition to the performance differences in the absence of misspeculation, the adaptive strategy also models the re-execution penalty to predict the best-performing method. Figure 7 shows the performance of each method (involving re-execution) and the method selected by the adaptive strategy under Ice Lake. Note that when $|Q| < |\mathcal{K}|$, we apply enumerative execution, spec(Q), that achieves 100% speculation hits; for example, the 128-bit shuffle speculates 7 states under Div7, with 9/16 wasted vector slots. Cases (c) and (d) in the graph search the input for substrings matching the following regex. The inputs are the Yelp reviews in JSON format [9]; they differ in how frequently the matches are found. The input is rich with matches in (c) while has few matches in (d).

```
/"city":"Las Vegas"|"stars":[0-9]\.[0-9]|"GoodForKids":"True"|"NoiseLevel":"u'quiet'"/
```

First, except for (a) Div7, whose states are visited equally likely as in Fig. 4, the state frequency sampling helps improve the speculation success rate (shown on top of bars) when compared to random selection (whose success rate is on average $|\mathcal{K}|/|Q|$). Second, the higher the speculation success rate, the closer the performance to the profiling result; for example, cases (a), (b), and (d) approximately reflect the performance differences of the 128- and 512-bit shuffle's shown in Fig. 5, where the 128-bit version beats the 512-bit version when $|Q| \leq 32$ or $64 < |Q| \leq 128$, but is beaten when $32 \leq |Q| < 64$. Third, the best choice in several cases is easy to predict solely from FSM; when $|Q| \leq 16$, the 128-bit shuffle is always the best choice as it can speculate all states without merging; similarly, when $32 < |Q| \leq 64$, we can firmly choose the 512-bit shuffle; when $16 < |Q| \leq 32$, however, it depends on the speculation success rate with $|\mathcal{K}| = 16$, since the throughput of the 128-bit shuffle is higher than the 512-bit version, while the former cannot speculate all states, but the latter can. Fourth, there are cases when the best method depends on not only the FSM but also the input text. As noted, (c) and (d) apply the same FSM to different inputs, with rich

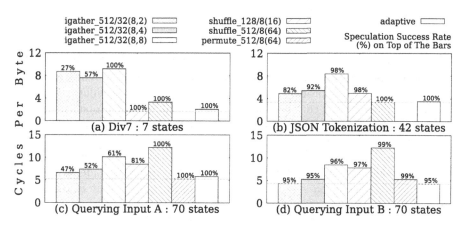

Fig. 7. Best Performing Method Selection Based on The Profiling Data (Ice Lake)

matching substrings in (c) but not in (d). In (d), the FSM mostly stays in a relatively small number of states corresponding to characters outside the sought pattern, rendering the speculation easy to succeed. In this case, the best method is igather_512/32(8,2) since $|\mathcal{K}| = 2$ attains sufficient speculation success rate and the SIMD lanes were utilized for processing eight chunks. In (c), on the other hand, a good speculation rate is difficult to come by small $|\mathcal{K}|$'s, and the best method is permute_512/8(64) which achieves 100% speculation hit by $|\mathcal{K}| = 64$.

Most notably, the adaptive strategy can predict the best-performing method with tiny overheads in all cases. We have described some intuitive selections if $|Q| \leq 64$. Table 5 shows how it actually works for case (c). Each row in the table represents an iteration of the inner loop of Listing 1.2, and the column($T_{|\mathcal{K}|}$) is the profiled reciprocal throughput of each method when speculating $|\mathcal{K}|$ states. In each row (inner loop iteration), it calculates the data of column($R_\mathcal{K}$) based on the $\mathcal{K}$ built in the outer loop and the state frequency sampling; specifically, the 512-bit shuffle and permute use the same $\mathcal{K}$. It updates the optimal method (null $\rightarrow$ igather_512/32(8,2) $\rightarrow$ permute_512/8(64)), with $\mathcal{K}$ memorized each time if it finds a lower reciprocal throughput ($+\infty \rightarrow 6.57 \rightarrow 5.98$).

6   Related Work

The Parallelization of FSMs is motivated by their broad usability. The multicore representative spec($\mathcal{K}$) produces redundant sub-results to hit the only correct target [14,16]. The SIMD methods apply data parallelism to each thread in spec($\mathcal{K}$), which brings significant performance improvement [4,6]. Similarly, SFA [12] embeds the data-parallel nature into the FSM during the FSM generation process.

Speculation Techniques rely on static/dynamic analysis to improve the speculation success rate. Looking back at part of the previous chunk [16] can achieve more accurate speculation based on the convergence property [4,6,16].

7   Conclusion

This paper presents SimdFSM that incorporates many vectorization methods for FSM speculative execution and performance profiling under different FSM sizes, vector extensions, and processor microarchitectures. It encapsulates low-level processor-specific details that are hard to maintain and error-prone.

Through profiling, we show that a wrong method selection not considering FSM properties and execution environment can lead to poor performance. Thus, we design an adaptive strategy for optimal method selection. It considers not only the throughputs of SIMD instructions used but also the trade-off between them and the speculation success rate. The results show that it can correctly choose the best method in all cases.

References

1. Abel, A., Reineke, J.: Uops.info: characterizing latency, throughput, and port usage of instructions on intel microarchitectures. In: ASPLOS 2019, pp. 673–686 (2019)
2. Dlugosch, P., Brown, D., Glendenning, P., Leventhal, M., Noyes, H.: An efficient and scalable semiconductor architecture for parallel automata processing. IEEE Trans. Parallel Distrib. Syst. **25**(12), 3088–3098 (2014)
3. Intel Guide. https://intel.com/content/www/us/en/docs/intrinsics-guide/index.html
4. Jiang, P., Agrawal, G.: Combining SIMD and many/multi-core parallelism for finite state machines with enumerative speculation. SIGPLAN Not. **52**(8), 179–191 (2017)
5. Li, L., Sato, S., Liu, Q., Taura, K.: Plex: scaling parallel lexing with backtrack-free prescanning. In: 2021 IEEE International Parallel and Distributed Processing Symposium (IPDPS)
6. Mytkowicz, T., Musuvathi, M., Schulte, W.: Data-parallel finite-state machines. In: ASPLOS 2014, Association for Computing Machinery (2014)
7. Jiang, P.: (2022). https://github.com/jiangohiostate/ppopp17_artifact
8. uops.info. https://uops.info/table.html
9. Yelp Dataset. https://www.kaggle.com/yelp-dataset/yelp-dataset
10. Ren, G., Wu, P., Padua, D.: Optimizing data permutations for SIMD devices. In: PLDI 2006, pp. 118–131 (2006)
11. Reps, T.: Maximal-munch tokenization in linear time **20**(2), 259–273 (1998)
12. Sinya, R., Matsuzaki, K., Sassa, M.: Simultaneous finite automata: an efficient data-parallel model for regular expression matching. In: ICPP 2013, pp. 220–229 (2013)
13. Wadden, J., et al.: ANMLzoo: a benchmark suite for exploring bottlenecks in automata processing engines and architectures. In: IISWC 2016, pp. 1–12 (2016)
14. Xia, Y., Jiang, P., Agrawal, G.: Scaling out Speculative Execution of Finite-State Machines with Parallel Merge. Association for Computing Machinery, New York, NY, USA (2020)
15. Yu, F., Chen, Z., Diao, Y., Lakshman, T.V., Katz, R.H.: Fast and memory-efficient regular expression matching for deep packet inspection. In: ANCS '06
16. Zhao, Z., Shen, X.: On-the-fly principled speculation for FSM parallelization. SIGPLAN Not. **50**(4), 619–630 (2015)

Privacy

Broad Learning Inference Based on Fully Homomorphic Encryption

Xinru Deng, Yingpeng Sang$^{(\boxtimes)}$ ⃝, and Zhaojue Li

School of Computer Science and Engineering, Sun Yat-sen University,
Guangzhou, China
{dengxr3,lizhj33}@mail2.sysu.edu.cn, sangyp@mail.sysu.edu.cn

Abstract. Distributed big data computing environments such as machine learning are widely deployed and applied on the cloud. However, since cloud servers can easily access user data, it leads to serious data leakage problems. As a potential technology, Fully Homomorphic Encryption (FHE) is often used in the field of privacy-preserving machine learning. However, in order to reduce the multiplicative depth of FHE, the neural network prunes the number of network layers, resulting in low inference accuracy. A learning model named Broad Learning System (BLS) has the characteristics of shallow model depth and low complexity. Based on this mode, we propose a privacy-preserving inference algorithm with low multiplicative depth, namely broad learning inference based on fully homomorphic encryption. We also extend the algorithm to the BLS model with incremental learning. We implement the privacy-preserving BLS for the first time using TENSEAL's CKKS scheme, and also verify the effectiveness of BLS inference with incremental learning. Experimental evaluations demonstrate the inference accuracy of 0.928 and 0.672 for datasets of MNIST and NORB, respectively.

Keywords: Fully Homomorphic Encryption · Homomorphic inference · Broad Learning System

1 Introduction

With the advent of the era of cloud computing and big data, distributed big data computing environments such as batch processing, stream computing, and machine learning have been widely deployed and applied on the cloud, bringing great convenience to cloud users. However, in this environment of outsourced computing, due to the large amount of data mining and data sharing, data leakage triggers a new privacy crisis, because cloud servers can easily access raw data containing sensitive user information, such as account password information, financial transaction information, health data, etc. Therefore, effective solutions that guarantee data privacy and availability at the same time are needed to solve the privacy protection problem in machine learning.

There are two typical approaches for privacy preserving machine learning research: Differential Privacy (DP) based and Homomorphic Encryption (HE)

© The Author(s), under exclusive license to Springer Nature Switzerland AG 2023
H. Takizawa et al. (Eds.): PDCAT 2022, LNCS 13798, pp. 497–508, 2023.
https://doi.org/10.1007/978-3-031-29927-8_38

based approaches. The former scrambles the data to protect sensitive information, and the latter encrypts the data before performing the computation. This paper focuses on HE-based privacy-preserving methods. HE provides a secure solution to the problem of data leakage in cloud servers. It allows blind processing of encrypted data in cloud servers, i.e., the third parties cannot obtain any information through input data or output results.

Many studies have demonstrated the feasibility of using FHE [4] in machine learning inference tasks. CryptoNets [14] demonstrated that cloud servers are able to apply neural networks to encrypted data to make encrypted predictions and return the predictions in encrypted form. However, since the Sigmoid activation function is directly replaced by a square function, the prediction accuracy decreases. Chabanne et al. [8] were the first to implement homomorphic inference in deep neural networks and tried to solve the performance-limited problem of CryptoNets by adding normalization layers. The introduction of CryptoDL [15] demonstrated the possibility of approximating activation functions with low-order polynomials. AlexNet [2] made encrypted predictions in 1% of the time taken by CryptoNets, demonstrating the effectiveness of using GPUs for homomorphic inference acceleration. Based on AlexNet, Ishiyama et al. [17] used a polynomial approximation of the activation function and added a normalization layer before the activation layer, which provided a new idea for improving the classification accuracy of MNIST dataset and CIFAR-10 dataset. Compared to CryptoNets, Brutzkus et al. [7] provided more than 10 times improvement in latency.

The biggest limitation of current reasoning based on FHE is the high complexity of operations (such as bootstrapping), making it infeasible in reality. Some studies applied leveled homomorphic encryption (LHE) [2,17] to inference tasks, which can avoid bootstrapping operations by determining the multiplicative depth in advance. However, previous studies were often limited by the multiplicative depth, and had to reduce the multiplicative depth by reducing the number of the neural network layers. The reason is that, the greater the multiplicative depth, the slower it runs and the higher the memory usage. Reducing the multiplicative depth by reducing the number of network layers affects the inference accuracy. The important thing is to find a balance between the time cost and inference accuracy.

Therefore, we propose an LHE-based algorithm for inference processing with low multiplicative depth, based on the BLS. BLS was proposed by [9], as a learning model that can improve training efficiency of data set, which has a shallow model depth and low complexity. When combining with LHE, it can effectively reduce the number of multiplications without affecting the inference accuracy. The contributions of this paper can be summarized as following:

1) To the best of our knowledge we are the first one to implement BLS inference processing using LHE.
2) We replace the activation function in the BLS approximately by a second-order polynomial. Due to its non-linearity, the activation function is not computable by LHE, and generally substituted by a square function. Due

to the low depth of BLS, its activation function can be approximated by a second-order polynomial which improves the inference accuracy.
3) We conduct BLS inference experiments with incremental learning. According to the experimental results, BLS with incremental learning can also be used for homomorphic inference.

The rest of the paper is organized as follows. The related work of HE, the inference of machine learning over LHE and privacy preserving broad learning is summarized in the Sect. 2. In Sect. 3 three methods are proposed, including the HE-based broad learning system, BLS inference with incremental learning, and a polynomial approximation method. In Sect. 4 the experimental data sets and results are demonstrated. Section 5 summarizes the whole paper.

2   Related Work

2.1   Homomorphic Encryption

Homomorphic Encryption (HE) is a problem raised by the cryptography community a long time ago. As early as 1978, Rivest et al. [18] proposed this concept in the context of banking applications. HE is an important tool in the field of privacy protection and secure multi-party computing. It means that the result obtained after decrypting the encrypted data is the same as the unencrypted original data processed in the same way.

Gentry [13] first proposed the concept of fully homomorphic encryption and constructed a homomorphic encryption scheme that allows bootstrapping. The reason why FHE keeps data secure is that it adds noise to the plaintext data when encrypting it to ensure that an attacker cannot decrypt it. However, this noise will increase with the increase of the number of homomorphic operations. Once the noise exceeds the allowable threshold, the encryption party cannot decrypt it correctly. The bootstrapping operation of Gentry's proposed scheme can reduce the noise in the ciphertext, is not limited by the depth of multiplication, and allows the ciphertext to undergo numerous homomorphic operations. Although Gentry's proposed scheme looks very attractive, the high computational cost and complex implementation make it impractical in reality.

Therefore, using LHE is appropriate when applying homomorphic encryption to inference tasks. It can avoid bootstrapping operations by determining the multiplicative depth in advance. However, the more homomorphic multiplication operations allowed by ciphertext, the longer the computation time and the larger the space occupied by the ciphertext. Therefore, there is a trade-off between multiplicative depth and performance.

2.2   Leveled Homomorphic Encryption Inference

Leveled Homomorphic Encryption (LHE) defines the maximum allowable depth of homomorphic multiplication in advance under the premise of known neural network framework. This avoids expensive bootstrapping operations and safely completes the task of homomorphic inference.

There are three traditional LHE schemes: BFV, BGC and CKKS schemes. BFV ([3,5,12]) and BGV ([6]) schemes are suitable for representing integers. CKKS ([10,11]) scheme can represent real numbers approximately, making it suitable for inference tasks in machine learning. The CKKS-based LHE scheme mainly includes four algorithms: *KeyGen*, *Encrypt*, *Decrypt* and *Evaluate*. *KeyGen* sets the parameters that meet the security level to generate encryption and decryption keys according to different requirements. *Encrypt* and *Decrypt* are encryption and decryption algorithms respectively. *Evaluation* is an operation on the ciphertext. The specific algorithms can be referred to in [10,11].

2.3   Privacy Preserving Broad Learning

BLS is a type of model that does not require deep neural network layers. In BLS, the training of parameters such as weights and biases do not require iterations of gradient descent, which makes the model training much faster. Yuan et al. [19] proposed a scheme using federated learning combined with broad learning to solve the data sharing problem in the vehicle networking. This scheme provides a balance between the efficiency and privacy of data sharing. To the best of our knowledge, there is no existing research on privacy protection in BLS using HE schemes.

3   Our Method

We propose an inference algorithm using LHE on BLS. Firstly, we use second-order polynomials of different approximation domains to substitute the ReLU activation function to improve inference accuracy. Secondly, in some cases, the BLS after one training may not achieve the expected effect, and the performance can be improved by adding some additional enhancement nodes. Therefore, we also adapt the LHE-based BLS with incremental learning.

3.1   LHE-Based Broad Learning System

Different from the traditional deep neural network, BLS (proposed by [9]) is a shallow learning model. In BLS, parameter training does not need to be iteratively generated by gradient descent, but is directly solved by pseudo-inverse of matrix, which makes the model training much faster.

According to [9], the BLS includes a mapped feature layer of n nodes and an enhancement layer of m nodes as shown in Fig. 1. $X \in \mathbb{R}^{N \times C}$ and Y are input data and output results, respectively. The mapped feature nodes are generated by:

$$M_i = f(XW_{m_i} + \beta_{m_i}), i = 1, 2, \ldots n \tag{1}$$

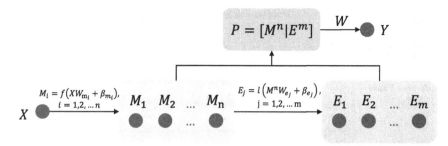

Fig. 1. The BLS structure.

Two sets of random parameters are defined as the weights $W_{m_i} \in \mathbb{R}^{C \times k}$, where k is the parameters we need to initialize, and the biases β_{m_i}. The activation function is denoted by f.

The output of the mapped feature nodes layer is $M^n = [M_1, M_2, \ldots, M_n] \in \mathbb{R}^{N \times nk}$, which is one of the important parameters for generating enhancement nodes.

$$E_j = l(M^n W_{e_j} + \beta_{e_j}), j = 1, 2, \ldots m \qquad (2)$$

The enhancement nodes layer consists of m nodes, where $W_{e_j} \in \mathbb{R}^{nk \times k}$ and β_{e_j} are random weights and biases, and the activation function is denoted by l.

Therefore, the output of BLS can be expressed as fellow:

$$Y = [M_1, M_2, \ldots, M_n | E_1, E_2, \ldots, E_m]W = [M^n | E^m]W \qquad (3)$$

where Y is the network output, $W = [M^n | E^m]^+ Y$ is the desired weight, and $()^+$ is the pseudo-inverse operator. Let $P = [M^n | E^m]$, which represents the final input of BLS. The ridge regression algorithm of [16] can be used to get the value of W by Eq. (4):

$$W = (\lambda I + P^T P)^{-1} P^T Y \qquad (4)$$

Then:

$$P^+ = \lim_{\lambda \to 0}(\lambda I + P^T P)^{-1} P^T \qquad (5)$$

where λ is the regularization coefficient.

HE can perform computations directly on encrypted data. We name the broad learning system that performs inference operations on encrypted data as HE-based broad learning system. As shown in Fig. 2, our system is divided into two phases: training and inference. The specific steps of HE-based broad learning system are as follows:

1) *Training Phase:* Let X_{train} and Y_{train} be the plaintext training sets used as the input data and output result of the BLS, respectively. We then compute the random weights W_{m_i}, W_{e_j} and biases β_{m_i}, β_{e_j}, and the weight W of the BLS.

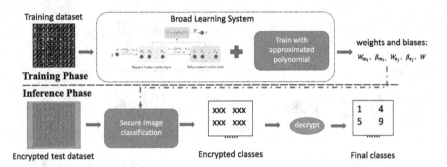

Fig. 2. Two phases of HE-based broad learning system.

2) *Inference Phase:*

  2.1) Let X_{test} be the plaintext test data. We get X_{enc} by $Encrypt(X_{test})$, and use Eq. (1) and (2) to obtain the encrypted input P_{enc} which is composed of the mapped feature nodes layer M^n and enhancement nodes layer E^m.

  2.2) We use $Y_{enc} = P_{enc} * W$ to get the encrypted prediction output Y_{enc}.

  2.3) The predicted output Y_{test} is obtained using $Decrypt(Y_{enc})$.

3.2   HE-Based Broad Learning System with Incremental Learning

By [9], if the BLS cannot achieve the desired performance after direct training, the performance can be improved by adding some enhancement nodes. Suppose p enhancement nodes are added, as shown in Fig. 3.

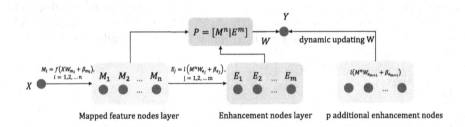

Fig. 3. The BLS structure withe incremental learning.

Denote P^{m+1} as:

$$P^{m+1} = [P|l(M^n W_{e_{m+1}} + \beta_{e_{m+1}})] \tag{6}$$

where $W_{e_{m+1}} \in \mathbb{R}^{nk \times p}$ and $\beta_{e_{m+1}}$ are randomly generated weights and biases for generating p enhancement nodes.

The pseudo-inverse of the new matrix as:

$$(P^{m+1})^+ = \begin{bmatrix} P^+ - HK^T \\ K^T \end{bmatrix} \tag{7}$$

where $H = [P^+|l(M^nW_{e_{m+1}} + \beta_{e_{m+1}})]$, $K^T = \begin{cases} (C)^+ & \text{if } C \neq 0 \\ (1 + H^TH)^{-1}K^TP^+ & \text{if } C = 0 \end{cases}$,

and $C = l(M^nW_{e_{m+1}} + \beta_{e_{m+1}}) - PH$.

Then, the updating weights:

$$W = \begin{bmatrix} W - HK^TY \\ K^TY \end{bmatrix} \tag{8}$$

The specific steps of HE-based broad learning system with incremental learning are as follows:

1) *Training Phase:*
   1.1) Let X_{train} and Y_{train} be the plaintext training sets used as the input data and output result of the BLS, respectively. We then compute the random weights W_{m_i}, W_{e_j} and biases β_{m_i}, β_{e_j} of the BLS.
   1.2) We use Eq. (6) to generate additional p enhancement nodes, and obtain the random weights $W_{e_{m+1}}$ and biases $\beta_{e_{m+1}}$, and the updating weights W.
2) *Inference Phase:*
   2.1) Let X_{test} be the plaintext test data. We get X_{enc} by $Encrypt(X_{test})$, and use Eq. (1), (2) and (6) to obtain the encrypted input P_{enc} which is composed of the mapped feature nodes layer M^n, enhancement nodes layer E^m and additional p enhancement nodes.
   2.2) We use $Y_{enc} = P_{enc} * W$ to get the encrypted prediction output Y_{enc}.
   2.3) The predicted output Y_{test} is obtained using $Decrypt(Y_{enc})$.

3.3 Polynomial Approximation of Activation Function

In the original BLS of [9], to generate the mapped feature nodes and enhancement nodes, the activation functions f and l are both implemented by ReLU, i.e., $ReLU = max(0, x)$. However, when building the HE-based broad learning system, a key limitation of the HE scheme is that it cannot support division and comparison, neither can it compute activation functions commonly used in BLS.

Therefore, it is necessary to find suitable polynomials, which are computable by HE, to approximate the ReLU activation function. The reason for choosing polynomials instead of a square function to approximate activation function is that the square function has unbounded derivative, which affects performance. Therefore, we use the least squares method to fit second-order polynomials in the domains $[-3,3]$, $[-4,4]$, $[-5,5]$ and $[-6,6]$, respectively. Specific polynomial approximation results are shown in Table 1. The comparison of ReLU activation function and its approximate polynomials is shown in Fig. 4.

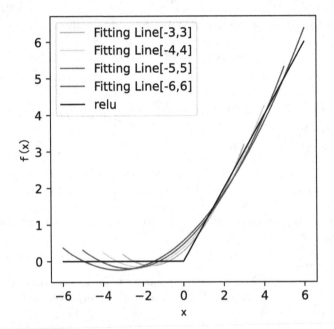

Fig. 4. Comparison of Relu and its polynomial approximations.

Table 1. Approximations of ReLu.

Activation function	Fitting domain	Polynomial approximated
ReLU	$[-3,3]$	$0.156093906x^2 + 0.5x + 0.281531532$
	$[-4,4]$	$0.117070429x^2 + 0.5x + 0.375375376$
	$[-5,5]$	$0.093656344x^2 + 0.5x + 0.469219212$
	$[-6,6]$	$0.078046953x^2 + 0.5x + 0.563063066$

4 Experimental Evaluation

We conduct experiments on plaintext training, plaintext inference, and ciphertext inference on the MNIST dataset and NORB dataset. The activation function used by the experimental baseline is a square function. The experiments are implemented in PyCharm on a platform with Intel i5-9400, 2.90-GHz.

4.1 Datasets

FHE can encrypt various types of data, such as text, images, audio, etc., which can effectively protect user privacy. Since Chen et al. used MNIST and NORB datasets in [9] to verify the validity of BLS, in order to better compare the relevant performance, we also use these two datasets to validate the proposed method, where MNIST is the grayscale image dataset and NORB is the RGB image dataset. In the plaintext experiment, the MNIST dataset is composed of 33,600 training images and 8,400 test images. The pixel size of each image is 28 × 28. Each handwritten digitized image is labeled with one of 10 numbers from 0 to 9. The NORB dataset consists of 24,300 training images and 24,300 test images labeled as one of ten categories. The pixel size of each picture is 2 × 96 × 96. In the ciphertext evaluation experiments, in order to save evaluation time, the test sets of both datasets were reduced to 1,000.

4.2 Network Architecture

In our experiments, the BLS network is constructed by 10 × 250 mapped feature nodes and 10 × 250 enhancement nodes, and the activation functions f and l are both approximated by the second-order polynomials in Table 1. In the BLS network with incremental learning, additional 1×250 enhancement nodes are added.

Table 2 shows the accuracy of the plaintext test. The highest classification accuracy of MNIST dataset is 0.92631, and for the NORB dataset it is 0.85169. The minimum training time is 59.925427 s and 47.469498 s, respectively. Due to hardware limitations, our accuracy does not reach the highest accuracy 0. 9874 and 0.8927 in [9].

4.3 Evaluation Method

We implement the LHE-based BLS inference using the Microsoft's TENSEAL [1] for the CKKS scheme. Each image is encrypted by the CKKS scheme into an encapsulated ciphertext. The parties other than the image owner cannot view the specific data content, which protects data privacy. CKKS's parameters used in the experiment are shown in Table 3. In this table N, Scale factor and $\log Q$ are parameters of the CKKS scheme which can be referred to in [10,11]. Depth is the multiplicative depth, which is the height of the multiplication dependency tree in the model of LHE-based BLS inference.

Table 2. Plaintext test results for MINST and NORB.

Dataset	Polynomial approximated	Accuracy	Training time (s)
MNIST	x^2	0.91738	**59.925427**
	$0.156093906x^2 + 0.5x + 0.281531532$	0.92143	60.787904
	$0.117070429x^2 + 0.5x + 0.375375376$	0.92571	60.129638
	$0.093656344x^2 + 0.5x + 0.469219212$	0.92429	60.297178
	$0.078046953x^2 + 0.5x + 0.563063066$	**0.92631**	61.145145
NORB	x^2	0.83329	47.607225
	$0.156093906x^2 + 0.5x + 0.281531532$	0.83041	49.596471
	$0.117070429x^2 + 0.5x + 0.375375376$	**0.85169**	57.917109
	$0.093656344x^2 + 0.5x + 0.469219212$	0.84251	**47.469498**
	$0.078046953x^2 + 0.5x + 0.563063066$	0.84877	48.077327

Table 3. CKKS parameters.

	Activation function	Order	N	Scale factor	$\log Q$	Depth
Baseline	Square	–	16384	60	200	5
Ours	Second-order polynomial	2	16384	60	280	7

4.4 Evaluation Results

For the consideration of time efficiency, the first 1000 records of the MNIST and NORB test set are taken as new test sets in the LHE-based BLS inference. The results of MNIST and NORB test sets on ciphertext inference are shown in Table 4. According to the experimental results, the highest accuracy of MNIST ciphertext inference is 0.928. Compared with the baseline method of directly replacing the activation function with a square function, the accuracy of the proposed method is increased by 0.015. On the NORB dataset, its best classification accuracy is 0.672, with an improvement of 0.004 compared to the baseline method.

Table 4. Encrypted test set results for MINST and NORB.

Dataset	Polynomial approximated	Plaintext accuracy	Ciphertext accuracy
MNIST	x^2	0.926	0.913
	$0.156093906x^2 + 0.5x + 0.281531532$	0.925	**0.928**
	$0.117070429x^2 + 0.5x + 0.375375376$	0.927	0.927
	$0.093656344x^2 + 0.5x + 0.469219212$	0.927	0.926
	$0.078046953x^2 + 0.5x + 0.563063066$	**0.932**	0.927
NORB	x^2	**0.821**	0.668
	$0.156093906x^2 + 0.5x + 0.281531532$	0.783	0.631
	$0.117070429x^2 + 0.5x + 0.375375376$	0.809	**0.672**
	$0.093656344x^2 + 0.5x + 0.469219212$	0.797	0.615
	$0.078046953x^2 + 0.5x + 0.563063066$	0.762	0.627

To verify whether BLS with incremental learning in [9] can improve performance, we conduct LHE-based BLS inference experiments with incremental learning. The results show an accuracy of 0.912 on the MNIST dataset and 0.616 on the NORB dataset. Neither can compare with the highest accuracy of LHE-based broad learning inference. Two reasons can be explained here. Firstly, by [9], not all BLS with incremental learning will certainly improve performance. In addition, since we replaced the non-linear activation function with approximate polynomials, the performance can be decreased by the errors induced.

5   Conclusions

In this paper we propose an LHE-based scheme for broad learning inference, avoiding the problems of high multiplicative depth. We further extend the scheme to LHE-based BLS with incremental learning. Approximate second-order polynomials are utilized to replace the non-linear activation function, which makes the LHE computations feasible and improve the inference accuracy. Experiments demonstrate that our proposed method achieves the highest classification accuracy of 0.928 and 0.672 on the MNIST and NORB dataset, respectively, which can compare with broad learning inference using plaintext data. In the future, we will extend the LHE-based scheme to more models and take more measures to balance the trade-off between inference accuracy and time efficiency.

Acknowledgement. This work was supported by the Key-Area Research and Development Program of Guangdong Province (No. 2020B010164003).

References

1. https://github.com/OpenMined/TenSEAL
2. Al Badawi, A., et al.: Towards the AlexNet moment for homomorphic encryption: HCNN, the first homomorphic CNN on encrypted data with GPUs. arXiv e-prints pp. arXiv-1811 (2018)
3. Bajard, J.-C., Eynard, J., Hasan, M.A., Zucca, V.: A full RNS variant of FV like somewhat homomorphic encryption schemes. In: Avanzi, R., Heys, H. (eds.) SAC 2016. LNCS, vol. 10532, pp. 423–442. Springer, Cham (2017). https://doi.org/10.1007/978-3-319-69453-5_23
4. Bost, R., Popa, R.A., Tu, S., Goldwasser, S.: Machine learning classification over encrypted data. Cryptology ePrint Archive (2014)
5. Brakerski, Z.: Fully homomorphic encryption without modulus switching from classical GapSVP. In: Safavi-Naini, R., Canetti, R. (eds.) CRYPTO 2012. LNCS, vol. 7417, pp. 868–886. Springer, Heidelberg (2012). https://doi.org/10.1007/978-3-642-32009-5_50
6. Brakerski, Z., Gentry, C., Vaikuntanathan, V.: (Leveled) fully homomorphic encryption without bootstrapping. ACM Trans. Comput. Theory **6**(3), 1–36 (2014)
7. Brutzkus, A., Gilad-Bachrach, R., Elisha, O.: Low latency privacy preserving inference. In: International Conference on Machine Learning, pp. 812–821. PMLR (2019)
8. Chabanne, H., De Wargny, A., Milgram, J., Morel, C., Prouff, E.: Privacy-preserving classification on deep neural network. Cryptology ePrint Archive (2017)
9. Chen, C.P., Liu, Z.: Broad learning system: an effective and efficient incremental learning system without the need for deep architecture. IEEE Trans. Neural Netw. Learn. Syst. **29**(1), 10–24 (2017)
10. Cheon, J.H., Han, K., Kim, A., Kim, M., Song, Y.: A full RNS variant of approximate homomorphic encryption. In: Cid, C., Jacobson, Jr., M. (eds.) Selected Areas in Cryptography (SAC 2018). LNCS, vol. 11349, pp. 347–368. Springer, Cham (2019). https://doi.org/10.1007/978-3-030-10970-7_16

11. Cheon, J.H., Kim, A., Kim, M., Song, Y.: Homomorphic encryption for arithmetic of approximate numbers. In: Takagi, T., Peyrin, T. (eds.) ASIACRYPT 2017. LNCS, vol. 10624, pp. 409–437. Springer, Cham (2017). https://doi.org/10.1007/978-3-319-70694-8_15
12. Fan, J., Vercauteren, F.: Somewhat practical fully homomorphic encryption. Cryptology ePrint Archive (2012)
13. Gentry, C.: A fully homomorphic encryption scheme. Stanford University (2009)
14. Gilad-Bachrach, R., Dowlin, N., Laine, K., Lauter, K., Naehrig, M., Wernsing, J.: CryptoNets: applying neural networks to encrypted data with high throughput and accuracy. In: International Conference on Machine Learning, pp. 201–210. PMLR (2016)
15. Hesamifard, E., Takabi, H., Ghasemi, M.: CryptoDL: deep neural networks over encrypted data. arXiv preprint arXiv:1711.05189 (2017)
16. Hoerl, A.E., Kennard, R.W.: Ridge regression: biased estimation for nonorthogonal problems. Technometrics **12**(1), 55–67 (1970)
17. Ishiyama, T., Suzuki, T., Yamana, H.: Highly accurate CNN inference using approximate activation functions over homomorphic encryption. In: 2020 IEEE International Conference on Big Data (Big Data), pp. 3989–3995. IEEE (2020)
18. Rivest, R.L., Adleman, L., Dertouzos, M.L., et al.: On data banks and privacy homomorphisms. Found. Secure Comput. **4**(11), 169–180 (1978)
19. Yuan, X., Chen, J., Zhang, N., Fang, X., Liu, D.: A federated bidirectional connection broad learning scheme for secure data sharing in internet of vehicles. China Commun. **18**(7), 117–133 (2021)

Application of Probabilistic Common Set on an Open World Set for Vertical Federated Learning

Hiroshi Someda[1]([envelope]) [ORCID], Shigeyuki Osada[2] [ORCID], and Yuya Kajikawa[1] [ORCID]

[1] School of Environment and Society, Technology and Innovation
Management/Department of Innovation Science, Tokyo Institute of Technology,
Tokyo, Japan
`someda.h.aa@mtitech.ac.jp`, `kajikawa@titech.ac.jp`
[2] The Japan Research Institute, Limited, Shinagawa-ku, Tokyo, Japan
`osada.shigeyuki@jri.co.jp`

Abstract. Vertical federated learning (VFL) is a distributed machine learning technology that is suitable for model building in organizations across different industries. It enables the identification of a common set of data that co-occur across organizations. However, VFL uses private set intersection (PSI) protocols, which requires making all data shareable, and satisfying the data minimization principle in the General Data Protection Regulation is difficult. To mitigate noncompliance in privacy regulations, we propose a new VFL method that uses horizontal federated learning to identify the common set instead of PSI. The method consists of two concepts: The first is to use a common data structure between organizations to avoid using PSI. The second is to identify the common set from machine learning classifiers of unseen data of a certain class. Our proposed method considers that the data labeled as the desired class is unseen data and it is not in the common set. Experimental results show that the F-measure is 0.8 or higher in 40% of the common set ratios.

Keywords: Federated Learning · private set intersection · open set recognition · information sharing · privacy

1 Introduction

Data use beyond organizations and industry can produce new insights and new value. However, according to privacy regulations, it is also important to obtain the clear consent of the customer, while sharing information in a way wherein the identification of an individual can be inferred among different organizations. There is a need for a method to analyze data while protecting privacy.

Among privacy enhancing technologies, federated learning [5–7,13] has been proposed as a method using a deep learning model without sharing data between organizations.

H. Takizawa et al. (Eds.): PDCAT 2022, LNCS 13798, pp. 509–519, 2023.
https://doi.org/10.1007/978-3-031-29927-8_39

A model using vertical federated learning (VFL) is particularly well-suited for different industries. To use VFL, it is necessary to identify samples that co-occur in the data held across organizations.

Private set intersection (PSI) [4,9], which has encrypted set operations, has also been proposed as a way to obtain co-occurring samples in data. However, PSI requires a setting that all data be shareable with other data; this makes it difficult to satisfy the data minimization principle in General Data Protection Regulation.

In this study, we propose a new VFL method that uses probabilistic set operations by horizontal federated learning to identify the common set instead of PSI.

This paper is organized as follows. Section 2 describes the problem to be solved and federated learning. In Sect. 3, we apply federated learning to propose a method for verifying the existence of common customers between two organizations with a common data structure without sharing the data. In Sect. 4, we evaluate the proposed method by its implementation. In Sect. 5, we summarize and discuss future work.

2   Background

2.1   Collaboration Between Different Industries and Privacy Care

There are challenges with privacy in sharing data between organizations. Each organization may have unseen class data that is private because by regulation, organizations are not allowed to share all data. These unseen class data present a challenge because models trained for classification often assume that all test class data have been seen at the training stage. Open set recognition (OSR) research is ongoing to detect unseen class data that are different from the data used for training. One-class SVM classification, OpenMAX [1] and garbage data are available for OSR [3]. However, there are currently no proposals that apply methods using one classification to federated learning [11]. OpenMAX has been proposed for image classification tasks. OpenMAX uses a deep learning convolutional neural network model to classify unseen classes. Shu et al. have proposed a text classification method for open-set classification. They found a significant drop in F-measures with an increasing number of classes even though their proposed method had better F-measures than OpenMAX using 20 classes and 50 classes data classification [12]. The resultant F-measures showed a drop with an increase in the number of classes from 20 to 50. In this paper, more than 1000 classes are used in all cases to classify the unseen and seen classes. These classified classes are used to identify the sample probabilistically. To identify the sample of the common set of P and Q probabilistically, we propose a method that uses garbage data, which is a method that has long been used, and we over-fit a model on trained classes, as suggested by Matan et al. [3,8]. According to Matan, the classifier should predict the class of data belonging to the untrained/unseen class with a bias toward a few specific classes. In addition, an

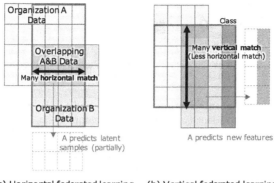

(a) Horizontal federated learning   (b) Vertical federated learning

Fig. 1. Horizontal and vertical federated learning. Vertical federated learning is suitable for model building with organizations between A and B in different industries.

N-gram-based compression method is proposed to match the infinite number of data possibilities as OSRs in deep learning.

Our proposed method probabilistically determines whether third-party data contains an organization's customers, without the third-party data being shared.

2.2 Federated Learning

Federated learning is a client–server system of machine learning that maintains a data distribution state. The federated learning approach depends on the degree of similarity in the data structures of a collaborating organization [13]. For example, when sharing data between different medical organizations that provide the same type of medical care, or when sharing data within industries such as finance and construction that have predetermined data structures due to industry regulations, it can be assumed that there are many overlapping data columns with the same meaning, as shown in Fig. 1(a).

Analysis based on the assumption that the overlapping data spread horizontally is called horizontal federated learning (HFL).

Conversely, if the collaborating organizations are in a relationship between different industries (such as the relationship between a bank and a web service), the overlapping data do not spread horizontally because the data structures are different. The vertical overlap data of the same target held by each organization enable researchers to build models using previously unknown classes and correlations. This method is called vertical federated learning (Fig. 1(b)).

To use vertical federated learning, it is necessary to identify samples that co-occur in the data held by the collaborating organizations. To achieve this, a method has been proposed to use private set intersection (PSI), a communication protocol that securely computes common data of different sets while protecting the privacy between organizations [4,9]. Although this method uses encryption for privacy protection, it may be subject to regulation against providing personal information to a third party.

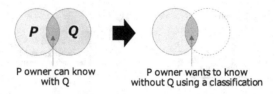

P owner can know
with Q

P owner wants to know
without Q using a classification

Fig. 2. Common set is the intersection between P and Q. To have vertical federated learning, it is necessary to identify samples of the common set in the data P and Q.

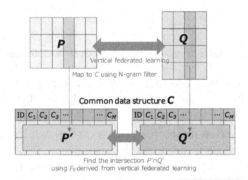

Fig. 3. Vertical federated learning using a common data structure C. The data structures between training and test data must match because the proposed method uses deep learning.

3 Proposed Method

3.1 Basic Idea

On the two data sets P and Q, as shown in Fig. 2, the owner of P wants to obtain the common set $P \cap Q$ without obtaining Q.

Common Data Structures. The owners of P and Q calculate the frequency of string occurrence using N-grams for the common data in the metadata. As shown in Fig. 3, the frequency of string occurrences is calculated. This is done by preparing a matrix with N columns of a variety of characters. This occurrence frequency is then expressed by turning bits on and off as in the Bloom filter [2]. For example, if we consider data consisting of numbers from 0 to 9, such as a telephone number or a credit card number, the result of the N-gram calculation is shown in Fig. 4. We use N-grams to construct a common data structure, C, to fit deep learning processing in a closed space (the Nth power of 10 in this case). The set of P and Q transformed into the C are called P' and Q', respectively. Because P' and Q' are comparable, the owner of P can identify the common set by federated learning on C.

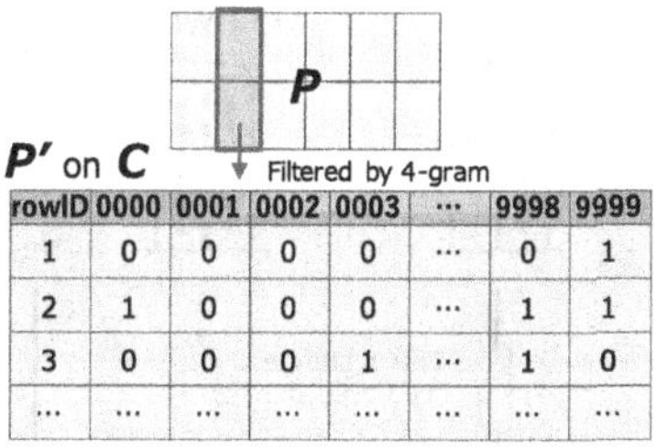

Fig. 4. Example of mapping P to P'. Our proposed common data structure, C, is built using N-grams to fit deep learning processing in a closed space (using the Nth power of 10 in this case).

Reduction of False Positives. The proposed method, which uses data concatenation based on the frequency of string occurrence, increases the possibility of false positives, as well as the Bloom filter, which is a probabilistic data structure. Therefore, to improve the classifier precision for $P \cap Q$, we insert the data G belonging to the garbage class with random values using the MT19937 that do not exist in Q into Q, and thus improve the classifier precision for $P \cap \bar{Q}$.

It is also suggested by Matan *et al.* that when making a classifier with a neural network specifying Softmax as the activation function, if data belonging to a uniformly distributed class is used for the training data, the classifier will predict the class of data belonging to the untrained or unseen class with a bias toward a few specific classes [3,8].

We use this bias to improve the precision of $P \cap \bar{Q}$ by assuming that the data, for which multiple samples are predicted to be in the same class, are data that do not exist in Q, the training dataset for the classifier.

3.2 Procedure

Under the restriction that each owner of P and Q cannot refer to each other's datasets, we propose a method for identifying the common dataset $P \cap Q$. The method is described from the view of the owner of the dataset P.

STEP 1: Definition of Common Data Structure. The owners of P and Q disclose the data structure of P and Q, respectively, and the data summary information, such as the number of samples, the number of columns, the name and meaning of each column, and the input rules to the extent possible. The owners of both P and Q check the other's data summary information. They specify one or more columns from each of P and Q that are likely to overlap. The owners of P and Q define the common data structure C for overlap columns that are quantified into a uniform distribution.

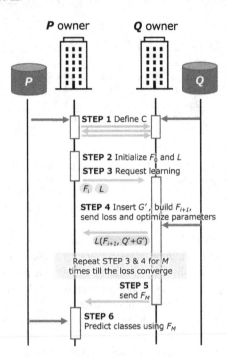

Fig. 5. Procedure of STEP 1 to 6.

STEP 2: Initialization. When the owner of P sends a request to train the classifier to the owner of Q, the owner of P creates a prototype F_0 of the classifier as well as a loss function L to evaluate the parameter optimization of the classifier that will be worked on by the owner of Q. F_0 is an untrained neural network with: nodes in the number of columns of C as the input layer; nodes in the number of samples of P plus the offset as the output layer; a hidden layer; and an activation function.

STEP 3: Classifier Building. The owner of P sends the F_0 and L created in STEP 2 to the owner of Q, and makes a request to execute deep learning using Q'.

STEP 4: Classifier Optimization. The owner of Q generates a dataset G belonging to the garbage classes with random values that do not exist in Q. G's classes are assigned from a specific range of classes. Each G's samples have a unique class from G's range of classes. The range of G's classes is shared between P and Q owners. Therefore, it is possible to remove G's classes. Although G's class data are not the common set between P and Q, it makes the boundary to classify the common set finer.

The owner of Q executes deep learning using G', Q', and F_i, which is the transformation of G on C, to obtain the classifier F_{i+1}. The owner of Q also calculates the value of F_{i+1} using L, and then only sends this value to the owner of P. The owner of P repeats the request to the owner of Q to execute deep learning as well as to evaluate F and this is done M times until the values received from the owner of Q converge.

STEP 5: Completion of the Classifier. The owner of Q sends the classifier F_M to the owner of P at the request of the owner of P. The owner of P decides whether to request more of the classifier F_M according to the status of convergence of the values fed to it by Q.

STEP 6: Data Consolidation The owner of P predicts the class of all samples in P using F_M. If only one class corresponds to one sample, then it predicts the sample is in both P and Q. If a relation appears that corresponds to more than one class in a sample, then the sample is either a garbage class or an untrained class. A specific class where multiple samples belong is regarded as an untrained sample class. Consequently, the samples in the multiple sample class are considered to be samples that exist in P but not in Q.

In this way, the owner of P can obtain the probabilistic common set $P \cap Q$ without directly being provided the data by the owner of Q.

4   Evaluation

4.1   Evaluation Environment

For the evaluation of the proposed method, we built an evaluation environment using `OpenMined PySyft 0.3.0` [10], which is a free and stable version. `PyTorch 1.6.0` and `Python 3.6.9` were used for the deep learning platform and the `Ubuntu 18.04.5` Linux distribution was used as the operating system.

A prototype of classification F_0 initialized by owner P is described as follows. The number of nodes of the input and output layers equals the number of columns in C. The F_0 deep learning model used in the evaluation environment had four layers, 10^4 nodes in the input layer, two hidden layers and 1000 nodes in each hidden layer. The activation function of each hidden layer was ReLu, and the output layer's activation function was Log SoftMax.

The loss function was specified as a negative log-likelihood function. This combination of the loss function and activation function computed the same result as SoftMax. For optimization, the learning rate was set to 0.01 using Adam, and the number of epochs was set to 30. The other parameters used in the evaluation environment are shown in Table 1.

Table 1. Parameters of the evaluation environment. Five datasets with differing combinations of P and Q giving the ratio of common set samples against P. For every evaluation, five samples of G datasets, 0, 100, 1000, 2000, and 3000, were added to Q.

	Datasets		Common sets ratio					
	P	Q	0.01	0.1	0.2	0.3	0.4	0.5
	2000	2000	20	200	400	600	800	1000
	2000	3000	20	200	400	600	800	1000
Samples	3000	2000	30	300	600	900	1200	1500
	1000	3000	10	100	200	300	400	500
	3000	1000	30	300	600	900	N/A	N/A

Average F-measures were evaluated for 1400 cases with a combination of 5 dataSets (P, Q), five garbage, six common sets, and ten random seeds. It was assumed that P and Q had phone numbers in the evaluation environment.

The phone numbers used in the evaluation environment were randomly generated using the Mersenne Twister algorithm (MT19937), which consists of 11 digits characters starting with "090."

In STEP 1, we assumed that each owner of P and Q was able to agree to construct a common data structure using a sequence of meaningful phone numbers by disclosing the data summary information to each other.

The common data structure was constructed using N-grams with $N = 4$, where each phone number was a character of length one. In other words, the common data structure C was a matrix indicating either co-occurrence or non-cooccurrence of strings of length 4 (strings from 0000 to 9999) appearing in the phone number and was obtained by running N-grams with $N = 4$.

To construct a common data structure, randomly generated 11-digit numbers were used as telephone numbers.

For practical business data use, one or more columns of P and Q, which are likely to overlap must convert to uniformly distributed quantification as part of preparation.

4.2   Results and Discussion

Using the evaluation environment of Table 1, the effects of the number of common sets between P and Q, the amount of data in the garbage class, and the presence or absence of the bias that Matan et al. described in Sect. 3 are shown in Fig. 6, averaged over the F-measure of each classifier. Legend "w/o B" shows the case where the bias is removed to improve the precision of $P \cap \bar{Q}$ detection.

Figure 6(a) shows that the F-measure increases as G increases when the bias of Matan et al. is included. This indicates that the amount of garbage class data inserted by the owner of Q contributes to improvement in the precision of the classifier.

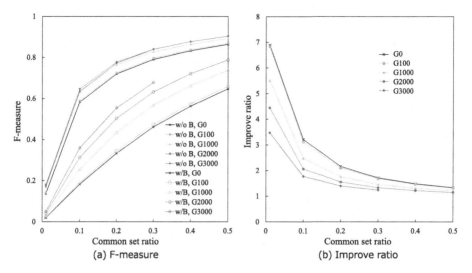

Fig. 6. F-measure of classifications and improvement ratio removing bias. The case uniformly distributed class is used for the training data with the SoftMax activation function. The classifier will predict the class of data belonging to the untrained/unseen class with a bias toward a few specific classes. [3,8]. The legend "w/ B" indicates the case where the bias is included, while "w/o B" shows the case where the bias is removed. The more G, the better is the F-measure both in "w/ B" and "w/o B". An improvement rate is defined as the value obtained by dividing the F-measure of "w/o B" and "w/ B". The improvement rate tends to decrease as the number of G increases.

Suppose that all combinations of bit sequences appearing on C could be covered by inserting garbage class data. Then, P could be a subset of $Q + G$. Therefore, using an over-trained discriminator, the F-measure is expected to be as close to 1 as possible. However, to achieve this, the owner of Q is forced to use a large amount of their computing resources to generate garbage classes and create classifiers. Hence, it may be necessary to design incentives for the owner of Q.

It can also be observed that removing the bias of Matan *et al.* improves the F-measure regardless of the number of G.

Conversely, if we define the "improvement ratio" as the value obtained by dividing the F-measure of "w/o B" and "w/ B". We can confirm that the "improvement ratio" decreases as the number of G increases, as shown in Fig. 6(b). Figure 6(b) also shows that the "improvement ratio" of the F-measure decreases as the samples of the common set increase. This may be because of the number of samples in the common sets in P and Q increases. The larger data in training, the better classifier we can build. Thus less effect of the set $P \cap \bar{Q}$ that is removed as bias.

F-measure standard deviation from "w/ B" (a) and "w/o B" in (b) in Fig. 7. The proposed method, without bias, has a higher standard deviation in evaluation cases, shown in (b). In future study, stability needs to be improved.

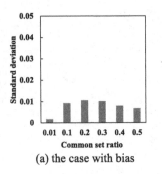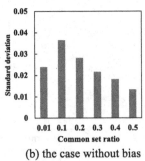

(a) the case with bias (b) the case without bias

Fig. 7. Standard deviation F-measure. (a) is the F-measure with bias, "w/ B", and (b) is the F-measure without bias, "w/o B".

The Q data owner gives the same class type on multi-samples of Q' in STEP4 for Q' data anonymization. This additional operation may enable the Q data owner to control k-anonymization for the common set of Q' and P' that train the model. In a future study, the k-anonymize and differential privacy methods should be considered to avoid identifiability of a specific individual by referring to other information and business practices and by usable accuracy tuning.

5   Conclusion

In this paper, we proposed a new VFL method that uses probabilistic set operations by horizontal federated learning to identify the common set instead of PSI.

We evaluated the F-measure of the models obtained by the proposed method using an evaluation environment. We confirmed that the proposed method could probabilistically predict the existence or non-existence of correspondence between the common set and the samples in the common set without share data.

In the future, we plan to extend the proposed method to the case where there are more than three parties; to add generality to the method of constructing the common data structure and incorporate k-anonymity to further reduce the "identifiability of a specific individual by referring to other information."

References

1. Bendale, A., Boult, T.E.: Towards open set deep networks. In: 2016 IEEE Conference on Computer Vision and Pattern Recognition (CVPR), pp. 1563–1572. IEEE Computer Society, Los Alamitos, CA, USA (2016). https://doi.org/10.1109/CVPR.2016.173
2. Bloom, B.H.: Space/time trade-offs in hash coding with allowable errors. Commun. ACM **13**(7), 422–426 (1970). https://doi.org/10.1145/362686.362692
3. Dhamija, A.R., Günther, M., Boult, T.E.: Reducing network agnostophobia. In: NeurIPS, pp. 9175–9186 (2018). https://proceedings.neurips.cc/paper/2018/hash/48db71587df6c7c442e5b76cc723169a-Abstract.html

4. Egert, R., Fischlin, M., Gens, D., Jacob, S., Senker, M., Tillmanns, J.: Privately computing set-union and set-intersection cardinality via bloom filters. In: Foo, E., Stebila, D. (eds.) ACISP 2015. LNCS, vol. 9144, pp. 413–430. Springer, Cham (2015). https://doi.org/10.1007/978-3-319-19962-7_24

5. Jiang, J.C., Kantarci, B., Oktug, S., Soyata, T.: Federated learning in smart city sensing: challenges and opportunities. Sensors **20**(21), 6230 (2020). https://doi.org/10.3390/s20216230

6. Kairouz, P., et al.: Advances and open problems in federated learning (2019). https://doi.org/10.48550/ARXIV.1912.04977

7. Kholod, I., et al.: Open-source federated learning frameworks for IoT: a comparative review and analysis. Sensors **21**(1), 167 (2021). https://doi.org/10.3390/s21010167

8. Matan, O., et al.: Handwritten character recognition using neural network architectures. In: the 4th USPS Advanced Technology Conference, pp. 1003–1011 (1990)

9. Miyaji, A., Nagao, Y.: Privacy preserving data integration protocol. In: 2020 15th Asia Joint Conference on Information Security (AsiaJCIS), pp. 89–96 (2020). https://doi.org/10.1109/AsiaJCIS50894.2020.00025

10. OpenMined: Pysyft (2022). https://www.openmined.org/

11. Perera, P., Oza, P., Patel, V.M.: One-class classification: a survey. arXiv preprint arXiv:2101.03064 (2021)

12. Shu, L., Xu, H., Liu, B.: DOC: deep open classification of text documents. In: Proceedings of the 2017 Conference on Empirical Methods in Natural Language Processing, pp. 2911–2916. Association for Computational Linguistics, Copenhagen, Denmark (2017). https://doi.org/10.18653/v1/D17-1314

13. Yang, Q., Liu, Y., Chen, T., Tong, Y.: Federated machine learning: concept and applications. ACM Trans. Intell. Syst. Technol. **10**(2), 1–19 (2019). https://doi.org/10.1145/3298981

Workflow

Towards a Standard Process Management Infrastructure for Workflows Using Python

Wael Elwasif[1(✉)], Thomas Naughton[1], and Matthew Baker[1,2]

[1] Oak Ridge National Laboratory, Oak Ridge, TN, USA
`{elwasifwr,naughtont}@ornl.gov`
[2] Voltron Data, Mountain View, CA, USA
`matthew@voltrondata.com`

Abstract. Orchestrating the execution of ensembles of processes lies at the core of scientific workflow engines on large scale parallel platforms. This is usually handled using platform-specific command line tools, with limited process management control and potential strain on system resources. The PMIx standard provides a uniform interface to system resources. The low level C implementation of PMIx has hampered its use in workflow engines, leading to the development of Python binding that has yet to gain traction. In this paper, we present our work to harden the PMIx Python client, demonstrating its usability using a prototype Python driver to orchestrate the execution of an ensemble of processes. We present experimental results using the prototype on the Summit supercomputer at Oak Ridge National Laboratory. This work lays the foundation for wider adoption of PMIx for workflow engines, and encourages wider support of more PMIx functionality in vendor provided system software stacks.

1 Introduction

Scalable workflows based on the use of many tasks or *ensemble computing* for large scale High Performance Computing (HPC) applications have become an important paradigm for scientific discovery in many domains [1,4,8]. In such applications, the execution of many instances of a core simulation is orchestrated to carry out the desired simulation campaign (typically in a parameter sweep campaign) via a top level driver engine. This paradigm represents an alternative to "classical" large scale HPC workloads where applications are built using a tightly coupled parallel programming model, with processes that make up a running application using message passing libraries to exchange data and coordinate overall application execution.

Notice: This manuscript has been authored in part by UT-Battelle, LLC under Contract No. DE-AC05-00OR22725 with the U.S. Department of Energy. The United States Government retains and the publisher, by accepting the article for publication, acknowledges that the United States Government retains a non-exclusive, paid-up, irrevocable, world-wide license to publish or reproduce the published form of this manuscript, or allow others to do so, for United States Government purposes. The Department of Energy will provide public access to these results of federally sponsored research in accordance with the DOE Public Access Plan (http://energy.gov/downloads/doe-public-access-plan).
M. Baker's work was performed while at ORNL.

By their very nature, loosely coupled workflows build on top of a "coordinated processes" abstraction as the foundation for orchestrated execution on large scale parallel platforms. As a result, at the core of workflow engines, such as Radical-Pilot [2,5] and Fireworks [7], lies a process management layer that provides the means for process lifetime management on behalf of high level workflow control logic. This process management layer, in turn, usually builds upon platform-specific (typically vendor provided) system software as the means for managing the scheduling, instantiation, monitoring and error handling of processes executing on behalf of the workflow engine.

Reliance on command line tools requires the workflow engine to implement custom process management logic to support different system software stacks, and/or support changes introduced by different versions of the same stack as a result of continuous development or different site configuration policies. Another drawback of this approach is the lack of a flexible programmatic interface for use by the workflow engine, as system "native" process management is exposed via command line tools that rely on the limited operating system (OS) process management system calls abstraction. This approach leads to an $O(N)$ growth of resources consumed by the workflow engine as the number of managed processes N grows, potentially exhausting OS resources on the compute node where the workflow engine executes (especially if it is a shared batch node). These drawbacks suggest that a standard, resource efficient, programmatic interface to process management would alleviate the need for workflow engines to develop and support a separate solution for separate platforms, thus focusing more on the workflow management aspect itself. Process Management Interface for Exascale (PMIx) is an effort to provide such a common layer.

PMIx is an application programming interface (API) standard to provide HPC libraries and programming models with portable and well-defined access to commonly available distributed computing system services. OpenPMIx [10] is the reference C implementation of PMIx that is used in many projects, including the PMIx Reference RunTime Environment (PRRTE) used in the Open MPI library. The low level nature of the PMIx interface, and the use of C as the implementation language has impeded the use of PMIx in higher level tools such as workflow engines, which are dominated by Python. Starting in version 4.0 of OpenPMIx, a Python binding was included to address this gap. However, this binding has yet to gain wide use by tool developers.

In this paper, we present our work to harden the Python binding of PMIx and study its usability as an API for orchestrating the execution of large ensemble of processes. We describe the development of a prototype Python driver (`Pyrun`) that is used to exercise the PMIx Python client API, and demonstrate the use of Python's high level data structures as a means to drive a PMIx compliant implementation, alleviating the need for using the low level, error-prone C interface. We report our results running various synthetic workloads on the Summit supercomputer at the Oak Ridge National Laboratory, using OpenPMIx/PRRTE as the basis implementation for the PMIx standard. In Sect. 2 we present an overview of PMIx and the main APIs used for process management. Our work to harden the PMIx Python client and the design of the `Pyrun` prototype driver are presented in Sect. 3. Experimental results are presented in Sect. 4 and we present our conclusions and future work in Sect. 6.

2   Background

The Process Management Interface for Exascale (PMIx) standard [11,12] is an open specification that provides an application programming interface for clients to interact with system management software in a consistent manner. The PMIx standard extends the earlier PMI-1 and PMI-2 definitions [6]. The OpenPMIx [10] project provides a reference implementation of the PMIx standard [11], which includes both a client library implmentation (`openpmix`) and a server implementation called the PMIx Reference RunTime Environment (PRRTE).

The PMIx standard seeks to provide a common programming interface for managing distributed processes in a portable manner in much the same way as scientific applications use the Message Passing Interface (MPI) [9] to write portable programs. There are three "roles", or viewpoints, within the PMIx interface [12]: client, server and tool. The PMIx server provides an interface to the native resource management system. The PMIx client is a task started by the PMIx server that may have a parallel context defined. The PMIx process has all needed information placed in its execution context to identify itself, e.g., rank, and to enable communication with peers in the parallel application. A tool is an auxillary software utility that can be used to request new processes be created by the server, and possibly to co-locate additional executables to support the tool itself, e.g., debuggers for parallel applications.

In PMIx, each application (serial or parallel) is assigned a unique '*job identifier (jobId)*' that is used to track the lifecycle of the instance (e.g., mapping to resources, launching task(s), termination). A PMIx *namespace* is a string that uniquely identifies the job and all applications within that job have the same namespace. PMIx uses a key-value approach to send directives for APIs and to pass qualifiers that may provide restrictions. The PMIx standard defines the recognized keys and their associated meaning/semantics, while the concrete values may be implementation specific. The standard also defines the data type for the information associated with the key, e.g., `PMIX_BOOL` (boolean value), `PMIX_STRING` (string value).

The PMIx interface is defined to be highly flexible and uses the attributes (key-value) system to define what features are being requested. This enables variation in the underlying resource management systems as to what features are supported. The caller can probe for supported features using a query interface, or use a try/re-try approach to backoff.

The PMIx interface makes heavy use of callback functions. These asynchronous callbacks are typically invoked by dedicated progress thread(s) associated with the progress engine of the underlying PMIx implementation. The callbacks are used to asynchronously notify the completion of tasks, or occurance of events, e.g., input/output events, signals. The standard includes details on what events are generated and their associated semantics. For example, process lifecycle can be monitored by registering for events like `PMIX_EVENT_JOB_START` (spawned first process in job), `PMIX_EVENT_JOB_COMPLETE` (spawned all processes in job), `PMIX_EVENT_JOB_END` (all processes in job terminate) [12].

The focus of this paper is on the use of PMIx in a Python based environment. Therefore, our examples use the Python bindings that were introduced in v4.0 of the PMIx standard. We have removed error handling from the examples to save space.

In Listing 1.1, a tool instance is initialized and connects to the server specified in a file (*dvm_file*); a callback handler (done_cb) is registered that is invoked when a job ends.

```
1  def done_cb(evhdlr:int, status:int, source:dict, info:list, results:list):
2      with done_var:
3          done_var.notify()
4      return pmix.PMIX_EVENT_ACTION_COMPLETE,None
5
6  tool = pmix.PMIxTool()
7  rc,my_proc = tool.init( [{'key': pmix.PMIX_SERVER_URI,
8                            'value': "file:{}".format(dvm_file),
9                            'val_type':pmix.PMIX_STRING}] )
10
11 rc,handle = tool.register_event_handler( [pmix.PMIX_EVENT_JOB_END], None, done_cb)
```

Listing 1.1. Example of tool initialization and registration for job termination to trigger a done_cb callback that uses a condition variable to notify the Python program.

```
1  job_info = [ {"key": pmix.PMIX_MAPBY, "value": "core", "val_type": pmix.PMIX_STRING},
2               {"key": pmix.PMIX_BINDTO,"value": "core", "val_type": pmix.PMIX_STRING} ]
3  exe = Path("/home/sgrundy/bin/sleeper").resolve()
4  app = { "cmd": str(exe), "argv": [str(exe), "-n", "180"], "maxprocs": 8, "my_id": 1 }
5  rc, nspace = tool.spawn(job_info, [app])
```

Listing 1.2. Example of tool requesting to spawn an 8 process job that takes a command-line argument, with all processes mapped & bound to by cores.

```
1  def iof_cb(iofhdlr:int, channel:int, source:dict, payload:dict, info:list):
2      buf = payload['bytes'][:int(payload['size'])].decode('UTF-8').strip()
3      #...process buffer in Python as appropriate...
4
5  tool.iof_pull( [{'nspace':nspace,
6                   'rank': pmix.PMIX_RANK_WILDCARD}],
7                 pmix.PMIX_FWD_STDOUT_CHANNEL |
8                 pmix.PMIX_FWD_STDERR_CHANNEL,
9                 [], iof_cb)
```

Listing 1.3. Example of a tool requesting to have all stdout and stderr from a remote set of processes routed to the callback handler iof_cb.

The *spawn* operation creates process, which may be a single core (serial) task, or a parallel application spanning thousands of compute nodes. Listing 1.2 shows an example of tool.spawn() that creates a job with 8 processes and *sleeper -n 180* as the command-line argument. The 8 processes in the job are mapped to the available resources based on compute cores, and each instance is bound to a single compute core.

Listing 1.3 shows an example of the tool requesting to receive the output from remote processes. When data from the remote processes is generated on the standard output and error file descriptors, the contents will be delivered to the registered callback handler (iof_cb()) where the data may be extracted from the buffer and processed accordingly by the calling Python process. The source of the data is also provided with the callback so the data can be recorded on a per-job basis, which might be printed at the end or written to a common file in order to reduce the number of file descriptors.

The OpenPMIx project's reference library and runtime environment are the most feature complete PMIx implementation available publically. There are commercial vendors with varying degrees of support for PMIx. IBM's LSF, used on the Summit supercomputer, uses portions of PMIx for the internal system but is not generally exposed for direct end-user interactions. SchedMD's SLURM resource manager includes support of a subset of the PMIx interface, and there are PMIx community efforts working to extend the supported feature set. Altair's PBS Pro leverages PRRTE in an allocation to provide a broad spectrum of PMIx services. The PMIx standard includes active participants from a number of commericial, university and national laboratories from around the world [11].

3 Approach

3.1 PMIx Python Bindings

The Python binding for PMIx was introduced starting in version 4.0. The binding relies heavily on the Cython[1] C-extension for Python as the backbone for the implementation. The Cython language is a superset of the Python language that additionally supports calling C functions and declaring C types on variables and class attributes. The use of Cython greatly simplifies the task of wrapping the low level API exposed by the native C PMIx API in OpenPMIx into a more usable Pythonic API and data structures.

As part of our work we improved the error handling of the existing OpenPMIx Python bindings to ensure output Python variables were set to appropriate values in all cases. We also resolved a problem related to encoding of string arguments when using modern versions of Python. These enhancements enabled us to use PMIx to prototype the many task workflow engine that is presented in Sect. 3.2.

Most of our work to harden the PMIx Python binding addressed the interplay between the Global Interpreter Lock (GIL) in Python which is held by any Python thread while executing Python code, and the locks that are part of the multithreaded C code that implements PMIx backends. Proper locking protocal is needed to avoid deadlock, which may happen even if the Python code is not multithreaded. For example, the OpenPMIx library creates an event thread that will invoke callbacks asynchronously while the main Python thread will call PMIx functions synchronously, leading to potential deadlock due to the wrong lock ordering between locks on the two sides.

Figure 1 shows the proper lock ordering of a PMIx+Python program. The Python interpreter starts with the GIL acquired in the main thread and the GIL is released on calls into the PMIx

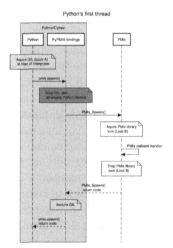

Fig. 1. Sequence diagram showing how Python and PMIx locks interact.

library. When a PIMx event triggers a call (from the C PMIx side) to a Python callback, it is necessary to hold both PMIx locks and the Python GIL. Since the event callbacks

---

[1] https://cython.org/.

are called from the OpenPMIx event loop before entering a Python context and taking the GIL, the locks will need be acquired in the reverse order from the order in the main program loop. For this reason the PMIx Python bindings must drop the GIL before calling a library function that may invoke callbacks to avoid ABBA deadlocks.

3.2 Pyrun Prototype

To exercise the functionality of the PMIx Python client, we developed *Pyrun*, a proto-type Python driver for executing an ensem-ble of tasks on a collection of computational resources provisioned via a PMIx compliant server. The code makes no assumptions about the targeted PMIx implementation as long as it supports the APIs used in the prototype, except for the need to instantiate and connect to such an implementation during startup. For that purpose, we use the Distributed Vir-tual Machine (DVM) mode of PRRTE which

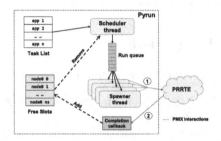

Fig. 2. Architecture of *Pyrun* driver proto-type.

allows remote connection to PRRTE servers using a uniform resource identifier (URI). This URI is used to instantiate an instance of the PMIx tool object that is used for all interactions with the PMIx backend implementation. Figure 2 shows the architecture of the *Pyrun* prototype.

At the core of the *Pyrun* prototype lies the scheduler thread in Fig. 2, which manages the execution of a task list that is defined during the initialization of the code. The task list definition includes the binaries to be executed, the number of processes that make up a running application (MPI processes), and any command line arguments used by the application. The scheduler also uses a *free slots* data structure to keep track of available resources to dispatch any outstanding tasks. When process placement is left to the PMIx backend, this data structure can be a simple counter for the number of available free slots. When the scheduler takes on the responsibility for controlling process placement, then *free slots* will require a more sophisticated data structure.

The scheduler implements a simple FIFO scheduling policy with back-fill. Ready tasks (for which free slots are readily available) are inserted into a Python *Run queue*, with a configurable number of worker *spawner threads* consuming tasks from the other end of the queue. Each spawner thread implements a simple loop, where tasks removed from the queue are spawned using the spawn() call on the PMIx tool object, as was shown in Listing 1.2. It should be noted that for scheduler-controlled placement of tasks, an additional entry is needed in the app dictionary that defines details about the applications to be launched. Similar to the job_info list of dictionaries in Listing 1.2, the app dictionary includes an 'info' entry that contains a list of dictionaries with additional application specific launching directives. This application 'info' dictio-nary contains the same trio of keys, 'key', 'value_type' and 'value', which are used to pass a string with a comma-seperated set of target host names as the value for the pmix.PMIX_HOST key. The pmix.PMIX_HOST is used to control the placement of the processes for the associated application.

The spawner threads communicate with the PMIx backend using a single connection via the PMIx tool object ((1) in Fig. 2), with the `spawn()` call returning immediately with an error code denoting whether the backend has successfully started the target set of processes. The prototype also registers a completion callback method (*completion callback*) to be invoked upon completion of any task running on the PMIx backend. When invoked ((2) in Fig. 2), this callback function updates *free slots* using data from the just completed application, and performs other logging operations, particularly updating the number of finished tasks.

The prototype terminates normally when all tasks from the initial task list have finished execution. We should note that for this simple prototype, we do not attempt to resubmit a task that fails to terminate normally (as reported by the data included in the `pmix.PMIX_EVENT_JOB_END` callback). We also note that we use an IO callback analogous to the one in Listing 1.3 to handle all standard output and standard error traffic from all executed tasks. Those outputs are gathered into a single file, to be later post-processed into separate per-job file if there is such a need. This approach avoids the creation of unnecessarily large number of file descriptors during the ensemble execution, which would be inevitable if command line tools are used to execute the same workload. The reduced number of required file descriptors at the frontend tool level is important in HPC environments because the service nodes where the tool runs are often shared among many users.

4   Evaluation/Demonstration

To evaluate the Python binding for PMIx, we carried out several experimental campaigns to execute ensembles of synthetic workloads on the Summit super computer at Oak Ridge National Laboratory[2]. These campaigns used the prototype Python launcher client described in Sect. 3.2 to exercise various aspects of the PMIx interface and demonstrate the ability to use Python to orchestrate the execution of many tasks workloads on a PMIx compliant server backend. Each execution instance was submitted as a separate batch job. All executables were staged on node-local storage to avoid parallel filesystem overhead. With the Power9 CPU on Summit supporting 168 hardware threads in SMT4 mode, the single core workload for each job consisted of an ensemble of tasks, with three tasks per hardware thread for a total of $3 * 168 * N$ for a run on N Summit nodes. In these campaigns, we used the PMIx Reference RunTime Environment (PRRTE) that is part of the openmpi/5.0.0rc6 release candidate as the backend for process execution on N Summit nodes, with $1 \leq N \leq 45$. We tested using both single core and parallel MPI tasks, with each task calling `sleep()` for a random duration uniformly distributed in the interval $(150, 180)$ s. In these experiments, no explicit nodes were assigned to individual tasks, and task placement was left up to the PMIx backend (PRRTE).

It should be noted that the focus of this evaluation is to exercise the capabilities exported via the PMIx Python interface, and to demonstrate the viability of using such

---

[2] https://www.olcf.ornl.gov/summit/.

an interface as a foundational process management layer for workflow engines. Implementation details, performance characteristics and scalability limitations of the underlying PMIx implementation will, by definition, impact the overall execution of the workload. Deep analysis of errors and/or performance limitations of the PRRTE backend used to execute these workloads is beyond the scope of this work. When such errors result in failure to execute a particular experiment, this is reported as a missing data point in the corresponding plot.

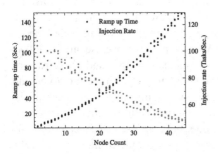 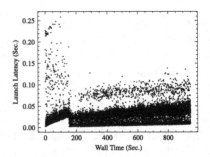

Fig. 3. Ramp up time & Injection rate Scalability

Fig. 4. Task Launch Latency time evolution for 45 nodes

4.1 Single Core Task Injection

In this experiment, we evaluate the robustness of the Python client and API by executing three independent sweeps across the targeted range of Summit nodes. Each execution instance targets a set of single core tasks generated using a different random distribution of task runtimes. Figure 3 shows the ramp up time (total time needed to fill all available slots with tasks) and the corresponding task injection rate for the three sweeps. The figure shows that in general, task injection rate decreases as the client dispatches tasks to a larger pool of nodes. Preliminary analysis suggests that this stems primarily from the overhead in the Pyrun prototype of managing the internal data structures and dispatching a new task after receiving PMIx acknowledgment that the prior task has been successfully instantiated.

Figure 4 shows the task launch latency for all tasks launched in a single 45 node experiment for all tasks in the ensemble, as observed by the Python client. The initial ramp up phase can be easily identified in the plot, where task launch latency increases as more tasks are launched, coupled with a larger variability in the task launch latency. This behavior can be attributed to PRRTE using a linear search algorithm to identify an available slot for each incoming task.

4.2 Comparison with Command Line Tools

In this experiment, we explore the use of the Python PMIx API to launch task ensembles compared to the use of the PRRTE command line tool prun to execute the same workload across the range of nodes. We use two different drivers to execute the prun ensembles. One driver written in `bash` (shell-prun in Fig. 5) that is part of the PMIx test suite, and one that uses a modified version of the Pyrun prototype that launches tasks via the `prun` command-line utility (Pyrun-prun in Fig. 5). We compare the total ensemble runtime for these two variants against the runtime for the same ensemble launched using the PMIx Python API (Pyrun-spawn in Fig. 5).

The theoretical ideal maximum runtime of three iterations of tasks with runtime uniformly distributed between 150 s and 180 s is 540 s (as indicated by the dotted horizontal line in Fig. 5). It can be seen that all execution mechanisms introduce overheads that increase as the number of tasks and the size of the target pool of nodes grows. However, Pyrun-spawn using the PMIx Python interface introduces the least overhead of the three variants. It should be noted that only 40 of the 45 jobs that constitute the shell-prun sweep completed successfully, as did only 28 jobs out of 45 from the Pyrun-prun sweep. When command line tools are used to instantiate PMIx processes, $O(N)$ OS resources such as file descriptors on the launch node are consumed for an ensemble of N processes. Alternatively, using the Pyrun-spawn launcher, only $O(1)$ such resources are utilized, alleviating resource pressure on the launch node and increasing the reliability of the overall workflow.

4.3 Multithreaded Launch Capability

In this experiment, we use the multiple launcher threads in Pyrun to exercise the robustness of the PMIx Python client when it is invoked from multithreaded Python code. The goal is primarily to test the functionality of the client code and to confirm that no deadlock occurs due to the interaction between locks on the Python and C side of the PMIx Python client. A secondary goal is to explore the impact of multithreaded launch clients on the overall performance using the PRRTE backend. Towards those goals, we run the same workload sweep from Sect. 4.2 using different numbers of threads in Pyrun. Figure 6 shows the total runtime for the task ensemble sweep using 2, 4, and 8 threads in addition to the default single launcher thread configuration. The plot shows that total runtime decreases as more launcher threads are used, with the most dramatic reduction occurring with the move from 1 to 2 threads. It should be noted that in this experiment, 5, 2 and 6 jobs failed when using 2, 4 and 8 launcher threads, respectively. Failures were

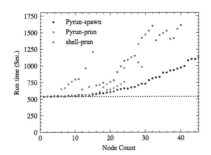
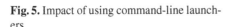
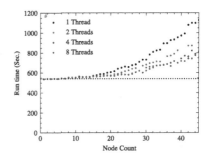

Fig. 5. Impact of using command-line launchers

Fig. 6. Total runtime for multiple launch threads

due to connections and/or binding and mapping errors in the PRRTE backend, and not due to any deadlock or other issues in the PMIx Python client.

4.4 Heterogeneous Parallel MPI Tasks

In this experiment, we exercise the ability to launch a heterogeneous ensemble of parallel MPI tasks using the PMIx Python API via Pyrun. In these runs, we use two task configurations, with the number of ranks in each task uniformly distributed in the range $(1, 6)s$ and $(1, 20)s$ and each task calling `MPI_Init()` and `MPI_Finalize()`, with an intervening call to `sleep()` for a random duration in the interval $(150, 180)s$. For a job launched on N nodes, we used M tasks, where $M = 3 * 168 * N/S$, where $S = 4$ and 11 for the two configurations, respectively. The entire sweep was repeated three times for each configuration. In these experiments, all jobs finished normally with no errors from the PRRTE backend. Figure 7 shows the task injection rate for the two sweeps, showing overall a higher task injection rate for the configuration with smaller number of MPI ranks per task. This can be partially attributed to the simple back-fill scheduling algorithm we use in Pyrun, which attempts to find tasks that would fit all available empty slots - a task made easier when task sizes are smaller.

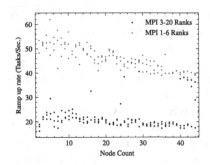

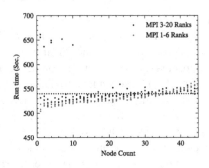

Fig. 7. MPI ramp up time   **Fig. 8.** MPI tasks total runtime

Figure 8 shows the total runtime for the two configurations. The plot shows that, as was observed before with single core tasks, total runtime increases as we target a larger node count and number of tasks. However, the increase is not as dramatic in this case, primarily due to the reduction in the total number of tasks executed for each node count.

5 Related Work

The focus of our work is on exposing the capabilities of PMIx, which are generally accessed through C language interfaces, to a broader set of users via the Python bindings. Other efforts also provide access to process management for improved productivity using Python. Flux [3] is a hierarchical resource management system, akin to

SLURM[3], that offers a rich set of interfaces for describing jobs, their dependencies and notifications during stages of job lifecycle. Flux and SLURM are primarily workload management and scheduling systems. Flux offers several Python based interfaces that can be used to embed the scheduler into workflows [3]. Our work seeks to provide a lightweight approach to interface with PMIx, that is (to our knowledge) the only generic interface for distributed process management that is under active maintenance/development. Dask[4] is another widely used Python library for parallel computing with support for distributed dynamic task management and scheduling. It however lacks support for individual parallel tasks and provides a higher level API and abstraction than the low level PMIx we target with this work as a foundational layer for process management.

6   Conclusion

The many tasks use case presents a number of challenges when used on typical high-performance computing systems. A programmatic interface alleviates the need for ad hoc measures when using command-line tool, e.g., arbitrary delays between task launches. The PMIx Python bindings enable a more effective use of the fine-grained control provided by PMIx events, e.g., process lifecycle introspection and management of errors.

In this paper, we presented work to harden the PMIx Python bindings, with the goal of enabling its use as a standard process management layer for workflow engines. We developed a prototype many task Python execution driver, and used it to demonstrate the viability of the PMIx Python binding and the ability to orchestrate the execution of ensembles of single core and parallel tasks on the PRRTE reference implementation of the PMIx standard. Our experimental results show the advantages of using the PMIx API relative to the often used command line tools approach to manage process lifetime in workflows. While studying the performance and reliability of PRRTE was not the main focus of this work, we illustrated the current scalability and robustness of PRRTE that may be enhanced for to more effectively support large scale tasks ensembles. To the best of our knowledge, no other PMIx implementation exports the process management API used in the Pyrun prototype. We hope this work motivates implementers to support and export a more complete subset of the PMIx specification, allowing wider and novel uses by workflows engines and alleviating the need for platform specific tooling. More work is needed to exercise a larger set of PMIx capabilities, e.g., error managment, and to further refine support in PRRTE for many-task workloads.

Acknowledgements. The original Python bindings were developed by Ralph Castain and Danielle Sikich with support from Intel and Argonne National Laboratory. We would like to thank Ralph Castain for his continued efforts and hard work spearheading the PMIx project. This research used resources of the Oak Ridge Leadership Computing Facility at the Oak Ridge National Laboratory, which is supported by the Office of Science of the U.S. Department of Energy under Contract No. DE-AC05-00OR22725. This research was partially supported by the Exascale Computing Project (17-SC-20-SC), a collaborative effort of the U.S. Department of Energy Office of Science and the National Nuclear Security Administration.

---

[3] https://slurm.schedmd.com.

[4] https://dask.org.

References

1. Acharya, A., et al.: Supercomputer-based ensemble docking drug discovery pipeline with application to COVID-19. J. Chem. Inf. Model. **60**(12), 5832–5852 (2020)
2. Merzky, A., Turilli, M., Maldonado, M., Santcroos, M., Jha, S.: Using pilot systems to execute many task workloads on supercomputers. In: Klusáček, D., Cirne, W., Desai, N. (eds.) Job Scheduling Strategies for Parallel Processing (JSSPP 2018). LNCS, vol. 11332, pp. 61–82. Springer, Cham (2019). https://doi.org/10.1007/978-3-030-10632-4_4
3. Ahn, D., et al.: Flux: overcoming scheduling challenges for exascale workflows. Futur. Gener. Comput. Syst. **110**, 202–213 (2020)
4. Ossyra, J., Sedova, A., Tharrington, A., Noé, F., Clementi, C., Smith, J.C.: Porting adaptive ensemble molecular dynamics workflows to the summit supercomputer. In: Weiland, M., Juckeland, G., Alam, S., Jagode, H. (eds.) ISC High Performance 2019. LNCS, vol. 11887, pp. 397–417. Springer, Cham (2019). https://doi.org/10.1007/978-3-030-34356-9_30
5. Turilli, M., et al.: Characterizing the performance of executing many-tasks on summit. In: IEEE Workshop on Emerging Parallel and Distributed Runtime Systems and Middleware (IPDRM), pp. 18–25 (2019)
6. Balaji, P., et al.: PMI: a scalable parallel process-management interface for extreme-scale systems. In: Keller, R., Gabriel, E., Resch, M., Dongarra, J. (eds.) EuroMPI 2010. LNCS, vol. 6305, pp. 31–41. Springer, Heidelberg (2010). https://doi.org/10.1007/978-3-642-15646-5_4
7. Jain, A., et al.: FireWorks: a dynamic workflow system designed for high-throughput applications. Concurr. Comput. Pract. Exp. **27**(17), 5037–5059 (2015)
8. Lee, H., et al.: Scalable HPC & AI infrastructure for COVID-19 therapeutics. In: Platform for Advanced Scientific Computing Conference (PASC 2021), pp. 1–13. ACM (2021)
9. MPI-Forum: MPI: a message-passing interface standard version 4.0 (2021)
10. OpenPMIx: Reference implementation of the process management interface for Exascale. https://openpmix.io/
11. PMIx: Process management interface for Exascale (2022). https://pmix.io/
12. PMIx-ASC. PMIx: Process management interface for Exascale standard v4.1 (2021)

Author Index

H. Takizawa et al. (Eds.): PDCAT 2022, LNCS 13798, pp. 535–537, 2023.
https://doi.org/10.1007/978-3-031-29927-8

Printed in the United States
by Baker & Taylor Publisher Services